Feudal Coats
of Arms

EFFIGY OF GEORGE PERCY, PREBENDARY OF BEVERLEY 1474,

drawn by Thomson Foley.

FEUDAL COATS
OF ARMS

JOSEPH FOSTER

SENATE

Feudal Coats of Arms

First published as *Some Feudal Coats of Arms*
in 1902 by James Parker & Company, London

This edition published in 1995 by Senate, an imprint of
Studio Editions Ltd, Princess House, 50 Eastcastle
Street, London W1N 7AP, England

Copyright © this edition Studio Editions Ltd 1995

ISBN 1 85958 153 6

Printed and bound in Guernsey by
The Guernsey Press Co. Ltd

INTRODUCTION.

M Y book, "Some Feudal Coats of Arms," published in the autumn of 1901, was at least a disinterested attempt to revive some of the ancient charm of Heraldry. The result seems to have pleased all, save two enthusiasts, who had fondly cherished conflicting, if not indeed barren, hopes of a compilation of their own. Fatuous to the bitter end, the Hope heraldic springs eternal in the Barron's breast.

By these the work was received in the true spirit of "the charlatan and the smatterer," and that Heraldry which all students desire to uphold in its pristine glamour was unchivalrously used as a handle for peevish personalities, after the best traditions of the Elizabethan Heralds. Their two-of-a-trade tirade is very tiresome, for it is neither calculated to enhance the characters of our visionaires, nor to advance the interests of the study of Heraldry, but rather to be-little them professionally, as it certainly has done, with right-thinking men, and be-foul the heraldic nest, which we all love so well.

The columns of the *Athenæum*, under its new editor, were specially utilised to serve the purposes of my opiniative opponents ; and, pitiable to add, other periodicals revealed, though in a minor degree, the mark of the "dirty bird." For the sake of armorial amenities it is undesirable to say more in this place, for, after all, such "reviews are no longer taken seriously either by authors or the public," especially when engineered by "the unspeakable Scot." To all lovers of fair play I commend the following appreciative excerpt from the *Morning Post* :—

"The friends of —— are fairly entitled to laugh at their foes over the discovery that the much-discussed article in the —— was eked out with long unacknowledged extracts from two criticisims which had already appeared in other periodicals, and to put forward this fact as a proof that all three articles were produced by the same critic. In the perennial argument on the great question of mutual assistance in the rolling of logs it has often been declared that certain persons possess, and exercise, the power of anonymously reviewing the same book in half a dozen quarters. But that an article written by a particular man should be quoted in support of another article from the same pen seems a more distressing matter. No doubt it saves a great deal of time if we fill up our 'new' articles by digging bits out of old ones, and there are cases in which the process might be justifiable. When three strong opinions, whether friendly or otherwise, are proved to be merely one, and the critic is shown to be a species of literary Spenlow-Jorkins and Gamp-Harris combination, there can be little enough to say in its favour."

This smaller edition of "Some Feudal Coats of Arms" will, it is hoped, place the contents of the Rolls of Arms, with the accompanying Heraldic illustrations, within the reach of all who are interested in early coat armour and in the uplifting of the Art Heraldic.

As the mode of differencing arms in feudal times is of considerable importance, I have included Chart Pedigrees of Astley, Fauconberg, Le Strange, Nevill and Venables, each of which affords some interesting examples. But I would call especial attention to the pedigree of Geoffrey de Mandeville and his kinsfolk, which I have reproduced on page 162 from the Chart compiled by Mr. Round, and to which I have added blocks of the arms. It is by an historical example such as this that we realise how clear and precise is the language of Feudal Heraldry.

Then, a differenced coat was evidence of actual affinity by blood or by marriage ; now, a coat of arms is so adroitly differenced as often to be a colourable and shameless imitation of an ancient one to which the grantee has no other claim nor pretence than an accidental similarity of name ; such a modern coat is evidence of nothing more than a vain imposture. From simple truth the language of Heraldry often degenerates in these later times to the language of Ananias.

A good friend kindly sends me "The Boast of Heraldry," which immediately follows this page. It is so singularly apposite that I am constrained to print it for the edification and perchance the entertainment of my heraldic *confrères*.

For the frontispiece to this volume, the excellent representation of Prebendary Percy's beautiful effigy in Beverley Minster, in all probability our finest example of Ecclesiastical Heraldry, I have to thank Mr. Thomson Foley, Architect, of that town, who has specially drawn it for this edition.

J. FOSTER.

21 BOUNDARY ROAD, N.W.,
July, 1902.

A TOURNAMENT, CIRCA 1500 ; BRITISH MUSEUM,
ADD. MS. 24,098.

"THE BOAST OF HERALDRY."

Well do I recollect that distant day
When I was taught the Elegy of Gray
And learnt by heart through many a grudging hour
"The boast of Heraldry, the pomp of Pow'r,"
My wont to sit in boyish discontent
And wonder wanly what on earth it meant;
Nor do I find, though older I have grown,
That I can call much clearer views my own.
I know, of course, that pomp of Pow'r implies
A vast importance in one's own two eyes,
Importance which, too vast at least by half,
Is apt to make less potent persons laugh;
But Providence not yet vouchsafes to me
To know what is this "boast of Heraldry."
    Is it, I ask myself, a secret cult,
Taboo unto the average adult;
A thing to whisper of with reverent air,
And lock up in some dim, recondite lair;
A thing to hide from ordinary life
" Far from the madding crowd's ignoble strife"?
Is it a weird and occult branch of knowledge
Confined to favourites of a fee-famed College?
Is this to claim the sole and secret stores
Of mysteries which the man of mind ignores—
Stores which, unlike some others, fail to give
A service civil and co-op'rative?
Or is this Heraldry the private prey
Of each and every callow F.S.A.?
    Tell me, ye shelves of Bloomsbury, Bodley, Queen's,
Rich fields wherein the student freely gleans,
Stored with those royal muniments of old
To Heralds trusted and by Heralds sold,
Can these things be?   And must the man who seeks
To bring it rescue from the grip of cliques
Prepare himself to face fierce Magazines
Intent to smash him into smithereens,
And must he find himself upon the brink
Of raging torrents of vain-glorious ink?

Must he, because he is no myrmidon,
Become a target for the hanger-on
And note the angry and anonymous
Attentions of a new-laid arquebus
Aimed from some grim Barronial mausoleum
By *Ancestor* or eke by *Athenæum*?
May he not ever seek to sift the wheat
From out the chaff of Queen Victoria Street,
Or pierce the obscuring crust that ever hardens
Upon the tumid tomes of Whitehall Gardens,
Or dare to doubt the dictum of a sage
Who decorates Archæologia's page,
Or mention e'en with modified aspersions
Th' "originality" of "spurious versions," *
Without the feeling that behind his back
There is developing some brave attack
From those who try to further private aims
Without appending their illustrious names?
Must he in humble wise lay bare his breast
To fangs from Burlingtonia's "Viper's Nest," †
A nest still smarting from its sad bereavement,
The loss of Mowbray's fabulous Atchievement? ‡
     Is this, again I ask, what is to be
The oft-repeated "boast of Heraldry"?
If it indeed be so, I gravely doubt
If Heraldry has much to boast about !

                        OXONIAN.

* See next page.
† "Archæologia," vol. xxxi., page 247.
‡ "Archæologia," vol. xxix., App., page 387 ; " Some Feudal Coats of Arms," 4to edn.,
pp. xx, 144 : 8vo. edn., page xv.

PREFACE.

"SOME Feudal Coats of Arms" is primarily a collection, from the Heraldic Rolls, of the names, with the personal insignia displayed on their banners or vestments, of the combatants at the battle of Falkirk, 1298, and at the siege of Carlaverock, 1300, at the tournaments of Dunstable in 1308 and 1334, at the battle of Boroughbridge, 1322, or at the siege of Calais, 1345–8, and before Rouen, 1418. With these have been incorporated the names and blasons in the so-called Heraldic Rolls or Lists, some of which I have re-named (*see* page xx *et seq.*), concluding with the Arundel or Military Roll, emblasoned *circa* Hen. VI.

How far these Heraldic Rolls or Lists were compiled from originals and added to by Heralds or Herald-painters of later date must remain a moot point. Of those which are generally accepted as contemporary with the persons whose arms are blasoned therein I may at least refer to the Military Rolls before mentioned, 1298–1418. The copy of the Dering Roll, which is considered to be the earliest of the Rolls assigned to the reign of Hen. III., agrees to a remarkable extent with the Howard or Planché Roll. The Ashmole copy of this same Dering Roll, No. 1120, made by that notorious Elizabethan Herald Ralfe Brooke (when Rouge Cross, 1580–93), is by him recklessly described as "the names and armes of those Knightes as weare w^t Kinge Richard the firste at the assigge of Acon or Acres," 1191 (*see* Black's Ashmolean Catalogue), another noteworthy instance, I am afraid, of the malpractices displayed by the officious Elizabethan Heralds, secure in their re-incorporation of 1555. For the convenience of the student I have distinguished the majority of these "Dering" blasons by a double dagger, ‡ ; and those interested in the Roll will find a short article thereon in the "Reliquary," vol. xvi. p. 135.

Probably the most interesting of the series, Historically and Heraldically, is the Boroughbridge Roll (1322), still in the possession of the family of Colonel Williams-Wynn, of Coed-y-Maen. Other original Rolls, of my period, are rarely to be met with ; in the British Museum is the Camden Roll, and a third, the Bodley Roll, is in the Ashmolean Collection at Oxford, No. 15 (A). The Society of Antiquaries boasts of one or two "Originals," admittedly spurious versions of older Rolls,* reprinted in the "Archæologia." Traced facsimiles of the Boroughbridge and Camden Rolls will be found on pages xviii and xix.

As is the case nowadays their compilers are to be caught tripping—in the Boroughbridge Roll the arms of Sir Edmond and Sir Geoffrey Cornwall are correctly assigned to them, but the same arms are also ascribed, though erroneously, to Sir Edmond and Sir Geoffrey Curteny. Other slips have been detected in the Falkirk and Carlaverock Rolls, even the simple coat De Vere was a notable stumbling-block to the early armorists. A volume of facsimiles of these Rolls which have all been edited and printed, some many a time and oft (the Parliamentary Roll half a dozen times), would be more welcome to the Heraldic student who is unable to consult the originals than a *réchauffée*, on modern-antique lines, with which we seem to be threatened.

---

* See "The Boast of Heraldry," preceding page.

In addition to the Roll authority for each coat, the Christian as well as the Surname of its original holder is here given, information not to be found in any of the printed Books of Arms ; the blasons and tricks of the various Rolls—the foreign coats usually excepted—have been collated and the whole alphabetically arranged, as in my other works. The voracious hack-editor of kindred works will doubtless calmly appropriate, " out and out," for any new edition of his armoury what I have arranged at infinite pains, in precisely the same way as all the original matter in my Peerage, and more especially in my Baronetage of 1880, was appropriated in 1881 and later years, without a breath of acknowledgment, unsuspected and therefore unnoticed by their reviewers and the public.

Annotation or identification was no part of my original plan in producing a series of blasons referring for the most part to well-known persons of ancient repute, the identity of whose coat armour has hitherto been carefully obscured in the published armouries, in perpetuation of the occult—and the inexact. In order to minimise repetition it will be noticed that I have combined under their respective names those who are named at Falkirk, 1298, and at Carlaverock, 1300, and those who sealed the celebrated Letter from the Barons to the Pope, 1301. Those who accompanied Prince Edward (E. 1.) in the last of the crusades, 1269–70, are distinguished with a cross, † ; the Dering Roll (‡), which is (sceptically) said to refer to the siege of Acre, 1191, has already been mentioned. The asterisk denotes those whose descendants are singled out by Mr. Shirley in " Noble and Gentle Men of England," and those (Shirley) names whose ancestors do not occur in these Rolls are included in square brackets, so *[ ] Shirley. For any who wish to annotate further much valuable information may be readily found in (1) the alphabetical section of the "Parliamentary Writs," by F. T. Palgrave, and in (2) the "Seals in the British Museum," published by the Trustees, under the editorship of Dr. de Gray Birch.

As " Hungry time hath made a glutton's meal on this Catalogue of Gentry " I have compiled, for ready reference, a somewhat tentative list of those named on the Rolls who are still represented in the male line. These families are in very deed the *Ancienne Noblesse* of this realm. See page xxv.

Perhaps more remarkable still is the exhaustion of the lineal descendants of the Knights of the Garter, for of all those (about 270) created before the reign of Henry VIII. only 13 are now represented in direct male descent.

(1) Lord Wrottesley represents Sir Hugh Wrottesley, a founder, 1344 ; a unique distinction.
(2) Marquis of Abergavenny, K.G., represents John, Lord Neville, of Raby, 1369.
(3) Lord Clifford of Chudleigh represents Sir Lewis Clifford, 1378.
(4) Rev. Robert Myles Stapylton, Rector of Lolworth, represents Sir Bryan Stapleton, 1382.
(5) The Earl of Derby, K.G., represents Sir John Stanley, 1405.
(6) The Earl of Shrewsbury represents John, Lord Talbot, 1424 (1st Earl of Shrewsbury).
(7) Simon Conyers Scrope of Danby represents John, 5th Lord Scrope of Bolton, 1461.
(8) The Earl of Huntingdon represents William, Lord Hastings, 1462.
(9) The Duke of Norfolk, K.G., represents John, Lord Howard, 1472 (1st Duke of Norfolk).
(10) The Viscount Hereford represents Walter, Lord Ferrers of Chartley, 1472.
(11) The Earl of Stamford represents Thomas, Marquis of Dorset, 1476.
(12) The Duke of Beaufort (c. 1490) and (13) the Duke of Leinster (1504) represent the creations of Henry VII.

My interest in the art side of Heraldry (so little appreciated), derived to some extent from my relative, the late Birket Foster, has led me critically to investigate and examine, for the best examples, a host of Heraldic MSS. in the British Museum, which contain the work of the older Herald painters ; and I trust that my critics and supporters will agree that my labour has not been in vain ; indeed, I shall be well pleased if this work but afford a starting point for future enquirers. How often, alas ! has a manuscript suffered by its change of owner, exquisite tricks all but obliterated by the coarsest daubs of colouring, so much so, that the ordinary consultation of a MS. for aught but the art-Heraldic would probably fail to reveal the artistic gems beneath. The chief among modern Heraldic art students was, without doubt, the late Mr. James E. Doyle, examples of whose exquisite work may be seen in "the Official Baronage." The late Frater Anselm, of Mount S. Bernard Abbey, greatly enhanced the attractiveness of my "Peerage and Baronetage," 1880–3. Of what is now the old school of Heraldry Mr. John Henry Metcalfe alone remains, his delicate physique, as with Mr. Doyle and Fr. Anselm, precluding continuous work ; the drawings of the arms of the Oxford Colleges, made for "Alumni Oxonienses," quite fifteen years ago, are his.

It may also appear singular that a work such as this, dealing with the beginnings of Heraldry, can be compiled quite outside the College of Arms,* and without the assistance in any shape or form of a Herald or Officer of Arms. That the period covered is prior to the incubation of the College is an insufficient retort, the fact really being that the older Heralds, having sold their books of arms and pedigrees, which are now in the British Museum and elsewhere, the present Heralds are largely indifferent to this early period ; moreover, is it not ultra-official, and therefore outside the pale of easily-gotten fees ?

" It is recorded by W. Segar, Somerset, afterwards Garter, that ' Cooke, Clar. made many profitable Visitations, both by hymself and his deputyes, whoe, notwithstanding they were well entertayned, feasted and richly rewarded by the gent of yᵉ cuntrey, hath left no memory of them in the Generall Office. These were upon deceasse attached by arrests, alienated and sould. Two Norroys Kings of Armes, two Windesors, Richmond, Lancaster, Somersett and Yorke, deceassed, have done the like to the great sclaunder and decaye of the office and officers present.'"—Cott. MS. Faustina, E. I., fo. 263.

I frankly appeal in this work to those who belong to our old families, or who take an intelligent interest in the history of our *ancienne noblesse.* My standpoint is the very opposite to that of those who seek to foist on the newly-armigerous person a "nobility" obtained by him in return for a cash payment. Nothing I know could be more grotesquely repellant to those to whom I appeal than this debased attitude, this absolute levelling of the claims of ancestry and high breeding in order to complete a business deal. Surely in the times in which we live these efforts to exalt the *novus homo* because he has paid fees to the heralds as not only the equal of all, but actually the superior of some of our old territorial families, whose social position is undoubted, and whose history is entwined all through the centuries with the story of their country, calls for an official protest, and invites the publication of such a work as this, in which those who are descended from our older houses will at least have heraldic justice.

The toil in such a work as this is as nothing to the pleasure which is evoked, as one Heraldic milestone after another is passed ; and with an enthusiast, is not the *fait accompli* his sole reward ? I boast no publisher, nor sponsor in any

* " The present movements in favour of the intelligent study of the science (Heraldry), of the pure and artistic design, and of the new honest genealogy, have all originated not within, but without, the walls of the Heralds' College." *Studies in Peerage and Family History,* Preface, XXVI, by J. H. Round.

shape; as with the "Alumni Oxonienses," the costs as well as the toil are wholly mine, but even so, without outside aid, I could never have produced this book in its present form. It is my most agreeable duty gratefully to acknowledge the very highly valued privileges and assistance I have received officially from Sir Edward Thompson, Director of the British Museum, from the Keeper of the MSS., and the chiefs of the Reading Room. For literary help and guidance I have been almost hourly indebted to the ever courteous Mr. F. B. Bickley, of the MSS. Department, whose knowledge and experience of ancient documents are probably unrivalled. My thanks are also due to Dr. Birch, whose unsurpassed Heraldic knowledge has ever been available and of the utmost value in clearing up many abstruse points. It is indeed difficult to avoid being invidious where all are so uniformly courteous and helpful.

Even though 'tis "forty years on" since the appearance of my first Genealogical work, and I have been responsible for many volumes in the interval, I must still claim indulgence for errors, which, in spite of every care, I feel sure must have been committed, as any one who knows aught of the babel of blazon will most readily understand and condone. Let me at least pray to have been delivered from the snare of the forger.*

J. FOSTER.

21 BOUNDARY ROAD,
    LONDON, N.W.

---

* "The Hughenden Effigies" of Wellesbourne and Montfort, temp. H. VIII. See *Peerage and Family History*, page 84, by J. H. Round.

SIR GEORGE WAUTON AND WIFE,
In the Church of Stoughton, Hunts.

HERALDIC INTRODUCTION.

—◆—

CONFUSION of the symbols and devices of the ancients with Heraldry as an exact system has led to much aimless discussion as to its origin and history, and also to much vague theory, as if, forsooth, Heraldry were really an occult science.

Surely in the nature-worshipper we detect the Heraldic protoplasm, the primeval king of arms. He it was who painted the object of his veneration on his skin as a charm against the evil one when at peace, and on his shield in defence of his person when at war ; the presence or whereabouts of his chieftain or tribal head he distinguished by a standard, ensign, or banner, as all writers testify, from Moses downwards ; in this simple statement may not the Heraldic prototype be surely discerned? Further down the ages it may well have been the bards of every clime who handed down in turn these mystic emblems in their own weird way, inventing as they went the almost forgotten chimera and other monstrosities which were calculated to strike terror into the hearts of the adversary. Later still, the vases of the Greeks (550, 500 B.C.) are eloquent in examples of the Hellenic equivalent of our Heraldic system.

Passing over the *quasi*-Heraldic aspect which some attribute to Totems and other personal distinctions so commonly employed among nations of imperfect civilisation, I may instance the usage of the Celtic tribes of Gaul and Britain who carried symbols or badges on their shields. Their national symbol—the boar—occurs on one such shield, found in the river Witham, and dates from the beginning of our era, see " Archæologia," xxiii. 95, and the larger edition of this work.

The symbols of the Normans, at the Conquest, represented in the much-debated Bayeux Tapestry next claim our notice. Mr. Fowke, the latest historian of the Tapestry, recites at length the opinions of Bolton Corney, M. Thierry, Dr. Lingard, Mr. Freeman, and many others, with whom he agrees in regarding it as a contemporary work, but in no way associated with Queen Matilda, though probably made under the orders of Bishop Odo by Norman workpeople at Bayeux for their church of Bayeux.*

Of its pre-heraldic devices I may, perhaps, be allowed to quote Mr. Fowke's own words :—

" As a nearer approach is made to the ages of Chivalry the realistic representations of natural objects give place to those of geometrical figures which were soon systematized as ordinaries, whilst the animals assume the more conventional form in which they were subsequently borne. Thus the place of the wild beasts is taken by crosses, roundles, or besants, interlacing bands, and simple tinctures, and this stage is most clearly shown in the tapestry. We do not here find any particular or distinguished person represented twice as bearing the same device ('Archæology,' xix. 188), and we must therefore conclude that they

* See *The Bayeux Tapestry: a Description and History*, by Frank Rede Fowke, first published by the Arundel Society in 1875, under the sanction of the Science and Art Department of the Committee of the Council on Education, and secondly by George Bell & Sons in 1897.

are not intended to represent the arms of any individual, or only in some cases and that appropriately, but their representation at all, of course, implies the existence of a system of bearings by which the wearer was known.   And this we gather also from Wace, who says—

> ' E tuit ovent fet cognoissances
> Ki Norman alter conust
> El ke l'autre portuer neuet.'

These were cognizances to distinguish one Norman from another, and no man dared to use another's—showing that the assumption of arms was not the subject of mere caprice.

With the spread of Feudalism, then, came the introduction of the linear, or geometrical, and from the imaginary per pale, per fess, per chevron, per saltire, &c., would naturally be evolved, the pale, the fess, the chevron, the saltire.* Out of this fortuitous combination of some of the elements of Euclid with the objects of the nature-worshipper, sprang that system we call Heraldry.

Although there is evidence that Heraldic bearings were assuming a definite form in the reign of Stephen (1135–54)† it is not a little remarkable that Richard I. is the first English king who is known to have adopted an heraldic bearing.   On his great seal (1189) he bore the two lyons for the Duchies of Normandy and of Poictou or Maine.   In his second great seal (1198)‡ he added a third lyon for the Duchy of Aquitaine, or, as some say, for Anjou; this has since been our national arms of dominion ; according to Sir Henry Spelman ("Aspilogia," page 67), the earlier kings of England had marks and tokens painted on their shields, which they altered at pleasure.   In this connection it would be interesting to know on what authority, if any, Brooke, York Herald, described the Dering Roll as " the names and armes of those Knightes as weare wᵗ Kinge Richard the firste at the assigge of Acon or Acres," 1191 (Ashmole MS. 1120).

Early instances of these symbols or badges are generally found on standards or banners, and it is worthy of note that in the Crusade of (2 and 3 R. I.) 1191, Richard "had a standard of yᵉ Dragon which he delivered to Peter de Preaus to beare notwithstanding yᵗ Robert Trusbut chalenged yᵉ carrying thereof as his hereditary right " (Ro. Hoveden, fo. 397, *n*. 10).

" These symbols or badges were not only borne on shields, but were also paynted on silken surcotes worne over their shirts of mail " (and also upon the caparisons of their horses).   See the Arundel or Military Roll and seals.   " But these surcotes of silke, being at firste made wide and girt close to them at ye waist, did, by reason of their pleates, oftimes confound the marks paynted on them, which being discerned they were afterwards made straight and plaine, so that ye same marks which stood eminently to be seen on the shield was also as visible on the surcote both before and behind, and being thus depicted on them gave ye first occasion of calling them cotes of armes " (Stowe MS. 662, fo. 16).

Does not this defect of the early "pleates" supply a clue to the origin of many of the variations in Heraldry ?   The appearance of a plain fess or a plain bend on a standard would vary, according to the point of view or the strength of the breeze, from different directions ; it might suggest, even if it did not appear as, undée, wavy, or dancettée ; add to this the proclivities of each arms painter, or the momentary illusion of, say, an engréle for a lozenge, fusil, dancet, indent, and even a mascle, and their evolution therefrom may be readily accounted for.   In Cole's copy of the Parliamentary Roll occurs the ominous note of warning, " Take Hede of his wordes endented and engrayled, and examine such cotes with older Presydents."   Nor must we omit to mention the

---

* See also *Antiquities of Heraldry*, by W. Smith Ellis, and "Heraldry, its Laws and its Humours," by Jane MacNeal, *Munsey's Magazine*, September 1901.
† *Geoffrey Mandeville*, by J. H. Round, Appendix A, pp. 388–396.
‡ Richard the First's change of Seal, see *Feudal England*, by J. H. Round, page 545.

cross moline, patonce, patée and flory, which are often confused, or imperfectly drawn, by the Herald-painter. So with the cross moline, cercellé and recercellé, which are equally confounded in blason and in trick ; even crosses crosslet are often drawn as crosses botonnée in early tricks, probably because it was easier so to do. In a less degree the bend, bendlet or baston, the quarter and the canton, fret and fretty, flory and florettée, often represent the caprice or indifference of the Herald or the Herald-painter of each particular roll. So, too, whether a mullet had 5 or 6 points, pierced or not, whether a label had 3 or 5 pendants ; and yet the theory has gone forth that the label of three denotes a son, and that a label of five denotes a grandson.

Perhaps a more interesting feature of these early Rolls is the quaint Norman-French blason ; I specially except such illiterate jargon as obtained under the Gartership of the two Dethicks, and of some succeeding kings-of-arms. The rising generation of Heraldic editors, whether of a Family Armorial or of a County History, hardly seem to justify the " out-of-the-mouths-of-babes-and-sucklings " theory by their eagerness to adopt in lieu of universally recognized formulæ the A-B-C of the " Accedens of Armoury." With equal intelligence might they rehabilitate the author of " Little Jack Horner," and present him to their admirers as the superior of Rudyard Kipling.* But, to be serious, who will solve the blasons of Berkeley and Cromwell in the Boroughbridge Roll or reconcile the "wyfers" (wiure, or, viure), which occur not only in the arms of Benhale and of Crek, but also in the arms of Sir Edmond de Mauley ; for Meyrick, in the " Archæologia," vol. xxxi. page 247, unable to resist a thrust at the expense of the Heralds and their College, supposes the "wyfers" to be vipers' nests ! evidently by confusing viure with guiuré. " Tertoleres " in Criel, " voyderis anabeles " in Dolerd, " p'my " in Constable, Dacre and Raynsford, "amptie " in Wellesby, or the " temoyles," " feuilles," " mailles," &c., of Bosville, are also curiosities in their way and worth consideration. The " undée en lung" of the Boroughbridge Roll and " ounde de longe " of Jenyns' Roll seem to have bifurcated and become sometimes palets nebulée, and at others the modern emasculate wavy, in lieu of the bold undulating lines of the old tricks. In this connection the blason of Theobald de Valoines suggests further complications. The " chevron et demi," of Strecche— " une barre et demi " of Twyford, and " une fees et demi " of Pipard, suggest the accommodation of the size of a repetition of charges to artistic effect, 2 chevrons or 2 bars to be equal to $1\frac{1}{2}$.

An early instance of a quarterly coat occurs in the Falkirk Roll, 1298 ; the coat of Sir Simon de Montagu quartered with Monthermer, which may be considered coeval with the oft-quoted coat of Castile quartered with Leon, borne by Eleanor, Queen of Edward i., who died in 1296.

The last point to which I will here refer is the ancient practice of adopting the arms, though not the name, of an heiress, and with the further object of drawing attention to this interesting point I append the few instances that occur to me of old families who do not bear the arms of their original paternal family :

Abney assumed Ingwardby ; disallowed to Lord Mayor Abney (1701), Harl. MS. 6179, fo. 66.
Congreve assumed Campion.

Coles assumed Knightley.
Croke assumed Blount.
(Croke claimed male descent from Blount.)
Fleming assumed Hudleston.

* See " Archæological Nomenclature," *Literature*, Nos. 194, 5, 6, July 6, 13, 20 (1901).

Harpur (Bart.) assumed Rushall.	Prideaux assumed Orcharton.
Hesketh (Bart.) assumed Fytton.	Stanley (E. Derby) assumed Bamville.
Leigh assumed Lymme.	Wallop (E. Portsmouth) assumed Barton.
Lumley (E. Scarborough) assumed Thwenge.	Wrottesley (E.) assumed Basset.

Contemporary with the early Rolls of Arms are the Seals of the Barons who signed and sealed the famous letter to the Pope (12 Feb. 1300–1) on his pretensions to the crown of Scotland. These hundred seals present the earliest and most authentic evidence of the armorials used by the Barons of England in the fourteenth century, or perhaps in the thirteenth century. From the plaster casts in the British Museum it would seem as if many of the seals had been engraved by the same man for the very purpose of this sealing; that used by John de Hastings, lord de Bergavenny, is supposed to be hypothetical, or perhaps a very early example of the fictitious in Heraldry; that of Brian FitzAlan is not heraldic, and that of John de Botetourt is of the nature of a badge or heraldic emblem, while Edmond de Hastings evidently adopted for the occasion the territorial or baronial arms (?) of Drummond, encircling them with a Hastings legend. The majority of the shields are of the triangular or heater shape. William Paynell affords the earliest example of arms on a lozenge, and Robert FitzPayne bore his arms on an oval shield. On fourteen seals, those to whom they belonged are represented on horseback in complete armour, but only three of them—namely, Thomas Plantagenet, Earl of Lancaster; Ralph de Monthermer, Earl of Gloucester and Hertford; and John de St. John—are represented as bearing crests on their helmets. The first named was of the blood royal; the second married Joan, the King's daughter, widow of Gilbert de Clare, Earl of Gloucester, &c; the last named, John de St. John, had distinguished himself in the wars of Gascony, France, and Scotland, and was therefore in high military repute. From this fact it is supposed that the bearing of a crest on a helmet was originally limited to those connected with the blood royal, or of the highest military renown, and was in effect the precursor of a much greater honour, eventuating in the Order of the Garter itself. See the " Archæologia."

" These great commanders in the wars in France and Scotland, who held of the King *in capite*, had numerous tenants who served under them, and, for the regular marshalling of their marks and badges, had each a peculiar Herald to ascertain that each (tenant) had a full and clear distinction from the other. These heralds had their titles either from some of the great seigniories belonging to the crown or from those unto whom they were retained." See also the "Complete Peerage," by G. E. C., vol. ii. p. 270, note *b*.

Notwithstanding these precautions some heraldic improprieties seem to have occurred subsequent to the battle of Agincourt, for in 5 Hen. v. it was proclaimed that " all such who had taken ye liberty of wearing cotes of armes in any former expedition where neither they nor their ancestors had ever used any were thenceforth prohibited yᵉ farther enjoyment of them unless they could produce a title thereto by Grant from some person who had authority for that purpose, excepting those only who had been with that warlike King in battell of Agincourt (1415), did then bear them in that memorable service." Close Roll 5 H. v. (1417), *in dorso* m. 15.

CONTENTS.

CHART PEDIGREES.

(? WILLIAM) BEVILL AND WIFE.
In the Church of Walton, Hunts. 3 *H.* 7, 1487.

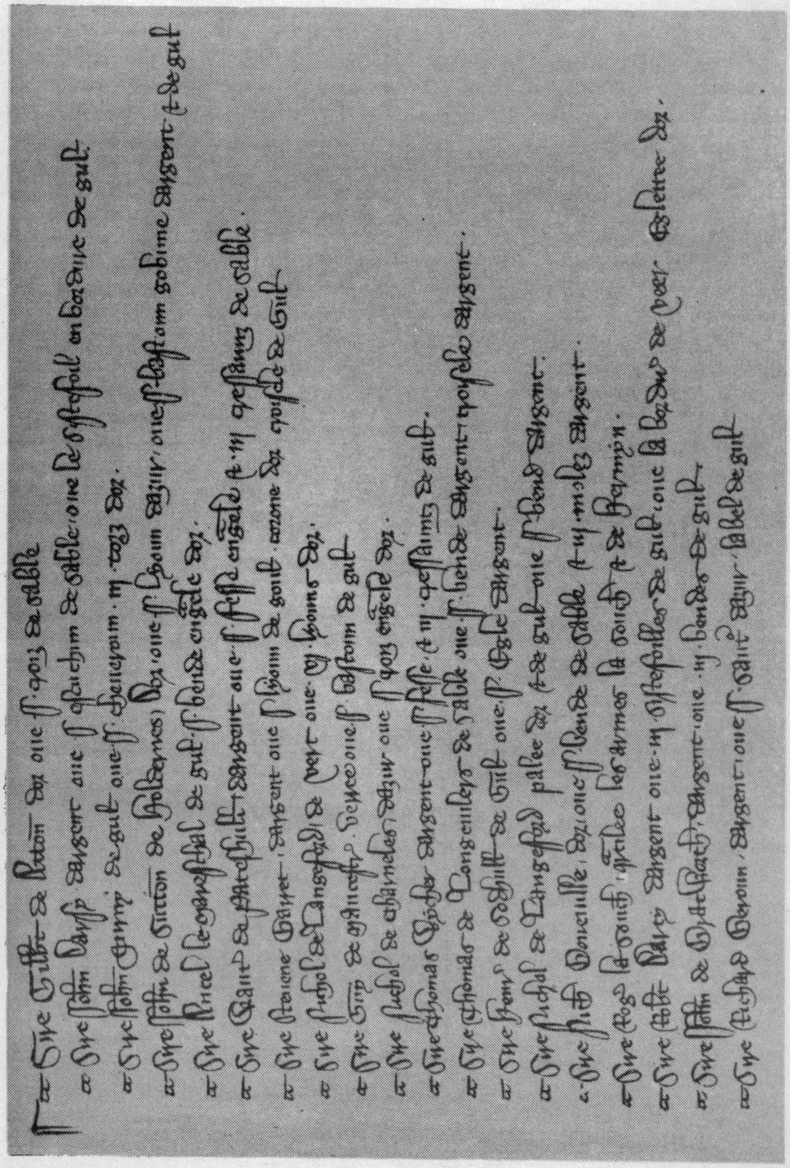

Facsimile of a Tracing from the Boroughbridge Roll 1322.

Facsimile of a Tracing from the Camden Roll temp E. I.

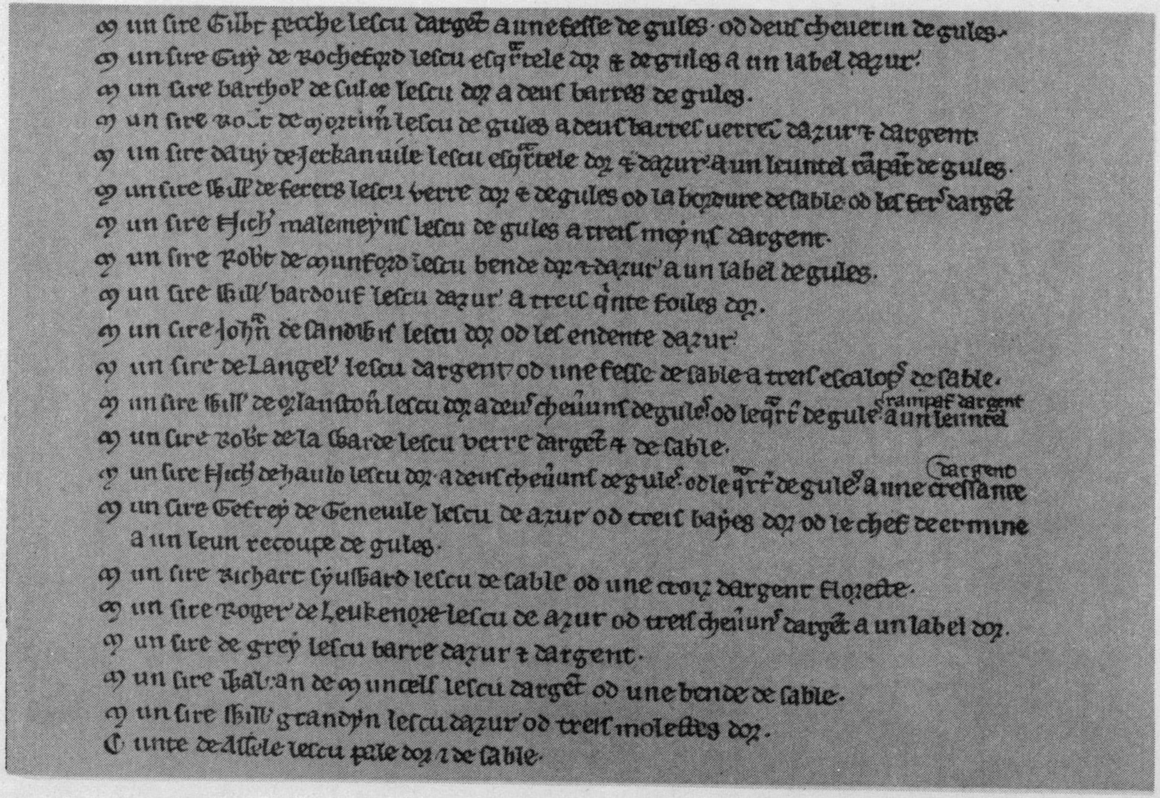
M un sire Gilbt pecche lescu darget a une fesse de gules · od deus cheuerun de gules.
M un sire Guy de Rochefford lescu esqrtele dor & de gules a un label dazur.
M un sire barthol de sulee lescu dor a deus barres de gules.
M un sire Robt de mortim lescu de gules a deus barres verrez dazur & dargent.
M un sire dauy de Jerkanuile lescu esqrtele dor & dazur a un leuntel rampant de gules.
M un sire Will de ferers lescu verre dor & de gules od la bordure de sable od les fers dargent
M un sire Hich malemeyns lescu de gules a treis meyns dargent.
M un sire Robt de munford lescu bende dor & dazur a un label de gules.
M un sire Will bardouf lescu dazur a treis qnte foiles dor.
M un sire John de sandwich lescu dor od les endente dazur.
M un sire de Langel lescu dargent od une fesse de sable a treis escalops de sable.
M un sire Will de glanston lescu dor a deus cheuruns de gules od le qrtr de gules a un leuntel rampant dargent
M un sire Robt de la Warde lescu verre darget & de sable.
M un sire Hich de haulo lescu dor a deus cheuruns de gules od le qrtr de gules a une cressante dargent
M un sire Gefrey de Geneuile lescu de azur od treis bayes dor od le chef de ermine a un leun recoupe de gules.
M un sire Richart Gyulsard lescu de sable od une croiz dargent florette.
M un sire Roger de Leukenore lescu de azur od treis cheuruns darget a un label dor.
M un sire de grey lescu barre dazur & dargent.
M un sire Walran de Muncels lescu darget od une bende de sable.
M un sire Will grandyn lescu dazur od treis molettes dor.
C unte de Alsele lescu pale dor & de sable.

ROLLS OF ARMS

INCORPORATED IN THIS VOLUME,

With references to British Museum Manuscripts, in which they are either tricked or blasoned, and to printed works in which they have already been printed; based on the lists given in the " Genealogist," Volume V.

The maladroit naming, by former editors, of many of these Rolls has led me to substitute Arden, Arundel, Ashmole, Howard, Norfolk and Surrey, for such names as Charles, Military, Planché, Powell, Walford and Willement—my regret is in not having carried substitution still further.

T = *trick.*   (B) = *blason.*   (C) = *coloured.*

Manuscripts	Printed Books
Arden (late *Charles*), H. III.	
H. 6137, ff. 45 (10)-57 (15). T.	1. *Archæologia* (1863), xxxix. 399.
Add. 4965, ff. 10 (1)-25 (5). T.	2. G. J. Armytage (1869) !
Arundel (late *Military*), H. VI.	
H. 4205, ff. 9-40ᵇ, in colours.	
Ashmole (late *Powell*), E. III.	
Ashmole 804, in colours on vellum.	
Add. 26,677, in colours.	
Atkinson, H. VI.	
H. 1408, ff. 105-109 (B).	*Genealogist* (1876), i. 226.
Cott. Cleop. C. III. ff. 201ᵇ, 202 (B).	
Ballard, E. IV.	
H. 2076, ff. 78ᵇ-82. T.	
Boroughbridge, E. III.	1. Parliamentary Writs (1830), ii. Appendix
A. W. Williams-Wynn (B).	196, by Sir F. T. Palgrave.
Ashmole 831, ff. 100-106ᵇ. T.	2. *Genealogist*, N.S., vols. i and ii.
Calais, E. III.	
H. 246, ff. 6ᵇ-14ᵇ. T.	
H. 3968, ff. 112-127. T.	
H. 6589, ff. 51ᵇ (B).	Rowe Mores, Oxford (1749), 4to.
H. 6595, ff. 1-15ᵇ, colours.	
Cott. Tib. E. IX., ff. 81, 89. T and (B).	
Ashmole 1120, ff. 150ᵇ-162ᵇ. T.	
Calais (knighted there), E. III.	
H. 1068, ff. 156-163ᵇ, 183 (B).	*Notes and Queries*, 23 Oct. and 13 Nov., 1875
H. 1156, ff. 82-83 (B).	
H. 6589, f. 11 (B).	
Calais (slain there), E. III.	
Add. 29,502, fragment, colours on vellum.	
Camden, E. I.	
Cotton Roll, xv.-8 (B).	*Genealogist* (1879), iii. 216, 260.
H. 6137, ff. 66ᵇ (1), 72ᵇ (13). T.	

Manuscripts	Printed Books

Carlaverock, E. I.
  H. 1068, ff. 1–6 (B).
  H. 1408, ff. 142–143ᵇ (B).
  H. 2213, ff. 28–29ᵇ. T and (B).
  H. 4033, ff. 58–60, coloured and (B).
  H. 4270, ff. 28–30ᵇ. T and unnamed.
  H. 6137, ff. 37ᵇ (6)–40 (12). T.
  H. 6589, ff. 13ᵇ, 50, 51 (ʀ).
  Cotton, Calig. A. xviii., ff. 23ᵇ, 30ᵇ (B).
    "The Poem."
  Lansd. 209, ff. 257–271. T.
  Add. 5848, pp. 155–159ᵇ (c).

Sir Harris Nicolas, London (1828), 4to. &c., &c.

Charles (here called *Arden*).

Cotgrave, might be described as a spurious version of *Jenyns' Ordinary*, with which it can, however, be easily corrected.

Dering, H. III.
  Harl. 6137, ff. 89ᵇ (13)–97ᵇ (16). T.
  H. 6589, ff. 52–53, fragment. T.
  Lansd. 260, ff. 216–220 (B). "Mr. Knyvett's."
  Ashmole 1120, ff. 171ᵇ–174. T.

The Reliquary, 1876–8, xvi. 135, 237; xvii. 11, 209; xviii. 23, 89, 171.

Dunstable (1), E. II.
  H. 1068, ff. 6ᵇ–18 (B)
  H. 1408, ff. 141, 141ᵇ, 144–147ᵇ (B)
  H. 2213, ff. 24–27ᵇ.
  H. 4033, ff. 53–57, coloured and (B)
  H. 4270, ff. 24–28. T, unnamed.
  H. 6137, ff. 31ᵇ (3)–37ᵇ (4). T.
  H. 6148, ff. 144ᵇ–149.
  H. 6589, ff. 8ᵇ, 41–43ᵇ (B).
  Add. 5848, ff. 145–154 (c).

"Collectanea Topographica" (1837), iv. 61.

Dunstable (2), E. III.
  H. 6589, ff. 49–49ᵇ, fragment (B).
  Cott. Otho. D.4 xxx., ff. 187–192ᵇ (B).
  Lansd. 860 A., ff. 11 and 11ᵇ, fragment (B).
  Sloane 1301, ff. 257–261ᵇ (B).

"Collectanea Topographica" (1837), iv. 389.

Falkirk, E. I.
  H. 6589, ff. 9, 9ᵇ (B).

Reliquary (1875), xv. 27, 68.
Gough, H. (1888), London, 4to.

Glover, H. III.
  H. 6589, f. 11ᵇ (B).
  Add. 29,796, *part*, colours on vellum.

1. Sir Harris Nicolas, London (1829), 8vo.
2. G. J. Armytage (June 1869)!

Grimaldi, E. III.
  Stacy Grimaldi, colours on vellum.

"Collectanea Topographica et Genealogica" (1834), ii. 320.

Guillim, E. I.
  H. 6137, ff. 57 (19)–61 (4). T.
  H. 6589, ff. 44, 45. T.

Genealogist (1877), i. 325, 355.

Harleian, E. I. or II.
  H. 337, ff. 12–31, in colours on vellum.

Genealogist, N.S., iii. 37, 118.

Holland, E. I. or II.
  H. 1068, ff. 22·24 (B).
  H. 2213, ff. 29ᵇ–30 (ʀ).
  H. 4033, ff. 60ᵇ–61, coloured and (B).
  H. 4270, ff. 30ᵇ–31ᵇ. T, unnamed.
  H. 6137, ff. 40 (14)–41 (20). T.
  Add. 5848, ff. 159–161 (c).

Howard (late *Planché*).
  H. 1068, ff. 156–183 (B).

Genealogist, N.S., iii., iv., v.

Manuscripts   **Printed Books**

Jenyns'—   Ordinary. | *Roll—Jenyns'.*
H. 872 (B). | (B).
H. 1068, ff. 79–136ʰ | ff. 136ʰ–155ʰ (B).
(B). |
H. 1577. T. | T.
H. 6589, ff. 21ʰ-34ʰ | ff. 37–40, 48–48ʰ
(B). | (B).
Add. 12,224, ff. 1– | ff. 39–51. T.
39. T. |
Cott. Tib. E. ix., ff. | ff. 133–138, 251,
236-251 (B). | 251ʰ (B).

Jenyns' Ordinary.—A corrupt copy of this Ordinary was made by Hugh Cotgrave (Richmond Herald, 1566–1585), and unfortunately edited by Sir Harris Nicolas, London (1829).
Jenyns' Roll.—*Antiquary* (1880), i. 205 ; ii. 97, 238.

Military Roll (here called *Arundel*).

Nativity Roll, E. I.
H. 6589, f. 10 (B).

Reliquary Roll (1875), xv. 228.

Nobility Rolls, E. I. and II.
I. to V., Mr. Hovenden's Collection. T.
VI. *Nob.* Add. 29,505, colours on vellum.

Notes and Queries.

Norfolk (late *Walford*), H. III.
H. 6589, ff. 12, 12ʰ (B).

Archæologia (1863), xxxix. 380.

Parliamentary, E. II.
H. 1068, ff. 18–22 and ff. 25, 78 (B).
H. 1386, ff. 38–82ʰ. T.
H. 2106, ff. 95–104 (B).
H. 2116, ff. 23–57, colours.
H. 2210, ff. 81–107ʰ. T.
H. 2213, ff. 1–23ʰ (B).
H. 4033, ff. 30–52, colours and (B).
H. 4270, ff. 1–23. T, unnamed.
H. 5803, ff. 272–283 (B).
H. 6137, ff. 1–31ʰ (2). T.
H. 6589, ff. 1–8 (B).
Cott. Calig. A. xviii. 3–21ʰ (B).
Lansd. 855 (B).
Add. 5848, pp. 100–144 (c).

1. Rowe Mores (1749).
2. *Antiquarian Repertory* (1780), iii. 86 ;
3.   ,,   2nd ed. (1807), vol. i., p. 81.
4. Parliamentary Writs (1827), i. 410, ed. by Sir F. T. Palgrave.
5. Sir H. Nicolas, London (1828), 8vo.
6. *Genealogist*, 2nd S., vols. xi., xii.

Planché (here called *Howard*).

Powell (here called *Ashmole*).

Rouen, H. v.
H. 1386, ff. 84ʰ (1)–86 (12). T.
H. 6137, ff. 41ʰ (2)–44 (11). T.
Ashmole 1120, ff. 175, 176. T.

Notes and Queries, 11 Dec., 1880 ; 22 Jan., 1881.

St. George, H. III.
H. 246, ff. 22ʰ (1)–43ʰ (5). T.
H. 6137, ff. 73 (16), 89ʰ (10). T.
H. 6589, ff. 15–20. T.

Archæologia (1863), xxxix. 418.

Segar, E. I.
H. 6137 ff. 61 (6)–66 (17). T.

Genealogist (1880), iv. 50, 90.

Surrey (late *Willement*), R. II.
Newling Collection.

Willement, London (1829), folio.

Walford (here called *Norfolk*).

Willement (here called *Surrey*).

A further account of Rolls of Arms occurs in the "English Cyclopædia," Arts and Sciences Supplement, page 1267, "Heraldic Literature," by Dr. de Gray Birch. British Museum Reading Room, shelf 2106 E.

ILLUSTRATIONS.

ANCIENNE NOBLESSE.

SOME FAMILIES WHOSE ANCESTORS APPEAR ON THE HERALDIC ROLLS IN THIS WORK.

Bedfordshire—
St. John.

Buckinghamshire—
Harcourt.

Cheshire—
Baskerville.
Davenport.

Cornwall—
Molesworth.
Prideaux.

Cumberland—
Pennington.
Musgrave.
Huddleston.

Derbyshire—
Gresley.
Curzon.
Vernon.
Burdett.
Cave.
Colvile.
Menill.

Devonshire—
Courtenay.
Carew.
Pole.
Champernown (*née* Harington).
Acland.
Bellew.
Clifford.
Upton.

Dorset—
Digby.

Durham—
Lumley.
Salvin.

Essex—
Waldegrave.

Gloucestershire—
Berkeley.
Trye.

Hants—
Wallop.
Cope.

Huntingdon—
Thornhill.

Kent—
Neville.
Dering.
Toke.

Lancashire—
Stanley.
Molyneux.
Hoghton.
Radcliffe.
Clifton.
Chadwick.
Trafford.

Leicestershire—
Turvile.
Beaumont.
De Grey.
Babington.

Lincolnshire—
Alington.
Dymoke.

Norfolk—
Howard.
Astley.
Bedingfeld.

Northamptonshire—
Wake.

Northumberland—
Grey.
Haggerstone.
Ogle.
Swinburne.
Middleton.
Selby.

Notts—
Willoughby.
Clinton.

Oxfordshire—
Stonor.
Blount.
Annesley.
Villiers.

Rutland—
Manners.
Harington.
Wingfield.

Salop—
Corbet.
Cornewall.
Lingen.
Manwaring.
Sandford.
Tyrwhit.

Staffordshire—
Wrottesley.
Arden.
Okeover.
Bagot.
Broughton.

Suffolk—
Hervey.
Bernay.

Sussex—
Ashburnham.
Pelham.

Warwickshire—
Shirley.
Bracebridge.
Chetwynd.
Stanton.

Westmorland—
Lowther.
Strickland.
Fleming.

Worcestershire—
Talbot.
Winnington.

Yorkshire—
Fitzwilliam.
Scrope.
Stapleton.
Stourton.
Grimston.
Hamerton.
Hotham.
Tempest.
Boynton.
Waterton.
Rokeby.
Savile.
Meynell.
Saltmarshe.
Worsley.
Wyvill.

"SOME FEUDAL COATS OF ARMS."

By JOSEPH FOSTER, Hon. M.A., OXON. Royal 4to. PRICE 3 GUINEAS nett.—8vo. Edition, 12s. 6d. nett.

NOTICES OF THE PRESS.

The Times.—"Mr. Joseph Foster has given us for the Middle Ages a work of reference, the usefulness of which no one will deny."

Spectator.—"Labour so disinterestedly undertaken deserves a substantial reward, and we hope that the titled and untitled nobles of the United Kingdom will take care that Mr. Foster does not miss it."

Literature. "It has a distinct value for students of both heraldry and genealogy."

Saturday Review.—"We welcome *Some Feudal Coats of Arms* as a work of art."

Academy.—"This latest stone of the monument which the indefatigable Mr. Foster is building to his own heraldic fame is as prodigal of record as an Assyrian brick."

Notes and Queries.—"His work has profound interest for all who indulge in the study of heraldry."

Vanity Fair.—"The Bayeux Tapestry supplies a quaint running accompaniment all through the pomp of the pages, where shields and seals and effigies, curious and beautiful, make glad the heart and the eyes of the student."

The Speaker.—"A work which tends to revive the fame of English heraldry . . . the great atchievements are magnificently rendered."

The Guardian.—"We wish it to be distinctly understood that this is a good book. Mr. Foster has produced a work of real interest and of permanent value."

Annual Register.—"*Some Feudal Coats of Arms* is a work of marvellous industry and erudition."

The Standard.—"Mr. Joseph Foster has compiled a volume of singular value to the student, as well as of great artistic charm. . . . It would be difficult to praise too highly the skill, care, and artistic taste with which the book has been prepared."

The World.—"So far as we are able to form an opinion of the work, it is one of conspicuous merit as regards both design and execution."

Morning Post.—"With rare enthusiasm for an ancient art, Mr. Foster has been at much pains to investigate the old heraldic Rolls. . . . As a work of reference for those interested in genealogical inquiry or heraldic study, the uses of the book are obvious."

Daily Chronicle.—"Altogether it is a very remarkable work."

The Daily News.—"Mr. Foster gives us an admirably compiled and profusely illustrated work."

The Record.—"We can imagine no more interesting volume. . . . Mr. Foster's patience and care as an investigator and chronicler are familiar to all who work in his fields, and his devotion deserves the warmest recognition."

Pall Mall Gazette.—"Some fine full page examples of many quartered atchievements."

The Westminster Gazette.—"Mr. Foster may claim to have produced with infinite care and loving pains a most admirable and attractive book."

Tatler.—"Mr. Foster has been a very laborious worker in the field of Genealogy, for it is over forty years since his first genealogical work appeared."

The Field.—"The coats of arms, the copies of the different brasses and the seals, are as beautiful as art can make them, and the author is to be complimented on having produced so magnificent a work."

Journal of the British Archæological Association.—"Mr. Foster has not stinted anything, and the result is a reliable book."

The Irish Times.—"A monument of research. Splendidly reproduced facsimiles of early armorial seals."

The Observer.—"A handsome volume, full of interest for students of heraldry."

The Scotsman.—"Turning to his book, we may say that it is in many respects delightful and admirable."

APPRECIATIVE COMMENTS BY SUBSCRIBERS.

Your handsome volume *Feudal Arms* is richly illustrated, and I am glad to see our effigies and brasses so well utilised . . . the facsimile tricking of Arms from Rolls, Visitations, &c., is an immense advance on the ordinary heraldic books, and most valuable for the correct representation of charges. It must have been a heavy labour to collect so much original work.—DILLON (*Viscount*), President Society of Antiquaries.

. . . A most beautiful volume that I would have paid any price for ten years ago—nothing can be more valuable and helpful than your collection of early and sound work.—P. L.

I have since been enjoying this very beautiful and most useful volume, for which all who care for armoury should owe you a debt of gratitude.—F. P. BARNARD.

I cannot refrain from letting you know how exceedingly I admire your *Feudal Coats of Arms*, both in the manner in which the work is produced, and from the evidence of great and careful research which must have been made.—W. D.

I opened *Feudal Arms* as soon as it came, with the intention of only just giving a glance at its contents until I had more time to examine it, but spent two hours before I realised how time was passing.—T. F.

The volume is handsome in its get up, but more than that, the contents are of extreme interest, and the book is much appreciated here.—D. H. CRUSE (*Librarian*), The Leeds Library.

Your learned book, *Feudal Coats of Arms*, safely to hand.—ARUNDELL OF WARDOUR (*Baron*).

Your beautiful book.—THE PRESIDENT OF QUEEN'S COLLEGE, OXFORD.

I must write you a line to say how delighted I am with my *Some Feudal Coats of Arms*. It is really a splendid book, and what it means in research is beyond one's comprehension.—G. R. PRIDEAUX-BRUNE.

I have seen nothing to equal your *Feudal Coats of Arms.*—C. B. LYSTER.

The book has come, and I like it very much, I think it a wonderful performance.—WINCHILSEA (*Earl*).

I have been examining your work, and the more I look into it the more I wonder at your great industry, and the book is charming. The illustrations are far beyond anything I expected ; it promises me a great deal of pleasure.—C. E. HAIG.

A most charming book, and we are all (even Dorothy, aged seven) in love with it already.—S. STAKES.

Feudal Arms arrived safely, and I beg to offer you my congratulations on the magnificent work you have produced. All students of heraldry owe you a deep debt of gratitude. It is difficult to imagine how one pair of hands could have accomplished so much, and it speaks volumes both for the marvellous industry and for the brain which guided them.—L. GERALD DILLON.

The facsimile reproduction from the Boroughbridge Roll, and indeed all the other plates in the book, seem to me admirably executed.—A. W. WILLIAMS-WYNN.

Your *magnum opus* has come, and promises many a happy hour for me ; also, I hope, a delight to many others in the days to come—(Rev.) E. G. PUNCHARD.

It is a grand book.—(Sir) R. P. EDGCUMBE.

Your last fascinating book.—J. L. LAMBE.

MR. FOSTER'S
PRINCIPAL PUBLISHED WORKS,
1862-1902.

1. SOME FEUDAL COATS OF ARMS (and some Chart Pedigrees), Illustrated with 2,000 Zinco Etchings from the Bayeux Tapestry, Greek Vases, Seals, Tiles, Effigies, and Brasses. 4to., price 3 guineas nett. See notices of the Press, on opposite page.

2. SOME FEUDAL COATS OF ARMS, Illustrated with upwards of 830 Coats of Arms and 47 Effigies and Brasses. 8vo. price 12s. 6d. nett.

3. ALUMNI OXONIENSES. Eight Vols. 1500–1886. See Sonnenschein's "The Best Books."

4. OXFORD MEN AND THEIR COLLEGES. Two Vols. 1880-92. See Sonnenschein's "The Best Books."

5. THE BRITISH PEERAGE AND BARONETAGE, including "Chaos." Two Vol. 1880-1-2-3.

6. OUR NOBLE AND GENTLE FAMILIES of Royal Descent. Two Vols.

7. NOBLE AND GENTLE FAMILIES entitled to Quarter Royal Arms. Folio.

8. LANCASHIRE COUNTY FAMILIES. One Vol.

9. YORKSHIRE COUNTY FAMILIES. Three Vols.

10. COLLECTANEA GENEALOGICA. Two Vols.

11. MEN AT THE BAR. 1885.

12. SCOTS M.P.'S. 1357–1882.

13. LONDON MARRIAGE LICENCES. 1521–1869.

14. GRAY'S INN ADMISSION REGISTER. 1521–1889.

15. INDEX ECCLESIASTICUS. 1800-1840.

Heralds' Visitations.

16. YORKSHIRE. 1584-5, 1612.
17. DURHAM. 1575, 1615, 1666.
18. MIDDLESEX. 1663.

19. CUMBERLAND. 1615, 1666.
20. WESTMORLAND. 1615, 1666.
21. NORTHUMBERLAND. 1615, 1666.

Noble and Gentle Families.

22. PENNINGTONIANA.

Family Genealogies.

23. WILSON of High Wray.
24. FOX of Devon and Cornwall.
25. HARRIS of Fordingbridge.

26. PEASE of Darlington.
27. BACKHOUSE of Darlington.
28. FOSTER of Cold Hesledon (1862).

THE KING OF ARMS, an Illustrated Quarterly for the Herald and Genealogist. Devoted to Archæology, Heraldry, and Genealogy. Each of these subjects to be under the editorship of experienced students. Literary contributions are invited. Part 1, January, 1903. 21 Boundary Road, N.W.

SIR WILLIAM DE ALDEBURGH, c. 1360.   33 Ed. III.

Aldborough Church, Yorkshire.

After Stothard.

SOME FEUDAL ARMS

F = Facsimile in this edition, or in the original work, 4to.

† = *took up the Cross, i.e., a Crusader* 1270.   ‡ *Dering Roll, see Preface, page* ix.

* = *probable ancestors of extant Noble and Gentle Families of the name.*

Abbehall, Sir (——) de (ABENHALL), of Gloucestershire – (E. II. Roll) bore, or, a fess gules ; Parliamentary Roll.

Abberbury, Richard—(R. II. Roll) bore, or, a fess crenellée ("embattled on the top") sable ; Surrey Roll. See ADDERBURY.

Abbetot, see D'ABBETOT.

Abell, Sir John, of Kent – (E. II. Roll) bore, argent, a saltire engrailed azure ; Parly. Roll.

Abell, John (ABLE) - (E. III. Roll) bore, sable, two bars or, in chief three torteaux (plates, in blason) ; Jenyns' Ordinary. F.

Abelyn, Nicholas (ABLYN) – (E. III. Roll) bore, gules, on a cross patonce argent five escallops azure ; Jenyns' Ordinary. F.

‡**Abelyne, Nicholas**—(H. III. Roll) bore, or, on a cross sable five eaglets argent , Dering Roll &c. F.

Abernoun *v.* **Dabernon.**

‡**Abingdon, Philip de**—(H. III. Roll) bore, argent, on a bend gules three eaglets or ; Dering Roll.

Aburgavenny, Le Sr. (BEAUCHAMP)— bore, at the siege of Rouen 1418, gules, crusily and a fess or, a crescent (sable) for difference.

Acclon, Henry—(E. III. Roll) bore, gules, a maunch between six cinquefoyles argent ; (blasoned, gules, a maunch ermine) ; Jenyns' Ordinary. F.

Achard *v.* **Archard.**

Achard, Piers - (E. III. Roll) bore, undée (barry wavy of ten) argent and gules. Jenyns' Roll : another, undée (6) and a label (3) azure ; Arden Roll, &c. F.

Acherton, William de – (R. II. Roll) bore, argent, two bendlets and a bordure sable ; Surrey Roll. See also ATHERTON.

▸**Ackland, John**—(R. II. Roll) bore, checquy argent and sable, a fess gules ; Surrey Roll. F.

Acton (——), an Essex Knight—(H. VI. Roll) bore, gyronny (12) argent and gules, *quarterly with*, gules, on a cross moline argent five escallops of the field ; Arundel Roll.

Acton, Sir John de (AKETON)— bore, at the battle of Boroughbridge 1322, quarterly indented azure and argent ; probably per fess indented is intended, as in the next.

Acton, Sir John de— bore, at the siege of Calais 1345-8, quarterly per fess indented argent and sable (*vel azure*) also ascribed to RICHARD ACTON in Surrey Roll R. II. F.

*[**Acton, Edward de,** of Aldenham, Salop, 1387—bore, gules, crusily or, two lyons passant in pale argent.—Shirley.] F.

[**Acton, Sir Roger,** of Sutton, 1410—bore, gules, a fess ermine within a bordure engrailed of the second. - Shirley.] F.

Acworth (——), a Suffolk Knight – (H. VI. Roll) bore, argent, a gryphon segreant per fess sable and azure ; Arundel Roll.

Adam, Sir John ap, baron 1299 – bore, at the battle of Falkirk 1298, argent, on a cross gules five mullets or ; (pierced vert, Jenyns' Ordinary). (F.) The name is often written Badham. He signed, but did not seal, the Barons' letter to the Pope 1301.

Adderbury, Sir John—slain at the siege of Calais 1347, bore, argent, a fess crenellée sable. See also ABBERBURY.

Aglionby, John—(E. II. Roll) bore, argent, two bars and in chief three martlets sable ; Jenyns' Ordinary.

‡**Aguillon, Robert** (AGILLUN, AGUILUN or AGULON) - (H. III. Roll) bore, gules, a fleur-de-lys argent. (F.) - WILLIAM (‡) bore it with an azure field ; Dering and Glover Rolls, &c.

de Akeny *v.* **Dakeny.**

Alanby, Thomas—(E. III. Roll) bore, argent, a chevron within a bordure engrailed azure ; Jenyns' Roll. F.

Albemarle, see also AUBEMARLE.

Albemarle, Earl of (H. III. Roll) bore, gules, a cross patonce vair ; Glover Roll, &c. F.

Albini *v.* **Daubeny,** and **de Albini.**

Aldam, Sir Francis, of Kent fil. John— (E. II. Roll) bore, azure, a pile or, Parliamentary Roll ; a sun in Harl. 4033 ; see ALDEHAM.

[**Aldeburgh, William de,** baron 1371-1386—bore, azure, a fess argent between three crosses crosslet or ; Nobility Roll.]

[**Aldeburgh, Sir William de,** of Aldeburgh, Yorkshire, 1360—bore, a fess dancettée from point to point, between three crosses crosslet (now called botonnée) an annulet for difference. See Monumental Brass.]

Aldefelde, Robert - (E. III. Roll) bore, gules, a lyon rampant argent debruised by a bend sable charged with three crosses crosslet fitchée argent ; Jenyns' Ordinary. F.

‡**Aldeham, Thomas de**—(H. III. Roll) bore, azure, a sun (16 rays) in his glory or ; Dering Roll.

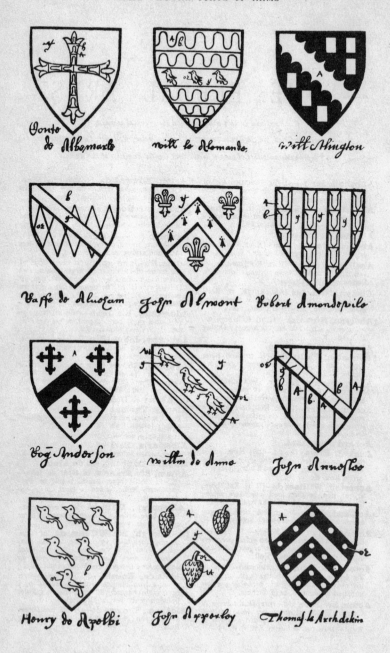

Conte de Albemarle   will le Alemand   Will Alington

Vasse de Alnetam   John Almont   Robert Amondevile

Roq Anderson   willm de Anne   John Annesleo

Henry de Apelbi   John Apperley   Thomas le Archdekin

Alderby, Sir Walter—(E. III. Roll) bore, gules, three bulls' heads cabossed argent, horned azure ; Ashmole Roll.

*[**Aldersey, Hugh de,** temp. H. III.—bore, gules, on a bend engrailed argent between two cinquefoyles or three leopards' faces vert—or more anciently, sable, three chargers or dishes argent. - Shirley.]

Alemande, William le—(H. III. Roll) bore, vair, on a fess gules three martlets or, Arden Roll ; the field, undée argent and azure, in St. George Roll. F.

Alexander (Count Allisander, doubtful if a surname) - (H. III. Roll) bore, barry (6) or and azure, a bordure gules ; Arden Roll.

Alneham, Raffe de—(E. III. Roll) bore, azure, five fusils in fess or, a bend gules ; Jenyns' Ordinary. F.

Alwent, John—(E. III. Roll) bore, gules, a chevron ermine between three fleurs-de-lys of the last ; Jenyns' Ordinary. F.

✦**Alyngton (——),** an Essex Knight - (H. VI. Roll) bore, sable, billettée and a bend engrailed argent ; Arundel Roll.

‡**Ambras, William** (AMBESAS) — (H. III. Roll) bore, or, three dice sable, each charged with an annulet argent, Howard Roll ; a plate in Dering Roll.

Amondevill, Robert—(E. III. Roll) bore, vair, three palets gules ; Jenyns' Ordinary. F.

Amyas, Drewe de (or AMYAS DE DREWE?) - (H. III. Roll) bore, gules, three palets sable (azure in trick) ; Howard Roll.

*[**Anderson, Roger,** of Wrawby, co. Linc. 14th cent.—bore, argent, a chevron between three crosses flory sable.—Shirley.] F.

Andrew, Sir John, of Suffolk—(H. VI. Roll) bore, argent, on a bend engrailed sable three mullets pierced of the field ; Arundel Roll.

Angelley, del—(rather DE LANGLEY) (E. I. Roll) bore, argent, a fess and in chief three escallops sable ; Camden Roll.

Anger, Sir Thomas (AWGER), of Kent - (H. VI. Roll) bore, ermine, on a chief azure three lyonceux rampant or ; Arundel Roll.

Angervile, Sir John de, of co. Leicr.— (E. II. Roll) bore, gules, a cinquefoyle ermine, within a bordure sable bezantée ; Parliamentary Roll. HUGH, took up the cross 1269.

Angevyn, Robert (AUNGEVYN) - (H. III. Roll) bore, gules, un florette (a fleur-de-lys) or ; Norfolk Roll.

Angus, Gilbert, Earl of—bore, at the battle of Falkirk 1298, gules, a cinquefoyle pierced or, within an orle of crosses crosslet of the last—more probably, crusily. See also UMFRAVILLE.

Anlaby, Halnath de—(R. II. Roll) bore, argent, a fess between six fleurs-de-lys sable ; Surrey Roll.

Ane or **Ano, Drew de** (ANO DE DREW or DREW DEANE - H. III. Roll) bore, gules, a saltire ermine ; Arden Roll.

Anno, Alysaunder de (? DEANE) - (H. III. Roll) bore, gules, frettée argent ; Howard Roll.

Anne, Sir William—(E. III. Roll) bore, or, three popinjays between two cotises sable ; Ashmole Roll. The arms borne by ANNE (of Burghwallis) were, gules, three bucks' heads cabossed argent.—Yorkshire Visitations, ed. FOSTER.

Anne, William de—(E. III. Roll) bore, gules, on a bend argent cotised or three popinjays vert beaked and legged gules ; Jenyns' Ordinary. F.

***Annesley, John de**—(R. II. Roll) bore, paly (6) argent and azure a bendlet gules, Jenyns' and Surrey Rolls, (F.)—with a bend vaire argent and sable in Cotgrave Roll E. III.—and paly (6) azure and argent a baston gobony or and gules, in Jenyns' Ordinary, E. III. &c. &c. F.

Antingham, —— (E. III. Roll) bore, sable, a bend argent ; Ashmole Roll.

Ap Adam v. **Adam.**

‡**Apeldrefeld, Henry de**—(H. III. Roll) bore, ermine, a bend gules ; HENRY LE FITZ (‡) bore the bend vaire or and gules. WILLIAM (‡) bore, or, a fess lozengy gules and vair ; Dering and Howard Rolls.

Apperley, John de—(E. III. Roll) bore, argent a chevron gules between three pine-apples vert, slipped or ; Jenyns' Ordinary. F.

Appelby, Sir Henry of Staffordshire—bore, at the first Dunstable tournament 1308, azure, six martlets or ; the same are ascribed to Sir WILLIAM (with a label of three), and to EDMUND in other Rolls. (F.) - 14 martlets to Sir EDMUND in Ashmole. See also JOHN LE MOINE.

Appleby, Sir Robert—bore, at the battle of Boroughbridge 1322, azure, the bordure of martlets or—tricked as 8 martlets in orle.

Applegarth, Robert—(E. III. Roll) bore, argent, three apples slipped gules ; Jenyns' Ordinary. F.

Apr(e)'sby, Christopher de—(R. II. Roll) bore, sable, a cross and in the first quarter a cinquefoyle pierced argent ; Surrey Roll.

Arcalowe, Sir William—bore, at the battle of Boroughbridge 1322, argent, three (bars) gemelles sable. F.

Arcas, Sir Alexander, of co. Leicr.— (E. II. Roll) bore, sable, three fleurs-de-lys argent ; Parly. Roll. HARCHAS in Harl. Roll.

Archard, Sir Robert of Berkshire—(E. II. Roll) bore, or, a bend engrailed sable ; Parliamentary Roll.

Archat, Sir Richard—(E. I. Roll bore, argent, on a bend cotised gules three fleurs-de-lys or, a bordure of the second ; Nativity Roll.

Archedeckne, John, baron 1343—bore, at the second Dunstable tournament 1334, argent three chevronels sable ; the same is ascribed (1) to ADAM (‡) in the Howard and Dering Rolls, and (2) to Sir THOMAS of Cornwall (in the Parly. Roll) GEFFREY, differenced with a label (5) gules, Arden and St. George Rolls.

Archedekin, Thomas—(H. III. Roll) bore, argent, three chevronels sable bezantée ; Glover Roll. F.

Archer, Nicol le—(H. III. Roll) bore, sable, a lyon rampant or ; St. George Roll. F.

John de Argentine   will Arcgob   Gilo's Argentom

John de Ardern   Wablin   Ago. Artchur
                      de Ardern

Jamis de Arbogo   Voim̄ de Arundel   Appnab Asdalo

Barth   Vobt de Asheton   Adam
Asheburnham   Asheurst

Arches, Alexander de—slain at the siege of Calais 1347, bore, gules, three arches argent.

Arches, William—bore, at the siege of Rouen 1418, gules, three double arches argent. F.

*****Arden, Sir Thomas** and **Sir Robert** (ARDERNE) of Warwickshire—(E. II. Roll) bore, ermine, a fess compony or and azure; Parliamentary and other Rolls. In Jenyns' Ordinary, E. III., a fess "Garen" (*i.e.*, Warren) is tricked chequy for John. F.

†**Arderne, Sir John**, of Salop—bore, at the first Dunstable tournament 1308, gules, crusily and a chief or; (F.) Another Sir JOHN—bore, at the siege of Calais 1345-8, gules, crusily fitchée and a chief or (F.), which is also ascribed to HUGH in Jenyns' Ordinary and to WILLIAM with crest in Ballard Roll temp. E. IV.

Arderne, Rauf de—(H. III. Roll) bore, ermine, on a fess gules three lozenges or; Arden Roll. F.

†**Arderne, Randulph de**—(H. III. Roll) bore, or, crusily a lyon rampant sable; Arden Roll. F.

Arderne, Wakeline de—(E. III. Roll) bore, or, a lyon rampant vert, in Segar Roll, colours reversed, Jenyns' Ordinary (F.) RICHARD, junior, bore, vert, a lyon rampant or debruised by a fess gules.—SIRE DE ARDERNE (‡) bore, argent, a lyon rampant azure, debruised by a bend gules; Dering Roll.

Arderne, William de—(H. III. Roll) bore, sable, three lyons passant or; Arden Roll.

Arfois or **Arforce**, —— (E. III. Roll) bore, argent, three castles triple-turretted gules; Ashmole Roll.

Argentine, Sir Giles of Cambridge — bore, at the first Dunstable tournament 1308, gules, crusily and three covered cups argent.

Argentine, Sir John, Knight banneret, 2nd baron—bore, at the first Dunstable tournament 1308, gules, three covered cups argent. (F.) WILLIAM bore the reverse.

Argentine, Reynold de, a baron 1297 —bore, gules, crusily fitchée and three covered cups argent, Nobility Roll; father of Sir JOHN, before named, see facsimile GILES.

Armine, *v.* **Ayrmine** and **Ermine**.

Arnes, Robert de—(H. III. Roll) bore, azure, two bends or; Howard Roll.

Arras, Rafe de—(H. III. Roll) bore, argent, on a cross azure five fleurs-de-lys or; Arden Roll. (F.) The Castellan of Arras in Normandy (‡), bore, gules a chief ermine; Dering Roll. See also DARRES.

Arthur, Sir Thomas—bore, at the siege of Rouen 1418, gules, a chevron argent between three clarions or.

Artoys, Janico de—(E. III. Roll) bore, gules, four bars wavy argent; Jenyns' Roll. (F.) See D'ARTOIS.

Arundel, Richard, Earl of, banneret—bore, at the battle of Falkirk 1298, at the siege of Carlaverock 1300, gules, a lyon rampant or; sealed the Barons' letter to the Pope 1301. Borne also by Earl EDMUND at the first Dunstable tournament 1308, and by another Earl RICHARD at the siege of Calais 1345-8.

MOUNSYER RICHARD DE ARUNDELL and (Earl JOHN) LE SR. MATRAVERS bore, at the siege of Rouen 1418, ARUNDEL, *quarterly with*, MATRAVERS, sable, a fret or. (F.) See also FITZALAN.

*****[Arundell, Reinfred de**, temp. H. III.— bore, sable, six martlets (*vel* hirondelles) argent. —Shirley.] F.

Asdale, Thomas—(E. III. Roll) bore, gules, a cygnet passant argent; Jenyns' Roll. F.

*****Ashburnham, Sir Bartholomew de**— bore, at the battle of Boroughbridge 1322, gules, a fess (between) six moles (mullets of 6) argent. (F.)—Sir JOHN bore the same with martlets in lieu of mullets, and another SIR JOHN, bore plates instead of mullets; Parliamentary Roll E. II.

‡**Ashburnham, Richard de**—(H. III. Roll) bore, gules, a fess and in chief three spurrowells argent; Dering Roll.

Ashbye, Sir Robert de—(E. II. Roll) bore, argent, billettée gules and a lyon rampant sable; in another trick the lyon (and not the field) is billettée or; Parliamentary Roll.

Asche, Sire de—(E. I. Roll), bore, argent, a fess azure over all a saltire gules. JOHN DE ASSE, bore, or, a saltire gules over all a fess sable. Camden Roll.

Ashebaston, Sir Richard (ECHEBASTON) of co. Leicester—bore, at the battle of Boroughbridge 1322, argent, a lyon rampant gules, on his shoulder a cinquefoyle of the first, over all a baston azure (in another trick the cinquefoyle is on the baston); Parliamentary Roll. See also EDGBASTON. For same coat without the baston, see Sir ANDREW ASTLEY.

Asherst, Sir Adam—bore, at the siege of Calais 1345-8, gules, a cross engrailed between four fleurs-de-lys argent.

Ashfeld (——), a Suffolk Knight—(H. VI. Roll) bore, sable, a fess engrailed between three fleurs-de-lys argent; Arundel Roll.

As(h)ton, Richard de—(E. IV. Roll) bore, per chevron sable and argent—with crest; Ballard Roll.

Aske, Conan de—(E. III. Roll) bore, or, three bars azure; Grimaldi Roll. F.

Askeby, Sir Robert—(E. III. Roll), bore, argent, a lyon rampant sable billettée or; Ashmole Roll. F.

Aspall, Sir Robert of Suffolk—(E. III. Roll) bore, azure, three chevronels or; Arundel and Parliamentary Rolls. The field gules in Ashmole Roll.

Asse, John de, *v.* ASCHE.

Asseles, Alan de—(H. III. Roll) bore, gules, a saltire and a chief argent; Arden and St. George Rolls. See LASSELLS.

*****[Assheton, Sir Robert de**, E. III.—bore, argent, a mullet pierced sable.—Shirley.] F.

Assi, Sir Robert de—(E. III. Roll) bore, gules, a bend cotised between six martlets or, Ashmole Roll.

Astinn (—— ?an Essex), Knight—(H. VI. Roll) bore, argent, a chevron between three fleurs-de-lys sable; Arundel Roll.

SIR HENRY BACON.
IN GORLESTON CHURCH, SUFFOLK.
C. 1335.   AFTER STOTHARD.

Astley, Sir Andrew, a baron 1295—bore, at the battle of Falkirk 1298, argent, a lyon rampant gules, on his shoulder a cinque-foyle of the first ; (F.) (Borne with a baston by Sir RICHARD ASHEBASTON.) Borne with a cinquefoyle ermine by THOMAS (F.) in Jenyns' Ordinary, and with a billet ermine in place of the cinquefoyle by Sir NICHOLAS, banneret in Arundel Roll (F.) ; Sir GILES of co. Leic. ƒ Thomas, 3rd lord—bore the cinquefoyle or and a label (3) and azure ; Parly. Roll E. II.

Astley, Thomas—bore, in the second Dunstable tournament 1334, azure, a cinquefoyle pierced ermine. (F.) Ascribed also to ANDREW, JOHN, and Sir THOMAS in St. George and Ashmole Rolls and Jenyns' Ordy. *THOMAS, of (Hill) Morton, differenced with a bordure engrailed or ; in Surrey Roll R. II. Sir RAUFF—a bordure argent—in Ashmole Roll E. III. ; and THOMAS DE—with a label (3) or, on each point two bars gules, in Surrey Roll R. II.

[**Astley, Giles**—bore, gules, a cinquefoyle pierced ermine between three mullets or ; Harl. MS. 1481 fo. 75ᵇ.]

Astley, Robert—(E. III. Roll) bore, azure, crusily or and a lyon passant gardant argent ; Jenyns' Ordinary. F.

Aston, Sir John de, of Northants—(E. II. Roll) bore, sable, a saltire argent ; Parliamentary Roll.

Aston, Sir Richard de, of Gloucestershire —(E. II. Roll) bore, gules, a lyon rampant or, debruised by a bend vair ; Parliamentary Roll.

Aston, Sir Richard of Hants or Wilts.—(E. II. Roll) bore, azure, crusily or, and a bend argent cotised of the second. Parliamentary Roll. One of these names took up the cross 1270.

Aston, Roger de—(E. III. Roll) bore, argent, a dancette (embelif) sable ; Jenyns' Roll. F.

Atherton, —— (E. IV. Roll) bore, gules, three hawks or—with crest ; Ballard Roll.

Atherton, William, see ACHERTON.

†**Athol, (David) Earl of**—(H. III. Roll) bore, paly or and sable, in Norfolk and Grimaldi Rolls (F.)—paly (6) in Arden Roll—or, 4 palets sable, in Howard Roll and, or three palets azure, in Segar, Camden and St. George Rolls. ADOMAR of Suffolk, younger brother of DAVID DE STRABOLGY, differenced with a bendlet argent. Harl. MS. 1481 fo. 74.

Aton, Sir Gilbert de, a baron 1324—bore, at the battle of Boroughbridge 1322, or, a cross passant sable (F.) ; (borne also by Sir WILLIAM, 2nd baron, in Ashmole) ; and gules, a cross patonce argent (F.), in Parliamentary Roll, &c., another (? platey at the points) in Ashmole.

Atte Hethe v. Hethe.

Attwater, William, Bishop of Lincoln (6 H. VIII. 1515) bore, undée (barry wavy of six) ermine and gules, on a chevron between three shrimps embowed or, a rose gules seeded argent and leaved vert enclosed by two flowers ; Nobility Roll.

Attewode, John—(R. II. Roll) bore, gules a lyon rampant tail fourchée argent ; Surrey Roll, and as ATWOOD in Ashmole Roll.

Aubemarle, Sir Geffrey of Devon and Hants—(E. II. Roll) bore, gules, crusily or and a bend lozengy ermine ; Parliamentary Roll.

Aucher, Henry—(H. III. Roll) bore, ermine, on a chief azure three lyons rampant or ; Arden Roll.

Audley, Hughe de, Earl of Gloucester, 1337-47—bore, or, three chevronels gules, Nobility Roll H. VI. See also CLARE.

Audley, Sir Nicholas de, of Heligh, baron 1297—bore, at the battle of Falkirk 1298, gules, a fret (*vel* fretty) or ; so borne also by his son JAMES, K.G. (a founder), one of the heroes of Poictiers, and by WILLIAM DE AUDLEY (‡) ; Dering Roll. Sir HUGH of co. Gloucr. differenced with a label (5) azure (F.) ; HUGH and JOHN, a bordure argent (F.), Cotgrave and Jenyns' Ordinary E. III. JAMES, with, a label gobony argent and azure, Cotgrave ; and Sir JAMES of co. Gloucr. with a label (3) azure, on each point a lyoncel of the second ; Parliamentary Roll E. II. where Sir NICHOLAS first named, appears among the bannerets. Another JAMES took up the cross 1270.

Auke, Gregory de—(E. III. Roll) bore, gules, two bars and in chief three annulets all argent ; Jenyns' Ordinary. F.

Aunsell, Alexander—(E. III. Roll) bore, ermine, on a fess gules three crosses crosslet or ; Jenyns' Ordinary. F.

Auntesheye, Sir Richard (DAUNTSEY) of Gloucestershire—(E. II. Roll) bore, per fess or and argent, a fess undée gules. (F.) Parliamentary Roll.

Austre(y), William de—(H. III. Roll) bore, gules, a fess argent, a label (5) or ; or AUSTRY *vel* DAUTREY ; Arden Roll.

Autrey, William de (DAUTREY)—(H. III. Roll) bore, azure, a fess dancettée (5) argent, a label (5) gules ; Arden Roll.

Avenbury, Osbern de—(H. III. Roll) bore, gules, three lyons rampant tails fourchée argent ; Arden Roll.

Avene, Sir Leyson de (DAVENEY), of co. Glouc.—(E. II. Roll) bore, gules, three chevronels argent ; Parly. Roll. See VENE.

Avenel, Sir John de—(E. III. Roll) bore, argent, a fess between six annulets 3 and 3 gules ; Ashmole Roll—the same for Sir WILLIAM of Cambridgeshire in Parliamentary Roll E. II. F.

Awger, Sir Thomas (AUGER) of Kent—(H. VI. Roll) bore, ermine, on a chief azure three lyonceux rampant or ; Arundel Roll.

Awillers v. Davelers.

Ailesbury, Sir Robert de—bore, at the battle of Boroughbridge 1322, azure, a cross argent and a label (3) gules. JOHN, bore it undifferenced, and another JOHN, with a baston gules, instead of the label ; Jenyns' Ordinary E. III. F.

Ayrmyn, William—(E. III. Roll) bore, argent, a saltire engrailed and a chief gules ; Jenyns' Ordinary. (F.) WM. DE ERMINE, bore, ermine, a saltire engrailed gules, on a chief of the last a lyon passant gardant or. Surrey Roll.

SIR WILLIAM BAGOT, 8 HEN. IV. 1407.
BAGINTON CHURCH, WARWICKSHIRE. *After Boutell.*

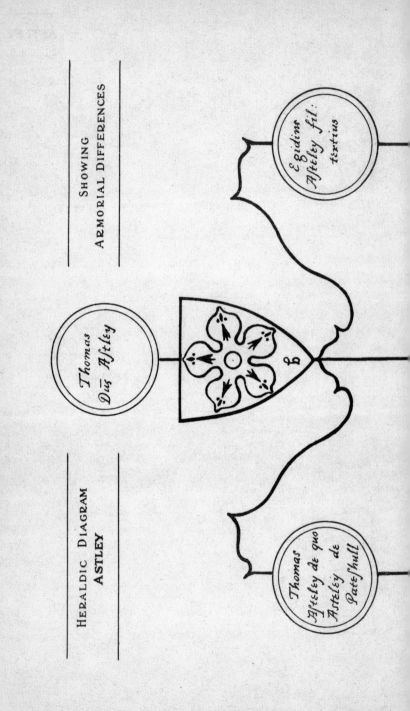

HERALDIC DIAGRAM
ASTLEY

SHOWING
ARMORIAL DIFFERENCES

Thomas
Duͦ Aſtley

Egidius
Aſtley fil:
tertius

Thomas
Aſtley de quo
Aſtley de
Pateſhull

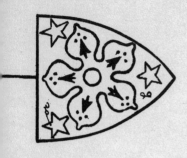

Gulielmus Astelley filius primus.

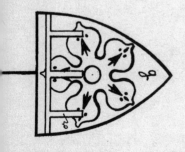

B

Baa, Sir Walter de of Bedfordshire – (E. II. Roll) bore, gules, a chevron argent between three plates ; Parliamentary Roll.

Babington, Sir John de, of Dorset or Somerset - (**E.** II. Roll) bore, gules, platey, though tricked as torteaux in Harl. MS. 4033 ; Parliamentary Roll.

*[**Babington, Sir John** (E. III.) – bore, argent, ten torteaux and a label (3) azure.— Shirley.] F.

Babthorpe, Sir R.—(H. VI. Roll) bore, sable, a chevron or between three crescents ermine ; Atkinson Roll.

Bacon, Sir Edmond—bore, at the first Dunstable tournament 1308, gules, on a chief argent two mullets sable pierced or ; the same was borne by another EDMOND at the second Dunstable tournament, 1334 - by ROBERT, within a bordure or—and by JOHN within a bordure engrelée or (F.); borne also by EDWARD in Jenyns' Ordinary. Sir EDMUND, of Hants. or Wilts. bore the mullets unpierced. (F.) Parliamentary Roll.

[**Bacon, Sir Henry,** of Gorleston, Suffolk, temp. E. III. (1335)—bore, gules a bend fusily sable, on a chief argent two spur-rowells of the second.] Add. MS. 19,116 fo. 129. See Monumental Effigy.

Badewe, Sir Hugh—(E. III. Roll) bore, argent, on a bend azure three eaglets displayed or ; Ashmole Roll. Probably intended for Sir HUGH DELAMARE.

Badham, Sir John, see ADAM-AP-ADAM.

Badlesmere, Sire Bartholomew de; banneret (baron 1309)—bore, at the siege of Carlaverock 1300, argent, a fess double cotised gules with a label (5) azure, his father GUN-CELME being then alive (F.), but without the label at the first Dunstable tournament 1308, and at the battle of Boroughbridge 1322 ; so borne by Sir GILES, Ashmole Roll ; and by GUNCELME (‡) and RAFE (‡) in the Arden Roll—another RAFE bore the field ermine, Camden and St. George Rolls.

Bagod, William - (H. III. Roll) bore, argent, two chevronels azure ; Arden Roll. F.

Bagot, Sir William, of co. Cambridge— (E. III. Roll) bore, ermine a bend gules. Ashmole Roll. Another Sir WILLIAM bore three eaglets or on the bend, at the first Dunstable tournament 1308. F.

*Bagot, John**—(R. II. Roll) bore, argent, a chevron gules between three martlets sable ; Surrey Roll. Sir WILLIAM, of Bromley— temp. H. IV., differenced with a crescent. See Monumental Effigy.

Bagpuze, John de—(H. III. Roll) bore, azure, crusily or, a fess vaire of the second and gules ; Arden Roll. (F.) Sir JOHN, of Rutland, bore, E. II., gules, two bars argent, in chief three horse-shoes or ; RAFE, bore, H. III., azure, crusily a chevron or. (F.) St. George Roll ; and another coat under this surname, paly (6) argent and gules, on a chief azure three horse-shoes of the first, occurs in the Ashmole Roll.

Bagworth, —— (E. III. Roll) bore, sable a fess engrailed ermine between three boars' heads couped of the last, tusked argent ; Ashmole Roll.

Baiggingedene, Richard de—(H. III. Roll) bore, or a pile sable and nine mullets (6 points) counterchanged 3, 3, 3 ; St. George Roll. (F.) See also ROBERT DE CHANDOS.

Bakwell, Sir John de, of Middlesex— (E. II. Roll) bore, paly (6) argent and azure, on a chief gules a lyon passant gardant or ; Parliamentary Roll.

Baldreston, Richard de—(E. III. Roll) bore, argent a lyon rampant purpure - same as Sir ROBERT FITZROGER ; Jenyns' Ordinary.

*[**Baldwin, Roger,** of Diddlebury, Salop, 1398 – bore, argent, a saltire sable.—Shirley.] F.

Baliol, Sir Alexander de, a baron 1300 —bore, at the battle of Falkirk 1298, and at the siege of Carlaverock 1300, argent, a faux escocheon (an orle) gules, and many of his name bore the same. (F.) JOHN of Barnard Castle, another ALEXANDER and others bore the reverse the field of the banner borne at Carlaverock is by some stated to have been, or.

†**Baliol, Eustace de**—(H. III. Roll) bore, azure, crusily and an orle or ; Glover Roll.

Baliol, Hugh de, of Bywell—(E. III. Roll) bore, argent, on an inescocheon azure, a lyon rampant argent crowned or, all within a bordure gules, Jenyns' Ordinary ; without the border in Grimaldi Roll ; a somewhat different coat assigned to EUSTACE DE BALLIOL DE TEAS in Glover Roll. See EUSTACE DE TOURS.

Baliol, Ingram de—(H. III. Roll) bore, gules, an orle ermine, a label (5) azure. Arden and St. George Rolls. F.

Baliol, William de—(H. III. Roll) bore, or, an orle vair, a label (5) gules. Another WILLIAM —bore, or, an orle azure, a lab:l (5) gules. Arden and St. George Rolls.

Alex. Balioll   Hugh Baylioll   north de Balnye

John Balun   Bam   John Bamfylde

Thomas de   Adam Banestre   John de Bar
Banribare.

John de Bars   Robt.   will. Bonnak.
                      Barbesworz

Balnye, William de—(E. III. Roll) bore, argent, an eagle displayed azure, beaked and membered gules. Jenyns' Ordinary. F.

‡**Balun, John,** and **Walter de**—(H.III. Roll) bore, barry dancettée (6 or 8) argent and gules (F.) St. George, Howard and Dering Rolls; THOMAS, gules and or, in Jenyns' Ordinary.

Balun, John—(E. III. Roll) bore, per fess indented argent and gules. Jenyns' Roll. F.

Bam (me), ——, a Kentish Knight—(H. VI. Roll) bore, ermines on a chief pily argent two trefoyles sable; Arundel Roll. F.

Bamnye v. **Bawnd** or **Bownd.**

*[**Bampfylde, John** (BAUMFIELD), E. I.— bore, or, on a bend gules, three mullets argent.—Shirley.] F.

Banastre, Sir Adam, of Lancashire—bore, at the first Dunstable tournament 1308, argent, a cross patonce sable, and also by Sir WILLIAM, who was knighted at the capitulation of Calais 1348, and by Sir THOMAS K.G. 1376; the cross is variously tricked or blasoned, patée, patonce, and flory, according to the humour of the Herald or his painter, for they were evidently interchangeable, or one and the same. F.

Banastre, Sire William—(E. I. Roll) bore, argent, three chevronels gules, Guillim Roll, and the reverse in the Parliamentary Roll.

Banbury, Gilbert de, and **Sir Thomas de,** of Oxon—(E. I. Roll) bore, argent a cross patonce (or flory) gules, between four torteaux; Parliamentary Roll.

Banbury, Thomas de—(E. I. Roll) bore, argent, a cross between four mullets (6) pierced gules; Segar Roll. F.

Band, Sir Walter le—(E. II. Roll) bore, gules, three pairs of eagles' wings, or; Parliamentary Roll. See also BAUDE.

Banke, John de—(E. II. Roll) bore, sable a cross between four fleurs-de-lys argent, *quartering* argent a chevron between three annulets gules, Jenyns' Roll. F.

Bardolf, Sir Hugh, a baron 1299—Sealed the Barons' letter to the Pope 1301; bore, at the battle of Falkirk 1298, and at the siege of Carlaverock 1300, azure, three cinquefoyles or; as also did (1) Sir THOMAS at the first Dunstable tournament 1308, (2) Le Sr. BARDOLPHE at the siege of Rouen 1418, and (3) WILLIAM (‡) in the Dering Roll. A Bardolf coat w thin a bordure engrailed argent in the Ashmole Roll.

Bardolf, John—bore, at the second Dunstable tournament 1334, azure, three cinquefoyles argent (as did Sir WILLIAM, of Norfolk, in Parly. Roll, E. II.), but his cousin JOHN, also of Norfolk, bore a red field.

Bardolfe, Sir Thomas, banneret—(E. II. Roll) bore, or, three cinquefoyles azure. (F.) Parliamentary Roll; the Surrey Roll (R. II.) ascribes argent three cinquefoyles pierced or, to LE SR. DE BARDOLF.

Bardolfe, Thomas—(H. III. Roll) bore, azure, crusily and three cinquefoyles or. Glover and Norfolk Rolls.

Bardwell, William—bore, at the siege of Rouen 1418, gules, a goat saliant, or, *quarterly with,* or, an eagle displayed vert. One Sir WILLIAM bore the goat argent horned or. F. as Bedwell.

Bare, Sir John de—bore, at the battle of Falkirk 1298, and at the siege of Carlaverock 1300, azure, crusily and two barbes or, a bordure indented gules, engrailed in the Carlaverock Roll—the "barbes" blasoned "poissons" in Harl. 6589 fo. 3ᵇ, and "barbeaux" fo. 50; correctly tricked only in Add. 5848 fo. 79, as two barbels addorsed embowed or; in all other MSS. erroneously blasoned or tricked as Heraldic bars. F. RALPH BARRY took up the cross in the last Crusade 1270.

Bare, John de—(E. III. Roll) bore, azure two bars or, a bordure engrailed gules; Jenyns' Ordinary. (F.) See also BARRE and BARRY.

Barkeworth, Robert (BARCEWORTH) —(E. III. Roll) bore, argent, a saltire sable a label (3) gules; Jenyns' Ordinary and Roll. (F.) See also BRAKWORTHE.

Barksworth, Sir Robert de, of Suffolk—(E. II. Roll) bore, chequy argent and gules, on a bend azure three lyonceux passant of the first (F.); Parliamentary Roll.

Barlow, —— (H. VI. Roll) bore, sable, a double-headed eagle displayed argent; Arundel Roll.

(Barlye ?), of Essex — (H. VI. Roll) bore, undeé (6) sable and ermine (*i.e.* barry nebulée); Arundel Roll.

Barnake, Sir William, of co. Leic.—(E. II. Roll) bore, argent a fess between three barnacles sable; Parly. Roll; and in Jenyns' Roll, argent three barnacles sable are ascribed to WILLIAM B., shovellers in lieu of barnacles, are also ascribed to both these names. F.

Barnam, Henry le—(H. III. Roll) bore, France, and a chief paly argent and gules; Norfolk Roll.

Barnard, John—(H. VI. Roll) bore, argent, a bear passant sable muzzled, or, *quarterly with,* gules three lucies naiant (? argent). Arundel Roll, in which two other BARNARD coats appear, (1) gules, three chevronels ermine, (2) argent a chevron sable, on a chief gules three mullets or, a crescent for difference.

Barnastone, Thomas—(E. III. Roll) bore, azure, crusily (5, 5) argent and a fesse dancettée ermine; (F.) Jenyns' Ordinary. This coat seems to have been allowed to, or appropriated by, BARNSTONE of Cheshire and BARNARDISTON of Suffolk.

‡**Barnes, Rauf de**—(H. III. Roll) bore, quarterly or and azure; Dering Roll -or, and vert in St. George Roll; called also BERNERS, see that name.

Barre v. **Bare** and **Barry.**

Barre, Robert—(R. II. Roll) bore, gules, three bars crenellée argent; Surrey Roll.

Barre, Thomas—(R. II. Roll) bore, gules, three bars compony argent and azure, *quarterly with,* barry (6) or and azure, a bend gules; Surrey Roll.

Barre, William—(R. II. Roll) bore, azure two lyons passant gardant and a bordure engrailed or; Surrey Roll.

Barres, (——) de (H. III. Roll) bore, lozengy or and gules; Arden Roll.

Barrett, John, of Suffolk—(Hen. VI. Roll) bore, argent, three buckles lozengy gules, tongues to the sinister; another JOHN bore the same between a bend azure thereon an annulet or; Arundel Roll.

Adam de
Bartholot

Stevene Barel

Witt Barantin.

Robt d. Barri

John de Basinges

Emo de Basset

Walter de
Baskevillo

Edmonde de
Basset.

Rich.d Basset

Gilec Vauf
Basset

Vauf Basset

Witt Basset

Barret, Sire Stevene—bore, at the battle of Boroughbridge 1322, argent, crusily and a lyon rampant gules crowned or.

Baret, Sire Stevene—bore, at the battle of Boroughbridge 1322, argent, crusily potent (tricked fitchée in Ashmole) and three fleurs-de-lys sable within a bordure engrailed of the second. F.

Barrentine, Sir Drew de, of Bucks— (E. II. Roll) bore, sable, six eaglets, 3, 2, 1, argent; Parliamentary Roll. Three eagles in the Segar Roll; eaglets or, in the Glover Roll. F.

Barrington, Sir Nicholas de, of Essex— (E. II. Roll) bore, argent, three chevronels gules, a label (3) azure; Parliamentary and Arundel Rolls.

Barington, Sir Philip, of co. Leic.— bore, at the first Dunstable tournament 1308, argent, a lyon rampant sable tail fourchée, on the shoulder a fleur-de-lys or. Parly. Roll.

Barowe, William—(E. III. Roll) bore, argent, on a fess dancettée sable three besants; (F.) Jenyns' Ordinary.

Barry, John—(E. III. Roll) bore, gules two gemelles argent, *en manere de barres*; (F.) Jenyns' Ordinary.

Barry, Sir Robert, of Bucks—(E. II. Roll) bore, azure, two lyons passant gardant or; Arden, St. George, and Parly. Rolls. F.

***[Bartelott, Adam de,** 1428—bore, sable, three falconers sinister gloves pendant argent, tasseled or.—Shirley.] F.

Barton, Geoffrey, of Tatton—is heir to the cote of Sir GEOFFRY MASSY of Tatton and also of MASSY—(Ed. IV. Roll) bore, quarterly gules and argent, a label (5) azure. Ballard Roll.

***Barton, John de**—(R. II. Roll) bore, argent, a bend wavy sable; Surrey Roll. See RICHARD DE WALLOP.

Barton, John, of Friton—(E. III. Roll) bore, ermine, on a fess gules three annulets or; Grimaldi Roll and Jenyns' Ordinary. F.

Bartram, Roger, baron of Mitford—(E. III. Roll) bore, gules, crusily and an orle or; Jenyns' Ordinary. See also BERTRAM. F.

Barwick, see BERWICK.

Basan, Stephen—(H. III. Roll) bore, undée argent and gules, a quarter sable; Glover Roll.

‡**Basemes, Godfrey de** (called also BASE-VILE)—(H. III. Roll) bore, gules an inescocheon argent within an orle of cinquefoyles or; Dering Roll.

Basford, Sir John, knighted at the capitulation of Calais 1348—gules a lyon rampant ermine. F.

Basynges, John—(R. II. Roll) bore, gules, seven barrulets argent; Surrey Roll.

Basing, Sir John, of Middlesex—(E. II. Roll) bore, azure, a cross recercelée voided or. (F.) Sir WILLIAM, of Kent, bore the same with a baston gules; Parliamentary Roll. A cross moline in Jenyns' Ordinary. F.

Baskerville, Andrew de—(H. III. Roll) bore, argent, a chevron azure between three torteaux; Arden Roll.

Baskerville, Sir Richard de, banncret — (E. II. Roll) bore, argent, a chevron gules between three hurts; Parliamentary Roll. JOHN and WALTER bore torteaux instead of hurts; Arden and Glover Rolls. F.

***Baskervile, Sir Walter,** of co. Glouc.— bore, at the first Dunstable tournament 1308, argent, on a chevron gules between three hurts as many mullets (fleurs-de-lys in Cotgrave Roll) or; in the Parly. Roll, crosses crosslet are substituted for mullets, and in another MS. 5 instead of 3 crosses crosslet are blased crusily. JOHN took up the cross in the last Crusade 1270.

‡**Baspes, Sire de**—(H. III. Roll) bore, gules, three palets vair, on a chief or a demi fleur-de-lys issuant sable; Dering Roll. F.

Basset, Rauf—(H. III. Roll) bore, or, three piles gules; Arden Roll.

Bassett, Richard, of Weldon, a baron 1299—bore, or, three palets gules, and a bordure azure. RAUFF, also baron, bore the bordure besantée; Surrey Roll.

Basset, Rauff, of Drayton, 1st baron 1264— (E. I. Roll) bore, or, three piles meeting in base gules, a canton ermine. Segar and St. George Rolls (F.)—and so also RALPH 4th Baron K.G. 1369. RALPH 2nd baron bore, at the battle of Falkirk 1298, paly (6) or and gules, a canton ermine. F., probably father of the next named.

Basset, Sir Rauf, banneret—bore, at the first Dunstable tournament 1308, or, three piles meeting in base gules, a canton ermine. Sir SIMON bore them, with a label (3) azure, at the siege of Calais 1345-8, and RAUF LE FITZ also, at the second Dunstable tournament 1334. In tricks for Sir ROBERT or ROGER of Worcestershire the piles are sometimes azure sometimes sable; Parly. Roll. ROGER bore them sable and the canton gules; Segar Roll.

‡**Basset, Sir Rauf**—(H. III. Roll) bore, or three piles meeting in base gules, a canton vair; Arden and St. George Rolls. JOHN, bore on the canton argent, a gryphon segreant sable armed or; Surrey Roll.

Basset, Lord, slain at the siege of Calais 1347—bore, gules, three piles meeting in base argent, a canton ermine.

Basset, Rauff—(H. III. Roll) bore, paly (6) or and gules, on a canton argent a cross patée sable; Parliamentary Roll.

Basset, Sir Richard—bore, at the first Dunstable tournament 1308, paly (6) or and gules, a bordure sable besantée; (F.) Another Sir RICHARD (E. II.) bore the bordure azure; Parliamentary Roll.

Basset, Sire Rauf—(E. I. Roll) bore, argent, three bars undée sable; Guillim Roll. F.

Basset, Rauf, of Sapcote, a baron 1264, and **Simon**—(H. III. Roll) bore, undée (6) argent and sable; St. George and Harl. Rolls. Sir JOHN bore the same besantée; Ashmole Roll.

Basset, H.—(H. III. Roll) bore, undée argent and sable a canton gules; St. George Roll.

THOMAS BEAUCHAMP, 4TH EARL OF
WARWICK, K.G. 1406.
IN S. MARY CHURCH, WARWICK. *After Waller.*

Basset, Lawrence—(H. III. Roll) bore, undée (6) argent and gules ; Arden and St. George Rolls. PHILIP bore, or and gules, St. George Roll ; and WILLIAM the reverse in Jenyns' Ordinary. SYMON (‡) bore argent and azure in Howard Roll ; and or and azure in Dering Roll.

*[**Basset, Sir William**, of Tehidy, Cornwall, E. III.—bore, or, three bars undée gules —wavy, in Shirley.] F.

Bassett, Simon—bore, at the second Dunstable tournament 1334, ermine, un partie gules, a mullet or ; Collect. and Top., IV. 390.

Bassett, Sir Lawrence and **Thomas**, of Cornwall.—(E. III. Roll) bore, barry dancettée (6) argent and gules Ashmole Roll and Jenyns' Ordinary.

Bassett, Philip—(H. III. Roll) bore, quarterly or and gules ; Glover Roll.

Bassett, Sir Richard, of Rutland, and **Sir William**—(E. II. Roll) bore, argent, two bars azure, in chief three chaplets gules ; Parly. and Ashmole Rolls.

Bassett, Simon—(E. III. Roll) bore, ermine, on a canton gules an orle argent ; another a mullet (6) pierced or on the canton ; Ashmole and Jenyns' Rolls. F.

‡**Bassett, Anscel**—(H. III. Roll) bore, ermine, a chief dancettée gules ; Dering Roll. F.

Bassett, Sir John—bore, at the siege of Carlaverock 1300, ermine, on a chief dancettée (*vel* indented), gules, three spur rowells or. Sir EDMONDE, of co. Gloucester, his brother, bore escallops in lieu of the spurrowells. F.F.

Bassett, Osmond—(E. III. Roll) bore, ermine, on a chief indented gules, two mullets or pierced vert.

Bas(s)ingbourne, Sire Mayeu de—bore, at the battle of Boroughbridge 1322, quarterly or and gules, four crescents counterchanged. F.

‡**Bassingbourne, Baldwin**, or **Jordan**—(H. III. Roll) bore, gyrony (12) vair and gules ; Arden Roll ; the same for WARREN, in Cotgrave Roll, and for RAFFE in Jenyns' Ordinary.

Bassingbourne, Giles ƒ HUMPHREY—(E III. Roll) bore, gyrony (6) argent and gules, a baston azure ; Cotgrave Roll.

Bassingbourne, Sir Humphrey, of co. Cambridge—(E. II. Roll) bore, gyrony (8) argent and gules, Parliamentary Roll ; tricked also 6 and 12 for other Humphreys.

Bassingbourne, Sir John, of Herts—(E. II. Roll) bore, gyrony (8) or and gules ; Parliamentary Roll.

Bassingbourne, Sir Warren, of co. Lincs.—(E. II. Roll) bore, gyrony (8, sometimes 12 and 16), or and azure, Parliamentary Roll and Jenyns' Ordinary. F.

*[**Bastard** (——), of Kitley, Devon—bore, or, a chevron azure.—Shirley.] F.

Battott, —— (H. VI. Roll) bore, gules, a gryphon segreant or, a bordure engrailed sable ; Arundel Roll.

Bause, Sire William, see GAUSE.

Baud, Sir Thomas le—(E. III. Roll) bore, azure, a lyon passant or ; Ashmole Roll.

Baud, Sir Walter le, of Essex—(E. II. Roll) bore, gules, three eagles' wings or ; Parliamentary Roll.

Bawde, William, of Essex—(E. III. Roll) bore, gules, three chevronels argent ; Cotgrave and Surrey Rolls.

Bavent, Sir Roger, a baron 1313—bore, at the first Dunstable tournament 1308, argent, a chief indented sable. (F.) See BAMNYE in margin ; bore also by ADAM (‡) in Howard and Dering Rolls. Another ROGER bore it with 3 besants ; Jenyns' Ordinary. F.

Bavent, Sir John de—bore, at the battle of Boroughbridge 1322, argent, a chevron gules within a bordure sable besantée ; another JOHN bore this coat with the bordure engrailed, at the second Dunstable tournament 1334. F.

Bavant, William—(E. III. Roll) bore, ermine, two bars gules each charged with three spur-rowells or ; Jenyns' Ordinary. F.

Bavesar, Walter de—(H. III. Roll) bore, argent, a lyon rampant tail fourchée gules ; Dering Roll.

Baynard, Sir Robert, of Norfolk—(E. II. Roll) bore, sable a fess between two chevronels or ; Parly. Roll. Ascribed also to JOHN in Jenyns' Ordinary. F.

Bayning, William de—(H. III. Roll) bore, argent, three fleurs-de-lys azure ; Howard Roll.

Baynton, Sir Robert, knighted at the capitulation of Calais 1348—bore, sable a bend fusily argent.

Bayous, Sir John, knighted at the capitulation of Calais 1348—bore, gules, two bars and in chief three escallops argent (F.) ; the same coat was borne by Sir WILLIAM, of co. Linc., at the first Dunstable tournament 1308.

Bayouse, Herbert de, of Merkington—(E. III. Roll) bore, gules, an inescocheon voided argent over all a bend vair ; Jenyns' Ordinary. F.

Bayouse, Sir Robert, of Hunts.—(E. II. Roll) bore, argent three water-bougets purpure ; Parliamentary Roll ; lyonceux rampant in Harl. MS. 6137 ƒ 22. F.

Beauchamp, William, de Elmeley—(E. I. Roll) bore, gules, a fess or—Grimaldi Roll ; JAMES differenced with a label (5) argent (or azure) ; Arden and St. George Rolls. F.

‡**Beauchamp, Water de**—(H. III. Roll) bore, gules, a fess and in chief three martlets or ; Dering and Howard Rolls.

Beauchamp, Sir Walter de, banneret, (3rd son of WILLIAM, 5th Baron of Elmeley)—Sealed, as Dominus de Alcestre, the Barons' letter to the Pope 1301, bore, at the battle of Falkirk 1298, and at the siege of Carlaverock 1300, gules, a fess between six martlets or ; a Sir WALTER bore the same at the battle of Boroughbridge 1322. They were also borne by Sir GILES, at the siege of Calais 1345-8. (F.)

(1) Another Sir GYLES differenced at the battle of Boroughbridge with a bordure engrelée argent ; endentée in Parly. Writs App.

(2) Sir JOHN, son of Sir GILES, differenced at the siege of Calais 1345-8, with a label (3) points argent (or azure).

(3) Sir EDWARD (or Sir GILES) who was knighted at the capitulation of Calais 1348, differenced, with a label (5), pendants gobony argent and azure.

THOMAS BEAUCHAMP, 3RD EARL OF
WARWICK, K.G. 1369.
IN ELSING CHURCH, NORFOLK. *From the Hastings Brass.*

Beauchamp—

(4) ROGER differenced, with a mullet pierced sable ; Surrey Roll.

(5) Sir WILLIAM, of co. Gloucester, differenced at the first Dunstable tournament 1308, with a bordure indented or, Parliamentary Roll.

(6) Another WILLIAM bore, at the second Dunstable tournament 1334, for difference, " sur le melot devaunt," three chevrons gules ; Sloane MS. 1301 fo. 260^b.

(7) Sir WALTER (*f* 2) JOHN of Powick bore Sir WALTER'S coat within a bordure argent ; Harl. MS. 1481 fo. 41.

Beauchamp, Guy, 2nd Earl of Warwick— bore, at the battle of Falkirk 1298, at the siege of Carlaverock 1300, and at the first Dunstable tournament 1308, gules crusily (3.3) and a fess or, and these were borne by his son THOMAS, 2nd Earl, at the second Dunstable tournament 1334. (F.) They are ascribed to WILLIAM, banneret, 1st Earl, 24 E. 1., 1295-6 in the Parly. Roll. (F). Earl WILLIAM and Earl GUY also bore it, *quarterly with* ' Le Veyl escu,' (de Warwike), chequy or and azure, a chevron ermine—F.—(the latter sealed the Barons' letter to the Pope 1301) ; Nobility Roll ; borne quarterly also by THOMAS, 3rd Earl, at the siege of Calais 1345-8, and RICHARD, 5th Earl, at the siege of Rouen in 1418 ; tricked crusily (7, 6) in Jenyns' Ordinary. See Monumental Effigies of the 3rd and 4th Earls.

Beauchamp, Sir John, K.G., brother of Guy, 2nd Earl—bore, at the siege of Calais 1345-8, gules, crusily (3.3) and a fess or, and for difference, a mullet sable ; WILLIAM differenced with a crescent sable, Surrey Roll ; as did RICHARD, Lord Abergavenny, at the siege of Rouen 1418 ; Sir GUY differenced with a label (3) azure ; and Sir THOMAS differenced with an annulet azure, both in Ashmole Roll ; and another JOHN differenced with a bordure engrelée or.

Beauchamp, Sir John, del County de Warwike—bore, at the first Dunstable tournament 1308, gules billettée and a fess or ; 12, 11, 10, 9 and sometimes 6 billets. (F.) Ascribed also to JOHN (‡) in Dering Roll and to Sir JOHN of Essex in Parly. Roll. Another Sir JOHN (6 billets) differenced with a label (3) azure ; Harl. Roll.

Beauchamp, Sir John de, of Hache in county Somerset, baron 1299, and banneret— Sealed the Barons' letter to the Pope 1301 ; and bore, at the battle of Falkirk 1298, and at the siege of Carlaverock 1300, **vair** ; borne also by Sir ROGER at the siege of Calais 1345-8, ascribed to ROBERT in Glover Roll. (F.) Ascribed to JOHN (‡) in Dering Roll. Sir MILES, of Bucks, differenced with a label (3) gules, and Sir HUMPHREY with the label or, in Parliamentary Roll. Sir WILLIAM, "frere" (probably of Sir ROGER), knighted at the capitulation of Calais 1348, bore, vair, on an inescochoen argent, the arms of MORTIMER. (F.) For other differences see Harl. MS. 1481 fo. 89.

Beauchamp, William de, of Eton—(H. III. Roll) bore, gules fretty argent ; Glover Roll. RAFE bore, for difference, a label (3) vert ; same as THOMAS FLEMING, of Westmorland ; Jenyns' Ordinary.

Beauchamp, John, Walter, and **William,** of Bedford—(H. III. Roll) bore, quarterly or and gules a bend of the last ; Parliamentary, Norfolk, and St. George Rolls (F.) ; in other MSS. a bend sable occurs.

Beauchamp, John de—(H. III. Roll) bore, sable, an eagle argent, beaked and legged or ; Glover Roll. A second JOHN bore, H. III., undée (6) argent and azure ; St. George Roll. F.

Beauchamp, Sir John, of Fyfield in Essex —(E. II. Roll) bore, argent (*vel* or) a lyon rampant sable, crowned gules ; Parly. Roll.

Beauchamp, Sir John (BESCHAMP), of Somersetshire—(H. VI. Roll) bore, vert, three besants ; Arundel Roll.

Beauchamp, William, of Cumberland— (E. III. Roll) bore, argent on a bend gules three plates ; Jenyns' Roll. F.

Beaufitz, Henry—(E. III. Roll) bore, quarterly per fess indented argent and gules ; Jenyns' Ordinary.

Beaufort, John—(R. II. Roll) bore (before his legitimation), per pale argent and azure on a bend gules, three lyons passant gardant or, a label (3) azure, on each pendant three fleurs-de-lys of the fourth ; Surrey Roll.

Beaufoy, John and **William** — (E. III. Roll) bore, argent a chevron between three eaglets gules ; Jenyns' Ordinary. F.

Beaulieu, William—(E. III. Roll) bore, same coat as DALSTONE, LASSELLS, of South Cowton, &c., argent a chevron dancettée (i.e. indented) between three daws' heads erased sable ; Jenyns' Roll. F.

Beauly, John, of the South—(E. III. Roll) bore, gules and argent embelif battaillée ; Jenyns' Roll. See also BEULEE.

Beaumays, Sir (——) de, of Hunts—(E. II. Roll) bore, azure, three garbs banded or ; Parliamentary Roll.

*Bea(u)mond, Le Sr.—bore, at the siege of Rouen 1418, azure, florettée and a lyon rampant or, *quarterly with,* azure, three garbs or. (F.) BEAUMONT, of Cole Orton, bears the first quarter as his coat at the present day.

Be(a)umond, Godfrey de—(H. III. Roll) bore, sable, six martlets 3, 2, 1, or, in St. George Roll (F.) ; sable nine martlets in orle argent in Arden Roll.

Be(a)umond, Sire Henry de, banneret— bore, at the battle of Boroughbridge 1322, azure, florettée and a lyon rampant or, over all a baston gobony argent and gules ; this coat is also ascribed to LEWES BEAMMOND in Jenyns' Ordinary. (F.) See BOHN.

Beaumond, John, of Devonshire - (E. III. Roll) bore, barry of six ermine and gules in Jenyns' Ordinary (F.) ; another JOHN, according to Surrey Roll, bore barry (6) vair and gules.

Beaumont, Sir Thomas—bore, at the siege of Calais 1345-8, gules, entoyre of crescents and a lyon rampant argent (F.) ; his son, Sir THOMAS, junior, bore them at the same time, with a label (3) or.

Robt. Beaupoyl   michol Berke   John Beeston

Antd. de Bek
Enesq̃z. Duram   Prod Bokard.   Oñr. Bekerinz

Jgo. Bekeringe   walter Bekunt   John de Belhuse

Tebaud d' Belhuse   John Bellasyse   John Bolome

Be(a)umond, William de—(H. III. Roll) bore, gyrony (12) or and gules; Arden Roll.

Beaupell, John (or BEAUPLE)—(E. III. Roll) bore, gules, a bend cotised argent; Jenyns' Ordinary. F.

Beaupeyl, Sire Robert—bore, at the battle of Boroughbridge 1322, gules, a bend vair (F.); another Sir ROBERT BEAUPLE, of Cornwall (E. II.) bore the same between six escallops argent; Parliamentary Roll.

Beaupré, Ralph de—(E. III. Roll) bore, vert, a lyon rampant or, a baston gules; Jenyns' Ordinary.

Becard (Sir) Piers—(E. II. Roll) bore, or a saltire between four eaglets azure; the saltire is gules in some tricks (F.); Parliamentary Roll.

Beche, Sir John de la, of Berks.—bore, at the first Dunstable tournament 1308, argent, on a bend gules three bucks' heads erased or, in the cantell a martlet sable; Parliamentary Roll.

Beche, John de la, a baron 1342—bore, vaire argent and gules; NICHOL bore the same, and on a canton of the first a martlet sable; Jenyns' Ordinary. F.

Beck, Sire Philip de (Bek)—bore, at the battle of Boroughbridge 1322, argent on a fess gules three bucks' heads cabossed or (F.); his son, Sir JOHAN, bore the same with a martlet sable for difference, but hinds' heads couped, in Ashmole Roll. See also BEK.

Beckebury, Sir William - (E. III. Roll) bore, azure, an eagle or; Ashmole Roll.

Beckham, Roger de, see PECKHAM.

Bedford, John, Duke of, K.G. 1399, bore France and England quarterly, a label (5) per pale ermine and azure, the latter florettée or; K. 400 fo. 6.

*****Bedingfeld, Piers de**—(H. III. Roll) bore, gules, an eagle ermine; Howard Roll; the reverse is now borne by the baronet's family.

Beeston, John—(E. III. Roll) bore, vert, a lyon rampant argent crowned gules; Jenyns' Ordinary. F. The same as MENVILE.

Beeston, W.—(E. I. or II. Roll) bore, sable, crusily fitchée and a bend or; Harl. Roll.

‡**Beices, Hameris** (LEICES or LEITES—(H. III. Roll) bore, or a lyon rampant gules crowned azure; a bordure sable besantée, Ashmole Roll; the field argent, and the bordure platey in the Dering Roll.

†**Bek, Antony de**, Bishop of Durham—bore, at the battle of Falkirk 1298, and at the siege of Carlaverock 1300, gules a fer-du-moulin ermine. (F.) The Bishop's name appears among the bannerets in Parliamentary Roll. Brother of the next named.

Bek, John, a baron 1295—(E. III. Roll) bore, gules, a cross moline argent in Jenyns' Ordinary (F.); the cross recercelée in the Arden Roll. Father of the next named.

Bek, Sir Waut de—(E. I. Roll) bore, gules, a cross recercelée argent; Guillim Roll.

Bekeyring, Thomas de—(E. I. Roll) bore, checquy argent and gules; Nativity Roll.

Bekering, Sir Christofer de, knighted at the capitulation of Calais 1348 — bore, checquy argent and gules, a bend sable (F.); THOMAS, bore it with the baston (or bend) azure; Jenyns' Ordinary. F.

Bekering, Thomas—(R. II. Roll) bore, checquy argent and gules, on a chevron sable three escallops of the first; Surrey Roll. Another THOMAS, bore, E. III., same as a JOHN DE LA RIVER, lozengy or and gules; blasoned "masclée," in Jenyns' Ordinary. F.

Bekuns, Walter—(E. III. Roll) bore, argent, a bend engrailed sable, a label of three gules; Jenyns' Ordinary. F.

Bekynham, Sir (——), a Kentish Knight—(H. VI. Roll) bore, argent, a chevron gules between three bucks' heads cabossed of the last, attires or; Arundel Roll.

Belchamp, Geffry de—(H. III. Roll) bore, quarterly, argent and sable; Glover and Howard Rolls.

Belet, Sir Ingram, of Norfolk—(E. II. Roll) bore, argent, on a chief gules three cinquefoyles argent; Parliamentary Roll. WILLIAM took up the cross in the last Crusade 1270.

Belett, Michael—(E. III. Roll) bore, argent, a fess and in dexter chief point a greyhound courant gules; Jenyns' Ordinary. F.

Belhous, Sir John, of Essex—bore, at the first Dunstable tournament 1308, argent, three lyonceux rampant gules (F.); and Sir WILLIAM (E. II.) bore the same, within a bordure indented sable; Parliamentary Roll.

Belhuse, Sir John de; knighted at the capitulation of Calais 1348—bore, or, on a saltire gules another vair. F.

Belhuse, Roger de—(E. III. Roll) bore, or, on a saltire gules five bezants (F.); another bore, sable, a fret enfruct or (F.); Jenyns' Ordinary.

Belhuse, Tebaud de—(H. III. Roll) bore, or, on a bend gules five lozenges vair (F.); St. George Roll.

Belkamore, John de—(E. III. Roll) bore, gules, a bordure engrailed argent, over all a bend of the last (F.); Jenyns' Ordinary. See ROBERT DE BILLEMORE.

Bellasyse, John, of Eltoftes—(E. III. Roll) bore, argent, three chess-rooks sable (F.); Jenyns' Roll.

Bellenden, Sir John de, of co. Glouc.—(E. II. Roll) bore, azure, entoyre of martlets (3, 3, 2, 1) argent; Parliamentary Roll.

Bellers, James—(R. II. Roll) bore, per pale gules and sable, a lyon rampant argent; Surrey Roll.

*****Bellewe, John**—(E. III. Roll) bore, sable, fretty or; Jenyns' Roll. F.

Bell ston, —— (E. III. Roll) bore, or, on a chevron gules, three crosses recercelée argent; Ashmole Roll.

[**Bellomont, Robert**, Earl of Leicester—"Fitz Pernell" SEAL, a cinquefoyle ermine.]

Belsede, Sir (——), of Norfolk—(E. II. Roll) bore, argent, four bars sable, a canton of the first; Parly. Roll. Harl. MS. 6137.

Beltoft, Les Armes de—(E. III. Roll) bore, or, fretty and a chief azure; Ashmole Roll.

THOMAS DE BERKELEY, 1243.

IN THE WALL OF THE SOUTH AISLE OF THE CHOIR
OF BRISTOL CATHEDRAL.

Beltoft, Sir Roger de, of co. Linc.—(E. II. Roll) bore, argent, fretty and a chief azure; Parliamentary Roll. ROBERT bore it, fretty engrailed, in Jenyns' Ordinary. F.

Beltoft, Symon de—(E. III. Roll) bore, argent, three chevronels interlaced azure, a chief of the last; blasoned, argent a frette and a chief azure; Jenyns' Ordinary. F.

[**Bendish,** alias **Westley, Ralph,** of Barrington, co. Cambridge, E. I.—bore, argent, a chevron sable between three rams' heads erased azure.—Shirley.] F.

Beneville, John—(E. III. Roll) bore, or, on a bend sable three mullets pierced argent; Jenyns' Ordinary. See BONEVILE. F.

Bengham, Sire Thomas de—bore, at the battle of Boroughbridge 1322 party, gules and vert, a lyon (rampant) argent. This coat is wrongly ascribed to Sir JOHN DE HOLAND in Bodley's Copy.

Benhale, Robert de—bore, at the second Dunstable tournament 1334, sable, a bend deux wyfres argent—Stowe; six wyfres in Sloane; (cotised wavy) Jenyns' Ordinary (F.) For wyfres=vipers' nests! see "Archæologia," vol. 31, p. 247; see also CREK, post.

Benhale, Sir Robert de, a baron 1360; knighted at the capitulation of Calais 1348—bore, argent, a bend between three fizures (cotises) wavy sable; in another cotises undée.

Benhalle, Robert—(E. III. Roll) bore, gules a cross recercelée (moline in blason) argent, a baston azure (F.); Ashmole Roll and Jenyns' Ordinary; another with a bordure instead of a baston.

"Bennes DE HAMPTON**"**—(H. III. Roll) bore, azure, three lyons passant gardant or; Howard Roll.

Bennet, Sir John, of Norfolk—(E. II. Roll) bore, argent, a chevron gules, a bordure sable bezantée; Parl. Roll, Harl. MS. 6137.

Benet, Sir Richard—(E. III. Roll) bore, gules, a lyon rampant ermine, a bordure engrailed of the last; Ashmole Roll.

Benstede, —— (H. VI. Roll) bore, gules, three bars argent; Arundel Roll.

Benstede, Sir John de, a Justice Common Pleas 1309-20—bore, at the battle of Falkirk 1298 [. . . .] a cross pierced and patée and botonné argent. F.

Benstede, Sir William, of Essex—(E. II. Roll) bore, azure, a fess between two chevronels or; Parliamentary Roll. F.

‡**Berbling, Walter** or **William de**—(E. III. Roll) bore, argent, three fleurs-de-lys sable; Dering Roll.

Berbroune, Thomas—(E. III. Roll) bore, or, a cross patée flory gules; Jenyns' Ordinary. F.

Berdone, Walter de—(E. III. Roll) bore, argent, an eagle azure beak and claws gules; Jenyns' Ordinary. F.

Bere, see DE LA BERE.

Bereford, Robert de—bore, at the second Dunstable tournament 1334, sable, a bend engrelée argent. F.

Bereford, Sir Symon, of co. Warwick—(E. II. Roll) bore, argent, three fleurs-de-lys sable; Parliamentary Roll. These arms are ascribed to Sir HENRY DE BERFELD, in the Boroughbridge Roll. See DE BOREFELD.

Bereford, Sir Symon—bore, at the battle of Boroughbridge 1322, argent crusily potent and three fleurs-de-lys sable, a bordure engrailed gules; crusily fitchée in Ashmole Roll.

Bereford, Sir William, of Northants—(E. II. Roll) bore, argent, crusily and three fleurs-de-lys sable; Parly. Roll. BAWDWIN and JOHN—bore crusily fitchée (F.); Surrey Roll and Jenyns' Ordinary.

Berfield v. BORFIELD.

Berhalgh, Richard—(E. III. Roll) bore, argent, three bears passant sable muzzled or (F.); Jenyns' Ordinary.

Beringer, Sir Ingram, of Hants.—(E. II. Roll) bore, or, a cross vert and a bend gules; Parliamentary Roll and Jenyns' Ordinary. F.

Beringham v. **Bermingham.**

*[**Berington, Thomas de**—(E. III.) bore, sable, three greyhounds courant in pale argent, collared gules, within a bordure of the last.—Shirley.] F.

‡**Berkeley, Morris** and **Thomas de**—(H. III. Roll) bore, gules, a chevron argent; Arden and St. George Rolls.

Berkele, Sir Thomas—bore, at the battle of Boroughbridge 1322, gules "queyntée de la mermounde" for a similar crux, see Sir JOHN DE CROMWELL: Queynty d'argent fretty de ses armes d'ermyne. Parliamentary Writs (Vol. 23), 1830, ii. app. 196. The shields for these coats are left blank in Bodley's Copy of the Roll: their Heraldic interpretation was evidently beyond Brooke, York Herald of that day.

*Berkeley, Sir Thomas,** baron 1295—Sealed the Barons' letter to the Pope 1301, and bore, at the battle of Falkirk 1298, gules, crusily patée and a chevron argent, Nobility Rolls; and so borne by Sir MORRIS or THOMAS at the siege of Calais 1345-8, and in Surrey and other Rolls. See Monumental Effigy. Baron THOMAS was father of Sir MAURICE and Sir JOHN, in the next par., and of Sir THOMAS 1308.

Berkeley, Sir Maurice de, banneret, baron 1308—bore, at the battle of Falkirk 1298, and at the siege of Carlaverock 1300, gules, crusily patée and a chevron argent (with a blue label of 3 because his father Thomas was then alive); Parly. Roll. Lord BERKELEY bore it also at the siege of Rouen 1418 (F.). The shield of Sir MORYS, H. VI., has nine crosses patée, in the Arundel Roll; and that of Sir JOHN (brother of Sir MAURICE 1308), of co. Glouc., three (or) in the Parly. Roll; he served also at the battle of Falkirk. JAMES (R. II.) differenced with a crescent azure; Surrey Roll.

Berkeley, Maurice de—bore, in the second Dunstable tournament 1334, gules, crusily argent and a chevron ermine (F.); in Surrey Roll (R. II.), crusily patonce. THOMAS bore the chevron argent in Segar Roll &c. F.

Berkeley, Sir Maurice, of Uley, co. Glouc., a baron 1308—bore, gules, crusily formée argent, a chevron ermine; Atkinson Roll.

Berkeley, Sir Maurice OF OM'—(H. VI. Roll) bore, gules, crusily formée and a chevron argent, all within a bordure of the last; Atkinson Roll.

Gile d Berkelaie

John Barkley

Rich.
de Beringham

BLENKINSOPP.
MONUMENTAL SLAB—HALTWHISTLE CHURCH.

wal.
Bernyngham

walt de Botton

Volt de Botune

Berkley, Sir John—bore, at the siege of Calais 1345-8, gules, a chevron between ten cinquefoyles argent (F.); ascribed to another JOHN in Surrey Roll, the cinquefoyles pierced.

Berkeley, Sir Thomas—bore, at the first Dunstable tournament 1308, gules, a chevron between ten roses, 6, 4, argent; he served at the battle of Falkirk 1298. In the Parly. Roll as Sir THOMAS, banneret of co. Glouc. (E. II.) he bore, the chevron between 6 roses. Brother of Sir MAURICE 1308 and of Sir JOHN.

Berkeley, Giles de—(H. III. Roll) bore, quarterly or and azure, a bendlet gules in Arden Roll (purpure in St. George); quarterly per fess indented in Harl. MS. 6137 fo. 79. F.

Berkrolls, Sir Roger and **Sir William de**, of co. Glouc.—(E. III. Roll) bore, azure, a chevron between three crescents or; Ashmole and Parly. Rolls.

Berley, John—(E. III. Roll) bore, gules, three mullets pierced or, a quarter ermine; Jenyns' Ordinary. F.

Berlingham, Sir Richard—(E. II. Roll) bore, gules, three bears unmuzzled passant argent; Parliamentary Roll.

Bermingham, Sir Richard de (BERING-HAME)—bore, at the first Dunstable tournament 1308, gules, three owls or. F.

Bermingham, Sir Foulke and John de—(R. II. Roll) bore, per pale dancettée argent and sable; Surrey and Ashmole Rolls. F.

Bermingham, Sir Thomas—bore, at the first Dunstable tournament 1308, azure, a bend engrelée or. (F.) Sir WILLIAM, banneret (a baron 1326) also bore it at the battle of Boroughbridge 1322; the bend tricked as fusily in the Arden, Guillim and St. George Rolls (F.); and, perhaps wrongly, tricked as a bordure in the Arundel Roll, fo. 102b. Sir THOMAS, of co. Worcester, bore it with a label of three gules for difference; Parliamentary Roll.

Bermingham, Sir Walter de (BERYNG-HAM)—bore, at the first Dunstable tournament 1308, argent on a bend gules cotised sable, two escallops or (F.). Jenyns' Roll places three escallops on the bend, and the Parliamentary Roll in addition gives or, as the field. F.

*Bernay (——), a Suffolk Kt —(H. VI. Roll) bore, per pale gules and azure a cross engrailed ermine; Arundel Roll.

Berners, John and **Rauf de**—(H. III. Roll) bore, quarterly or and vert (F.); Arden, St. George, and Howard Rolls. Another JOHN bore the same with a label gules; Glover and Norfolk Rolls.

Beroun, see also BYRON.

Beroun, Sire John de—bore, at the battle of Boroughbridge 1322, argent, three bendlets gules—and Sir JAMES also, in Parly. Roll.

Beron, Nicholas, of Claiton—(E. IV. Roll) bore, argent, three bendlets enhanced gules and *quarterly with*, argent on a bend azure three annulets or, a cross crosslet fitchée of the second, with crest; Ballard Roll.

Beronden, Sir Walter de, of Northumberland—(E. II. Roll) bore, argent three roses sable. Parly. Roll.

Beronden, Sir Gilbert de, of Northumberland—(E. II. Roll) bore, gules on a bend argent three roses sable; Parliamentary Roll.

Bertout, —— (H. III. Roll) bore, or, three palets gules, on a canton sable a lyon rampant of the field; Howard Roll. See BERTRANT.

Bertram, Sir Roger, feudal baron of Bothal — (E. II. Roll) bore, or, "a false escocheon" voided (an orle) azure; Parliamentary Roll (F.). Sir JOHN bore the same, H. VI., *quarterly with*, argent, a fess between three crescents gules; Atkinson Roll. See also BARTRAM.

Bertram, Roger—(H. III. Roll) bore, gules, crusily and an orle or; Glover Roll. See also BARTRAM.

Bertram, Robert—(H. III. Roll) bore, gules a fess or; Howard Roll.

Bertram, Robert—(H. III. Roll) bore, or, a lyon rampant vert (F.); St. George Roll; crowned azure in Howard Roll.

Bertrant, Walter—(H. III. Roll) bore, per pale or and gules, on a canton azure a rowell argent; Norfolk Roll. See BERTOUT.

Bertto, Hamont de, slain at the siege of Calais 1347 - bore, argent, on a chief gules a dexter and sinister hand appaumé pileways of the field. F.

Berwicke, Hugh of—(E. IV. Roll) bore, argent, three bears' heads couped sable muzzled or; with crests; Ballard Roll. One of these names took up the cross in the last Crusade 1270.

Beschamp, Sir John (or BEAUCHAMP), of Somersetshire—(H. VI. Roll) bore, vert three bezants; Arundel Roll.

Besille, John de—(H. III. Roll) bore, argent three torteaux (F.); Arden and St. George Rolls. [JOHN, the nephew, bore the same within a bordure azure (F.); Jenyns' Roll.] Sir THOMAS, E. III, bore a mullet of five or on the first torteaux; Ashmole Roll.

Beslingthorpe, Sir Richard, of co. Linc. —(E. II. Roll) bore, argent, a chevron gules a chief indented sable; Parliamentary Roll.

Besonn, Sir Thomas de, of Cumberland—(E. II. Roll) bore, lozengy argent and sable; Parly. Roll. See BOSON.

*[Betton, Walter de, of Salop—bore, argent, two palets sable, each charged with three crosses crosslet fitchée or.—Shirley.] F.

Betune, Baudewyn de, lord of the manor of Skipton in Craven, brother of the Count of Flanders and Count of Albemarle and Ile; who married Hawisia, Countess D'Albemarle —E. III. Roll, bore, bendy (6) argent and gules (*sic*) a chief or (F.); Jenyns' Ordinary.

‡Betune, John de—(H. III. Roll) bore, azure, on a chief argent a lyon passant gules; Dering Roll.

Betune, Robert de—(E. I. Roll) bore, or, a lyon rampant sable (F.); Camden Roll.

Betune, William de—(E. I. Roll) bore, argent, a fess gules and in dexter chief point a lyon passant regardant sable (F.); Camden Roll.

Beulee, Richard de—(R. II. Roll) bore, quarterly argent and gules a rose counterchanged seeded or; Surrey Roll. See also BEAULY.

SIR JOHN DE BITTON,

12 HEN. III., 1227.

IN BITTON CHURCH, GLOUCESTERSHIRE. *After Boutell.*

Bevercote, Sir John de—bore, at the battle of Boroughbridge 1322, argent a cross patée (patonce) azure, a label (3) gules. F.

Beynham, Edmund de—(R. II. Roll) bore, sable three mullets, two and one argent; Surrey Roll. See also REYNHAM.

Beyton, Sir William de (BOYTON or BRITTON)—(E. II. Roll) bore, azure, six escallops 3, 2, 1, or ; Parliamentary Roll.

Biblesworth, Sir Hugh de, of Herts.— (E. III. Roll) bore, azure, three eaglets or; (F.) St. George and Parliamentary Rolls. Sir JOHN bore six eaglets, 3, 2, 1, or; Ashmole Roll ; both are also ascribed to WALTER. Another WALTER took up the cross in the last Crusade 1270.

Bicklond, John, see BUCKLAND.

‡**Bicknore, John de**—(H. III. Roll) bore, argent a chief azure ; Howard Roll.

Bicknore, Sir John de, of Kent—(E. III. Roll) bore, argent, on a chief azure three lyonceux rampant of the first (crowned or, Dering Roll); Parly. Roll. Sir THOMAS bore the coat with a baston gules ; Ashmole and Parliamentary Rolls.

∗[**Biddulph (Thomas de)**, of Staffordshire (H. III.)—bore, vert, an eagle displayed argent; another coat—argent, three soldering irons sable.—Shirley.] F.

Bigod, Roger le, (4th) Earl of Norfolk— (H. III. Roll) bore, or, a cross gules ; Glover and St. George Rolls.

Bigod, Roger, Earl of Norfolk, Earl Marshal of England—bore, at the battle of Falkirk 1298, per pale or and vert a lyon rampant gules, and so sealed the Barons' letter to the Pope 1301. (F.) RAUF bore it oppressed by a baston argent ; Arundel Roll.

Bigod, Hugh—(H. III. Roll) bore, gules a lyon passant or ; Norfolk and Glover Rolls.

Bigod, Rauff, of Settrington, Yorks—(H. III. Roll) bore, or, on a cross gules five escallops argent. Glover Roll, &c. Ascribed also to JOHN (F.) in the St. George Roll, and to Sir RAFFE, of Norfolk, in the Parly. Roll.

Bigod, John (BYGOOD), of Essex, Knight— (H. VI. Roll) bore, argent, on a chief gules two crescents of the first (? or); Arundel Roll.

Billemore, Robert de—bore, at the second Dunstable tournament 1334, argent a bend gules a bordure engrelé or. (F.) See JOHN DE BELKAMORE.

Billynge, Nicol—(R. II. Roll) bore, gules, three fish naiant (in pale) or, a bordure engrailed argent ; Surrey Roll.

Bilney, Sir Roger de, of Norfolk—bore, at the first Dunstable tournament 1308, argent an eagle vert, borne also by WILLIAM ; (F.) Jenyns' Ordinary.

Binchestre, Robert de—(E. III. Roll) bore, gules, a chief battaylé argent, tricked. gules a fess crenellée argent ; (F.) Jenyns' Roll.

ᵃ[**Bingham, Robert de**, of Melcombe Somerset (H. III.)—bore, azure, a bend cotised between six crosses patée or.—Shirley.] F.

Bingham, Sire Thos. de, see BENGHAM.

Bingham, John and **Richard**—(E. III. Roll) bore, or, on a fess gules, three water-bougets argent ; (F.) Surrey Roll, Jenyns' Ord.

Bingham, Sir Richard—(E. III. Roll) bore, or two bars gules, charged with three water-bougets 2 and 1 argent ; Ashmole Roll.

Birland, William—(R. II. Roll) bore, gules, a chevron between three bears' heads couped argent, muzzled of the field ; Surrey Roll.

Bishopbury, Henry—(E. III. Roll) bore, argent a fess double cotised sable; Jenyns Roll. F.

Bishopdonne, John de—(E. III. Roll) bore, or, four bendlets azure, a quarter ermine ; Jenyns' Ordinary. F.

Bishopsdonne, William—(H. III. Roll) bore, bendy (10) or and sable; (F.) Arden and St. George Rolls ; and the same with a canton ermine was borne by Sir JOHN BISHOPSTONE, of Warwickshire, in Ashmole Roll ; bendy of 8 in Parliamentary Roll.

Bissett, Sir John, of co. Worcester—(R. II. Roll) bore, azure bezanty (3, 3, 2, 1) ; Parliamentary Roll.

Bittone, Sir John—(R. II. Roll) bore, ermine a fess gules ; Parly. Roll. See incised slab.

Blaen, Sir Raffe (or BLOAN) of Cornwall— (R. II. Roll) bore, sable, a saltire engrailed argent ; Parliamentary Roll. See BLOYON.

Blakeburne, John de—(H. III. Roll) bore, paly (6) argent and azure; St. George Roll. F.

Blaked, Sir John, of Bucks—(R. II. Roll) bore, gules, a chevron vair ; Parly. Roll.

Blakenham, Benet de—(H. III. Roll) bore, barry (6), sable and or, another sable, two bars or. (F.) St. George Roll ; called BEGES DE BLAKELIG in Arden Roll.

Blakenham, Sir Thomas, of Suffolk— (R. II. Roll) bore, azure, crusily and two bars or ; Parly. Roll.

Blanchminster, Sir Renaud, Sir Richard and William—(H. III. Roll) bore, argent, fretty gules ; Glover and Nativity Rolls. F.

Blande, John—(E. III. Roll) bore, gules, two bars and 8 martlets in orle or, 3, 2, 2, 1 ; Jenyns' Ordinary. F.

Blare, Adam de—(H. III. Roll) bore, sable, crusily argent and six crescents, 3, 2, 1, or; Arden and St. George Rolls (which latter gives another coat, crusily fitchée); (F.) Howard Roll gives three (not six) crescents.

Blaunfroun, Sire Thomas—bore, at the battle of Boroughbridge 1322, ermine, on an inescocheon, the arms of MORTIMER or, and azure, the MORTIMER inescocheon argent. See also TURPINTON or TRUMPINGTON.

Blencowe, John de—(E. III. Roll) bore, gules, a quarter argent ; Jenyns' Roll. F.

Blenkinsopp, Thomas—(E. III. Roll) bore, argent a fess between three garbs sable ; (F.) Jenyns' Ordinary. See also incised slab in Pedigree.

Blenkinsopp, Thomas, of Helbeck — (E. III. Roll) bore, gules, six annulets 3, 2, 1, or, a bordure engrailed argent. Jenyns' Ordinary.

Bleverhassett, John de—(E. III. Roll) bore, gules, three dolphins embowed argent; Jenyns' Roll. F.

Blewett, see BLUET.

. . . BOHUN, WIFE OF SIR PETER ARDERNE,

Chief Justice temp. H. vi. and E. iv., and Justice of the
King's Bench.

In Latton Church, Essex, 1465—5 Ed. iv.

After Drummond.

*[**Blois, Thomas,** of Norton, Suffolk (10 E. IV.)
—bore, gules, a bend vair between two
fleurs-de-lys or.—Shirley.] F.

Blonde v. **Blande.**

Blothow, ——(H. III. Roll) bore, argent, a
saltire gules between four torteaux ; St.
George Roll. F.

*[**Blount, Sir William le,** of Warwickshire
— bore, at the first Dunstable tournament 1308,
undée (6) or and sable (F.) ; borne by another
WILLIAM at the second Dunstable tournament
1334, by a Sir WILLIAM at the battle of
Boroughbridge 1322, and by Sir WILLIAM,
knighted at the capitulation of Calais 1348,
also by THOMAS, a baron, 1 E. III. ; Parly.
Roll ; and by JOHN, K.G., at the siege of Rouen
1418 ; another JOHN bore it, with a label of the
arms of " Mons. THOMAS BLOUNT," at the
second Dunstable tournament 1334. (F.)
WALTER BLOUNT bore, undée (8) or and sable ;
Surrey Roll. The modern form of undée, is
barry nebulée. One WILLIAM LE BLOUNT
took up the cross in the last Crusade 1270.

Blount, Sir Hugh le, of Essex, and **Thomas**
—(E. II. Roll) bore, quarterly argent and gules
on a bend sable three eaglets displayed or (F.) ;
Surrey and Parly. Rolls ; and another THOMAS
bore crosses crosslet fitchée in the place of
eaglets ; Jenyns' Roll. F.

Blount, Sir Thomas, of Warwickshire—
bore, at the first Dunstable tournament 1308,
gules, a fess between six martlets argent (F.).
Borne also by Sir THOMAS, who was knighted
at the capitulation of Calais 1348, and by Sir
WILLIAM ; Ashmole Roll. This coat was
adopted by the family of NICHOLAS LE
BLOUNT who assumed the name of CROKE.

Blount, Thomas—(E. III. Roll) bore, gules,
a fess between six spur-rowells 3 and 3 argent ;
Jenyns' Ordinary.

Blount, John—(R. II. Roll) bore, azure, a
saltire engrailed or ; Surrey Roll.

Blount, Thomas - (E. III. Roll) bore, azure,
three leopards' faces jessant-de-lys or, a bendlet
ermine ; Jenyns' Roll. F.

Blount, William—(E. III. Roll) bore, chequy
argent and gules, a baston sable ; Jenyns' O. F.

Bloy, Sire Adam de—bore, at the battle of
Boroughbridge 1322, argent, a chevron azure,
between three gryphons segreant gules. F.

Bloy, Sir Run'ard de—(E. I. Roll) bore,
gules, two (3) mullets or, a canton ermine ;
Nativity Roll.

Bloyon, John or **Robert—**(E. III. Roll)
bore, argent, a saltire engrailed sable ; Jenyns'
Ordinary. F. See BLAEN.

Bloys, the Castellan of—(H. III. Roll)
bore, gules, three palets vair, a chief or ; Arden
Roll. F.

Bluet, Sir John, of Hants —bore, at the first
Dunstable tournament 1308, or, a double-
headed eagle gules. F.

Bluet, Sir Walter, of co. Gloucester—(E. II.
Roll) bore, or, a chevron between three eaglets
vert ; Parliamentary Roll.

Bluet, William - (H. III. Roll) bore, or, two
wings conjoined in fess gules. F.

Blunde, William—(H. III. Roll) bore,
masculée or and sable ; Grimaldi and Glover
Rolls ; lozengy in Howard Roll and Jenyns'
Ordinary. F.

Blundell, Robert—(H. III. Roll) bore, azure,
billettée or, on a canton of the second a raven
ppr. ; Arden and St. George Rolls. F.

Blondeville, Randolf, Earl of Chester
ƒ Hugh Kevelioke, Earl of Chester (*whom see*)
1180–1231, bore on his seal, a lyon or a wolf
saliant ; Journal Brit. Arch. Ass. vol. v. p. 235,
but the Rolls (temp. H. III.) assign him, azu e,
three garbs or banded gules ; St. George Roll. F.

Blyg'feld, Thomas—(R. II. Roll) bore, argent,
on a bend sable three plates ; Surrey Roll.

Bocking, John—(E. III. Roll) bore, argent,
crusily (12) and a bend undée gules ; Jenyns'
Ordinary. F.

‡**Bocton, Stephen de**—(H. III. Roll) bore,
azure, on a chief dancettée (4) or, three torteaux ; Dering Roll. F.

*[**Bodenham, Hugh de,** lord of Bodenham
in Herefordshire—bore, azure, a fess between
three chess- ooks or.—Shirley] F.

‡**Bodiham, William de—**(H. III. Roll) bore,
gules, an inescocheon argent, and eight besants
in orle ; Dering Roll. F. ROBERT took up
the cross in the last Crusade 1270.

Bodiham, William de—(H. III. Roll) bore,
argent, a bend indented per bend indented
or and azure, within a bordure gules ; Howard
Roll. F.

Bodrugan v. **Botringham.**

Bodrugan, Sir Henry, and **Otes,** of Cornwall—(E. II. Roll) bore, argent, three bendlets
gules ; Parly. Roll and Jenyns' Ordinary. F.

Boer, Robert le—(H. III. Roll) bore, azure,
three boars' heads or ; Howard Roll.

Bohun, Humphrey de, Earl of Hereford,
Constable of England—bore, at the battle of
Falkirk 1298 (with a label gules), at the siege
of Carlaverock 1300, and at the first Dunstable
tournament 1308, as did his father HUMFREY
also at Falkirk, azure a bend argent cotised or,
between six lyonceux rampant of the last (F.)
[the bend is often blasoned Hereford cotised
(*i.e.* argent cotised or), and for HENRY, gules
cotised or]. Sir HUMPHREY of Herefordshire,
bore the bend ermine cotised argent ; Parliamentary Roll.

Bohun, Sire Edmund de—bore, at the
battle of Boroughbridge 1322, " Hereford
without the cotises " *i.e*, azure, a bend argent
between six lyonceux rampant or.

Bohun, Edward de—bore, at the second
Dunstable tournament 1334, the arms of the
Earl of Hereford with, un enisele (an inescocheon) of the arms of England. WILLIAM
DE BOHUN—bore, at that tournament
(1334) the arms of Hereford (with three mullets gules pierced vert on the bend) ; and so
also did WILLIAM, Earl of Northampton, K.G.,
at the siege of Calais 1345-8, with three mullets
(6) unpierced.

Bohun, Sir Gilbert de, of co. Herefordshire - (E. II. Roll) bore, azure on a bend
cotised argent between six lyonceux rampant
or, three escallops gules ; Parly. and St. George
Rolls. JOHN bore the same without the escallops ; St George Roll.

Bohun, Sir Edmond de, of Herefordshire—
(E. II. Roll) bore, azure, a bend per bend indented argent and gules plain cotised of the
second, between six lyonceux rampant or ;
Parly. Roll.

Jo de Bolturo   Robert de Bolton   Robt Bond

nicol de
Bonetby   will Booth   John Borehont

Robt de Borewd   John de   Hugh de
                     Boscawen   Bossard

Roger Bosseville   Allayn Botoler   Rauf Bozun

‡**Bohun, John de**—(E. I. Roll) bore, or, a cross azure (F.) Dering Roll; another JOHN, of Midhurst, a baron 1363, bore the same, Segar and Ashmole Rolls; ascribed also to ROBERT in Surrey Roll.

Bohun, Foulke and **Franke**, see BOUN.

Bokkesworthe, Sir William de (or BOLKWORTHE)—bore, at the first Dunstable tournament 13 8, or, a lyon rampant purpure collared or. F.

Bolde, Sir Henry, of Bold, Lancashire, Kt. —(H. VI. Roll) bore, argent, a gryphon segreant sable beaked and legged gules, *quarterly with* sable five fusils conjoined in fess argent, a label of three gules; Arundel and Ballard Rolls.

Bolebec, Hugh—(H. III. Roll) bore, vert, a lyon rampant ermine, Glover Roll; Sir HUGH, the feudal lord, bore (E. III.), vert, a lyon rampant argent; Jenyns' Ordinary. F.

Bolesby, William de—(R. II. Roll) bore, sable, a saltire or; Surrey Roll.

Bolmer, see BULMER.

Bolron,——(E. IV. Roll) bore, argent, a bend sable between five lozenges in chief and three picks in base sable; with crest; Ballard Roll F.

Bolron, Thomas—(E. III. Roll) bore, sable, on a chief argent a fer-de-moulin of the first; Jenyns' Roll. F.

Boltesham, Sir Thomas, of Rutland— (E. II. Roll) bore, gules, three besons or bird-bolts erect argent; Parliamentary Roll.

Bolton, John de—(E. I. Roll) bore, argent, on a bend sable three eaglets, or; Segar Roll. F.

Bolton, Robert de—(E. III. Roll) bore, argent, on a chevron gules three lyons passant gardant or; Jenyns' Ordinary. Borne also by THOMAS HESLARTON.

Bond, John de—(H. III. Roll) bore, gules, billettée or, and three lyons rampant argent; St. George Roll. F.

*[**Bond, Robert**, of Beauchamp Hache, Somerset (9 H. VI.)—bore, sable, a fess or.— Shirley.] F.

Bonetby, Nicol de—(H. III. Roll) bore, azure three estoiles argent; Glover Roll.

‡**Bonett, Hamon de**—(H. III. Roll) bore, checquy or and gules on a chief azure two spur-rowells argent; Howard and Dering Rolls. See BOWETT.

Bonevile, Sire Nichol—bore, at the battle of Boroughbridge 1322, or, on a bend sable three mullets (6) argent. F. See BENEVILE.

Bonevile, Sir William, of Sponton, Yorks. —(H. VI. Roll) bore, sable six mullets argent, *quarterly with* gules, three lyonceux gold; Atkinson Roll. WILLIAM, Lord BONVILE, K.G., bore the first coat, with the mullets pierced gules; K. 402 fo. 46.

Bonner, Sir Robert de, of Essex—(E. II. Roll) bore, ermine, a chief indented sable; Parliamentary Roll.

Booth, Sir John (BOUTHE), of Barton— (E. IV. Roll) bore, argent, three boars' heads erect and erased sable; with crest; Ballard Roll.

Booth, Sir William, knighted at the capitulation of Calais 1348—bore, vaire argent and gules, a bendlet sable. F.

Bordeux, Peter de, *v.* Burdeux.

Bordelys, Sir Geoffrey de, of co. Cambs. —(E. II. Roll) bore, ermine, on a chief gules a lyon passant gardant or; Parly. Roll.

Bordon, see BURDON.

Bordonn, Sir Walter—(E. III. Roll) bore, argent three cinquefoyles pierced sable; Ashmole Roll. See also BUROWDON.

Borefield, John—(E. III. Roll) bore, argent, a chevron gules between three pellets 2 and 1; Jenyns' Ordinary. F.

Borfeld, Sire Henry de (or BERFIELD)— bore, at the battle of Boroughbridge 1322, or, a chevron sable between three pellets (F.); in Ashmole Roll, or, three fleurs-de-lys sable.

Borgate, Sir Peers de, of Suffolk—(E. II. Roll) bore, paly (6) argent and sable; Parliamentary Roll.

Borges, Sir Thomas, of Kent—(H. VI. Roll) bore, argent, a fess counter-compony or and gules in chief three crosses crosslet of the last; Arundel Roll.

Borhont, Sir John, of Hants—bore, at the siege of Calais 1345-8, argent a fess between six martlets gules; (F.) Sir RICHARD, of Wilts., bore the same, E. II.; Parly. Roll.

[**Borowe, Robert de**, 1418—bore, gules, a bough erect and eradicated argent. Shirley.] F.

Borowell, (——**)** Kt.—(H. VI. Roll) bore, paly (6) argent and azure a bend gules; Arundel Roll. See BROWELL or BURWELL.

Borways *v.* **Burghersh.**

*[**Boscawen, John de** (E. III.) — bore, ermine, a rose gules; and more anciently, vert, a bull-dog argent!—Shirley.] F.

Bosco, Sir John de (1297)—bore, sable, crusily and three leopards' faces or; Nobility Roll.

Boson, Sir John and **Sir Piers**, of Norfolk —(E. III. Roll) bore, argent, three besons (or bird-bolts) erect gules; Ashmole, Parliamentary, and Surrey Rolls.

Boson, Raf—(H. III. Roll) bore, argent, three bird-bolts, one in pale erect between two pileways gules headed sable; Arden and St. George Rolls. F.

Bossard, Sire Hugo—bore, at the battle of Boroughbridge 1322, argent, two bars and in chief three mullets (6) within a bordure, all sable. F.

Bosville, Roger—(E. III. Roll) bore, argent, four fusils in fess gules; Jenyns' Ordinary. F.

Bosvile, Thomas, of Dayvile, in Yorks— (E. III. Roll) bore, argent, five fusils conjoined in fess gules, a crescent sable; Jenyns' Roll. F.

Bosville, Thomas—(E. III. Roll) bore, argent, five fusils in fess gules, in chief three leaves (feuilles in Cotgrave and temoyles in Jenyns' Ordinary) slipped sable (F.); crosslets in Cotton MS. & Harl. 6589; foyles or fer-mailes in Harl. 1068 and 1577.

Bosvill, John—(R. II. Roll) bore, argent, five fusils in fess gules, in chief three martlets sable; Surrey Roll.

Boteler, Allayne, of Berdon—(E. III. Roll) bore, azure, three covered cups or; Jenyns' Ordinary. F. See also incised slab.

SIR JOHN DE BOTILER, 1285.
IN S. BRIDE'S CHURCH, CO. GLAMORGAN.
After Boutell.

Boteler, Andrew (BUTLER)—bore, at the siege of Rouen 1418, argent six covered cups, 3, 2, 1, sable, *quarterly with*, gules a cross moline argent within a bordure engrailed or; Harl. 6137, reverses the quarterings. F.

Boteler, William de—baron, of Warrington, WILLIAM, of Wem, and Sir THOMAS, of Beausay—(E. II. Roll) bore, azure a bend between six covered cups or; Parliamentary, ballard, and Ashmole Rolls. JOHN, R. II., bore the bend argent in Surrey Roll. This is not the usually accepted coat—see below.

Boteler, James, of Rawcliff, in Lancs., also Sir NICHOLAS, and JOHN—(E. III. Roll) bore, azure, a chevron between three covered cups or; Surrey, Ballard, Ashmole, and Arundel Rolls. WILLIAM, of Kirkland, bore three mullets gules on the chevron; Ballard Roll.

Boteler, Sir William le, of Warrington, a baron, 27 E. I.—bore, gules, crusily or a fess counter-compony (checquy in H. 4033) argent and azure; Parliamentary Roll. RAUF bore this argent and sable, in St. George Roll.

Boteler, William of Wemme, baron 1308, bore, gules, a fess checquy argent and sable, between six crosses patée fitchée at the foot argent; Nobility Rolls. Another, gules, a fess checquy (counter-compony in trick), argent and sable between three crosses potent of the second (F.); Jenyns' Ordinary.

Boteler, William — bore, at the second Dunstable tournament 1334, gules, crusily argent, a fess checquy of the last and sable. RAUF bore this crusily or, in Glover Roll. F.

Boteler, Edward and **Sir William**—(E. I. Roll) bore, gules, crusily argent a fess counter-compony or and sable; Arden, Guillim, and Surrey Rolls.

Boteler, Sir Raffe le, of Salop—(E. II. Roll) bore, gules, a fess checquy or and sable (azure, sometimes), in chief two mullets or the second; Parliamentary Roll.

Boteler, Sir William—(E. III. Roll) bore, gules, a chevron counter-compony sable and argent; Ashmole Roll.

Botiler, Theobald, Earl of Ormond—(E. I. Roll) bore, or, a chief dancettée (3) azure; Segar and Ashmole Rolls, &c. (F.) JAMES, 5th Earl, K.G., bore it at the siege of Rouen 1418.

Botiler, Sire Rauf le—bore, at the battle of Boroughbridge 1322, argent, two bendlets gules (F.) RAF bore the bendlets azure (Arden Roll); ermine in Ashmole Roll.

Botiler, Sir Henry le—(E. I. Roll) bore, or, two bends gules a chief sable; Guillim Roll.

Botiler, Sir John (BOALER or BOYLER), knighted at the capitulation of Calais 1348, gules, four mascles in fess quarterly argent and sable, between three crosses flory or, H. 6589 (F.); between six crosses crosslet or, in H. 1068.

Botiller DE ST. LYS; le—(E. I. Roll) bore, quarterly argent and gules; Holland Roll.

Botelsham v. **Boltesham.**

Boter, Thomas—(E. III. Roll) bore, gyrony (8), ermine and gules; Jenyns' Ordinary. F.

Boterels, Sir William de, banneret—(E. II. Roll) bore, checquy or and gules a chevron azure; Parliamentary Roll. Sir REYNAUD, of Cornwall, bore, three horse-shoes argent on the chevron; Parliamentary Roll.

Boterels, Thomas—(H. III. Roll), bore, gules, bezantée, on a canton argent a cinquefoyle pierced sable; Arden and St. George Rolls. F.

Botetourt, Bartholomew de and **Sir Guy,** of Norfolk—(H. III. Roll) bore, ermine, a saltire engrailed gules; Arden and Parly. Rolls. Sir WILLIAM, of Norfolk, bore a mullet or, for difference at the first Dunstable tournament 1308 (F.); and Sir RALF, also of Norfolk, E. II., bore, a label (3) vert, for difference in Parly. Roll.

Botetourt, Sir John, a baron 1305—bore, at the battle of Falkirk 1298, and at the siege of Carlaverock 1300, or, a saltire engrailed sable; a banneret in the Parliamentary Roll. (F.) Sealed the Barons' letter to the Pope 1301 with a cinquefoyle pierced, on each (fcyle) a saltire engrailed.

Botetourt, Sir Thomas, of Norfolk—bore, at the first Dunstable tournament 1308, and at the battle of Boroughbridge 1322, or, a saltire engrailed sable, a label (5) gules. Sire JOHAN LE FIZ, bore the same at Boroughbridge, the pendants of the label platey.

Botreaux, Renaud (BOTR'WS)—(H. III. Roll) bore, checquy (also vaire) or and gules, on a chevron azure three horse-shoes argent (F.); Arden and St. George Rolls. Sir WILLIAM reversed the chequy; Harl. Roll.

Botreaux, Le Sire (NICHOLAS)—(E. III. Roll) bore, checquy or and gules, a bend vair. Jenyns' Ordinary. F.

Botreaux, William (BOTREWE)—(R. II. Roll) bore, argent, a gryphon segreant gules armed azure, Surrey Roll; gules and argent in Ashmole Roll.

‡**Botresham, Sire de**—(E. I. Roll) bore, or, three mascles two and one . . . . a chief paly (6) argent and gules; Dering and Camden Rolls. F.

Botringham v. **Bodrugan.**

Botringham, Sire Otes de—bore, at the battle of Boroughbridge 1322, argent three bendlets gules (F.) Sir HENRY bore the same; Harl. Roll.

Botringham, William de (BUTTRINGHAM)—bore, at the second Dunstable tournament 1334, argent a bend gules.

Botune, Steven de—(H. III. Roll) bore, azure, on a chief indented or three torteaux; Howard Roll.

Boues v. **Bucy.**

Boughton, Piers de—(R. II. Roll) bore, gules, a goat saliant or; Surrey Roll.

*[**Boughton, Robert de** (BORETON) E. III.—bore, sable, three crescents or.—Shirley.] F.

‡**Boulers, Baudwyn de**—(H. III. Roll) bore, sable billettée and a bend argent; Dering and St. George Rolls (F.). See also BULLER.

Boun, see BOHUN.

Boun, Foulke de—(E. III. Roll) bore, sable, three crescents argent; Jenyns' Roll; called JOIR, or JORCE, in the Arden Roll.

Boun, Frank de—(H. III. Roll) bore, gules, a crescent ermine within an orle of martlets ermine; Glover Roll. See BOHUN, of Tressingfield, Suffolk.

‡**Bourchalle, Henry de** (BORCHELLE)—(H. III. Roll) bore, paly (6) argent and azure, a fess gules, Dering Roll; tricked also or and azure. See also BURGHILL and BURRELL.

HENRY BOURCHIER, EARL OF ESSEX, 1483.
IN LITTLE EASTON CHURCH, ESSEX.
After Waller.

Robert Bonsor   Ogr de Bourno   Will Bourt

Egade Bointon   Henry de Boys   will d Boinile
                   del psburno

Bourchier, Robert (BURSOUR) – bore, at the second Dunstable tournament 1334, argent, a cross engrelée or. Lord BARNESSE or BERNERS.

‡**Bourchier, Hugh de** (BUCY or BOUES)— (H. III. Roll) bore, or three water-bougets azure; Dering and Howard Rolls. LE SIR BOWCEER, bore, H. VI., azure three water-bougets or; 6th Nobility Roll.

Bourchier, Sir Robert, a baron 1342, knighted at the capitulation of Calais 1348 — bore, argent, a cross engrailed gules, between four water-bougets sable (F.), as did Le Sire DE BOUCER, at the siege of Rouen 1418—where WILLIAM B. bore the same (differenced with a martlet or an annulet) *quarterly with* LOVAYNE, gules, billettée or and a fess argent. F.

Bourchier, Bartholomew (BOUSER) — (R. II. Roll) bore, argent, a cross engrailed gules between four water-bougets sable, a label (3) azure; Surrey Roll. WILLIAM, bore, three fleurs-de-lys or on the pendants, and his brother JOHN, 1st Lord Berners, K.G., bore on each pendant a lyon rampant or. Harl. MS. 1418 fo. 52ᵇ.

Bourgyloun, Sir Robert, of Norfolk— (E. II. Roll) bore, quarterly or and gules, in the second and third an annulet argent, over all a bend sable; Parliamentary Roll.

Bourne, Sir Thomas—bore, at the siege of Calais 1345-8, argent, a chevron gules between three lyons rampant sable, ascribed to NICHOLAS (F.) and Richard E. III.; Jenyns' Ordinary.

Bourne, Sir Christopher, knighted at the capitulation of Calais 1348—bore, gules, a lyon rampant argent a bordure engrailed or.

Bourne, Thomas de—bore, at the second Dunstable tournament 1334, gules, a lyon rampant or tail fourchée, a bordure engrelé argent.

‡**Bourne, John de**—(H. III. Roll) bore, ermine on a bend azure three lyons rampant or; Dering Roll; no lyons in Ashmole MS.

Bourneham, Sir Thomas de, of co. Linc. —(E. II. Roll) bore, or a maunch vert; Parliamentary Roll.

Bourt, William de—(H. III. Roll) bore, sable a cross patonce argent; Arden and St. George Rolls. F.

Boutevilain, Sir Robert, of Northants- —bore, at the first Dunstable tournament 1308, argent three crescents gules (F.), and Sir WILLIAM bore the same; Ashmole Roll and Jenyns' Ordinary.

Boutevilain, John–(R. II. Roll) bore, argent, a chevron between three crescents gules; Surrey Roll. ROBERT, bore, a fess in lieu of the chevron; St. George Roll. F.

Bovile, Herbert, and **Sir William de**– of Suffolk—(H. III. Roll) bore, quarterly or and sable (F.), and Sir JOHN, of Suffolk, a martlet, gules for difference; St. George and Parly. Rolls. WILLIAM bore, a lyon passant gules in the first quarter; Norfolk Roll.

Bovile, Sir John, le fys—(E. III. Roll) bore, gules, four bendlets argent; Ashmole Roll.

Bowes, Robert de, and **William** — (E. III. Roll) bore, ermine, three long bows "tenduz" gules; Jenyns' and Surrey Rolls.

Bowett, Thomas — (E. III. Roll) bore, argent, three reindeers' heads cabossed sable; Jenyns' Roll. F. See BONETT.

Bowles, Sir John–(H. III. Roll) bore, gules, a fess ermine, a bordure engrailed or; Ashmole Roll.

Bownd, Sir Roger — bore, at the first Dunstable tournament 1308, argent, a chief indented sable.

Box, Sir Henry de, of Essex—(E. II. Roll) bore, or, a bendlet between six lyonceux rampant gules; Parliamentary Roll. The lyonceux debruised by the bendlet, H. 6137 fo. 9.

Boxhull, see BUCKESHALL and BUXHULL.

Boxstede, Sir Raffe de, of Essex - (E. II. Roll) bore, quarterly argent and gules, on a bend sable three besants; Parliamentary Roll.

Boxworth, Sir William de, of co. Cambridge—(E. II. Roll) bore, or, a lyon rampant gules, collared argent; Parliamentary Roll.

Boydell, —— (E. IV. Roll) bore, quarterly 1 and 4, vert, a cross patonce or—2, gules, fretty argent a fess or—3, argent, on a fess azure three mullets of the field · and crest; Ballard Roll.

Boyland, —— (E. III. Roll) bore, sable an eagle displayed argent; Ashmole Roll.

Boyland, Sir John, of Norfolk—(E. II. Roll) bore, azure, a saltire engrailed or; Parliamentary Roll.

Boyler, Sir John, see BOTELER.

*****Boynton, Thomas de** - (R. II. Roll) bore, or, a fess between three crescents gules; Surrey Roll. F.

Boys, Sir John, v. BOSCO.

Boys, Sir Robert de, of Suffolk -- bore, at the first Dunstable tournament 1308, ermine a cross sable. Another ROBERT bore it at the second Dunstable tournament 1334, as did JOHN, of the South. (F.) Jenyns' Roll.

Boys, Ernald de, Henry, and **James** (H. III. Roll) bore, argent, two bars and a quarter (or canton) gules; Norfolk Roll, Jenyns' Ordinary, &c. F. Ascribed also to JOHN(‡) in Dering Roll.

Boys, Nicol de—(H. III. Roll) bore, ermine two bars and a quarter gules. Sir JOHN of co. Linc. and ROGER bore, over all, a bendlet sable; Parliamentary and Surrey Rolls.

Boys, Henry du - (E. III. Roll) bore, barry (8) gules and or (or and argent in blason) on a chief indented (3) sable, as many escallops of the second; Jenyns' Roll. F.

Boys, Sir Nichol de, of Bucks, and **John** – (E. III. Roll) bore, argent, a chevron sable bezanty (3 or 5); Parliamentary Roll and Jenyns' Ordinary. F.

Boys, Richard de—(H. III. Roll) bore, MORTIMER'S arms sable and or, the inescocheon argent billettée of the first; Arden, St. George, and Howard Rolls. One of these names took up the cross in the last Crusade 1270.

Boyton, see BEYTON.

‡**Boyville, William de** (E. I. Roll), and SIR WILLIAM, of Northants—(E. II. Roll) bore, gules, three saltorelles argent (F.), Dering and Parliamentary Rolls, &c.; colours reversed in St. George Roll. ROBERT took up the cross in the last Crusade 1269.

Boyvile, John—(R. II. Roll) bore, gules a fess or between three saltorelles argent; Surrey Roll.

THOMAS LORD BRAOSE.

Brabason, Sir Roger, of co. Leic.—(E. II. Roll) bore, gules, on a bend or three martlets sable ; Parly. Roll. One of these names with these arms slain at the siege of Calais 1347.

*****Bracebridge, Sir John de**, of co. Linc.— bore, at the first Dunstable tournament 1308, vaire argent and sable a fess gules (F.) ; Parly. Roll. Borne also by RAFFE at the siege of Rouen 1418.

Bracebridge, John—(H. III. Roll) bore, or, a cross azure ; St. George Roll. F.

Brackonbridge, Sir William, of Arden —(E. III. Roll) bore, argent, a cross pattée voided (*i.e.* quarter pierced) gules; Ashmole Roll.

Brace, William de—(H. III. Roll) bore, gules, a fess argent in chief two mullets (6) or ; Arden Roll [pierced gules St. George]; borne also by ROBERT, with a label (4) azure; St. George Roll. F.

Brace, Sir Robert—(E. III. Roll) bore, gules, a fess or, in chief two mullets argent; Ashmole Roll.

Bradburne, John de—(E. III. Roll) bore, argent, on a bend gules three mullets or voided (*i.e.* quarter pierced) vert; Jenyns' Ordinary. F.

Braddone, Sir Gefferay le, of Northants —(E. II. Roll) bore, sable, a bend engrailed argent- (F.) ; Parliamentary Roll. The bend fusily for WILLIAM, E. I., in Segar Roll. F.

Bradley, John de—(H. III. Roll) bore, argent, a chevron counter-compony or and sable between three ducks "swartish" (black) billed and legged or ; Howard Roll.

Bradley, Roger de—(H. III. Roll) bore, or, a fess gules between three buckles azure (F.) ; St. George Roll and also in Jenyns' Ordinary, where the buckles are blasoned, gules.

Bradshaw, Thomas—(E. III. Roll) bore, argent two bendlets enhanced sable ; Jenyns' Roll. F.

Bradshaw, William, of Haw (Haigh)— (E. IV. Roll) bore, argent two bendlets sable ; with crest ; Ballard Roll.

Bradstone, Roger—(E. III. Roll) bore, argent, an estachés engrailed (5) gules ; Jenyns' Roll. F.

Bradeston, Thomas de, baron 1322—bore, at the second Dunstable tournament 1334, argent on a quarter gules a rose or (F.). Sir THOMAS bore this at the siege of Calais 1345–8.

Braibef, John de—(H. III. Roll) bore, gules, a bend fusily or, a label (5) argent ; St. George Roll. F.

Brampton, John de—(E. III. Roll) bore, gules, a saltire between four crosses crosslet fitchée argent ; Arden Roll. F. BRYAN took up the cross in the last Crusade 1269. See BRUMTONE.

Branche, Piers—(H. III. Roll) bore, ermine, fretty gules ; Glover Roll.

Brandon (——), a Suffolk Kt.—(H. VI. Roll) bore, sable, two lyons' gambs per saltire between as many lyons' heads in pale, all erased argent ; Arundel Roll.

Branson, Sir John, see BRYANSON.

Braose, see also BREWES and BRUS.

Braose, Sir William de, banneret, baron of Gower 1299, sealed the Barons' letter to the Pope 1301—bore at the battle of Falkirk 1298, azure, crusily and a lyon rampant or tail fourchée ; and so for WILLIAM (‡) in Dering Roll; [crusily fitchée and not fourchée in Guillim and Nobility Rolls, &c.] not fourchée in Surrey and Parly. Rolls (F.)—see Monumental Effigy. So borne by THOMAS, baron 1342 ; Surrey Roll.

Braose, Sir Giles, de of Bucks—(E. II. Roll) bore, azure, crusily and a lyon rampant or, charged on the shoulder with a fleur-de-lys gules ; Parly. Roll. Sir JOHN bore the lyons crowned gules, at the siege of Calais 1345–8, and so also PETER, as the last, with a crescent for difference.

Braose, Sir Giles de, banneret—(E. II. Roll) bore, argent, crusily and a lyon rampant gules, tail fourchée renowée ; Parly. Roll.

Braose, Sir John, knighted at the capitulation of Calais 1348—bore, gules crusily and a lyon rampant or.

Braose, Sir Peers, of Gloucestershire— (E. II. Roll) bore, or, crusily and a lyon rampant sable, tail fourchée et renowée ; Parly. Roll.

Braose, John—(R. II. Roll) bore, argent crusily fitchée and a lyon rampant gules, tail fourchée ; Surrey Roll.

Braose, Robert de (BRUIS), of Brecknok, baron 1297—bore, barry (6) vaire (potent counter-potent) ermine and gules, and azure; Nobility Roll. Ascribed also to WM. DE BREWS.

‡**Braose, Reynald le** (BREWES)—(H. III. Roll) bore, azure, two bars vaire gules and ermine ; Howard and Dering Rolls; tricked the reverse (same as JOHN GRESLEY) in Jenyns' Ordinary. F.

Bratworthe, Sire Richard—bore, at the battle of Boroughbridge 1322, argent, a saltire azure, and a label (3) gules ; in this roll the arms of Sir JOHN DE BYRON are erroneously applied to him. See BARKSWORTH.

*****[Bray, Thomas** (9 E. III.)—bore, argent, a chevron between three eagles' legs sable à la cuisse.—Shirley.]

Bray, de —— (Oxon)—(E. III. Roll) bore, quarterly argent and azure, on a bend gules three fleurs-de-lys or ; Cotgrave Roll.

Braye, Sir Robert de, of Northants— (E. II. Roll) bore, vair, three bendlets gules ; Parly. Roll.

Braybrook, Sir Gerard, of Bucks—(E. II. Roll) bore, argent, seven mascles conjoined 3, 3, 1, gules ; Parliamentary Roll ; another GERARD bore it with a label of three azure; Surrey Roll ; and another GERARD and a THOMAS - bore, six mascles, 3, 2, 1, gules; Ashmole Roll and Jenyns' Ordinary. F.

Braylesford, Henry de—(E. III. Roll) bore, or, a cinquefoyle sable ; Jenyns' Ordinary. F.

Bredenhill *v.* **Brudenhill.**

Brenley, Sir Lawrence (or BRYNDALE)— (E. III. Roll) bore, gules, a gryphon segreant or ; Ashmole Roll.

Brent, Sir Robert de, of Somerset—(E. II. Roll) bore, gules, a gryphon segreant argent ; Parliamentary Roll.

Brentislee, John de—(E. III. Roll) bore, argent, on a bend engrailed gules three lyonceux passant of the field ; Jenyns' Ordinary. F.

SIR WILLIAM DE BRUCE, Kt.,
LORD OF UGGLEBARNBY, YORKSHIRE.
IN PICKERING CHURCH, C. 1226. *From Drummond.*

Brereleghe, Thomas—(E. III. Roll) bore, argent, a cross crosslet gules; Jenyns' Ordinary. F.

Brereley, Sir Thomas—(E. III. Roll) bore, argent, a cross potent gules; Ashmole Roll.

Brereton, Andrew of—(E. IV. Roll) bore, argent, two bars sable; with crest; Ballard Roll.

Bretagne, John de, nephew of K. Edward (8th Earl of Richmond, *f* John, Duke of BRITANNY)—bore, at the battle of Falkirk 1298, and at the siege of Carlaverock 1300; DREUX, with a quarter of Britanny and a bordure of England, viz., checquy or and azure, **a** bordure gules poudré with leopards or (*i.e.*, eight lyons of England passant gardant or), over all a canton ermine (F.). Borne also by DE MONTFORT, Earl of Richmond, K.G., 1376.

Breton, Sire Robert—bore, at the battle of Boroughbridge 1322, azure, a bend between six mullets (6) or ; spur-rowells in Jenyns' Ordinary and Surrey Roll ; borne also argent and gules, by PEIRES and Sir WILLIAM, of co. Linc. F.

‡**Breton, John**—(E. II. Roll) bore, quarterly or and gules, a bordure azure; Dering Roll; and for SIR JOHN, of Essex, in Parliamentary Roll. JOHN LE BRETON, D'N's. DE SPORLE appears to have sealed, with these arms, the Barons' letter to the Pope 1301.

Breton, Sire John, of Essex—(H. VI. Roll) bore, azure, two chevronels or, in chief two mullets pierced argent; Arundel Roll.

Breton, Philip de Cobburne—(E. III. Roll) bore, sable, fretty argent, a chief or ; Jenyns' Ordinary. F.

Breton, Robert de—(H. III. Roll) bore, per pale gules and azure, a fess between two chevrons argent; Arden and St. George Rolls.

Breton, Roger—(E. III. Roll) bore, argent, a chevron between three escallops gules; Jenyns' Ordinary. F.

Brett, Sir Amyan—bore, at the siege of Calais 1345-8, gules, in chief a lyon passant gardant or. F.

Brett, Sir Eumenious (or AMANEU), de la—bore, at the battle of Falkirk 1298, and at the siege of Carlaverock 1300, " gules" ; the arms of the French family of ALBRET, tricked as the next in Harl. MS. 6137 fo. 38ᵇ.

Brett, Sir John and **Sir Roger,** of Leicestershire—(E. II. Roll) bore, gules billettée and a fess dancettée or. (F.) Ashmole and Parly. Rolls.

Brewes, see also BRAOSE and BRUSE.

Brewes, John de—(E. II. Roll) bore, ermine, a cross lozengy sable; Jenyns' Roll. F.

Breysy, Sir Piers de—bore, at the first Dunstable tournament 1308, or a lyon rampant azure langued gules. (F.) See BRAOSE.

Bridelshall, Sir Gilbert de, of county Lincoln—(E. II. Roll) bore, argent, two gemelles azure, in chief three mullets gules; Parliamentary Roll.

Bridmanstone, Sir Stephen de, of Dorset—(E. II. Roll) bore, argent seven mascles conjoined sable; another trick, six lozenges, 3, 2, 1 ; Parliamentary Roll. See CROUPES.

Brygge (——), an Essex Kt.—(H. VI. Roll) bore, argent, three owls passant sable. beaked and legged or ; Arundel Roll. F.

Brightmere (——), of Essex—(H. VI. Roll) bore, gules, a chevron between three swans' heads and necks erased argent; Arundel Roll.

Brinton, Adam de—(H. III. Roll) bore, gules, a lyon rampant ermine tail fourchée; Arden and St. George Rolls. F.

*[**Brisco, Isold,** of Crofton, Cumberland, 1390—bore, argent, three greyhounds courant sable.—Shirley.] F.

Britby, Robert de—(E. II. Roll) bore, gules, billettée and a fess dancettée argent; Jenyns' Roll. F

Britehebury, Avery—(R. II. Roll)·bore, argent, two bars azure, on a canton of the last, a martlet or; Surrey Roll.

Britton, Sir William de (BEYTON or BOYTON), of Suffolk—(E. II. Roll) bore, azure, three escallops or; Parliamentary Roll.

Brius, or **Briwys,** see BRAOSE and BRUSE.

Broc, Laurence de—(H. III. Roll) bore, gules, on a chief argent a lyon passant of the field; St. George Roll. F.

Brocas, Bernard—(R. II. Roll) bore, sable, a lyon rampant gardant or ; [another BERNARD bore it with a label (3) gules, Surrey Roll]; and Sir JOHN also bore it at the siege of Calais 1345-8. F.

Brockhill, Sir Thomas (or BROKETT), of Kent—(H. VI. Roll) bore, gules crusily fitchée or and a cross engrailed argent; Arundel and Ashmole Rolls.

Brockhole, Thomas de—(H. III. Roll) bore, or, crusily and a chevron gules ; St. George Roll. (F.) Called also HOLEBROOKE. which see.

Brockholes, Geffrey—(R. II. Roll) bore, argent, a chevron between three brocks' or badgers' heads erased sable; Surrey Roll.

Brocking, Sir Ralffe, of Suffolk—(H. VI. Roll) bore, argent, crusily and a fess undée gules; Arundel Roll.

Broke, Nele de—(H. III. Roll) bore, gules, a chief indented or ; Howard Roll.

Broome, Sir Nicholas, of Norfolk—(E. II. Roll) bore ermine, a fess dancettée gules ; Parly. Roll.

Brome, Sire William de—bore, at the battle of Boroughbridge 1322, sable a cross passant argent. F.

Brome, Roger de—(H. III. Roll) bore, argent, a chief dancettée gules ; St. George Roll. F.

Bromley, Sir John of—(E. IV. Roll) bore, quarterly per fess dancettée gules and or ; with two crests; Ballard Roll.

(**Bromley?**), —— (R. II. Roll) bore, argent, on a chevron gules three besants, a bordure engrailed of the second; Surrey Roll.

Brompton, see BRAMPTON and BRUMTON.

Brontone, Piers de—(H. III. Roll) bore, argent, on a chief gules three escaliops or ; Arden Roll.

SIR GUY BRYAN, K.G. 1391,

IN THE ABBEY CHURCH OF TEWKESBURY. *After Stothard.*

Brony (——), a Suffolk Knight—(H. vi. Roll) bore, argent, a chief indented gules ; Arundel Roll.

*[Brooke, Adam de, lord of Leighton (H. iii.) —bore, or, a cross engrailed per pale gules and sable.—Shirley.] F.

Brooke, Sir Thomas (or Bork)—(E. ii. Roll) bore, argent, a fess dancettée (3) sable, bezantée at the points ; Parliamentary Roll.

*[Brooke, William de la, of Brooke, Somerset, 1231—bore, gules, on a chevron argent, a lyon rampant sable.—Shirley.]

Brotherton, Thomas of, Earl Marshal— bore, at the second Dunstable tournament 1334, England and a label (3) argent. F.

*Broughton, John de—(E. ii. Roll) bore, argent, two bars gules, on a quarter of the last a cross of the first ; Jenyns' Roll. F.

Broughton, Thomas de—(R. ii. Roll) bore azure, a cross engrailed argent ; Surrey Roll.

Browe, Hugh de—(R. ii. Roll) bore, gules, on a chevron argent, three roses of the field seeded or ; Surrey Roll.

Browne, Sir Thomas, of Kent, Kt.— (H. vi. Roll) bore, sable three lyonceux between two bendlets engrailed argent, in the sinister chief point an eagle's head erased or ; Arundel Roll.

Bruce, see Braose, Brewes and Bruse, Earl of Carrick.

Bruce, Robert, lord of Annandaie, a baron 1295—bore, or, a saltire and chief gules. (F.) See Bruse.

*[Brudenell, *alias* Bredenhill, William de, of Dodington, Oxon (E. i.)—bore, argent, a chevron gules between three morions azure.—Shirley.] F.

‡Bruere, Robert de la—(H. iii. Roll) bore, checquy argent and gules, a chief or and a demi-lyon issuant (sable ?) ; Dering Roll.

Bruges (——), of Gloucestershire - (E. ii. Roll) bore, argent, on a cross sable a leopard's face or, in the first quarter a crescent of the second ; Parliamentary Roll.

Bruges, Hue de (or Heggios)—(H. iii. Roll) bore, gules, bezantée and a chief ermine ; St. George Roll ; called Kenmays, Harl. 246 fo. 33.

Bruili, Roger de—(H. iii. Roll) bore, ermine on a bend gules three chevronels or ; St. George Roll. F.

Brumtone, Brian de (or Brompton)— (E. iii. Roll) bore, or, two lyons passant gules (F.) ;- Arden Roll and Jenyns' Ordinary. Walter bore it with a label (5) sable ; Arden and St. George Rolls. F. Brian de Brampton took up the cross in the last Crusade 1270.

Brumton, John de—(H. iii. Roll) bore, or, two lyons passant gules, a baston sable (F.), St. George Roll ; Baudwin bore, three escallops or on a bend ; Arden Roll.

Brune. Sir Morys le, a baron 1315—bore, at the first Dunstable tournament 1308, azure, a cross moline or ; 8 E. ii. (F.). Parly. and Harleian Rolls, and Jenyns' Ordinary ; recercelée (in Harl. 337), pearled or, in Ashmole Roll (F.); the cross sarcelée in Jenyns' Ordinary. F. William took up the cross in the last Crusade 1270.

Brune, Sir Richard le—(E. iii. Roll) bore, azure, a lyon rampant argent guttée de sang ; Jenyns' Ordinary. F.

Brune, Thomas—(E. iii. Roll) bore, azure, guttée de sang, a lyon rampant argent tail "estans" ; Jenyns' Ordinary.

Brune, William—(E. iii. Roll) bore, azure, billettée and a lyon rampant or ; Jenyns' Ordinary. F.

Bruse, Sir Barnarde, of Hunts., Ingram de(‡), and le frère, Sir Robert le—(H. iii. Roll) bore, azure, a saltire and a chief or ; Howard, Dering, and Holland Rolls.

‡Bruse, Richard de—(H. iii. Roll) bore, gules, a saltire and a chief or, Dering Roll ; and Robert (E. i.) bore the reverse (F.), and another Robert (E. i.) bore it with a spur-rowell argent ; Camden Roll and Harl. MS. 1481 fo. 43ᵇ.

†Bruse, Robert de, Earl of Karric, 1292— bore, or, a saltire gules, on a chief of the second a lyon passant gardant or ; Guillim Roll and Jenyns' Ordinary. F. He and his father took up the cross in the last Crusade 1269, 1270.

Brus, Sire William de—bore, at the battle of Boroughbridge 1322, gules, a saltire engrailed and a chief dancettée argent. See Monumental Effigy, Sir William 1226. In Jenvns' Ordinary the arms are tricked, gules, a saltire engrailed argent, a chief of the second, dancettée throughout gules F.

Brus, Piers, of Skelton, Yorkshire—(E. iii. Roll) bore, argent, a lyon rampant azure ; Grimaldi and Glover Rolls.

Brus, Richard (Brys)—bore, at the second Dunstable tournament 1334, argent a lyon rampant gules tail "double tresses et croissele," —fourchée et renowée. Sir Richard Breouse, of Norfolk (E. ii.), bore, the field ermine ; Parliamentary and Ashmole Rolls. F.

Brus, John—(H. iii. Roll) bore, or, three chevronels gules, a bordure engrailed azure ; St. George Roll. F. Indented in Norfolk Roll.

Brus, Robert de (Bruis or Briwys)— (H. iii. Roll) bore, gules, a lyon passant gardant ermine ; St. George Roll. F.

Brussele, Sire de—(E. i. Roll) bore, or, a saltire gules ; Camden Roll. (F.) See the "Genealogist," xiv. n.s. 10.

Brut, Richard le—(H. iii. Roll) bore, checquy argent and sable a bend gules. St. George Roll. F.

Bruton, Robert le, and Joan le—(H. iii. Roll) bore, quarterly or and gules a bordure engrailed azure ; St. George Roll (F.). H. 6137 ff 75, 80, see Breton.

Bryan, Sir Guy de, K.G., a baron 1350—bore, at the siege of Calais 1345–8, or, three piles meeting in base azure—the colours are often reversed. F. and Effigy.

Bryane, William le—(R. ii. Roll) bore, or, three piles meeting in base azure, on a canton paly (4) argent and azure, a bend gules charged with three eagles or ; Surrey Roll.

†Bryanson, Bartholomew—(H. iii. Roll) bore, gyrony (8 or 12) argent and azure ; Parly. and Dering Rolls, Jenyns' Ordinary, &c. F.F. Ascribed also to Sir John, banneret, and Otes.

Bryndale, Sir Lawrence—(E. iii. Roll) bore, gules a gryphon segreant or ; Ashmole Roll. See Brenley.

SIR ROBERT DE BURES, CIRCA 1302.
IN ACTON CHURCH, SUFFOLK. *After Waller.*

Bryne (——), of Tervaine—(E. IV. Roll) bore, argent an eagle displayed sable; with crest; Ballard Roll.

Buch, Sr. Captal de—bore, at the battle of Falkirk 1298, paly or and gules, a canton ermine and a bordure sable besantée. Buch or Bucher, the name of a fort near Bordeaux. See BURDEUX, DE FOIX, and GRAILLY. See also pedigree in Anstis' "Order of the Garter" vol. 1, Introduction, page 8.

Buchan, the Earl of—(E. III. Roll) bore, azure, three garbs or banded gules; Jenyns' Ordinary. (F.) See COMYN.

Buchard, Sire Thomas—bore, at the battle of Boroughbridge 1322, gules, and a label (5) sable. See next entry.

Buchard Sire Will Latymer (BOCHARD) —bore, at the battle of Boroughbridge 1322, gules, a cross (patée or) " Les Armes Latymer"; a label (5) sable charged with a martlet argent (indistinct).

Buckham, Roger de (BOKEHAM)—(E. III. Roll) bore, chequy or and sable, a fess ermine; Jenyns' Ordinary. F.

Buckland, John, de—(E. III. Roll) bore, gules, two lyonceux rampant argent, a quarter sable fretty or; Jenyns' Ordinary. F.

Buckeshall, Walter (BUKESHALL) — (E. III. Roll) bore, argent, crusily and a lyon rampant gules; Jenyns' Ordinary. F. See also BUXHULL.

Buckminster, Sire William—bore, at the battle of Boroughbridge 1322, argent, crusily and a lyon rampant sable (F.); florettée instead of crusily in Ashmole, Cotgrave, and of Lincolnshire in Parliamentary Rolls.

Buckton, John de—(E. II. Roll) bore, argent a goat saliant sable, horned vert; Jenyns' Roll. F

Buckton, Pyers—bore, at the siege of Rouen 1418, quarterly argent and gules, on the gules quarters three goats passant 2 and 1 of the first horned or. F.

Buckworth v. **Bokkesworthe.**

†**Bucy, Hugh de** (or BOUES)—(H. III. Roll) bore, or, three water-bougets azure; Dering and Howard Rolls. See BOURCHIER.

Bulkley (——), of Aidon - (E. IV. Roll) bore sable a chevron between three bulls' heads couped argent; with crest; Ballard Roll.

Buller, Baldwyn de—(H. III. Roll) bore, sable, billettée and a bend cotised argent; Howard Roll. See also BOULERS.

*[**Buller, Ralph**, of Woode, in Somerset, 14th cent.—bore, sable, on a plain cross argent quarter pierced, four eaglets of the field.—Shirley.] F.

Bulmer, Ansketell, of Sheriff Hutton, Yorkshire—(E. III. Roll) bore, gules, a lyon rampant or billettée sable; Jenyns' Ordinary.

Bulmer, Sir Raffe, a baron 1342—bore, gules, billettée and a lyon rampant or; Parliamentary, Surrey, Ashmole Rolls, &c.

Bulmer, John de—(E. I. Roll) bore, gules guttée d'or and a lyon rampant of the last (F.), Segar Roll; billettée instead of guttée in Jenyns' Ordinary.

*[**Bunbury, Alexander de** (15 H. III.)— bore, argent, on a bend sable three chessrooks of the field.—Shirley.] F.

Bur, William—(R. II. Roll) bore, azure, billettée and a lyon rampant or; Surrey Roll.

Burdeux, Sir Peres, banneret—bore, at the battle of Falkirk 1298, or, a greyhound gules, collared sable, a bordure of the last bezantée. (F.) Sometime Captal de Buch, a fort near Bordeux. See BUCH and GREILLY.

Burdet, Richard. and **Sir William**, of co. Leic.—(E. III. Roll) bore, azure, two bars or; Jenyns' Ordinary and Parly. Roll.

***Burdett, Sir Robert**, of co. Leic.— (E. II) bore, azure, two bars or, on the sovereign bar three martlets gules; Parliamentary Roll.

Burdet, John, (R. II. Roll) and **Roger**— (E. III. Roll)—bore, azure, two bars or, on each three martlets gules; Surrey and Parliamentary Rolls and Jenyns' Ordinary. F.

Burdon, Sir John, of Notts—(E. II. Roll) bore, gules, three burdons or pilgrims' staves pileways argent (F.), Parliamentary Roll; reversed in Howard and Jenyns' Rolls (F.); borne reversed by WILLIAM, in Arden Roll.

Burdon, William, or **Walter**—(E. II. Roll) bore, azure crusily and three pilgrims' staves or; Jenyns' and Arundel Rolls.

Bures, Sir Andrew (BOURES)—(E. III. Roll) bore, ermine on a chief dancettée sable two lyonceux rampant or; Ashmole and Parliamentary Rolls. See Monumental Brass for Sir ROBERT.

Burgh, Walter de, Earl of Ulster—(E. III. Roll) bore, or, a cross gules, the ancient arms of BIGOD, Earl of Norfolk; Ashmole Roll and Jenyns' Ordinary.

Burgh, Hubert de, Earl of Kent—(E. I. Roll), bore, lozengy gules and vair (F.), Segar Roll; the same for JOHN (‡), in Camden and Dering Rolls; and also (1) masculy vair and gules, Norfolk Roll; and (2) gules, seven mascles, 3, 3, 1, vair; Howard Roll.

Burgh, Sir John de—(E. III. Roll) bore, argent, on a fess dancettée sable three besants; Ashmole Roll. F.

Burgh, Thomas de, of Richmondshire— (E. III. Roll) bore, argent, on a fess sable three besants; Grimaldi Roll. F.

Burgh, Roald de, and **William de**— (E. III. Roll) bore, argent, on a saltire sable five cygnets of the field; Grimaldi Roll and Jenyns' Ordinary. F.

Burgh, Walter de—(H. III. Roll) bore, quarterly, argent and gules, a cross passant of the second; Norfolk Roll.

Burgh, William de (BURC)—(H. III. Roll) bore, quarterly, or and azure; Arden and St. George Rolls. F.

Burghersh, Sir Bartholomew, of Kent, the King's Chamberlain. a baron 1330—bore, at the battle of Boroughbridge 1322, and at the siege of Calais 1345-8, gules, a lyon rampant tail fourchée or (the tinctures reversed in Surrey and other Rolls). Sir STEPHEN bore the same at the first Dunstable tournament 1308 (F.); JOHN bore the same, Jenyns' Ordinary (F.); BARTHOLOMEW or HERBERT (‡) bore it with a label (5) azure, Dering Roll; and HERBERT bore, gules, a lyon rampant or; Howard Roll.

John Burdon   willm de Burgh   Robert Burlay

Sim. Burlay   Philip Burnell   John de Burnovill

Le Counte de Bouggan   Hugh de Burninghill   John de Birton

Roy d Burhhulle   Jho. Burton   Ralfe Boughill

†**Burghill, Henry de**—(H. III. Roll) bore, paly (6) or and azure, over all a fess gules ; Dering and Howard Rolls. See also BURRELL.

Burgoine, Osteleins de—(H. III. Roll) bore, azure, billettée and a lyon rampant or, crowned of the last ; Howard Roll.

Burley (——), a Suffolk Knight—(H. VI. Roll) bore, ermine on a bend or 4 chevronels gules ; Arundel Roll. F.

Burley, Robert, of Wherlsdale — (E. III. Roll) bore, gules, a besant ; Jenyns' Ordinary.

Burley, Simon—(E. II. Roll) bore, barry (6) sable and or, on a chief of the first two palets between as many esquires based of the second, over all an inescocheon gules three bars argent. (F.) Jenyns' Ordinary.

Burley, Sir Simon, K.G., **Sir Richard,** K.G., and **Sir John,** K.G., 1378—bore, or, three bars and in chief two palets sable, on an escocheon of pretence, gules, three bars ermine, a crescent for difference of the second. K. 399 ff. 21, 24, 26.

Burnaby, Sir Nicholas (BRONEBY) — (E. III. Roll) bore, argent, two bars and in chief a lyon passant gules ; Ashmole Roll.

Burne, John de—(H. III. Roll) bore, ermine on a bend azure three lyons rampant argent ; Howard Roll.

Burnell, Sir Edward, banneret, a baron 1311—bore, argent a lyon rampant sable, crowned or, a bordure azure ; Parliamentary and Surrey Rolls. In Jenyns' Ordinary this coat occurs *quarterly with,* or, a saltire sable. F. ; and so borne by HUGH, Lord BURNELL, K.G.,temp. H. IV., the saltire engrailed ; K. 400 fo. 20.

Burnell, Philip—(E. I. Roll) bore, argent, a lyon rampant sable crowned or ; Segar Roll. Sir EDWARD bore this H. VI. – and LE SR. B. also bore (H. VI.) argent, a lyon rampant tail fourchée sable.

Burnell, William—(H. III. Roll) bore, argent, a lyon rampant sable, a label (5) gules ; Howard Roll. ROBERT took up the cross in the last Crusade 1270.

Burnell, Philip—(H. III. Roll) bore, argent, a lyon rampant sable, on a bend gules three escallops or ; St. George Roll. Three mullets argent in Arden Roll. ROBERT took up the cross in the last Crusade 1270.

Burnell, Hugh, and **Philip**—(H. III. Roll) bore, argent, a lyon rampant sable, debruised by a baston gules ; Howard, Camden, and St. George Rolls. F.

Burnell, Sir Richard—(E. III. Roll) bore, argent, a lyon rampant azure guttée d'or crowned of the last, langued and armed gules ; Ashmole Roll.

Burneville, Sir John de—bore, at the battle of Boroughbridge 1322, gules, a saltire engrailed (argent) between four cinquefoyles or (F.) ; ascribed also to Sir ROBERT, of Suffolk, in Parliamentary Roll.

Burnham, Sir Thomas, *v.* **Bourneham.**

Burnham, Sir Walter, of Norfolk—(E. II. Roll) bore, sable, a cross between four crescents argent ; Parliamentary Roll.

Burninghill, Hugh de—(E. II. Roll) bore, sable three bats (or rere-mice) argent ; Jenyns' Roll. F.

Burowdon, Thomas - (E. III. Roll) bore, argent three cinquefoyles sable ; Jenyns' Ordinary. (F.) See also WALTER BORDOWN.

Burrell —— (H. III. Roll) bore, paly (6) or and azure, over all a fess gules ; St. George Roll. See BURGHILL. F.

Burrell, Roger de—(H. III. Roll) bore, paly (10) argent and sable, a bend gules ; St. George Roll. F.

Burton, Sir Rauf de—bore, at the battle of Boroughbridge 1322, paly (6) or and gules on a bend sable three water-bougets argent ; borne also by JOHN ; see Surrey Roll and Jenyns' Ordinary. F.

Burton, Sir John de—(E. III. Roll) bore, gules, three plates on each a chevron sable ; Ashmole Roll.

Burton, Sir Roger de—(E. III. Roll) bore, argent, a fess sable fretty or ; Ashmole Roll.

Burton, Sir William—(E. III. Roll) bore, sable, a chevron between three owls argent (F.); Ashmole Roll. THOMAS, R. II., bore, the owls crowned or ; Surrey Roll.

Buslingthorpe *v.* **Beslingthorpe.**

Bussy, Sir Hugh, of co. Linc. and **John** —(E. III. Roll) bore, argent three barrulets sable ; Parliamentary and Surrey Rolls and Jenyns' Ordinary. F.

Buterley, Roger or **Stephen**—(H. III. Roll) bore, or, a fess gules in chief three torteaux ; Arden and St. George Rolls. (F.) And another, in Arden Roll, with cinquefoyles pierced gules in lieu of torteaux.

Butler, see BOTELER.

Button, John de—(E. III. Roll) bore, ermine, a fess gules ; Jenyns' Roll. F.

Buttringham, William de—bore, at the second Dunstable tournament 1334, argent, a bend gules. See also BODRUGAN and BOTRINGHAM.

Buxhull *v.* **Boxhull.**

Buxhull, Sire Alayn de (BOXHULL) of Kent—bore, at the battle of Boroughbridge 1322, or, a lyon rampant azure fretty argent (F.), (or, in H. 6137 *f* 10ᵇ), Parliamentary Roll ; RAPHE in Jenyns' Ordinary.

Bycovyleyn, William—(R. II. Roll) bore, argent, three crescents 2 and 1 gules ; Surrey Roll. See BOUTEVILAIN.

Byron, Sire John de—bore, at the battle of Boroughbridge 1322, argent, three bendlets gules ; so also Sir JAMES, of co. Linc. R. II., Parliamentary Roll, and Sir RICHARD, E. II., Surrey Roll. In the Boroughbridge Roll, the arms of Sir RICH. BRAKWORTH or BRATWORTH are erroneously assigned to this Sir JOHN.

Byron, Sir John, LE FITZ—knighted at the capitulation of Calais 1348 —bore, argent, three bendlets gules and a label (3) azure. So also RICHARD, E. I., Nativity Roll. JAMES (‡), H. III., bore, a label (5), azure (F.), the tinctures reversed in the Dering Roll.

Byron, James de - (H. III. Roll) bore, bendy (10) argent and gules, a label (5), azure ; Howard Roll.

Byron, Nicholas, E. IV. See BERON.

Byye, Sir William—(H. VI. Roll) bore, three azure crescents or ; Arundel Roll.

SIR HUGH CALVELEY, of Lea
In Bunbury Church, Cheshire, temp. E. iii.
After Stothard.

C

Cabery, Alan de, of Hippeswell—(E. III. Roll) bore, gules, a fess vair ; Jenyns' Ordinary.

Caili, Adam de (CAILLY)—(H. III. Roll) bore, checquy or and gules, an inescocheon ermine ; St. George Roll. F.

Caili, Thomas, baron 1309—bore, checquy gules and or, a bend ermine ; Nobility Roll. Ascribed to Sir ADAM DE CAYLE, of Norfolk, in Parliamentary Roll.

Caili, Walter de (CAYLE)—(H. III. Roll) bore, checquy or and azure, on a fess gules three mullets argent ; St. George Roll.

Caili, Sir William (CALY)—(E. III. Roll) bore, quarterly argent and sable, over all on a baston gules three mullets pierced or ; Ashmole Roll.

Caldecott, Richard—(E. III. Roll) bore, per pale argent and azure, a chief gules ; Jenyns' Ordinary. SIRE DE CALDECOTT of Norfolk, bore, per pale or and azure, on a chief gules three leopards' faces of the first ; Parliamentary Roll.

Calkin, Sir Hugh, of Flanders—bore, at the siege of Calais 1345-8, argent, a pale between two greyhounds erect sable, (F.) ; respecting each other, in Stowe.

Calthorpe, Sir William, of Norfolk—(E. II. Roll) bore, checquy or and azure a fess ermine, Parliamentary Roll and Jenyns' Ordinary ; also borne, or and sable—another with the fess argent and yet another—chequy or and gules on a fess argent three martlets sable, in the Ashmole Roll.

Calthorpe (——), of Orthenley, Norfolk—(E. III. Roll) bore, ermine, a maunch gules ; Ashmole Roll and Jenyns' Ordinary. See GALTHORP.

Caltofte, Sir John de, of co. Linc.—(E. III. Roll) bore, argent, three roses gules—Parliamentary Roll—this surname occurs also in Cotgrave Roll and for coat "argent, a lyon vaire and a."

Calverley, Sir John—(E. III. Roll) bore, sable, an inescocheon within an orle of owls argent ; Ashmole Roll.

Calverley, Hue, John, and **Walter**—(R. II. Roll) bore, argent, a fess gules between three calves passant sable, see Effigy ; JOHN bore a crescent and HUGH bore a mullet, for difference ; Surrey Roll and Jenyns' Ordinary.

Calvert, Sir Richard (or CULVET)—(E. III. Roll) bore, gules, a bend nebulée argent ; Ashmole Roll.

‡**Cam, Richard**—(H. III. Roll) bore, argent, six eaglets 3, 2, 1, displayed sable ; Dering Roll. F.

Camoyes, Le Sr.—bore, at the siege of Rouen 1418, or, on a chief gules three plates—borne also by Sir RAPHE and Sir THOMAS, K.G. In Howard and Dering Rolls, two plates only are ascribed to JOHN (‡)—in the Camden Roll the (3) plates are in fess—in Grimaldi Roll three torteaux are ascribed to RAUF.

Camoyes, Sir Rauf, banneret—bore, at the first Dunstable tournament 1308, argent, on a chief gules three besants. F.

†**Campaine, Pers de**—(H. III. Roll) bore, argent, a chief gules ; Arden and St. George Rolls. See CHAMPAINE.

Camvile, Sir Geoffrey de, banneret, a baron 1295—bore, azure, three lyons passant in pale argent ; Nobility and Parliamentary Rolls, &c. So ascribed also to HUGH, ROBERT (‡), and WILLIAM. (F.) In the Dering and Howard Rolls the tinctures are reversed for GEOFFREY (‡).

Cantelo, Philip de—(H. III. Roll) bore, argent, a fess gules fretty or ; Howard Roll.

‡**Cantelou, Sire Johan de**—(E. I. Roll) bore, azure, three fleurs-de-lys or ; Dering Roll, &c. —leopards' faces jessant-de-lys in Ashmole MS.

Cantelou, George (E. I. Roll) and **William**—bore, gules, three fleurs-de-lys or (F.) ; Camden Roll, &c. Ascribed also to JORIS *vel* PRES DE, in Howard Roll ; Sir WILLIAM of Salop bore it with a baston argent, in Parliamentary Roll.

Cantelupe, Sir John, banneret—bore, at the battle of Falkirk 1298, azure, three leopards' faces jessant-de-lys or. (F.)—perhaps of Snitterfield ; the leopards' faces are often reversed. Sir H. bore a red field in the Atkinson Roll, and so did WILLIAM, with the faces reversed, in the Segar Roll.

Cantelupe, Sir William, of Ravensthorpe, banneret, a baron 1299, bore, at the battle of Falkirk 1298, and at the siege of Carlaverock 1300, gules, a fess vair between three leopards' faces jessant-de-lys or ; Parliamentary Roll—faces reversed in Jenyns' Ordinary, &c. F.

Cantelupe, Sir William—(E. I. Roll) bore, gules, a fess vair between three fleurs-de-lys or ; Guillim Roll.

Capelle, Sir Richard de, of co. Hereford—bore, at the first Dunstable tournament 1308, argent, a chevron gules between three torteaux. F.

SIR THOMAS CAWNE, OF NULCOMB.
IN IGHTHAM CHURCH, KENT, TEMP. E. III. *From Stothard.*

Capon, Sir Robert—(E. III. Roll) bore, gules, three capons and a bordure engrailed argent ; Ashmole Roll.

Capps or **Cappus** (——), a Kentish Knight— (H. VI. Roll) bore, argent, a chevron between three trefoyles sable, an escallop of the first ; Arundel Roll.

Caraunt (——), an Essex Knight—(H. VI. Roll) bore, argent, three hurts each charged with as many chevronels gules (*sic*) ; Arundel Roll.

Carbonell, John—(E. III. Roll) bore, gules, a cross argent, a bordure or ; Jenyns' Ordinary.

Carbonell, William—bore, at the second Dunstable tournament 1334, gules, a cross argent, a bordure engrailed or. (F.) Ascribed also to ROBERT in Surrey Roll, and to Sir JOHN in Ashmole Roll ; tricked indented for Sir JOHN, of Suffolk, in Parliamentary Roll.

Carbonell (——), a Suffolk Knight—(H. VI. Roll) bore, gules, a cross argent lozengy sable ; Arundel Roll.

Cardelecke, Henry—bore, at the siege of Rouen 1418, azure, a castle triple turretted or. F.

Cardeston, John de—bore, at the second Dunstable tournament 1334, gules, a saltire argent, a label besantée (*sic*). (F.) See also KERDESTON.

Caresville, Sir William—(E. III. Roll) bore, argent, three gemelles sable ; Ashmole Roll, ascribed to JOHN in Jenyns' Roll, with the remark—same as PERS DE CAREW.

Careswelle, William de—bore, at the second Dunstable tournament 1334, argent fretty gules, a fess azure. F.

***Carew, Nicholas de**, banneret—bore, at the siege of Carlaverock 1300, or, three lyons passant sable (F.) ; and by Sir JOHN, at the siege of Calais 1345-8, on which occasion Sir JOHN, junior, of co. Glouc., differenced with a label (3) gules. See Baron DE CAREW in Jenyns' Ordinary.

Carew, Pers de—(R. II. Roll) bore, argent, three gemelles sable ; Surrey Roll, same as JOHN CARESVILLE.

Carington ——, (E. IV. Roll) bore, sable, on a bend argent three lozenges of the field ; with crest ; Ballard Roll.

Carlyell, Sir William de, of Cumberland— (E. II. Roll) bore, or, a cross patonce gules ; Parliamentary Roll.

Carminow, Thomas—(E. III. Roll) bore, azure, a bend or, and a label (3) gules ; Jenyns' Ordinary.

Carnaby, William—(E. III. Roll) bore, argent, two bars azure in chief three hurts ; Jenyns' Roll.

Carrick, Earl of—(H. III. Roll) bore, sable, three cinquefoyles 2 and 1, or, Howard Roll ; argent in Camden Roll. (F.) This coat probably appertains to the name of Carrick rather than to an Earl of that name.

*[**Cary, Sir Robert,** of Cary, Devon (H. V.) —bore, argent, on a bend sable three roses of the first.—Shirley.] F.

Casa Nova, Otha de, banneret, *v.* **Sassenau.**

Cassynges, Sir William—bore, at the first Dunstable tournament 1308, azure, a cross moline voided or, over all a bendlet gules. F.

Castell, Sir William (or DE CHASTEL), of co. Glouc. — (E. II. Roll) bore, gules, two bars argent on a canton of the last a castle sable ; Parly. Roll. ALAN, of the city of London, took up the cross in the last Crusade 1270.

Castelmyne *v.* **Gasceline.**

Castilton, Sire de (——), a Knight, banneret, —bore, at the battle of Falkirk 1298, gules, a castle or. F.

Castre, Sir John de—bore, at the first Dunstable tournament 1308, azure, an eagle displayed barry (10), argent and gules, (F.) ; (8) in Ashmole MS.

Castre, Sir John de, of Norfolk—(E. II. Roll) bore, sable, an eagle displayed barry (12) argent and gules ; Parly. Roll. THOMAS, bore, the field argent and the eagle barry of 14 ; Jenyns' Ordinary.

Caterall, Thomas—(E. II. Roll) bore, azure, three mascles or, in trick—blasoned, lozenges pierced ; Jenyns' Roll ; of Garstang, in Lancs. with crest ; Ballard Roll.

Catesbury, Sir Richard de—(E. II. Roll) bore, gules, a fess vair between three goats' heads erased argent ; Parliamentary Roll. See GOTESBURY.

Caundysh, Andrew—(R. II. Roll) bore, sable, three crosses botonnée fitchée 2 and 1 or ; Surrey Roll.

Caunton, Sir John de, of co. Leic.—(E. II. Roll) bore, gules, two bars and in chief as many mullets argent ; Parliamentary Roll.

Causton, Robert de—(E. III. Roll) bore, argent, on a bend sable three crosses crosslet fitchée of the field ; Ashmole Roll and Jenyns' Roll and Ordinary. Another in Ashmole, argent, a bend between six crosses crosslet fitchée 3 and 3 sable.

***Cave, William**—(E. III. Roll) bore, azure, fretty argent ; Jenyns' Ordinary.

*[**Cavendish, Sir John,** Chief Justice E. III. —bore, sable, three bucks' heads cabossed argent.—Shirley.] F.

[**Cawne, Sir Thomas,** of Melcomb, Kent, E. III.—bore, a lyon rampant ermine—see Monumental Effigy.]

Cayville, John—(E. II. Roll) bore, argent, a fess florettée (flory counterflory), gules ; Jenyns' Roll.

Cayle, Walter de—(H. III. Roll) bore, chequoy or and azure, on a fess gules three mullets argent. (F.) Arden and St. George Rolls ; sometimes written CAPEL. See also CAILI.

Ceinteyno, John de (or ST. IVE)—(H. III. Roll) bore, or, three lyons passant gules ; Arden Roll.

Cerne, Philip de—(H. III. Roll) bore, per fess argent and gules, a lyon rampant within a bordure all counterchanged. (F.) St. George, Dering and Howard Rolls.

***Chadwick, Sir J.,** of Chadwick and Healey, co. Lanc.—(H. VI. Roll) bore, gules, an inescocheon within an orle of martlets argent ; Atkinson Roll.

Chalers, Ralph—(E. II. Roll) bore, argent, a fess between two chevronels sable ; Jenyns' Ordinary. An (Essex ?) Knight of the name (H. VI. Roll) bore, argent, a fess between three annulets gules ; Arundel Roll.

John Cavendiſʒ

Perſe Chalune

ffelipe Chamberlaʒn

m̄ī̃lo Chamberleng

Rob̄ de Champaine

Here d̄ Chaberun

John Chandos

Rōg. Chandos

Emari d̄ Chaſeul

Edw̄d Charlis

Lo̅ Sir Charloton.

Nicolad̄ d̄ Charneles.

†Chaluns, Piers de—(H. III. Roll) bore, gules, five fusils conjoined in fess ermine, a label (3 or 5), azure. (F.) Arden and St. George Rolls, Jenyns' Ordinary.

Chamberlain, Herbert le and Martin (H. III. Roll) bore, gules, three escallops or; Glover Roll. Sir JOHN bore the same (E. I. or II.); Holland Roll.

Chamberlain, Sir Richard, of Lincolnshire—(E. II. Roll) bore, gules, a chevron between three escallops or; Sir ROBERT bore a fess, Parliamentary and Surrey Rolls; and for JOHN in Jenyns' Roll.

Chamberlain, Simon—(E. III. Roll) bore, quarterly gules and or, in the first a fer-de-moulin argent; Jenyns' Ordinary.

‡Chamberlain, Philip—(H. III. Roll) bore, gules, two crossed keys wards to the sinister; Howard Roll. Wards inward in the Dering Roll. F.

†Chamberlain, William le—(H. III. Roll) bore, azure, three keys erect wards to the dexter 2 and 1 or. (F.) Dering Roll.

Chammon, John (CHANNON or CHAUMOND), of Colthorpe—(E. III. Roll) bore, gules, a lyon rampant argent within a bordure engrailed gobony or and argent (in some azure); Jenyns' Ordinary.

†Champaine, Pers de—(H. III. Roll) bore, argent, a chief gules; Arden and St. George Rolls. See CAMPAINE.

‡Champaine, Robert de—(H. III. Roll) bore, argent, three bars undée gules. (F.) Sometimes blazoned wavy, and in others nebulée; Howard and Dering Rolls. Sir JOHN of Kent bore the same (E. II.); Parliamentary Roll.

Champayne, Sir William—(E. III. Roll) bore, or, fretty sable crusily fitchée at the joints argent; Ashmole Roll.

‡Champernon, Henry de—(H. III. Roll) bore, gules, a saltire vair; Howard and Dering Rolls.

Champernoun, Sir Richard—bore, at the battle of Boroughbridge 1322, gules, billettée or, a saltire vair. (F.) JOHN also bore this coat; Jenyns' Ordinary. HENRY and RICHARD bore the coat crusily (F.) instead of billettée; St. George Roll and Jenyns' Ordinary.

‡Champernoun, John—(H. III. Roll) bore, gules, a chevron or; Dering Roll; the field azure in Ashmole Roll.

Chancellor, Walter—(E. II. Roll) bore, ermine, on a quarter argent a saltire engrailed sable; Jenyns' Roll.

Chanceux (Hugh) de *v.* Chauncy.

Chandos, Edward—(E. III. Roll) bore, argent, a pile gules; Jenyns' Ordinary. JOHN bore the reverse; Jenyns' Roll.

Chandos, Sir John, of co. Cambridge—bore, at the first Dunstable tournament 1308, argent, a pile gules, a label (3) azure (F.); Parliamentary Roll. So also did EDWARD at the second Dunstable tournament 1334.

Chandos, Sir John, K.G. (a founder), and Walter—(R. II. Roll) bore, or, a pile gules; Surrey Roll.

Chandos, Sir Robert or Roger of Cheshire —(E. III. Roll) bore, or, a lyon rampant gules, tail fourchée. (F.) Parliamentary Roll; ascribed also to JOHN, in Jenyns' Ordinary.

Chandos, Robert de—(H. III. Roll) bore or, a pile gules, nine estoiles 3, 3, 3 counterchanged. (F.) St. George Roll. See also BAIGGINGEDENE.

Chanscyre, John (probably a misreading)— (E. III. Roll)—bore, azure, an eagle barry of six argent and gules; Cotgrave Roll.

Chanseus, John de (or Thomas)—(H. III. Roll) bore, gules, three eagles displayed 2 and 1 argent. (F.) EMERY DE CHASEUS bore the same sable and or; Arden and St. George Rolls.

Chansi, Thomas de—(E. I. Roll)—bore, burrulée (22) sable and argent, a lyon rampant gules. (F.) Segar Roll. See MONCHENSI.

Charles, Sir Edward, of Norfolk—(E. III. Roll) bore, ermine, on a chief gules three lozenges of the first; Parly. Roll. EDWARD, of Cliffe and Briggenhall, bore his coat with five lozenges conjoined. (F.) Jenyns' Roll and Segar; and as a fess lozengy in Grimaldi Roll.

Charleston, Sir John de, banneret— (E. II. Roll) bore, or, on a chevron vert three eagles displayed of the field; Parliamentary Roll.

Charleton, Le Sr. de (Edward, K.G., a baron 1401-22)—bore, at the siege of Rouen 1418, or, a lyon rampant gules. F.

Charlworth (——), a Suffolk Knight—(H. VI. Roll) bore, ermine on a chief gules five lozenges or; Arundel Roll.

Charnells, Sire Nichol de—bore, at the battle of Boroughbridge 1322, azure, a cross engrailed or. (F.) Sir GEORGE, of Warwickshire, bore the same; Parliamentary Roll. Sir WILLIAM (fys) differenced with a mullet sable; Ashmole Roll.

Charneles, Thomas de—(H. III. Roll) bore, gules, two chevrons and a bordure or. (F.) St. George Roll.

Charnell, Sir John de—bore, at the first Dunstable tournament 1308, or, a fess ermine between two chevronels gules. (F.) Sir JOHN of Warwickshire, bore the reverse—gules and or; Parliamentary Roll and Jenyns' Ordinary.

Charron, Sir Richard de—(E. II. Roll) bore, gules, a chevron between three escallops argent; Parliamentary and Grimaldi Rolls.

Charteray, John—(E. III. Roll) bore, argent, a chevron between three six-foyles gules; Jenyns' Ordinary.

Chaseus, Emery de—(H. III. Roll) bore, sable, three eagles displayed or. (F.) Arden Roll.

Chaston, Thomas—(E. III. Roll) bore, gules, three barrulets vair; Jenyns' Ordinary.

Chaucombe, Sir Thomas de, of Wilts— (E. III. Roll) bore, or, on a cross vert five mullets pierced argent; Ashmole Roll. The mullets or, in Parliamentary Roll.

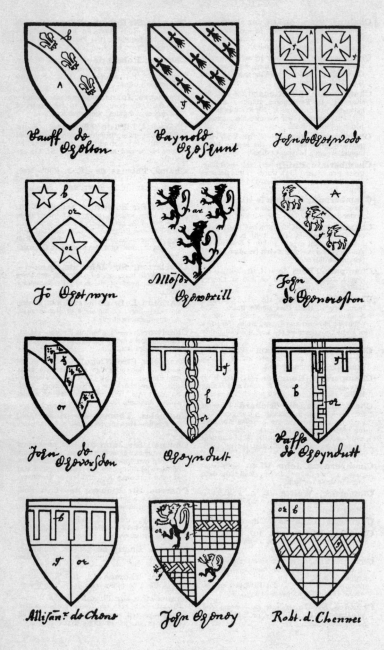

Rauff de Ogolton

Raynold Ogogunt

John de Ogotwode

Jo Ogotwyn

Mos'r Ogowxill

John de Ogonoroston

John de Ogovorsdon

Ogoyndutt

Rauff de Ogoyndutt

Allisan'r de Chono

John Ogonoy

Robt. d. Chenneu

Chauncy, Thomas, baron of Skirpenbeck in co. Linc.—(E. III. Roll) bore, argent, a chevron gules, a bordure sable besantée (Jenyns' Ordinary); as did Sir PHILIP, also of Lincolnshire; Parliamentary Roll.

Chauncy, Sir Philip de, of Essex—(E. II. Roll) bore, argent, a chevron between three annulets gules; Parliamentary and Cotgrave Rolls. F.

Chavent, Sir Peter, a baron 1299—bore, at the battle of Falkirk 1298, paly (6) argent and azure a fess gules. (F.) Sir JOHN of Somerset bore the same, Parliamentary Roll; azure and argent in Guillim Roll.

Chauvigny, William de—(H. III. Roll) bore, argent, "a fess engrele" (five fusils in fess) gules, a label sable; Norfolk Roll. See next name.

Chaveney, Sr. de—(H. III. Roll) bore, lozengy argent and gules; Arden Roll.

Chaworth, Sir Christopher, knighted at the capitulation of Calais 1348, bore, azure, two chevrons or (F.); borne also by JOHN, THOMAS (‡), Dering Roll, and Sir WILLIAM; for Sir THOMAS' quarterly coat see Atkinson Roll, Harl. MS. 1048 fo. 108.

Chaworth, Thomas de, of Norton, baron 1299; sealed the Barons' letter to the Pope 1301, with two chevrons; bore, barry (10), argent and gules, an orle of martlets (10), sable; Nobility Roll.

†**Chaworth, Patrick de** (CHAURCY)—(H. III. Roll) bore, burrulée (14), argent and gules, Glover and Howard Rolls. HENRY bore, (E. III.) burrulée (10, 12), argent and gules, a bend (or baston), sable; Jenyns' Roll.

†**Chaworth, Pain de** (CHAURS)—(H. III. Roll) bore, burrulée (16), argent and gules, an orle of martlets, 4, 2, 2, 1, sable; Arden Roll. Sir PATRICK (14) and 8 martlets; Ashmole Roll; also (14), and 13 martlets (F.), Camden Roll; and another (10 or 12) and 8 martlets, Jenyns' Ordinary. In the Arden, St. George, and Parliamentary Rolls there are coats with four and with six bars, probably tricked in error.

†**Chaworth, Hervieus de** (HEREUI DE CHAURS)—(H. III. Roll) bore, gules, crusily and a bend or; Arden Roll.

Chaworth, William de—bore, burrulée (20) argent and gules three martlets 2 and 1 sable; Harl. MS. 1481 fo. 47.

Checker v. **De la Checker.**

Chelton, Rauf de—bore, at the second Dunstable tournament 1334, argent on a bend azure three fleurs-de-lys (sic). F.

Cherleton v. **Charleton.**

Cheshunt, Sir Raynold—bore, at the siege of Calais 1345-8, gules, three bendlets ermine. F.

Chester, Earl of—bore, azure, three garbs, or, in most of the earliest Rolls. RANDOLPH DE BLONDEVILLE, the last earl, died 26 October 1232, and bore on his seal a lyon or wolf saliant. See BLONDEVILLE and KEVELIOK.

Chester, Earl of—bore, England within a bordure azure; Jenyns' Ordinary. THOMAS HOLLAND, Earl of Kent, bore the bordure argent.

Chester, William—(E. III. Roll) bore, gules, a chevron argent between three arming-buckles tongues to the dexter or; Jenyns' Ordinary.

*[**Chetwode, John de** (E. III.) — bore, quarterly argent and gules, four crosses patée counterchanged; Shirley.] F.

***Chetwynd, Sir John**—bore, at the battle of Boroughbridge, azure, a chevron between three mullets or. (F.) This coat was also borne by WILLIAM, in the Surrey Roll, the mullets also pierced.

Chetwynd, Sir John de, of Salop—(E. II. Roll) bore, azure, a chevron or between three besants; Parliamentary Roll.

Cheverell, Sir Alexander, of Wilts—bore, at the first Dunstable tournament 1308, argent, three lyonceux rampant sable. F.

Cheveresden, John de—bore, at the second Dunstable tournament 1334, or, on a bend gules three chevrons ermine. F.

Cheveresden, John de—(E. III. Roll) bore, argent, on a bend gules, three "chevres" passant of the field. (F.) Jenyns' Ordinary.

Chevouse, Henry de—(H. III. Roll) bore, argent, a cross gules between four lyons rampant azure; Norfolk Roll.

Cheyndutt, Sir Ralph, of Bucks—(E. II. Roll) bore, azure, a cheyne or, a label of three gules; Parliamentary Roll. F.F.

Che(y)ney (——), de, a Buckinghamshire Knight—(E. II. Roll) bore, argent, a fess and in chief three martlets gules; Parliamentary Roll.

Cheyne (——), an Essex Knight—(H. II. Roll) bore, quarterly sable and argent, six lozenges conjoined in bend sinister (sic); Arundel Roll.

†**Che(y)ne Alexander de**—(H. III. Roll) bore, quarterly or and gules, a label (5) azure (F.); Dering Roll—label vert in Ashmole Roll.

Che(y)ney, John — (R. II. Roll) bore, quarterly or and azure, a fess gules fretty ermine; Surrey Roll.

Che(y)ney, John—bore, at the siege of Rouen 1418, checquy or and azure, a fess gules fretty ermine; *quarterly with*, or, a lyon rampant per fess gules and sable; Ashmole Roll—the quarters sometimes reversed. F.

Che(y)ney, John, Henry and **Robert de**—(H. III. Roll) bore, checquy or and azure, a fess gules fretty argent. (F.) Arden and St. George Rolls. In Jenyns' Ordinary the tinctures are sometimes reversed.

Cheyne, John—(E. III. Roll) bore, gules, four fusils in fess argent, on each an escallop sable; Jenyns' Ordinary—RAUFF bore this coat within a bordure of the second; Surrey Roll.

Che(y)ney, William—bore, at the siege of Rouen 1418, azure, a cross patonce or, *quarterly with*, gules five fusils conjoined in fess argent, on each an escallop sable—evidently for CHEYNEY. F.

Cheyny, Robert—(E. III. Roll) bore, azure, semée of estoiles and two lyons passant or; Jenyns' Ordinary.

In Memoriam.

GILBERT DE CLARE,

LORD OF CLARE, EARL OF GLOUCESTER AND HERTFORD, ob. 1230.

After John Carter.

See GLOUCESTER, 110.

Cheyne, Thomas—(R. II. Roll) bore, azure on a fess nebulée between three crescents or, a fleur-de-lys gules ; Surrey Roll.

Che(yny), Sir William—bore, at the battle of Boroughbridge 1322, gules, frettée or, a label (5) argent. F.

*[**Chichester, Richard,** of Devon (E. III.)—bore, checquy or and gules, a chief vair ; Shirley.] F.

Chicker, see DE LA CHICKER.

Chideoke, Sir John—(E. II. Roll) bore, gules, an inescocheon within a double tressure argent ; Parliamentary Roll, as a northern Knight.

Chidiock, John—(E. III. Roll)—bore, gules, a false escocheon within an orle of martlets argent ; Jenyns' Ordinary.

Chilton *v.* **Chelton.**

Chilton —— (E. III. Roll), bore, argent, a chevron gules ; Ashmole Roll.

Chirchingham, Sir Walter de, knighted at Calais 1348—bore, argent, three bars gules in chief as many torteaux, over all a bendlet sable. F.

Chiston, Robert de—bore, at the second Dunstable tournament 1334, argent, three bends sable crusily fitchée of the field. F.

*[**Cholmondeley, Sir Hugh,** of Cholmondeley in Cheshire (H. III.)—bore, gules, two helmets in chief argent, and in base a garb or ; Shirley.] F.

Chowne, Andrew, slain or drowned at the siege of Calais 1345-8—bore, argent, a fess and in chief three martlets gules.

Chra(c)heth —— (H. III. Roll) bore, gules, five fusils in bend or, a label (5) argent ; Arden Roll. Perhaps CRACHERODE.

Christmas (——), a Kentish Knight—(H. VI. Roll)—bore, gules, on a bend sable three covered cups argent ; Arundel Roll.

Chycheley (——) an Essex (?) Knight — (H. VI. Roll) bore, or, a chevron between three cinquefoyles pierced gules ; Arundel Roll.

Cifrewast, Richard de—(H. III. Roll) bore, azure, two bars gemelles and a chief or. (F.) St. George and Arden Rolls. Three bars gemelles (H. VI. Nobility Roll) and the chief argent in Jenyns' Roll. See SYFFREWAST.

Cir(en)cester, Sir Thomas de, of Glouc. —(E. II. Roll) bore, argent, a chevron azure, a label (3) gules ; Parliamentary Roll.

Clapham, Robert—(E. II. Roll) bore, argent, on a bend sable three covered cups of the first, in chief a quatrefoyle slipped of the second ; Jenyns' Roll.

Clare, Le Seigneur de—(E. II. Roll)—bore, argent a quarter gules ; Jenyns' Roll ; this coat was borne by LYONEL —— at the second Dunstable tournament in 1334.

Clare (——), **de** (E. III. Roll) bore, ermine, three chevronels gules ; Cotgrave Roll ; some are of opinion that the original arms of CLARE were clarions. THOMAS, brother of the Earl of Gloucester, took up the cross in the last Crusade 1270.

Clare, Gilbert de, Earl of Hertford and Gloucester — bore, at the first Dunstable tournament 1308, or, three chevronels gules (see Monumental Effigy). Sire GILBERT and

THOMAS differenced with a label (5) azure ; Guillim and Camden Rolls. Sir RICHARD differenced with a label (3) azure at the first Dunstable tournament 1308. (F.) WILLIAM DE CLARE differenced with a label azure ; Glover Roll. See also Audley and Gloucester.

Clare, Robert, 4th brother of Earl Gilbert—bore or, a fess between two chevronels gules — " antecessor" Baron de Fitzwater ; Harl. MS. 1481 *ff* 15, 28.

Clare, Sir Nicholas, of co. Glouc.—bore, at the first Dunstable tournament 1308, or, three chevronels gules, a bordure indented sable—engrailed in Harl. 6137 fo. 31*b.* F.

Clarence, Lionel of Antwerp, Duke of—bore, France and England quarterly, a label (3) argent on each pendant a canton gules ; Jenyns' Ordinary ; a billet in dexter base of pendant, K. 398 fo. 32 ; 400 fo. 5.

Clarendon, Roger de—(R. II. Roll) bore, gules, a bend or ; Surrey Roll.

Claron, Sir John—(E. I. Roll) bore, gules, a cross recercelée argent, over all a bendlet azure charged with three mullets (6) of the second ; Harleian Roll.

Clavering, Sir John de, 2nd baron, FITZROBERT LE FITZROGER—bore, at the battle of Falkirk 1298 and at the siege of Carlaverock 1300 (when he assumed the name of Clavering by the King's command), quarterly or and gules, a baston sable, a label (3) azure at Falkirk and vert at Carlaverock (F.) wrongly blasoned in Harl. MS. quarterly or and gules fretty argent. See FITZ ROGER. The antient coat, vair, a chief gules ; Nobility Roll 1299.

Clavering, Sir John, banneret—(H. VI. Roll) bore, quarterly or and gules a bend sable, Arundel Roll ; a baston in Ashmole Roll. ROBERT bore a bendlet ; Surrey and Grimaldi Rolls.

Clavering, Sir Allen—bore, at the siege of Calais 1345, quarterly argent and gules, on a bend sable three mullets of the first. The metal is altered to *or* in the Ashmole MS. (F.) in which the mullets are both argent, and or. Sir ALEXANDER, an Essex Knight, bore this coat (E. II. Roll), with the metal or, in the Parliamentary Roll.

Clederow, Roger, a Kentish Knight—(H. VI. Roll) bore, argent, three covered cups and a bordure engrailed sable ; Arundel Roll.

Clere, John de—(H. III. Roll) bore, argent a fess azure and in chief a lyon passant gules ; Howard Roll.

Clervaux, —— (CLAREVAUX), of Croft—(E. III. Roll) bore, sable, a saltire or, Grimaldi Roll and Jenyns' Ordinary, where the coat is tricked, or, a saltire engrailed gules for JOHN CLAREVAUX. See also JOHN TROMYN.

Cleseby, Asculphus de (HURSQUI)—(E. III. Roll) bore, gules, a fess between three lozenges 2 and 1 argent, Grimaldi Roll (F.) ; JOHN and ROBERT bore the same, Jenyns' Ordinary. F.

Cleseby, John de—(E. II. Roll) bore, gules, "a bend et demi" argent, a quarter ermine, tricked as 2 bends ; Jenyns' Roll.

Cleuisby (or **Clemsby**), **Sir John,** of co. Leic.—(E. II. Roll) bore, argent, a lyon rampant purpure crowned or ; Parliamentary Roll.

Clevedon, see CLIFTON.

Roɣ d' Clifford   Joan d' Clifford   John de Olifdons

Jorn de Olovodon   Jorn de Olivodon   Roɣ de Clistone

Joan d' Clinton   Johan de Olinton   will de Olynton

warm de Olido   wal. Oloyton   Robt de Colboɫam

Cleville, Sir Thomas (or CHEVILLE)—(E. II. Roll) bore, sable, crusily and a cinque-foyle argent ; Holland Roll.

Cliffe, John OF THE WOLD—(E. II. Roll) bore, argent, three popinjays ppr., Jenyns' Roll ; the Count of Cliffe, de Alemain (H. III. Roll), bore, gules, an orle argent within an escarbuncle or ; Arden Roll.

∗**Clifford, Sir Robert de,** baron 1299—bore, at the battle of Falkirk 1298, at the siege of Carlaverock 1300, and at the first Dunstable tournament 1308, checquy or and azure a fess gules ; sealed, as Castellan of Appleby, the Barons' letter to the Pope 1301. Sire ROGER, banneret, bore the same at the battle of Boroughbridge 1322 (F.), and so also ROGER (‡) in the Dering Roll. Another ROBERT differenced, with a crescent or, Surrey Roll ; and ROGER le fiz, with cinquefoyles pierced argent on the fess (F.) Arden and St. George Rolls ; roses in the Camden Roll. F. ROBERT took up the cross in the last Crusade 1270.

Clifford, Lewys de—(R. II. Roll) bore, checquy or and azure a fess and bordure gules, Surrey Roll ; borne also by CLIFFORD, a Kentish Knight (H. VI.) Arundel Roll.

†**Clifford, Roger, Sir John,** of Somerset, **Reinaud,** and **Walter**—(H. III. Roll) bore, checquy or and azure, a bend gules (F.), Parliamentary, St. George, Grimaldi, Arden, St. George, and Glover Rolls.

Clifford, John de—(H. III. Roll) bore, checquy or and azure on a bend gules three lyons rampant argent, (F.) St. George Roll. RICHARD of Frampton-upon-Severn, bore the lyons passant or ; Harl. MS. 1481 fo. 37.

Clifton, Adam de—(E. III. Roll) bore, checquy or and gules, a bend ermine, Jenyns' Roll ; in Jenyns' Ordinary, a mullet azure for difference. In Ashmole Roll (E. III.) occurs, checquy or and gules, a bordure ermine.

Clifton, Sir John de—bore, at the first Dunstable tournament 1308, or, a lyon rampant sable crowned gules (F.) ; borne also by Sir EDMUND (E. III.) and RENAUD (H. III.), Ashmole and St. George Rolls ; Sir JOHN bore the lyon azure, according to the Parliamentary Roll (E. II.).

Clifton, Gervase de—(E. III. Roll) bore, argent, a lyon rampant azure, on its shoulder a fleur-de-lys gules ; Jenyns' Ordinary.

Clifton, Sir Gervase—(E. III. Roll) bore, sable, a lyon rampant within an orle of six-foyles pierced argent ; Ashmole Roll. Ancestor of the baronets, who bore cinquefoyles.

Clifton, John—(R. II. Roll) bore, argent, a lyon rampant within an orle of cinquefoyles sable ; Surrey Roll.

Clifton (——), of Hodsock, Notts.—(E. III. Roll) bore, argent, a lyon rampant sable tail fourchée ; Jenyns' Ordinary ; same as THOMAS CRECY v. CRESSY.

Clifton, John de (CLIVEDON)—bore, at the second Dunstable tournament 1334, argent, three escallops gules (F.) ; Sir JOHN, who was knighted at the capitulation of Calais 1348, bore mascles (F.) alii escallops.

Clifton, Roger de—(H. III. Roll) bore, argent, a chevron sable between three six-foyles pierced gules (F.) ; Arden and St. George Rolls ; roses in Jenyns' Ordinary.

∗**Clifton, James,** of Clifton—(E. IV. Roll), **John** (E. III. Roll), **Robert de** (R. II. and **W.,** E. II. Rolls) bore, sable, on a bend argent three mullets gules ; Ballard and Surrey Rolls ; mullets pierced in Harl. Roll and Jenyns' Ordinary.

Clifton, Nycol de—(R. II. Roll) bore, sable, on a bend argent three crescents gules, in the cantel a crescent of the second ; Surrey Roll.

∗**Clinton, Sire William de** (a baron 1330) —bore, at the battle of Boroughbridge 1322, argent, on a chief azure two mullets (6) or. (F.) JOHN, baron de Clinton 1299, bore the mullets pierced ; Nobility and Parliamentary Rolls. THOMAS (R. II.) differenced with a label of three points ermine ; Surrey Roll.

Clinton, Le Sr.—bore, at the siege of Rouen 1418, quarterly or and gules, for SAY, *quarterly with* CLINTON, argent, on a chief azure two mullets pierced or. F.

Clinton, Sir John, of Warwickshire—(E. II. Roll) bore, argent on a chief azure two fleurs-de-lys or ; Parliamentary Roll.

Clinton, Sir Thomas de, of Warwick-shire—(E. II. Roll) bore, ermine, on a chief azure two mullets or ; Parliamentary Roll.

Clinton, Sir John de—bore, at the battle of Boroughbridge 1322, argent, crusily sable, on a chief azure two mullets or ; crusily fitchée in Ashmole Roll (F.), and was so borne by WILLIAM at the second Dunstable tournament 1334, and as Earl of Huntingdon at the siege of Calais 1345-8.

Clinton, John de—(E. III. Roll) said to bear the same arms as William de St. Omer—azure a fess between ten crosses crosslet 5 and 5 or ; Jenyns' Ordinary.

Clinton, John de—(H. III. Roll) bore, paly (6) or and azure, a canton ermine. (F.) HUGH bore a fess in lieu of the canton. (F.) St. George Roll.

Clinton, Sir John de, of Warwickshire—(E. II. Roll) bore, or, three piles meeting in base azure, a canton ermine ; Parly. Roll.

Clitherow v. **Clederow.**

Clivam, William de—(R. II. Roll) bore, argent, a fess gules between three eagles displayed sable armed of the second ; Surrey Roll.

∗⌈**Clive, Warin de** (H. III.)—bore, argent, on a fess sable three mullets or.—Shirley.⌉ F. ROGER ATTE CLIVE took up the cross in the last Crusade 1270.

Clopton (——), a Suffolk Knight—(H. VI. Roll) bore, sable on a bend argent between two indents vert, an ermine spot ; Surrey Roll.

Clopton, Walter—bore, at the siege of Rouen 1418, sable, a bend argent cotised or. F.

Clovile (——), an Essex Knight—(H. VI. Roll) bore, argent, two chevronels sable each charged with five nails erect or ; Surrey Roll.

Cobham, Sire Stevene de, a baron 1326—bore, at the battle of Boroughbridge 1322, gules, a cross argent ; so borne also by THOMAS and Sir HENRY, of Kent, uncle of Sir STEPHEN, who differenced with a label (3), azure ; Surrey and Parliamentary Rolls. ROBERT (H. III. Roll) bore, gules, a cross ermine. (F.) Arden and St. George Rolls.

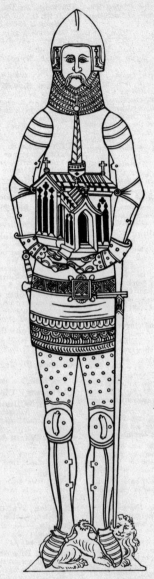

SIR JOHN COBHAM.

IN THE CHANCEL AT COBHAM, 1375–1407. *After Gough.*

‡**Cobham, Henry de**—(H. III. Roll) bore, gules, florettée or a cross argent. (F.) Dering and St. George Rolls.

Cobham, Sire Rauf de, a baron 1324—bore, at the battle of Boroughbridge 1322, argent, a lyon (rampant) checquy or and sable. (F.) Sir JOHN *f* RAUF bore it checquy or and azure ; Ashmole Roll.

Cobham, Thomas—(E. II. Roll) bore, ermine, three crescents gules each charged with a besant ; Jenyns' Roll.

Cobham, Le Sr. de (Sir JOHN OLDCASTLE)—bore, at the siege of Rouen 1418, gules, on a chevron or three lyonceux rampant sable, *quarterly with*, argent, a castle sable. F.

Cobham, Sir John, a baron of the Exchequer 1297—bore, gules, on a chevron or three lyonceux rampant sable. Nobility Roll ; ascribed to another JOHN (‡) in Dering Roll.

Cobham, Sir Henry de, of Kent—(E. II. Roll) bore, gules, on a chevron or three fleurs-de-lys azure ; Parliamentary Roll. (Ascribed also to JOHN in Howard Roll and Jenyns' Ordinary). Sir RICHARD, of Kent, bore mullets in lieu of fleurs-de-lys.

Cobham, John de—(E. III. Roll) bore, gules, on a chevron or between three fleurs-de-lys azure (*sic*), as many estoiles sable ; Cotgrave Roll.

Cobham, Reginald, a baron 1342, K.G.—bore, at the second Dunstable tournament 1334, gules, on a chevron or three estoiles sable. (F.) Sir JOHN bore the same at the siege of Calais 1345-8, differenced with a label (3) or.

Cobham, Sir Reginald—bore, at the siege of Calais 1345, argent, on a chevron sable three estoiles or ; Cotton MS.

Cobham, Sir John—bore, at the siege of Calais 1345-8 ; gules, on a chevron or three martlets sable ; see Monumental Brass. Borne also by STEPHEN, Bishop of Lincoln, Harl. MS. 1481 fo. 64.

Cobham, John, of Blackburgh in Devon—bore, gules, on a chevron or three eaglets sable ; and THOMAS *fil* Henry of Beluncle in Hoo, Kent, differenced with crescents in lieu of eaglets ; Harl. MS. 1481, fo. 64.

Cobham, Sir Reynold or **Richard de**, of Kent—(E. II. Roll) bore, gules, on a chevron or three mullets azure ; Parly. Roll.

***Codrington, John**, of Codrington, co. Glouc.—arms confirmed 5 July 1441, or 1 July 1442, per R. Leigh clar., altered 23 May 1445, "as worne by him in the service (as standard bearer) of Henry V. in battaile watch and warde," to argent, a fess between three lyonceux passant gules ; and for augmentation 19 Hen. VI. the fess was embattled counter-embattled sable fretted gules (F.) ; in 1473 an additional coat was granted him as a supporter of the House of Lancaster, viz., vert, on a bend argent three roses gules, a dexter hand couped of the second ; Add. MS. 6297 fo. 139, Harl. MS. 1359 Ashmole MS. 857 *ff* 520—1, copy of confirmation in Bodleian Library.

Cokesalton John de, (*v.* KOKESALTON)—(H. III. Roll) bore, argent, fretty gules ; Arden Roll.

Coderinge, Baudewyn de (or CODERUGGE)—(H. III. Roll) bore, gules, three lyonceux rampant or, a label (3 or 5), argent (F.) ; Arden, St. George and Jenyns' Ordinary.

Cogan, John de—(H. III. Roll) bore, lozengy argent and gules ; Howard Roll, same as THOMAS FITZTHOMAS. THOMAS bore gules, three lozenges (2 and 1), argent ; Jenyns' Ordinary.

Cogan, Sir Richard—(E. III. Roll) bore, gules, three leaves vert ; Ashmole Roll.

Cogeshall, William—(R. II. Roll) bore, argent, a cross between four escallops sable ; Surrey and Parliamentary Rolls for an Essex Knight.

Cokayn, John—(R. II. Roll) bore, argent, three cocks (2 and 1) gules ; Surrey Roll. Argent, three cocks' passant sable, in Ashmole Roll. See also THOMAS DE COKEFIELD ; HENRY DE COKINGTON bore the reverse.

*[**Coke, Hugh**, of Trusley, co. Derby (E. III.)—bore, gules, three crescents and a canton or.—Shirley.] F.

Cokke, Thomas (or COLKE)—(E. III. Roll) bore, sable three bendlets argent ; Jenyns' Ordinary.

‡**Cokefeld, Robert** and **Adam**—(H. III. Roll) bore, gules, a fleur-de-lys ermine. (F.) Dering and Howard Rolls.

Cokefeld (? Adam) de—(H. III. Roll) bore, gules, six fleurs-de-lys argent ; St. George Roll. F.

Cokefeld, Thomas de—(H. III. Roll) bore, argent, three cocks (passant) gules ; Jenyns' Ordinary. See COKAYN.

Cokefeld, Sir John de, of Norfolk—E. II. Roll) bore azure, a cross checquy argent and gules ; Parly. Roll and Jenyns' Ordinary.

Cokefield, Sir Richard, of Suffolk—(E. II. Roll) bore, azure, a cross between four cocks' passant or ; Parliamentary Roll.

Cokefeld, Sire Henry de (COCFELD)—bore, at the battle of Boroughbridge 1322, argent, a saltire engrailed sable, a label (3) gules. (F.) Sir SIMON, of Suffolk, bore the same at the first Dunstable tournament 1308 ; they are ascribed also to ROBERT in Jenyns' Ordinary.

Cokerell, —— (H. III. Roll) bore, gules, crusily, three cocks' argent. (F.) St. George Roll.

Cokerell, Robert (KOKERELL)—(H. III. Roll) bore, or, a cross between four cocks gules. (F.) Arden Roll.

Cokerington, Gilbert de—(E. III. Roll) bore, argent, on a cross sable a mullet or ; Jenyns' Ordinary.

Cokerington, John de—(E. III. Roll) bore, argent, a chevron between three cocks' passant gules ; Jenyns' Roll and Ordinary.

Cokesey, Walter de—(H. III. Roll) bore, gules, crusily and a fess argent. (F.) Arden and St. George Rolls.

Cokesey, Walter—(R. II. Roll) bore, argent on a bend azure three cinquefoyles pierced or ; Surrey Roll.

Henri de Cockington

mason de Columbers

Thomas Colvile de Codrvald

Philip d' Colevile

Robt. Colevile

Will d. Colevile

John Coumbe

Vic de Coombe

Robt. Compton

John Comyn

Will Congreve

John Constable

‡**Cokington, Henry de**—(H. III. Roll) bore, gules, three cocks, 2 and 1, argent ; Arden Roll—nine cocks, 3, 3, 2, 1. (F.) in Howard and Dering Rolls.

Cokyn, Sir Renard or **Roland de**—bore, at the first Dunstable tournament 1308, bendy (6) gules and ermine. (F.) Sir RENARD bore the reverse (E. II.) Parliamentary Roll ; and THOMAS bore bendy (6) argent and gules ; Jenyns' Roll.

Coldington *v.* **Goldington.**

Collay, Sir Robert, of Kent—(H. VI. Roll) bore, sable, three swans' heads and necks erased argent ; Arundel Roll.

Collingborne (COLYNGBORN)——an (Essex ?) Knight—(H. VI. Roll) bore, quarterly or and azure, a cross moline counterchanged ; Arundel Roll.

Colne, William—(E. III. Roll) bore, sable, a fess between two chevronels argent ; Jenyns' Ordinary.

Colpeper, Thomas — (R. II. Roll) bore, argent, a chevron sable between five martlets in chief and two in base gules, *quarterly with*, argent, a bend engrailed gules ; Surrey Roll.

Colshill, Thomas—(R. II. Roll) bore, checquy argent and sable (on the second chequée), a crescent or, a chief of the last ; Surrey Roll. F.

Columbers, Maheu de—(H. III. Roll) bore, (1) argent, a chief gules, Glover Roll ; (2) (E. III.) gules a chief argent, a cross-recercelée (moline in trick) counterchanged ; Jenyns' Ordinary. In St. George and Arden Rolls the chief becomes per fess argent and gules, and the cross moline counterchanged. F.

*****Colvyle, John**—(R. II. Roll) bore, azure, a lyon rampant argent ; Surrey Roll. (F.) Sir GEOFFREY, of co. Linc. (Parliamentary Roll), bore this coat differenced with a label (3) gules ; and JOHN, of Mershland (Jenyns' Ordinary) bore the reverse with the same label.

Colvile, John and **Osmond,** of Bytham, in Lincolnshire—(E. III. Roll) bore, or, a fess gules ; Jenyns' Roll and Ordinary. Sir SYMON or EMOUN, of co. Linc. and WALTER bore the same, and another WALTER differenced his coat with a mullet argent.

Colvile, Sir Thomas—bore, at the siege of Calais 1345-8 ; or, on a fess gules three lyonceux rampant of the field. (F.) Borne, with the lyonceux argent, by Sir Thomas and Thomas, of Codwald, or Cokewald ; Jenyns' Ordinary, Parliamentary Roll.

Colvile, Sir John (and **William**)—(E. III. Roll) bore, or, on a fess gules three crosses crosslet argent ; Ashmole Roll ; fitchée in Jenyns' Ordinary. PHILIP took up the cross in the last Crusade 1270.

Colvile, Sir Robert de, of Yorkshire—E. II. Roll) bore, or, a fess gules in chief three torteaux ; Parliamentary Roll. Borne also by JOHN in Surrey Roll and ROBERT of Dale, in Jenyns' Ordinary.

Colvile, William de—(H. III. Roll) bore, gules, billettée or 4, 5, 4, 3, 2 Arden and St. George Rolls. Six billets and colours reversed in Howard Roll. F.

Colvile, Sir Robert—(E. III. Roll) bore, azure, two bars or, in chief three bezants ; (F.) Ashmole Roll.

Colvyle, Sir J.—(H. VI. Roll) bore, or, three chess rooks gules *quarterly with*, azure a lyon rampant argent collared and armed gules ; Atkinson Roll.

Colevile, Sir Robert of Blakamor—(E. III. Roll) bore, azure two bars or and in chief three bezants ; Ashmole Roll.

Colvile, Henry, of Cambridgeshire—(E. III. Roll) bore, argent a cross patonce gules, borne also by WALTER PERCEHAYE, and are in dispute "et son en debate" ; Jenyns' Ordinary. These arms are also ascribed to Sir HENRY (or ROBERT) in Parliamentary Roll, PHILIP (F.), in Arden Roll, and ROBERT and HENRY in Jenyns' Ordinary ; in this last BERENGAR LE MOYNE is said to bear the same arms—the cross is variously tricked as moline and flory, patée or patonce and is also blasoned recercelée.

Colwyk (——) a Suffolk Knight—(H. VI. Roll) bore, argent, on a bend azure three besants, in the cantel a cross crosslet fitchée of the second ; Arundel Roll.

Colworthe, Richard de—(H. III. Roll) bore, vaire argent and gules. (F.) St. George Roll. ROBERT or RICHARD in Jenyns' Ordinary.

Comale, Robert de—(H. III. Roll) bore, azure, a semée of escallops or, a lyon rampant argent ; Howard Roll. (F.) See CORMAYLE.

Combe, Sir John (COUMBE)—(E. III. Roll) bore, argent, a chevron engrailed gules between three black birds proper ; Ashmole Roll. F.

Combe, Richard de—(E. III. Roll) bore, ermine three ("leopardes lyonceux passant") lyons passant gardant gules ; Jenyns' Ordinary. F.

Compton, Sir Robert—bore, sable, three esquires helmets visors up, or ; Cotton MS. Tib. D. 10. F.

*****[Compton, Thomas de** (H. III.)—bore, on a chevron—three fleurs-de-lys—THOMAS, of Fenny Compton, bore, sable three esquires helmets 2 & 1 argent.—Shirley.] F.

Comyn, John—(E. I. Roll) bore, gules three garbs or. (F.) Ascribed also to Sir JOHN in the Guillim Roll. See BUCHAN.

Comyn, Sir John, of Lincolnshire—(E. II. Roll) bore, argent, crusily and three garbs gules ; Parliamentary Roll.

Comyn, —— (H. III. Roll) bore, azure, semée of estoiles or, a chief argent, over all three garbs argent (*sic*) (? counterchanged) banded gules. (F.) St. George Roll. Harl. MS 6137 fo. 78.

*****[Congreve, William,** E. II.—bore the arms of CAMPION, sable, a chevron between three battle axes argent.—Shirley.] F.

Conquest, Sir John, of Beds.—(E. II. Roll) bore, quarterly argent and sable, a label (3) gules ; Parliamentary Roll.

Constable, Sir William—(E. I. Roll) bore, quarterly vair and gules ; Sir ROBERT bore the same with a bend "engréle" or ; Nativity Roll, though gules and vair in the Parliamentary Roll. This coat is more often blasoned in the Rolls—quarterly gules and vair a bendlet (*vel* baston) or, for Sir JOHN, Sir MARMADUKE, RICHARD and ROBERT.

JOHN OF ELTHAM,
EARL OF CORNWALL, 2ND SON OF EDWARD II.
IN ST. EDMUND CHAPEL, WESTMINSTER ABBEY, 1334. *After Stothard.*

Constable (——), of Flamborough, in Yorks.—(E. III. Roll) bore, quarterly gules and vair a baston argent " parmy "(across) " le gules " ; Cotgrave Roll. For parmy see also DACRE and RAYNSFORD.

Constable, Sir John—Knighted at the capitulation of Calais 1348, bore quarterly vair and gules a border engrailed or. F.

Constable, Roald le, de Richmond—(H. III. Roll), bore, gules, a chief and two gemelles or, Glover Roll : possibly intended to be the same as in the next.

Constable, Robert, of Holderness—(E. III. Roll) bore, barry of six or and azure ; Jenyns' Ordinary.

Constantyn v. Costantyn.

Conway, Henry—(R. II. Roll) bore, sable, on a bend argent cotised ermine a rose gules between two annulets or ; Surrey Roll.

Conyers, Sir John and **Robert**—(E. II. and E. III. Roll) bore, azure, a maunch or ; Parliamentary Roll and Jenyns' Ordinary (Sir ROBERT bore the reverse—Parliamentary Roll) ; CHRISTOPHER and another, ROBERT, bore the coat differenced with an annulet sable ; Surrey Roll and Jenyns' Ordinary.

Conyers (——), a Yorkshire Knight—(H. VI. Roll) bore, azure, a maunch or charged with a torteaux, *quarterly with* St. Quintin, or, a chevron gules and a chief vair ; Arundel Roll.

Conyers, Sir Robert—(E. III. Roll) bore, azure, a maunch ermine ; Ashmole and Cotgrave Rolls and Jenyns' Ordinary. Cotgrave also blasons, azure a maunch argent for CONYERS.

Conyers, Robert—(E. II. Roll) bore, or five fusils conjoined in fess sable, *quarterly with* or, a maunch azure ; Jenyns' Roll.

Coote (——), a Suffolk Knight—(H. VI. Roll) bore, argent, three coots 2 and 1 sable : Arundel Roll.

***Cope, William,** of Essex, gentleman—(H. VI. Roll) bore, argent, on a chevron azure between three roses gules slipped and leaved vert as many fleurs-de-lys of the field ; Arundel Roll.

Copuldick, John—(R. II. Roll) bore, argent, a chevron between three crosses crosslet gules ; Surrey Roll. F.

†**Corane, Sire de**—(H. III. Roll) bore, argent, an inescocheon sable, a label (5) gules ; Dering Roll. F.

***Corbet, Peter,** Baron of Caux 1297—bore, or, a corbyn (or raven) sable ; Nobility, Parliamentary and Ashmole Rolls. This latter gives the same coat also for CORBET within a bordure engrailed gules.

Corbet, Sir Peter—bore, at the battle of Falkirk 1298, or two corbeaux (corbyns) sable (F.), probably son of the Baron of Caux, to whom the same arms are ascribed in the Parliamentary Roll. THOMAS DE CAUX, ROBERT (‡) and Sir THOMAS, of Herefordshire, bore the same ; Dering and Parly. Rolls.

Corbet, Sir Roger—(E. III. Roll) bore, two corbyns sable a bordure engrailed gules ; Ashmole Roll.

Corbet, Sir Thomas—bore, at the first Dunstable tournament 1308, or three corbyns 2 and 1 sable. (F.) Borne also by RAFE (E. II.), ROGER (E. I.), and WILLIAM (H. III.) ; Jenyns', Segar and Arden Rolls.

Corbet, Thomas—(H. III. Roll) bore, or, six corbyns 3, 2, 1 sable, on a quarter gules two lyons passant argent ; Arden Roll ; three lyons in St. George Roll. F.

Corbet, Sire Johan—bore, at the battle of Boroughbridge 1322, argent, two bars and a quarter gules, a label argent. F.

Corbet, William—bore, at the second Dunstable tournament 1334, argent two bars gules " un fece d'asure."

Corbet, Sir Roger—Knighted at the capitulation of Calais 1348, bore, argent two bars gules on a canton of the last a cinquefoyle argent. F.

Corbet, Robert—(R. II. Roll) bore, argent, two bars and a canton gules, ROBERT son fitz, differenced with a label (3) argent ; Surrey Roll. This coat ascribed to Sir ROBERT (E. III.) in Ashmole Roll.

Corbridge, —— (E. III. Roll) bore, ermine, a fess fusily gules and vair (a better blason may be, ermine on a fess gules five lozenges vair) ; Ashmole Roll.

Corder, Sir Galyon (altered to Sir WILLIAM in Ashmole Roll)—bore, at the siege of Calais 1345-8, or, on a chief indented (or dancettée) azure, three crosses crosslet of the field. F.

Cormayle, Sir John—bore, argent, three crows proper ; Ashmole and Parliamentary Rolls ; See also COMALE.

Cormmale, Richard de—(H. III. Roll) bore, argent, on a fess sable three bezants ; Howard Roll.

Cornerth, Sir Richard, of Suffolk—Knighted at the capitulation of Calais 1348, when he bore, azure a fess between two chevronels or. (F.) Borne also by THOMAS (R. II.) ; Surrey Roll ; and by Sir THOMAS GRAY in Ashmole Roll.

Cornwall, John of Eltham, EARL OF ; *f 2* EDWARD II. bore, at the second Dunstable tournament 1334, England within a bordure of France. See Effigy.

Cornwall, Piers Gaveston, Earl of—(E. II. Roll) bore, vert six eagles displayed 3 and 3 or ; Arundel Roll (H. VI.).

Cornewall, Sir Edmond de—bore, at the first Dunstable tournament 1308, and at the battle of Boroughbridge 1322, argent, a lyon rampant gules crowned or debruised by a baston sable thereon five bezants. (F.); Add. MS. 5848—(no baston in Harl. MS. 6137 fo. 37). Sir EDMOND, of Oxon. bore, three bezants on the bend ; Parly. Roll ; as did SYMON in Cotgrave Roll. Sire GEOFFREY bore it at the battle of Boroughbridge 1322, with three mullets (6) or, on the bend. (F.) These two Boroughbridge coats are also ascribed to Sir EDMOND and Sir GEFFREY CURTENEYE in that Roll — an instructive blunder.

Cornwall Richard and **Edmund,** Earls of -(E. I. Roll) bore, argent, a lyon rampant gules crowned or, within a bordure sable bezantée (F.) in all the Rolls. Sir EDWARD bore the same (E. III.); Ashmole Roll. Sir JOHN, K.G. (H. IV.), bore the bordure engrailed, K. 400 fo. 21.

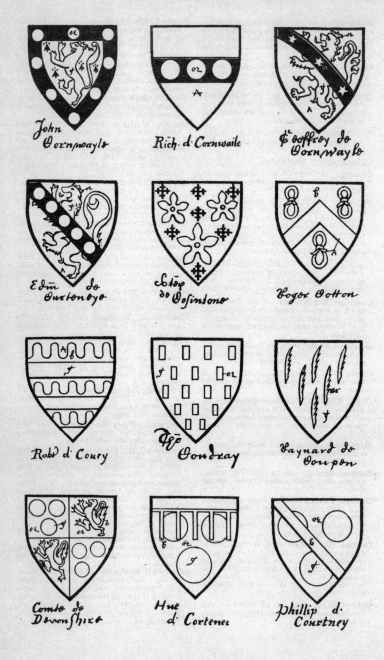

John
Cornwayle

Rich· d· Cornwaile

Ç. Goffroy de
Cornwayle

Edm   de
Curtenoye

Step
de Cosintone

Roger Cotton

Robt d· Coury

Gondray

Faynard de
Coupen

Comte de
Devonshire

Hue
d· Cortenei

Phillip d·
Courtney

Cornwall, John, a baron 1433 – bore, at the siege of Rouen 1418, ermine, a lyon rampant gules crowned or within a bordure sable bezantée. Borne also by *BRYAN ; Surrey Roll.

Cornwall, John de—(R. II. Roll) bore, argent. three fusils in bend between six crosses crosslet fitchée sable ; Surrey Roll.

Cornwall, Richard de—(H. III. Roll) bore, argent on a fess sable three besants (plates in the Dering Roll). (F.) Arden and St. George Roll. ROBERT (‡) bore the same in the Ashmole Copy of the Dering Roll.

Cornwall, Sir Richard—Knighted at the capitulation of Calais 1348 – boré argent, on a bend sable three plates ; a marginal note adds *puto* or, *i.e.* besants.

Cornwall, Sir Walter de, of the West – (E. II. Roll) bore, argent, a cross sable bezantée (5, 9) ; Parliamentary Roll. Sir LAURENCE of the North, bore, argent a cross patonce sable bezantée ; Parliamentary Roll and Jenyns' Ordinary, in which latter the cross is tricked flory.

Corry, Sir Walter de, of Cumberland— (E. II. Roll) bore, argent, a saltire sable, on a chief azure three cinquefoyles or ; Parly. Roll.

Cospatrick, Thomas, of Workington— (E. III. Roll) bore, argent, fretty gules, a chief azure, according to the blason, but tricked, argent, three chevronels interlaced in base gules, a chief azure, same as CHRISTOPHER CURWEN. Jenyns' Ordinary.

Cossington, Stephen—(H. III. Roll) bore, azure three roses or ; Howard Roll (a single rose in Jenyns' Ordinary). Ascribed also to Sir WILLIAM of Hants in the Parliamentary and Surrey Rolls.

‡**Cossington, Stephen**—(H. III. Roll) bore, azure, crusily and three cinquefoyles pierced or. (F.) Dering Roll. No crosslets in the Ashmole Copy.

Costantyn, William, of Essex—(H. VI. Roll) bore, argent, a chevron gules between three hurts ; Arundel Roll.

Cotel, Sir Ellis, of Somerset – (E. II. Roll) bore, or, a bend gules ; Parliamentary Roll. THOMAS also bore it ; Jenyns' Ordinary.

Cotenham, John de—(E. III. Roll) bore, barry dancettée (8) argent and gules, tricked as barry dancettée (6) gules and argent ; Jenyns' Ordinary.

*[**Cotes** (——) of Cotes, co. Stafford, wrongfully bore the arms of KNIGHTLEY which see,— Erdeswick ; Shirley.]

Cotingham, —— (E. IV. Roll) bore, sable, two hinds (perhaps colts) passant counterpassant argent ; with crest ; Ballard Roll.

Cottingham, John de – (E. III. Roll) bore, sable, a chevron engrailed between three quills (? plumes) argent ; Jenyns' Roll.

*[**Cotton, Roger,** of Alkington, Cheshire (R. II.)—bore, azure, a chevron between three hawks' lures (or cotton hanks) argent.—Shirley.] F.

†**Cotun, Raffe de**—(H. III. Roll) bore, barry (6) argent and azure, in chief three buckles gules tongues to the dexter ; Arden and Jenyns' Roll, where it is also tricked argent two bars azure, &c.

Coucy, Robert de (H. III. Roll) and **Thomas**—(E. III. Roll) bore, barry (6) vair and gules (F.); St. George Roll and Jenyns' Ordinary ; with a bend or for THOMAS in Norfolk Roll. INGELRAM, Earl of Bedford, K.G., 1366, bore it quarterly with, gules, a fess argent ; K. 398 fo. 43.

Coudray, Sire Thomas de, of Berks— bore, at the first Dunstable tournament 1308, and at the battle of Boroughbridge 1322, gules, billettée or. (F.). Borne also by PIERS and WILLIAM ; Arden, St. George, Parly., Cotgrave, and Jenyns' Rolls. Sir THOMAS differenced with a label of three azure ; Ashmole Roll.

Coudray or **Caundray,** ——(E. III. Roll) bore, gules. billettée or, and a bend vair ; Ashmole Roll.

Coupen, Sir Raymond—(E. II. Roll) bore, gules, six pens erect argent ; Parliamentary Roll. F.

Coupland, Sr. de—(E. II. Roll) bore, argent, a chief gules ; Jenyns' Roll. Same as WILLIAM FORS, Earl of Albemarle.

Coupland, John de—(R. II. Roll) bore, argent, on a cross sable a mullet of the field ; Surrey Roll. The mullet is pierced in Jenyns' Roll.

*_Courtenay, Sir Hugh de,_ banneret ; a baron 1299, Earl of Devon 1335—bore, at the battle of Falkirk 1298, or, in chief three torteaux, a label azure. The label distinguished the English from the elder branch settled in France.

Courtenay, Hugh de, banneret—bore, at the siege of Carlaverock 1300, or, three torteaux (2 and 1) a label azure (F.) (with a label of five in NICOLAS) ; as also did Sir PHILIP at the first Dunstable tournament 1308 (F.); borne also by Sir HUGH, K.G., a founder, and Sir PIERS, K.G. Another HUGH bore the same at the second Dunstable tournament 1334, on which occasion THOMAS bore it with a baston azure ; Guillim, St. George, and Howard Rolls.

Courtenay, Sir Hugh—bore, at the siege of Calais 1345-8, or, three torteaux, a label (3) azure, each pendant charged with as many crescents of the field – besants, in Cotton MS.— annulets in Harl. MS. (F.) Sir HUGH, who was knighted at the capitulation of Calais 1348, bore, or, three torteaux, a label (5) azure, on each pendant a fleur-de-lys argent (F.); and PHILIP of Powderham. differenced with plates in lieu of fleurs-de-lys ; Harl. MS. 1481 fo. 55.

Courtenay, (Hugh 4th), Earl of Devon— bore, at the siege of Rouen 1418, or, three torteaux *quarterly with,* or, a lyon rampant azure (for REDVERS). (F.) In the Grimaldi Roll the Earl of Devonshire's coat is blasoned or three gastrels gules (besants) a label azure.

Courtenay, Monsyer—bore, at the siege of Rouen 1418, or, three torteaux, a label (3) azure, on each pendant as many annulets argent (F.); plates in the Ashmole MS., and so borne by Mons. PHILIP (R. II.) Surrey Roll, and Sir PETER, K.G., 1388 K. 399 fo. 25.

Courtenay, Sir Philip, of Somersetshire – (E. II. Roll) bore, or, three torteaux, a bend gobony argent and azure ; Parliamentary Roll ; Harl. MS. 6137 fo. 7ᵇ ; a bend azure in Harl. MS. 4033 fo. 33. See Sir PHILIP, 1308.

SIR JOHN DE CREKE.

IN WESTLEY WATERLESS CHURCH, IN CAMBRIDGESHIRE, 1325.

After Waller.

Courtenay, Sir Edmond and **Sir Geoffery.** See Sir EDMOND and Sir GEOFFERY CORNEWAYLE.

*[**Courthope** (——), of Goudhurst, Sussex *c.* 1413—bore, argent, a fess azure between three estoiles sable - Shirley.] F.

Cove, Sir John, of Norfolk—bore, at the first Dunstable tournament 1308, gules, a bend argent cotised or; written as COUE, COWE, and TONYE. Parly. Roll, &c.

‡**Covert, Roger le**—(H. III. Roll) bore, gules, a fess ermine, in chief two mullets pierced or, (F.); Dering and Howard Rolls. The fess is between three mullets, or in the Ashmole MS.

Couffolds —— (H. VI. Roll) bore, argent five barrulets and a quarter gules; Arundel Roll.

Cowley, Sir Robert (COVELEY)–(E. III. Roll) bore, argent, on a chevron sable, three leopards' faces or; Ashmole Roll.

Cozans, Sir William — Knighted at the capitulation of Calais 1348, bore, argent, a bend fusily sable, a label (5) gules. F.

Craddok, Richard — (R. II. Roll) bore, argent, on a chevron azure three garbs or; Surrey Roll.

Craili, John—(H. III. Roll) bore, or, a cross between four mullets gules. (F.) St. George Roll. See TRAYLEY.

Crameville, Sire Johan de—bore, at the battle of Boroughbridge 1322, gules, an inescocheon and a bordure molliettée argent—*i.e.* mullets in orle. F.

Crane (——), a Suffolk Knight—(H. VI. Roll) bore, argent, a fess between three crosses crosslet fitchée gules · Arundel Roll.

Crawcestre, John — (E. II. Roll) bore, quarterly or and gules in the first a martlet sable; Jenyns' Roll.

Crek, Walter de — bore, at the second Dunstable tournament 1334, argent a bend azure three "wyfres" *i.e.* cotises wavy. (F.) See also BENHALE *ante* and "Archæologia," Vol. 31, 247, where they are quaintly defined as vipers' nests.

[**Creke, Sir John de,** bore or, on a fess sable three lozenges vair. See Monumental Brass.]

Creon, Maurice de—bore, at the siege of Carlaverock 1300, gules, seven mascles conjoined 3, 3, 1 or. F.

Crepin, William—(H. III. Roll) bore, argent three bars gules "engrélles"; Norfolk Roll. See also CRISPIN.

Creppinge, Sir John de, of Lincolnshire—(E. II. Roll) bore, gules, billettée or, and a lyon rampant argent; Parly. Roll. Guttée d'or in Segar Roll.

Creppings, Richard de—(H. III. Roll, bore, chequy or and azure, a crescent gules. (F.) St. George Roll.

Cressner, John—(E. II. Roll) bore, azure on a chief argent three chaplets gules; Jenyns' Roll.

Cressy, William de, banneret, a baron (25 E. I. 1297)—bore, argent, a lyon rampant tail fourchée sable. (F.) Nobility and Arundel Rolls (borne also by CLIFTON, of Hodsall, Notts)—Sir ROGER, of Yorkshire bore it with a label (3) gules; Parliamentary Roll.

Creston, Sir Thomas (or CRISTON) - (H. VI. Roll) bore, gules, a saltire engrailed argent; Atkinson Roll.

Cretinges, John de, a baron 1332—bore, at the siege of Carlaverock 1300, argent, a chevron between three mullets gules. (F.) Borne also by ADAM, JOHN, OSMOND and ROBERT; in some tricks the mullets are pierced, in others they become spur-rowells.

Cretinge, Sir John, of Suffolk – (E. II. Roll) bore, argent, a chevron gules between three torteaux; Parliamentary Roll.

‡**Crevequer, Robert** and **Hamon**—(H. III. Roll) bore, or a cross voided gules. (F.) Glover. Dering and Arden Rolls; the cross voided of the field in Camden and Howard.

Creveker, Sir Robert, of Kent–(E. II. Roll), bore, gules, a cross or; Parliamentary Roll.

Crey, Sir Robert de la—bore, at the first Dunstable tournament 1308, argent, an inescocheon gules over all a bendlet sable. F.

Crey, Sir Simon de, of Kent–(E. II. Roll) and **John de** (E. III. Roll) bore, gul s, a cross engrailed or. (F.) Parliamentary Roll and Jenyns' Ordinary—a copy of the Dering Roll adds—for SIMON (‡) "in dexter chief an eagle displayed, Harl. MS. 6137 *f* 90^b."

Crey, Sir William de (KROY), of Kent—bore, at the first Dunstable tournament 1308, gules, a cross engrailed or, over all a baston azure. (F.) See also Parliamentary Roll.

Criketoft, John—(E. III. Roll) bore, lozengy or and sable (F.); Ashmole Roll and Jenyns' Ordinary; blasoned mascles, tricked lozengy—same as WILLIAM BLUNDE.

‡**Criell, Nicholas de,** baron 1297—bore, gules, a chief or, Nobility Roll—per fess or and gules, in Dering Roll.

Criel, Nychole de (CRYEL)—(H. III. Roll) bore, per fess or and gules, three annulets counterchanged "tertoleres"; Vincent MS. No. 165, 151^u and Harl. MS. 1068 fo. 172 (F.). Perhaps ORIEL, which see.

Criol, John (KYRIEL)—bore, at the second Dunstable tournament 1348, or, three chevronels and a canton gules. F.

Criol, Sir Thomas, K.G.—(H. VI. Roll) bore, or two chevronels (a chevron et demye) and a quarter gules; Atkinson Roll. BERTRAM (‡) (F.) or ROBERT, JOHN and Sir NICHOLAS of Kent bore the same; Dering, Parly., Howard, Jenyns' and Surrey Rolls.

+**Crispin, William**—(H. III. Roll) bore, lozengy argent and gules (or, in Dering Roll). (F.) JOHN differenced it with a label (5) azure; Howard Roll. See also CREPIN.

Cristemasse. See CHRISTMAS.

Croft, Sir Hugh, of Salop—bore, at the first Dunstable tournament 1308, quarterly per fess indented azure and argent (in the first quarter) a lyon passant gardant or (F.) and Parly. Roll—H. 6137 fo. 27^b. In Harl. MS. 4033 the tinctures are reversed, the lyon appearing in the second quarter. In the Ashmole Roll it is erroneously tricked per pale and a chief indented, &c.

Perd Crok   Simon d Crombe.   John de Crumwell

Hict de Crombewell   Basse Crophill   Rich. d Cronpes

Croxford   Johan de Cudemore   John Curson.

Robert Curson   Roger de Curson   Tho. d Coxowen

Crofte, Nicholas de—(E. III. Roll) bore, lozengy argent and sable (mascles in blason) ; Jenyns' Ordinary and Ballard Roll ; borne also by Sir PETER LEE of co. Lanc.

Croke v. **Sir Thomas Blount.**

Croke, Piers—(H. III. Roll) bore, azure three crooks or ; St. George Roll. Birds' heads in Harl. MS. 6137, fo. 86ᵇ. F. NICHOLAS and ROBERT took up the cross in the last Crusade 1270.

Crokedayke, Sir Adam de, 1297—bore, ermine three pellets ; Nobility Roll.

Crombe, Simon de—(H. III. Roll) bore, argent, a chevron gules on a chief of the last three escallops of the first (F.) ; St. George Roll. In the Arden Roll, the field ermine and the escallops or, sometimes argent.

Cromwell, John de—bore, at the siege of Carlaverock 1300, azure, a lyon rampant argent tail fourchée, ducally crowned or. F.

Cromwell, Sir John de, banneret—(E. I. Roll) bore, gules, six annulets or ; Nativity and Parliamentary Rolls, and Jenyns' Ordinary.

Cromwell, Sire Rauf de—(E. I. Roll) bore, argent, a chief azure, surmounted by a bendlet gules, (F.) ; (SIMON bore the same, E. III. Roll) ; Guillim and St. George Rolls.

Cromwell, John, of Tatishall, baron 1308—RAUFE (E. I. Roll) and THOMAS of Lamlay (E. III. Roll) bore, argent, a chief gules surmounted by a baston azure ; Segar and Arundel Rolls and Jenyns' Ordinary.

Cromwell, Sire Richard de—bore, at the battle of Boroughbridge 1322, argent, a chief gules surmounted by a baston gobony or and azure, (F.) and in Jenyns' Ordinary.

Cromwell, Sir Raulf le (DE TATERSALE) —(R. II. Roll) bore, checquy or and gules, a chief ermine, *quarterly with,* argent a chief gules surmounted by a baston sable ; Surrey Roll.

Cromwell. Sire John de—bore, at the battle of Boroughbridge 1322, "Queynty d'argent frettée de ses armes d'Ermyne" ; not tricked in the Ashmole Copy, made by BROOKE, York Herald, the blason has yet to be solved, though it rather points to the quarterly coat of RAUF. See also BERKELEY.

Crophill, Raffe—(E. III. Roll) bore, argent, a saltire gules fretty or ; Ashmole Roll and Jenyns' Ordinary.

Croupes, Richard de—(H. III. Roll) bore, argent, six lozenges 3, 2, 1 gules ; Arden Roll. Sir RICHARD bore mascles (E. II. Roll) with a label (3) azure ; Parliamentary Roll ; and in the St. George Roll it appears with a label of five also azure. F. See BRIDMANSTONE.

Croxford, —— (E. III. Roll) bore, argent a chevron between three buckles sable garnished with mascles, tongues to the sinister ; Ashmole Roll. F.

Crull, —— (E. III. Roll) bore, gules, a chevron between three eagles displayed argent ; Ashmole Roll.

Cudemers, John de—(E. I. Roll) bore, gyronny (12) or and sable, (F.), (in the centre what might be mistaken for a pellet) ; Segar Roll.

‡**Cudham, Oliver and Robert de**—(H. III. Roll) bore checquy gules and argent a fess azure (F.) ; Dering Roll ; reversed, *i.e.* argent and gules, in the Ashmole MS.

Cuffolds (——), an Essex Knight (? COW-FFOLDS)—(H. VI. Roll) bore, argent, five barrulets and a quarter gules ; Arundel Roll.

Cuggeho, Nicol de—(E. I. Roll) bore, gules, a fess between three lozenges argent (F.) ; Camden Roll.

Cuggeho, William—(H. III. Roll) bore, gules, a fess and in chief three mascles argent (F.) ; St. George and Parliamentary Rolls ; COGGENHO, Northants.

Cuilly, Hugh de—(E. III. Roll) bore, argent a chevron between three mullets sable ; Cotgrave Roll. Written TUYLEY in Jenyns' Ordinary. Sir HUGH of Notts bore (E. II. Roll) ogresses in the place of mullets ; Parliamentary Roll.

Culcheth, Randolph, alias HINDLEY—(E. IV. Roll) bore, sable, a gryphon segreant argent ; with crest ; Ballard Roll.

Curson, Sire Roger de—bore at the battle of Boroughbridge 1322, checquy or and sable, a fess argent. (F.) JOHN (E. III. Roll) bore, chequy or and azure, a fess argent, a label (3) gules ; Jenyns' Ordinary.

Curson, John—bore, at the siege of Rouen 1418, ermine a bend counter-compony argent and sable (F.) MONSYER CURSON bore on the same occasion this coat differenced with a martlet gules.

Curson, Robert—bore, at the siege of Rouen 1418, gules, on a bend between six billets or, three escallops sable. F.

Curson, Sir John, of Norfolk—(E. II. Roll) bore, or, on a bend gules three besants ; Parliamentary Roll.

***Curson, Roger**—(R. II. Roll) bore, argent, on a bend sable three popinjays or, collared and membered gules—a crescent of the last ; Surrey Roll.

Curteis (——), an Essex Knight (CORTEYS)—(H. VI. Roll) bore, ermine on a canton gules an orle argent ; Arundel Roll.

Curwen, Thomas de—(H. III. Roll) bore, gules, fretty argent (F.) ; Arden and St. George Rolls.

Curwen, Christopher—(E. III. Roll) bore, argent, fretty gules, a chief azure ; THOMAS bore, argent fretty and a chief gules, Jenyns' Ordinary, but they are tricked, probably in error, argent three chevrons interlaced in base gules, a chief azure for CHRISTOPHER ; the chief of the field, for THOMAS ; Jenyns' Roll. See COSPATRICK.

Cusance, William—(E. III. Roll) bore, argent, a bend engrailed sable, in chief an escallop of the last ; Jenyns' Ordinary.

SIR JOHN D'ABERNON.

IN STOKE DABERNON CHURCH, SURREY, 1277.   *After Waller.*

D

D'Abernon, Sir John de, of Surrey—(H. III. Roll) bore, azure, a chevron or ; St. George and Howard Rolls ; see Mon. Brass ; his son Sir JOHN differenced with a label (3) argent, at the first Dunstable tournament 1308, and at the battle of Boroughbridge 1322. F.

D'Abitot, Geoffrey, of Hindlip, co. Worc.—(H. III. Roll) bore, per pale gules and vert two lyons passant gardant argent—another, or, two lyons passant gardant that in chief gules, that in base azure. (F.) Arden and St. George Rolls.

D'Abitot. Sir William, of co. Worc.—(E. II. Roll) bore, ermine, a chief bendy (6) or and sable ; Parliamentary Roll.

Dabridgcourt, Sir John (K.G. 1413)—bore, at the siege of Rouen 1418, ermine three bars humettée gules. (F.) Borne also by NICOL and by SANCHET, K.G., a founder ; Surrey Roll (R. II.). This coat by an heraldic illusion may be blasoned the reverse, viz., gules two bars and a bordure ermine.

Dabridgecourt, John de—(R. II. Roll) bore, ermine, three bars humettée gules each charged with as many escallops or ; Parly. Roll.

Dacre, Sir William, of Cumberland—(E. I. Roll) bore, gules, three escallops argent. (F.) Segar, Ashmole and Parliamentary Rolls.

Dacre, Sir Edward, of Cumberland—(E. II. Roll) bore, gules, florettée or, three escallops argent ; Parliamentary Roll.

Dacre, Randolph—(H. III. Roll) bore, azure on a cross or five escallops gules. (F.) Arden and St. George Rolls ; (same as NICHOL VILLERS) ; in Jenyns' Ordinary the cross is described as p'my. See CONSTABLE and RAYNSFORD.

Dagnall, Robert—(H. III. Roll) bore, paly (6) or and azure, a chief gules ; Howard Roll.

Dagworth, Thomas, a baron 1347—bore, ermine on a fess gules three besants. Borne also by Sir JOHN of Suffolk, Parly. Roll—and RALPH, in Ashmole Roll ; torteaux in lieu of besants for NICHOLAS in Surrey Roll (R. II.).

Dagworth, Thomas—(E. III. Roll) bore, ermine on a chevron gules three besants ; Jenyns' Ordinary.

Dakeneye, Sir Baldwin, of Cambridge—(E. II. Roll), **John** and **William** (H. III. Roll) bore, azure, a cross between four lyonceux rampant or. (F.) Parliamentary, St. George and Glover Rolls.

Dakeney, Sir Thomas, of Norfolk—(E. II. Roll) bore, argent, a cross between four lyonceux rampant gules ; Parliamentary Roll.

Dalden, Jordan de—(E. II. Roll) bore, argent, a cross patée (patonce in trick) gules, between four daws proper ; Jenyns' Roll.

Dale, Sir Thomas—(E. III. Roll) bore, gules, a swan close argent, membered sable ; Ashmole and Surrey Rolls.

Dallingridge, MOUNSYER—bore, at the siege of Rouen 1418, argent, a cross engrailed gules (F.), and in Jenyns' Roll. See Monumental Brass.

D'Alry, Johan (DE ALRE)—(H. III. Roll) bore, argent, three escallops gules ; Howard Roll.

Dalston, John de—(E. II. Roll) bore, argent, a chevron engrailed sable between three daws' heads erased of the last ; Jenyns' Roll.

Dalton, Sire Robert de—bore at the battle of Boroughbridge 1322 and at the siege of Calais 1345-8, azure, crusily or, a lyon rampant gardant argent.

Dalton, Robert de—(E. III. Roll) bore, azure, a leopard rampant argent—*i.e.* a lyon rampant gardant ; Jenyns' Ordinary.

Dalton (——), a Yorkshire Knight—(H. VI. Roll) bore, azure, florettée or, a lyon rampant gardant argent. (F.) Arundel Roll.

Dammerell, William—(E. III. Roll) bore, azure, on a chief gules two crescents and another in base argent ; Ashmole Roll.

Damory, Sir Richard—bore, at the first Dunstable tournament 1308, undée (6) gules and argent—possibly an error for argent and gules ; another Sir RICHARD of Oxon bore, at the siege of Calais 1345-8, undée (6 or 8) argent and gules—also in Parliamentary Roll. ROBERT bore the same with a label (5) sable ; Arden Roll ;—In Dering Roll the labels azure, each file being charged with three bezants. (F.) Said to be vairy (modern) argent and gules, &c., in Howard Roll.

Damory, Sir Roger, baron 1317—bore, at the first Dunstable tournament 1308, undée (6) argent and gules a bend azure. (F.) See also Parliamentary Roll.

Dancastre, Robert—(E. III. Roll) bore, or, on a bend azure, three castles triple turreted argent. (F.) Jenyns' Ordinary.

Daneston, John, a Suffolk Knight—(H. VI. Roll) bore, argent three Danish axes gules *quarterly with,* argent, on a chevron sable, a cross patée of the first ; Arundel Roll.

Dangervile, Sir John, of co. Leic.—(E. II. Roll) bore, gules, a cinquefoyle ermine, a bordure sable bezantée ; Parly. Roll. HUGH took up the cross in the last Crusade 1269.

SIR — DALYNGRUGGE.

IN FLETCHING CHURCH, SUSSEX, 1395 ; 8 RIC. II.   *After Boutell.*

D'Angle, Sir Guichard, K.G. 1372, Earl of Huntingdon 1377 for life—bore, or, billettée and a lyon rampant azure, K. 398 fo. 44.

Danny, Sir John—(E. III. Roll) bore, argent, on a bend cotised azure three six-foyles pierced or ; Ashmole Roll ; cinquefoyles argent in Jenyns' Ordinary.

Danny, Nicholas—(E. III. Roll) bore, argent, on a bend vert cotised azure three cinquefoyles or ; Jenyns' Ordinary.

Danvers, Sir Thomas (DE ANVERS) of Cheshire, Kt.—(E. II. Roll) bore, gules, a chevron or between three besants ; Parliamentary Roll. An Essex (?) Knight bore the same (Hen. VI.); with pierced mullets in lieu of besants ; Arundel Roll.

Danyell, (——) of Danby-upon-Yore, in Yorkshire—(E. III. Roll) bore, argent seven mascles 3, 3, 1 gules (blasoned as lozenges pierced) ; Jenyns' Ordinary.

Danyell, Hugh—(E. III. Roll) bore, azure, two bars argent a chief gules ; Jenyns' Ordinary.

Daniell, John—(H. III. Roll) bore, azure, a bend between six escallops or. (F.) St. George Roll.

Danyell, Thomas—(E. III. Roll) bore, argent a pile indented of five points sable. (F.) Jenyns' Ordinary.

Danyell (——), of Cheshire—(E. IV. Roll) bore, argent, a pale lozengy sable, *quarterly with*, argent, a fox regardant sable – with crest ; Ballard Roll.

Darcy—The cinquefoyles are often tricked as six-foyles and roses.

Darcye, Sir Adomar (AMOR)—bore, at the siege of Calais 1345-8, argent, an inescocheon within an orle of cinquefoyles gules.

Darcy, Sir John—bore, at the first Dunstable tournament 1308, argent an inescocheon sable between three cinquefoyles gules. F.

Darcy, Sir John—bore, at the battle of Boroughbridge 1322, argent, an inescocheon sable within an orle of six-foyles gules (blasoned in Jenyns' Ordinary for DARCY DE PARKE as sable, a bordure of the arms of DARCY). Sire JOHAN le fiz, bore on the same occasion—argent, on an inescocheon sable an estoile or, all within an orle of cinquefoyles pierced gules.

Darcy, Sir John (of co. Lincoln), knighted at the capitulation of Calais 1348—bore, argent, an inescocheon sable within an orle of cinquefoyles (roses in Parliamentary Roll) gules ; also blasoned, as argent, an orle of six-foyles gules and a false escocheon sable. Ascribed to ROBERT in Cotgrave Roll.

Darcy, Sire Norman, le fiz—bore, at the battle of Boroughbridge 1322, argent the bordure of roses (gules) a label (3) azure. F.

Darcy, Sir Rauff—(E. III. Roll) bore, argent, on an inescocheon gules, three crosses crosslet fitchée or, all within an orle of (8) seysfoyles pierced of the second ; Ashmole Roll.

Darcy, Sir John, of Knaith, a baron 1332— bore, argent, a cinquefoyle and a bordure indented gules ; Nativity Roll.

Darcy, Philip, baron 1299 - bore, at the battle of Falkirk 1298, argent, three cinquefoyles gules (incorrectly blasoned as crosses crosslet) ; Nobility Roll — the cinquefoyles were borne pierced by (1) Sir PHILIP, Knight banneret, (2) NORMAN(‡) (F.), and also (3) by an Essex Knight ; Dering and Howard Rolls.

Darcy, Sir Norman, knighted at the capitulation of Calais 1348 - bore, argent three cinquefoyles gules a label (5) azure. F. Roses for Sir NORMAN, of co. Linc., in Parly. Roll.

Darcy, Sir Robert — bore, at the first Dunstable tournament 1308, argent three cinquefoyles gules a bordure indented sable— engrailed in Harl. MS. 6137 fo. 31b.

D'Arcy, Sir William—bore, at the siege of Calais 1345-8, azure, crusily and three cinquefoyles argent. (F.) See also Cotgrave. (Sir JOHN, of co. Lincoln, bore roses ; in Parliamentary Roll). The same coat was borne at the siege of Rouen 1418 by Le Sr. DE DARCYE —and by DARCY *le nepueu* ; Jenyns' Ordinary. (ROGER, 2nd son of JOHN of Knaith, in Yorkshire, bore it within a bordure or, Harl. MS. 1481 fo. 88) and by Le Sr. DARCY (R. II. Roll) bore it *quarterly with*, azure three gemelles and a chief or ; Surrey Roll.

Darcy, Norman—bore, at the second Dunstable tournament 1334, argent, three six-foyles gules ; Segar Roll. Borne al·o by JOHN in Jenyns' Ordinary. Another NORMAN differenced with a label azure ; Jenyns' Ordinary. ROBERT bore it (E. I.) within a bordure engrailed sable. (F.) Segar and Harleian Rolls. In Segar tricks roses may be intended.

Darcy, Sire Robert—bore, at the battle of Boroughbridge 1322, argent three six-foyles gules a bordure vair eglettée or. (F.) Tricked in the Ashmole MS. rather like - vert, on an inescocheon gules three six-foyles gules all within an orle of eaglets displayed or.

Darcy. Sir John—bore, at the siege of Calais 1345-8, argent three roses gules. (F.) (See also 6th Nobility Roll, H. VI.) Sir JOHN, the son, bore the same arms at this siege differenced with a label (3) gules. Borne undifferenced by Sir PHILIP, a baron (25 E. I.) and reversed by Sir WILLIAM, of co. Linc., in Parly. Roll.

Darcy, Sir William, of co. Linc.—(E. II. Roll) bore, argent, three roses gules ; and Sir ROBERT, also of co. Linc. bore it within a bordure indented sable ; Parliamentary Roll.

Darcy, Nicol—(H. III. Roll) bore, sable, a fess or. (F.) St. George Roll.

Darres, Sir Robert—(E. III. Roll) –bore, argent on an orle gules eight escallops or ; Ashmole Roll. See Sir JOHN and ROBERT DARCY ; see also ARRAS.

D'Artois, Janico (DE ARTOYS)—(E. III. Roll) bore, gules four barrulets wavy argent ; Jenyns' Roll (F.).

Dassy, Sir Robert (DE ASSI)—(E. III. Roll) bore, gules, a bend cotised or between six martlets of the last ; Ashmole Roll.

Daubeney, Le Sr.—(E. II. Roll) bore, gules, three fusils conjoined in fess argent ; Jenyns' Roll.

SIR JOHN DAUBENY.

In Norton Brize Church, Oxon., 1346.

After Boutell.

Daubeny, Elias (DE ALBINIACO), baron 1295–1305 –bore, gules four lozenges conjoined in fess argent ; Nobility Roll. Borne also by Sir GILES, of Devon or Cornwall, Parly. Roll, PHILIP and RAUF, the latter in Segar Roll (E. I.). See also Monumental Slab.

Daubeny, Sir John, of OXOII, 1346—bore, four fusils conjoined, each charged with a mullet (5) pierced ; surrounded by three different Daubeny coats here named and a fourth lozengy argent and gules, a bordure of the first. See Monumental Slab.

Daubeny, Elys—(E. I. Roll) bore, gules four fusils conjoined in fess argent, a baston azure. (F.) Segar Roll. WILLIAM bore the same at the second Dunstable tournament 1334, though blasoned as a fess engréle. F.

Daubeny, Felipe—(E. I. Roll) bore, gules four fusils conjoined in fess argent and in chief three martlets or ; Segar Roll—five fusils in the St. George Roll, &c. (F.) And so also for RAUFE and WILLIAM (‡) in the Howard and Dering Rolls.

Dawbeney, Sir Ellis, banneret—bore, at the siege of Carlaverock 1300, gules five fusils conjoined in fess argent. (F.) Drawn as a fess engrailed in NICOLAS — *Gent's. Mag.* xcvi. pt. 1, p. 400—an " engréle" is differently interpreted by the earlier arms painters. Sir JOHN, who was knighted at the capitulation of Calais 1348, bore the same coat. So also ELIAS, Baron DAUBENEY, Parly. Roll and RAUF (‡) Dering Roll, the latter blasoned as a fess engrailed in Glover Roll.

‡Dawbeny, Philip—(E. III. Roll) bore, gules, a fess fusily (*vel* lozengy *vel* 5 fusils in fess) argent, and in chief three mullets pierced or ; Dering and Howard Rolls.

Dawbneye, Sir John—(E. II. Roll) bore, gules a fess lozengy argent (another ermine, and in a third trick a fess indented ermine) in chief three mullets or. (F.) See also Monumental Slab. Parly. Roll.

Dawbeney, Sir Ralph—(E. III. Roll) bore, gules five fusils conjoined in fess (another a fess engrailed) argent, in chief three escallops or. (F.) Holland and St. George Rolls. WILLIAM bore the same, over all a bend azure ; St. George Roll.

Dawbeny, William, de Belvoir—(E. III. Roll) bore, or two chevronels and a bordure gules ; Glover and Grimaldi Rolls ; the bordure engrailed, on the Monumental Slab.

Daubeny, William (DE AUBENY)—(E. III. Roll) bore, sable, three helmets 2 and 1 argent. (F.) Arden Roll.

Daundelegh, Philip—(E. III. Roll) bore, argent, two bars gules each charged with three crosses crosslet or ; Jenyns' Roll and Ordinary.

Daundely, Sir Robert—(E. III. Roll) bore, argent, three bars gules crusily 3, 2, 1 or ; Ashmole Roll.

Dauntesey, John (DANDESEYE)—(R. II. Roll)—bore, per pale or and argent three bars undée gules ; Surrey Roll.

Dauntesey, Sir Richard (AUNTESHEYE), of co. Glouc.—(E. II. Roll) bore, per fess or and argent a fess undée gules ; Parly. Roll. F.

Dautrey, Geffrey (DE ALTA RIPA)— (E. III Roll) bore, azure five fusils conjoined in fess argent, a baston gules ; Jenyns' Ordinary.

Dautrey, Lyon—(E. III. Roll) bore, gules, a bend argent between two cotises engrailed or ; Jenyns' Ordinary.

Dautrey, John—(R. II. Roll) bore, sable, five fusils conjoined in fess argent ; Surrey Roll. WILLIAM (‡) differenced it with a label (5) gules. (F.) Arden, Dering and Howard Rolls—blasoned also as a fess dancettée of five. In Cotgrave Roll the fusils are gules for DAWTRYNE.

Dautrey, Richard—(E. III. Roll) bore, or five fusils conjoined in fess sable ; ARNOLD PERCY, bore the same ; Jenyns' Ordinary.

Daveney *v.* **Avene** and **Vene.**

***Davenport, William** – (E. IV. Roll) bore, argent, a chevron between three crosses crosslet fitchée sable—with crest ; Ballard and Arundel Rolls.

Daventree, John — (E. III. Roll) bore, ermine, a fess chequy (counter compony in trick) or and azure ; Jenyns' Ordinary.

Daventry, Robert—bore, at the second Dunstable tournament 1334, ermine, a fess gules. (F.) A cross in Jenyns' Ordinary.

Daveye, Philip—(R. II. Roll) bore, argent, on a chevron sable between three mullets pierced gules, a crescent of the field ; Surrey Roll.

Davelers, Sire Bartholomew, of Suffolk —bore, at the battle of Boroughbridge 1322, argent, three inescocheons gules. (F.) DE AWILLERS in Parliamentary Roll.

Davereignes. See DE VALOIGNES.

***[Dawnay, John**, 17 E. II.—bore, argent, on a bend cotised sable three annulets of the field. —Shirley.] F.

Dawney, John — (E. III. Roll) bore, per decision of Earl Percy, or five fusils conjoined in fess azure, a bordure azure besantée " per Darell (*sic*) Earl Percy"; Jenyns Ordinary.

Dawtrey *v.* **Dautrey.**

***[Dayrell, Richard**, of Lillingston, Bucks, *c* 1200 — bore, azure, a lyon rampant or crowned argent.--Shirley.] F.

de Albini, Nigel (of whom the MOWBRAYS) —(H. I. Roll) bore, gules, a lyon rampant argent ; his brother WILLIAM, chief butler of England (father of WILLIAM, Earl of ARUNDEL) bore, gules, a lyon rampant or — Harl. MS. 1481 fo. 34[b].

De Alta Ripa, Geoffray—(E. III. Roll) bore, azure, five fusils conjoined in fess argent, a baston gules ; Jenyns' Ordinary. See also DAUTREY.

Deane, Sir William (DE DEN), of Essex— (E. II. Roll) bore, argent, a fess dancettée gules ; Parliamentary Roll.

Deane, Sir Henry (DE DEN), of Northants —bore, at the first Dunstable tournament 1308, argent, a fess dancettée between three crescents gules. (F.) See also Parly. Roll.

Deen, Sire Johan de—bore, at the battle of Boroughbridge 1322, argent, two bars sable crusily patée or ; three on each bar in Ashmole MS.—in Parliamentary Roll for DEN, of Hunts. Knight (E. II.), the bars gules, and the crosses patonce.

Dreu deane

Henry de Don

John de Doon

Robert Dono

Simon d' la here

John la Boro

Adam
de la fforde

nich de la Hosse

John de la Hay

John de la Linde

Pers d' la Mare

Richard
de la mare

Deane (ALYSAUNDER DE ANNO) – (E. III. Roll) bore, gules, fretty argent ; Howard Roll.

Deane, Drew (DE ANE) – (E. III. Roll) bore, gules a saltire ermine ; another coat—argent guttée de poix. (F.) Arden and St. George Roll.

Dene, Sir John de, of co. Leic. —(E. II. Roll) —bore, argent, a lyon rampant purpure ; Parliamentary Roll.

Dene, John – (E. III. Roll) bore, gules, three bars a quarter argent and a torell de sable ; tricked as, barry (6) gules and argent, on a quarter of the last a bull passant gardant sable ; Jenyns' Ordinary.

Deane, Robert (DENE) of Sussex – (E. II. Roll) bore, per bend sinister enhanced azure and gules, a maunch argent (also tricked with the maunch over all) ; Jenyns' Roll.

Deincourt *v.* **Deyncourt.**

De Insula, Sir John, 1297 —bore, or, a fess between two chevrons sable ; Nobility Roll. He signed, but did not seal, the Barons' letter to the Pope 1301.

Deiville *v.* **Deyville.**

De la Beche, John, a baron 1342—bore, vaire, argent and gules. NICHOL, added, on a canton of the first, a martlet sable ; Jenyns' Ordinary. F., vide BECHE.

De la Beche, Sir John, of Berks. – (E. II. Roll) bore, argent, on a bend gules three bucks' heads erased or (cabossed in Harl. 4033) ; in the cantell a martlet sable ; Parliamentary Roll. See DE LA VACHE.

De la Bere, John – (E. II. Roll) bore, azure, crusily fitchée and three boars' heads couped or. (F.) Jenyns' Roll. One of these names took up the cross in the last Crusade 1270.

De la Bere, Simon – (E. III Roll) bore, azure, a bend cotised argent between six martlets or. (F.) Surrey Roll. Cotised or, in St. George Roll.

De la Checker, Sir Laurence – (E. II. Roll) bore, checquy argent and azure ; Holland Roll.

De la Ferret, Sir John – (E. I. Roll) bore, gules, a double-headed eagle displayed or ; Holland Roll.

De la fforde, Sir Adam, of Wilts. —bore, at the siege of Carlaverock 1300, azure, three lyonceux rampant 2 and 1 crowned or. (F.) Parliamentary Roll. Sir RICHARD bore the same ; Holland Roll.

De la Freign, Sir Foulk, of Ireland —bore, at the siege of Calais 1345-8, azure on a saltire or, a saltorelle gules. F.

De la Hacche, Sir Eustace, banneret, a baron 1299 – bore, at the battle of Falkirk 1298 and at the siege of Carlaverock 1300, a cross engrailed gules ; Guillim and Parliamentary Rolls.

De la Hay,—— (E. III. Roll) bore, argent, a fess sable between six mullets 3 and 3 gules ; Ashmole Roll.

De la Haye, Piers, one of the founders of Swine Abbey, postea Melton modo Darcij— bore, argent three escallops in bend gules between two cotises sable ; Jenyns' Roll.

‡**De la Haye, John**—(E. I. Roll) argent, a sun in his splendour gules. (F.) 12, 13, 16, and 24 rays ; Dering and St. George Rolls.

De la Hav, Rauf—(H. III. Roll) bore, argent a ray (of the sun) gules ; Glover Roll. Called a ruell in Norfolk Roll.

De la Hoese, Sir John (or HESE), a Berkshire Knight —(E. II. Roll) bore, argent, a fess sable between three lyonceux rampant gules ; Parliamentary Roll and Jenyns' Ordinary.

‡**De la Hose, Nicholas** (HESE or HEUSE)— (E. I. Roll) bore, argent three hose (men's) 2 and 1 gules ; Camden, Dering, and other Rolls (F.) ; or and sable, in the illustration.

De la Launde, Henry – (E. I. Roll) bore, per pale gules and azure three lyons passant gardant in pale or. (F.) Segar Roll.

De la Lee, Sir John, of Herts – (E. II. Roll) bore, argent, a cross checquy or and azure ; Parliamentary Roll.

De la Lee, John, of Herts—(E. III. Roll) bore, gules, billettée argent a fess counter compony or and azure. (F.) St. George Roll.

De la Leye, Gilbert of Kilvington—(E. III. Roll) bore, or, a fess crenellée between six mullets 3 and 3 gules ; Jenyns' Ordinary.

De la Leye, Thomas—(E. III. Roll) bore, azure, three chevronels argent (F.) ; St. George Roll.

De la Ley, Wauter (LEEY)—(R. II. Roll) bore, argent, a fess between three crescents sable ; Surrey Roll.

De la Lynde, John (E. III. Roll) and **Sir Walter,** of Sussex—(E. II. Roll) bore, argent, a cross engrailed gules (F.) ; St. George and Parliamentary Roll. Borne also by JOHN LE FITZ HENRY, ANDREW LEVAAT, and PAINE TIBTOT.

De la March —— (H. III. Roll) bore, " burulée de argent et d'azure de un menue burules ; " Norfolk Roll.

De la Mare, Sir John, banneret, baron 1299—bore, at the battle of Falkirk 1298, and at the siege of Carlaverock 1300, gules, a maunch argent (F.) ; Dering and Arundel Rolls. Sir JOHN of Oxon (E. II.) bore the maunch ermine ; Parly. Roll. JOHN and ROBERT (E. I.) bore it issuing from the sinister chief (F.) ; Segar Roll.

De la Mare, John—(E. III. Roll) bore, gules, a leon leopard rampant argent, *i.e.* a lyon rampant gardant ; Jenyns' Ordinary.

De la Mare, Sir Piers, knighted at the capitulation of Calais 1348—bore, gules, two lyons passant gardant argent (F.), as also did JOHN and Sir ROBERT of Hants ; Surrey and Parliamentary Rolls.

De la Mare, Sir Geoffrey, of Surrey or Sussex—(E. II. Roll) bore, or a fess double cotised azure ; Parliamentary and Ashmole Rolls. PIERS (E. III.) bore the field argent ; Jenyns' Ordinary.

De la Mare, William—(E. III. Roll) bore, argent, a fess between three fleurs-de-lys 2 and 1 gules ; Jenyns' Ordinary.

Jakes de la Plaunc

Guy de la Boce

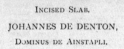

INCISED SLAB.

JOHANNES DE DENTON,

DOMINUS DE AINSTAPLI.

Le Dount de Eryfolbe

Roger d' la Ware

De la Mare, Daland—(E. III. Roll) bore, azure, a bend between six crosses crosslet fitchée 3 and 3 or ; Jenyns' Roll.

De la Mare, Sir John, of Essex –(E. II. Roll) bore, argent on a bend azure three eaglets displayed or ; Parliamentary Roll.

De la Mare, Piers (*c* R. II. Roll) and **Sir Reginald** (E. III. Roll)—bore, barry dancettée (6) or and gules ; Surrey and Ashmole Rolls.

De la Mayne *v.* **MacMoylin.**

De la More, Bartholomew—(E. III. Roll) bore, argent seven barrulets azure, a chevron gules ; Arden and St. George Rolls.

De la More, John—(E. II. Roll) bore, gules a cross patée (patonce in trick) and an escallop argent ; Jenyns' Roll.

De la More, Richard—(E. III. Roll) bore, quarterly indented argent and azure ; Norfolk Roll. One of these names took up the cross in the last Crusade 1270. See also ACTON, page 1.

De la More, William—(E. III. Roll) bore, sable a cross argent ; Jenyns' Ordinary.

De la Mote, William—(E. III. Roll) bore, vair, a bend engrailed gules ; another, vair, a bend gules and a label (3) argent ; Jenyns' Ordinary.

De la Penne, Sir John of Bucks—(E. II. Roll) bore, argent, on a fess sable three plates ; Parliamentary Roll. F.

De la Penre, Sir Guy (surname illegible)— (E. III. Roll) bore, or three bendlets gules a label (3) azure ; Ashmole Roll.

De la Pipe *v.* **Pipe.**

De la Planche, Sir James of Bucks, Kt.— (E. II. Roll) bore, argent, billettée and a lyon rampant sable crowned or (F.) ; Parliamentary Roll. In Segar the billets resemble guttée de poix, and they suggest ermine.

De la Pole *v.* **Pole.**

De la Pole, John—(R. II. Roll) bore, or, a stag's head cabossed gules, between the antlers a fleur-de-lys of the last ; Surrey Roll.

De la Pole, Michel and **Simon**—(R. II. Roll) bore, azure, a fess between three leopards faces or ; Surrey Roll. (F.) Borne also by WILLIAM, K.G., Earl of Suffolk, at the siege of Rouen 1418 ; *quarterly with*, WINGFIELD, K. 401 fo. 22

De la Pole, Sir Walter—bore, at the siege of Calais 1345-8, azure two bars wavy or (F.) Not wavy in Cotton MS. ; argent two bars, nebulée azure, in Parliamentary Roll, for POOLE, a Norfolk Knight.

De la Poyle, Sir John of Middx. Kt.— (E. II. Roll) bore, argent, a saltire gules, a bordure sable besanty ; Parliamentary Roll. WALTER bore the reverse ; Arden and Howard Rolls.

De la River, Sir Richard—bore, at the battle of Boroughbridge 1322, argent, a fretty sable and an inescocheon gules (F.) ; Jenyns', Ashmole, and Arundel Rolls.

De la Ryver, Sir Nicholas—(E. II. Roll) bore, vaire argent and gules, a bordure azure besantée ; Parliamentary Roll.

De la River, Sir John (of Berks)—bore. at the first Dunstable tournament 1308, azure two dancets or (F.) (two bars dancettée in Parly. Roll). He signed but did not seal the Barons' letter to the Pope 1301. Another JOHN bore this coat at the second Dunstable tournament 1334 ; RICHARD bore it also ; St. George and Arden Rolls. Sir R. bore three dancets ; Atkinson Roll. H. VI.

‡**De la Roce, Guy**—(E. III. Roll) bore, or, three bends azure, within a bordure gules entoyre of fleurs-de-lys argent. (F.) Dering Roll.

De la Roch, Thomas, a baron 1300—bore, sable, two lyons passant gardant argent ; Nobility Roll ; (ascribed to JOHN in Jenyns' Ordinary). Sealed the Barons' letter to the Pope 1301.

De la Roche, William—(H. III. Roll) bore, gules, two bends argent, each charged with as many lozenges bendways azure ; Howard Roll.

De la Vache, Hugh *v.* **Vache.**

De la Vache, Sir John (of Berks)—bore, at the first Dunstable tournament 1308, argent on a bend gules three (" deym ") deer heads erased or, in the cantell a martlet sable. Called DE LA BECHE in the Parly. Roll, where the heads are cabossed.

De la Vach, Sir Richard, of Bucks, K.G. 1356—bore, at the siege of Calais 1345-8, gules, three lyonceux rampant argent crowned or. (F.) Ashmole Roll ; as did Sir PHILIP, K.G. 1399 ; K. 399 fo. 19. Sir RICHARD bore it (E. II.) differenced with a label (3) gobony or and argent ; Parly. Roll. See also DELAFFORDE.

De la Vale, Gilbert, de la Marche—(H. III. Roll) bore, argent a cross fourchée gules ; Glover Roll.

De la Val, Guy—(H. III. Roll) bore, or, eglettée 4, 4, 3, 3, azure on a cross gules five escallops argent ; Howard Roll.

De la Val, John—(E. II. Roll) bore, ermine two bars vert ; Jenyns' Roll. Another, ermine two gemelles and a chief or ; Jenyns' Ordinary.

De la Ward, Sir Robert, baron 1299—bore, at the battle of Falkirk 1298, and at the siege of Carlaverock 1300, vaire argent and sable. (F.) Dering and Camden Rolls. Sealed the Barons' letter to the Pope 1301. Ascribed also to JOHN in Jenyns' Ordinary.

De la Warde, Robert—(E. III. Roll) bore, undée (6) argent and sable ; Jenyns' Ordinary.

De la Warr, Roger—bore, at the siege of Carlaverock 1300, gules, crusily (fitchée in NICOLAS, but wrongly) and a lyon rampant argent ; Dering and Howard Rolls. Ascribed also to JOHN (E. III.) Sir JOHN, a baron (27 E. I.) and Sir JOHN, Kt. banneret. For JOHN, second baron, see next entry also.

(De) La Warr, Roger, baron, of Isfield, signed, but did not seal, the Barons' letter to the Pope 1301. He bore (E. I. Roll) gules, crusily fitchée and a lyon rampant argent. (F.) (See preceding entry.) Ascribed also to a JOHN and a ROBERT ; the latter perhaps took up the cross in the last Crusade 1270. JOHN, son of ROGER, differenced with a label (3) azure, at the first Dunstable tournament 1308 ; Nobility Rolls.

EDWARD, LORD DESPENCER.

IN THE ABBEY CHURCH AT TEWKESBURY, 1375.

After Carter.

De la Warre, Sir William, knighted at the capitulation of Calais 1343—bore, gules crusily fitchée argent a lyon rampant or.

Delefend, Sir Gilbert—bore, at the first Dunstable tournament 1308, undée (6) sable and argent a label (3) gules. JOHN bore or two bars undée sable. F.

De Le Fend, Sir John—bore, at the first Dunstable tournament 1308, "argent two barres unde de sa."

De L'Isle, Gerard—(E. III. Roll) bore, gules, a lyon passant argent or; Jenyns' Ordinary. Same as WARIN DEL IDLE, whom see.

De Lisle, Sir John, banneret—(E. II. Roll) —bore, or, on a chief azure three lyons rampant of the first; Parliamentary Roll.

De Lisle, Sire John—bore, at the battle of Boroughbridge 1322, ermine two chevrons sable. F.

De Lisle, Sir John, K.G., a founder, and **Robert**—(E. III. Roll) bore, or a fess between two chevronels sable. (F.) St. George Roll and Jenyns' Ordinary. See also (1) Sir ROBERT DEL IDLE, who bore the same at the battle of Boroughbridge,1322, and (2) JOHN, Baron Lisle.

De Lisle, John, of Hants—(E. III. Roll)— bore, gules, a chevron between three "foyles de gletvers" gules; Parly. Roll, (leaves slipped) or in Jenyns' Ordinary.

Delves, —— (E. IV. Roll) bore, argent, a chevron gules between three billets (delves) sable; with crest; Ballard Roll.

Dengayne v. **Engayne.**

Denham, Sir John (DENOM)—(E. III. Roll) bore, argent, a bend sable lozengy or cotised gules; Ashmole Roll.

Dennardeston, Sir Peers de, of Suffolk— (E. II. Roll) bore, azure, two bars argent, on a chief gules a lyon passant (gardant in H. 4033 fo. 15) or; Parly. Roll.

Dennis (——), a Kentish Knight—(H. VI. Roll) bore, argent, a fess undée gules between six fleurs-de-lys 3 and 3 azure; Arundel Roll.

Dennis —— (R. II. Roll) bore, sable three hatchets erect 2 and 1 argent; Surrey Roll.

Dent, William de—(E. II. Roll) bore, vert, a buck's head cabossed or, a bordure engrailed of the last; Jenyns' Roll.

Denton, John de, of Ainstable—bore, two bars in chief three martlets. See Incised Slab.

Denton, Richard—(E. III. Roll) bore, gules, a chevron between three crescents argent.

Denton, Sir Richard—(E. III. Roll) bore, argent, two bars gules in chief three cinque-foyles pierced sable; Ashmole Roll.

De Ore, Nicole—(H. III. Roll) bore argent a cross gules frettée or between four jackdaws proper. (F.) Dering Roll.

De Ore, Richard—(H. III. Roll) bore, barry (6) argent and azure on a bend gules five bezants. (F.) Dering Roll.

Depden, John—(R. II. Roll) bore, argent, on a chief azure three lyons rampant or; Surrey Roll.

Depham, Sir Stephen of Norfolk, Kt.— (E. II. Roll) bore, argent on a fess gules three lyonceux passant gardant or; Parliamentary Roll.

Derby (Henry) Earl of (E. II.)—bore, England and a baston azure; Cotgrave Roll. According to the 6th Nobility Roll, temp. H. VI., bore England undifferenced.

Derby, Henry "of Bolingbroke," EARL of— (R. II. Roll) bore, France and England quarterly, differenced with a label (5) per pale (2)ermine and (3) azure florettée or; Surrey Roll.

*[**Dering, Richard,** fil.; de Haute, bore, SEAL, 19 Hen. IV.— argent, a fess azure in chief three torteaux.—Shirley.] F. Said to be father of the next-named.

*‡**Dering, Ric.** le fiz—(H. III. Roll) bore, or, a saltire sable (F.); Dering Roll. The arms of DE MORINIS.

De River. See RIVER.

Dernford, William—(H. III. Roll) bore, sable, an eagle displayed argent (F.); Arden and Howard Rolls. Another WILLIAM bore argent two wings conjoined sable (F.), and a third WILLIAM bore three fish haurient con-joined in triangle (Y)—(F.); Arden and St. George Rolls.

Derward (——) an Essex Knight—(H. VI. Roll) bore, ermine on a chevron sable three crescents or; Arundel Roll.

Derwentwater, John—(E. III. Roll) bore, argent ("a fez et demy") two bars gules on a quarter of the last a cinquefoyle pierced of the first; Jenyns' Roll and Ordinary; pierced or, in Surrey Roll.

‡**Despencer, Sir Hugh le,** banneret (baron 1265-1326)—bore, at the battle of Falkirk 1298, F.; and at the siege of Carlaverock 1300, argent, *quarterly with*, gules a fret or over all a baston sable; [his son Sir HUGH banneret (baron 1314-1326) differenced with a label (3) azure at the first Dunstable tournament 1308.] HUGH (Earl of Gloucester) bore the same at the second Dunstable tournament 1334, and at the siege of Calais 1345-8. PHILIP, 2nd lord, also bore this at the siege of Rouen 1418; another HUGH, differenced with a martlet sable, in Surrey Roll; Sir GILBERT, with a bend engrailed; Ashmole Roll. Sir HUGH LE and Sir PHILIP bore it at the siege of Calais 1345-8, over all on a bend sable three mullets of the first; Sir PHILIP differenced with a label (3) azure. See Monumental Effigy of EDWARD 5th lord.

Dethike, Robert—(E. III. Roll) bore, argent, a fess vaire or and gules between three water-bougets azure (sable in trick); Jenyns' Ordy.

‡**Detling, William de**—(E. I. Roll) bore, sable, six lyonceux rampant 3, 2, 1 argent (F.); Dering and Camden Rolls. Called ECLYNGE or OCLYNE in Jenyns' Ordinary.

Devereux (——) bore, at the siege of Rouen 1418, argent, a fess gules and in chief three torteaux (F.); also attributed to WALTER in Arden and St. George Rolls, and to Sir JOHN, K.G., baron 1384-94, differenced with a mullet pierced or; K. 399 fo. 22. JOHN differenced it with a mullet or (R. II.); Surrey Roll.

Devereux, John (E. III. Roll) and **Sir William,** of Cheshire—bore, the reverse *i.e.* gules, a fess argent, in chief three plates; Ash-mole, Glover and Parliamentary Rolls; besants in Harl. MS. 4033 fo. 49b, probably an error for the first coat.

MONUMENTAL SLAB.

—— DISNEY,

IN KINGERBY CHURCH, LINCOLNSHIRE, C. 1350

After Boutell.

Devonshire, Earl of. See COURTENAY and REDVERS.

Deyncourt, Sir Edmund, baron, 1299 — bore, at the battle of Falkirk 1298, azure, billettée and a fess dancettée or (F.)—sealed the Barons' letter to the Pope 1301,—his sons EDMUND and JOHN bore the same at the siege of Carlaverock 1300, and also WILLIAM, baron, (1310) in Nobility Roll, and Sir HENRY, baron, at the siege of Calais 1348. Le Sr DAYN-COURTE bore them at the siege of Rouen 1418 ; Sir JOHN, baron (1 E. II. 1308) and Sir JOHN, banneret, bore the same ; Parliamentary and Arundel Rolls. WILLIAM, brother of ED-MUND of Granaby differenced with a baston gobony argent and gules ; Harl. MS. 1481 fo. 42.

Deyncourt, Sir William (of Yorkshire) — bore, at the first Dunstable tournament 1308, and Sir JOHN, who was knighted at the capitulation of Calais 1348, bore, argent, billettée and a fess dancettée sable ; also borne by JOHN (R. II.) and Sir ROGER of Essex, Kt. ; Surrey and Arundel Rolls.

Deyncourt, Hugh – (H. III. Roll) bore, checquy or and azure on a fess gules three roses argent ; St. George Roll — buckles (F.) in Harl. MS. 6137 fo. 78[b].

Deyncourt, Raf - (H. III. Rcll) bore, gules, billettée and a fess dancettée or ; Arden and St. George Rolls.

Deyncourt, Sir William—(E. I. Roll) bore, ermine a fess dancettée sable ; a note in Jenyns' Ordinary, an earlier coat than the, argent billettée dansey sable. See Sir WILLIAM above.

Deyvill, Sir John—bore, at the battle of Falkirk 1298, or, a fess gules, floretée counterchanged—3, 3, 2, 1 - 3, 2, 1 (F.) 2, 2, 2. Borne also by ROBERT ; Jenyns' Ordinary.

Deyvill, Roger—(E. III. Roll) bore, or, a fess sable, floretée counterchanged ; Jenyns' Ordinary.

Deyvile, Sir John, banneret—bore, at the battle of Boroughbridge 1322, gules, floretée and a lyon rampant argent. (F.) Parliamentary Roll.

‡**Deyvile, Ansele** (DE VILE)—(H. III. Roll) bore, argent a fess between six mullets (6) pierced gules ; (F.) Dering Roll ; three pierced mullets (5) in chief only, in Ashmole MS.

Dichant, John and **Robert**—(E. III. Roll) bore, ermine two gemelles and a chief gules— tricked as two bars cotised ; Jenyns' Roll and Ordinary.

***Digby, Sir John de,** of co. Leicester— (E. II. Roll) bore, azure, a fleur-de-lys argent ; Parliamentary Roll.

Digges (——), a Kentish Knight - (H. VI. Roll) bore, gules, on a cross argent five eaglets displayed sable ; Arundel Roll.

Dinant, Sire Oliver, banneret, a baron 1295 - bore, gules, five fusils conjoined in fess ermine ; Nobility Roll ; ascribed to another OLIVER (‡) in Dering Roll ; blazoned also as a fess dancettée, a fess of fusils and a fess fusily— four lozenges conjoined in Parliamentary Roll. ROBERT bore 3 escallops in chief ermine ; Howard Roll. Another ROBERT (‡) bore the fess between four escallops 3 and 1 ermine. (F.) Dering Roll.

Dinant, Roillans de - (H. III. Roll) bore, gules five fusils conjoined in fess between six roundles ermine ; Howard Roll.

Dinant, Geoffrey de - (H. III. Roll) bore, gules, crusily or five fusils conjoined ermine. (F.) St. George Roll.

Dinawesbran, Sr. (——) **de** - (H. III. Roll) bore, azure, crusily an orle or ; Arden Roll.

Dinham v. **Dynham.**

Disney, William—(R. II. Roll) bore, argent, three lyons passant in pale gules ; Surrey and Cotgrave Rolls.

*[**Disney, Sir William** (H. III.)—bore, argent, on a fess gules three fleurs-de-lys or. Shirley.] F. See Monumental Slab.

D'Obehale v. **Obehale.**

Dockseye, Sir Richard de, of Salop— (E. II. Roll) bore, argent, a lyon rampant azure, a baston gobony or and gules ; Parliamentary Roll.

‹[**Dod, Hugo,** of Cloverly, Salop (H. IV.) – bore, argent a fess gules between two cotises wavy sable. DOD of Edge bore, three crescents or, on the fess.—Shirley.] F.

Doddingsells, John (v. ODINGSELLS)— (R. II. Roll) bore, argent, a fess gules ; Surrey Roll.

Dodingsells, Sir John (v. ODINGSELLS), banneret—bore, at the first Dunstable tournament 1308, argent, a fess and in the dexter chief point a mullet (6) gules ; Parliamentary Roll. (—— ODINGSELLS, le filz, differenced with a label azure, at the second Dunstable tournament 1334); borne also (F.) by HUGH (E. I.) and RALF (E. III.) in Jenyns' Ordinary. Another HUGH and WILLIAM of Long Ichendon, bore two mullets (6) in chief (F.) Jenyns' Ordinary and Segar Roll ; spur-rowells in Dering Roll, but in the Ashmole Copy the fess is between three spur-rowells.

Dodingsells, Nicolas (v. ODINGSELLS) (f WILLIAM)—(H. III. Roll) bore, argent on a fess gules three escallops or in chief two spur-rowells of the second. (F.) St. George Roll ; the fess between three spur-rowells, in Harl. MS. 1481 fo. 87[b].

Dointon, John de—(H. III. Roll) bore, azure two trumpets (vel hautboys) pileways or. (F.) Arden and St. George Rolls.

Dokesworth, Sir John, of co. Cambridge —(E. II. Roll) bore, azure, a cross between four lyonceux rampant argent ; Parliamentary Roll.

Dolerd, Sir H.—(H. VI. Roll) bore, gules, two flaunches (voyderis anabelees) argent, a bordure sable ; Atkinson Roll. F.

Domare, John de (? DONMARE)—(H. III. Roll) bore, azure, billettée and a crescent or. (F.) St. George Roll.

Donneworthe, Robert de—(E. I. Roll) bore, gules a cross argent between four besants. (F.) Segar Roll.

Dordant, Sir John, fell at the siege of Calais 1348—bore, per fess indented azure and argent a pipe gules.

SIR JOHN DRUMMOND.

In the Choir of Inchmahome. Ob. 1301. *After Drummond.*

Dovedale, Sir John (or DE UVEDALE) of Surrey or Sussex (E. II. Roll) bore, argent a cross moline gules in trick, blasoned, recercelée; Parliamentary and Jenyns' Rolls. THOMAS bore it (E. III. Roll) *quarterly with*, azure fretty or; Jenyns' Roll.

Dovre, Richard de—(H. III. Roll) bore, gules, two leopards (*i.e.* lyons) passant or; Glover Roll.

Doyley, John—(E. III. Roll) bore, or, two bends gules; Jenyns' Ordinary.

Draicott, Richard de, baron—bore, 1297 paly (6) argent and gules a bend ermine; 1st Nobility Roll. BERTRAM took up the cross in the last Crusade 1270.

Drayton, Sire Symon de—bore, at the battle of Boroughbridge 1322, argent a cross engréle gules. F.

*[**Drewe, William,** of Orcheston, Devon, *c* 1300—bore, ermine a lyon passant gules— Shirley.] F.

Drewell, Sir John (or DURWEL) of Bucks —(E. II. Roll) bore, quarterly argent and sable, in the first a crescent gules; Parliamentary Roll.

Driffield, William, of the Wold—(E. III. Roll) bore, argent, a chevron between three lyons' heads erased sable; Jenyns' Roll.

Drokenesford, John de (DROCHFORD)— bore, at the battle of Falkirk 1298, quarterly or and azure (4) roses counterchanged (F.); Keeper of the Wardrobe, Bishop of Bath and Wells 1309–29.

Dronsfield, Christopher—(E. II. Roll) bore, gules, two bastons couped in " guise du chevron " or, tricked, gules a chevron raguly fracted in the centre argent (F.); Jenyns' Roll.

Drummond, Sir John, of Inchmahome, 1301—bore, three bars wavy. See Monumental Slab. He was taken prisoner in the Scottish wars, his lands were conferred on Sir Edmuud Hasting, who signed the Barons' letter to the Pope 1301, and sealed it with this Sir John's seal. See *post.*

Drury (——) a Knight—(H. VI. Roll) bore, argent on a chief vert two mullets or; Arundel Roll. Mullets pierced in Ashmole Roll; NICHOLAS of Saxham. Suff. bore a cross Tau between the mullets; Harl. MS. 1481 fo. 84.

Dryby, William—(E. II. Roll) bore, argent, three quartrefoyles and a quarter gules—tricked argent three cinquefoyles pierced and a quarter gules; Jenyns' Roll.

Dryland (——) a Kentish Knight—(H. VI. Roll) bore, gules guttée d'eau, on a fess undée (nebulée) argent an ermine ipot; Arundel Roll.

Du Bois, James. See BOYS.

Duckinfield —— (R. II. Roll) bore, argent, a cross voided sable, *quarterly with*, argent six annulets 3 and 3 gules, for PLECY; Surrey Roll.

Dunbar, Patrick, Earl of—bore, at the battle of Falkirk 1298, gules, a lyon rampant argent, a bordure of the second charged with

roses of the first; he bore this also at the siege of Carlaverock 1300, when he was styled " Conte de Laonis " (Lothian); at the same siege his son PATRICK differenced the arms with a label (3) gules (F.); though according to NICOLAS a blue label of 5 points; most of the Rolls blazon the roses (fraises) as cinquefoyles. The bordure is omitted from the Norfolk Roll.

‡**Dunstanville, Walter de**—(H. III. Roll) bore, argent, fretty (6) gules, on a quarter of the second a lyon passant gardant or (F.); Dering, Glover, and Howard Rolls.

Dunsta(n)ville, Sir Robert, K.G.—(R. II.) bore, argent a fret gules within a bordure engrailed sable, over all on a canton of the second a lyon passant or; K. 399 fo. 30. This K.G. is doubtful.

Dunyton, Reynald de—(E. III. Roll) bore, argent three crosses moline gules—fer-demoline in trick; Jenyns' Ordinary.

Durace v. Derace, le Conte—(E. III. Roll) bore, gules, three palets vair, on a chief or a demi fleur-de-lys issuant sable; Jenyns' Ordinary.

Duresme, Sir Emon (or GELEM) of Essex —(E. III. Roll) bore, argent on a cross of St. George (gules) five fleurs-de-lys or; Parliamentary Roll and Jenyns' Ordinary; six fleurs-de-lys in Ashmole Roll. F.

Durevassal, John (DURON-ASPAL)—(H. III. Roll) bore, vert, three fleurs-de-lys or (F.); Arden and St. George Rolls. The field also azure in the latter roll.

Durwell v. Drewell.

Dutton, Laurence de—(R. II. Roll) bore, argent *quarterly with*, gules a fret or; Surrey Roll (F.); ascribed to Sir PIERS in the Atkinson Roll. See also ALAYN DE ELLESFELD.

*[**Dykes, William de,** of Dovenby in Cumberland (E. III.)-bore, or, three cinquefoyles sable; Shirley.] F.

Dyk(e s, William de—(R. II. Roll) bore, argent, a fess vaire or and gules between three water-bougets sable; Surrey Roll. F.

*[**Dymoke, John**—(R. II. Roll) bore, sable, two lyonceux passant in pale argent crowned or; Surrey Roll and Jenyns' Ordinary. F.

Dymot, Sir David, of co. Lanc.—(E. II. Roll) bore, gules, on a chief or a lyon passant sable (another of the field); Parliamentary Roll.

Dyne, Sir John of Oxon—(E. II. Roll) bore, or a fess sable; Parliamentary Roll.

Dynham, Sir Oliver, knighted at the capitulation of Calais 1348 – bore, gules, four fusils conjoined in fess erminé, a bordure engrailed argent (F.) JOHN bore the arms without the bordure; Surrey Roll and Jenyns' Ordinary. Sometimes five fusils and sometimes ermines.

Dynham, Oliver de—(E. III. Roll) bore, gules, three bezants; Jenyns' Ordinary.

Dyve (-——) a Suffolk Knight—(H. VI. Roll) bore, gules, a chevron between three dyvers sable, the breasts argent; Arundel Roll. F.

A:LA:MEMOIRE:DE:

𝕲 𝕭

MARGUE:DE:GROUVILLE:A:L'ABBAYE:DE:S:GRINGE:DE:LESSAY:A:D:1149

MASSIRE:GEOFFREY:DE:BUISSON:CHEVALIER:QUI:DONNA:LE:PAQRON

AGE:DE:L'EGLISE:DE:S:

GEOFFREY DU BUISSON.

In Grouville Church, Jersey, 1149.

E

[**Eam, Sir Henry,** K.G., a founder – doubtful arms, or, a fess sable, issuant therefrom a demi-lyon rampant gules; K. 398 fo. 28. F.]

Eccleshall, Sir Robert de—(E. II. Roll) bore, gules, a bend between six martlets 3 and 3 argent; another sable and or; Parliamentary Roll.

Echebaston, Sir Richard (or ASHEBASTON). See EDGEBASTON.

Echingham, William de, a baron, 8 E. II. —(E. I. Roll) bore, azure fretty argent. (F.) Camden Roll. Borne also at the siege of Rouen 1418. Ascribed also to another WILLIAM(‡) in the Dering Roll.

Echingham, Sir Robert de, of Kent— (E. II. Roll) bore, azure, fretty argent, a bordure indented or; Parliamentary and Ashmole Rolls. Le Sir DE E. bore the bordure engrailed in Jenyns' Ordinary.

Eclynge, William de (or OCLYNE)—(E. III. Roll) bore, sable, six lyonceux rampant argent; Jenyns' Ordinary. Called DETLING in the Camden Roll.

Eden (——), a Suffolk Knight – (H. VI. Roll) bore, a chevron between three close helmets or; Arundel Roll.

Edenham, Robert, of Swaledale—(E. II. Roll) bore, azure, on a bend gules three dolphins embowed argent. (F.) Jenyns' Roll.

*[**Edgcumbe, Richard,** 1292 – bore, gules, on a bend ermine cotised or, three boars' heads couped argent.—Shirley.] F.

Edgebaston, Sir Richard de, of co. Linc. —bore, at the battle of Boroughbridge 1322, argent, a lyon (rampant) sable, a baston azure a cinquefoyle ermine. (F.) The lyon gules and the cinquefoyle argent in the Parliamentary Roll—the cinquefoyle sometimes on the lyon's shoulder and at other times on the baston.

Edlington v. **Erdington.**

[**Edwardes (——)** of Kilhendre, Salop—bore, gules, a chevron engrailed between three tygers' heads erased argent.—Shirley.] F.

*[**Egerton, Uryan,** of Egerton, in Cheshire 14th cent.—bore, MALPAS, argent (a lyon rampant gules between) three pheons sable.—Shirley.] F.

Eglescliff, Walter de—(E. III. Roll) bore, or, on a saltire azure five plates; Jenyns' Ordinary.

Eglesfield, John de—(E. I. Roll) bore, argent, three eaglets displayed gules; Jenyns' Roll.

Eglestone, Adam de, of Wilberfosse— (E. I. Roll) bore, argent an eagle displayed sable, membered purpure; Jenyns' Roll.

Ekont v. **Glanvile.**

Elande, Sir Hugh—(E. II. Roll) bore, argent, on a bend gules three escallops or; Parliamentary Roll.

Elande, Thomas de—(R. II. Roll) bore, gules two bars argent between eight martlets 3, 2, 3 of the last; Surrey Roll.

Ellerton, Roger de, of Swaledale—(E. III. Roll) bore, argent, a chevron between three bucks' heads cabossed sable; Jenyns' Roll.

Ellesfield, Sire Gilbert de (or ELMESFIELD), of Oxon—bore, at the battle of Boroughbridge 1322, undée (6) argent and sable (F.) (Three bars in Ashmole Roll.) Sir JOHN of Oxon bore the same; another Sir GILBERT differenced it with a label (3) gules; Parliamentary Roll.

Ellesfeld, Sir John (ELCHESFIELD) of Oxon—(E. II. Roll) bore, argent two bars undée sable; Parliamentary Roll.

Ellesfeld, Alayn de—(E.' I. Roll) bore, DUTTON, over all on a bendlet sable three mullets (6) of the third (or). (F.) Segar Roll.

Ellis (——), of Thornton Rust, Yorks.—(E. III. Roll) bore, sable, three ("haches batantz") battle axes argent; Grimaldi Roll.

Ellis, Sir Henry, of Yorkshire—(E. II. Roll) bore, or, on a cross sable five crescents argent; Parliamentary Roll. JOHN bore escallops; Surrey Roll.

Elmbride (ELMINDBRIGHT) **——,** (E. III. Roll) bore, gules, on a chief or three tremoyles vert; Cotgrave Roll. See next blazon.

Elmeden, William—(E. II. Roll) bore, argent, on a bend sable three crescents of the first. (F.) Jenyns' Roll.

Elmerugge, Adam de—(H. III. Roll) bore, checquy argent and sable on a chief or three elm leaves slipped vert. (F.) Arden and St. George Rolls.

Elmham, Sir W., of Elingham or Elmham, in Norfolk, Knight — (H. VI. Roll) bore, argent a fess gules between three eagles displayed sable; Atkinson and Arundel Rolls. THOMAS bore it also; Jenyns' Ordinary.

Eltham, Thomas de - (H. III. Roll) bore, azure, an estoile of 15 points or; Howard Roll.

KING

*From
a rubbing
of the
Hastings Brass,*

EDWARD III.

*in
Elsing Church,
Norfolk.*

Emerike, John—(E. III. Roll) bore, barry (6) or and sable, a baston ermine ; Cotgrave Roll.

Empryngham, Sir Johan de—bore, at the battle of Boroughbridge 1322, vert, an inescocheon within an orle of (am'oles) martlets argent ; the field sable in the Cotgrave Roll. See also ERPINGHAM.

†**Eneby, Robert**—(H. III. Roll) bore, paly (6) argent and gules, a bend sable. (F.) Dering and Howard Rolls.

Enfende, Sir Bartholomew de, of Middlesex – bore, at the first Dunstable tournament 1308, argent, on a canton sable a mullet or—the canton gules (F.) in the Parliamentary Roll ; the mullet pierced in the Cotgrave Roll.

Enfield, Sir Henry de, 1297—bore, gules, an inescocheon within an orle of martlets or ; 1st Nobility Roll ; also borne by HUGH in Jenyns' Roll, and thus blazoned – gules, an orle of martlets or, a false escocheon of the same.

Engayne, Sir John de and **Sir Thomas de**—both knighted at the capitulation of Calais 1348, the latter bore, or a fess dancey sable ; the former bore, gules, a fess dancey or (F.), which is also ascribed to RAFE in Jenyns' Ordinary, in which MS. azure, a fess dancettée argent, occurs for WILLIAM.

Engayne, John de, banneret, a baron 1299—bore, at the battle of Falkirk 1298 and at the siege of Carlaverock 1300, gules, crusily and a fess dancettée or ; he signed, but did not seal, the Barons' letter to the Pope 1301. Sir HENRY bore this also at the siege of Calais 1345–8 (F.), and they are ascribed to WILLIAM in Howard Roll and Jenyns' Ordinary.

Engayne, Eustace (DENGAYNE)—(E. III. Roll) bore, azure, billettée and a fess dancettée or, a label (3) gules ; Jenyns' Ordinary.

Engayne, John—(R. II. Roll) bore, azure, on a fess dancettée between six escallops argent, a mullet pierced gules ; Surrey Roll.

Engaine, Sir Nicholas de, of Essex— (F. II. Roll) bore, azure, crusily and a fess dancettée or, over all a bend gules ; Parliamentary Roll.

Engham, Oliver de (see INGHAM)—(E. III. Roll) bore, per pale or and vert, a cross moline gules ; Jenyns' Ordinary.

England, Kings of—See SEALS.

England, Edward I. King of—bore, at the battle of Falkirk 1298, and at the siege of Carlaverock 1300, gules, three leopards passant or—*i.e.* lyons passant gardant.

England, Edward II. King of—bore, as Edward le Fitzroy, at the siege of Carlaverock 1300 ; England with a label (3, sometimes 5) azure.

England, Edward III. King of—bore the arms of France and England quarterly— see Monumental Brass. EDWARD THE BLACK PRINCE bore them with a label (3) at the siege of Calais 1345–8 ; see Monumental Effigy.

England, Henry V. King of—bore, at the siege of Rouen 1418, France and England quarterly.

England, Princes of—See Bedford, Chester, Clarence, Cornwall, Derby, Exeter, Gloucestr, Huntingdon, Kent, Lancaster, Richmond, Rutland, York, &c. &c.

Englefield, Sir Roger de, of Berks.— (E. II. Roll) bore, barry (6) argent and gules, on a chief or a lyon passant azure ; Parliamentary Roll ; argent, three ·bars gules &c., in Arundel Roll.

Englethorpe (——), an Essex Knight— (H. VI. Roll) bore, gules, a cross engrailed ermine, an annulet argent ; Arundel Roll. See INGLETHORPE.

Englishe, Sir John le (ENGLEYS), of Cumberland –(E. II. Roll) bore, sable, three lyonceux rampant 2 and 1 argent ; Parliamentary Roll. Sir ROBERT and WILLIAM bore the same ; a second trick in Ashmole Roll makes the lyons ermine. See also INGLOWE.

Englosse, Sr. (——) bore, at the siege of Rouen 1418, gules, three gemelles or, and a canton argent billety sable ; Ashmole Roll.

Enneyse, Sr. (——) de, of Bucks—(E. II. Roll) bore, gules, a fess dancettée ermine ; Parliamentary Roll.

Erde (——), a Kentish Knight—(H. VI. Roll) bore, ermine three saltorelles gules ; Arundel Roll.

Erdern, (——) de—(H. III. Roll) bore, checquy azure and or, a chevron gules ; Arden Roll. See also MAURUS, *post*.

Erdington, Thomas de—(R. II. Roll) bore, azure, two lyons passant in pale or ; Surrey Roll.

Erdington, Sir Henry (EDRINGTON) of Warwickshire, a baron 1336—bore, azure, two lyons passant or a bordure gules ; Parliamentary and Arden Rolls. ? Same as PERCEVALL DE SOMERI, in St. George Roll.

Ere, Nichole de—(H III. Roll) bore, ermine, a cross gules fretty or ; Howard Roll. See ORE.

Erington, John de—(E. III. Roll) bore, argent, two bars and in chief three escallops azure ; Jenyns' Roll.

Ermine, William de—(R. II. Roll) bore, ermine, a saltire engrailed gules, on a chief of the last a lyon passant gardant or ; Surrey Roll. See also AYRMYN.

Erpingham *v.* **Empringham.**

Erpingham, Sir Thomas, K.G. 1401—bore, at the siege of Rouen 1418, vert, an inescocheon within an orle of martlets argent (F.), and so ascribed to Sir THOMAS of Norfolk, in Parliamentary Roll.

Erpingham, Thomas de—(R. II. Roll) bore, azure an inescocheon within an orle of (8) martlets argent, another or ; Surrey Roll.

Ertingdene, Bartholomew de—(H. III. Roll) bore, gyronny (12) or and sable (F.) ; St. George Roll.

Eryholme, William—(E. III. Roll) bore, argent, a chevron between three martlets sable ; Jenyns' Ordinary.

Eschallers, John - (E. III. Roll) bore, argent, a fess between two chevronels sable ; Jenyns' Ordinary.

EDWARD, THE BLACK PRINCE. Ob. 1376.

In the Chapel of S. Thomas Beckett, Canterbury Cathedral.

After Stothard.

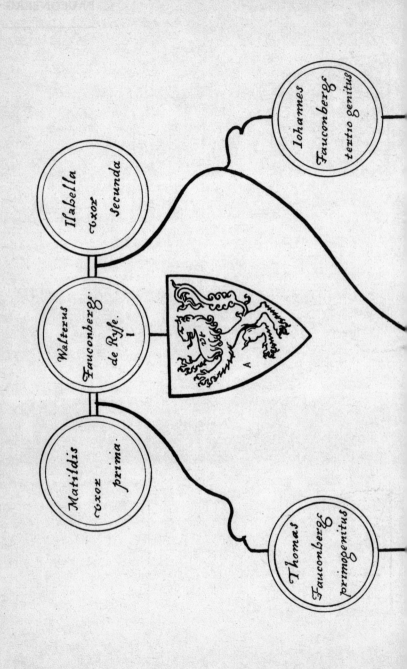

Isabella uxor secunda

Walterus Fauconbergs de Ryfe. I.

Matildis uxor prima

Iohannes Fauconbergs tertio genitus

Thomas Fauconbergs primogenitus

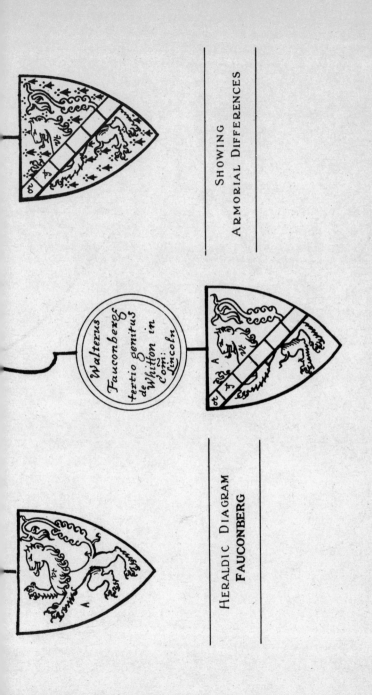

Walterus Fauconbergs tertio genitus de Whitton in Com: Lincoln

HERALDIC DIAGRAM
FAUCONBERG

SHOWING
ARMORIAL DIFFERENCES

Eschallers, Sir Thomas of Cambridge-shire—(E. II. Roll) bore, argent a fess between three annulets gules; Parliamentary Roll. ESCALES, Harl. MS. 6137 fo. 18ᵇ.

Escote *v.* **Estcote.**

‡**Eslynge, Raufe de**—(H. III. Roll) bore, azure, a bend gules cotised or between six boars' heads 3 and 3 couped of the last (F.); Dering and Howard Rolls.

Eslynton, John de—(E. III. Roll) bore, argent, two bars and in chief three mullets azure; Jenyns' Ordinary.

Essex and **Gloucester, Earl of.** See GEOFFREY DE MANDEVILLE.

Estave, Sir Bawdewyn de (or ESTONWE), of co. Cambridge—(E. II. Roll) bore, sable, a cross patonce argent; Parliamentary Roll.

Estcote, Hugh de—(E. II. Roll) bore, sable six escallops 3, 2, 1 or; Jenyns' Roll. 4, 3, 2, 1 (F.) in Arden and St. George Rolls.

[**Estcourt, Walter de la,** *c* 1326 - bore, ermine, on a chief indented gules, three estoiles or; Shirley.] F.

Esterling, John de—(E. I. Roll) bore, paly (6) argent and azure on a bend gules three fleurs-de-lys or (F.); Segar Roll.

Estonwe *v.* **Estave.**

Estotevile, Sir Nicholas de, of Norfolk —(E. II. Roll) and **Walter** (H. III, Roll)— bore, burulée argent and gules over all three lyonceux rampant sable; Parliamentary and Norfolk Rolls. Sir ROBERT, banneret (E. II. Roll) and ROBERT LE NORMAND (H. III. Roll) bore one lyon only; Parliamentary and Glover Rolls.

Estotevile, William, de la March—(H. III. Roll) bore, burulée, argent and gules, over all three cocks sable; Glover Roll.

‡**Estotot, Robert l'**—(H. III. Roll) bore, ermine on a cross gules five martlets or (F.); Arden and St. George Rolls. Written also SCOTHE, SCOTTO and STOTOT.

Estrateshull, Sir Nicholas de (EST'U-SHULLE), of Norfolk—(E. II. Roll) bore, argent, three cinquefoyles gules; Parliamentary Roll.

Estun (——), an Essex (?) Knight—(H. VI. Roll) bore, or, three covered cups gules, a label (3) azure; Arundel Roll.

Etone *v.* **Stone.**

Etton, Sir J.—(H. VI. Roll) bore, burulée gules and argent on a quarter sable a cross patée or; Atkinson Roll and Jenyns' Ordinary, differenced by a label (3) azure in Surrey Roll for — DE ETTON.

Eure, Henry de, Sir John de, and Raufe de—(H. III. Roll) bore, quarterly or and gules, on a bend sable three escallops argent (F.); St. George and Parliamentary Rolls, &c. See FITZ-JOHN.

Everard, Osmond—(E. II. Roll) bore, argent, on a chief gules three mullets pierced of the field; Jenyns' Roll.

Everingham, Adam, baron 1310—bore, gules a lyon rampant vair; Nobility Roll. Borne also by Sir ADAM, knight banneret; Arundel, Nativity, and Parliamentary Rolls, and by JOHN, in Jenyns' Ordinary; an ADAM bore the lyon crowned or (F.) in St. George Roll; EDMUND bore it charged with an annulet gules, Ashmole Roll; and THOMAS bore the original coat with a baston or; Cotgrave Roll.

Everingham, Reynold de—(R. II. Roll) bore, gules, a lyon rampant vair *quarterly with*, sable, a bend between six crosses crosslet argent; Surrey Roll.

Everingham, Adam de, of Birkin, Yorkshire, and **John**—(E. III. Roll) bore, argent, a fess azure, a label (3) gules (azure, in Nativity Roll); Jenyns' Ordinary and Ashmole Roll.

Everingham, Sir Adam, and **John** of Rockley - (E. III. Roll) bore, quarterly argent and sable a baston gules. LAURANCE bore the baston sable; Surrey Roll.

Everley, Walter de—(H. III. Roll) bore, or on a bend azure three escallops of the first (F.); Arden and St. George Rolls. WILLIAM took up the cross in the last Crusade 1270.

Evington, Sir John de (QUINGTON)— bore, at the first Dunstable tournament 1308, argent, on a chief azure two fleurs-de-lys or. See also OVINGTON.

Ewen, John, an Essex Knight—(H. VI. Roll) bore, sable a chevron between three fleurs-de-lys or; Arundel Roll.

Exeter, Duke of, THOMAS BEAUFORT, K.G. 1400—bore, France and England quarterly, within a bordure gobony ermine and azure. K. 400 fo. 8.

Eynes, Sir (——) of Salop—(E. II. Roll) bore, argent, on a fess gules between three hounds (talbots) courant azure, as many besants; Parliamentary Roll.

Evnesford, John and **William**—(E. III. Roll) bore, gules, a fret ermine at each joint; Arden, Ashmole, and Surrey Rolls.

Eynesford, William—bore, at the second Dunstable tournament 1334, gules, a fret engrailed ermine at each joint (F.), ascribed also to JOHN in the Surrey Roll, and to Sir JOHN in the Ashmole Roll, where the trick as an illusion appears as ermine, semée of quatrefoyles gules. THOMAS bore the same differenced with a bordure azure in Jenyns' Ordinary.

Eynegrove, Walter de—(H. III. Roll) bore, ermine, a chief dancettée gules (F.); St. George Roll.

*[**Eyre, William le,** of Hope (H. III.)—bore, argent on a chevron sable three quatrefoyles or.—Shirley.] F. RICHARD LE EYR took up the cross in the last Crusade 1270.

*[**Eyston, John** (H. VI.)—bore, sable, three lyons rampant or.—Shirley.] F.

*[**Eyton, John de,** 1394—bore, or, a fret azure, *quarterly with,* gules, two bars ermine.— Shirley.] F.

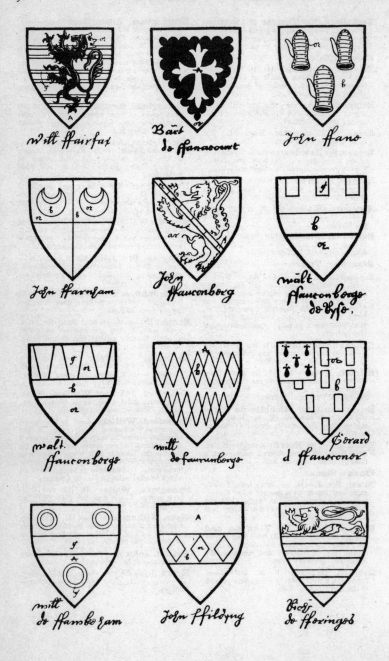

will ffairfax

Bart
de ffancourt

John ffano

John ffarnham

John
ffauconberg

walt
ffauconborge
de Bysto.

walt.
ffauconborge

witt
de ffauconborge

Gorard
d ffauconor

witt
de ffambergam

John ffildyng

Ricts
de fforinges

F

*[Fairfax, William (H. III.)—bore, argent, three bars gemelles gules, surmounted by a lyon rampant sable crowned or.—Shirley.] F.

*[Fane, John (VANE), of Hilden, Kent (H. VI.)—bore, azure, three dexter gauntlets or.—Shirley.] F.

Falvesley, John de (FAWSLEY) a baron 1383—bore, or, two chevron gules; Surrey Roll.

Fanecourt, Sire Bartholomew de—bore, at the battle of Boroughbridge 1322, sable a cross patonce (flory) argent a bordure indented or—engrailed in Ashmole MS. (F.); and Jenyns' Ordinary.

†Fanecourt, Gerard de—(H. III. Roll) bore azure, billetée or, a quarter ermine (F.); Arden Roll and Jenyns' Ordinary. The field gules in St. George Roll; another argent, billetée sable, Harl. MS. 6137 fo. 56.

Fannell, John—(E. III. Roll) bore, sable a cross or; Jenyns' Ordinary.

Fannell, Sir William, of Rutland (E. II. Roll) and Roger (E. III. Roll) bore argent, a bend gules, a bordure sable bezantée; Parliamentary Roll an 1 Jenyns' Ordinary. Allowed to FAVELL, of Northants.

‡Farynges, Richard de (FERINGES) — (H. III. Roll) bore, argent two (bars) gemelles and in chief a lyon passant gules. (F.) Dering and Howard Rolls.

Farington, William—(R. II. Roll)—bore, gules, three cinquefoyles 2 and 1 or; Surrey Roll. FFARINGTON of ffarington, Kt., bore the same (K. IV.) *quarterly with,* argent, a chevron gules between three leopards' faces sable; Ballard Roll.

Farmingham *v.* Framlingham.

Farnham, Sir Robert de, of co. Staff.—(E. II. Roll) bore, quarterly argent and azure four crescents counterchanged; Parliamentary Roll.

*[Farnham, John, 1393 - bore, quarterly or and azure, in the first and second quarters a crescent counterchanged.—Shirley.] F.

Farnhill, John—(E. II. Roll) bore, bendy (6) ermine and azure; Jenyns' Roll.

Fastolf, John—(R. II. Roll) bore, quarterly or and azure on a bend gules three escallops argent; Surrey Roll. Ascribed to Sir JOHN, K.G. temp. H. VI.; K. 402 fo. 6.

Faucombe, Walter de—(H. III. Roll) bore, sable, a cinquefoyle within an orle of martlets argent; Glover Roll. See also FAUKEHAM.

Fauconberg, Sir Walter, banneret, a baron (27 E. I. Roll)—bore, argent, a lyon rampant azure; Parly., Arundel, Surrey, and Ashmole Rolls (same as PIERS BRUS, of Skelton). ROGER bore the lyon differenced on the shoulder with a fleur-de-lys; Surrey Roll.

Fauconberg, John—bore, at the second Dunstable tournament 1334, argent, a lyon rampant azure, a baston gobony or and gules. (F.) The same coat is ascribed to Sir WALTER, the baron, in the Nobility, Parliamentary and Nativity Rolls. JOHN bore the field ermine; Harl. MS. 1481 fo. 44.

Fauconberg (——) of the South—(E. III. Roll) bore, argent three leopards passant gules *i.e.* three lyons passant gardant gules; Jenyns' Ordinary.

Fauconberge, Peres, of Ketelwell—(E. III. Roll) bore, azure, a cinquefoyle between five martlets 3 and 2 or; Jenyns' Ordinary.

Fauconberge, Walter de—(H. III. Roll) bore, sable, a cinquefoyle within an orle of martlets argent; Norfolk Roll.

Fauconberge, Walter, of Ryse—(E. III. Roll) bore, or, a fess azure, in chief three palets gules —St. George Roll, and so sealed the Barons' letter to the Pope 1301; in Jenyns' Ordinary, the trick and blazon is three "peus recoupée" (piles couped). F.

Fauconbridge, Sir Henry—(E. II. Roll) bore, argent, ten lozenges (or fusils) conjoined 5, 5 barways sable (azure for WILLIAM). (F.) Parliamentary Roll and Jenyns' Ordinary ff. 21, 32b—but in folio 18b tricked as argent, two bars engrailed sable.

Fauconer, Sir John le, of Notts - (E. II. Roll) bore, argent, three falcons close, belled gules; Parliamentary Roll.

‡Faukeham, William de - (H. III. Roll) bore, argent, a fess between three annulets gules. (F.) Dering and Howard Rolls. See also FAUCOMBE.

*[Feilding, John (FILDYNG), of Newnham (12 H. VI.) - bore, argent, on a fess azure three fusils or. Seals E. III., R. II.—Shirley.] F.

SIR GEORGE FELBRIGGE.

IN PLAYFORD CHURCH, SUFFOLK, 1400.   *After Boutell.*

Felbridge, Sir Roger, of Norfolk, knighted at the capitulation of Calais 1348—bore, or, a lyon rampant gules (F.), and so also did a knight and an esquire of the family at the siege of Rouen 1418. Borne also by Sir ROBERT and Sir SIMON, K.G., the Standard bearer, see Monumental Brass; Parliamentary, Guillim and Ashmole Rolls. GEORGE bore the lyon differenced with a mullet pierced argent on his shoulder. See Monumental Brass, Sir GEORGE.

Felbrigge, John—(E. III. Roll) bore, or a lyon "embelife" rampant gules—*i.e.* saliant. (Jenyns' Ordinary), and so blasoned for Sir ROGER, of Norfolk, in the Parliamentary Roll.

Feltgrave, John—(E. II. Roll) bore, or, three chevronels gules each charged with as many fleurs-de-lys argent ; Jenyns' Roll. Same as Sir WM. FITZRAFFE.

Felton, John de—(E. III. Roll) bore, gules, a buck's head cabossed or ; Jenyns' Roll.

Felton, Sir Amand and **William**—(E. III. Roll) bore, gules two lyons passant ermine ; Ashmole Roll and Jenyns' Ordinary. Sir ROBERT and Sir THOMAS, K.G., bore the lyons crowned or as in the next ; Gloucester and Ashmole Rolls.

Felton, Sir John de, le filz—bore, at the first Dunstable tournament 1308, gules, two lyons passant ermine crowned or. Sir WILLIAM bore it also at the siege of Calais 1345–8, and Le Sr. DE FELTON bore it at the siege of Rouen 1418 [one MS. gives two lyons argent (F.) another three uncrowned lyons argent.] Sire ROGER bore it also differenced with a mullet (6) or on the cantel, at the battle of Boroughbridge 1322. F.

Felton, Sir Robert de, of co. Gloucr,—(E. II. Roll) bore, gules two lyons passant ermine, a baston gobony or and azure. Sir WILLIAM bore the lyons argent ; Parliamentary Roll. Sir JOHN, also of Gloucester, bore the lyons crowned or.

Felton, John and **Will de**—(E. III. Roll) bore, gules, two lyons passant argent within a double tressure flory counterflory of the second ; Jenyns' Roll and Ordinary. In Surrey Roll the tressure is *or*, for JOHN.

Fenes, Sir John de—(E. II. Roll) bore, or, a lyon rampant sable ; Parliamentary Roll ; the field argent for the Sire (‡) DE FENES in the Dering and Camden Rolls, and the lyon rampant regardant in the latter. F.

Fenes, Sir R. and **Sir J.** (with difference)—(H. VI. Roll) bore, argent two lyons passant azure ; Atkinson Roll.

Fenes, Sir Gyles de, of Sussex—(E. II. Roll) bore, azure, three lyonceux 2 and 1 rampant or, a label (3, 5) gules ; Parliamentary and Howard Rolls. ROGER bore the coat undifferenced in Jenyns' Ordinary. GILES, WILLIAM, and INGRAM took up the cross in the last Crusade 1270.

Fenton, Thomas de—(E. III. Roll) bore, argent, a cross between four fleurs-de-lys sable ; Jenyns' Ordinary.

Fenwick, Sir John—(E. III. Roll) bore, argent a chief gules, six martlets 3, 2, 1 counterchanged (F.) ; Ashmole Roll and Jenyns' Ordinary ; blasoned as, per fess gules and argent, six martlets 3, 2, 1 counterchanged, in Surrey Roll.

Feringes *v.* **Faringes.**

Ferlington, Henry—(E. III. Roll) bore, sable, five fusils in fess or ; Jenyns' Ordinary.

Ferlington, Henry—(E. III. Roll) bore, gules, three palets vair and a chief or ; Jenyns' Ordinary and Grimaldi Roll.

Ferne *v.* **Cerne** and **Frene.**

‡**Ferne, Philip de**—(H. III. Roll) bore, per fess argent and gules a lyon rampant within a bordure all counterchanged (F.) ; Ashmole copy of Dering Roll. Called also CERNE.

Ferre, Sir Guy (FERE) of Suffolk—(E. II. Roll) bore, gules, a fer-de-moulin argent, a baston azure ; Parliamentary Roll ; a cross recercelée in Segar and Harleian Rolls. F. JOHN took up the cross in the last Crusade 1270.

Ferrers, (William 7th) Earl of Derby—(H. III. Roll) bore, vaire or and gules (F.) ; Glover, Arden, and Howard Rolls ; argent and gules in St. George Roll. ROBERT (called RALF) baron of Chartley, bore the same arms at the siege of Calais 1345–8, also as Sir ROBERT when knighted at the capitulation of Calais 1348, by Sir JOHN, banneret, 1st baron of Chartley (1299), and WILLIAM (E. II.) ; Nobility and Parliamentary Rolls.

Ferrers, Sir Thomas de, of Herefordshire—(E. II. Roll) bore, vaire or and gules, a baston azure : Parliamentary Roll.

Ferrers, Hugh de—(H. III. Roll) bore, vair ; Glover Roll.

Ferrers, Sir William of Groby, banneret, a baron 1297—bore, the DE QUINCI coat, viz. : argent, seven mascles conjoined 3, 3, 1 or (F.), at the battle of Falkirk 1298, and at the siege of Carlaverock 1300, Nobility and Parliamentary Rolls ; he sealed the Barons' letter to the Pope 1301. Perhaps grandfather of Sir RALPH who differenced them with a label (3) argent at the siege of Calais 1345 8. Another Sir WILLIAM, knighted at the capitulation of Calais 1348, differenced them with a baston azure. WILLIAM, 5th Lord FERRERS of Groby, bore the undifferenced coat at the siege of Rouen 1418, ascribed also to HENRY in Jenyns' Ordinary ; another Sir RAUFF also bore them (E. III.) within a bordure engrailed argent ; Ashmole Roll. The BADDESLEY-CLINTON line added a canton ermine to the DE QUINCI coat. F.

Ferrers, Sir John de—bore, at the first Dunstable tournament 1308, vaire or and gules, (Add. MS. 5848) a lyon passant of the first, Harl. MS. 6137 fo. 32 ; ROBERT of Wem, baron 1375, bore the coat with a lyon passant gardant or, in the sautreme point ; Jenyns' Ordinary.

Ferrers, Sir Thomas de—bore, at the first Dunstable tournament 1308, vaire or and gules, on a quarter the arms of BOHUN, azure, a bend argent cotised or between six lyonceux rampant of the last. F.

JOHN FITZ ALAN, EARL OF ARUNDEL.

<small>In the FitzAlan Chapel, Arundel, 1434. *After Stothard*.</small>

Ferrers, William—(H. III. Roll) bore, vaire (old form) or and gules a bordure azure; Arden Roll. F.

Ferrers, William—(E. III. Roll) bore, vaire or and gules, a bordure azure, entoyre of de-crescents or; Jenyns' Ordinary.

Ferrers, Richard (E. III. Roll), **William** (H. III. Roll) bore, vaire, or and gules, a bordure azure, entoyre of horse-shoes argent; Jenyns' Ordinary, St. George Roll, and Harl. MS. 1481 fo. 46; in the Howard and Camden Rolls the bordure is sable for WILLIAM. F.

Ferrers, Sir John and **William** of Cornwall—(E. III. Roll) bore, or, on a bend sable three horse-shoes argent; Ashmole Roll and Jenyns' Ordinary. F.

Ferret, Sir John de la—(E. I. Roll) bore, gules, a double headed eagle displayed or; Holland Roll.

Fetheir, William—(E. II. Roll) bore, gules, a chevron ermine between three plumes (feathers in trick) argent; Jenyns' Roll. Harl. MS. 6589 gives a single ermine spot on the chevron.

Fifehead *v.* **Fishead.**

Fyffe, Earl of—(E. III. Roll) bore, paly gules and or; Grimaldi Roll.

*[**Filmer (Robert)**, of Herst, in Otterden (E. II.)—bore, sable, three bars and in chief as many cinquefoyles or.—Shirley.] F.

*[**Finch**, alias **Herbert, Vincent** (E. II.)—bore, argent, a chevron between three gryphons sable.—Shirley.] F.

Fineux, Sir John, of Kent, Kt.—(H. VI. Roll) bore, vert, a chevron between three eagles displayed or, *quarterly with*, gules, a lyon rampant argent; Arundel Roll.

Fishacre —— (E. III. Roll) bore, azure six lucics or; Cotgrave Roll.

Fishacre, William—(E. II. Roll) bore, gules, a dolphin hauriant embowed argent; Jenyns' Roll.

Fisheade, William—(E. III. Roll) bore, or, three water-bougets azure; Jenyns' Ordinary.

Fisseburn, Giles de—(H. III. Roll) bore, gules, a dolphin naiant embowed argent; St. George Roll. F. Called FISSHMAN in Arden Roll.

Fytton, Richard — (R. II. Roll) bore, argent on a bend azure three garbs or, a crescent of the second; Surrey Roll. See HESKETH.

Fitton, Sir Thomas, of Gawsworth—(E. IV. Roll) bore, argent, two chevronels and a quarter gules; with crest; Ballard Roll.

Fitz Alan, Sir Bryan le, banneret, baron of Bedale 1295, sealed the Barons' letter to the Pope 1301, with a strange device. He bore, at the battle of Falkirk 1298, and at the siege of Carlaverock 1300, barry or and gules (F.) blasoned (1) as barry (10) in the Nobility Rolls 1297, 1299, 1300; (2) as barry (8) at Carlaverock; these arms are said to be the same as HUGH POINTZ and to be disputed, see also Glover, Grimaldi, Howard and St.

George Rolls and Jenyns' Ordinary; (3) attributed to BRYAN (‡) as barry (6) in Dering and Guillim Rolls, and (4) as, or three bars gules in the Arundel and Parly. Rolls.

Fitz Alan, Sir Richard, Earl of ARUNDEL, banneret—sealed the Barons' letter to the Pope 1301, and bore, at the battle of Falkirk 1298, and at the siege of Carlaverock 1300, gules, a lyon rampant or; ascribed to JOHN (‡) in the Dering Roll (F.); another Earl JOHN bore it at the siege of Rouen 1418 *quarterly with* MALTRAVERS, sable a fret or; fretty in Monumental Effigy. See also ARUNDEL.

Fitz Aleyne William—(E. III. Roll) bore, azure, three boars' heads erect couped paly (8) azure and or; F. Ashmole Roll.

Fitz Aucher, Henry—(E. III. Roll) bore, ermine, on a chief azure three lyons rampant or; Jenyns' Ordinary. See FITZ HENRY.

Fitz Barnard, John—(E. II. Roll) bore, vair a fess gules in chief two mullets pierced or; Jenyns' Ordinary.

Fitz Barnard, Ralf le—(H. III. Roll) bore, vair, on a chief gules a cross patonce argent. (F.) St. George Roll. See FITZ ROGER.

Fitz Bernard, Sir Thomas le, of Kent, baron (8 E. II.)—bore, vair, on a chief gules two mullets or; Parly. Roll. RAFE also bore this coat; Arden Roll. JOHN and RAFE bore the mullets pierced in Jenyns' Ordinary and Parl. Roll.

Fitz Ellis, Robert, of Newton-(E. III. Roll) bore, argent, a dancettée in chief azure. (F.) Grimaldi Roll and Jenyns' Roll.

Fitz Edmund, Athelward—(H. III. Roll) bore, argent, an eagle displayed azure on a chief of the second a lyon of the first. REYNAUD bore it or and azure. WYCHARD bore the reverse, and RICHARD bore it sable and or. Howard Roll.

Fitz Ernys (or FITZ ERMYS), **Sir Philip,** of Hunts—(E. II. Roll) bore, argent, three torteaux; Parliamentary Roll.

Fitz Eustace, Sir Thomas, of Lincolnshire—(E. II. Roll) bore, azure, crusily or, a bend argent; Parliamentary Roll.

Fitz Geffrey, John le—(H. III. Roll) bore, quarterly or and gules a bordure vair; Glover and Grimaldi Rolls, Jenyns' Ordinary. Same as RICHARD LE FITZ JOHN. HENRY, of Horsede, took up the cross in the last Crusade 1270.

Fitz Gerald, Maurice, 4th Earl of Kildare —bore, at the siege of Calais 1345-8, argent, a saltire gules. (F.) Howard, Camden and other Rolls. Ascribed to another MAURICE (‡) in Dering Roll.

Fitzgerald, Sire Thomas, Earl of Desmond—(E. I. Roll) bore, ermine a saltire gules; Guillim Roll and Jenyns' Ordinary.

Fitz Gerald, Warine le—(H. III. Roll) bore, gules a leopard (a lyon rampant) argent, crowned or; Glover Roll.

Fitz Henry, Sir Aucher le, of Essex, baron 1310—bore, ermine on a chief azure three lyonceux rampant or; Nobility and Parliamentary Rolls; borne also by ROBERT, son of HENRY in Parly. Roll. See FITZ AUCHER.

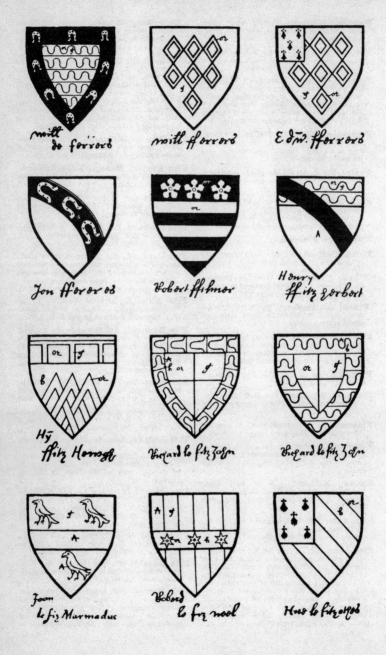

Will
de ferrers

will fferrers

E dw. fferrers

Jon fferrers

Robert ffshmor

Henry
ffitz herbert

Hij
ffitz Hensgh

Richard le fitz Johan

Richard le fitz Johan

Joan
le fiz Marmaduc

Robert
le fiz noel

Hue le fitz otes

Fitz Henry, Conan, of Kelfield, in Yorkshire—(E. III. Roll) and THOMAS (R. II. Roll)
bore, argent a cross engrailed sable ; Jenyns'
Ordinary and Surrey Roll. JOHN LE FITZ
HENRY bore the cross gules (St. George Roll),
where it is said that the same arms were borne
also by ANDR. LEVAAT and JOHN DE LA
LINDE. HENRY. of Sconebrok, took up the
cross in the last Crusade 1270.

Fitz Henry, Hugh, lord of Ravenswath
1294, sealed the Barons' letter to the Pope
1301 ; SIR HENRY, knighted at the capitulation
of Calais 1348 ; and RANDOLPH (E. III.) all
bore azure fretty and a chief or. (F.) St.
George and Grimaldi Rolls. See FITZ HUGH.

Fitz Henry, Adam, of Ellerton, Yorkshire
—(E. III. Roll) bore, argent seven mascles
conjoined 3, 3, 1 gules, on a quarter ermine a
covered cup or ; Jenyns' Ordinary.

Fitz Herbert, —— (E. III. Roll) bore, gules,
three lyonceux rampant or ; Ashmole Roll.
See FITZ PIERS and FITZ REGINALD.

Fitz Herbert, Thomas—(E. II. Roll) bore,
argent, six martlets and two cotises engrailed
sable—tricked as argent a plain bend between
two cotises engrailed sable ; Jenyns' Roll.

*[Fitz Herbert, Sir Henry (E. I.)—bore,
argent, a chief vaire or and gules, over all a
bend sable.—Shirley.] F.

Fitz Hugh, Sir Henry le, banneret—bore,
at the battle of Falkirk 1298, azure fretty and
a chief or. His son Sir HENRY differenced
with a label (3) gules at the first Dunstable
tournament 1308 ; Ashmole Roll and Jenyns'
Ordinary ; azure, a fret or, in Cotgrave Roll.
See FITZ HENRY.

Fitz Hugh, Sir Henry le, banneret and
a baron 1321—bore, azure, three chevronels
interlaced in base and a chief or ; Arundel,
Parliamentary and Surrey Rolls. F.

Fitz Hugh, Edmond—(R. II. Roll) bore,
gules, three lyons rampant 2 and 1 or, a
bordure engrailed argent ; Surrey Roll. See
Sir REYNOLD FITZ REGINALD.

Fitz Hugh, Jernegan, of Tanfelde—(E.
III. Roll) bore, or three bars azure, over all an
eagle displayed gules ; Grimaldi Roll—barry
(6) in Howard Roll, and (14) azure and or
in Jenyns' Ordinary.

‡Fitz Humfrey, Walter—(E. II. Roll) bore,
quarterly argent and sable. (F.) Parly.,
Dering and Howard Rolls. Ascribed also to
Sir WALTER, of Essex, in Parly. Roll. Same
as HANITUNE.

Fitz John, Richard le, a baron 1295
(*f* JOHN, baron 1264)—bore, quarterly or and
gules, a bordure vair. (F.F.) Borne also by
MATTHEW fil, JOHN, Parliamentary Roll, and
by JOHN (‡) in Dering, Howard and Norfolk
Rolls. Same as JOHN LE FITZ GEFFREY.

Fitz John, Roger le, de Evre—(H. III.
Roll) bore quarterly or and gules, a bend
sable ; Glover Roll. (THOMAS FITZ NICOL
bore the bendlet argent in Surrey Roll.) Same
as Sir ROBERT LE FITZ ROGER.

Fitz John, Mathew, D'n's de Stokeham
1297, sealed the Barons' letter to the Pope
1301, and bore, per pale (azure and gules)
three lyonceux rampant (or) ; ascribed to
HERBERT and JOHN LE FITZ MAHEU in
Glover and Segar Rolls. (F.) See FITZ MAHEU.

Fitz John, Sir Robert le—(E. I. Roll) bore,
checquy or and gules ; Holland Roll. RICHARD
bore it with a chief ermine in Jenyns' Ordinary.

Fitz John, Randolf, of Woodhall—(E. III.
Roll) bore, azure a chief indented or ; Grimaldi
Roll ; dancettée in Surrey Roll. See FITZ
RANDOLPH.

Fitz John, Sir Adam de, of Lincolnshire—
(E. II. Roll) bore, sable, two bars argent, in
chief three plates ; Parliamentary Roll.

‡Fitz Lee or Fitz Lel, William—(E. III.
Roll) bore, sable, crusily and three crescents
2 and 1 argent. (F.) Dering Roll.

Fitz Maheu, Philip le—(H. III. Roll)—
bore, per pale gules and azure three lyon-
ccux rampant ermine. (F.) Arden and St.
George Rolls. See FITZ JOHN.

Fitz Marmaduke, John le, banneret
(eldest son of Marm. Fitz Geoffry, lord of
Hordern *vel* Hawthorne, co. Durham)—bore,
at the siege of Carlaverock 1300, gules a fess
between three popinjays argent (F.) ; sealed the
Barons' letter to the Pope 1301 ; ascribed also to
THWENG of Lumley in Jenyns' Roll and Ordinary. (F.) Sir RICHARD bore it (E. II.) with
a baston, over all, azure ; Parliamentary,
Jenyns' and Glover Rolls. See also THWENGE.

Fitz Martin, Nicol le—(H. III. Roll) bore,
argent, two bars gules, a label (3) azure ;
Glover and Jenyns' Rolls.

Fitz Michaell, Michael, of Siggeston—
(E. III. Roll) bore, barry (8) or and gules, a
quarter ermine ; Jenyns' Ordinary.

Fitz Nele, Sir Robert—bore, at the first
Dunstable tournament 1308, paly (6) argent
and gules ; borne also (E. II.) by Sir RAUF of
Bucks, Parliamentary Roll ; and THOMAS
(E. III.) Jenyns' Ordinary.

‡Fitz Nel, Robert—(H. III. Roll) bore, paly
(6) argent and gules a fess azure ; Dering Roll
three bezants on the fess in the Ashmole
Copy ; three spur-rowells or (F.) in the Howard
and Segar Rolls.

Fitzneel, Thomas—(E. II. Roll) — bore,
argent, three palets gules, on a fess azure as
many martlets or ; Jenyns' Roll. JOHN in
Cotgrave, the martlets argent.

Fitz Nicol, Rauf le—(H. III. Roll) bore,
gules, semée of escallops argent, a cinquefoyle
or ; Glover Roll. Ascribed also to RICHARD
in the Norfolk Roll.

Fitz Nicol, Thomas—(R. II. Roll) bore,
quarterly or and gules, a bendlet argent ;
Surrey Roll. See also ROGER LE FITZ JOHN.

Fitz Oberne, Sir Roger—(E. II. Roll)
bore, three gemelles and a canton argent ;
Parliamentary Roll.

‡Fitz Otes, Hugh le—(H. III. Roll) bore,
bendy (6) or and azure a quarter ermine. (F.)
St. George and Camden Rolls—three bends in
the Howard Roll—bendy (8) argent and azure
a quarter ermine, in Jenyns' Ordinary.

(SIR WILLIAM) FITZ RALPH.

In Pebmarsh Church in Essex, 1323. *After Waller.*

Fitz Payne, Robert le, a baron 1299, sealed the Barons' letter to the Pope 1301—bore, at the battle of Falkirk 1298, and at the siege of Carlaverock 1300, gules, three lyons passant in pale argent, a baston azure. (F.) Parliamentary, Segar and other Rolls (save the Nobility Rolls, in which, as Baron of Lammer 1297–1308, he has only two lyons). Sir ROBERT, Kt., banneret, bore the same without a baston; Arundel Roll (H. VI.) and SIR JOHN or ROBERT of Gloucestershire bore, the baston gobony or and azure; Parliamentary Roll and Jenyns' Ordinary.

Fitz Payne, John le—(E. II. Roll) bore argent, a hawk's lure gules; Jenyns' Roll.

Fitzpiers, Reginald (REYNALD, REYNARD or RENAUD LE—(H. III. Roll) bore, gules, threelyonceux rampant or. (F.) Howard, Glover, St. George and Camden Rolls. See FITZ HERBERT and FITZ REGINALD.

Fitz Rauff, Sir Robert le—bore, at the first Dunstable tournament 1308, burulée (10) argent and azure three buckles 2 and 1 gules tongues to the sinister.

Fitz Raffe, Sir Robert, of Yorkshire—(E. II. Roll) bore, barry (8) argent and azure three chaplets gules, a label (3) or; Parly. and Nativity Rolls; WILLIAM bore, burulée (14) in Arden Roll. Some MSS. assign him buckles, in lieu of chaplets gules, tongues to the dexter. F. See FITZ WILLIAM.

Fitz Rauffe, Raffe, of Multon in Richmondshire, founder of the Abbey of Egglestone—(E. III. Roll) bore, barry (6) or and azure, tricked as or two bars azure, in Jenyns' Ord.

Fitz Rauff, Hugh le—(H. III. Roll) bore, gules, a fess vair; Glover Roll. WILLIAM took up the cross in the last Crusade 1269.

Fitz Raffe, Sir William of Essex—(E. II. Roll) bore, or, three chevrons gules on each as many fleurs-de-lys argent; Parliamentary Roll. See Monumental Brass. Same as JOHN FELTGRAVE, in Jenyns' Roll.

Fitz Rauf, Sire Randolf—bore, at the battle of Boroughbridge 1322, purpure a chief indented or (F.); Ashmole Roll.

Fitz Randolph, John, of Spenythorne, and **Randolph Fitz John,** of Woodall—(E. III. Roll) bore azure a chief indented or, and **Rauf** of Midleham bore the reverse; Jenyns' Ordinary. HENRY bore azure a chief fretty or; Glover Roll. See also FITZ ROBERT.

Fitz Reginald, John, baron of Blenleveny in Wales (25 E. I.) sealed the Barons' letter to the Pope 1301—bore, gules, three lyonceux rampant or; Nobility and Parliamentary Rolls; called FITZ RAYMOND in Arundel Roll. See FITZ HERBERT and FITZ PIERS.

Fitz Reginald, Sire Reynald le—bore, at the battle of Boroughbridge 1322, gules, three lyonceux (rampant) or within a bordure indented argent (F.); tricked engrailed in Ashmole Roll; and so ascribed to EDMOND FITZ HUGH in Surrey Roll.

Fitz Reynarde, Sir John, of Bucks—(E. II. Roll) bore, or, two chevrons gules, on a canton of the last a lyon passant argent; Parliamentary Roll. Called JACOB in Harl. MS. 4033 fo. 36b.

Fitz Richard, Sire Hamond le—bore, at the battle of Boroughbridge 1322, gules, a chevron (between) three unicorns argent. F.

Fitz Richard, Sire Rauf—bore, at the battle of Boroughbridge 1322, ermine, a chief bendy (10) or and azure. F.

Fitz Robert, Randolph (of Midleham) or RANDOLPH DE MIDLEHAM—(E. III. Roll) bore, or, a chief azure; Grimaldi Roll. See FITZ JOHN and FITZ RANDOLPH.

Fitz Robert, Sir Walter le, of Rutland—(E. II. Roll) bore, or two chevrons gules; Parliamentary Roll. Another WALTER bore it with a fess gules; Grimaldi Roll. See FITZ WALTER.

Fitz Roger, Sir Robert le, banneret, lord of Clavering—bore, at the battle of Falkirk 1298, and at the siege of Carlaverock 1300, quarterly or and gules a baston sable (F.); signed, but did not seal, the letter to the Pope 1301; Nobility, Parliamentary, and other Rolls. Ascribed also to JOHN(‡), in the Ashmole Copy of the Dering Roll; same as Sir ROGER LE FITZ JOHN. See also Sir JOHN DE CLAVERING.

Fitz Roger, Sire Robert le—(E. I. Roll) bore, argent a lyon rampant purpure (sable in Dering and Howard Rolls) (F.); Guillim Roll and Jenyns' Ordinary. RICHARD BALDERSTON bears the same.

Fitz Roger, Rauf le—(H. III. Roll) bore, vair, a chief gules, (F.); St. George Roll; ascribed also to JOHN, Baron FITZ ROGER, in the 2nd Nobility Roll 1299. See also CLAVERING and FITZ BARNARD.

Fitz Simon, Sir Hugh and John—(E. III. Roll) bore, gules, three false escocheons argent (F.); Ashmole and St. George Rolls. RICHARD, K.G., a founder, bore the reverse in Arundel and Surrey Rolls.

Fitz Simon, Sir John of Norfolk—bore, at the battle of Boroughbridge 1322, sable, a fess (between) three crescents argent (F.); Parliamentary Roll; another Sir JOHN bore the same, knighted at the capitulation of Calais 1348.

Fitz Simon, Sir John, of Herts—(E. II. Roll) bore, azure three eaglets displayed or a canton ermine; Parliamentary Roll; four eaglets 2 and 2 in Harl. MS. 6137 fo. 13.

Fitz Symond, Richard le—bore, at the second Dunstable tournament 1334, gules, a chief or (F.); THOMAS bore the reverse in Surrey Roll.

Fitz Simon, Sir Raffe, of Lincolnshire—(E. II. Roll) bore, azure, a lyon rampant ermine; Parly. Roll. ROBERT DE WY' took up the cross in the last Crusade 1270.

Fitz Simon, Simon le—(E. III. Roll) bore, gules, three roses ermine; Jenyns' Ordinary. Another SIMON (H. III.) bore gules, three chess-rooks ermine (F.); St. George Roll.

Fitz Stevens, Raffe of Thornton Rust, Yorks—(E. III. Roll) bore, azure, three martlets or, tricked as martels (hammers with claws); Jenyns' Roll. See MATHEW of Thornton Steward.

Robt le ffitzrauf

Simon le fitz Simon

Rog ffitz-urse

Mayn ffitz warin

Rauf fitz william

Jon ffitz william

will ffitz willia

Baldwin de fflanders

will fflemingo

John ffloyer

The ffoggo

Tho Fole gambe

Fitz Thomas, Thomas le—(H. III. Roll) bore, lozengy argent and gules (F.); St. George Roll, called FITZ COLOM, in Arden Roll; same arms as JOHN COGAN. See also FITZ WILLIAM. JOHN, of Wrastulingwrth, took up the cross in the last Crusade 1270.

Fitz Urse, Reginald—(H. III. Roll) bore, or, a bear passant sable, muzzled argent; Howard Roll. F.

Fitz Walter, Sir Robert le, banneret, a baron 1295, sealed the Barons' letter to the Pope 1301 - bore, at the battle of Falkirk 1298 and at the siege of Carlaverock 1300, or a fess between two chevronels gules. (F.) Nobility and Parliamentary Rolls ; borne also by Sr. —— FITZ WALTER, knighted at the capitulation of Calais 1348, and by Sir RICHARD, Kt. banneret in the Arundel Roll (H. VI.) also by Le Sr. —— FITZ WALTER at the siege of Rouen 1418, he probably WALTER 7th Lord. Ascribed also to ROBERT(‡) in the Dering Roll. See FITZ ROBERT.

Fitwaryn, Sir Fouke, of Whittington, banneret and baron 1295—bore, quarterly per fess indented (tricked, dancettée) argent and gules, Nobility Roll, (quarterly indented in the Parly. Roll); asdribed also to FOUK(‡) in Dering Roll; sealed the Barons' letter to the Pope 1301. Another Sir FOUKE bore it at the first Dunstable tournament 1308 differenced with a mullet sable. (F.) See also WM. FITZ WILLIAM, in Cotgrave. Sir WILLIAM, baron, bore it (undifferenced) at the siege of Calais 1345-8, on which occasion Sir JOHN bore it differenced with a label (3) azure, and so ascribed to PHILIP in the Norfolk Roll (H. III.)—reversed for Sir FOUKE in the Ashmole Roll, where tricked per pale with a chief indented counterchanged—probably in error.

Fitzwarren, Sire William—bore, at the battle of Boroughbridge 1322, quarterly per fess indented (tricked, dancettée) argent and sable. (F.) Parliamentary, Arden, St. George and Segar Rolls; reversed in Guillim Roll. This Sir WILLIAM may be identical with the preceding Sir WILLIAM of Calais. Another WILLIAM and EUDO took up the cross in the last Crusade 1270.

Fitz Waren, Alayn—bore, at the second Dunstable tournament 1334, quarterly argent and gules, on a canton of the first a martlet sable. F.

Fitz Warren, Sir Foulke, K.G.—(E. III. Roll) and **Sir William,** a baron 1342—bore, quarterly per fess indented (tricked, dancettée) ermine and gules; Cotgrave, Surrey and Arundel Rolls; reversed in Jenyns' Ordinary, and in the Ashmole Roll; where tricked per pale with a chief indented counterchanged —probably in error.

Fitz William, Sir Rauffe le, banneret, baron 1295, sealed the Barons' letter to the Pope 1301—bore, at the battle of Falkirk 1298 and at the siege of Carlaverock 1300, burulée (12) argent and azure, three chaplets gules (F.) —barry (6) &c., in the Nobility Rolls 1297-1310, and Segar Roll; argent four bars azure, &c., Parliamentary Roll; barry (10) Arundel and Jenyns' Roll; burulée (18) in Guillim Roll. WILLIAM, of Coleston, took up the cross in the last Crusade 1270. See FITZ RAFFE and GREYSTOCK.

*Fitz William, Sir William,** a baron 1327—bore, at the first Dunstable tournament 1308, lozengy argent and gules. (F.) Parliamentary, Ashmole and Surrey Rolls —masculée in Nativity and Parliamentary Rolls and Jenyns' Ordinary. See also FITZ THOMAS.

Fitzwilliam, Sir John—(E. III. Roll) bore, lozengy gules and argent; Ashmole Roll. F.

Fitz William, Thomas le—(H. III. Roll) bore, masculée ermine and gules; Glover Roll.

Fitzwilliam, Sir William—bore, at the battle of Falkirk 1298, or, a fess gules. F. Called FLUMAN in the Wrestpark Copy of the Falkirk Roll.

Fitz Wyth, Sir Geoffrey, of Norfolk— (E. II. Roll) bore, azure, three gryphons passant or; Parliamentary Roll. See WYTHE.

Fitz W(——), John le—(H. III. Roll) bore, ermine, two bars gules; Arden Roll.

Flamville, Sir William—(E. III. Roll) bore, argent, a maunche azure; Ashmole and Surrey Rolls.

Flamville, Sir Roger, of co. Leicr.—(E. II. Roll) bore, argent, a maunche gules, besantée ; Parliamentary Roll.

‡**Flandres, Baudwin de**—(H. III. Roll) bore, or, a lyon rampant sable within a bordure gules. (F.) Dering Roll—bordure engrailed in Ashmole MS. The Constable of Flanders bore, argent, an inescocheon gules, in Dering Roll.

Flaunder, Sir Henry, of Flanders—bore, at the siege of Calais 1345-8, sable, fretty or.

Fleming, Sir Baldwin and Robert— (E. III. Roll) bore, vair, a chief checquy or and gules ; Ashmole Roll and Jenyns' Ordinary ; in the latter tricked per fess, &c.

Fleming, John, of Layland—(E. III. Roll)— bore, the arms of RICHARD GRAY (azure, two bars argent on a chief of the last) with three cushions erect gules ; Jenyns' Ordinary.

*Fleming, John, and Thomas,** of Westmorland—(E. III. Roll) bore gules, fretty argent, a label (3) vert; Jenyns' Ordinary. Same arms as RAUFE BEAUCHAMP.

Flemyng, Sir William, of Gloucestershire —bore—at the first Dunstable tournament 1308, and at the battle of Boroughbridge 1322, gules, fretty argent and a fess azure. (F.) Parliamentary Roll.

Fleming, Thomas—(R. II. Roll) bore, barry (6) argent and azure in chief three lozenges gules ; Surrey Roll. Compare this JOHN F. of Layland.

Fletham, John de—(E. II. Roll) bore, sable, three unicorns' heads couped argent ; Jenyns' Roll.

Flitwick, Sir David, of Beds.—(E. II. Roll) bore, argent, two lyons passant gardant sable; Parliamentary Roll and Jenyns' Ordinary.

*[**Floyer, John,** of Floyer Hayes, E. I.—bore, sable, a chevron between three arrows argent. —Shirley.] F.

Fluman, Sir William—bore at the battle of Falkirk 1298, or, a fess gules. See FITZ WILLIAM.

Fogge (——), a Kentish Knight—(H. VI. Roll) bore, argent, a fess between three annulets sable ; Arundel Roll.

ELIZABETH,
2ND WIFE OF SIR ROGER NORTHWOODE, WIDOW OF RICHARD FOLLIOTT
AND DAUGHTER OF SIR JOHN DE SEGRAVE.
MONUMENTAL BRASS IN MINSTER CHURCH, ISLE OF SHEPPEY, 1361.
After Stothard.

Fogge, Thomas—bore, at the siege of Rouen 1418, argent on a fess between three annulets sable as many spur-rowells of the field. (F.) Surrey Roll.

Foix, Gaston de, K.G. 1438–9, Earl of Longueville, and his son, JOHN, K.G. 1445, Earl of Kendal, Captal de Buch—bore, or, three palets gules, *quarterly with*, or, two bulls passant gules, a riband round the neck vert, over all a label (3) the pendants cruceiform sable, each charged (for JOHN) with 5 escallops in cross argent ; K. 402 fo. 22. See also BUCH, BURDEUX, and GRAILLY. Pedigree in Anstis' " Order of the Garter," vol. I. Introduction, page 8. F.

Foljambe, Godfrey—(R. II. Roll) bore, sable a bend or between six escallops argent ; Surrey Roll. THOMAS bore the bend or (F.) ; St. George Roll.

Folkeram, Sir Richard, of Berks—(R. II. Roll) bore, or, a bend engrailed azure ; Parliamentary Roll—a bend of fusils (F.), in St. George Roll—a bend endentée *vel* lozengy in Jenyns' Ordinary.

Folliot, Jordan, a baron 1295—bore, gules, a bend argent (F.) as did Sir RICHARD (of Norfolk) at the first Dunstable tournament 1308.

Foliott, Sr. Edmond or OSMOND, of Lincolnshire - (E. II. Roll) bore, gules, a bend argent, a label (3) or ; Parliamentary Roll (called SIMON in Harl. MS. 4033 fo. 43) another OSMOND bore it, with the bend between six crescents argent ; Jenyns' Ordinary.

Folliott, Osmonde—(E. III. Roll) bore, gules, a bend argent between six increscents 3 and 3 or ; Jenyns' Ordinary.

[**Folliott, Richard,** Ed. III., bore, undée. See Monumental Brass of his widow, who became the second wife of Sir Roger Northwood.]

Folliott, Samson (or SAUNSUIN)—(E. III. Roll) bore, argent, two lyons passant gardant gules (F.) ; St. George Roll.

Folvile, Sir Christopher—(E. III. Roll) bore, per fess ermine and or a cross moline (recercelée) gules ; Sir JOHN bore it per fess argent and or ; Ashmole Roll.

Folvile, John—(E. III. Roll) bore, or, a chief argent, over all a cross recercelée (tricked moline) gules ; Jenyns' Ordinary.

Folvile, Sir Matthew—(E. III. Roll) bore, argent, two bars undée sable a canton gules ; Ashmole Roll.

Folvile, Philip—(E. III. Roll) bore, undée (6) argent and sable, a quarter gules.

*[**Forester (Richard),** of Willey (*c* 1325)— bore, quarterly per fess dancettée argent and sable, in the first and fourth quarters a bugle horn of the last.—Shirley.] F.

Forde *v.* **de la Forde.**

Forneus, Sire John de—bore, at the battle of Boroughbridge 1322, sable a pile engrelée argent (F.) as also did another Sir JOHN ; who was knighted at the capitulation of Calais 1348, then blasoned as a pale fusily ; as a pile indented of five, in Jenyns' Ordinary ; and as a pale lozengy of three pieces, in Ashmole Roll.

Forneus, Sir Robert, of Norfolk—(E. II. Roll) bore, argent, a pile engrailed sable ; Parliamentary Roll.

Forneus, St. Maheu—(E. I. Roll) bore, gules, crusily and bend or ; Harleian Roll.

Forneus, Maheu de—(E. I. Roll) bore, gules, a bend between six martlets or (F.) ; Segar Roll.

Forneus, Sir Simond—(E. III. Roll) bore, or, a bordure indented gules and a label of three azure ; Ashmole Roll.

Fors, William de, Earl of Albemarle, and Sr. de Coupland—(E. III. Roll) bore, argent, a chief gules ; Glover, Grimaldi, and Jenyns' Rolls.

*[**Fortescue, (Adam)** (31 E. I.)—bore, azure, a bend engrailed argent plain cotised or.— Shirley.] F.

Fossard, Amaund—bore, at the second Dunstable tournament, gules six bendlets or. F.

Fossard, Robert—(E. II. Roll) bore, or, a bend sable ; Grimaldi and Jenyns' Rolls, borne also by BIGOD and Le Sire MAULEY.

Fotheringay, John—(E. III. Roll) bore, argent, two lyons passant rere-regardant sable, reversed in the trick ; Jenyns' Ordinary.

‡**Fouche, Roger la**—(H. III. Roll) bore, ermine, on a fess gules three bezants ; Dering Roll.

Fouleshurst, Robert—(R. II. Roll) bore, gules, fretty or, on a chief argent two spur-rowells sable ; Surrey Roll.

Fox ——, an (?) Essex Knight—(H. VI. Roll) bore, per pale vert and sable a cross potent argent ; Arundel Roll.

Foxley, Sir John de, of Bucks—(E. II. Roll) bore, gules two bars argent ; Parliamentary and Surrey Rolls. See Monumental Brass.

Framlingham (——), a Suffolk Kt.—(H. VI. Roll) bore, argent, a fess gules between three ravens proper *quarterly with*, argent, a chevron between three crescents sable ; Arundel Roll.

*[**Frampton, John de,** (E. III.)—bore. argent, a bend gules cotised sable.—Shirley.] F.

Franceis, Adam — (R. II. Roll) bore, per bend sinister sable and or a lyon rampant counterchanged, Surrey Roll ; per bend or and sable &c., in Jenyns' Ordinary.

Frances, Sr. (——), of Norfolk—(E. II. Roll) bore [. . . .] a saltire between four crosses crosslet fitchée all argent ; Parliamentary Roll.

Fraunceys, Robert — (R. II. Roll) bore, argent, a chevron between three eagles displayed gules ; Surrey Roll.

Franks, Sir William—bore, at the siege of Calais 1345-8 (knighted at the capitulation 1348) vert, a saltire engrailed or (F.) ; Ashmole Roll and Jenyns' Ordinary.

Fraser, Sir Symond—summoned to Scotland among the barons 1298, served at Falkirk and Carlaverock. See FRYSELL.

Freford, John de—(E. III. Roll) bore, gules, a bend between six mascles argent ; Jenyns' Ordinary.

SIR JOHN DE FOXLEY.

In Bray Church, in Berkshire, 1378. *After Boutell.*

Frembaude, Sir Nicholas, of Bucks—(E. II. Roll) bore, gules, crusily and a cross or ; Parliamentary Roll.

Frene, Sir Gerard (FRENYE) (E. II. Roll) bore, or, a fleur-de-lys sable and a bordure gules ; Parliamentary and Harleian Rolls. See also DE LA FREIGN.

Frene, Hugh de (a baron 1336)—bore, at the second Dunstable tournament 1334, gules two bars "endente" argent and azure—indented from point to point (F.) ; Ashmole Roll and Jenyns' Ordinary ; the bars, per fess indented in St. George Roll ; bends, per bend indented, in Parliamentary Roll, and for Sir WALTER, of Herefordshire, also, one bend only ; H. 6137 fo. 27.

Freschville, Raff de, Baron of Stavely 1297—bore, azure, a bend between six escallops argent ; Nobility Roll ; ascribed also to AUKER and JOHN in Howard Roll and Jenyns' Ordinary ; RAUFF differenced with a mullet gules ; Surrey Roll.

Frevile, Alexander—(H. III. Roll) bore, or, a saltire lozengy vair and gules. (F.) ; Arden and St. George Rolls.

Frevile, Sir Alexander de, of co. Worc.—(E. II. Roll) bore, or, a cross lozengy gules and vair. (F.) Sir BALDWIN bore or, on a cross gules five lozenges vair ; Parliamentary Roll ; (cross flory in Jenyns' Ordinary) ; 12 lozenges (F.) in St. George Roll.

Frevile, John—(E. III. Roll) bore, or, on a cross vair 9 lozenges in cross gules ; Jenyns' Ordinary. Although the blason of these crosses differ, it should probably be the same in all.

Frevile, Sir Baldwin—(E. III. Roll) bore, or, a cross patonce gules ; Ashmole and Surrey Rolls. Sir PIERS differenced with an annulet azure ; Ashmole Roll.

Frevile, Baudwin de—(H. III. Roll) bore, vair, a cross " passant" gules ; Norfolk Roll.

Frevile, Sir John de, of Cambridgeshire, and RICHARD and ROBERT—(E. II. Roll) bore, gules, three crescents ermine. (F.) Parliamentary, Arden, St. George, and Jenyns' Rolls. Another RICHARD (E. I.) bore, or three crescents gules. (F.) Segar Roll, see FREISLE and FRIVILE.

Fritherby, Edmond de — (R. II. Roll) bore, argent, three fleurs-de-lys 2 and 1 gules ; Surrey Roll.

Frodsam (——), an Essex Kt.—(H. VI. Roll) bore, argent, on a cross engrailed sable five mullets (8) gules ; Arundel Roll.

Frognal (——), a Kentish Kt.—(H. VI. Roll) bore, sable, two bars or, a chief argent ; Arundel Roll.

Frowick (——), a Suffolk Kt.—(H. VI. Roll) bore, azure, a chevron between three leopards faces or ; Arundel Roll.

Frysell, Sir Symond (FRESELL or FRÁSER)—bore, at the battle of Falkirk 1298, sable, six roses (fraises) argent (F.) ; and nine roses (fraises) 3, 3, 2, 1 at the siege of Carlaverock 1300.

Fulborne, Sir John de, of Cambridgeshire—(E. II. Roll) bore, argent, a chevron between two wyverns (tails nowed) sable ; Parliamentary Roll—tricked in Harl. MS. 6137 fo. 18, or a chevron and in chief two wyverns sable.

*[**Fulford, Sir Henry,** (E. III.)—bore, gules, a chevron argent.—Shirley.] F.

Fulthorp, Alan—(E. III. Roll) bore, argent, a cross moline sable. WILLIAM differenced with a crescent argent ; Surrey Roll and Jenyns' Ordinary.

Furneus *v.* **Forneus.**

Furnivall, Thomas, D'nus de Sheffield, a baron 1295 and a banneret, sealed the Barons' letter to the Pope 1301 ; bore, at the battle of Falkirk 1298 and at the siege of Carlaverock 1300, argent, a bend between six martlets gules. (F.) Nobility, Parliamentary and Arundel Rolls. borne also by GERARD (of Munden), Sir THOMAS and WALTER ; Glover, Guillim and Norfolk Rolls. WILLIAM differenced with a label azure ; Glover Roll. In the Glover Roll the field is tricked or for GERARD (Harl. MS. 1481 fo. 38) and also for THOMAS in the St. George Roll.

Furnivall, Le Sr.—(E. III. Roll) bore, gules, on a cross patonce or five mullets of the field ; Ashmole Roll and Jenyns' Ordinary. Same as Sir THOMAS UGHTRED.

*[**Fursdon, Walter,** (E. I.)—bore, argent, a chevron azure between three fire-balls proper. —Shirley.] F.

†**Fyliol, Richard**—(H. III. Roll) bore, sable three covered cups or. (F.) St. George Roll.

Fyliol, Sir Thomas, of Essex—(E. II. Roll) bore, or, on a fess between two chevronels gules, three trefoyles argent ; Parliamentary Roll.

Fyliol, Sir John, of Essex—(E. II. Roll) bore, vair, a canton gules (F.) ; Parliamentary and Arden Rolls. His son Sir JOHN differenced with a mullet (on the canton) or, at the first Dunstable tournament 1308.

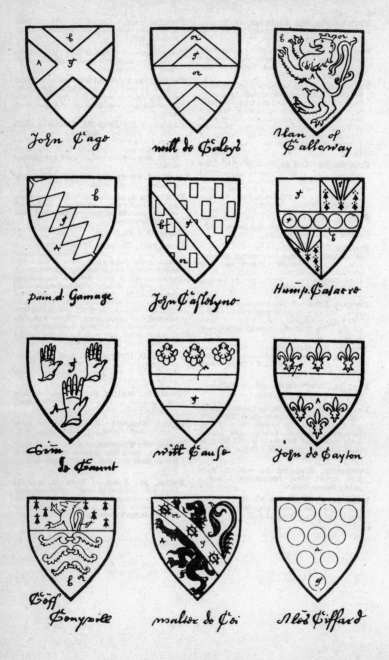

John S^c ago   roilt do S^c aloyd   Alan   of
                                               S^c alloway

pain d Gamage   John S^c aflolyno   Hump S^c alacre

Giue   rortt S^c auso   John do S^c ayton
   do S^c aunt

S^c off   mattor do S^c oi   Alco S^c iffard
   S^c onyrille

G

Gabriell, Bartholomew—(E. III. Roll) bore, or billety (6) sable ; Cotgrave Roll.

*[**Gage, John** (9 H. IV.)—bore, per saltire argent and azure a saltire gules.—Shirley.] F.

Gainsforde (——) an Essex? Knight—(H. VI. Roll) bore, argent, a chevron gules between three greyhounds courant sable ; Arundel Roll.

Galeys, William de—(E. I. Roll) bore, gules, a fess between two chevronels or ; Segar Roll. (F.) See also WALEIS.

Galloway, Alan, lord of—(E. III. Roll) bore, azure, a lyon rampant argent, crowned or ; Jenyns' Ordinary.

Galthorp, Bartholomew, of Orthenley, Norfolk—(E. III. Roll) bore, ermine, a maunch gules ; Ashmole Roll and Jenyns' Ordinary.

Gammage, Payne de—(H. III. Roll) bore, argent, a chief azure, over all five fusils in bend gules (F.) ; ADAM, differenced with a label (5) of the first ; a label or, for NICHOL ; Arden and St. George Rolls. In Jenyns' Ordinary the bend is engrailed.

Gant, Gilbert de, baron (of Lindsey) 1295—bore, barry (6) or and azure a bend gules ; Nobility and Parliamentary Rolls. Ascribed also to GEOFFREY (H. III.,) Norfolk Roll ; WILLIAM (H. III.), Glover Roll ; and to GILBERT of Swaledale (E. II.) in Jenyns' Ordinary.

Gard, Hugh, of Denmark—(E. III. Roll) bore, azure, a sun or ; H. 6589 fo. 37. See ANDREW HUGARDE.

Gardyn, Sir Thomas de, of Cambridgeshire—(E. II. Roll) bore, argent, two bars sable, a label (3) gules ; Parly. Roll.

Gargrave (——) of Suffolk, Kt. (Sir JOHN, Master of the Ordnance to King Henry in France)—(H. VI. Roll) bore, lozengy argent and sable on a bend of the last three crescents of the first ; Arundel Roll.

Garshall, Sir Thomas, of Warwickshire—(E. II. Roll) bore, quarterly argent and sable on a bend gules three fleurs-de-lys of the first ; Parliamentary Roll.

Gascoigne, William—(E. III. Roll) bore, argent, on a pale sable a lucie's head couped hauriant of the first ; Jenyns' Ordinary.

Gaselyn, Sire Edmond, of Hants—bore, at the battle of Boroughbridge 1322, or, billettée sable (F.) (azure, in Parliamentary Roll.) An-

other EDMOND bore it with a label (5) gules fretty of the second ; Arden and St. George Rolls, and GEOFFREY bore it with a label gules. Another GEFFREY took up the cross in the last Crusade 1270.

Gaselyn, Sir Walter, of Hants—bore, at the first Dunstable tournament 1308, or billettée azure with a label (3) gules ; no label in Parliamentary Roll. Sir JOHN of Hants bore it with a bend gules (F.), Parliamentary Roll ; and Sir SIMOND bore the first coat with a label (5) gules ; Guillim Roll.

*[**Gatacre, Humphrey,** esquire of the body to Hen. VI.—bore, quarterly gules and ermine a fess azure bezantée between in the second and third quarters three piles meeting in base of the first.—Shirley.] F.

‡**Gatton, Hamon de**—(H. III. Roll) bore, checquy argent and azure (F.) ; Dering and Camden Rolls. GARTUNE in the Howard Roll.

Gaunte, Le Chastelyn de—(E. III. Roll) bore, azure, a false escocheon argent (an inescocheon) ; Jenyns' Ordinary.

Gaunt, Simon de—(E. II. Roll) bore, gules, three dexter gauntlets apaumée argent (F.) ; Jenyns' Roll.

Gause, Sire William—bore, at the battle of Boroughbridge 1322, gules, two bars and (in chief) three escallops argent. (F.)

Gaveston, Piers, Earl of Cornwall 1308, banneret—bore, vert, three eaglets displayed or ; six eaglets, 3, 2, 1, in Parly. Roll ; 3 and 3 in Arundel Roll ; the field azure, both in Jenyns' Roll and Ordinary.

Gayton, Sir John de, of Rutland, Kt.—(E. II. Roll) bore, argent a fess between six fleurs-de-lys 3 and 3 gules ; Parliamentary Roll ; the fess between three in Arden Roll.

Gayton, Sir Philip de, of Rutland—(E. II. Roll) bore, argent, crusily and three fleurs-de-lys azure ; Parly. Roll. HAMOND, JOHN, WILLIAM and WALTER took up the cross in the last Crusade 1270.

Geddinge, Sir John de, of Suffolk—(E. II. Roll) bore, checquy argent and gules on a fess azure three round buckles or, tongues to the dexter ; Parliamentary Roll.

Geddinge (——) a Kentish Knight—(H. VI. Roll) bore, gules, a chevron argent between three gryphons' heads erased or ; Arundel Roll.

PETER GERARD, Esq.

IN WINWICK CHURCH, LANCASHIRE, 1492. *After Waller.*

Gelres, The Count de (or GUELDRES in Flanders)—(E. III. Roll) bore, azure, billettée and a lyon rampant or ;- Jenyns' Ordinary. Possibly of the family of the author of the famous "Armorial de Gelres."

Genevill, Geffray de, a baron 1299—bore, azure, three pairs of barnacles expanded in pale or, on a chief ermine a demi lyon rampant issuant gules (F.); Nobility Roll, &c. (the barnacles argent in the Harl. Roll). Attributed to another GEFFREY (‡) in Dering Roll. A GEFFREY and WILLIAM took up the cross in the last Crusade 1270.

Genevile, Simon de (or JOINVILLE)—(H. III. Roll) bore, sable three pairs of barnacles expanded or, on a chief argent a demi lyon rampant issuant gules ; Glover Roll.

‡**Genne, William le**—(H. III. Roll) bore, argent, three lyons rampant 2 and 1 sable (F.) ; Dering Roll.

Genney, Sir Roger, of Norfolk—(E. II. Roll) bore, paly (4) or and gules a chief ermine ; Parly. Roll. See also GENY.

*[**Gent (John),** of Wymbish, in Essex, 1328— bore, ermine, a chief indented sable (F.), and, adds Shirley, a chevron sable is sometimes borne on the shield.]

Gentill, Sir Nicholas—(E. II. Roll) bore, argent, two bars sable on a chief of the last two mullets pierced of the first ; Parliamentary Roll.

Gentill, Sir Nicholl, of Sussex or Surrey— bore, at the first Dunstable tournament 1308, or, on a chief sable two mullets argent pierced gules (F.); pierced argent, in Parliamentary Roll, and gules in Jenyns' Ordinary.

Geny, Sir Thomas—(E. III. Roll) bore, azure, a false escocheon within an orle of martlets or ; Ashmole Roll, an orle *vel* inescocheon voided.

Gerard, Sir Thomas of the Bryne—(E. IV. Roll) bore, azure, a lyon rampant ermine, ducally crowned or ; with crest. Ballard Roll —see Monumental Brass for PETER, 1492.

Gerard, Thomas — (E. III. Roll) bore, gules, three inescocheons ermine ; Jenyns' Ordinary. See WILLIAM GERMINE.

*[**Gerard, William** (16 E. I.)—bore, argent, a saltire gules, in Shirley.] F.

Gerberge, John and **Raffe**—(E. III. Roll) bore, ermine, on a chief gules, three lozenges or ; Jenyns' Roll and Ordinary—the lozenges vair, in Ashmole Roll.

Gerberge, Thomas — (R. II. Roll) bore, sable, a fess between two chevrons or ; Surrey Roll.

Gercomvile v. Jerkavile and **Marconvile.**

Germyn v. Jermyn.

Germine, William—(E. III. Roll) bore, gules three false escocheons ermine a mullet (6) argent. (F.) Jenyns' Ordinary. See THOMAS GERARD.

Gernons, see BLUNDEVILE, Earl of CHESTER.

Gernoun, Sir William de, of Essex— (E. II. Roll) bore, argent, three piles undée meeting in base gules ; Parliamentary Roll. Wavy in Harl. 6137 fo. 14ᵇ—paly wavy argent and gules in Glover Roll.

Gerthestone, Robert de—(E. III. Roll) bore, argent, on a fess sable three crosses patonce or ; Jenyns' Ordinary.

Gerveys, Robert—(E. II. Roll) bore, argent, a chevron azure between three escallops sable ; Jenyns' Roll.

Gery, Sir John—(E. III. Roll) bore, paly (6) or and gules, a chief ermine ; Ashmole and Surrey Rolls.

Getingdon, Nicholas—(E. III. Roll) bore, gyronny (8) or and sable ; Jenyns' Ordinary.

Gey, Walter de—(H. III. Roll) bore, argent a lyon rampant sable debruised of a bend gules (Arden Roll); charged with three buckles or. (F.); in St. George Roll.

Ghisnes, Ingelram de, a baron 1295— bore, gules, a chief vair (potent counter potent); Nobility Roll.

Giffarde, Sir John, of co. Worc.—(E. II. Roll) bore, argent, nine torteaux 3, 3, 2, 1 ; Parliamentary Roll. ALEXANDER, JOHN and RAFFE bore ten torteaux. (F.) St. George and Surrey Rolls and Jenyns' Ordinary.

Giffard, William—(E. III. Roll) bore, argent, three stirrups and straps gules ; Jenyns' Roll—the reverse in Howard Roll (H. III.). Sir PEIRS bore, at the battle of Boroughbridge 1322, azure, three stirrups within a bordure indented all or. (F.) Tricked engrailed in Ashmole MS. *PETER GIFFORD (H. III.) bore the last coat without the bordure.—Shirley.

Giffard, John de, banneret, a baron 1295— bore, gules, three lyons passant in pale argent. (F.) Nobility, Parliamentary and Arundel Rolls—ascribed also to WILLIAM in Jenyns' Ordinary. Sir JOHN LE BOEF, of Oxon, bore it (E. II.) differenced with a label (3, 5) azure ; Parliamentary Roll. Ascribed to another JOHN (‡) in Dering Roll. Sir EDMUND, of co. Glouc. (E. II.) bore the same difference— but sable in Harl. MS. 4033 fo. 48, and so also one OSBERT, baron 1297 ; Nobility Roll.

‡**Giffard, Ellis**—(H. III. Roll) bore, gules, three lyons passant in pale argent within a bordure or ; Dering Roll—the bordure engrailed in Howard Roll.

‡**Giffard, Walter**—(H. III. Roll) bore, azure, three lyons passant in pale argent crowned or ; Dering and Howard Rolls.

Giffard, William—(H. III. Roll), bore, argent, crusily and a lyon rampant gules. (F.) Jenyns' Ordinary ; (WALTER BUKESHALL bears the same)—crusily sable in Arden and St. George Rolls. A WILLIAM took up the cross in the last Crusade 1270.

Giffard, Osberne—(H. III. Roll) bore, ermine, two bars gules on a chief of the last a lyon (of England) passant gardant or ;- St. George Roll and Jenyns' Roll—(a fess in lieu of the bars (F.) Segar Roll); attributed to another OSBERNE (‡), the field and lyon or, in the Dering Roll ; the field argent in the Ashmole MS.

Giffard, Osburne—(H. III. Roll) bore, argent, two bars gemelles and a chief gules; Howard Roll.

In Memoriam.
———
ROBERT the CONSUL,
EARL OF GLOUCESTER, 1119, II. F.NAT. II. I.
In the Choir of Tewkesbury Abbey, ob. 1147. *After J. Carter.*
See also Clare 52.

Giffard, Robert de—(H. III. Roll) bore, or a cross engrailed sable. (F.) St. George Roll ; blasoned fusily and tricked dancettée in Arden Roll.

‡**Gifford, Robert**—(H. III. Roll) bore, argent, a cross engrailed sable, over all a gorge azure. (F.) Dering Roll.

Gifford, Hugh—(E. III. Roll) bore, gules, fretty engrailed ermine ; Jenyns' Ordinary. WAREYN DE VALOYNES bears the same.

Gilder, Sir Gawayne—(E. III. Roll) bore, gules, three estoiles or, a bordure engrailed argent. Ashmole Roll.

Gillott, Nicholas DE MERKINGTON—(E. II. Roll) bore, per bend indented sable and argent ; Jenyns' Roll.

Gise *v.* **Guise.**

Gisell or **Oysell, Roger**—(E. III. Roll) bore, argent, a saltire engrailed between four birds (oiseau) sable ; Jenyns' Ordinary.

Gissing, Sir Thomas—(E. III. Roll) bore, argent on a fess (between two crosses crosslet fitchée) azure three eagles displayed or ; Ashmole Roll—a bend in lieu of a fess and without crosslets in Surrey Roll.

Gistell, Walter de—(H. III. Roll) bore, gules, a chevron ermine ; Norfolk Roll.

Glamville, Randolf de (or GLANVILE)—(E. III. Roll) bore, or, a chief indented (4) azure ; Jenyns' Ordinary.

[**Glanville (——)**, of Catchfrench (*c* 1400), bore azure, three saltorelles or.—Shirley.]

Glanville, *sive* **Ekont** —— (H. III. Roll), bore, azure, crusily three crescents argent. (F.) St. George Roll.

Glastonbury, Sir Henry de, of Somerset —bore, at the first Dunstable tournament 1308, argent a bend engrailed sable (F.) blasoned as fusily for the Sir HENRY who was knighted at the capitulation of Calais 1348 ; ascribed as lozengy to JOHN (E. III.) in Jenyns' Ordinary—probably engrailed ; fusily and lozengy are synonymous.

Gloucester, Earl of, GILBERT DE CLARE—bore, at the first Dunstable tournament 1308, or three chevronels gules (F.) ; Nobility and Arundel Rolls, &c. See AUDLEY and CLARE.

Gloucester, Duke of, THOMAS of Woodstock K.G.—(R. II. Roll) bore, quarterly 1, England 2 and 3, France, all within a bordure argent, 4, azure, a bend argent between two cotises and six lyons rampant or ; Surrey Roll ; K. 399 fo. 4.

[**Gloucester, Robert** (of Caen), Earl of ; surnamed CONSUL, fil. nat. Hen. I.—to him is improperly ascribed gules three clarions or. See Monumental Effigy.]

Gloucester, Sire Walter de (of co. Glouc.) —bore, at the battle of Boroughbridge 1322, argent three lyonceux (rampant) gules, within a bordure indented azure (F.) ; Parliamentary Roll ; tricked engrailed in Ashmole MS. ; blasoned " cersele " in Cotgrave Roll.

Gobaud, Sire Johan, of co. Linc.—bore, at the battle of Boroughbridge 1322, gules, a fess and in chief three besants (F.) ; Holland Roll ; two bars or, &c., in Jenyns' Ordinary and Parliamentary Roll.

Gobion, Sir Hugh, of Yorkshire—(H. III. Roll) bore, barry (8) argent and gules a label (3, 5) azure ; St. George (F.) and Parliamentary Rolls ; burulée (18) in Arden Roll.

Godard, Sir Hugh, of Cheshire—(E. II. Roll) bore, ermine, a cross patonce sable ; Parliamentary Roll.

Godard, John—(E. III. Roll) bore, quarterly gules and argent, in the second and third quarters an eagle displayed sable ; Jenyns' Ordinary.

Goddyston, Sir John, of Essex—(H. VI. Roll) bore, ermine, a saltire engrailed gules ; Arundel Roll.

Godemontone, John de—(H. III. Roll) bore, argent, an eagle displayed gules (F.) ; Arden and St. George Rolls.

Goderiche, William—(R. II. Roll) bore, argent, two lyons passant gardant in pale sable ; Surrey Roll.

Goldesborow, Richard de—(R. II. Roll) bore, azure, a cross patonce argent ; Surrey Roll ; cross, tricked flory in Jenyns' Ordinary.

Goldingham, Sir Allen de, of Suffolk— (E. II. Roll) bore, undée (6) argent and gules, a label (3) azure ; Parliamentary Roll. Argent a bend nebulée gules is ascribed to another Suffolk Knight ; Arundel Roll.

Goldingham, Alexander—(R. II. Roll) bore, barry nebulée (6) ermine and gules ; Surrey Roll.

Goldingham, William de—(H. III. Roll) bore, ermine, three bars wavy gules ; Howard Roll.

Goldington, Sire John de—bore, at the battle of Boroughbridge 1322, or, two lyons passant sable, a label (3) gules ; borne without the label but with the lyons gardant by Sir JOHN, who was knighted at the capitulation of Calais 1348. F.

Goldington, Sir Raffe de, of Beds—(E. II. Roll) bore, argent two lyons passant in pale azure ; Parliamentary Roll.

Golofree, Sir John—(E. III. Roll) bore, undée (6) argent and gules on a baston sable four besants, Ashmole Roll ; three besants for JOHN and THOMAS, in Surrey Roll and Jenyns' Ordinary.

Gondronville, Gerard de, of Loreyne— bore, at the siege of Carlaverock 1300, vair ; sometimes called HUNTERCOMBE. See NICOLAS edn.

Gonnis, Bryan de (E. III. Roll) bore, vair, a bend lozengy (*vel* engrailed) gules (F.) ; St. George Roll and Jenyns' Ordinary, where it is blasoned vaire or and azure a bend gules.

Gonnis, Walter de—(E. III. Roll) bore, quarterly vair and gules ; Jenyns' Ordinary.

Brian
do Conua

Ada Furdun

Vasso
do Gorges

John do Goring

mal
de Segalo

miH de Sower

Hy. de Graham

wal. d' Graucure

wm Grandin

Otes
Grandison

will
Grantsonn

Guillaume
de Graundsonn

Gonnyes, de —— (E. III. Roll) bor , gules, a chevron ermine; Jenyns' Roll and Ordinary; borne also by LODBROOKE.

Gonvile, Sir Nicholas—(E. III. Roll) bore, or, on a bend sable three mullets argent pierced gules; Ashmole Roll.

Gordon, Sir Adam, of Hants or Wilts— (E. II. Roll) bore, gules, three leopards' faces jessant-de-lys argent; Parliamentary Roll.

‡**Gordon, Adam**—(H. III. Roll) bore, or, a fleur-de-lys gules; Dering and Howard Rolls.

Gordon, Adam de—(H. III. Roll) bore, gules, three fleurs-de-lys argent (F.); Arden and St. George Rolls. See also Sir ADAM GORDON.

Gordon, Sir Thomas, or GARDYN, of co. Cambridge—(E. II. Roll) bore, argent, two bars sable, a label (3) gules; Parliamentary Roll.

Gorges, Raffe de—bore, at the siege of Carlaverock 1300, and at the first Dunstable tournament 1308, lozengy or and azure (F.); this coat appears in many rolls, sometimes the tinctures are reversed, at others six lozenges 3, 2, 1 are tricked for lozengy; the mascles are tricked five lozenges for Sir RAFFE, banneret, in Parliamentary and Arundel Rolls; masculée argent and azure is ascribed to JOHN, in Jenyns' Roll.

Gorges (——), a Suffolk Knight—(H. VI. Roll) bore, lozengy or and azure a chevron gules (F.), *quarterly with,* argent, on a chief gules three bezants; Arundel Roll.

Gorges, Rafe de—(H. III. Roll) bore, argent, a gorge azure (F.); Arden, Jenyns', Howard and Glover Rolls; (successfully claimed by WARBURTON of Cheshire); a RAFE took up the cross in the last Crusade 1270.

*[**Goring, John de** (E. II.)—bore, argent, a chevron between three annulets gules.— Shirley.] F.

Gornay *v.* **Gurnay.**

Goschalle, Walter de—(E. III. Roll) bore, or, a hurt charged with a cinquefoyle of the first, on a chief dancettée (4 indents) azure, two besants (F.); Ashmole Roll. In the Dering Roll the coat is tricked per fess dancettée, &c., for RAFFE or WALTER (‡).

Gotesbury, Sir Richard de, of Herts— (E. II. Roll) bore, gules, a fess vair between three goats' heads erased argent: Parliamentary Roll.

Gounis *v.* **Gonnis.**

Gousell, John—(E. III. Roll) bore, argent, a fess between six martlets 3 and 3 sable; Jenyns' Ordinary.

Gousell, John—(E. III. Roll) bore, paly (6) argent and gules on a chief azure a fess dancettée or, RAFE bore it with the colours of the chief and fess reversed; Jenyns' Ordinary.

Gousell, Thomas (GAUSILL)—(E. II. Roll) bore, argent, on a bend sable three trefoils or; Jenyns' Roll.

Goushull, Nicoll—(R. II.) bore, barry (6) or and gules, a canton ermine, his son NICHOLL differenced with a label (3) azure; Surrey Roll.

Gower, Sir Robert—(E. III. Roll) bore, argent, on a chevron sable three leopards' faces or; Ashmole Roll. JOHN DE GUER took up the cross in the last Crusade 1270.

Gower, Thomas, of Stittenham (? Stainsby) (E. III. Roll) bore, ermine, a cross flory gules, blasoned as patée; Jenyns' Ordinary.

*[**Gower, Sir Nicholas,** of Stittenham (12 E. III.)—bore, barry (8), argent and gules, a cross flory gules — blasoned patonce by Shirley.] F.

Grabom, William (or GABOM) — (H. III. Roll) bore, argent, on a bend gules three eagles displayed or; Arden Roll.

Graham, Henry de, banneret—bore, at the siege of Carlaverock 1300, gules, a saltire argent on a chief of the last three escallops gules. F.

Grailly *v.* **Buch, Greilly.**

Gramary, Henry—(E. III. Roll) bore, gules, crusily botonnée and a lyon rampant argent; Jenyns' Ordinary.

Gramary, Sir William—(E. III. Roll) bore, gules, billettée or, and a lyon rampant argent, Ashmole Roll; billettée argent in the coat ascribed to WILLIAM; Jenyns' Ordinary.

Grancourt, Walter de (GRAUNCURT) — (H. III. Roll) bore, sable, florettée or, (F.); St. George Roll and Arden Roll sable, six fleurs-de-lys 3, 2, 1, or.

Grandall *v.* **Grendole.**

†**Grandin, William**—(E. I. Roll) bore, azure, three mullets 2 and 1 or, (F.); Dering and Camden Rolls.

Grandison, de —— (E. III. Roll) bore, paly (6) argent and azure on a bend gules a castle or. Another (see OTHO)—azure, on a bend argent three escallops gules; Cotgrave Roll.

Grandison, Oto de, a baron 1299—bore, paly (6) argent and azure on a bend gules three escallops or, (F.); Nobility Roll, &c. (ascribed to another OTES (‡) in Dering Roll); paly (4) Harl. Roll; paly (8) in Jenyns' Ordinary; azure, three palets argent, &c.; Guillim Roll.

Grandison, Sir Otho de, knighted at the capitulation of Calais 1348—bore, paly (6) argent and azure, on a bend gules three buckles, tongues erect bendwise or (F.); Ashmole Roll.

Grandison, Sir William de, banneret, a baron 1299—bore, at the battle of Falkirk 129?, and at the siege of Carlaverock 1300, paly (6) argent and azure, on a bend gules three eaglets displayed or (F.); Nobility, Parliamentary, and Arundel Rolls. Borne also by Sir PIERS at the battle of Boroughbridge 1322, by Sir WILLIAM at the siege of Calais 1345-8, by another WILLIAM at the siege of Rouen 1418, and by Sir THOMAS, K.G., 1370.

Granem, William (or GRAVEM)—(H. III. Roll) bore, azure, six spur-rowells or, a label (5) gules; Howard Roll. See GRANDIN.

Vic de Gronvile Euſt. Gronville Gefrai d. Greſelere

Joan de Fraundon Perſ d. Grete Will Ḡ'o'ȯl

Henry de Grey Johṅ d. Grey. Johan de Grey

nichol de Grey Joan d. Grey Lo Baſtard de Grey

Granville, Richard de—(H. III. Roll)
bore, argent three clarions gules garnished
argent (F.); Arden Roll. It is surmised that
the clarions were originally the canting coat
of CLARE, and that their arms were erroneously
ascribed at an early period to GRANVILLE.

‡**Gras, Nicole le**—(H. III. Roll) bore, azure,
three lyonceux rampant 2 and 1 or, a chief
argent (F.); Dering and Howard Rolls.

Grauncurt v. **Grancourt.**

Gravesend, Sir Stephen, of Kent—(E. II.
Roll) bore, or, four eagles displayed sable, a
canton ermine; Parliamentary Roll.

Greece; The Palialologi; Emperors of
—(H. III. Roll) bore, or a sea lyon sable.
Segar Roll. F.

Greenacre, Richard—(R. II. Roll) bore,
sable, three covered cups 2 and 1 argent
(ROBERT bore it with an annulet argent),
Surrey Roll; ascribed, colours reversed and a
torteux for difference, to another RICHARD
in Jenyns' Ordinary.

Greene (——), a Knight—(H. VI. Roll) bore,
argent, a bugle horn between th ee gryphons'
heads erased sable; Arundel Roll.

Greene, Henry—(R. II. Roll) bore, argent,
a cross engrailed gules; Surrey Roll.

Greene, John—(E. II. Roll) bore, chccquy or
and azure, a bordure gules; Jenyns' Roll.
THOMAS MAUDUIT bore these arms.

Greene, Richard — (E III. Roll) bore,
argent, a fess dancettée sable, in chief three
leopards' faces of the last; Jenyns' Ordinary.

Greene, Thomas – (R. II. Roll) bore, azure
three bucks passant (perhaps statant) 2 and 1
or; Surrey Roll.

Greenford, John - (E. III. Roll) bore, vert a
lyon rampant tail estant or; Jenyns' Ordinary.

Greet v. **Grete.**

Gregory, Sir Henry, Knight banneret—
(H. VI. Roll) bore, azure two bars double
cotised or, in chief a lyon passant of the last;
Arundel Roll.

*[**Gregory, John** (E. I.)—bore, or, two bars
and in chief a lyon passant azure.—Shirley.]
F.

Greilly, Piers de (GRELY)—(H. III. Roll)
bore, or, on a cross sable five escallops
argent; Howard Roll; and so in Surrey Roll
for MONS. PIERS LE CAPITOU DE BOUCH,
K.G. and a founder. See pedigree Anstis'
"Order of the Garter," vol. I. Introduction,
page 8. See also BUCH *ante.*

Grelle, Thomas de, banneret, and a baron
1308 – bore, gules, three bendlets enhanced or
(F.), a bend and two bendlets above; Nobility
Roll 1303, Gresley 131c, borne also by JOHN,
ROBERT, and Sir THOMAS. (Another JOHN
bore the field argent, JOHN MAUVEISIN carried
the same). Another ROBERT bore four bendlets. The coat for Sir THOMAS is tricked in
Harl. 6137, fo. 40', probably erroneously, as
bendy (8) or and gules.

Greley, Sir William, Knight banneret—
(H. VI. Roll) bore, gules three bars or;
Arundel Roll.

Grendale, Sir Walter de, of Yorkshire—
(E. II. Roll) bore, ermine, a cross patonce
gules; Parliamentary Roll.

Grendon, Raffe de, banneret, a baron 1299,
sealed the Barons' letter to the Pope 1301—
bore, at the battle of Falkirk 1298, argent, two
chevrons (a chevron et demy) gules (F.);
Nobility, Parliamentary, and Arundel Rolls.
Ascribed also to a ROBERT in Arden and St.
George Rolls.

Grendon, Sir Robert de, of co. Leic.—
(E. II. Roll) bore, argent, two chevronels gules,
a label (3) vert, Parliamentary Roll—(ascribed
also to a JOHN, in Jenyns' Ordinary)—a label
(3) argent, each point vaire of the last and
sable; Ashmole Roll.

Grendon, Sir John, of Warwicks.—bore, at
the first Dunstable tournament 1308, vaire
argent and sable a baston or (F.); Ashmole
and Parliamentary Rolls.

Grensted v. **Grimsted.**

[**Grenville, Sir Eustace,** of Wootton
(E. I.)—bore, vert, on a cross argent five torteaux.—Shirley.] F.

*Gresley, Sir Piers** and **Geffray**—(E. II.
Roll) bore, vaire, ermine and gules; Parly.,
Arden and St. George Rolls. Sir PIERS DE
GREYLLIE, Knight banneret (H. VI. Roll), and
JOHN (E. II. Roll) bore the reverse; another
JOHN bore, vaire argent and gules; Surrey
Roll.

Gresley, John—(E. III. Roll) bore, barry (6)
azure and ermine, tricked, vaire ermine and
gules, two bars azure; Jenyns' Ordinary.
RAYNELL DE BREWES bears the same arms.

Grete, Pers de—(H. III. Roll) bore, argent,
a saltire engrailed azure (F.); Arden and St.
George Rolls.

*[**Grevel, William,** of Milcote 1401—bore,
sable, on a cross engrailed or five pellets, a
bordure engrailed argent; borne by WILLIAM
of Campden, with the addition of a mullet in
the first quarter, and his son JOHN bore 10
annulets in lieu of the pellets.—Shirley.] F.

Grey—For differences see Harleian MS. 1481
folios 17, 19, 20, 21, 23, 25, 26, 27.

Grey, Henry le, of Codnor, banneret, a baron
1299, sealed the Barons' letter to the Pope
1301—bore, at the battle of Falkirk 1298, and
at the siege of Carlaverock 1300, barry (6)
argent and azure (F); Nobility and Parliamentary Rolls; borne also by JOHN, K.G.
(? of Rotherfield, a founder, see), in Surrey,
Arden and St. George Rolls; by REGINALD
or REYNAUD in the Segar Roll; by Sir
RICHARD, Kt. banneret in Arundel, Parliamentary, Dering, Glover and Howard Rolls.
Le Sr de GRAYE also bore these arms at the
siege of Rouen in 1418 (? Baron DE WILTON).
The Camden Roll affords the solitary example
of the colours reversed, Harl. MS. 6137 fo. 70.

Grey, Sir Reginald de, of Wilton, banneret,
a baron 1297, sealed the Barons' letter to the
Pope 1301—bore, at the battle of Falkirk 1298,
barry (6) argent and azure a label (3, 5) gules;
Nobility and Dering Rolls. Sir HENRY
bore the same at the battle of Boroughbridge
1322 (F.); Segar Roll; also ascribed to Sir
JOHN, Knight banneret; Parliamentary Roll.

ROGER,
LORD GREY
DE RUTHYN,
1352-3.

*From a Rubbing
of the
Hastings Brass
in
Elsing Church,
Norfolk.*

Grey, John DE SANDIACRE—bore, at the second Dunstable tournament 1334, barry (6) argent and azure a label gules besantée ; borne also by RICHARD of Sandiacre, in Ashmole Roll and Jenyns' Ordinary.

Grey, Sir John de—bore, at the first Dunstable tournament 1308, barry (6) or and azure in chief three torteaux (F.), borne also by ADAM (H. III.) ; St. George Roll, and Le Sr DE RYTHYNE temp. (H. VI.) ; Nobility and Surrey Rolls (R. II.). See Monumental Brass for ROGER, 1st Lord Grey de Ruthyn. See Sir THOMAS.

Grey, Sir John de, banneret, of Rotherfield, Oxon—bore, at the battle of Falkirk 1298, and at the siege of Carlaverock 1300, barry (6) argent and azure a baston gules (F.) ; as did his son JOHN, of Rotherfield. K.G. and a founder (a baron in 1338), at the second Dunstable tournament 1334 ; the same arms are ascribed with a baston, bendlet or bend to Sir JOHN of Essex, RICHARD, and ROBERT in the Parliamentary, Surrey, and Arden Rolls. In the Carlaverock Roll the arms for Sir JOHN are argent four bars azure a bend engrailed gules. F.

Grey, Sire Nichol de—bore, at the battle of Boroughbridge 1322, barry (6) azure and argent, a baston gobony of the second and gules (F.), (gobony or and gules in Nativity Roll) ; tricked, barry argent and azure in the Ashmole MS.

Grey, Sir Nichol, of Essex—(E. III. Roll) bore, barry (6) argent and azure a baston gobony or and gules ; gules and or for ROBERT of Barton in Rydal ; Parliamentary Roll and Jenyns' Ordinary.

Grey ——, (E. III. Roll) bore, barry (6) argent and azure on a bend gules three fleurs-de-lys or ; Ashmole Roll.

Grey, John de—(H. III. Roll) bore, barry (6) argent and azure, a bend of lozenges gules (F.) Howard Roll ;—argent, a bend fusily gules, St. George Roll.

Grey, Sir Richard—(E. I. Roll) bore, barry azure and argent florettée or ; Nativity Roll.

Grey, Reginald de—(H. III. Roll) bore, argent, three bars azure, a label (5) gules, probably a mistake for barry, as before ; Howard Roll.

Grey, Richard de—(H. III. Roll) bore, argent, three bars azure over all a bend gules bezantée, probably a mistake for barry, as before ; Howard Roll.

Gray, Sir R.—(H. VI. Roll), and **Sir Thomas**—(E. III. Roll) bore, gules, a lyon rampant and a bordure engrailed argent ; Atkinson and Ashmole Rolls. Borne also by Sir JOHN, K.G., temp. H. V.

*****Gray, Thomas,** of Heton—(E. III. Roll) bore, gules, a lyon rampant argent and a bordure engrailed or ; Jenyns' Ordinary. See HETON.

Grey, Sr (——) LE BASTARD—Knighted at the capitulation of Calais 1348, bore, gules, a lyon rampant and a border engrailed argent, a baston sable. F.

Grey, Sir Thomas—(E. I. Roll) bore, gules, a lyon rampant and a bordure indented argent, a baston azure ; Nativity Roll.

Gray (——), a Knight—(H. VI. Roll) bore, gules, a lyon rampant argent a bordure engrailed gobony of the second and or ; Arundel Roll.

Grey, Sir Thomas, of co. Lancs.—(E. II. Roll) bore, gules, seven mascles 3, 3, 1 conjoined or, a baston gobony argent and azure ; Parliamentary Roll.

*****[Grey, Sir Thomas de,** of Suffolk, E. I.—bore, barry (6) argent and azure, in chief three annulets gules.—Shirley.] F. Ancestor of the Earls of Stamford, who discarded the annulets ; this family also bore the coat of CORNERTHE, as in the next entry.

Gray, Sir Thomas, of Cambridgeshire—(E. III. Roll) bore, azure, a fess between two chevronels gules ; Ashmole Roll. The coat of CORNERTHE.

Grey, Sir Thomas, of Suffolk—(E. II. Roll) bore, azure, a fess between two chevronels or a label (3) gules ; Parliamentary Roll.

Greystoke, Sire Rauf de (formerly FITZ WILLIAM)—bore, at the battle of Boroughbridge 1322, burulée (12) azure and argent, three chaplets gules (F.), also burulée (14, 16) argent and azure, &c. ; Ashmole and Surrey Rolls and Jenyns' Ordinary ; grandson of RALPH FITZ WILLIAM. See that name.

Greystoke, John de, a baron 1295, sealed the Barons' letter to the Pope 1301, with 3 lozenges ; see also Monumental Slab—according to the Rolls he bore, gules, three cushions or (F.) Nobility Roll ; (? argent), in St. George Roll ; or and gules in Jenyns' Roll, and apparently in the Holland Roll.

Greyton, Sir John v. **Gayton.**

Griffith, Evan ap, of Wenunwyn—(H. III. Roll) bore, or, a lyon rampant gules (F.) ; Arden and St. George Rolls.

Griffith, David ap—(H. III. Roll) bore, quarterly or and azure four lyonceux passant gardant counterchanged (F.) ; St. George Roll.

Griffith, Llewellin ap—(H. III. Roll) bore, quarterly or and gules four lyons passant counterchanged ; St. George and Norfolk Rolls.

Griffin, John (E. III. Roll) and **Thomas** (R. II. Roll)—bore, sable, a gryphon segreant argent, armed or ; Cotgrave and Surrey Rolls.

Griffith, Ydon, lord of—(H. VI. Roll) bore, azure, a gryphon segreant armed and membered gules ; "his daughter married to Lord Hoo" ; Atkinson Roll.

Griffith, Owen ap—(H. III. Roll) bore, gules, a cross or between four eagles displayed argent ; Arden Roll.

Griffith, Rees, ap—bore, at the second Dunstable tournament 1334, gules on a fess dancettée argent between three lyonceux passant or as many martlets sable (F.) ; six lyonceux passant in the Surrey Roll. F.

Grimeles, Robert de—(H. III. Roll) bore, argent, on a cross gules five spur-rowells or ; Howard Roll.

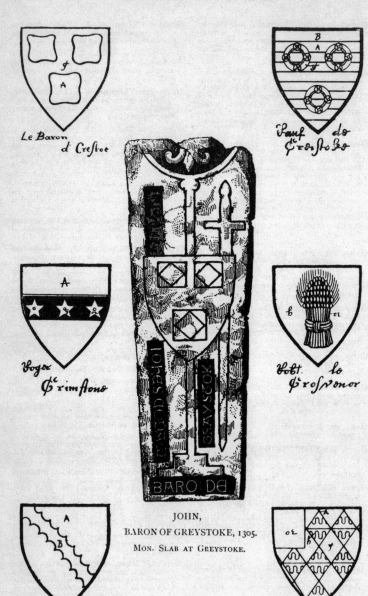

Le Baron
d' Crestoc

Rauf de
Greystoke

Roger
Grimstone

Robt. le
Grosvenor

JOHN,
BARON OF GREYSTOKE, 1305.
MON. SLAB AT GREYSTOKE.

Will Cronoy

Auncel d' Gise

Grimsby, John de—(R. II. Roll) bore, per chevron sable and argent in chief two cinquefoyles pierced of the field; Surrey Roll.

Grimsted, Sir Andrew (or GRENSTED), of Somerset—(E. II. Roll) bore, gules three barrulets vair; Parliamentary Roll.

*****Grimston, Gerrard de** and **Roger de**— (E. III. Roll) bore, argent on a fess sable, three mullets (6) or pierced gules (F.); Surrey Roll and Jenyns' Ordinary.

Grimston, Roger—(E. III. Roll) bore, argent, on a fess vert three mullets pierced or; Jenyns' Ordinary.

Grindale, John—(E. III. Roll) bore, burulée (12) argent and gules a cross patonce (flory in trick) sable; Jenyns' Ordinary.

Groney, Sir William, of Normandy—bore, at the siege of Calais 1345-8, argent, a bend engrailed azure (F.); surname uncertain, perhaps BORNEY or GORNEY.

*****[Grosvenor, Sir Robert le,** 1389—bore, azure, a garb or, on the determination of the Scrope and Grosvenor controversy.—Shirley.] F.

Grose *v.* **le Grose.**

Guise, Auncell de (GYSE)—(H. III. Roll) bore, lozengy gules and vair a canton (sometimes a quarter) or (F.); St. George and Howard Rolls—tricked vair and gules in the Dering Roll (perhaps erroneously tricked paly for lozengy as in facsimile from Camden Roll) —masculée in Jenyns' Ordinary, &c., blasoned by Jenyns as the arms of the Earl of Kent reversed and a canton or. In Arden Roll another AUNCEL bears a spur-rowell sable, on the quarter, see Sir JOHN.

Guyse, Walter de—(F. II. Roll) bore, masculée vair and gules, on a quarter or a fleur-de-lys azure; tricked, lozengy gules and vert, &c.; Jenyns' Roll.

Guise, Sir John (GYSE), of Bucks—(E. II. Roll) bore, gules, six lozenges 3, 2, 1, vair, on a canton or a spur-rowell sable.

Gu(y), Imberd—(H. III. Roll) bore, azure, three pheons 2 and 1 argent; St. George Roll. Names doubtful. See also GEY.

Guldeford, Sir John de, of the North— (E. II. Roll) bore, argent, two bars gemelles sable; Parliamentary Roll; three bars H. 6137 fo. 28[b].

Gurney, Sir Thomas de, of Somerset— bore, at the first Dunstable tournament 1308, paly (6) or and gules; paly (8) or and azure in Parliamentary Roll. F.; and so ascribed to AUNCELL and MAHEU, in St. George and Surrey Rolls.

Gurnay, Sir John, of Essex, Knight— (H. VI. Roll) bore, azure, on a bend cotised argent, three leopards' faces gules jessant-de-lys or; Arundel Roll.

†**Gurney, Johan de**—(H. III. Roll) bore, argent, a cross engrélée gules; Norfolk Roll.

Gurnay, Maheu—(E. II. Roll) bore, or, three piles meeting " in poynt " gules; Jenyns' Roll. Sir MATHEW said by some to have been a Companion of the Garter 1386.

Gurney, Robert de—(H. III. Roll) bore, or, a lyon rampant sable a border gules; Glover Roll.

Gurney, Sir William (BORNEY or GORNEY), of Normandy—bore, at the siege of Calais 1345-8, argent, a bend engrailed azure; name doubtful.

SIR ROBERT HARCOURT, K.G. 1461, DIED 1471; AND HIS WIFE MARGARET, DAU.
OF SIR JOHN BYRON, OF CLAYTON, CO. LANC., KT., A LADY OF THE ORDER.
TOMB IN THE CHURCH NEAR STANTON HARCOURT, OXON.
From Anstis' History of the Garter.

H

Habervile, Henry—(H. III. Roll) bore, azure, in dexter chief point a lyon passant gardant or, in sinister chief point and in base a cinquefoyle pierced of the last ; Arden and St. George Rolls. (F.) See TUBERVILLE.

Hacche, Sir Eustace de, banneret, baron 1299, sealed the Barons' letter to the Pope, 1301—bore, at the battle of Falkirk 1298, and at the siege of Carlaverock 1300 or, a cross engrailed gules (F.) ; ascribed also to JOHN in Jenyns' Ordinary.

Haccombe, Sir Stephen, of Devon— (E. II. Roll), and JOHN (E. III. Roll) - bore, argent, three bendlets sable ; Parliamentary Roll and Jenyns' Ordinary.

Ha(c)ket, Henry—(H. III. Roll) bore, or, three bendlets gules, a label (5) azure ; Arden Roll.

‡**Hacket, Rauf de**—(H. III. Roll) bore, sable, crusily and three hake-fish hauriant 2 and 1 (F.), Dering Roll ; hauriant in pale in Ashmole MS. ; ascribed to WILLIAM in Howard Roll.

Ha(c)ket, Sir Walter, of Derbyshire—bore at the first Dunstable tournament 1308, argent, two bend gules (F.), Parliamentary and Ashmole Rolls ; ascribed also to JOHN in Jenyns' Ordinary.

Ha(c)kley (——), armiger ; slain at the siege of Calais 1347—bore, azure, a chevron between three bugles argent, a crescent for difference.

Ha(c)klute, Sir Edmond, of Salop— (E. II. Roll) bore, argent, on a (plain) bend between two cotises dancettée gules three mullets or. Sir RICHARD bore it with trefoyles in place of mullets on the bend ; Parliamentary and Ashmole Rolls.

Hacklute, Sir Richard—bore, at the first Dunstable tournament 1308, argent, on a bend gules cotised sable three fleurs-de-lys (F.), LEONARD (R. II. Roll) bore, mullets or pierced azure, instead of fleurs-de-lys, on the bend — another trick makes the bend and cotises sable, both in Surrey Roll.

Hacklute, John de—(E. III. Roll) bore, argent, a fess gules and another in chief dancettée of the last ; Jenyns' Ordinary.

Ha(c)kelute, Sir Walter, of Salop - (E. II. Roll) bore, gules, a fess dancettée between three Danish hatchets erect or, Parly. Roll ; fess indented argent, Harl. 6137, fo. 27ᵇ.

Hacon, Sir Hubert (HAKON), of Norfolk —(E. II. Roll) bore, sable, two bars vaire argent and vert ; Parliamentary Roll.

Hadham, Thomas—(E. III. Roll) bore, argent a bend between six round buckles 3 and 3 azure, tongues to the base ; Jenyns' Ordinary.

*****Haggerston, Robert**—(E. III. Roll) bore, azure, on a bend cotised argent three chess-rooks (? rightly billets) in bend of the field (F.) ; Jenyns' Ordinary. Originally, a scaling ladder between two leaves in allusion to a Hazlerigg heiress ; Shirley.

Hake, Andrew—(E. III Roll) bore, azure, three bars or, a bordure engrailed argent ; Jenyns' Roll.

Hakenbeche, Reginald—(R. II.) bore, or two bars argent ; Surrey Roll.

Hales, Sir Stephen de—(E. III. Roll) bore, sable, a chevron between three lyonceaux rampant argent ; Ashmole and Surrey Rolls.

Hallys ——, (E. III. Roll) bore, burulée (12) argent and azure, on a canton gules a lyon passant or ; Ashmole Roll.

Halnsby (——), a Knight—(H. VI. Roll) bore, or, a saltire sable ; Arundel Roll.

Halouton, Sir Robert de, of co. Cambridge—(E. II. Roll) bore, argent on a bend gules three eaglets displayed or (F.) ; Parliamentary Roll and Harl. MS. 6137, fo. 63. ROBERT DE HAULTON took up the cross in the last Crusade 1270.

Hal(o)uton, Sir Thomas de, neyr.—bore, at the battle of Boroughbridge 1322, and another THOMAS bore at the second Dunstable tournament 1334, gules a lyon rampant argent crowned or, and so also did Sir THOMAS, knighted at the capitulation of Calais 1348 ; (F.) Ashmole Roll.

Hal(o)ughton, Thomas de —(H. III. Roll) bore, gules, three bucks' heads cabossed or (F.), St. George Roll ; one buck's head in Arden Roll.

Halowton, Thomas de—(E. II. Roll) bore, gules "a palme" argent - a sinister hand apaumée couped in trick ; Jenyns' Roll.

Halsham, Sir Henry—bore, at the siege of Rouen 1418, or, a chevron engrailed between three lyons' heads erased gules (F.)—the field argent and leopards' faces for a Suffolk Knight ; Arundel Roll.

Haltham, Sire Francis de—bore, at the battle of Boroughbridge 1322, azure an escarbuncle or (F.)

SIR JOHN HARSYCK.

IN SOUTHACRE CHURCH, NORFOLK, 1384, 8 R. II. *From Boutell.*

Halton, John de—(E. III. Roll) bore, argent, two bars azure in chief two escallops gules—ROBERT bore three hurts in chief; Jenyns' Ordinary. See HALOUTON.

Hameldene, Sir Laurence de. of Suffolk, Knight - bore at the first Dunstable tournament 1308, argent, fretty gules, florettée at the points or—a fret in Parliamentary Roll. F.

Hamerton, John—(E. III. Roll) bore, argent, a fess between three lyonceux rampant, tails fourchée, sable; Jenyns' Ordinary.

*****Hamerton, Lawrence**—(E. II. Roll) bore, argent, three martels (*vel* hammers) sable (F.); Jenyns' Roll.

Hamlowe *v.* **Hanlowe.**

Hamlyn, Sir John, of Leicestershire, Knight—bore at the first Dunstable tournament 1308, and at the battle of Boroughbridge 1322, gules, a lyon rampant ermine crowned or (F.); Parliamentary and Ashmole Rolls. Cotgrave gives—gul- s, a lyon or guttée de poix, for HAMLYN. F.

Hamme *v.* **Hawnes.**

Hamme, Sir John de, of Surrey—(E. II. Roll) bore, azure, a chevron between three demi lyons rampant or; Parliamentary Roll.

Hammon, Sir John (or HANLOWE), of Oxon (E. II. Roll) bore, argent, a lyon rampant azure guttée d'or; Parliamentary Roll.

Hampton, Sir John (HOPTON)—bore, at the siege of Calais 1345-8, argent, a fess counter compony or and azure, between six martlets gules. F.

Hancett, Hamond (or HAMO HAUTEYN)—(H. III. Roll) bore, gules, three bends or; Arden Roll; a label (5, 6) argent; St. George Roll. Compare with tricks in copies of the Arden Roll. F.

Haningfylde, Sir William, of Essex—(E. II. Roll) bore, or, a chevron sable; Parliamentary Roll.

Haninvile, Henry de—(H. III. Roll) bore, sable, crusily fitchée and a bend or (F.); St. George Roll. Surname doubtful. See also HANVILE.

Hanitune, John de—(E. I. Roll) bore, quarterly argent and sable (F.), same as FITZ UMFREY; Guillim and Segar Rolls.

Hankeford ——(E. III. Roll) bore, argent, two cotises dancettée sable; Ashmole Roll.

Hanley (——) a Kentish Knight—(H. VI. Roll) bore, vert, a saltire engrailed argent; Arundel Roll.

Hanle(y), Sir John (of Kent)—bore, at the first Dunstable tournament 1308, gules, three crescents or; argent in Parliamentary Roll. F.

‡**Hanlo, Nichole de**—(H. III. Roll) bore, or, two chevronels gules on a quarter of the second a crescent argent (F.); Dering, Howard and Camden Rolls.

Hanlowe, Sir John de (of Oxon)—bore, at the first Dunstable tournament 1308, argent, a lyon rampant azure guttée d'or (F.); Parliamentary Roll (as of Kent) and Jenyns' Ordinary. See also HAMMON.

Hansarde, Robert de—bore, at the siege of Carlaverock 1300, gules, three mullets argent (F.); ascribed also to GILBERT, JOHN, Sir JOHN, and to Sir ROBERT of co. Lincs., Parliamentary, Nativity, and Ashmole Rolls; in some the mullets are pierced, in others mullets of six pierced occur, *i.e.* spur-rowells; estoiles, not mullets for GILBERT are tricked in Glover Roll; and azure, not gules, for the field is ascribed to WILLIAM in Norfolk Roll.

Hansard, Sir John, of Lincolnshire—(E. II. Roll) bore, gules, a bend between six mullets 3 and 3 argent; Parliamentary Roll.

Hansted *v.* **Hausted—Hawsted.**

Hanvile, Sir Thomas de, of Bucks—(E. II. Roll) bore, azure, a fess dancettée between three " girfauks " (falcons) or, tricked as martlets; Parliamentary Roll—a plain fess gules in Ashmole Roll. See HANINVILE.

Harcla, Sir Andrew, of Cumberland baron 1321, Earl of Carlisle 1322—bore, at the first Dunstable tournament 1308, argent, a cross gules, in the cantel a martlet sable (F.) (as HARTECLEY); Parliamentary and Nativity Rolls.

Harcla, Sir Nicholas (or MICHEL HERTE-CLAWE) of Cumberland—(E. II. Roll) bore, argent, a cross gules; Parliamentary Roll; borne also by one of this name with a label (5) azure (F.) knighted at the capitulation of Calais 1348.

*****Harcourt, Sir John de**, of co. Leic. banneret—bore, at the first Dunstable tournament 1308, gules two bars or, as also did ROGER, K.G., slain at the siege of Calais 1347: (F.) Parliamentary Roll [borne by JOHN ƒ Sir JOHN, with a label (3, 5) azure] the reverse ascribed to another JOHN, RICHARD, THOMAS, and WILLIAM; Parliamentary, Segar, Glover, and St. George Rolls.

Harecourte, Robert de—(H. III. Roll) bore, gules, two bars ermine; Howard Roll.

Hardeshull, Sire Johan de—bore, at the battle of Boroughbridge 1322, and at the second Dunstable tournament 1334, argent, semée of martlets gules, a chevron sable (F.), in Ashmole MS.; 3 and 3 martlets at Dunstable, 7 and 4 in Ashmole Roll, and in Jenyns' Ordinary for THOMAS.

Hardeshull, Sir William, of co. Leic.— (E. II. Roll) bore, or a cross engrailed gules in the first quarter a martlet vert; Parliamentary Roll. See HARCLA.

Harding, Sir Edmond, of Kent, Kt.— (H. VI. Roll) bore, gules, a lyon rampant ermine over all a chevron or; Arundel Roll.

‡**Hardres, Robert de**—(H. III. Roll) bore, ermine, a lyon rampant gules debruised by a chevron or; Dering Roll; the field argent in Howard Roll. F.

Harlaston (——) a Suffolk Knight—(H. VI. Roll) bore, argent, a chevron sable, *quarterly with*, argent a fess ermine cotised sable; Arundel Roll.

Harleston, Thomas—(E. III. Roll) bore, argent, a saltire gules between four fleurs-de-lys azure; Jenyns' Ordinary; JOHN NEVILL, of Lincolnshire, bears these arms.

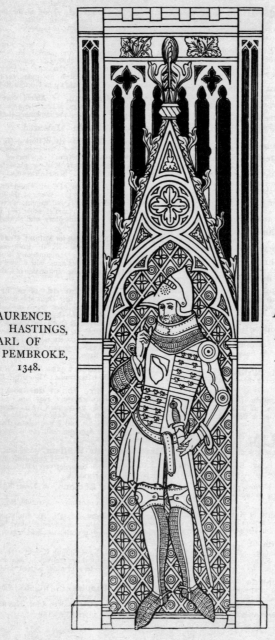

LAURENCE
HASTINGS,
EARL OF
PEMBROKE,
1348.

*From a Rubbing
of the
Hastings Brass
in
Elsing Church,
Norfolk.*

Harley, Sir Richard (HARLEE) of Salop—
(E. II. Roll) bore, or, a bend cotised sable ;
Parliamentary Roll. F.

Harling, ——, (E. III. Roll) bore, azure,
florettée argent ; Ashmole Roll.

Harlyns (——), a Suffolk Kt.—(H. VI. Roll)
bore, argent, a unicorn rampant sable horned
and unguled or ; Arundel Roll. F.

Harington v. **Haverington.**

*****Harington, Sir John de** (HAVERINGTON)
a baron 1324—bore, at the first Dunstable
tournament 1308, sable fretty argent (F.) ;
Parliamentary Roll, &c. ; this coat was also
carried at the siege of Rouen 1418. Sir JOHN,
Sir MICHAEL and Sir JOHN appear to have
differenced with a label (3) gules ; Ashmole,
Nativity, and Surrey Rolls.

Harington (——), a Knight—(H. VI. Roll)
bore, quarterly (1) sable fretty argent, a label
(3) gules ; (2) argent, a saltire gules ; (3) gules,
three escallops argent ; (4) argent, a cross
patonce sable ; Arundel Roll.

Harington, Sir T.—(H. VI. Roll) bore,
sable, a fret argent, a label (5) gules, *quarterly
with*, argent a cross patée sable ; Atkinson
Roll.

Harington, Sir James, of Hornby—(E. IV.
Roll) bore, argent, fretty sable ; with crest ;
Ballard Roll.

Harington, Sir John de—(E. II. Roll)
bore, or, a chief gules, over all a bend azure ;
Parliamentary Roll ; the field argent, Harl.
MS. 6137 fo. 19.

Harington, John de—(E. III. Roll) bore,
or, a chief gules over all a bend sable ; Jenyns'
Ordinary.

Harpden, Sir William de, of Oxon—
(E. II. Roll) bore, argent a mullet pierced
gules, Parliamentary Roll ; a Suffolk Knight
of this surname, bore (H. VI.) argent on a
mullet gules, a besant charged with a martlet
sable ; Arundel Roll.

[**Harpur** (——) of Rushall – a plain cross—but
bore the arms of Rushall, argent, a lyon
rampant within a bordure engrailed sable.—
Shirley.]

Harsick, John de—(E. III. Roll) bore, or,
a chief indented (4) sable ; Jenyns' Ordinary,
a fess in Ashmole Roll. See Monumental Brass.

Hartford v. **Hertford.**

Hartford, Robert—(E. III. Roll) bore,
argent, on a fess sable three harts' heads
cabossed or ; Jenyns' Ordinary.

Hartford, Thomas, of Badsworth—(E. III.
Roll) bore, argent, a lyon purpure masculy
or ; Jenyns' Ordinary.

Harthull, Sir Richard de, of co. Derby—
(E. II. Roll) bore, argent two bars vert ; Par-
liamentary Roll — also ascribed to JOHN
HERTHILL, though tricked vair, in Jenyns'
Ordinary.

Hartwell, —— (HAREWELL), an Essex?
Knight—(H. VI. Roll) bore, sable, a buck's
head cabossed argent between the attires a
cross patée of the last ; Arundel Roll. F.

Haseley (——) a Suffolk Knight—(H. VI. Roll)
bore, argent, a fess gules between three hazle
nuts or, husks and stalks vert ; Arundel Roll.
F.

*****[Hasilrig, Thomas,** of Fawdon — bore,
argent, a chevron between three hazel leaves
slipped vert.—Shirley.] F.

Haslarton v. **Heslarton.**

Hassell v. **Hansard.**

Hastang, Sir Robert de, of co. Staff., a
baron 1311—bore, at the first Dunstable
tournament 1308, azure, a chief gules, over all
a lyon rampant or – Guillim, Segar and Parliamentary Rolls. Sir ROBERT signed the
Barons' letter to the Pope 1301 and sealed
with a lyon fourchée over all a barrulet in
chief ; see also Jenyns' Ordinary and Parliamentary Roll).

Hastang, Sir John de (HASTINGES)—bore
at the first Dunstable tournament 1308, azure,
a chief gules over all a lyon rampant argent ;
ascribed also to HUMFRY in Arden and St.
George Rolls, and to Sir PHILIP, of Staff., in
Parliamentary Roll.

Hastang, Sire Thomas de—bore, at the
battle of Boroughbridge 1322, azure, a chief
gules over all a lyon rampant or, and a label
argent (F.) ; ascribed also to Sir JOHN, *f* Sir
ROBERT, of co. Staff., in Parliamentary Roll.

Hastang, Sir Nichol de (of co. Staff.)—
bore, at the first Dunstable tournament 1308,
azure, a chief gules, a lyon rampant or debruised by a baston argent (F.) ; Parly. Roll.

Hastang, Rafe de—(H. III. Roll) bore,
azure, a chief or and over all a lyon rampant
gules ; Howard Roll.

Hasthorp, Sire Johan de—bore, at the
battle of Boroughbridge 1322, argent on a
bend sable three martlets or. F.

Hasting [Drew de—bore, before the Conquest per fess or and vert, a bull rampant
counterchanged ! ! Jenyns' Roll, Add. MS.
12,224 fo. 48ᵇ.]

Hastings, John de, Baron of Bergeueny
1299, signed the Barons' letter to the Pope
1301 and sealed with a cross which with the
field is charged with fleurs-de-lys—He bore, at
the siege of Carlaverock 1300, or, a maunch
gules (F.) ; Nobility, Parliamentary and Arundel Rolls ; borne also by HENRY, Sir HENRY,
and by JOHN (*t*) in Dering Roll ; also by Le
Seigneur DE HASTINGES at the battle of
Boroughbridge 1322—and by LAURENCE, Earl
of PEMBROKE, at the siege of Calais 1345-8 ;
HASTINGS is borne quarterly with VALENCE on
the Monumental Brass.

Hastings, Sir Edmund de, banneret,
a baron 1299 (brother of JOHN, Baron of
Bergavenny)—bore, at the battle of Falkirk
1298, and also at the siege of Carlaverock 1300,
or, a maunch gules a label (5) sable (*argent,* in
Nobility Roll ; *vert* in Parly. Roll.) Sir EDMUND
had from Edward I. the Scottish Earldom of
Menteith on the deprivation of Earl ALAN.
On becoming surety for Sir JOHN DRUMMOND,
a prisoner in England, and having succeeded
to his lands and apparently his arms, barry
wavy of six, he so sealed the Barons' letter to
the Pope 1301 as "D'n's de Enchincholmok"
=Inchmahome ; see Sir JOHN's effigy *ante.*

SIR HUGH HASTINGS.

FROM THE HASTINGS BRASS IN ELSING CHURCH, NORFOLK, 1347.

Hastings, Sir Hugh, of Gressing, Norfolk, summoned to a council in 1342—bore, at the siege of Calais 1345, or a maunch gules a label (3) azure (F.) see Monumental Brass; borne also by Sir NICHOLAS at the first Dunstable tournament 1308; Cotgrave and Parliamentary Rolls, and by Sir WILLIAM (E. I.) Harl. Roll. Another Sir WILLIAM, banneret (E. II. Roll), bore, a label (3) charged with the arms of Pembroke, checquy argent and azure three martlets gules; Parliamentary Roll.

Hastings, Sir William de—bore, at the first Dunstable tournament 1308, or, a maunch within an orle of martlets gules, a label (3) argent, each pendant charged with four barrulets azure, for Valence.

Hastings, Le Sr. de (——) bore at the siege of Rouen 1418, or, a maunch gules, *quarterly with*, gules, a bend argent.

Hastings, Sir John, of co. Glouc. (brother of Sir WILLIAM)—bore, at the first Dunstable tournament 1308, HASTINGS within a bordure of Valence, also blasoned burulée argent and azure, eight martlets in orle gules, over all on an escocheon (of HASTINGS), or a maunch gules. (F.) Sir WILLIAM, banneret, bore it also (E. II.); Parliamentary Roll. See another Sir WILLIAM, who bore HASTINGS, with a label of PEMBROKE.

Hastings, Sir Edmund, bore (erroneously it is said) at the battle of Falkirk 1298, or, three maunches gules a label azure (F.) (see Sir EDMUND above); tricked without the label in Jenyns' Ordinary for OSMOND and EDMOND—the field argent for another EDMUND in Jenyns' and Arundel Rolls.

Hastyng (——) Knight (H. VI. Roll)—bore, argent a fess gules between three maunches sable; Arundel Roll.

Hastings, Sir Rafe — Knighted at the capitulation of Calais 1348, argent, a maunch sable. (F.) Ashmole and Cotgrave Rolls, &c.

Hastings, Sir Miles de, of Oxon—(E. II. Roll) bore, or, a fess in chief two mullets gules; Parliamentary Roll. Sir PHILIP bore it differenced with a label (3) azure at the first Dunstable tournament 1308.

Hastings, Sir Robert de, of Cambridge-shire—(E. II. Roll) bore, ermine, on a chief azure two mullets or; Parliamentary Roll.

‡**Hastings, William de**—(H. III. Roll) bore, argent, a fess between three lozenges azure. (F.) Dering, Howard and Camden Rolls.

Hatfeld, Thomas, Bishop of Durham—bore, at the siege of Calais 1345-8, ermine a chevron sable (sometimes gules) impaled on the dexter with the arms of the See of Durham. F.

Hatfeild, Thomas—(E. II. Roll) bore, sable, a chevron between three lyonceux rampant argent, Jenyns' Roll; the chevron or and a mullet sable in Jenyns' Ordinary.

Hatthorpe, Robert—(E. III. Roll) bore, sable, a chevron engrailed or; Jenyns' Ordinary.

Hauberk, John—(R. II. Roll) bore, argent on a bend sable three cinquefoyles pierced or, Surrey Roll.

Hausted, Sire John de, of Rutland, a baron 1322—bore, at the battle of Borough-bridge 1322, and at the second Dunstable tournament 1334, gules a chief checquy (counter-compony in trick) or and azure, a baston ermine; Jenyns' Ordinary, Parliamentary Roll and Ashmole MS. Sir ROBERT bore it at the first Dunstable tournament 1308 with a bend argent; Parliamentary and Harl. Rolls—ascribed with a bend sable to another JOHN in Jenyns' Ordinary.

Hausted, Sir John de—bore, at the first Dunstable tournament 1308, argent on a bend vert three eaglets displayed or. F.

Haute, Sir William, of Kent, Kt.—(H. VI. Roll) bore, per pale azure and gules, a lyon rampant argent, *quarterly with*, or, a cross engrailed gules; Arundel Roll. See HAWTE.

Hauteville, Sir Geffrey (of Devon or Cornwall)—bore, at the battle of Borough-bridge 1322, sable crusily and a lyon rampant argent. (F.) Parliamentary Roll —ascribed crusily fitchée to THOMAS in Jenyns' Ordinary.

Hauteyn, Hamo, *v.* **Hancett.**

Hautot, Richard de—(H. III. Roll) bore, ermine, on a chief gules three mullets (6) or. (F.) Arden and St. George Rolls. See HOTTOT.

Havering, Sir John de, banneret, baron of Grafton 1269—bore, at the battle of Falkirk 1298 (argent) a lyon rampant, gules collared or; tail fourchée and collared azure in Nobility and Parly. Rolls; on his seal affixed to the Barons' letter to the Pope, the lyon is fourchée but not collared.

Havering, Richard and **William de**—(H. II. Roll) bore, argent, a lyon rampant tail fourchée gules; St. George Roll and Jenyns' Ordinary.

Havering, Sir John—(E. III. Roll)—bore, argent, crusily fitchée and a lyon rampant tail fourchée and renowée all gules (F.); Ashmole Roll; ascribed in the same Roll with a label (3) azure to—HAVERINGHAM.

Havering, John ap, of Essex—(H. II. Roll) bore, argent, three lyons' heads erased sable. Arundel Roll. F.

Havering, John de—(H. III. Roll) bore, azure, on a fess argent, three escallops gules. (F.) St. George Roll.

Haveringham, *v.* **Sir John Havering.**

Haverington, Sir John de - (E. II. Roll) bore, argent, three hinds' heads couped gu es, a label (3) or; Parliamentary Roll.

Haverington, Sir John de (*v.* HARINGTON) - bore, at the first Dunstable tournament 1308, argent fretty argent; St. George and Nativity Rolls. Sir MICHAEL differenced with a label (3) or, at the first Dunstable tournament 1308 —but with a label gules (F.) in Nativity Roll.

Haversage, Matthew de (HAVERSEGGE) (H. III. Roll) bore, paly argent and gules, a chief of the first; Glover Roll.

Haversham, Nicol de—(H. III. Roll) bore, azure, crusily and a fess argent; St. George Roll.

Haward *v.* **Howard.**

Geoff   do
Hautevillo

Th. Hawkston

Hanimo

nich Hawto

Vic. Hoigdam

mald do Helinn

Herei
d. Hereford

Robt
d. Hereford

Vogdr
Horgam

Robt. Horowardo

Henri de Heriet

Joan Herun

Hawarde, Sire William, of Norfolk, baron 1296 bore, gules crusily and a bend argent ; Nobility and Parliamentary Rolls.— Sire WILLIAM HAUWARDE *v.* HAYWARDE, bore the same at the battle of Boroughbridge 1322. See also HOWARD.

Hawkewoode, John—(R. II. Roll) bore, argent, on a chevron sable three escallops of the field ; Surrey Roll.

Hawkston, Sir Thomas — bore, at the siege of Calais 1345–8 argent, on a fess gules three hawks or. F.

Hawley, Thomas — (R. II. Roll) bore, azure, a saltire engrailed argent ; Surrey Roll.

Hawnes —— (HAMME), of Suffolk, Kt.— (H. VI. Roll) bore, vert, two fish (lucies) hauriant addorsed and embowed argent; Arundel Roll. F.

Hawte, Nicholas — bore, at the siege of Rouen 1418 argent, on a bend azure three lyons passant or. (F.) Called HAWE in Ashmole MS. See HAUTE.

Haye, see **De la Haye.**

Heath *v.* **Hethe.**

Heaton *v.* **Heton.**

Heaton, William — (E. IV. Roll) bore, argent, on a bend engrailed sable three bulls' heads erased of the field, *quarterly with*, argent, a Moor's head wreathed ppr. between three fleurs-de-lys sable ; with crest ; Ballard Roll.

Hebden, William — (E. III. Roll) bore, ermine, five fusils conjoined n fess gules ; Surrey Roll and Jenyns' Roll and Ordinary.

Hedingham, Richard de (E. III. Roll) bore, argent a chevron between three fleurs-de-lys sable, ermine in blason ; Jenyns' Ordinary.

Heggios, Huge (*sive* BRUGES) (H. III. Roll) bore, gules, bezantée and a chief ermine ; St. George Roll.

*[**Heigham, Richard,** *c* 1340 –bore, sable, a fess checquy or and azure, between three horses' heads erased argent.—Shirley.] F.

Hekin, Sir Richard, knighted at the siege of Calais 1348—bore, sable, a gryphon segreant argent. F.

Hellifield, William de—(E. III. Roll) bore, argent, two bends undée sable - same as RIC. DE STAPLETON ; Jenyns' Ordinary.

Hellis, Raufe de—(H. III. Roll) bore, sable, a bend argent ; Howard Roll.

Helyon, Richard and **Walter**—(H. III. Roll) bore, or, a buck's head cabossed sable ; Arden Roll and Jenyns' Ordinary. F.

‡**Helyon, Walter**—(H. III. Roll) bore, or three bucks' heads couped sable. F. (azure in Ashmole MS.) ; Dering and Howard Rolls.

Heminghall, Sir Raffe de, of Norfolk— (E. II. Roll) bore, or, on a fess between two chevronels gules three escallops argent ; Parliamentary and Ashmole Rolls. THOMAS bore the escallops or ; Surrey Roll.

*[**Heneage, John,** 10 E. III.– bore, or, a greyhound courant sable between three leopards' faces azure, a border engrailed or.—Shirley.] F.

Hengrave, Sir Edward, of Suffolk - (E. II. Roll) bore argent, a chief dancettée (4) gules ; Parliamentary, Ashmole and Surrey Rolls, dancettée of 3 points in Jenyns' trick.

‡**Henre, William de**—(H. III. Roll) bore, gules, a cross argent, a label (5) azure ; Dering and Howard Rolls.

Henyngham (——), of Suffolk, Kt.—(H. VI. Roll) bore, quarterly or and gules a bordure sable poudré of escallops argent ; Arundel Roll.

Herbert, H—— (E. I. Roll) bore, ermine, a chief vaire or and gules over all a baston sable ; Harl. Roll.

Herbert, ——, (E. III. Roll) bore, per pale azure and gules three lyonceux rampant or ; Ashmole Roll. See FITZHERBERT.

Hercy, Sir Hugh, of Langford, co. Derby —(E. III. Roll) bore, gules, a chief argent ; Ashmole Roll. Sir HUGH, of co. Leic. (E. II.) differenced with a label (3) azure ; Parliamentary Roll—reversed in Jenyns' Roll. F.

Hercy, Henry del—(H. III. Roll) bore, azure, a cross or. (F.) St. George Roll.

Herdebye, John de—(E. III. Roll) bore, gules, billettée (5–5) and a fess dancettée argent ; Jenyns' Ordinary.

Hereford, Earl of, *v.* **Bohun.**

Her(e)ford, Sir Henry de—(E. III. Roll) bore, gules, three eaglets displayed argent ; Ashmole Roll. HENRY, differenced with a label (5) azure ; St. George Roll. F.

Hereford, Robert de—(H. III. Roll) bore, or on a chief dancettée azure three annulets argent. (F.) Arden Roll.

Hereford (——) **de**—(H. III. Roll) bore, or, a pair of wings conjoined gules ; Arden Roll.

Hereward, Sir Robert, of Norfolk—(E. II. Roll) bore, azure, a fess gobony gules and vert between three owls argent ; Parly. Roll. F.

Hereward, Sir Robert, of Cambridgeshire — (E. II. Roll) bore, checquy or and azure on a bend gules three eagles displayed argent ; Parly. Roll—in some checquy azure and or &c.

Herham, Sir Roger, Knighted at the capitulation of Calais 1348—bore, undée en lung argent and gules. F.

‡**Herice, Henry de**—(H. III. Roll) bore, or three hedgehogs passant in pale sable (F.) ; Howard Roll—2 and 1 passant sable in Dering Roll. Boars in Ashmole MS.

‡**Heringod, William,** and **Sir John,** of Sussex—(E. II. Roll) bore, azure, crusily and six herring hauriant 3, 2, 1, or (F.) ; Dering, Camden, Parly., and Howard Rolls.

Herle, Sir Robert—(E. III. Roll) bore, gules, a chevron between three drakes (shovellers) argent ; Ashmole and Surrey Rolls.

Heron, Sir Godard, Sir Roger, John, (F.), **Sir John,** of Essex, **Sir Odinel,** of Northumberland—(E. II. and E. III. Rolls) bore, azure three herons passant argent ; Nativity, Glover, Parly., and St. George Rolls—tinctures reversed in Parly. Roll for Sir ODINELL. See HERONVILE, THOS.

Heron, Sir Roger and **Sir William**— (E. II. Roll) bore, gules, three herons passant argent ; Parly. and Ashmole Rolls—GERARD differenced with an annulet, and WALTER with a cross crosslet, both in chief, or ; Surrey Roll.

Simon d: Herſwell

Horpy

Hēnʳ Hoſo

witt Hoſkoth

John Ałhо Hоtzo

Hoob do Hotzoman

Gilbert do Hixton

William Hill

Bogor Hillary

Robᵗ d Hilton

Bobort Hilton

Hodoy

Heron, John—(R. II. Roll) bore, gules, a chevron between three herons argent—WILLIAM bore the chevron engrailed; Surrey Roll and Jenyns' Ordinary.

Heron, William—(H. III. Roll) bore, gules, crusily or, a heron argent; Arden and St. George Rolls.

Herondel, John de—(H. III. Roll) bore, gules, billettée and three lyons' rampant or; Arden Roll.

Heronvile, John de—(H. III. Roll) bore, sable, two lyons passant argent crowned or; Arden Roll.

Heronvile, Thomas—(E. II. Roll) bore, azure, three herons passant argent, same as HERON; Jenyns' Roll.

Hersham, Simon de (or HERSTUN)—(H. III. Roll) bore, sable three spur-rowells gules; Arden Roll. Written HERSHEW in Harl. MS. 4965 fo. 10.

Herswell, Simon de—(H. III. Roll) bore, sable, three mullets (6) or (F.); St. George Roll.

Hertford, Earl of, v. **Clare.**

Hertford, ——, (E. III. Roll) bore, sable, five lozenges in bend or; Ashmole Roll.

Herthill, John—(E. III. Roll) bore, argent two bars vert; tricked vair; Jenyns' Ordinary. See HARTHILL.

Hertlington, Henry—(E. III. Roll) bore, argent, a lyon rampant crowned gules; Jenyns' Ordinary.

Hertlow, Sir William—(E. III. Roll) bore, argent, three gemelles gules; Ashmole Roll.

*****Hervy (——)**, an Essex Knight—(H. VI. Roll) bore, gules, on a bend argent three trefoyles vert; Arundel Roll, F. See HOUN.

Hese v. DE LA HESE, HOSE, and HUSSEY.

Hese, Henry—(H. III. Roll) bore, or, three eagles displayed 2 and 1 sable (F.); Arden and St. George Rolls.

Hesy, Hugh le—(R. II. Roll) bore, or, on a fess sable a lyon passant gardant argent; Surrey Roll.

Hese, John de la—(E. III. Roll) bore, argent, a fess sable between three lyonceux rampant 2 and 1 gules; Jenyns' Ordinary, and in Roll as HESSEE, and as Sir JOHN DE LA HOESE, a Berkshire Knight, in Parly. Roll.

Hesilton, Elynaud de—(E. III. Roll) bore, argent, a saltire gules between four torteaux; Jenyns' Ordinary.

*****[Heskayte, Sir William**, 1275—bore the arms of FYTTON—argent, on a bend sable three garbs or; Shirley.] F.

Heslarton, Sir Thomas de, of Yorkshire —(E. II. Roll) bore, gules, six lyonceux rampant 3, 2, 1, argent crowned or; Parly. Roll—borne also by WALTER in Jenyns' Ordinary and by Sir RAFFE in Ashmole Roll—in which is the same cont, within a bordure engrailed argent – but without Christian name.

Heslarton, Thomas—(E. II. Roll) bore, argent, on a chevron gules three lyonceux passant gardant or; Jenyns' Roll and Ordinary, borne also by ROBERT DE BOLTON.

Heslington, Richard de—(H. III. Roll) bore, argent, three crescents sable; Norfolk Roll.

Hethe, John Atte—(E. III. Roll) bore, gules, on a bend cotised argent three heathcocks sable; Ashmole Roll. F.

Hethersett, ——, (E. III. Roll) bore, azure, a lyon rampant gardant or—another with a mullet sable on the lyon's shoulder; Ashmole Roll.

Hethman, Sir Raol (or Roos) **de**—bore, at the first Dunstable tournament 1308, azure, fretty argent, a bordure indented or. F.

Heton, Sir Gilbert de—bore, at the first Dunstable tournament 1308, gules, a cross flory or (F.) same arms as Sir WILLIAM LATYMER.

Heton, Henry de—(R. II. Roll) bore, azure, a lyon rampant argent; Surrey Roll.

Heton, Sir John—(E. III. Roll) bore, argent, on a chief indented sable two fleurs-de-lys or; Ashmole Roll.

Heton, Thomas de—(E. III. Roll) bore, gules, a lyon passant argent; Jenyns' Ordinary.

Heton, Thomas de—(E. II. Roll) bore, vert, a lyon rampant and a bordure engrailed argent; Jenyns' Roll. See GREY of Heton.

Hevere, William de—(E. I. Roll) bore, gules, a cross argent and a label (5) azure. (F.) Camden Roll.

Heverley, Walter—(E. III. Roll) bore, or, on a bend azure three escallops of the first. Jenyns' Ordinary.

Hewes, Sir Richard, of Cornwall or Devon —(E. II. Roll) bore, gules, fretty and a quarter argent; Parliamentary Roll.

Hewys, Thomas—(E. IV. Roll) bore, argent, fretty gules, and a quarter ermine; Jenyns' Ordinary.

Hewick, Sir Nicholas—(E. III. Roll) bore, gules, bezantée and a lyon rampant argent; Ashmole Roll. MALTHAM RATCLIFFE carryes the same; Jenyns' Ordinary. NICHOLAS bore, vair (tricked vert), six besants 3, 2, 1, Jenyns' Ordinary.

Heworth, Thomas—(E. III. Roll) bore, argent, a saltire between four mullets pierced gules; Jenyns' Ordinary.

Heyham, Sir Roger de, of Beds.—(E. II. Roll) bore, paly (6) argent and azure on a chief gules three escallops or; Parliamentary Roll.

Heyham, Sir William—(E. I. Roll) bore, bendy (6) argent and gules a label (3) azure; Holland Roll—gules three bends argent and a label azure in Harl. MS. 6137 fo. 40.

Hildyard, Sir Robert—(E. I. Roll) bore, azure, three mullets or; Nativity Roll.

*****[Hill, William**, R. II.—bore, ermine, on a fess sable a castle argent.—Shirley.] F.

Hillarye, Sir Walter, of Norfolk—(E. II. Roll) bore, argent, a fess chequy or and sable, a mullet of the last; Parliamentary Roll. F.

Hillary, Roger—(E. III. Roll) bore, sable, crusily fitchée and three fleurs-de-lys argent; Ashmole and Surrey Rolls. F.

JOICE, Widow of Sir JOHN TIPTOFT, daughter of
EDWARD CHARLETON, LORD POWIS.
MON. BRASS IN ENFIELD CHURCH, MIDDLESEX, OB. 1446. *After Boutell.*
Arms of Holland and Charleton.

Hilton, Sir Robert de, banneret, a baron 1297—bore, at the battle of Falkirk 1298, argent, two bars azure. (F.) Nobility, Parliamentary and St. George Rolls.

Hilton, Sir Robert de—bore, at the battle of Boroughbridge 1322, argent, three chaplets gules. (F.) Borne also by ROBERT, of Swyne, in Holderness, one of the founders of the Abbey there ; Jenyns' Roll and Ordinary.

Hilton, John, of Westmorland — (E. III. Roll) bore, sable, three annulets or, in chief two saltorelles argent ; Jenyns' Roll.

Hincle(y), Sir John de—(E. III. Roll) bore, gules, a chevron engrailed argent ; Ashmole Roll.

Hindley, Randolph (*alias* CULCHETH)—(E. IV. Roll) bore, sable a gryphon segreant argent ; with crest ; Ballard Roll.

Hingham, Sir John, of Norfolk—(E. II. Roll) bore, per pale or and vert a fer de moulin gules ; Parliamentary Roll.

Hinlington, William de (HINELYNTON) —(H. III. Roll) bore, argent, a label (5) gules ; Howard Roll —probably a foreigner.

Hinton, John de—(E. III. Roll) bore, gules, on a bend argent cotised or three martlets sable ; Jenyns' Ordinary.

Hippeswell, Alan de—(E. III. Roll) bore, argent, a fer de moulin sable ; Grimaldi Roll.

Hodey (———), a Suffolk Kt.—(H. VI. Roll) bore, argent, a fess indented point in point, vert and sable, plain cotised counterchanged, a bordure engrailed of the second ; Arundel Roll. F.

Hodnet, Ede de — (H. III. Roll) bore, quarterly per fess indented argent and gules, a label (5) azure. (F.) Arden and St. George Rolls—as EDGAR.

Hoese, Sir John de la, *v.* **Hese.**

Hoggesharde, Sir Thomas—bore, at the siege of Calais 1345-8, vaire argent and gules, a bordure sable bezantée. (F.) ? HOGHSHEAD.

Hoggeshawe, Robert de (or SHIREBROK) (H. III. Roll) bore, vair, a chief or, over all a bend gules. (F.) St. George Roll—on the bend three mullets of six points ; Harl. MS. 6589.

Hoghton, Sir Alexander, of Hoghton, in Lancs.—(E. IV. Roll) bore, argent, three bars sable ; Ballard and Ashmole Rolls.

*Hoghton, Richard de—(E. I. Roll) bore, sable, three bars argent ; Arundel, Surrey and Jenyns' Rolls. JOHN (E. I.) differenced with a mullet sable ; Jenyns' Roll. Another RICHARD differenced with a label (3) gules ; Surrey Roll.

Hoghton, Sir Robert (or HOUGHTON), of Notts—(E. III. Roll) bore, azure, three bars humettée argent ; Ashmole Roll.

Holand *v.* **Holland.**

Holbech (———), an Essex ? Kt.—(H. VI. Roll) bore, argent, a chevron engrailed sable ; Arundel Roll.

Holebrooke, Sr. (———) **de,** a Suffolk Kt.— (E. II. Roll) bore, or crusily and a chevron gules ; Parliamentary and Ashmole Rolls ; as-cribed also to RICHARD in Arden and St. George Rolls—same as THOMAS DE BROKEHOLE in Glover Roll.

Holewell, Sire Walter—bore, at the battle of Boroughbridge 1322, ermine, on a bend gules three crescents or.

(Holester) ——— (E. I.) ; bore, or, a cross gules ; Harleian Roll ; OLWESTER or OLUNSTER.

Holford, Sir George—(E. IV. Roll) bore, argent, a greyhound passant sable ; with crest ; Ballard Roll.

Holgomb, John de (? HOLCOMBE)—(R. II. Roll) bore, or, on a bend sable three mullets argent ; Surrey Roll.

Holland *v.* **Hoyland.**

Holland, Sire Richard de—bore, at the battle of Boroughbridge 1322, azure, semée of escallops and a lyon rampant gardant, argent. F.

Holland, Richard—(E. III. Roll) bore, sable, semée of escallops and a lyon rampant argent ; Jenyns' Ordinary.

Holland, Thomas, K.G. 1376, a founder, Earl of Kent (1381) bore, England within a bordure argent. Seal 1371—represented without the bordure in the Monumental Brass to JOICE, Lady TIPTOFT.

Holland, John, K.G. 1381, Earl of Holland, Duke of Exeter 1443-7—bore, England within a bordure azure Holland ; or ; Surrey Roll.

Holand, Sir Robert de, banneret, a baron 1314—bore, at the first Dunstable tournament 1308, azure, florettée and a lyon rampant gardant argent (F.) ; Parly. and Arundel Rolls ; borne also by HENRY and JOHN, Surrey Roll and Jenyns' Ordinary, and by Sir OTES, K.G. (a founder), and Sir THOMAS, K.G., at the siege of Calais 1345-8, the former then differenced with a cross patée gules on the lyon ; ALAN (ancestor of HOLLAND of Denton) differenced with a bendlet gules ; Harl. MS. 1481 fo. 58[b].

Holand, Sir John—bore, at the battle of Boroughbridge 1322, gules, two bars, the martlets in bordure argent (F.) ; generally blasoned and tricked six martlets 3, 2, 1 argent, see next blason. This coat is wrongly ascribed to Sir THOMAS BENGHAM in the Ashmole MS.

Holande, Sir Hugh—(E. III. Roll) bore, argent, two bars and nine martlets in orle, 4, 2, 3 gules ; Ashmole Roll.

Hollingshed, Sir Hugh de—(E. II. Roll) bore, argent on a cross sable a mullet or ; Parliamentary Roll.

Holme, John, of North Holme—(E. II. Roll) bore, or, three fleurs-de-lys azure ; Jenyns' Roll.

Holteby, Sir Henry de, of Lincolnshire— (E. II. Roll) bore, azure, fretty argent, a chief of the last ; Parliamentary Roll.

Hondesacre, Rafe (E. III.) and **William** (H. III. Roll) bore, ermine, three chess-rooks 2 and 1 gules (F.) ; Jenyns', Arden, and St. George Rolls.

Honford, ———, (E. IV. Roll) bore, sable, an estoile argent ; with crest ; Ballard Roll.

*[Honywood, Edmund de, of Postling, Hen. III.—bore, argent, a chevron between three hawks' heads erased azure. —Shirley.] F.

Hoo, St. John (E. III. Roll) bore, gules, on a fess indented argent two mullets pierced sable ; Ashmole Roll.

Ł Ł̄
HoggoſŁ qʳ

Edm̄. de
Honywood

Ɓoɓī Hoplon

Wal d Hopetone

Jofn de Horbyrs

Jogn Horo

wiſt
de Horneb

Jogn
de Hoŋum

Will deHotot

Jofn Hovilo

wiſh Haward

Jognde Howard

Hoo, Sir Robert de, of Beds—(F. II. Roll) bore, quarterly argent and sable a bend gules; Parliamentary Roll.

Hoo, Robert de — (H. III. Roll) bore, quarterly sable and argent, a bendlet or; Arden and St. George Rolls.

Hoo, Thomas and **William de**—(E. II. Roll) bore, quarterly argent and sable (F.); Jenyns' and Surrey Rolls. To MOUNSYER Hoo (Sir THOMAS) the reverse are ascribed at the siege of Rouen 1418; borne also by THOMAS, Lord Hoo and HASTINGS, K.G. 1445; K. 402 fo. 27.

Hookes, Sir William, of Yorkshire—(E. II. Roll) bore, azure, a fess between three fleurs-de-lys or; Parliamentary Roll.

Hopeton (——), a Suffolk Knight—(H. VI. Roll) bore, argent, a chevron azure; Arundel Roll.

Hopton, Sir John (or HAMPTON)—bore, at the siege of Calais 1345–8, argent, a fess counter-compony or and azure between six martlets gules—blasoned checquy.

Hopton, Robert—(E. II. Roll) bore, argent, two bars sable each charged with three mullets pierced or; Jenyns' Roll. F.

Hopton, Walter de, of co. Glouc.—(H. III. Roll) bore, gules crusily and a lyon rampant or (F.); Arden, St. George, and Parliamentary Rolls. Sir WALTER bore it crusily fitchée (E III.) Ashmole Roll.

Horbourne, Sir John (or HORBURY), of Yorkshire—(F. II. Roll) bore, barry (8) argent and azure, a bend gules (F.); Parliamentary Roll; barry of six and a bendlet; Guillim and Camden Rolls.

Hore, John—bore, at the siege of Rouen 1418, sable, three cinquefoyles argent pierced gules. F.

Horkeslev, Sir William, of Essex, Kt.—(E. II. Roll) bore, ermine, on a chief indented azure three lyonceux rampant or; Parliamentary Roll.

Horne, Gerard, *v.* **Hournis.**

Horne, Sir John de, of Sussex—(E. II. Roll) bore, gules, a fret vair; Parliamentary Roll.

Horne (——), an Essex ? Knight—(H. VI. Roll) bore, gules, three bugle horns sable, another impaling, gules, crusily fitchée and three crescents argent; Arundel Roll.

+Hornes, William de—(H. III. Roll) bore, argent, three hunting horns in pale gules garnished sable. (F.) Dering Roll.

Horsley, Robert—(E. II.) bore, gules, three horses' heads erased argent bridled sable; Jenyns' Roll.

Horsele, Robert de—(R. II. Roll) bore, sable, three cinquefoyles 2 and 1 pierced argent —Surrey Roll and Jenyns' Ordinary.

Hoscarle, Sir Thomas—(E. III. Roll) bore, azure, three battle axes erect argent; Ashmole Roll—see HURSTAL; surname doubtful.

Hoscott, Sir Robert de, of Bedfordshire—(E. II. Roll) bore, azure, a cross patée ermine between four roses gules; (tricked patonce); Parliamentary Roll; a cross patée argent, Guillim Roll; and a cross formée argent; Surrey Roll.

Hose, Nichole de la (HESE or HEUSE)—(H. III. Roll)—bore, argent, three (men's) hose 2 and 1 gules; Arden and Howard Rolls. F.

Hoter, Thomas—(H. III. Roll) bore, gyronny (12) ermine and gules; Arden Roll.

Hotham, John de—(E. III. Roll) bore, or, on a bend sable three mullets argent pierced gules (F.), being the arms of DE MAULEY with three mullets on the bend; Jenyns' Ordy. Sir JOHN differenced it with a martlet gules, at the battle of Boroughbridge 1322.

*Hotham, John, of Boudlay—(E. III. Roll) bore, burulée (12) argent and azure, on a canton or a martlet sable; Jenyns' Ordinary.

Hotote (——), a Suffolk Kt.—(H. VI. Roll) bore, azure, a cross moline argent; Arundel Roll.

Hotot, Sir John, of co. Glouc.—(E. II. Roll) bore, azure, on a chevron cotised or between three crescents argent, two bars gemelles of the first; Parliamentary Roll—chevron plain in Harl. 6137 fo. 26.

Hotot, Richard *v.* **Hautot** and **Robert Hoscott.**

Hotot, Sir William de, of co. Glouc.—(E. II. Roll) bore, azure, a chevron or, between three crescents argent; Parliamentary Roll. F.

Houghton, Sir Robert, of Notts—(E. III. Roll) bore, azure, three bars humettée argent; Ashmole Roll. STEPHEN DE HOUTON took up the cross in the last Crusade 1270. See also HOGHTON.

Houn, Hervey de—(H. III. Roll) bore, vert, on a bend argent three escallops gules; Arden Roll.

Hournis, Gerard — (E. III. Roll) bore, argent, a lyon rampant gardant gules—another with a label (3) azure; Ashmole Roll—surname almost illegible.

Hovell, Sir Hugh, of Suffolk, **Richard, Robert** and **Sir Robert**—(H. III. Roll) bore, sable, a cross or; Arden, Parly. and St. George Rolls. Sir STEVEN, also of Suffolk, bore it at the first Dunstable tournament 1308, differenced with a label (3) argent (F.) in Parly. Roll.

Hovile, Hugh—(H. III. Roll) bore, argent, a bend azure, a label (5) gules. (F.) Arden and St. George Rolls.

Hovile, Sir John—bore, at the first Dunstable tournament 1308, quarterly or and gules, a martlet of the second. F.

*Howard, Sir John, of Norfolk—(E. II. Roll) bore, gules, crusily and a bend argent; Parliamentary Roll. Sir WILLIAM bore it at the battle of Boroughbridge 1322 (F.), tricked crusily fitchée in the Ashmolean MS.; Arden and St. George Rolls (F.) in Arundel Roll; WILLIAM in Jenyns' Ordinary.

*Howard, Sir William—bore (1297) gules, crusily fitchée and a bend argent; Nobility Roll; his son, Sir WILLIAM, bore it also at the battle of Boroughbridge 1322; Ashmole MS., as before mentioned. Sir JOHN, Admiral of the North fleete, bore it at the siege of Calais 1345–8 (F.); Surrey Roll, Jenyns' Roll and Ordinary (borne also by HUNTINGFIELD). This coat appears in the Ashmole Roll differenced with a fleur-de-lys azure and apparently with an ermine spot on the bend in Harl. MS. 1481 fo. 83.

Henry. Huband.

Will
d Hugeford

Robt. de Huggam

Joan d. Hulle

Ricꝰ de Hulton

Dns. de Hundiscote

John
Huntyngfeld

Malk. de
Hungerford

Will
d Hursthalo

Will Hurleton

Henri Houso

John de Huyse

Hoyland. Sir William de, of Lancashire —(E. II. Roll) bore, sable, a cross patonce or ; Parliamentary Roll.

Huband, Henry—(H. III. Roll) bore, sable three fleurs-de-lys argent. (F.) St. George Roll.

Huckford, Sir Walter de (HUKEFORD), of Gloucestershire—(E. II. Roll) bore, or, an eagle displayed sable, collared argent ; Parliamentary Roll.

Hudehovile, John de—(H. III. Roll) bore, per pale or and azure a saltire counterchanged. St. George Roll. See HUNTE.

*****[Hudleston, Sir John de,** banneret, sealed the Barons' letter to the Pope 1301—bore, at the battle of Falkirk 1298, and at the siege of Carlaverock 1300, gules, fretty (6) argent. (F.) Arundel, Parliamentary and Guillim Rolls—a fret for JOHN, in Surrey Roll. JOHN DE KOKESALTON bore the reverse ; Arden Roll.

Hudleston, Sir Adam—bore, at the first Dunstable tournament 1308, and at the battle of Boroughbridge 1322, gules, fretty argent, a label (3) azure ; Nativity Roll (in which RICHARD occurs without the label). Also ascribed to Sir RICHARD in the Parliamentary and Ashmole Rolls, and to Sir RICHARD, THE NEPHEW, also in Parliamentary Roll—the label is sometimes tricked or.

Hudleston, Sir Adam de—(E. II. Roll) bore, gules, fretty argent, a bordure indented or , Parliamentary Roll.

Hugarde, Andrew, of Danemarke —(E. III. Roll) bore, azure, a sun argent ; Jenyns' Roll. HUGH GARD bore, azure a sun or ; Harl. MS. 6589 fo. 37. See OGARD.

Hugford, William de—(H. III. Roll) bore, azure, three bucks' heads cabossed or. (F.) Arden and St. George Rolls.

Hugford, William de (or HUNGERFORD) —(E. II. Roll) bore, azure, three palmes (? quills in trick) 2 and 1 or. (F.) Jenyns' Roll.

‡Hugham, Robert de—(H. III. Roll) bore, argent, five chevronels sable. (F.) Dering Roll ; six in Ashmole MS., four in Howard Roll, are ascribed to ROBERT DE HUHAM.

Hull, Sir Edward, K.G. (H. VI.)—bore, argent three crosses crosslet fitchée in bend azure between two bendlets gules ; K. 402, fo. 35.

Hulle, John de—(H. III. Roll) bore, azure, an eagle displayed argent. (F.) Arden and St. George Rolls.

Hulls, Sir Richard de, of Cambridgeshire —(E. II. Roll) bore, azure an eagle displayed argent. a baston gules ; Parliamentary Roll.

*****[Hulton, Richard de,** (32 E. I.)—bore, argent, a lyon rampant gules.— Shirley.] F.

Hundescote, Sire de — (E. I. Roll) bore, ermine, a bordure gules. (F.) Camden Roll.

Hungerford, Walter, K.G., a baron 1426— bore, at the siege of Rouen 1418, sable, two bars argent, in chief three plates, *quarterly with,* per pale dancettée gules and vert a chevron or (F.) tricked in the Ashmole MS., gules, a chevron and in chief a dancettée (3) argent— the paternal coat in Jenyns' Ordinary. Sir E. with his proper difference (unnamed) and Sir R. with a label (5)—in Atkinson Roll. HUNGERFORD, THE BASTARD, slain at the siege of Calais 1345-8, bore, barry (6) sable and argent, in chief three plates.

Hunte, Sir Oswald, Kt. banneret—(H. VI. Roll) bore, per pale argent and sable a saltire counterchanged ; Arundel Roll.

Huntercombe, Sir Walter, banneret, a baron 1295, sealed the Barons' letter to the Pope 1301—bore, at the battle of Falkirk 1298, and at the siege of Carlaverock 1300, ermine two gemelles gules. (F.) Nobility, Arundel and Parliamentary Rolls—ascribed to RAUF in St. George Roll. WILLIAM took up the cross in the last Crusade 1270.

Huntercombe, Gerard de, of Loreyne— HONDERCOMBE, rightly GONDRONVILLE.

Huntingdon, Earl of. See SCOTT.

Huntingfield, Roger de, of Bradenham, a baron 1297, sealed the Barons' letter to the Pope 1301—bore, or, on a fess gules three plates ; Nobility Roll. Sir WILLIAM, banneret, (F.) bore the same ; Parliamentary, Arundel and other Rolls.

Huntingfield, Sir Piers de, of Kent— (E. II. Roll) bore, quarterly or and gules a bordure sable ; Parliamentary Roll.

‡Huntingfield, Peres de—(H. III. Roll) bore, quarterly or and gules, a label (5) sable ; Howard Roll—on each pendant three plates (F.) Dering Roll ; besants in Ashmole Roll.

Huntingfield, Sir Walter, of Herts— (E. II. Roll) bore, gules, on a bend three lyonceux passant sable. (F.) Parliamentary Roll. Ascribed also to JOHN in Jenyns' Roll and Ordinary. WILLIAM took up the cross 1270.

‡Huntingfield, Cael, Sael, or Saer de— (H. III. Roll) bore, gules, crusily fitchée and a bend argent. (F.) Dering, Howard, and St. George Rolls. Same arms as HOWARD.

Huntingfield, Sir William de—(E. I.) bore, argent, crusily (8, 13) and a bend gules ; Holland Roll.

Hurleton, William—(E. IV. Roll) bore, four ermine spots in cross (F.) with crest ; Ballard Roll.

Hurstal, William—(H. III. Roll) bore, azure, three axes argent. (F.) St. George and Arden Rolls—ascribed to Sir THOMAS HOSCARLE in Ashmole Roll.

Hussey, Henry de, of Sussex, baron 1295 —bore, ermine three bars gules ; Nobility, Parliamentary and Ashmole Rolls ; ascribed to another HENRY (‡) in the Dering Roll ; tricked, barry (6) in Arden and Norfolk Rolls.

Hussey, Sir John (of Hants or Wilts.), knighted at the capitulation of Calais 1348— bore, or, a cross vert. (F.) Ascribed also to Sir ROGER in Ashmole Roll — another Sir JOHN (E. II.) differenced with a label (3) gules ; Parliamentary Roll and Jenyns' Ordinary.

Hussee, John de la—(E. III. Roll) bore, gules, a fess between two chevronels ermine ; Jenyns' Ordinary.

Hutton, William, of the Forest—(E. II. Roll)—bore, gules, a fess sable between three cushions tasselled argent ; Jenyns' Roll.

*****[Huyshe, John de** (13th cent.), bore, argent, on a bend sable three lucies naiant of the first. —Shirley.] F.

Hyde ——, a Knight—(H. VI. Roll) bore, gules, a saltire engrailed or, a chief ermine ; Arundel Roll.

Hyde ——, (E. IV. Roll) bore, azure, a chevron between three lozenges or ; with crest ; Ballard Roll.

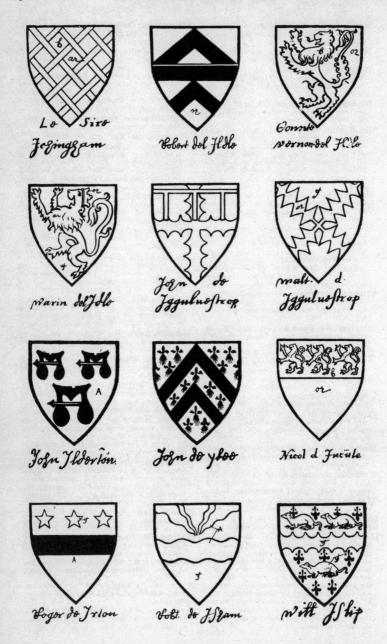

Lo Sire
Jeʒinggam

Robert del Hlo

Connte
vernon del Hlo

warin del Hlo

Jorn de
Jggulnestrop

walt. d.
Jggulnestrop

John Jldorton

John de yloo

Nicol d Jnsule

Roger de Jrton

Robt. de JSeam

Witt JSlip

I

Ichingham, le Sire—bore, at the siege of Rouen 1418, azure, fretty argent, (F.) See ECHINGHAM.

Idle, Sire John del—bore, at the battle of Boroughbridge 1322, gules crusily and a lyon passant argent ; not gardant in Ashmole MS.

Idle, Sire Robert del, banneret—bore, at the battle of Boroughbridge 1322, or, a fess between two chevrons sable ; and with the chevrons gules, ascribed to ROBERT in Camden Roll. Same as JOHN and ROBERT DE LISLE.

Idle, Count Vernon del - (E. I. Roll) bore, or, a lyon rampant azure. (F.) Camden Roll. See ISLE.

Idle, Sire Warin del, banneret—bore, at the battle of Boroughbridge 1322, gules, a lyon p.ssant (gardant) argent, crowned or (F.) ; not gardant in the Ashmole copy. Same as GERARD DE L'ISLE.

Ilderton, John—(E. III. Roll) bore, argent, three water-bougets sable ; Jenyns' Ordinary. F.

Illey, Sir Philip de, of Lincolnshire—(E. II. Roll) bore, gules, an eagle di-played or, a baston azure ; Parliamentary Roll. WILLIAM took up the cross in the last Crusade 1270.

Illey, John de - (E. III. Roll) bore, ermine, two chevrons sable. (F.) Ashmole Roll. Same as Sir JOHN DE LISLE.

Ilsley, Sir Robert de—(E. III. Roll) bore, or, two gemelles sable and in chief three ogresses ; Ashmole Roll.

Imberd, William or **Guy** - (H. III. Roll) bore, azure, three fleurs-de-lys 2 and 1 argent. Arden and St. George Rolls these names are usually reversed, and the surname written GU. F.

Incule, Nichol de—(H. III. Roll) bore, or, on a chief azure three lyonceux rampant argent. (F.) Arden and St. George Rolls; same as DE MENNE. See also LISLEY.

Inge, Sir William, of Beds.—(E. II. Roll) bore, or, a chevron vert ; Ashmole, Parliamentary and Nobility Rolls.

Inglefield v. **Englefield**.

Inglethorpe, John, of Norfolk—(E. II. Roll) bore, gules a cross engrailed argent ; Parliamentary, Ashmole and Surrey Rolls. Sir JOHN, differenced it with a label (3) or, at the battle of Boroughbridge 1322. (F.) An Essex Knight (H. VI. Roll) bore, gules, a cross engrailed ermine, an annulet argent Arundel Roll.

+**Inglethorpe, John**—(H. III. Roll) bore, gules a saltire engrailed or. (F.) Arden Roll.

Ingham, Robert—(E. III. Roll) bore, ermine, on a fess gules three escallops or ; Jenyns' Ordinary. Perhaps INGRAM.

Ingham, Oliver de, a baron 1328 - bore, per pale or and vert, a cross moline gules ; Jenyns' Ordinary.

Ingleby, John de—(E. II. Roll) bore, sable an estoile argent ; Jenyns' Roll.

Inglish and **Inglosse** v. **English** and **Englosse**.

Inglows, Henry — (R. II. Roll) — bore, quarterly or and azure in the first quarter a lyon rampant sable. Surrey Roll.

Ingram, John—(E. II. Roll) bore, ermine on a fess gules three escallops argent ; Jenyns' Roll. ROBERT bore the escallops or ; Grimaldi Roll and Jenyns' Ordinary.

Insula v. **de Insula**.

Ipre v. **Ypre**.

Irby, John de - (R. II. Roll) bore, argent, fretty sable, a quarter of the last ; Surrey Roll.

Irby, Sir Thomas, of Cumberland—(E. II. Roll) bore, argent, fretty sable, on a canton gules a cinquefoyle or ; Parliamentary Roll.

Ireland, John, of Hutt—(E. IV. Roll) bore, gules, six fleurs-de-lys 3, 2, 1, argent –with crest ; Ballard Roll.

+**Irie, Maheu de**—(H. III. Roll) bore, argent a bend azure ; Dering Roll.

[**Irton, Roger de**, 1292 - bore, argent, a fess sable in chief three mullet gules.—Shirley.] F.

*[**Isham, Robert de**, 2 R. II.—bore, gules, a fess and in chief three piles wavy meeting in the centre argent.—Shirley.] F.

**Iskynsall, —— ** (E. III. Roll) bore, or, a fess between two chevronels gules, a canton ermine ; Ashmole Roll.

Isle, Earl of the, Baldwin ; EARL OF DEVON or EXETER and LORD OF THE ISLE OF WIGHT –(E. I. Roll) bore, or a lyon rampant azure ; Segar and St. George Rolls. See also VERNON and WARREN DEL IDLE.

Islip, William, Keeper of the Privy Seal – bore, at the siege of Calais 1345-8 ermine, a fess engrailed between three weasels passant gules. F.

Edm Jonney

Dany Jorkavilo

Walt. Jorningham.

Thō Jocolyn

Robert Joreo

John Jod

John Golly

Alixand d Kenei

Vicħ Gondall

Will Gidosby

Will Gordoftono

Vicħ   do Kinardofteio

J—K

*[Jenney, Edmund, c 1400—bore, ermine, a bend gules cotised or.—Shirley.] F.

Jerkavile, Davy de—(E. I. Roll) bore, quarterly or and azure in the first quarter a lyon rampant gules. (F.) Camden Roll — called GERCOMVILE in Howard Roll. See also MARCONVILE in Dering Roll.

Jermyn, Sir John, of Suffolk, Kt.—(H. VI. Roll) bore, argent, a lyon rampant gardant gules; Arundel Roll.

*[Jerningham Sir Walter, (22 E. I.)—bore, argent, three buckles, tongues to the dexter gules.—Shirley.] F.

Joce, Sir John (or Jos)—bore, at the first Dunstable tournament 1308 argent, an eagle displayed sable a bendlet gobony or and gules. (F.) Sir JOHN, of Middlesex (E. II.) bore the baston gules; Parliamentary Roll.

*[Jocelyn, Thomas, (13 E. I.)—bore, azure, a circular wreath argent and sable with four hawks' bells affixed in quadrature or.—Shirley.] F.

John, Lewis (or JONES), an Essex Knight—(H. VI. Roll) bore, sable, a chevron between three trefoyles argent; Arundel Roll.

Jorce, John—(E. III. Roll) bore, per pale azure and gules, an eagle displayed argent membered of the second; Jenyns' Ordinary.

Jorcee, Robert—(E. III. Roll) bore, argent, on a bend or, three water-bougets azure. (F.) Jenyns' Ordinary.

Jove, William le — (H. III. Roll) bore, argent, three lyons rampant sable; Howard Roll.

Jumper, William (? INNPERE)—(H. III. Roll) bore, argent, a fess between three crescents gules; Arden Roll.

Justine, Adam de—(H. III. Roll) bore, barry (6) argent and azure, in chief three torteaux; Arden Roll.

*Kekitmore, Piers de—(E. III. Roll) bore, gules, three text S's 2 and 1 or; Arden Roll.

[Kelly, Sir John, (44 E. III.)—bore, argent, a chevron between three billets gules; Shirley.] F.

Kendale, Sir Edmonde de, of the North —(E. II. Roll) bore, argent, a bend vert cotised gules, all dancettée; Parly. Roll—cotises vert, in Glover Roll.

Kendale, Sir Robert de, of Herts.—bore, at the first Dunstable tournament 1308 argent, a bend vert, a label (3). Parly. Roll; EDWARD, bore it at the second Dunstable tournament 1334. (F.) Ascribed also to RICHARD in Jenyns' Ordinary.

Kendale, Robert—(R. II. Roll) argent, on a bend azure three mullets pierced or; Surrey Roll.

*[Kendall, Richard, 43 E. III. — bore, argent, a chevron between three dolphins naiant embowed sable.—Shirley.] F.

Kene (——) of Essex ? Knight—(H. VI. Roll) bore, ermine a cross florettée sable, *quarterly with*, azure, on a fess between two chevronels or three eaglets displayed gules; Arundel Roll. ROBERT LE KEN, took up the cross in the last Crusade 1270.

Kenney, Alexander de—(H. III. Roll) bore, quarterly or and gules a label (5) sable bezanty (F.); St. George Roll.

Kennings, Sir John, of Norfolk—(E. II. Roll) bore, azure, a fess engrailed between three escallops argent; Parly. Roll.

Kenette, Pers de—(H. III. Roll) bore, gules, three talbots-on-the-scent argent; Arden Roll.

Kent, Earl of—HUBERT DE BURGH 1227-43 —bore, lozengy *vel* masculy vair and gules; Grimaldi and Parly. Rolls; reversed in Arden and Nobility Rolls.

Kent, Earl of, EDMUND of Woodstock—bore, 1321, England within a bordure argent; Parly. Roll and Jenyns' Ordinary; borne also by HOLLAND, Earl of Kent; Surrey Roll.

‡Kent, Thomas de—(H. III Roll) bore, argent, a fess gules (F.); Dering and Howard Rolls.

Kentwode, John—(R. II. Roll) bore, gules, three roses ermine; Surrey Roll.

Kerdeston, Sir William de, of Norfolk, knighted at the capitulation of Calais 1348— bore, gules, a saltire engrailed argent (F.); Parly. Roll—ascribed also to JOHN, FOUKE, and WILLIAM in Arden and Norfolk Rolls and Jenyns' Ordinary Sir ROGER differenced with a label (3) or; Parly. and Ashmole Rolls.

Kerdeston, John—bore, at the second Dunstable tournament 1334, gules a saltire argent a label besantée (*sic*).

Kerdiff, Paul de—(H. III. Roll) bore, azure, a fess or (F.) (St. George Roll); between six martlets (3, 3) or, in Arden Roll.

Kevelioke, Hugh, EARL OF CHESTER—(E. III. Roll) bore, azure, six garbs 3, 2, 1, or; Jenyns' Ordinary, but see BLONDEVILLE.

Kidesby, Sir William—bore, at the siege of Calais 1345-8, sable, a fess or, between two chevrons argent. F.

Kidley, Thomas (KYDELEY)—(R. II. Roll) bore, sable, a saltire embattled argent; Surrey Roll.

Kighley, Sir Henry (KEIGHLEY)—(E. IV. Roll) bore, argent, a fess sable—with crest—Ballard Roll; ascribed to WILLIAM in Jenyns' Ordinary.

nigell de
ffing frote

Jofn kingoftone

will
d Kirkham

Piorb korban

will de
Kyrktoft

John de kirkton.

Rauf
d Kirkerone

John knatchbull

bobt knightley

Bogod de knovile

will de
kymbo

John de
kynafton

Kildare, Earl of—bore, argent, a saltire gules ; Jenyns' Ordinary. See FITZGERALD.

Kilkelely v. **Milkeley.**

Killom, Aleyn de—(E. III. Roll) bore, azure, three covered cups or—same as ALLAYN BOTELER ; Grimaldi Roll and Jenyns' Ordinary.

Kimbe, William de (KYMBALL)—(H. III. Roll) bore, or, a chevron gules, a bordure sable ; Glover Roll.

Kinardsley, Sir Hugh de, of Salop— (E. II. Roll) and RICHARD (H. III. Roll) bore, azure, crusily and a lyon rampant argent (F.); Parly. and St. George Rolls.

Kingesmede, Sir Walter de, of Salop— (E. II. Roll) bore, barry (8) or and azure, on a bend argent three escallops gules ; Parly. Roll.

*[**Kingscote, Nigell de,** E. I.—bore, argent, nine (perhaps 10) escallops shells sable, on a canton gules a mullet pierced or ; Shirley.] F.

Kingston, John, D'N'S DE KINGESTON, sealed the Barons' letter to the Pope 1301 with a lyon rampant tail fourchée ; another JOHN bore, at the second Dunstable tournament 1334, sable a lyon rampant tail fourchée or—ascribed also to Sir JOHN, banneret, and to THOMAS, in Arundel and Parly. Rolls. Sir NICHOLAS, of Yorkshire, differenced with a label (3) gules, and Sir JOHN with a label (3) argent, Sir WALTER, also of Yorkshire, differenced with a baston sable ; Parly. Roll. See KYNASTON.

Kirham, Nichol (or WILL) **de**—(H. III. Roll) bore, argent three lyonceux rampant gules, a bordure sable (F.) ; Arden and St. George Rolls.

Kiriell v. **Criol.**

Kirkan, Piers (KERKAN)—(E. II. Roll) bore, argent, three "clete" leaves vert (F.) ; Jenyns' Ordinary.

Kirkbride, Thomas—(E. III. Roll) bore, vert, a cross engrailed argent, tricked the reverse ; Jenyns' Ordinary.

Kirkbride, Sir Richard, of Cumberland —bore, at the siege of Carlaverock 1300, argent, a saltire engrailed vert ; Parly. Roll— a cross in NICOLAS.

Kirkby, Sir John and Richard de— (E. III. Roll) bore, argent 2 bars gules on a canton of the last a cross moline (recercelée) or ; Ashmole and Surrey Rolls.

Kirkby, Richard de—(E. II. Roll) bore, argent a fess et demy (2 bars) sable, on a quarter of the last a fer-de-moulin of the second ; Jenyns' Roll.

Kirkland, William (or RICHARD)—(E. III. Roll) bore, argent, three gemelles sable ; Jenyns' Ordinary.

Kirkton, John de, a baron 1362—bore, at the second Dunstable tournament 1334, barry ermine and gules (F.) ; gules, three bars ermine in Ashmole Roll and Jenyns' Ordinary.

Kirkton, Rauf de — (E. III. Roll) bore, azure, three water-bougets 2 and 1 argent ; Jenyns' Ordinary.

‡**Kirkton, Raufe de**—(H. III. Roll) bore, argent, six eaglets displayed 3, 2, 1 sable ; Dering and Howard Rolls—three eaglets (F.) in St. George Roll, and so ascribed to THOMAS in Jenyns' Ordinary.

Kirktott, William de (KIRKTOFT)—bore, at the second Dunstable tournament 1334, masculy or and sable (F.) ascribed also to Sir —— KIRKETOTT, knighted at the capitulation of Calais 1348.

Kirktot, Sir William, of Suffolk, Kt.— (E. II. Roll) bore, azure, on a cross argent five escallops gules ; Parliamentary Roll.

*[**Knatchbull, John,** (E. III.)—bore, azure, three crosses crosslet fitchée in bend between two cotises or.—Shirley.] F.

Knevet (——), an Essex Knight—(H. VI. Roll) bore, argent, a bend engrailed gules, *quarterly with*, argent three inescocheons each charged with a lyon rampant gules ; Arundel Roll.

*[**Knightley, Sir Robert de** (KNYTELEY), 30 E. I. - bore, ermine, *quarterly with*, paly (6) or and gules.—Shirley.] F.

Knolle, Ellis de—(E. III. Roll) bore, argent, a bend cotised sable ; Jenyns' Ordinary.

Knolles, Robert, K.G.—(E. II. Roll) bore, gules, on a chevron argent three roses of the field ; Surrey and Jenyns' Rolls. K. 399, fo. 20.

Knovill, Sir Bogo, a baron 1295—bore, argent, three spur-rowells gules ; Nobility Roll. Sealed the Barons' letter to the Pope 1301 (a label of three), (reversed — no label — in Dering and Ashmole Rolls — gules, three mullets or pierced vert in Cotgrave Roll).

Sir GILBERT, of co. Glouc., also bore argent, three spur-rowells gules ; Arden, Dering and Howard Rolls. Another BOGO, BOGES, or BEVIS differenced with a label (5) azure (F.) ; Howard and Camden Rolls ; and Sir JOHN, of co. Glouc. (*f* Sir GILBERT aforesaid) differenced with a label (3) azure at the first Dunstable tournament 1308 ; Parly. Roll.

Knovill, Bogo, or **Boege,** or **Beges**— (H. III. Roll) bore, gules, six spur-rowells or, a label (3, 5) azure ; Arden, St. George and Jenyns' Rolls.

Knoville, Thomas—(E. III. Roll) bore, gules, three water-bougets ermine ; Jenyns' Ordinary—borne also by JAMES ROOS.

Kokesalton, John de—(H. III. Roll) bore, argent fretty gules ; Arden Roll. See HUDLESTON.

Kymball v. **Kimbe.**

Kyme, Philip de, banneret, a baron 1295— sealed the Barons' letter to the Pope 1301 and bore, at the siege of Carlaverock 1300, gules crusily and a chevron or ; Ashmole and Dering Rolls – ascribed also to Sir SIMON, of Lincolnshire (E. II.) Parliamentary and Segar Rolls, and to Sir WILLIAM (E. II.) Parliamentary and Arundel Rolls - the crosses crosslet are omitted from the blason of the Howard Roll.

Kyme, Sir William de - bore, at the first Dunstable tournament 1308 and at the battle of Boroughbridge 1322, gules, crusily and a chevron or, a label (3) argent. (F.) ; azure in Nativity Roll.

[**Kynaston, Sir John de,** (E. II.)—bore, sable, a lyon rampant tail fourchée or.— Shirley.] (F.) See also KINGSTON.

Kynes, Sir John—(E. III. Roll) bore, barry (6) vair and gules ; Ashmole Roll.

Kyriel, Sir Thomas, K.G. 1460—bore, or, two chevrons and a quarter gules. K. 402, fo. 48. See CRIOL.

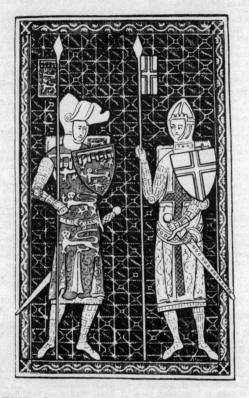

EDMUND, CROUCHBACK, EARL OF LANCASTER 1295

(BROTHER OF EDWARD I.),

AND PROBABLY HIS PATRON SAINT ST. GEORGE.

From an Illumination prefixed to a Missal, "Archæologia," xii. 200.

L

Lacy, Henry de, banneret, Earl of Lincoln 1257—bore, at the battle of Falkirk 1298 and at the siege of Carlaverock 1300, or, a lyon rampant purpure (F.) ; Nobility and Parliamentary Rolls. JOHN, his grandfather, bore, quarterly or and gules, a baston sable, a label (5) argent " Le veyl escu de Nicol." See Earls of LINCOLN.

Lacy, Adam de—(H. III. Roll) **and Sir John,** of Herefordshire—(E. II. Roll) bore, or, a fess in chief three martlets gules. (F.) Parliamentary and St. George Rolls.

Lacy, Sir John de, of Rutland—(E. II. Roll) bore, undée (6) gules and ermine ; Parliamentary Roll.

Lacy, Sir Robert de, of Cambridgeshire— (E. II. Roll) bore, argent an orle gules, over all a bendlet sable ; Parliamentary Roll.

Lacy (——), a Cornish Knight—(H. VI. Roll) bore, azure, three shovellers' heads and necks erased argent ; Arundel Roll.

Lakenham, William—(E. III. Roll)) bore, argent, a cross between four lyonceux rampant gules ; Jenyns' Ordinary.

Lakenheath, John (LAKYNGHYTHE) — (R. II. Roll) bore, argent, a chevron sable between three caps of the last, turned up gules ; Surrey Roll.

‡**Lambourne, Sir William de,** of Essex— (E. II. Roll) bore, argent, two chevrons sable (F.) ; Parly., Dering and Howard Rolls. Ascribed to MILES in Arden Roll—a trick with label (3) gules in Ashmole Roll.

Lambourne, William—(R. II. Roll) bore, argent, on a bend sable cotised gules three lyons' heads erased of the field (another or) ; Surrey Roll.

Lambton (——), a Kentish Knight—(H. VI. Roll) bore, a chevron between three lambs' heads couped argent, *quarterly with*, argent, a chevron sable between three ravens (? Cornish choughs) ppr. beaked and legged gules ; Arundel Roll.

[Lambton, Robert de,** 1314—bore, sable, a fess between three lambs passant argent.— Shirley.] F.*

Lampet, Sir John, of Bardwell, Suffolk, Kt.—(H. VI. Roll) bore, argent on a bend engrailed azure three rams' heads couped of the first horned or ; Arundel Roll.

Lampette, Sir John, of Suffolk, Kt.— (H. VI. Roll) bore, argent, on a cross engrailed gules between four escallops sable five besants ; Arundel Roll.

Lamplewe, Sir John de, of Cumberland —(E. II. Roll) bore, or (argent in Glover Roll) a cross florettée at the points sable ; Parliamentary Roll (peculiarly tricked in Harl. MS. 4033 fo. 50)—ascribed also to ROBERT (F.) and THOMAS in Segar and Surrey Rolls.

Lamplogh, Thomas—(E. II. Roll) bore, argent, a chevron between three lyons' heads erased sable ; Jenyns' Roll.

Lancaster, Edmund, Earl of (1267-75) — (*fil* H. III.) bore, England, with a label (3) France, a label (4) on his tomb ; Grimaldi Roll and Jenyns' Ordinary. Father of the next named.

Lancaster, Thomas, banneret, **Earl of** (1296-1322)—sealed the Barons' letter to the Pope 1301, bore at the battle of Falkirk 1298, at the siege of Carlaverock 1300, and at the first Dunstable tournament 1308, England, and a label (3) of France ; Arundel and Parliamentary Rolls—a label (5) in Guillim and St. George Rolls.

Lancaster, Sir Henry de, banneret (brother of THOMAS, last-named) bore, at the battle of Falkirk 1298 and at the siege of Carlaverock 1300 (Earl of LANCASTER, restored 1327)—England and a baston azure (F.) ; Parliamentary and Arundel Rolls ; sealed the Barons' letter to the Pope 1301 ; styled Baron of MONMOUTH in the Nobility Roll his son HENRY bore the same at the second Dunstable tournament 1334.

Lancaster, Henry, K.G., **Duke of** (1345-62) —bore, at the siege of Calais 1345-8, England with a label of France. (F.) See Monumental Brass.

Lancaster, John, OF GAUNT, Duke of (1362-99) bore, France and England quarterly ; over all a label (3) ermine on each pendant three ermine spots ; Surrey Roll and Jenyns' Ordinary.

Lancaster, John de, banneret, baron 1299 —bore at the siege of Carlaverock 1300, argent two bars gules, on a canton of the second a lyon passant gardant or, (sealed the Barons' letter to the Pope 1301) ; barry (6) in lieu of 2 bars, &c., ascribed to JOHN of Holgill in Jenyns' Ordinary and to ROGER and WILLIAM in St. George Roll. In the Nobility Roll the canton is charged with a cinquefoyle or.

Lancaster, Sir Thomas—bore at the siege of Calais 1345-8, argent, two bars gules, on a canton of the second a rose or - in the margin also gules, a lyon rampant gardant or, collared azure ; Ashmole Roll.

HENRY, DUKE OF LANCASTER, K.G., GRANDSON OF H. III.
IN ELSING CHURCH, NORFOLK, 1347, 21 E. III.
From a rubbing of the Hastings Brass.

Lancastre, John de—(R. II. Roll) bore, argent, a chevron between three eagles legs à la cuisse gules, a bordure engrailed sable; Surrey Roll.

Landles, John de—(E. III. Roll) bore, gules, an orle or; Nativity Roll and Jenyns' Ordinary. See also LAUNDELES.

Lane *v.* **Lone.**

Langford, Sir John de—bore, at the battle of Boroughbridge 1322, paly (6) argent and gules, on a chief azure a lyon passant or (F.); gardant in Ashmole and so borne by Sir CHRISTOPHER, knighted at the capitulation of Calais 1348. Ascribed also to THOMAS in Jenyns' Ordinary.

Langford, Sir Nichol de—bore, at the battle of Boroughbridge 1322, vert, six lyonceux rampant 3 2 1 or. (F.) See next entry for another.

Langford, Sir Nichol de—bore, at the battle of Boroughbridge 1322 and at the siege of Calais 1345-8, paly (6) or and gules, a bend bendlet or baston argent (F.); Ashmole Roll — and for Sir JOHN, of Derby or Notts, in Parliamentary Roll. Another NICHOL bore it at the second Dunstable tournament 1334 and he was probably knighted at the capitulation of Calais 1348.

Langford, Sir Rauff, see Longford.

Langley, Sir Edmonde de, of Warwickshire—(E. II. Roll) bore, argent, a fess and in chief three escallops sable; Parly., Camden, and Harl. Rolls. (WALTER bore ogresses in place of escallops (F.); St. George Roll. Ascribed to GEOFFREY (‡) in Howard Roll, and with the escallops 2 and 1 between the fess in Camden and Dering Rolls.

Langley, Sir Thomas—(E. III. Roll) bore, gules, two bars and in chief as many bucks' heads cabossed or; Ashmole Roll.

Langton (——) baron of Walton in Lanc., Knighted at the capitulation of Calais 1348— bore. argent, three chevronels gules (F.); ascribed (with crest) also to Sir JOHN, of Walton, E. IV., Ballard Roll, and also to THOMAS, baron of Newton, in Jenyns' Ordinary; CHRISTOPHER, differenced with a label (3) azure; Surrey Roll.

Langton (——) a Knight—(H. VI. Roll) bore, gules, a chevron argent between three lyonceux rampant or; Arundel Roll.

Langton, John de—(E. III. Roll) bore, per pale or and vert, a cross recercelée (moline, in trick) gules, over all a baston sable; Jenyns' Ordinary.

Langton, Raffe—(E. III. Roll) bore, gules, an orle argent, a bend sable; Jenyns' Ordinary.

Langton, Thomas, of Wingarde—(E. II. Roll) bore, or, a lyon rampant sable vulned on the shoulder proper; Jenyns' Roll.

*[**Langton** —— of Langton, co. Linc.—(temp. H. II.) bore, paly (6) argent and sable, a bend or.—Shirley.] F.

Langtree, Gilbert—(E. IV. Roll) bore, three ermine spots 2 and 1—with crest; Ballard Roll.

Lansladron, Serlo de, of Cornwall, baron 1299 bore, sable, three chevronels argent; Nobility and Parly. Rolls.

Lanthony, —— (E. I. Roll) bore, or, on a chief indented azure, three plates; Harl. Roll.

Lapare *v.* **Larpare, ——** (E. III. Roll) bore, gules crusily and a lyon rampant argent; Ashmole Roll. Name and blason doubtful.

Lapun, Robert de—(H. III. Roll) bore, gules, fretty vair (F.); St. George Roll. See LATHUN.

Lascelles, Allen—(E. III. Roll) bore, gules, a saltire and a chief argent (F.); Jenyns' Ordinary, where it is blasoned, probably in confusion with EGLESCLIFFE, gules on a saltire five besants argent. See also ASSELES.

Lasselles, John de, of Allerthorpe—(E. III. Roll) bore, sable, a cross patée (flory in trick) or; Jenyns' Ordinary.

*[**Lascelles, John de,** of Hinderskelfe (9 E. II.) 1315-16—bore, sable, a cross patonce and a bordure or.—Shirley.] F.

Lassels, John, of Langthorn—(E. III. Roll) bore, argent, six roses 3, 2, 1 gules; Jenyns' Ordinary.

Lascelles, Pigot—(E. II. Roll) bore, argent, three chaplets gules; Jenyns' Roll. ROGER, differenced with a bordure engrailed of the last; Jenyns' Ordinary.

Lascelles, Thomas, of South Cowton— (E. III. Roll) bore, gules, on a chevron sable between three eagles' heads erased as many mullets (6) all argent; Jenyns' Ordinary.

Lathom, Sir Thomas—bore, at the siege of Calais 1345-8, argent (? or) on a chief dancettée azure three plates (F.) besants in Ashmole MS.—the field or with besants in Ashmole Roll and Jenyns' Ordinary.

Lathom, Philip, of Knowesley—(E. IV. Roll) bore, or on a chief dancettée azure three plates, over all a bendlet gules; with crest; Ballard Roll and Harl. MS. 1481 fo. 82.

Lathun, Robert de—(H. III. Roll) bore, gules, fretty vair; St. George Roll. See LAPUN.

†**Latimer, William le**, of Corby, banneret, a baron 1299—bore, at the battle of Falkirk 1298 and at the siege of Carlaverock 1300, gules, a cross patonce or (F.); sealed the Barons' letter to the Pope 1301. His son WILLIAM, also a baron, having precedency over his father, bore the same at Falkirk 1298 with a label argent, but without at the first Dunstable tournament 1308, and probably at the battle of Boroughbridge 1322, then styled banneret, his son may, however, be intended, who certainly bore the same at the second Dunstable tournament 1334. JOHN and THOMAS differenced with a label (3, 5) azure; St. George and Surrey Rolls.

Latimer, John de—bore, at the battle of Boroughbridge 1322, and Sir THOMAS bore, at the first Dunstable tournament 1308, gules, a cross patonce or, a label (3) of France; Parly. Roll. Another THOMAS bore it also at the second Dunstable tournament 1334, and it is also ascribed in Jenyns' Ordinary to THOMAS, of Norfolk; it was also carried at the siege of Rouen 1418; and with a bordure argent at the second Dunstable tournament 1334.

Warine Latymer

Thos Latimer

Ger de Laton

will de Laton

Thos Lawley

Hugh Lawton

John Lee

Adam Lochmore

Oimle de Loycestro

John Loycestor

John Leigh

Ric Leighton

Latimer, Thomas de, of Braybrooke, a baron 1299—bore, gules, a cross patonce or, a label (sable); Nobility and Parly. Rolls. Sir THOMAS, LE BOURSARY, or BOUCHARI, differenced with a label (3) sable, on each pendant a plate (F.), at the first Dunstable tournament 1308. Ascribed also to Sir WILLIAM in the Parly. Roll. Sire WILLIAM LE BOCHARDE further differenced, at the battle of Boroughbridge 1322, with a martlet argent on the label. In the Nobility Roll the label is differenced bezantée for (1) Sir WILLIAM; and for (2) Sir JOHN sable florettée or (F. as THO.), and for (3) Sir THOMAS the label is azure.

Latimer, Sire John le—(E. I. Roll) bore, gules, on a cross patonce or five covered cups sable; Guillim Roll.

Latimer, Sir John le, of Yorkshire—(E. II. Roll) bore, gules, on a cross patonce or, four escallops sable; Parly. Roll (the father of Sir WARYN). Sir THOMAS bore five escallops; Harl. Roll and Harl. MS. 1481 fo. 86.

Latimer, Sir Waryn—bore, at the battle of Boroughbridge 1322, and another Sir WARYN, knighted at the capitulation of Calais 1348, bore, gules, on a cross patonce or five maunches of the field (F.); Jenyns' Ordinary and Harl. MS. 1481 fo. 86.

Latymer, Sire Nicholas—bore, at the battle of Boroughbridge 1322, LATYMER, and bend of France, *i.e.* on a bend azure three fleurs-de-lys or (F.) To Sir NICHOLAS, of Yorkshire, a later hand in Parly. Roll (E. II.) adds " Noe bende nor fleur-de-luces," Harl. MS. 613¹ fo. 22; for differences see Harl. 1481 fo. 85.

Laton, Sir Christopher de (LAYTON)—Knighted at the capitulation of Calais 1348, argent, crusily fitchée (3, 3) a fess sable (F.); ascribed also to THOMAS in Grimaldi Roll and Jenyns' Ordinary. ROBERT differenced with a cinquefoyle pierced of the field; Surrey Roll.

Laton, William de—(E. II. Roll) bore, argent, on a bend gules three escallops of the field; Jenyns' Roll. F.

Laton, William de—(R. II. Roll) bore, or, a cross moline gules; Surrey Roll.

Launde *v.* **De la Launde.**

Laundeles, Sir John de—(E. III. Roll) bore, azure an orle or; the field gules for LANDLES; Nativity Roll and Jenyns' Ordinary.

Laurence, Sir James, of Asheton—(E. IV. Roll) bore, argent, a cross ragulée gules—with crest; Ballard Roll. F.

La Ware *v.* **De la Ware.**

*[**Lawley, Thomas,** 1471—bore, argent, a cross formée checquy or and sable.—Shirley.] F.

*[**Lawton, Hugh,** Hen. VI.—bore, argent, on a fess between three crosses crosslet fitchée sable, a cinquefoyle of the first.—Shirley.] F.

Lebaud, Sir Thomas—(E. III. Roll) bore, azure, a lyon passant or; Ashmole Roll.

*[**Leche, John,** 1475—bore, ermine, on a chief indented gules, three crowns or.—Shirley.] F.

*[**Lechmere, Adam de**—bore, gules a fess, and in chief two pelicans or, vulning themselves ppr.—Shirley.] F.

Le Despencer, Hugh—bore, at the second Dunstable tournament 1334, quarterly argent and gules (*sic*) a bâston sable; the fret or in the 2nd and 3rd quarters is probably omitted. See DESPENCER and SPENCER.

Ledye, Roger—(R. II. Roll) bore, argent, a fess gules between three eaglets displayed sable; Surrey Roll.

Lee, Ley, *v.* **De la Lee** and **De la Ley.**

Leeham *v.* **Leigham.**

Leeke, Andrew de (LEYKE)—(R. II. Roll) bore, argent, a chief gules surmounted by a bend engrailed azure. ROBERT differenced it with a mullet pierced or; Surrey Roll.

Leeke, John de (LEYKE) — (R. II. Roll) bore, argent, on a saltire engrailed sable nine annulets or; Surrey Roll.

Leeke, John de (LEKE)—(E. III. Roll) bore, sable, six annulets 3, 2, 1, or; Jenyns' Ordinary.

Leem (——) a Norfolk Knight—(E. II. Roll) bore, or, a saltire engrailed vert; Parliamentary Roll, an addition. See LE MOYNE.

Legh, Sir Peter (LEE), of co. Lanc.—(E. III. Roll) bore, masculy argent and sable, tricked lozengy; Jenyns' Ordinary—*modo* NICHOLAS DE CROFTE.

Legh (William) of the Boothes—(E. IV. Roll) bore, azure, two bars argent, over all a bendlet counter compony or and gules—*with crest*; Ballard Roll; blasoned checquy but tricked counter-compony in Jenyns' Roll. Harl. MS. 1481 fo. 80.

Legh, Sir Piers á, of Bradley—(E. IV. Roll) bore, quarterly (1), argent, a cross sable a fleur-de-lys of the last, (2), gules, a cross engrailed argent (3), argent, a mullet sable (4), vert, a chevron between three crosses patonce or—*with crest*; Ballard Roll.

Legh, Thomas, of Adlington—(E. IV. Roll) bore, azure, a plate between three crowns or, a bordure argent; *quarterly with,* argent, a cross patonce sable, *with crest*; Ballard Roll.

*[**Legh, John,** 12 Hen. VI.—bore, gules, a cross engrailed and a fusil argent.—Shirley.] F.

*[**Legh, Thomas de,** H. III.—bore the arms of Lymme, gules, a pale fusily argent. Shirley.] (F.) Or, a lyon rampant gules, was subsequently allowed to LEIGH of West Hall and a silver lyon to LEGH of East Hall.

Le Grose, Sir Renaud, of Norfolk - (E. II. Roll), bore, quarterly, argent and azure, on a bendlet sable three martlets or; Parliamentary Roll—ascribed to Sir JOHN in the Ashmole Roll.

Leices or **Leites** *v.* **Beices.**

Leicester, Earl of, SIMON DE MONTFORT, 1230–65—bore, gules, a lyon rampant, tail fourchée argent. (F.) Arden, Glover, St. George and other Rolls; bore on his banner— per pale dancettée argent and gules; Glover, Grimaldi and other Rolls.

Leicester, John, of Cheshire - (E. IV. Roll) bore, azure, a fess gules fretty or between three fleurs-de-lys 2 and 1 of the last—with crest; Ballard Roll. See also LEYCESTER.

Le Strange.

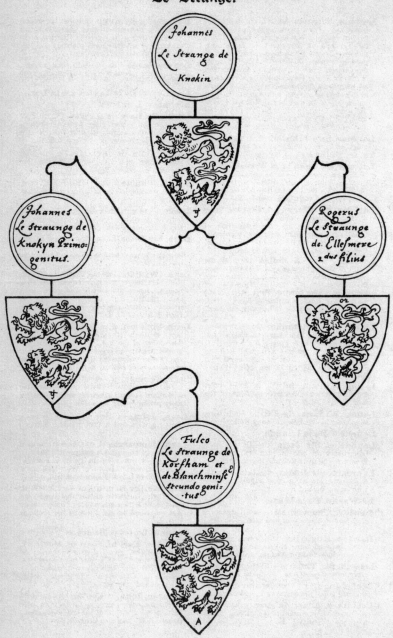

Leigham, Sir John de (LEEHAM), of Berks – (E. II. Roll) bore, sable, florettée (3, 2, 1) or ; Parliamentary Roll ; in another MS. 2, 2, 1.

[Leighton, Sir Richard,** 1313 bore (Seal) quarterly per fess indented or and gules, over all a bendlet.—Shirley.] F.*

Lekebourne, Sir Henry de—bore, at the first Dunstable tournament 1308, argent crusily and a fess dancettée sable. F.

Lekebourne, Sir Henry de, of co. Lincs. —(E. II. Roll), and **Hugh** (E. III. Roll) bore, argent, crusily (6, 4) and a chevron sable ; Nativity and Parliamentary Rolls and Jenyns' Ordinary.

‡**Le Leu, Nicole**—(H. III. Roll) bore, gules two heraldic wolves passant argent ; Dering Roll—greyhounds in Ashmole MS. See Low.

Le Mare *v.* **De la Mare.**

‡**Le Moy(n)e, Berenger**—(E. I. Roll) bore, gules, crusily and a cross patée argent. (F.) Segar Roll. See MOYNE.

Le Moyne, Sir John, of Suffolk—(E. II. Roll) bore, or a saltire engrailed gules ; Parliamentary Roll. See LEEM.

‡**Le Poer, Robert**—(H. III. Roll) bore, quarterly ermine and azure two leopards' faces or ; Dering Roll.

Le Sor, John—(H. III. Roll) bore, checquy or and gules a fess azure. (F.) St. George Roll.

Le Strange, Sir John, of co. Glouc.— (E. II. Roll) bore, gules, two lyons passant argent, a bordure indented or, over all a baston azure ; Parliamentary Roll.

Le Strange, Roger, of Ellesmere, baron 1295 – bore, gules, two lyons passant argent and a bordure engrailed or ; sealed the Barons' letter to the Pope 1301 ; Nobility, Howard and Arundel Rolls, &c. (F.) Ascribed also to Sir JOHN in Harleian Roll.

Le Strange, Sir Fouke, banneret, baron 1309—bore, at the first Dunstable tournament 1308, argent two lyons passant gules (F.) ; sealed the Barons' letter to the Pope 1301 ; borne also by (‡) JOHN, in Dering, Camden and St. George Rolls ; his son JOHN differenced with a label azure in Glover Roll.

L'Estrange, Sir John, of Knockyn, banneret, baron 1299—bore, at the siege of Carlaverock 1300, gules two lyons passant argent, sealed the Barons' letter to the Pope 1301. (His son JOHN, of Corsham and of Blanchminster, bore the reverse ; Harl. MS. 1481 ff. 16, 18) ; and by Sir ROGER at the siege of Calais 1345-8. Borne also by EUBULUS, Baron Strange 1325 and JOHN and HAMON, in Segar, Surrey and St. George Rolls and by LE SR.—at the siege of Rouen 1418. Another JOHN (brother of EUBULUS) differenced with a bendlet or ; Surrey Roll— as did his son HAMON, of Hunston, Norfolk. EUBULUS, younger brother of JOHN (the father of HAMON) differenced with a label (3) or, on each pendant a lyon rampant gules ; Harl. MS. 1481 fo. 19ᵇ.

L'Estrange, Sir John—bore, at the first Dunstable tournament 1308, gules, two lyons passant argent within an orle (8) martlets or. (F.) Of co. Gloucester in Parliamentary Roll.

L'Estrange, Fowke—bore, at the second Dunstable tournament 1334, gules, two lyons passant argent crowned or.

Le Strange, John—bore, at the siege of Rouen 1418, gules, two lyons passant on the shoulder of each a fleur-de-lys sable. F.

Le Strange, Sir Hamon—bore, at the first Dunstable tournament 1308, gules, two lyons passant argent oppressed by a baston or. (F.) ; of co. Glouc. in Parliamentary Roll.

Le Strange, Robert—(H. III. Roll) bore, gules crusily and two lyons passant argent ; St. George Roll – crusily fitchée in Harl. MS. 6137 fo. 77ᵇ. F.

Le Strunn John (or LE STURMY ?)—(H. III. Roll) bore, gules, a chevron between three mullets (6) argent. (F.) Arden and St. George Rolls.

Lesume, Adam—(E. II, Roll) bore, barry (10) argent and azure in chief three torteaux ; Jenyns' Ordinary.

Leu *v.* **Le Leu** and **Low.**

Levaat, Andrew — (H. III. Roll) bore argent, a cross engrailed gules ; St. George Roll. Borne also by JOHN LE FITZ HENRY and JOHN DE LA LINDE.

‡**Leveland, Raufe de**—(H. III. Roll) bore, sable, three bears' heads bendways couped 2 and 1 argent. (F.) Dering Roll ; boars' heads in Howard Roll.

Leventhorpe (——), Knight—(H. VI. Roll) bore, argent, a bend gobony gules and sable cotised sable ; Arundel Roll.

Leversage, ——, (E. IV. Roll) bore, argent, a chevron between three levers erect 2 and 1 sable—with crest ; Ballard Roll. F.

Levett *v.* **Livett.**

Levinton, John de--(E. II. Roll) bore, gules, on a chevron argent three cinquefoyles sable ; Jenyns' Roll.

Leving, Richard (LEWYNE)—(E. II. Roll) bore, ermine, on a bend gules three escallops or. (F.) Jenyns' Roll. WILLIAM DE LEOYN, of Brampton, took up the cross in the last Crusade 1270.

Lewknor, Sir John—bore, at the siege of Calais 1345-8 azure, three chevronels argent ; ascribed also to ROGER (‡) and Sir THOMAS, of Sussex ; Dering and Parliamentary Rolls. Another ROGER differenced with a label (5) or (F.) ; Camden Roll.

Lewknor, John—bore, at the second Dunstable tournament 1334, gules, two bends depressed by a chevron argent. F.

Lewknor, Sir John—(E. III. Roll) bore, gules, a chevron between three talbots passant argent ; Ashmole Roll.

Lexington, John de—(H. III. Roll) bore, argent, a cross fourchée azure—"au kanee" —Glover Roll.

Leyburn, Sir William, banneret, a baron 1299—bore, at the siege of Carlaverock 1300, azure, six lyonceux rampant 3, 2, 1, argent. (F.) ; Nobility, Parliamentary and Arundel Rolls ; sealed the Barons' letter to the Pope 1301—ascribed also to JOHN of Kent, ROGER (‡) and another WILLIAM (‡) ; Jenyns' Ordinary, Dering and Norfolk Rolls. ROGER took up the cross in the last Crusade 1270.

Symon de Leybourne

Will de Leyburne

John Leycester

Rauf de Limosey

Cu͡le de Nicol

Guto de Nicholo

Alex Lyndsey

Felipe de Lindesore

Will de Lindeseao

Raf de Lingoynt

Will de Lylle

John de Lisle

Leyburn, Sir Henry de—bore, at the first Dunstable tournament 1308, azure, six lyonceux rampant, 3, 2, 1, argent, a label (3) gules. Sir JOHN, knighted at the capitulation of Calais 1348, differenced with a bordure engrailed or; ascribed also to SIMON in Segar Roll (F.)—and in the Parliamentary Roll to Sir SIMON, of Kent, with a bordure indented or; ROGER and THOMAS a label (4) gules; Segar Roll. Sir HENRY of Kent, with a label gobony or and gules; Parly. Roll.

Leyborne (——), of the household of the Earl of Salisbury—(E. III. Roll) bore, azure, five lyons rampant 2, 2, 1 argent, a bordure engrailed or, over all a quarter ermine; Jenyns' Ordinary—ascribed to THOMAS, without the bordure; Jenyns' Ordinary.

Leyburn, Sir William, banneret—(H. VI. Roll) bore, argent, six lyonceux rampant 3. 2, 1 sable; Arundel Roll.

Leyburn, Sir de (? JOHN), knighted at the capitulation of Calais 1348 - bore, gules, six lyons rampant 3, 2, 1 argent—ascribed also to Sir RICHARD of Yorks, and THOMAS; Parliamentary and Surrey Rolls. Sir NICHOLAS of Yorks differenced with a label (3) azure.

Leyborne, John, of the North, banneret—(E. III. Roll) bore, or six lyonceux rampant 3, 2, 1 sable; Jenyns' Ordinary. Ascribed also to ROGER and Sir WILLIAM, of the North; Howard and Parly. Rolls (see WILLIAM above—the field argent)—THOMAS MALLORY bore the same; JOHN DE ST. MARTIN bore the reverse.

Leycester v. **Leicester**.

Leye v. **de la Leye**.

Leyland, Sir Thomas—(E. III. Roll) bore, argent a bend gules cotised sable; Ashmole Roll, surname doubtful.

Lille, Ancels de (LYLLE)—(H. III. Roll) bore, argent, a fess between six mullets (6) gules; Howard Roll— in other Rolls a label (5) azure.

Lillebon, Walter de—(H. III. Roll) bore, per pale argent and sable a chevron counterchanged. (F.) Arden Roll.

Lilleburne, John de—(E. III. Roll) bore, sable, three dossers (or water-bougets) argent; Ashmole and Surrey Rolls.

Limbury v. **Lymbury**.

Limesy, Sir Piers de (of Warwickshire)—bore, at the battle of Boroughbridge 1322, gules, an eagle displayed or. (F.) Ascribed to RICHARD in Segar Roll and to Sir RICHARD of Warwickshire, with a baston of MONTFORT, or four bendlets azure, in Parliamentary Roll—and in Jenyns' Ordinary to JOHN, with and without a bend azure, and another JOHN or an eagle purpure. membered gules.

Limesy, Raf de—(H. III. Roll) bore, gules, three eagles displayed or. (F.) Arden and St. George Rolls—another RAUF(‡) bore, six eagles 3, 2, 1 (F.) Dering and Holland Rolls (Sir RAFE)—and in a note, a label (5) azure for Sir RICHARD; Holland and Howard Rolls. See Harl. MS. 1481 fo. 67ᵇ.

Limsey, Sir Philip (LINDESEY) of the North—(E. II. Roll) bore, or, an eagle displayed purpure; Parliamentary Roll; ? azure and oppressed by a baston argent; Harl. Roll —(the eagle sable) oppressed by a baston gobony azure and gules (F.) (perhaps the baston of MONTFORT is intended); Segar Roll.

Limsey, Sir Simon de, of the North—(E. I. Roll) bore, or an eagle displayed purpure; Ashmole Roll; sable in Segar Roll and differenced with the baston (? MONTFORT) gobony argent and azure; Parliamentary Roll.

Lincoln, Earl of (JOHN DE LACY), 1232—(E. I. Roll) bore, quarterly or and gules a baston sable, a label (5) argent. (F.) " Le veyl escu de Nicol." Segar, Camden, Nobility and other Rolls; no label in Nobility Roll H. VI.

Lincoln, Earl of (HENRY DE LACY), 1257-1311—bore, at the battle of Falkirk 1298, and at the siege of Carlaverock 1300, or a lyon rampant purpure (F.); lyon sable in Howard Roll.

Lindsay, Sir Alexander—bore, at the battle of Falkirk 1298; gules, a fess chequy or (in error for argent) and azure. (F.) Jenyns' Ordinary.

Lindsay, Sir Gilbert de, of Hunts—(E. II. Roll) bore, gules, crusily or an orle vair; Parliamentary Roll; ascribed also to WILLIAM (F.) in St. George Roll.

Lindsay, Walter de—(H. III. Roll) bore, gules, an orle vair; Arden and Glover Rolls. WALTER le fitz, differenced with a label (3) azure; Jenyns' Ordinary.

*Lingayn, Sir Rauff—(E. III. Roll) bore, barry (6) or and azure, on a bend gules three cinquefoyles pierced argent; Ashmole Roll—escallops on the bend (F.) in Arden and St. George Rolls.

Lisle v. **De Lisle**.

Lisle, John de, of Wotton, baron 1299—bore, or, a fess between two chevronels sable ascribed also to his son JOHN, 2nd baron, K.G. (a founder), who served at the siege of Calais 1345-8; Nobility and Surrey Rolls—ascribed also to Sir ROBERT, Banneret, in Guillim, Parliamentary and Arundel Rolls; to another ROBERT (‡) in Dering Roll; to WARREN in Segar Roll, and to WILLIAM (F.) at the siege of Rouen 1418; another WILLIAM differenced with a martlet or.

Lisle, Sir Baldwin de, of Rutland—(E. II. Roll) bore, or, on a fess between two chevronels sable three roses argent; Parly. Roll.

Lisle, Robert de, of Rougemont, baron 1311, appears to be referred to in the first entry. Sir JOHN, his son or grandson, knighted at the capitulation of Calais 1348 —bore, gules, a lyon passant gardant argent crowned or (F.), one of the founders of the Order of the Garter, Sir GERARD and Sir WARIN, of Rutland, both bore the arms at the first Dunstable tournament 1308; Parly. Roll; ascribed to another GERARD in Dering Roll. They are also ascribed to Sir FOULK in Harleian Roll.

Lisle, Gerard de—(E. III. Roll) bore, gules, crusily fitchée or, a lyon passant gardant, argent; Parliamentary Roll and Jenyns' Ordinary. Sir ROBERT, of Rutland, bore it crusily in Parliamentary Roll.

SIR HUMPHREY LITTELBURY.

IN HOLBEACH CHURCH IN LINCOLNSHIRE. *After Stothard.*

Lisle, Sir Warren de, knighted at the capitulation of Calais 1348 –bore, argent, a lyon passant gardant gules crowned or.

Lisle –Le Count de le Ille–(H. III. Roll) bore, gules, three bars or "diaspres" (? diapered).–Norfolk Roll.

Lisley, Sir John de, banneret –(H. VI. Roll) bore, or, on a chief azure three lyonceux rampant of the first. (F.) Arundel and St. George Rolls. See also INCULE.

Lisley, Sir John de, of Hants - (E II. Roll) bore, or, a chevron between three leaves ("foyles of gletuers") gules; Parliamentary Roll. See also DE LISLE. F.

Lisley, John de, Seigneur of Laybourne – (E. I. Roll) bore, gules, a chevron between three "foyles" or; Grimaldi Roll. (F.) Sir WALTER bore the reverse and a label azure; Nativity Roll.

Lisoures, John–(E. III. Roll) bore, azure, two chevronels and a mullet or –tricked as a martlet; Jenyns' Ordinary and Roll.

Lisours, John–bore, at the second Dunstable tournament 1334, azure, a chief or. (F.) Ashmole Roll and Jenyns' Ordinary.

*****[Lister, John,** 6 E. II.–bore, ermine, on a fess sable, three mullets or.–Shirley.] F.

Littlebury, John de–(R. II. Roll) bore, argent, two lyons passant gardant gules; Surrey Roll. Sir ROBERT differenced, with a label (3) azure; Ashmole Roll. See Monumental Effigy of Sir HUMPHREY.

Littlebury, Humphrey and William– (E. III. Roll) bore, argent, two lyons passant gardant gules on a bend vert. three eaglets displayed or; Jenyns' Ordinary.

Littlebury, Robert–bore, at the second Dunstable tournament 1334, argent two lyons passant gules, a label azure (F.)–apparently not gardant.

‡**Livett, Robert**–(H. III. Roll) bore, argent, crusily gules a lyon rampant sable. (F.) Dering and Howard Rolls.

Lockton, Roger de (LOKINTONE)–(H. III. Roll) bore, argent, a chief azure, a label (5) gules. (F.) St. George Roll.

Lodbrooke, Sir John, of Warwickshire– (F. II. Roll) bore, azure, a chevron ermine. (F.) Harleian, Parliamentary, and St. George Rolls. See also GONNYES.

Lodiham *v.* **Bodiham.**

Londe, William de–(F. III. Roll) bore, argent, two bars sable, a bordure engrailed gules; Jenyns' Ordinary.

*º**[Lone, Richard de le,** DE HAMPTON– 1315 bore, per fess or and azure, a chevron gules between three mullets counterchanged.– Shirley.] F.

Longchamp, Henry–(E. III. Roll) bore, or, three crescents gules on each a mullet argent. See HENRY DE THANI; Jenyns' Ordinary.

Longe, Sir William–(F. I. Roll) bore, or, a saltire gules; Harl. Roll, Jenyns' Ordinary.

[Longespée, Mauld, dau. of WILLIAM, Duke of Normandy, and wife to HUGH MORTIMER, who came with the Conqueror–(Roll E. I.) bore, gules, three espées (swords erect), argent, Jenyns' Roll–a fable.]

Longespée, William, Earl of Salisbury– (H. III. Roll) bore, azure, six lyonceux rampant (3, 2, 1) or; Howard, Glover and Grimaldi Rolls; see Monumental Effigy. ESTIENN differenced with a label gules, Glover Roll–and another with a "cantell" ermine, Norfolk Roll.

Longford *v.* **Langford.**

Longford, Sir Rauff–(E. IV. Roll)–bore, paly (6) or and gules a bendlet argent, *quarterly with,* quarterly gules and argent–and crest; Ballard Roll.

Longueville, Sir Gerard–(E. III. Roll) bore, gules, crusily argent 4, 3, 2, 1, a fess dancettée ermine; Ashmole Roll. HENRY and Sir JOHN, of Hunts., bore the fess argent (F.); Segar, Parly., and Jenyns' Rolls.

Longvale, John–(E. I. Roll) bore, gules, three bends vair; Jenyns' Ordinary.

Longvilliers, Sir John, of Whatton– (E. III. Roll) and Sire THOMAS, who fought at the battle of Boroughbridge 1322, bore, sable, crusily and a bend argent (F.); Ashmole Roll and Jenyns' Ordinary.

Longe, Sir John de, of co. Linc.–(E. II. Roll) bore, chequy argent and azure, on a chief gules three mullets or; Parly. Roll.

*****[Loraine, William,** H. IV.–bore, quarterly sable and argent, a plain cross counterchanged. –Shirley.] F.

Loring, Nele, K.G. (a founder) 1344–bore, quarterly argent and gules, a bend sable; K. 398 fo. 24; at the siege of Calais 1345–8 the coat is blasoned, quarterly or and gules a bend of the last; and in the Surrey Roll (R. II.) quarterly argent and gules a bend engrailed of the last; Sir PIERS, of Beds, bore the bend plain; Parly. Roll; as did Sir WILLIAM at the siege of Rouen 1418.

L'Orti vel de Urtiaco, Henry de, baron 1299–bore, vert a pale or; Nobility Roll.

Lorty, Sir Henry de, of Somerset–(E. II. Roll) and JOHN (E. III. Roll) bore, azure a cross or; Parly. Roll and Jenyns' Ordinary.

Loudham, Sir John de, of Suffolk–(E. II. Roll) bore, argent, three inescocheons sable; Parly. and Ashmole Rolls. Ascribed to RAFFE in Jenyns' Ordinary.

Loudham, Sir John, of Derby–(E. II. Roll) bore, argent, on a bend azure, three crosses crosslet or; Parly. Roll. Crusily on the bend in Ashmole Roll and Harl. MS. 6137 fo. 19.

Lounde, Henry–(E. I. Roll) bore, argent, fretty azure; Jenyns' Roll.

Loundres, Robert de–(H. III. Roll) bore, per pale argent and sable, a chevron gules; Howard Roll. Sir ROBERT bore the chevron per pale gules and or; Ashmole Roll.

Louthe, Richard–(E. I. Roll) bore, "partie endentée" or and gules–tricked per pale dancettée or and gules; Jenyns' Roll.

WILLIAM LONGESPÉE, EARL OF SALISBURY,
SON OF HEN. II. BY FAIR ROSAMOND.
IN SALISBURY CATHEDRAL, 1226–7. *After Stothard.*

Lovayne, the Chastelain de—(E. I. Roll) bore, bendy (6) gules and or; Camden Roll. F.

Lovayne, Sire de—(E. I. Roll) bore, sable, a lyon rampant argent, crowned or (F.), Camden Roll; uncrowned in Howard Roll; his brother EDMUND differenced with a label (5) gules.

Lovain, Sire Thomas de, (of Suffolk)— bore, at the battle of Boroughbridge 1322, gules, billettée or a fess argent (F.); Parly. Roll and Jenyns' Ordinary. Ascribed to MATHEW (baron 1294); Glover, St. George, and other Rolls.

Lovedale, Sir John de, of Brabant—bore, at the siege of Calais 1345-8, sable, a bugle horn argent, on a chief of the second a lyon passant gardant or. F.

Lovedaye, Sir Richard, of Essex—(E. II. Roll) bore, azure, three bars dancettée or; Parly. Roll; colours reversed in Harl. MS. 6137 fo. 14. ROGER, bore dancée (6) or and sable (F.); St. George Roll.

Lovell, John, of Tichmarsh, banneret, baron, 1299—bore, at the battle of Falkirk 1298, undée (6) or and gules; Nobility, Parly., and Arundel Rolls. JOHN, Lord de Dackingg, sealed the Barons' letter to the Pope 1301, with these arms differenced with a label (3) on each pendant 3 mullets; see JOHN (2) below. Another JOHN bore them (undifferenced) at the second Dunstable tournament 1334; ascribed also to THOMAS, of Tichmarsh, in Jenyns' Ordinary; tricked or and azure in Ashmole Roll, and as, or three bars nebulée gules for Sir JOHN in Harleian and Guillim Rolls.

(1) JAMES, brother of JOHN, first-named, differenced with a quarter ermine, Harl. MS. 1481 fo. 43.

(2) JOHN, differenced with a label (5) azure, Camden and St. George Rolls; each charged with three mullets (6) or; Segar Roll. F.

(3) Sir WILLIAM, knighted at the capitulation of Calais 1348, differenced with a label (3) gobony argent and azure (F.); the label tricked in Ashmole MS. as barry (8) argent and azure, perhaps identical with trick of Sir WILLIAM, of Oxford, in Parly. Roll, who bore a label of VALENCE, viz., barry, argent and azure, on each pendant, a martlet gules.

(4) WILLIAM, differenced with a label of France at the second Dunstable tournament 1334.

(5) Sir JOHN, the bastard, (of Oxford), differenced with a label (3) azure, each charged with a mullet argent; Parly. Roll.

Lovell, Sir Thomas (of Oxon.), who tilted at the first Dunstable tournament 1308—bore undée (6) or and gules, a baston or azure (F.) in Parly. and Ashmole Rolls. JOHN LE FITZ bore the baston argent in Camden Roll, and another JOHN differenced with a baston sable in Arden Roll.

Lovell, Le Sr. (William) de—bore, at the siege of Rouen 1418, undée (6) or and gules *quarterly with,* azure, florettée and a lyon rampant gardant argent (F.); Surrey Roll, as LE SR. DE LOVEL and HOLLAND. Borne also by his grandfather, JOHN, K.G. 1405; K. 400 fo. 19.

Lovell, Sir Richard, banneret—bore, at the first Dunstable tournament 1308, or, crusily and a lyon rampant azure (F.); Parly. and Arundel Rolls. Not crusily in Glover Roll. JOHN took up the cross in the last Crusade 1270.

Lovetot, John de—(H. III. Roll) bore, argent, a lyon rampant per fess gules and sable, Arden and St. George Rolls; (sable and gules, Jenyns' Ordinary); NIGEL, of Hunts, bore the field or; Harl. MS. 1481 fo. 39.

*[**Lovett, Robert** (33 E. I.)—bore, argent, three wolves passant in pale sable.—Shirley.] F.

Low, Sir John le, of Bucks—(E. II. Roll) bore, argent, two bars and in chief three wolves' heads erased gules; Parly. Roll.

Low, Nichole le—(H. III. Roll) bore, gules, two wolves passant argent. (F.) Dering and Howard Rolls.

*Lowther, Henry**—(E. III. Roll) bore, argent, six annulets 3, 2, 1 sable; Jenyns' Ordinary— HUGH bore the field or; Jenyns' Ordinary and Ashmole Roll. Borne also by Sir JEFFRY, a Kentish Knight. See Incised Slab.

Lucien, Piers—(E. III. Roll) bore, argent, a lyon rampant gules, over all a baston gobony or and azure; Jenyns' Ordinary.

Luckyn, Sir Roland de (LOKYN)—bore, at the first Dunstable tournament 1308, bendy (6) gules and ermine. Surname doubtful; rather COKYN or QUKIN.

Lucre, William—(E. III. Roll) bore, argent, an orle sable; Jenyns' Ordinary.

Lucy, Sir Geffrey—(E. II. Roll) bore, gules, two lucies pileways argent; Holland Roll.

Lucy, Geffrey de, of Cockermouth, baron 1297—bore, gules, three lucies hauriant 2 and 1 argent (F.) Ashmole Roll; or, in Arden and Glover Rolls—ascribed to RICHARD in the Grimaldi Roll, and so carried at the siege of Rouen 1418. THOMAS, differenced at the second Dunstable tournament 1334 with a label azure and a bordure engrailed argent (F.); also by ANTHONY or AMERY in Jenyns' Ordinary—4 lucies in blason. Sir WILLIAM bore the paternal coat crusily argent; Harl. 1481, ff. 59–65.

Lucy, Sir Amery (AYMER or EMERY), of Kent—(H. III. Roll) bore, azure crusily and three lucies 2 and 1 hauriant or; Parliamentary, Howard, St. George and Dering Rolls. Sir THOMAS, of Kent, bore the lucies argent; Parliamentary Roll.

Lucy, Geoffrey, of Kent—(H. III. Roll) bore, gules, crusily three lucies hauriant 2 and 1 or (F.); Parliamentary Roll, &c. REYNOLD differenced with a label (3) azure; Surrey Roll. See Harl. 1481 ff. 59, 65.

Ludburgh, John de—(E. III. Roll) bore, gules, a chevron argent between three leopards' faces or; Jenyns' Ordinary.

Ludlowe, Sir Christopher de, knighted at the capitulation of Calais 1348—bore, or, a lyon rampant sable. (F.) So also JOHN, in Surrey Roll and Jenyns' Ordinary.

Ludlow, Sir Thomas, of Salop (E. II. Roll) and John (E. III.)—bore, azure, three lyons passant gardant argent; Parliamentary Roll and Jenyns' Ordinary.

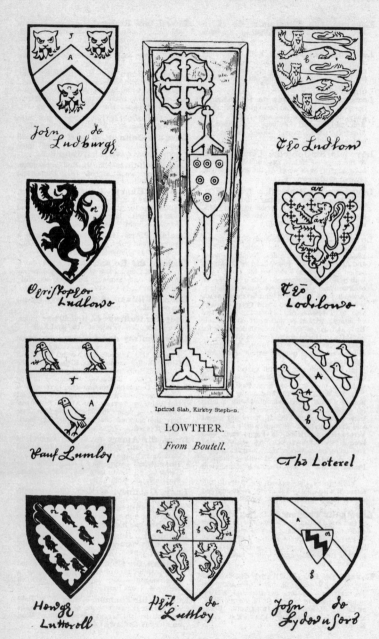

John de Ludburgh.

Christopher Ludlowo.

Paul Lumley.

Incised Slab, Kirkby Stephen.

LOWTHER.

From Boutell.

Tho Ludlow

Tho Lodilowo

Tho Loterel

Hondg Lutteroll

Phil de Luttley

John de Lydoviusford

Ludlow, Thomas—bore, at the second Dunstable tournament 1334, gules, crusily a lyon rampant and a border engrailed all argent (F.) (gardant in Parliamentary Roll); crusily or in Ashmole Roll.

Lukard ——, (E. III. Roll) bore, argent three (? wolves) heads couped gules; Ashmole Roll

*****Lumley, Rauf and Sir T.**—(R. II. Roll) bore, argent, a fess gules between three popinjays ppr. (F.); Surrey and Atkinson Rolls.

Lumley, Marmaduke (R. II. Roll) bore, gules, on a fess between three popinjays argent as many mullets pierced of the last. Sir ROBERT DE, of co. Durham (E. III) bore the mullets sable. (F.) Surrey and Parliamentary Rolls.

Lusignan, Sir Geoffrey—(H. III. Roll) bore, burulée (12) or and azure, a lyon rampant gules; Arden Roll. See also VALENCE and Harl. MS. 1418 fo. 29.

[**Luttley, Philip de**, 20 E. I.—bore, quarterly, or and azure four lyons rampant counterchanged.—Shirley.] F.

Luttrell, Andrew, and **Sir Geoffrey,** of co. Linc., **Robert** and **Thomas** (F.)—(H. III. Roll) bore azure, a bend between six martlets argent; St. George and Guillim Rolls. ALEXANDER took up the cross in the last Crusade 1270.

Luttrell, Sir Andrew, of co. Linc. (E. II. Roll), and Sir HUGH (H. VI. Roll) bore, or, a bend between six martlets sable; Parliamentary and Atkinson Rolls.

Luttrell, Hugh—bore, at the siege of Rouen 1418, or, a bend between six martlets sable a bordure engrailed of the second. (F.) Surrey Roll.

Lydevusers, Sir John, of France—bore, at the battle of Boroughbridge 1322, azure on a bend argent, an inescocheon or charged with a bend dancettée sable. F.

Lye (——), a Knight—(H. VI. Roll) bore, argent, a bend fusily sable, a crescent of the second; Arundel Roll.

Lymbury, Sir John, knighted at the capitulation of Calais 1348—bore, argent an escocheon sable within an orle of cinquefoyles gules. F.

Lymbury, Sire William de—bore, at the battle of Boroughbridge 1322, argent five cinquefoyles 2, 2, 1 sable. (F.) Six-foyles ascribed to JOHN in Jenyns' Ordinary.

Lynde *v.* **de la Lynde.**

Lyons, Sir John—bore, at the second Dunstable tournament 1334, argent, a lyon rampant gules. (F.) Ashmole Roll.

[**Lyster, John,** 6 E. II.—bore, ermine, on a fess sable three mullets or; Shirley.] See Bookplate.

Lythegranes, John—(E. III. Roll) bore, gules, an orle argent, over all a bend or; Jenyns' Ordinary.

*[**Lyttelton, Thomas**—bore (H. IV. Seal) argent, a chevron between three escallops sable.—Shirley.] F.

WILLIAM TAYLARD AND ELIZABETH ANSTEY, HIS WIFE;
in the Church of Dodington, Hunts.
37 H. VI.

John marshall.

Charles Vougo de la mayne

Cilo de maili

will Mailot

John malos

Baldwin malot

Rob Malet

michaell malovovori

will Maulare

M

M . . . seles, Edmond de—(H. III. Roll) bore, per pale argent and sable a fess counter-changed; St. George Roll—borne also by CUSACKE and FITZ PAINE. See WINCELES.

Mac Culloch, Patrick (MAKCOLAGH), of Scotland—(E. III. Roll)—bore, ermine, fretty gules ; Jenyns' Ordinary.

Mac Donnell, Sir Duncan, of Scotland—(E. I. Roll) bore, or, three lyonceux sable ; Nativity Roll.

Machell, John—(E. I. Roll) bore, argent, three greyhounds courant in pale sable collared (?gemelles) or. (F.) Jenyns' Ordinary.

Mac Moylin, Clarus (O'MOILLCHONRYE), Archdeacon of Elphin, founded the Abbey of Loughkee 1215 and also the Church of Deryndoyne, co. Roscommon, (ARCHDALE)—bore, argent, a dexter arm issuant from the sinister gules. (F.) Jenyns' Ordinary as CHARLES DE LA ROUGE MAYNE.

Madrestone, Philip de—(H. III. Roll) bore, gules, a double headed eagle displayed . . . . membered or ; Howard Roll.

Magnaby, Hugh de—(E. III. Roll) bore, argent, three bars sable, a maunch gules ; Grimaldi Roll. See MANBY.

‡**Maili, Giles de**—(H. III. Roll) bore, or, three mallets (or martels) gules. (F.) Dering Roll.

Mailott, William — (H. III. Roll) bore, gules, fretty or, a chief ermine. (F.) St. George Roll.

Mainwaring, John, of Pever—(E. IV. Roll) bore, gules, two bars argent, a crescent azure ——M. of Ightfield bore the same, *quarterly with*, checquy argent and sable ; Ballard Roll.

*****Man(waring), William**—(E. III. Roll) bore, argent, two bars gules ; Grimaldi Roll.

Malebys, Sir John — (E. II. Roll) bore, argent, three (heads " de bis ") hinds' heads couped gules ; Parliamentary Roll.

Malbys, Sir William—(E. III. Roll) bore, argent, a chevron between three hinds' heads erased gules ; Ashmole Roll—byses in Jenyns' Ordinary.

‡**Males, John**—(H. III. Roll) bore, gules, three Catherine wheels (F.) altered to round buckles, tongues to the dexter or ; Dering and Howard Rolls.

Malessour, Sir Thomas—(E. III. Roll) bore, per pale azure and gules, three crescents argent ; Ashmole Roll. ROBERT fil. HENRY took up the cross in the last Crusade 1270.

*****[Malet, Baldwin,** E. I.—bore, azure, three escallops or.—Shirley.] **F.**

‡**Malett, Robert**—(H. III. Roll) bore, sable, three round buckles, tongues to the dexter, 2 and 1, argent. (F.) Dering, Howard and St. George Rolls.

Mallet, Sir Thomas, of Notts—(E. II. Roll) bore, gules, a fess ermine between six buckles tongues to the dexter, or; Parliamentary Roll —the fess or, in Harl. MS. 6137 fo. 19ᵇ.

Malett, Richard and **Sir Robert,** of Bucks—(E. II. Roll) bore, sable, a chevron between three buckles tongues to the dexter argent ; Jenyns' and Parliamentary Roll.

Maleverer, John, Oliver, Robert — (E. III. Roll) bore, gules, three greyhounds courant in pale argent collared gemelles or ; Surrey Roll and Jenyns' Ordinary. (ROBERT bore the field sable—and the collar blasoned gobonée or and sable.) Sir THOMAS and Sir WILLIAM seem to have borne the greyhounds uncollared ; Arden, Parliamentary, Ballard and Arundel Rolls.

Maleverer, Sir John, Knight banneret— (H. VI. Roll) bore, sable, fretty or. Arundel Roll.

Maleverer, Sir Michael—bore, at the first Dunstable tournamen: 1308, argent, a bend engrailed gules—pɪrpure in Harl. MS. 6137. (F.) But see MALMAINS.

Maleverer, Sir John—(E. I. Roll) bore, gules, a chief or, over all a baston gobony (6) argent and azure ; Nativity and Parliamentary Rolls and Jenyns' Ordinary.

Malignee, Reynold — (R. II. Roll) bore, ermine, on a fess gules, three palets or ; Surrey Roll.

Malise, Roger de (MELESE)—(H. III. Roll) bore, argent, two bars and in chief three escallops gules ; Arden Roll. See also STRATHERNE.

Mallory, Antony and **Sir Peter** (1227)— bore, or, a lyon rampant tail fourchée gules ; Ashmole, Nobility and Surrey Rolls.

Mallory, Sir Piers, of co. Leicester—(E. II. Roll) bore, or, three lyonceux passant gardant sable ; Parliamentary Roll.

Mallory, Thomas—(E. III. Roll) or, bore, six lyonceux rampant, 3, 2, 1, sable ; Jenyns' Ordinary. JOHN DE LAYBOURNE bore the same, and JOHN DE ST. MARTIN bore the reverse.

Mallory, William (MAULARE)—(H. III. Roll) bore, or a demi-lyon tail fourchée in chief gules. (F.) St. George Roll.

MANDEVILLE AND DE VERE PEDIGREE.

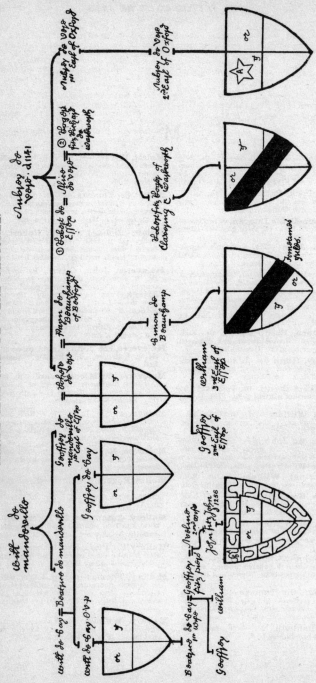

AN ILLUSTRATION OF

The Fundamental Principles of Heraldic Evolution which were based on Consanguinity or Alliance:

As shown in "Geoffrey de Mandeville," page 392, by J. H. Round, M.A.

Malmains (Sir) Thomas—bore, at the second Dunstable tournament 1334, gules (three dexter hands apaumée argent an), ermine (spot in each palm) ; Ashmole Roll.

‡**Malmains, Henry** — (H. III. Roll) bore, gules, three dexter hands apaumée 2 and 1 argent, Dering Roll ; hands, or (F.) in Howard Roll ; gules in Ashmole Roll ; NICOLE bore them argent in Dering and Howard Rolls. F.

Malmains, Sir Nicole, of Kent—(H. III. Roll) bore, gules, three sinister hands 2 and 1 couped ermine. (F.) Arden and St. George Rolls—argent in Camden Roll.

Malmains, Sir Nicholas—bore, at the first Dunstable tournament 1308, argent, a bend engrailed purpure (F.) (azure in Harl. MS. 6137 fo. 10) ; Parliamentary Roll and Jenyns' Ordinary—bend, plain in Nativity Roll.

Malmains, Thomas—(E. I. Roll) bore, sable, a bend lozengy argent. (F.) Jenyns' Ordinary.

Malolacu, Peter de, v. **Mauley.**

Maltham, Ratcliffe—(E. III. Roll) bore, gules, bezantée and a lyon rampant argent ; Jenyns' Ordinary.

Malton, Henry de—(E. I. Roll) bore, sable, a lyon rampant or, within an orle of annulets argent ; Jenyns' Ordinary.

Malton, Sir Henry de—(E. III. Roll) bore, sable, a lyon rampant argent crowned or, a bordure of the second charged with annulets (13) of the first ; Ashmole Roll.

Malton v. **Multon.**

Maltravers, Sir John, banneret, a baron 1330—bore, at the first Dunstable tournament 1308 (as le fitz) and at the battle of Boroughbridge 1322, sable, fretty or, a label (3) argent (F.) ; another Sir John bore it without the label (F.) at the siege of Calais 1345-8. Sire GAWYN bore the same, Howard Roll (H. III.) as often tricked and blasoned, a fret. See also ARUNDEL and FITZALAN. Ascribed to another JOHN (‡) in the Dering Roll.

‡**Maltravers, William**—(H. III. Roll) bore, sable, fretty or, on a quarter argent, three lyons passant in pale gules (F.) ; Dering Roll.

Malvesyn v. **Mavesyn.**

Man, the King, of the Isle of—bore, gules, three legs conjoined argent. (F.) Harl. MS. 6137 fo. 61ᵇ.

Manby, Hugh and **John de**—(E. III. Roll) bore, argent, three barrulets sable, over all a maunch gules ; Jenyns' Ordinary. MAGNABY in Grimaldi Roll.

Manby, Sir Walter de, banneret—(E. II. Roll) bore, azure, a cross or ; Parliamentary Roll.

Mancestre, Sir Grey de—bore, at the battle of Boroughbridge 1322, vair, a baston gules—vaire, argent and sable (F.) ; in the Ashmole MS., Harl. and Ashmole Rolls, and so also for JOHN in the St. George Roll.

Mancestre, Sir Simon de, of Warwickshire, bore, at the first Dunstable tournament 1308, vaire, or and sable on a bend gules three eaglets displayed or ; Parliamentary Roll.

Manclerk v. **Menclerk.**

Mandevile (Geffrey de) Earl of (Essex and Gloucester 1213-16)—bore, quarterly or and gules ; Glover and Grimaldi Rolls. See Mr. Round's GEOFFREY DE MANDEVILLE 392-6. Borne also by the family of DE SAY.

Mandevile, Sir John de, of Hants. or Wilts.—(E. II. Roll) bore, quarterly vair and gules ; Parliamentary Roll.

Mandevile, John de—(H. III. Roll) bore, quarterly argent and azure within a bordure vaire or and gules ; Howard Roll.

Mandevile, Sir John or **Richard de**, of Warwickshire (E. II. Roll) bore, azure, fretty or ; Parliamentary &c. (argent in Ashmole Roll). Sire RICHARD differenced it at the battle of Boroughbridge 1322 with a label (3) gules. F. Ascribed to another RICHARD in Dering Roll.

Mandevile, Richard de—(H. III. Roll) bore, azure, fretty argent a fess gules ; Glover and Grimaldi Rolls. RICHARD and THOMAS— the fretty *or* in Jenyns' Ordinary.

Mandeville, Sir Thomas de, of Essex— (E. II. Roll) bore, argent, on a chief indented gules, three martlets or ; Parliamentary Roll. JOHN in Harl. MS. 6137.

Mandeville, Thomas—(E. III. Roll) bore, or three barrulets azure ; Jenyns' Ordinary.

Manfee, Sir William, of Sussex—(H. III. Roll) bore, argent, a lyon rampant sable between nine escallops in orle gules. (F.) Dering (as MANBY), Camden and Parliamentary Rolls. Borne also by MANBY, of Elsham, in co. Linc.

Manners, Sir Bawdwyn de, of co. Cambridge—bore, at the first Dunstable tournament 1308. argent, a saltire engrailed sable. (F.) Ascribed also to HENRY, in Arden Roll (H. III.)—JOHN BLOYON bears the same ; Jenyns' Ordinary.

***Manners, John** and **Sir Robert**—(E. III. Roll)—bore, or, two bars azure and a chief gules (azure, in Nativity Roll) ; Ashmole and Jenyns' Ordinary.

Manningham (——), Knight (H. VI. Roll) —bore, argent a chevron between three moorcocks sable ; Arundel Roll.

Manny, Terry de—(E. III. Roll)—bore, or, three chevronels sable ; Ashmole Roll and Jenyns' Ordinary. RICHARD SUTTON, of Norfolk, bore the same.

Manny, Sir Walter de, K.B. 1331, K.G. 1359, a baron 1347—bore, at the second Dunstable tournament 1334, and at the siege of Calais 1345-8, or three chevronels sable, on the second a lyon passant of the first (F.) ; a lyon passant guardant on the premier chevronel, in K. 398 fo. 50—two chevronels only in Jenyns' Ordinary.

Mansell v. **Maunsell.**

Manston (——), a Kentish Knight—(H. VI. Roll) bore, gules, a fess ermine between three mullets pierced argent ; Arundel Roll.

Maneston, Richard de — (H. III. Roll) bore, argent, a fess gules between three eagles displayed sable ; Howard Roll.

Mantell (——), an Essex Knight—(H. VI. Roll) bore, argent, a cross engrailed between four martlets sable ; Arundel Roll.

Mapertishall, Sir John—(E. III. Roll) bore, argent, fretty sable, on a chief gules a lyon passant gardant or ; Ashmole Roll.

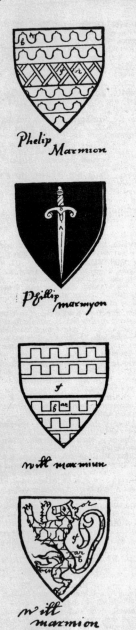

Phelip Marmion

Phillip marmyon

will marmiun

will marmion

Effigy of William Marshall, Earl of Pembroke 1219.
In the Temple Church. *From Richardson.*

March and Ulster, Earl of, *v.* **Edmund Mortimer.**

March *v.* **de la March.**

Marchington, Thomas—(R. II. Roll) bore, or, a fret sable, and a canton gules; Surrey Roll. See also MARKINGTON.

‡**Marconville, Raulf de**—(H. III. Roll) bore, quarterly argent (or, in Ashmole MS.) and azure, in the first quarter a lyon rampant gules. (F.) Dering Roll—same arms as DAVY GERCOMVILE alias JERKAVILE.

Mardestone, Sir Peers de, of Suffolk—(E. II. Roll) bore, azure, two bars argent, on a chief gules a lyon passant (gardant—H. 4033 ƒ 15ᵇ) or; Parly. Roll. See DENNARDESTON.

Mare, Mareli, Mareys, Mardac, *v.* **de la Mare, Marley, Smareys, Murdac.**

‡**Marines, Thomas de**—(H. III. Roll) bore, or, a cross engrailed gules. (F.) Dering and St. George Rolls.

Marke, Ingram, Robert and **William** (MERC or MERKE)—(H. III. Roll) bore, gules, a lyon rampant argent; Arden and Norfolk Rolls—"sautant embelif" (F.) in Jenyns' Ordinary. Sir JOHN of Essex bore it within a bordure indented or; Parly. Roll—engrailed (F.) in St. George Roll.

Markham, Sir Robert (ƒ Sir JOHN, King's Sergeant E. II.)—bore, azure, on a chief or a demi lyon rampant issuant gules. (F.) Sir JOHN of Sedbrooke bore it within a bordure (? argent). Harl. MS. 1481 fo. 84.

Markinfield, Andrew—(H. III. Roll) bore, argent, on a bend sable three besants; Jenyns' Ordy. (—) a Yorkshire Knight bore it—H. VI. Roll,—*quarterly with,* gules, three closed helmets argent, garnished sable—Arundel Roll.

Markington, Henry de—(E. III. Roll) bore, gules, an orle argent, over all a bend ermines; Jenyns' Ordinary.

Marley, Roger de (MERLEY)—(H. III. Roll) bore, barry, argent and gules, a bordure azure charged with martlets or; Glover Roll.

‡**Marley, Tebaud de** (MARELI)—(H. III. Roll) bore, or, a cross gules fretty argent, between four eaglets displayed azure. (F.) Dering Roll.

Marmaduke *v.* **Fitz Marmaduke.**

Marmion, John, banneret, baron 1297—bore, vair, a fess gules; Nobility Roll—as also did PHILIP (F.), Sir ROBERT in Norfolk, Ashmole and Arden Rolls; and WILLIAM (¿) in Dering Roll.

Marmion, Philip—(H. III. Roll) bore, vair, a fess gules fretty or. (F.) St. George and Glover Rolls.

Marmion, Sir John, Knight banneret—(H. VI. Roll)—bore, vert, a fess gules—and, added—between six lyons rampant 3 and 3 argent; Arundel Roll.

Marmion, Sir William—bore, at the siege of Calais 1345-8, vair, a fess gules, a label (3) or. (F.)

Marmion, Geoffrey, of Checkendon, Bucks, bore, vair, three mascles 2 and 1 gules—Harl. MS. 1481 fo. 71.

Marmion, Sir William—bore, at the first Dunstable tournament 1308, gules, a lyon rampant vair crowned or (F.); (uncrowned in Jenyns' Ordinary)—ascribed to a Suffolk Knight in Arundel Roll, and to Sir WILLIAM, of co. Leic. in Parly. Roll, though in Harl. MS. 6137 fo. 24, the field is argent and the lyon vert.

‡**Marmion, Philip** — (H. III. Roll) bore, sable, a sword erect in pale, point in chief argent; Dering and Howard Rolls—point in base (F.) Camden Roll.

Marnell, Stephen de—(H. III. Roll) bore, azure, on a chief or, a lyon passant gules; Howard Roll.

Marney, Robert—(R. II. Roll) bore, gules, a lyon rampant gardant argent; WILLIAM differenced with a label (3) or; Surrey Roll.

Marr, Earl of—(H. III. Roll) bore, azure, crusily fitchée and a bend or; Vincent 162 fo. 133ᵇ. In Norfolk Roll—azure, billettée and a bend or.

Marshall, The (Earl of Pembroke)—(H. III. Roll) bore, per pale or and vert a lyon rampant gules; Glover, Howard and Norfolk Rolls. See Monumental Effigy.

Marshall, William, banneret, baron 1309—bore, at the siege of Carlaverock 1300 (sealed the Barons' letter to the Pope 1301), and at the first Dunstable tournament 1308, gules a bend lozengy or (F.) (blasoned, engrailed); Parly. Roll. Sire ANCEL, of Norfolk, then differenced it with a label (3) argent. Another Sire ANCEL bore it undifferenced at the battle of Boroughbridge 1322 (Parly. Roll); Ascribed also to JOHN ‡ in Dering and Harl. Rolls—variously blasoned and tricked as, a bend fusily or lozengy, or a bend of fusils or lozenges conjoined—which last appears to be the recognised form. The Marshal of Ireland bore the bend argent; Jenyns' Ordinary.

Marshall, Sir Raffe le, of Hants—(E. II. Roll) bore, or, a cross moline gules, sometimes blasoned récercelée; Parliamentary Roll.

Martell, Sir John, of Essex, Kt.—(H. VI. Roll), and **Walter,** H. III.—bore, gules three martels (or hammers) argent. (F.) Arundel and Norfolk Rolls. Sir ADAM, of Berks, and RICHARD bore the field sable. (F.) Parly. and St. George Rolls.

‡**Martel, Richard**—(E. I. Roll) bore, or, three martels gules; Dering Roll.

Martel, Sir John—(E. I. Roll) bore, gules, a bend fusily or; Harleian Roll—same arms as MARSHALL.

Martell, Sir William—(E. I. Roll) bore, argent, two bars gules and in chief three torteaux.—Harleian Roll. See MOELS.

Martin, Sir William of Kemeys, banneret, baron 1295—bore, at the battle of Falkirk 1298, argent, two bars gules — (same as WILLIAM MAUDUYT) sealed the Barons' letter to the Pope 1301. Another Sir WILLIAM, differenced with a label (5) azure, bezanty. (F.) Guillim and Segar Rolls. See also St. MARTIN and WINTERSHULLE.

Martyne, Sir Waryne, of co. Glouc.—(E. II. Roll) bore, argent, two bars gules each charged with three bezants; Parly. Roll.

Martyn, Warryn—(H. III. Roll) bore, ermine three bars gules. WILLIAM differenced with a label (5) azure; Howard Roll. NICHOLAS and ROBERT took up the cross in the last Crusade 1270.

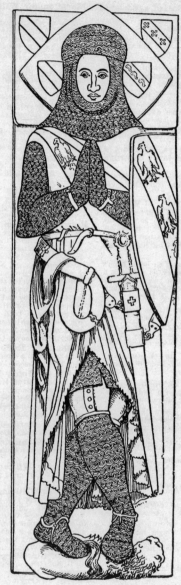

SIR ROBERT DE MAULEY.

(FORMERLY) IN YORK MINSTER, TEMP. E. II.   *From the "Archæologia."*

Martinaux, Anketyn—(E. III. Roll) bore, argent, a cinquefoyle gules ; Jenyns' Ordinary.

Martindale, William de—(E. I. Roll) bore, barry (6) argent and gules, a baston sable; Jenyns' Roll.

*[**Massie, Hugh,** of Coddington, R. II.—bore, quarterly gules and or, in the first and fourth three fleurs-de-lys argent, a canton of the third.—Shirley.] F

*[**Massingberd, Lambert,** (E. I.)—bore, azure, three quatrefoyles (two and one) in chief a boar passant or, charged on the shoulder with a cross patée gules.—Shirley.] F.

Massy, Sir Geoffrey, of Tatton—(E. IV. Roll) bore, quarterly gules and argent, a label (5) azure—with crest. GEOFFREY BARTON, of Tatton, is heir to this cote of MASSEY and also of MASSY ; Ballard Roll.

Massy, Hamond — (E. III. Roll) bore, quarterly gules and or n the first a lyon rampant argent ; Jenyns' Ordinary. Another cote is thus obscurely blasoned from the Howard Roll, bendy of lozenges conjoined or and gules a lyon rampant sable.

Massy, John—(R. II. Roll) bore, sable, a cross patonce or ; Surrey Roll.

Mateflon, Guy de—(H. III. Roll) bore, chevronny (8) gules and or ; Howard Roll.

Mathew (——), of Thornton Steward, Yorks. (E. I. Roll) bore, gules, three martlets argent, tricked as martels ; Jenyns' Roll. See FITZ STEVEN, of Thornton Rust.

Mauduit, Sir John—bore, at the first Dunstable tournament 1308, gules, three piles wavy meeting in base or. Undée or and gules "en lung" (F.) was carried by Le Sire . . . MAUDUYT at the battle of Boroughbridge 1322, *i.e.,* paly wavy (6) or and gules ; tricked as three palets nebulée in Ashmole Roll for Sir JOHN of Swinford, and as three piles dancettée meeting in base for Sir JOHN of Hants. or Wilts. in Parly. Roll. JOHN, carried "gules" (*sic*)—at the second Dunstable tournament 1334—and in Jenyns' Roll (E. I.) paly undée (6) or and sable is ascribed to another JOHN.

Mauduit, Sir Roger, of Northumberland—bore, at the battle of Boroughbridge 1322, ermine, two bars gules (F.) ; Parly. and Nativity Rolls. WALTER and WILLIAM bore the field argent ; Sir WILLIAM MARTYN bears the same ; Glover and Jenyns Rolls.

Mauduit, Sir John, of Warminster, and **Thomas**—(E. III. Rolls) bore, chequy or and azure, a bordure gules (F.) (tricked bezanty in Jenyns' Ordinary), Ashmole and St. George Rolls. THOMAS took up the cross in the last Crusade 1270.

Maulare, William v. **Mallory.**

Mauley, Piers de—(H. III. Roll) bore, vair, a maunch gules (F.) ; Glover and St. George Rolls.

Mauley, Sir Piers de, banneret, baron 1295—bore, at the battle of Falkirk 1298, or, a bend sable (F.) and sealed the Barons' letter to the Pope 1301. Sir ROBERT, or rather, perhaps, Sir PIERS (3rd baron) bore it at the siege of Calais 1345-8, and Sir PIERS, banneret (4th baron), bore it at the siege of

Rouen 1418 ; Arundel Roll. In Jenyns' Roll Le Sire MAULEY bore or, a bend sable *quarterly with* BIGOD, same as ROBERT FOSSARD. His brothers (1) ROBERT, bore, on the bend, three eaglets displayed argent and (2) JOHN, bore on the bend, as many dolphins embowed argent ; Harl. MS. 1481 fo. 87. See following entries.

Mauley, Sir Robert de, of Yorkshire—(E. II. Roll) bore, or, on a bend sable three eaglets displayed argent (F.) ; Segar and Harleian Rolls ; see Monumental Effigy, and "Archæologia," vol. 31, p. 47—the bend azure in Ashmole Roll.

Mauley, Sir John de, of Yorkshire—(E. II. Roll) bore, or, on a bend sable three dolphins embowed argent ; Parly. Roll.

Mauley, Sir Ed. de, of Yorkshire—(E. I. Roll) bore, or, on a bend sable between two lyons rampant of the second, three dolphins embowed argent, Harleian Roll ; another coat—or, on a bend sable, three eight foyles (imperfectly drawn) argent ; Harleian Roll.

Mauley, Sir Edmond de, of Yorkshire—(E. II. Roll) bore, or, on a bend sable, three wyverns, tails nowed, argent—F. (Harl. MS. 4033 fo. 43ʰ) ; three bunches of grapes argent ; Harl. MS. 6137, Parliamentary Roll. F.

Maunsell, John—(E. I. Roll) bore, sable, a chevron between three mullets pierced or ; Jenyns' Roll.

Maunsell, Thomas and **Sir William,** of co. Glouc.—(E. II. Roll) bore, gules, a fess argent, a label (3, 5) argent—sometimes or (F.) ; St. George and Parly. Rolls, Jenyns' Ordinary ; ascribed to another WILLIAM in Dering Roll.

*[**Maunsell, William le,** 1287—bore, argent, a chevron between three maunches sable.—Shirley.] F.

Maurus, Aumeri de—(H. III. Roll) bore, checquy or and azure, a chevron gules. (F.) St. George Roll. Variously called DE ERDERNE and DE MANES.

Maurewarde, Thomas—(R. II. Roll) bore, azure, a fess argent between three cinquefoyles pierced or ; Surrey Roll.

Mause, William—(R. II. Roll) bore, argent, semée of escallops gules and a lyon rampant sable ; Howard Roll.

Mautas, William—(H. III. Roll) bore, azure, seven mascles conjoined 3, 3, 1 or ; Howard Roll.

Maveysyn, Guy—(H. III. Roll) bore, or two bars gules ; Howard Roll.

‡**Maveysyn, Henry, John** and **Robert**—(H. III. Roll) bore, gules, three bendlets argent ; Dering, Howard and Surrey Rolls. JOHN GRELEY, carries the same.

Mawburney ——, (E. I. Roll) bore, masculy gules and ermine, on a quarter azure a cross recercelée or — tricked masculy and a cross moline ; Jenyns' Roll.

Medhope ——, (E. III. Roll) bore, ermine, a lyon rampant azure ; Jenyns' Ordinary.

Meldone, Sir William—(E. III. Roll) bore, argent, a saltire sable ; Ashmole Roll.

Melise, Roger de—(H. III. Roll) bore, argent two bars and in chief three escallops gules ; Arden Roll. See MALISE.

John
de moolton

Richard mexyll

nich de meynyll

Henry monyld

nichot
de monno

John   de
Moreworth

Jon̄
de motoham

Andr̄
m et stodo

Godfrey de
Mono

witt
d' Midleton

John de mitford

John d' Moles

Melsanby, Walter de—(E. I. Roll) bore, sable, two gemelles and a chief argent ; Jenyns' Roll.

Melton, John and **William de**—(E. III. Roll) bore, azure, a cross patonce voided argent ; Jenyns', Surrey, and Cotgrave Rolls, in which last it is not voided.

Melton, John de—(E. III. Roll) bore, argent, a cross patonce voided gules—pecé botonée. (F.) Jenyns' Ordinary.

Menclerk, Peres de—(H. III. Roll) bore, azure, three cinquefoyles argent ; Norfolk Roll.

*****Menell, Sir Hugh** (MENYLE, MENYLL, MEYNELL), of co. Cambridge—bore, at the first Dunstable tournament 1308, vaire argent and sable, a label (3) gules. (F.) Sir GYLES, bore it undifferenced, and RICHARD bore the label gobony or and gules. (F.) Jenyns' Ordinary.

*****Menill, Sir Nichol de**, of Whorlton, banneret, Baron Meinell, 1295—bore, at the battle of Falkirk 1298, azure, three gemelles and a chief or. (F.) St. George Roll and Jenyns' Ordinary ; sealed the Barons' letter to the Pope 1301 ; borne also (H. III. Roll) by TREMON (or TREVOR) DE MENYLL in Glover Roll ; two gemelles in Nobility, Guillim and Parliamentary Rolls.

Menell, Gilbert de—(E. III. Roll) bore, paly (6) argent and gules, on a bend sable three horse-shoes or ; Cotgrave Roll.

Menyle, Henry (E. III. Roll) bore, paly (12) and **William**, paly (8) argent and gules, on a bend azure three horse-shoes or. (F.) Jenyns' Ordinary.

Menell, Ralph (MENVILE)—(E. III. Roll) bore, vert, a lyon rampant argent crowned gules ; Jenyns' Ordinary. Same as JOHN BEESTON.

Menne, Nichol de—(H. III. Roll) bore, or, on a chief azure three lyonceux rampant argent. (F.) Arden and St. George Rolls ; same as D'INCULE.

Merc *v.* **Marke.**

Menteth, the Earl of—(E. III. Roll) bore, gules, a fess checquy or and azure—tricked compony ; Jenyns' Ordinary.

Meredith, Howell ap—(H. III. Roll) bore, paly (6) or and azure on a fess gules three mullets argent. (F.) St. George Roll.

‡**Meremond, Geffrey de**—(H. III. Roll) bore, argent two bars sable (F.) Dering Roll ; and in chief a mullet pierced gules, in the Ashmole copy.

‡**Mereworth, William** and **John**—(H. III. Roll) bore, argent, crusily sable and a chevron gules. (F.) Dering and Howard Rolls and Jenyns' Ordinary.

Meriett, Sir John de (MERYETT or MERIEL) of Hants or Wilts.—(E. II. Roll) bore, barry (6) or and sable (barry 8 in Ashmole). Sir JOHN, the nephew, differenced with a bend ermine ; Parliamentary Roll.

Merton, Sir Richard—(E. III. Roll) bore, vert, three bendlets argent ; Ashmole Roll ; argent and azure in Jenyns' Ordinary.

Merville *v.* **Henry le Sturmin.**

Meschines *v.* **Randolf Blondeville.**

Mesi, Robert de—(H. III. Roll) bore, gules, a fess argent. (F.) Arden and St. George Rolls ; reversed in Harl. MS. 6137 fo. 55, "Mezi" fo. 82.

Metford (——), an Essex Knight—(H. VI. Roll) bore, or, a fess gules, between three martlets sable, *quarterly with*, sable, a lyon rampant tail fourchée and renowée argent ; Arundel Roll.

Metham, Thomas — bore, at the second Dunstable tournament 1334, quarterly azure and argent a fleur-de-lys or. (F.) Surrey Roll and Jenyns' Ordinary. Sir THOMAS in Ashmole Roll, reversed in Howard Roll.

Metstede, Andrew—(E. III. Roll) bore, quarterly or and gules four escallops counterchanged ; Jenyns' Ordinary.

Mette, Semkyn, of Kent, Kt.—(H. VI. Roll) bore, azure, on a bend or three mascles gules ; a fleur-de-lys argent ; Arundel Roll.

Meus, Sir Godfrey de (MEUX)—bore, at the first Dunstable tournament 1308, azure, six gryphons segreant 3, 2, 1 or. (F.) Ascribed also to Sir GEFFREY and Sir JOHN ; Ashmole and Nativity Rolls.

Middleton (——) a Yorkshire Knight—(H. VI. Roll) bore, gules, a lyon rampant argent, on a bend azure three escallops or ; Arundel Roll.

*****Midelton, John** of Northumberland, and **William de**—(H. III. Roll) bore, quarterly gules and or, in the first quarter a cross patonce (patée in blason) argent ; St. George Roll and Jenyns' Ordinary. (F.) GILBERT took up the cross in the last Crusade 1270.

Midelton, Pieres de—(E. III. Roll) bore, argent, fretty and a quarter sable ; Jenyns' Ordinary.

Milkeley, Sir Robert de, of Herts, Kt.— (E. II. Roll) bore, gules, three chevronels argent ; Parliamentary Roll.

‡**Mingee, Adam de**—(H. III. Roll) bore, or, on a quarter azure, a cat-a-mountain's head erased argent ; Dering Roll.

Mynyot, John—(E. I. Roll) bore, gules, three helmets argent, crested or—ROGER of Calton differenced with a label (3) azure ; Jenyns' Roll.

Missenden, Edmond de—(R. II. Roll) bore, or, a cross engrailed gules, in the dexter canton a raven proper ; Surrey Roll. See MUSSENDEN.

*****[Mitford, John de**, R. II.—bore, argent, a fess between three moles sable.—Shirley.] F. ROBERT took up the cross in the last Crusade 1270.

Moels, Sir John, of Cadbury, banneret, baron 1299—bore, at the battle of Falkirk 1298 argent, two bars gules, in chief three torteaux (F.) sealed the Barons' letter to the Pope 1301 ; borne also by JOHN MULES at the second Dunstable tournament 1334 ; Arundel, Nobility, Parliamentary Rolls, and by ROGER in St. George Roll ; mullets ascribed to NICHOLAS in Glover Roll.

Mohaut *v.* **Monhaute** and **Monthalt.**

Jorn mohun

Will d Moun

Wai d Molecastre

Walt molosworth

Symon de moloun

Will mollynorb

Bertram do mountbocher

Bertram de mountbocher

Ada de monthaut

Will montaguo

Simon de montagu

Dino do mountford

Mohun, Sire John de, of Dunster, banneret, baron 1299—sealed the Barons' letter to the Pope 1301. He bore at the battle of Falkirk 1298, and at the siege of Carlaverock 1300, or, a cross engrailed sable (F.) ; when his son Sir JOHN (father of Sir JOHN, 2nd baron, K.G., and a founder) also bore it, with a label (3) gules ; Nobility, Arundel, and Ashmole Rolls. Sir REIGNOLD, knighted at the capitulation of Calais 1348—differenced it with a label (5) gobony argent and gules.

Mohun, Reginald de—(E. III. Roll) bore, gules, a maunch ermine ; Grimaldi Roll—the maunch argent, in Glover Roll—and so ascribed to WILLIAM differenced by a label (5) azure (F.) in St. George Roll.

Mohun, John de—(H. III. Roll) bore, gules, a maunch ermine, a fleur-de-lys issuant or. (F.) Howard Roll and Jenyns' Ordinary.

Moigne *v.* **Moyne.**

Molcaster, Sir Robert—(E. III. Roll) bore, barry (6) argent and gules, a baston azure ; Ashmole Roll. Burulée (12) ; as MONCASTRE in Surrey Roll.

Molcastre, Walter de—(H. III. Roll) bore, burulée (12) argent and gules, on a bend azure three escallops or. (F.) St. George and Parliamentary Rolls tricked in the latter, barry 8 and 10—the bend sable.

*****Molesworth, Sir Walter de**, of Hunts—(E. III. Roll) bore, vair, a bordure gules crusily or ; Parliamentary Roll. F.

Moleyns, Sir John and **Richard**—(E. III. Roll) bore, sable, on a chief azure three lozenges conjoined gules ; Ashmole Roll and Jenyns' Ordinary—the field azure, in the coat carried by Lord MOLEYNS, who was slain at the capitulation of Calais 1348.

Moleyns, John—(R. II. Roll) bore, **or,** three palets wavy gules ; Surrey Roll.

Molington, Sir John de, of Suffolk—(E. II. Roll) bore, argent, a fess between two chevrones azure ; Parliamentary Roll.

†**Moloun, Symon de**—(H. III. Roll) bore, azure, bezanty 3, 2, 1 (sometimes platey) on a chief argent (sometimes or) a demi-lyon rampant issuant sable. (F.) Dering Roll, gules in Ashmole MS.

Molton *v.* **Moton.**

*****Molyneux, William**—(E. III. Roll) bore, azure, a fer-de-moulin pierced or ; Jenyns' Ordinary and Ballard Roll ; on an escutcheon of pretence, the atchievement of Sir THOMAS of Sefton, in Ballard Roll.

Mompesson, Sir Giles, of Norfolk—(E. II. Roll) bore, argent, a lyon sable, on his shoulder a " pynzon " or ; Parliamentary Roll.

Mompesson, Giles de—(E. I. Roll) bore, argent twelve birds (? " pynzon") 3, 3, 3, 2, 1 azure, beaked vert and membered gules. (F.) Segar Roll.

Monbocher, Bertram de—bore, at the siege of Carlaverock 1300, argent, three pitchers sable, a bordure of the second bezanty (F.) (piles meeting in base gules (F.) in Harl. MS. 6137 fo. 39ᵇ) ; Sire BERTRAM bore the pitchers gules at the battle of Boroughbridge 1322 ; Surrey and Harleian Rolls ; piles as before in Parliamentary Roll.

Monbocher, Raffe—(E. I. Roll) bore, argent, three " possenetts " gules ; Jenyns' Roll.

Monchensi *v.* **Munchensi.**

Monceaux, Hamond—(E. I. Roll) bore, gules, a cross recercelée (tricked moline) and an escallop or ; Jenyns' Roll.

Moncell, William de—(H. III. Roll) bore, gules, a fess argent, a label (5) or ; Howard Roll.

Monhaute *v.* **Monthalt.**

†**Monhaute, Adam de**—(H. III. Roll) bore, argent, three gemelles over all a lyon rampant gules (F.) ; Howard Roll and Jenyns' Ordinary ; borne also by Sir JAMES, of Lincolnshire, in Parliamentary Roll. JOHN and SIMON also took up the cross in the last Crusade 1270.

Monmouth, Guy and **John de**—(H. III Roll)—bore, or, three chevronels gules, over all a vair (argent in Norfolk Roll and Jenyns' Ordinary) ; Arden and Glover Rolls and Jenyns' Ordinary.

*****[Monson, John**, 1378—bore, or, two chevronels gules.—Shirley.] F.

Montagu, Sir Simon de, baron 1300, bore, at the battle of Falkirk 1298, quarterly 1 and 4, argent, three lozenges conjoined in fess gules ; 2 and 3, azure, a gryphon segreant or ; one of the earliest examples of a quarterly coat. With the first he sealed the Barons' letter to the Pope 1301, and at the siege of Carlaverock 1300, he carried the gryphon only, which is supposed to be the original arms of the family ; a male gryphon is ascribed to OSMOND in Jenyns' Roll.

Montagu, Sir William, baron 1317-18—bore, at the first Dunstable tournament 1308, argent, three lozenges conjoined in fess gules, as did WILLIAM (Earl of Salisbury 1337-44) at the second Dunstable tournament 1334 ; when Lyonel differenced with, a quarter gules. F. Sir EDMUND bore it at the siege of Calais 1345-8, differenced with a label or on each pendant an eagle displayed vert ; JOHN bore it within a bordure sable in lieu of the label, Surrey Roll, and his son RICHARD of Stowe in Somerset differenced with three pellets 2 and 1 in lieu of the bordure, Harl. MS. 1481 fo. 45.

Montagu, William, 2nd Earl of Salisbury 1344, K.G., a founder—bore, argent three lozenges conjoined in fess gules, *quarterly with*, gules, three armed legs flexed and conjoined argent garnished or, for he lordship of Man, in Surrey Roll ; in the same Roll the quarters are also given in the reverse order. THOMAS, 4th Earl of Salisbury, 1409, K.G.—bore, at the siege of Rouen 1418, argent three lozenges conjoined in fess gules *quarterly with*, MONTHERMER, or an eagle displayed vert.

Montagu, Edward—(E. II. Roll) bore, ermine, three lozenges conjoined in fess gules ; Jenyns' Ordinary.

Montfichet, Richard de—(H. III. Roll) bore, gules, three chevronels or, a label azure ; Glover Roll.

Montfort, Simon de, Earl of Leicester 1230-65—bore, gules, a lyon rampant tail fourchée argent. (F.) ; Arden and Camden Rolls. PHILIP differenced with a label azure ; Norfolk Roll—a coat with the tinctures reversed in Ashmole Roll.

John montfort   Adam d Mungomeri   will de Montgomory

John montgomory   Rob de mungaut   Andrew mongault

Edward mountgermor   Edw. mountgermor   Saffo de Mountgermor

will mordaunt   will morolo   Robt Morley

Montfort, Sir Alexander, Sir John, of Dorset, **Sir Lawrence** and **Thomas**—(E. III. Roll) bore, argent, crusily gules and a lyon rampant azure ; Ashmole, Parliamentary, Grimaldi and Jenyns' Ordinary.

Montfort, Sir John de, banneret—bore, bendy (10) or and azure. (F.) Parliamentary and Jenyns' Rolls. PIERS (‡) has (1) bendy of 12 in Camden Roll (2) or, four bendlets sinister azure in Dering and Arden Rolls and (3) azure six bendlets or, in Segar Roll.

‡**Montfort, Robert** and **Sir William**—(F. III. Roll) bore, bendy (10) or and azure a label (5) gules (azure in St. George) ; Dering and Howard Rolls ; a label (3) gules for Sir WILLIAM, of Surrey or Sussex ; Parliamentary Roll.

Montfort, Sir John—(E. III. Roll) bore, azure, three bendlets or ; Guillim Roll ; another four bendlets or, a label (3) gules ; Ashmole Roll ; or, four bendlets azure ; Nobility Roll. H. 6.

Montfort, Sir John, banneret—(H. VI. Roll) bore, barry undée (10) argent and azure ; Arundel Roll. F.

Montfort, Sir W.—(H. VI. Roll) bore, argent, on a chief azure two fleurs-de-lys or ; Atkinson Roll.

Montford, John de (otherwise DE BRETAGNE), Duke of Britanny, Earl of Richmond 1372, K.G. 1376—bore, checquy or and azure a bordure of England, over all a canton ermine ; K. 398 fo. 35. See BRETAGNE.

Mon(tford), le Count de—bore, or four bendlets azure ; Nobility Roll, temp. H. VI. 1422-60 ; more like MONTHERMER in Roll.

Montgomery, Adam de—(H. III. Roll) bore, or, three lyons passant in pale sable (F.) ; Arden and St. George Rolls.

Montgomery, John—(E. III. Roll) bore, argent, a cross engrailed between four mullets gules ; Jenyns' Ordinary.

Montgomery, John—(F. III. Roll) bore, gules, a false escocheon ermine, within an orle of horse-shoes argent, nailed sable ; Jenyns' Ordinary ; the same is ascribed to WILLIAM in the Glover Roll, and is blasoned ermine, a bordure gules, entoyre of horse-shoes argent nailed sable ; in Arden Roll the tinctures are argent gules or and sable.

Montgomery, Sir William de (of Derby or Notts)—bore, at the battle of Boroughbridge 1322, or, an eagle displayed azure (F.) ; borne also by Sir JOHN at the siege of Calais 1345-8, and also by NICOL and Sir WALTER.

Monthalt, Sir Roger (MOHAUT, MUHATT, MUNHAUT) baron 1295 (H. III. Roll) —bore, azure, a lyon rampant argent ; Glover and Howard Rolls ; his brother Sir ROBERT, banneret, baron 1299, bore the same at the battle of Falkirk 1298, and at the siege of Carlaverock 1300 (sealed the Barons' letter to the Pope 1301) ; Nobility, Parliamentary and Arundel Rolls. (JOHN ORTON bore the same) JOHN differenced it with a label (3) or, Jenyns' Ordinary ; a label (5) gules, Arden and St. George Rolls, and so also with the field or, also in Arden Roll.

Monthalt, Sir Andrew (MONHAULT), of Masenden—bore, at the siege of Calais 1345-8, azure, a lyon rampant argent, a bordure or. F.

Monthaute v. Monhaute.

Monthermer, Sir Raffe, banneret, Earl of Gloucester and Hertford 1209—bore, at the battle of Falkirk 1298, or, an eagle displayed vert, and at the siege of Carlaverock 1300, or, three chevronels gules for CLARE, Earl of Gloucester, though he was then vested in his own arms as borne at Falkirk. Sealed, with an eagle, the Barons' letter to the Pope 1301.

Monthermer, Sir Edward, Knighted at the capitulation of Calais 1348—bore, or an eagle displayed vert, on a bordure gules 8 or 10 lyons of England (F.) ; Ashmole Roll. Ascribed also to another EDWARD (F.) without the bordure in Jenyns' Ordinary.

Montjoy v. Mountjoy.

Montmorency, John de—(H. III. Roll) bore, or, poudrée of eagles azure, a cross gules ; Norfolk Roll.

Montryvell —— (E. III. Roll)— bore, azure, a lyon tail fourchée or, armed and crowned argent ; Cotgrave Roll.

Moran, Sir Thomas—(E. III. Roll) bore, argent, on a fess sable three six-foyles pierced or, in chief a lyon passant gules ; Ashmole Roll.

Mordac v. Murdac.

*[**Mordaunt, William** (25 E. I.)—bore, argent, a chevron between three estoiles sable. —Shirley.] F.

More v. de la More.

More —— (F. III. Roll) bore, argent, a fess dancettée (3) paly (6) or and gules, between three spur-rowells sable ; Ashmole Roll.

More, Sir Thomas—(E. III. Roll) bore, gules, a bend paly billettée sable ; Ashmole Roll, Same as MORREWES.

Morell, Sir William—bore, at the battle of Boroughbridge 1322, azure, florettée or, a demi-lyon (rampant) couped argent, over all a bend gules. F.

Moresby, Sir Hu₂h—(E. III. Roll) bore, sable a cross or, a cinquefoyle pierced argent ; Ashmole Roll. A six-foyle tricked in Jenyns' Ordinary.

Morgan (——), a Kentish Knight—(H. VI. Roll) bore, sable, a chevron between three spear-heads erect argent ; Arundel Roll.

Morley, Sir William, of Norfolk, baron 1299—bore, at the battle of Falkirk 1298, argent, a lyon rampant tail fourchée sable—crowned or, in Parly. and Segar Rolls.

Morley, Sir Robert de—bore, at the battle of Boroughbridge 1322, argent, a lyon rampant sable crowned or (F.) Another Sir ROBERT bore the same at the siege of Calais 1345-8 ; borne also by THOMAS, 4th Lord, K.G., father of THOMAS (5th Lord) who bore it at the siege of Rouen 1418 ; Surrey Roll and Jenyns' Ordinary.

Morley, Robert de—(R. II. Roll) bore, argent, a lyon rampant sable, a label (3) gules ; Surrey Roll. Another ROBERT bore, sable, a lyon rampant argent, a baston gules ; Cotgrave Roll.

Barth̄ de
morston

Witt
d' Morriton

bobt
de morteygno

Dousf. de
mortimor

Gefray
d' Mortimer

Henꝛ de mortun

Howgᵉ
de mortimor

bobt de.
Mortimor

bogor
le mortimor

bogor
de mortoñ

bogor de
mortimor
le fitz

witt molton

Morley, John de, of Craven—(E. III. Roll)
bore, sable, a leopard's face or jessant-de-lys
argent ; Jenyns' Ordinary.

Mor(r)ice, John—(E. III. Roll) bore, sable, a
saltire engrailed argent - on an E. P. the arms
of the Earl of Ulster ; viz., or, a cross gules ;
Jenyns' Ordinary.

Morice, John (Morys or Norys)—(E. III.
Roll) bore, azure, billettée and a cross recercelée argent—moline in trick ; Jenyns' Ordinary.

Morieus, Sir Hugh de, of Suffolk, Kt.—
(E. II. Roll) bore, azure three meures (mul-
berry) leaves or ; Parly. Roll. See MURIELL.

Mor(r)eres, William de—(H. III. Roll)
bore, ermine, on a fess or four bendlets azure
(F.) ; Arden and St. George Rolls.

Morrewes, Thomas —(R. II. Roll) bore,
gules, a bend argent billettée sable ; Surrey
Roll. Same as Sir THOMAS MORE.

‡**Moristone, Bartholomew de**—(H. III.
Roll), bore, argent, on a chief gules three
birds or (F.) ; Dering and Howard Rolls.

Morritone, William de, *v.* **Morteyn.**

Morteyn *v.* **Norteyn, or Norton.**

Morteyn, Robert de, and **William de**
—(H. III. Roll) bore, ermine a chief gules ;
Glover and Jenyns' Rolls ; called MORRITONE
(F.) in St. George Roll. Sir JOHN, of Beds
(E. II. Roll) bore the chief indented ; Parly.
Roll.

Morteyne, Sir Roger, banneret—bore, at
the siege of Carlaverock 1300, azure three
lyonceux rampant 3, 2, 1. azure—sable (F.) in Harl. MS.
6137 fo. 39, and in Arundel and Parly. Rolls,
where the tails are fourchée.

Morteyn, Sir Roger—(E. I. Roll) bore,
azure, three lyons rampant argent (sometimes,
or) ; Guillim Roll.

Moton, Sir William—(E. III. Roll) bore,
argent, a cinquefoyle pierced azure ; Ashmole
and Surrey Rolls.

Mortimer, William, of Attleborough,
baron 1294—bore, or, florettée sable, Nobility
Roll ; his son, Sir CONSTANTINE, bore the
same 3, 2, 1 at the first Dunstable tournament
1308, and as florettée (F.) at the battle of
Boroughbridge 1322. Ascribed also to WIL-
LIAM in Arden and St. George Rolls. In the
Ashmole Roll, the coat also occurs differenced
with a label (3) gules ; another, with a bordure
engrailed argent.

Mortimer, John—bore, at the second Dunstable tournament 1334, as also, Sir WILLIAM,
Knighted at the capitulation of Calais 1348,
azure, florettée argent.

Mortimer, Henry de, of Foxcote—(H. III.
Roll) bore, argent on a cross azure five escallops of the field ; Arden Roll. WILLIAM,
bore the escallops or (F.), in St. George Roll.

Mortimer, Sir Hugh de, of Richard's
Castle, baron 1299—bore, at the (F.) battle of
Falkirk 1298. and at the siege of Carlaverock
1300, gules, two bars vair. (F.) Ascribed
also to JOHN in Jenyns' Ordinary and to
ROBERT (‡) in Dering Roll. F.

Mortimer, Robert de—(H. III. Roll) bore,
barry or and vert florettée ; Norfolk Roll.

Mortimer, Walron—(E. III. Roll) bore,
argent, two bars gules, on a chief of the last
three six-foyles of the first—cinquefoyles in the
trick ; Jenyns' Ordinary.

Mortimer, William de—(E. III. Roll) bore,
gules, crusily or, two bars vair ; Arden Roll.

Mortimer, Sir William, banneret—(H. VI.
Roll) bore, gules, a cross flory or, Arundel
Roll ; in which the name is doubtful, perhaps
LATYMER is intended.

Mortimer, Edmund, of Wigmore, baron
1295—bore, as did ROGER his father, barry (6)
or and azure, on a chief of the first three
palets between two esquires based of the
second, over all an inescocheon argent (sealed
the Barons' letter to the Pope 1301) ; Camden
and Guillim Rolls. [EDMUND, last Earl of
March and Ulster, K.B. ; quartered DE BURGH
or, a cross gules ; Surrey Roll.] His brethren
differenced
 (1) Sir WILLIAM with a baston, and
 (2) Sir GEOFFREY, with a saltire over all
gules (F.) ; ascribed also to Sir JOHN of
Herefordshire in Parly. Roll.

Mortimer, Sir Roger, of Chirke, a baron
1307, bore, MORTIMER'S arms with the inescocheon ermine (F.) (wrongly argent in the
Nobility Roll) at the battle of Falkirk 1298
and at the siege of Carlaverock 1300 ; sealed
the Barons' letter to the Pope 1301 ; see also
Harl. MS. 1481 *ff* 33, 66.
 The field is as often as not tricked the
reverse and bars (3) rather than barry. The
seals of EDMUND and ROGER show one palet
only on the chief.

Mortimer, Hugh, lord of Chilmarsh, uncle
to EDMUND above-named, bore, at the battle
of Boroughbridge 1322, MORTIMER's arms or
and gules—the inescocheon argent—Harl.
MS. 1481 *ff* 33, 66 ; ascribed also to Sir
HENRY of Herefordshire in the Parly. Roll ;
the reverse, gules and or, ascribed to JOHN,
in Norfolk and St. George Rolls.

Mortimer, Sir Roger de, le fiz (*f* ROGER,
2nd baron) of Herefordshire, bore, at the first
Dunstable tournament 1308, MORTIMER's arms
or and azure, the inescocheon (argent) charged
with a lyon rampant purpure (F.) ; Parly.
Roll. HENRY bore the reverse azure and or,
the inescocheon (argent) billettée sable ; Arden
Roll.

Mortimer, Raf de—(H. III. Roll) bore,
MORTIMER's arms sable and or—the inescocheon argent ; Arden Roll.

Mote *v.* **De la Mote.**

Moton, Sir William—(E. III. Roll) bore,
argent, a cinquefoyle pierced azure ; Ashmole
and Surrey Rolls.

Moton, Sir William (or MOLTON), knighted
at the capitulation of Calais 1348—bore,
argent, crusily and three fleurs-de-lys within a
bordure engrailed sable. F.

Moulton *v.* **Multon.**

Moulton, Sir Edmond—(E. III. Roll) bore,
azure a cross patonce voided argent ; Ashmole
Roll. See MULTON.

Moulton, Thomas de—bore, at the second
Dunstable tournament 1334, gules, a baston
azure. See MULTON.

Ḡḡᵒ do
Mountnoy

John do
mountony

John de m̃baẏ

John
mountnoy

John Mowin

Will moigno

Jon de moinos

John moyno

Borong lo moyo

mulfo

John do multon

John multon

Mounce, Sir Eble or **Ellis de**—(E. II. Roll) bore, or, a bend cotised gules, a label (3) azure ; Parliamentary Roll.

Mounceaux, Hamond—(E. I. Roll) bore, gules, a cross recercelée (moline, in trick) and an escallop or ; Jenyns' Roll.

Mounchensi v. Munchensi.

Mouncy, Sir Walter de, baron 1299—bore, at the battle of Falkirk 1298 and at the siege of Carlaverock 1300, chequy argent and gules. (F.) Nobility and Guillim Rolls ; sealed the Barons' letter to the Pope 1301.

Mounferant, Hubert—(E. III. Roll) bore, paly (6) argent and sable, on a chief gules three six-foyles or, cinquefoyles in trick ; Jenyns' Ordinary.

†**Mounteney, Sir Ernaud** (MUNCENI), of Essex, and †**Robert**—(H. III. Roll) bore, azure, a bend between six martlets or ; Glover and Howard Rolls. Sir JOHN, differenced with a mullet gules at the first Dunstable tournament 1308 ; St. George Roll, attributes a label (5) gules to ERNAUD.

Mounteney, Sir Thomas de—bore, at the battle of Boroughbridge 1322, gules, a bend between six martlets or. (F.) Parly. Roll ; ascribed to JOHN also in Surrey Roll.

Mounteney, Sir John de—bore, at the battle of Boroughbridge 1322, gules, a bend cotised or between six martlets of the last. (F.) Ashmole MS. and Parliamentary Roll. Ascribed to THOMAS in Jenyns' Ordinary.

‡**Mounteney, Robert de**—(H. III. Roll) bore, azure, a bend or. (F.) Dering Roll.

Mounteney, John and **Rauffe**—(E. III. Roll) bore, vaire argent and sable, a chief or over all a baston gules ; Jenyns' Ordinary. F.

Mountfort v. Montford.

‡**Mountjoy, Stephen de**—(H. III. Roll) bore, gules, three inescocheons or. (F.) Dering and Howard Rolls.

Mowbray, Sir John, banneret—bore, at the first Dunstable tournament 1308, gules, a lyon rampant argent (F.) ; borne also by his father, ROGER, of Axholme, baron 1295 ; Nobility and Parliamentary Rolls. Ascribed to ROGER (‡) in Dering Roll, in Arden Roll to ROBERT (possibly in error for ROGER), and in the Arundel Roll to Sir THOMAS, banneret. Sir PHILIP, of Scotland, differenced with a bend " engréle" sable ; Nativity Roll.

Mowbray, Sr. de, the Earl Marshal (THOMAS, K.G., Duke of Norfolk 1397-8)—bore, England, differenced with a label (5) argent *quarterly with*, gules a lyon rampant argent ; Surrey Roll. Another coat in the same Roll attributed to THOMAS MOWBRAY, is England differenced with a label (3) argent charged with three eagles displayed of the first *quarterly with*, gules, a lyon rampant argent, a label (3) azure.

‡ **Mowin, John**—(H. III. Roll) bore, argent, three cinquefoyles pierced and a quarter gules. (F.) Dering Roll.

†**Moyne, Berenger le**—(E. III. Roll) bore, argent, a cross patonce (*vel* patée) gules, flory in trick—same as HENRY COLVILE ; Jenyns' Ordinary ; colours reversed in Segar Roll, there called " LE MOYE." F.

Moyne, Jacques le and **Sir John**, of Suffolk—(F. II. Roll) bore, or a saltire engrailed gules ; Jenyns' Ordinary and Parliamentary Roll. F.

Moyne, Sir John—(E. III. Roll) bore, or, three bars vert ; Ashmole Roll. F.

Moyne (MOINS), **John le**—(H. III. Roll) bore, azure, six martlets 3, 2, 1 or ; Arden Roll. Ascribed to HENRY DE APPLEBY in St. George Roll.

Moyne, John—(E. I. Roll) bore,. argent, a bend between six mullets gules ; Jenyns' Roll. F.

Moyn, John, VEL MOYZ—(H. III. Roll) bore, argent a canton gules—the field diapered masculy ; Howard Roll.

Moyle, Sir Thomas le—(E. III. Roll) bore, argent, on a canton gules a lyon passant gardant or ; Ashmole Roll.

Moyle, Sir William le, of Hunts.—(E. II. Roll) bore, azure, crusily and a fess dancettée argent ; Parliamentary Roll.

Moyne, William (MOIGNE)—(E. III. Roll) bore, argent, two bars and in chief three mullets (6) sable ; Surrey Roll and Jenyns' Ordinary. F.

Mules, John—bore, at the second Dunstable tournament 1334, argent, two bars gules, on a chief of the last three torteaux. See MOELS.

Mulso (——), a Suffolk Kt.—(H. VI. Roll) bore, ermine on a bend sable three goats' heads erased argent, horned or ; Arundel Roll. F.

Multon, Sir Thomas de, of Egremont, banneret, baron 1299—bore, at the battle of Falkirk 1298, barry argent and gules (F.) ; sealed the Barons' letter to the Pope 1301, and bore, at the siege of Carlaverock 1300, argent, three bars gules (F.) ; (no doubt his banner was the same on both occasions, though Falkirk seems in error) ; Arundel, Glover and Nobility Rolls (reversed in Arden, Guillim and St. George Rolls). The latter coat borne also by RAFFE, of Egremont and Tebauld ; Howard Roll and Jenyns' Ordinary, and at the second Dunstable tournament 1334, by JOHN.

Multon, Thomas de, of Frankton, bore, at the second Dunstable tournament 1334 (argent three bars) gules, a baston azure (gules, three bars argen n Cotgrave Roll, and so in Ashmole, with the baston azure) ; THOMAS of Gillesland differenced with a label (3) vert (no baston), Jenyns' Ordinary (no label in Cotgrave Roll), and THOMAS LE FORRESTIER with a label sable ; Glover Roll.

Multon, John, of Frankton—(E. III. Roll) bore, gules, three bars argent, in chief as many crescents or ; Jenyns' Ordinary. F.

Multon, John de—(E. III. Roll) bore, sable three bars, in chief as many annulets all argent ; Jenyns' Ordinary. F.

Multon, Thomas—(E. III. Roll) bore argent, two bars gules, a label (3) vert ; Jenyns' Ordinary.

James
de moltune

maryn de
mounconsy

will
de mounconsy

Vand
mounconsio

John de
muneduo

þo de
mortror

þo muriell

Rauf Musart

Joh de
muchegros

þo musgravo

þo de
Mussenden

Henri Mustel.

Multon, Thomas de, of Gillesland, baron 1307 —bore (Vaux, *i.e.*), checquy or and gules ; Nobility Roll 1310 and Parliamentary Roll ; according to Cotgrave Roll he subsequently bore argent three bars gules ; a label (3) vert is added in Jenyns' Ordinary, see above; Arden and St. George Rolls ascribe the Vaux coat to HUBERT DE MOLETONE. F.

Multon, Sir James and **Sir Thomas,** both of Lincolnshire—(E. II. Roll) bore, checquy, or and sable (F.); Harleian, Parly. and Segar Rolls.

Multon, Sir Edmond—(E. III. Roll) bore, azure a cross patonce voided argent ; Ashmole Roll.

†Muncells, William, or **Walran** (MUN-CEUS, MUNCELTH) — (H. III. Roll) bore, argent, a bend sable (F.) ; Dering, Howard, and Camden Rolls. See MUNCY.

†Munceny, Ernulphus and **Robert** *v.* **Mounteney.**

Munchensi, Sir Richard de—bore, at the battle of Boroughbridge 1322, argent, a chevron between three billets azure (F.); ascribed to RAFFE, the billets sable in Jenyns' Ordinary.

Munchensi, Rauf de—(H. III. Roll) bore, quarterly sable and or (F.) ; St. George Roll ; differenced with a mullet (6) argent ; Arden Roll.

Munchensi, Randolph—(E. III. Roll) bore gyronny (8) sable and or, an inescocheon ermine, a mullet (6) gules, tricked sable ; Jenyns' Ordinary. F.

Munchensi, Sir William, of Herts—(E. II. Roll) bore, burulée (14) argent and azure. Sir RANDOLPH differenced with a label (3) gules, Parly. Roll ; barry of 8 Harl. MS. 6137 fo. 13 ; barry of 10 in Jenyns' Ordinary.

Munchensi, Walter—(H. III. Roll) bore, argent, seven barrulets azure (F.) ; Arden Roll, six in St. George Roll.

†Munchensi, William de—(E. I. Roll) bore, or, three inescocheons vair (F.) ; Camden Roll. In Dering Roll the inescocheons are [barry (6)] vair and gules, and are so ascribed to WARREN in Glover and Howard Rolls.

Munchensi, Sir Warren de—(E. I. Roll) bore, or, three inescocheons bendy (6) vair and gules ; Grimaldi Roll and Jenyns' Ordinary.

Munchensi, Sir William de—(E. II. Roll) bore, lozengy vair and gules (F.) Parly. Roll, Harl. MS. 4033 fo. 51.

†Muncy, John de—(H. III. Roll) bore, gules, a maunch or (F.) ; Dering and Howard Rolls.

Murdac, Sir Thomas, of Northants—bore, at the first Dunstable tournament 1308, or, fretty sable (F.) ; Parly. Roll. Borne also by Sir JOHN at the battle of Boroughbridge 1322, and by another Sir JOHN who was knighted at the capitulation of Calais 1348 ; Ashmole and Surrey and H. VI. Nobility Rolls ; ascribed to WILLIAM (F.) in St. George Roll.

Muriell, Thomas, of Scremby—(E. III. Roll) bore, argent a chevron between three " roses crochees " sable, Catherine wheels in trick ; Jenyns' Ordinary. F.

†Musard, Rauf de—(H. III. Roll) bore, gules three plates (F.) ; Dering, Howard and St. George Rolls.

Muscegros, John and **Robert**—(E. I. Roll) bore, or, a lyon rampant gules ; Camden Roll and Jenyns' Ordinary ; apparently borne also by GRIFFITH LE FITZ OWEN and by WILLIAM POLE.

Muscegros, John de—(E. I. Roll) bore, gules, a lyon rampant or, a label (6) azure (F.) ; Segar Roll.

*Musgrave, Sir Thomas—(E. III. Roll) bore, azure, six annulets 3, 2, 1 or ; Ashmole Roll and Jenyns' Ordinary. F.

Mussenden, Edmond de—(R. II. Roll) bore, or, a cross engrailed gules, a Cornish chough proper ; Surrey Roll. Sir THOMAS, slain at the siege of Calais 1347, bore the field argent and a martlet sable. F.

Mustell, Henry—(H. III. Roll) bore, sable, platey and a quarter ermine (F.) ; Arden and St. George Rolls.

Mustone, William de—(E. I. Roll) bore, argent, a chevron between three crosses patée sable —patonce in trick ; Jenyns' Roll.

Myland, Amary de—(H. III. Roll) bore, sable, billettée and a lyon rampant tail fourchée argent ; Norfolk Roll. See NEIRNWYST.

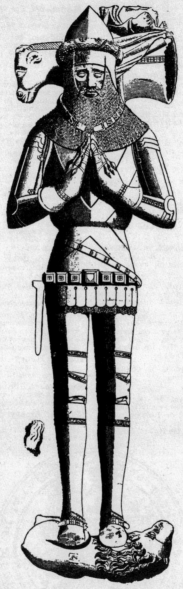

RALPH NEVILL, EARL OF WESTMORLAND.

IN STAINDROP CHURCH, CO. DURHAM, 1425. *After Stothard.*

N—O

Nalinghurst *v.* **Naylyngest.**

Namar, Sir Robert, K.G. 1370—bore, or, a lyon rampant sable, oppressed by a baston gules; K. 398 fo. 57.

Nancovenant, Sir Geoffrey, of Lincolnshire—(F. II. Roll) bore, argent, a bend sable, cotised gules; Parliamentary Roll and Jenyns' Ordinary.

Napton, John de—(F. III. Roll) bore, or, on a fess azure three escallops argent; Harleian Roll and Jenyns' Ordinary.

[**Narburgh** (——) bore, ermine a chief gules. (F.) Arden Roll—added in "a newe hand."]

Naunton, Bartholomew de—(E. I. Roll) bore, sable, three martlets argent; Ashmole and Jenyns' Rolls.

Nautur *v.* **Vautur.**

Naylyngest, Sir Hew, of Essex, Kt.— (H. VI. Roll) bore, gules, a cross engrailed or —*quarterly with*—argent, a bend sable cotised or; Arundel Roll.

Neirnwyst, Sir John (or NEYRMIST) of Bucks—(E. II. Roll) bore, sable, billettée and a lyon rampant argent; Parliamentary Roll.

Nele, John de—(H. III. Roll) bore, burulée (12) argent and azure, a bend gules; Howard Roll.

‡**Nele, Rauf de**—(H. III. Roll) bore, gules, two fish (? eel) hauriant addorsed argent. (F.) Dering Roll; or, in Ashmole MS.

Nelson, Henry le—(H. III. Roll) bore, paly (6) argent and purpure a bend (new put in with colours) vaire or and sable. (F.) Arden Roll—paly argent and sable in Add. MS. 4965.

Nerford, John de (or NEIRFORD)—bore, at the second Dunstable tournament 1334, gules, a lyon rampant ermine. F.) Borne also by Sir William of Norfolk (probably father of John), summoned to advise on the affairs of the realm 1294, 1297. See also WILLIAM in Dering Roll.

Nertoft, Sir Adam de, of Essex—(E. II. Roll) bore, sable, a lyon rampant or; Parliamentary Roll.

‡**Nervile, Laurence** and **Sir Jarvis** (or JAMES NEVILE), of Sussex—(H. III. Rolls) bore, gules crusily two hunting-horns addorsed or (F.F.)—trumpets or hautboys; Dering, Arden and Howard Rolls.

Nevesfeld, Sir Guy de, of Essex—(E. II. Roll) bore, vert, an eagle displayed or; Parliamentary Roll. See STEINEFELD.

Neville, Geffray de—(E. I. Roll) bore, or, une nief, maste, cables and phane sable. (F.) Grimaldi Roll.

Nevill, John de, of Hornby, Yorks.—bore, at the second Dunstable tournament 1334, argent, a saltire gules. (F.) Ascribed also to GEFFREY in St. George Roll, to ROBERT of Hornby, in Jenyns' Ordinary, and to Sir JOHN Guillim and Parly. Rolls. JOHN of Lincolnshire bore the same between four fleurs-delys azure; Jenyns' Ordinary—same as THOMAS HARLESTONE.

Nevill, Raff of Raby, baron 1295—bore, gules, a saltire argent; Nobility Roll—sealed the Barons' letter to the Pope 1301. Borne at the siege of Rouen 1418 by RALPH, Earl of Westmoreland, K.G., see Monumental Effigy; Ascribed also to Sir RANDOLPH banneret, in Arundel Roll, and to ROBERT of Raby, in Grimaldi Roll; and to another ROBERT‡ in Dering Roll. RICHARD, K.G. 1436, Earl of Salisbury (and his son RICHARD, K.G., Earl of Warwick), differenced, with a label (3) gobony argent and azure, his brother (a) WILLIAM, lord FUACONBERG, with a mullet sable, (b) his brother GEORGE, lord LATIMER with a pellet, and (c) his brother *EDWARD lord of Abergavenny, with a rose gules. (F.) Harl. MS. 1418 fo. 49ᵇ.

(1) ALEXANDER of Condal differenced with a mullet pierced sable; Surrey Roll and Jenyns' Ordinary.

(2) ALEXANDER of Raskelfe differenced with a martlet gules; Jenyns' Ordinary.

(3) Sir JOHN differenced with a label (3) azure; Ashmole Roll.

(4) Sir RALPH differenced with an annulet sable; Ashmole Roll

(5) Sir ROBERT differenced with a mullet sable; Ashmole Roll.

(6) THOMAS, differenced as ALEXANDER of Raskelf; Surrey Roll.

(7) WILLIAM, differenced with a saltire azure; Surrey Roll.

Nevile, Rauf de—bore, at the second Dunstable tournament 1334, gules, a saltire "engréle" argent. F.

Nevil, Robert, DE PYKALE—(E. III. Roll) bore, gules, a saltire ermine; Jenyns' Ordinary.

Nevil, John de—(E. I. Roll) bore, gules, a saltire or; Segar Roll—the reverse borne by JOHN DE VAUTUR.

Nevile, Sir Hugh, banneret, and **John,** of Essex—(H. III. Roll) bore, azure, a lyon rampant or. (F.) Arundel and Norfolk Rolls and Jenyns' Ordinary.

Nevill, John, "the forester" (E. III. Roll) bore, gules, a lyon rampant argent guttée de poix; Jenyns' Ordinary. See below.

Neville, Sir Philip, of Lincolnshire—(E. II. Roll) bore, argent, a fess dancettée gules, a bend sable. (F.) Parly. Roll—a bordure sable bezantée (no bend), Jenyns' Ordinary.

Joan d' Neiule

Peillip de nouile

Teband d' Neiule

Peillip de nouile

wat. d' noiuile

Robt. de now burgg

Adam d' Newenton

Robert noel

John norburyz

Ricard de norfolk

John de norays

Andr. north cote

Neville, Sir Philip, of co. Leic.—(E. II. Roll) bore, gules, five fusils conjoined in fess argent, in chief three mullets or. (F.) Sir RICHARD, differenced with a label (3) azure instead of the mullets ; Parliamentary Roll.

Nevile, Sir Roger (or ROBERT)—bore, at the siege of Calais 1345-8, gules, a fess dancettée argent, a bordure indented or. (F.) Ascribed to Sir ROBERT, of co. Leic., in Parly. Roll.

Nevile, Sir Philip—bore, at the battle of Boroughbridge 1322, gules, a chief engrailed (dancettée in trick) argent, within a bordure indented (engrailed in trick) or—a label (3) azure each file charged with 2 bars of the second, blasoned, barruly of the second and azure. F.

Nevill, Sir Thomas, of Lincolnshire—(E. II. Roll)—bore, argent, a chief indented vert, a bend gules ; Parliamentary Roll.

Nevylle, Raffe, of Cotham or Cletham—(E. III. Roll) bore, ermine, a chief indented azure ; Jenyns' Ordinary.

Nevile, Walter de (NEIUILE)—(H. III. Roll) bore, azure, two gemelles in chief a lyon passant gardant argent. (F.) St. George Roll.

Nevile, John de—(H. III. Roll) bore, paly (6) azure and or, on a chief gules three escallops argent ; Howard Roll.

Neville, Geoffrey, of Sheriff Hutton—(E. III. Roll) bore, masculy (tricked lozengy) or and gules, a quarter ermine ; Jenyns Ordinary—ascribed in the Glover Roll to JOHN DE NEVILL, cowerde.

Nevill, John le, LE FORRESTIER—(H. III. Roll) bore, or, crusily sable, a bend gules ; Glover Roll. See above.

Nevile, Tebaud de (NEIUILE)—(H. III. Roll) bore, azure, crusily three garbs argent banded gules (F.) ; St. George Roll—another crusily or, and a chief argent, added.

Nevile, Sir Theobald de, of Northants or Rutland—(E. II. Roll) bore, azure, crusily three fleurs-de-lys argent ; Parly. Roll—leopards' faces jessant-de-lys ; Harl. MS. 6137 fo. 23.

Nevile, Sir John de, of Northants or Rutland—(E. II. Roll) bore, gules, crusily and three fleurs-de-lys argent ; Parly. Roll.

Nevill, Henry—(H. III. Roll) bore, gules, crusily fitchée and three leopards' faces jessant-de-lys or, on the first, a crescent azure ; Surrey Roll.

Nevyll, John—(H. III. Roll) bore, gu'es, crusily fitchée or three leopards' faces of the last jessant-de-lys argent ; Surrey Roll.

Newborough, Robert de—bore, at the second Dunstable tournament 1334, bendy (6) or and azure, a bordure engrelée gules (F.) Borne also by Sir ROBERT, knighted at the capitulation of Calais 1348.

Newby, John de—(E. I. Roll) bore, sable on a fess argent three roses gules ; Jenyns' Roll.

Newenham, Sir John de, of Surrey—(E. II. Roll) bore, argent a cross gules over all a bendlet azure ; Parly. Roll.

Newenton, Sir Adam de, of Essex—(E. II. Roll) bore, azure, six eaglets displayed 3, 2, 1 or ; Parly. Roll—three eaglets (F.) in Arden Roll and Jenyns' Ordinary.

Newmarch, Adam and **Sir Thomas**—(E. III. Roll) bore, argent five fusils conjoined in fess gules ; Jenyns' Ordinary, Ashmole and Parly. Rolls ; (4 fusils in H. 6137 fo. 19) a fess engrelée in Nativity Roll.

Newmarch, Sir Adam, Sir John, and **Roger**—(E. II. Roll) bore, gules, five fusils conjoined in fess or (F.) ; Jenyns' Ordinary, Holland, Parly. and St. George Rolls—(a fess engrailed in Glover Roll)—the reverse ascribed to Sir ROBERT in Guillim Roll.

Newson, John de—(E. I. Roll) bore, azure, on a fess argent three crosses gules ; patée in trick ; Jenyns' Roll.

*****[Noel, Robert** (*c* H. III.)—bore, · or, fretty gules, a canton ermine.—Shirley.] F.

Noon, Edmond—(H. III. Roll) bore, or, a cross engrailed vert ; Surrey Roll.

Norbury, Hugh de (NORTHBURGH)—(H. III. Roll) bore, gules, crusily fitchée and three roses argent ; Surrey Roll.

Norbury, Sir John—bore, at the siege of Rouen 1418, sable, on a chevron between three bulls' heads cabossed argent, a fleur-de-lys of the field (F.) ; Arundel Roll.

Norfolk, Earl of, *v.* Bigod.

Norfolk, Richard—(E. I. Roll) bore, gules, a fess between two chevronels argent (F.) ; Segar Roll.

Norland, Richard—(H. III. Roll) bore, sable, a chevron argent between three wolves' heads of the second couped gules ; Surrey Roll.

‡**Normanvile, Rafe de**—(H. III. Roll) bore, gules, a fess double cotised argent ; Dering, Surrey, and Camden Rolls. F.

Normanvile, Rafe—(E. I. Roll) bore, argent, on a fess double cotised gules three fleurs-de-lys of the first ; Jenyns' Roll and Ordinary—being the arms of BADLESMERE with the fleurs-de-lys added.

Norris (NORAIS), **Sir John de**—bore, at the first Dunstable tournament 1308, sable, billettée and a cross florettée argent. F. In the Parly. Roll the cross ascribed to Sir JOHN, of co. Glouc. seems to be patée florettée fitchée at the foot in Harl. MS. 6137—differently tricked in Harl. MS. 4033, fo. 48. F.

Norrys, Sir John—(E. III. Roll) bore, azure, billettée and a cross recercelée argent—moline in trick ; Jenyns' Ordinary.

Northam, Thomas de—(E. III. Roll) bore, per pale gules and sable, a lyon rampant argent crowned or ; Jenyns' Ordinary.

*****[Northcote, Andrew** (17 E. I.)—bore, or, a chief gules fretty of the first.—Shirley.] F.

‡**Northey, William de**—(H. III. Roll) bore, quarterly argent and azure (F.) ; Dering and Howard Rolls.

Northwich, Northwood *v.* NORWICH, NORWOOD.

SIR ROGER NORTHWOODE.
IN MINSTER CHURCH, ISLE OF SHEPPEY, 1361.
After Stothard.   For his wife see Foliot, page 102.

NEVILL.

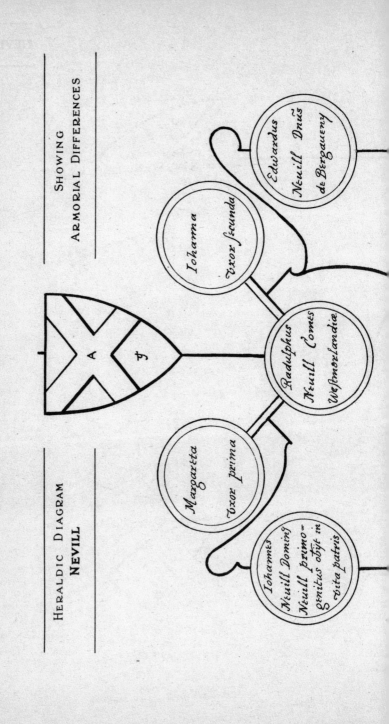

HERALDIC DIAGRAM
NEVILL

SHOWING
ARMORIAL DIFFERENCES

Margareta
Uxor prima

Iohanes
Neuill Dominj
Neuill primo-
genitus obijt in
vita patris

Radulphus
Neuill Comes
Westmorlandiæ.

Iohanna
Uxor secunda

Edwardus
Neuill Dñus
de Bergaueny

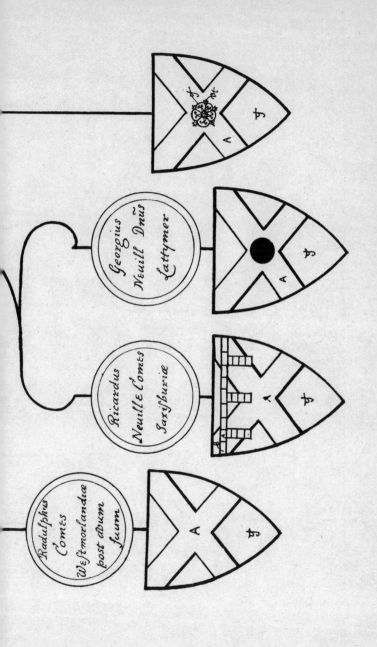

Norton, Sir —— (NORTEYN) — bore, at the siege of Rouen 1418, per pale gules and azure a lyon rampant ermine. (F.) same as NORWICH.

Norton, Sir James de, of Hants.—(E. II. Roll) bore, vert, a lyon rampant or; Parly. Roll. WILLIAM took up the cross in the last Crusade 1270.

Norton, Sir John, of Kent—(H. VI. Roll) bore, gules, a cross potent ermine; Arundel Roll.

Norton, Richard—(E. I. Roll) bore, argent, three cushions sable; Jenyns' Roll.

Norton, Robert de—(E. I. Roll) bore, sable, three piles florettée at the points, issuant from the sinister argent (F.); Jenyns' Roll.

Norton, Sir Robert de —bore, at the battle of Boroughbridge 1322, argent, a chevron between three buckles sable; tongues to the base in the Ashmole MS. F.

Norton, Roger—(E. III. Roll) bore, argent, a chevron between three cushions sable; Jenyns' Ordinary. RICHARD bore this without the chevron, as above.

* **Norton, Roger,** formerly CONYERS, E. III. —bore, azure, a maunch ermine, over all a bend gules.—Shirley.] F.

Norwich, Sir John de (NORTHWICH)— bore, at the battle of Boroughbridge 1322, per pale gules and azure a lyon rampant ermine, a label (3) or. (F.) Ascribed to . , . NORTEYN, undifferenced at the siege of Rouen 1418.

Norwich, John de (NORTHWYCHE)—bore, at the second Dunstable tournament 1334, per pale azure and gules, a lyon rampant ermine (F.), as did Sir JOHN, knighted at the capitulation of Calais 1348; Jenyns' Roll and Ordinary.

Norwoode, Sir John de—bore, at the first Dunstable tournament 1308, argent, a cross engrailed gules, a label (3) azure.

Norwoode, Sir John de, baron 1313— bore, ermine a cross engrailed gules (a saltire in Jenyns' Ordinary); Arundel and Howard Roll; ascribed to ROGER‡ in Dering Roll; see Monumental Effigy for Sir ROGER 1301. Sir JOHN, of Kent, differenced with a label of three azure (F.); and another, ermine a cross patonce gules; Harleian Roll.

Nowell, John—(E. III. Roll) bore, argent, three covered cups sable; Jenyns' Ordinary.

Nowers, John and **Sir Simon,** of Norfolk —(E. II. Roll) bore, vaire argent and gules; Parly. Roll and Jenyns' Ordinary. RICHARD COLEWORTH bears the same.

Nowers, Sir John and **Roger**—(E. III. Roll) bore, azure, a fess argent between three garbs or; Ashmole and Jenyns' Rolls. F.

Nowers, Sir (——), a Bucks Knight—(E. II. Roll) bore, argent, two bars and in chief three crescents gules; Parliamentary Roll.

Nunwike, Roger de—(E. III. Roll) bore, sable, an eagle displayed or; Jenyns' Ordinary. F.

Nutbeme, Thomas—(H. III. Roll) bore, gules, a fess undée ermine; Surrey Roll.

*[**Oakeley, Philip,** H. III.—bore, argent, on a fess between three crescents gules as many fleurs-de-lys or; Shirley.] F.

Obehale, Raufe d'—(H. III. Roll) bore, or, a fess gules. (F.) St. George Roll.

Oc —— v. Ok ——.

O'Clare'ce, Sir B.—(H. VI. Roll) bore, azure, a fleur-de-lys or, on a chief (? of the last) gussett gules, two lyons combatant or; another blason, per chevron gules and azure in the chief or two lyons rampant combatant or; and for the Honour of CLARE or CLARENCE, a fleur-de-lys of the third in base; Atkinson Roll.

Odingsells *v.* **Doddingsells.**

Offingtone, David de—(H. III. Roll) bore, azure, a saltire engrailed or. (F.) Arden and St. George Rolls.

Ogard (——), a Yorkshire (?) Knight—(H. VI. Roll) bore, azure, a mullet of seven points argent; Arundel Roll. See HUGARD.

[**Oglander, Roger,** H. III.—bore, azure, a stork between three crosses crosslet fitchée or. —Shirley.] F.

*[**Ogle, Robert** (or RICHARD) **de**—(E. I. Roll) bore, argent, a fess between three crescents gules (Jenyns' Roll) F.; *quarterly with,* or an orle azure; Surrey Roll.

*[**Oker, Philip de (OKEOVER)**—(H. III. Roll) bore, ermine, on a chief gules three besants. (F.) Surrey Roll.

Okham, Nicholas de—(E. III. Roll) bore, gules, a fess between three crescents, 2 and 1 argent; Jenyns' Ordinary.

Okindon *v.* **Wokindon.**

Okinton, John d'—(H. III. Roll) bore, or, three cinquefoyles pierced gules; St. George Roll; roses (F.) in Harl. MS. 6137 fo. 88.

Okinton (OLZETON) John de—(H. III. Roll) bore, or a fess vert between three cinquefoyles pierced gules. (F.) Arden Roll.

Okstede, Roland de—(H. III. Roll) bore or, a "kene" gules; Glover Roll.

‡**Okstede, Roland**—(H. III. Roll) bore, argent, an oak eradicated proper acorned or. (F.) Dering and Howard Rolls.

Oldcastle, Sir John, baron Cobham 1409— bore, at the siege of Rouen 1418, gules, on a chevron or three lyonceux rampant sable *quarterly with,* argent a castle sable.

Oldhall, —— (E. III. Roll) bore, per pale azure and gules, a lyon rampant ermine, a label (3) or; another with lyon ducally crowned or, but no label; Ashmole Roll. Sir WILLIAM in Atkinson Roll, without arms; Harl. MS. 1408 fo. 108ᵇ.

Olney, Sir John de, of Bucks.—(E. II. Roll) bore, azure, crusily and a fess argent; Parly. Roll; ?[another barry (6) argent and azure, a bordure indented gules; "Genealogist" XI. 181.]

*[**Ondeslow, Roger de,** E. I.—bore argent, a fess gules between six Cornish choughs proper.—Shirley.] F.

Opshale, Michel de—(H. III. Roll) bore, argent, a cross sable fretty or. (F.) Arden and St. George Rolls. See UPSALE.

Jon de Oxbobi

Jorn Oroylo

Oxbablin

Le Counto de Ormaund

Safe de Ottingdon

Vand de Ottoby

Sire de Ondeuardo

Jorn de Oufthorpo

william Onyngton

Jorn de Quingoton

Solomon Orondon

C' de Oxford

Orbebe, John de—(H. III. Roll) bore, argent, two chevrons gules, on a quarter of the second as many lyons passant of the first (F.) ; Arden Roll.

Ore, Nichol de (ERE)—(H. III. Roll) bore, ermine, a cross gules fretty or ; Howard Roll.

‡**Ore, Nicole de**—(H. III. Roll) bore, argent, a cross gules fretty or, between four daws ppr. ; Dering Roll.

‡**Ore, Richarde de**—(H. III. Roll) bore, barry (6) argent and azure, on a bend gules five besants ; Dering Roll. F.

Oreyle, John—(E. III. Roll) bore, argent, a cross between four martlets gules ; Jenyns' Ordinary. F.

Oriel, Nichole de (CRYEL)—(H. III. Roll) bore, " or and gules partie per fess three annulets counterchanged tertoleres " ; Howard Roll. See (F.) CRIOL.

Orkablin —— (H. III. Roll) bore, or, on a cross vert five escallops argent (F.) ; Arden Roll. See WALTAUBIN ; same arms as THORLEY.

‡**Orlaston, William de**—(H. III. Roll) bore, or, two chevrons gules, on a quarter of the second a lyon rampant or ; Dering Roll ; argent (F.) in Howard and Camden Rolls.

Ormonde, James Butler, Earl of—bore, at the siege of Rouen 1418, or, a chief dancettée (3) azure. F. See also BOTELER.

Ornesby, John—(E. III. Roll) bore, gules, crusily botonnée and a bend argent ; tricked, gules, a bend argent ; Jenyns' Ordinary.

Ornesby, Sir William de, of Norfolk —(E. II. Roll) bore, gules, crusily argent, a bend checquy or and azure (argent and azure Harl. 6137 fo. 17) ; Sir JOHN differenced with a mullet ; Parliamentary Roll.

Orphill *v.* **Crophill.**

Orreby, Sir John, of Dalby in Cheshire, baron 1309—bore, gules, two lyons passant argent, a label (3) or ; Parliamentary, Nobility and Ashmole Rolls (F.); undifferenced in Jenyns' Ordinary.

Orton, John de—(E. III. Roll) bore, azure, a lyon rampant argent ; Jenyns' Ordinary ; same as ROBERT DE MONHAUT.

Otteby, Sir Randolph de, of Lincs.— (E. II. Roll) bore, gules, two bars argent, in chief three plates ; Parliamentary Roll. F.

Otterburne, John—(E. III. Roll) bore, argent, on a chief dancettée (3) gules three crosses crosslet fitchée of the first ; Jenyns' Ordinary.

‡**Otringden, Rafe de**—(H. III. Roll) bore, ermine, a cross voided gules ; Dering and Howard Rolls ; a cross gules voided argent in Arden Roll, voided or (F.) in Camden Roll ; sometimes blasoned, a cross surmounted of another.

‡**Oudenarde, Sire de**—(H. III. Roll) bore, barry (6, 12) or and gules, a bend azure ; Dering and Camden Rolls.

Oughtred, Sir Thomas, K.G. 1356—bore, at the siege of Calais 1345-8, gules, on a cross flory (patonce) or five mullets pierced of the field ; K. 398 fo. 58. See UGHTRED.

Oulwenne, Gilbert—(H. III. Roll) bore, argent, fretty gules, a chief azure ; Surrey Roll.

Ousthorpe, John de—(E. I. Roll) bore gules, three " dewe " leaves argent ; Jenyns Roll. F.

Ovington, Sir John de (QUINGTON)— bore, at the first Dunstable tournament 1308, argent on a chief azure two fleurs-de-lys or. See also EVINGTON.

Ovington, William—(E. III. Roll) bore, gules, on a bend argent three martlets sable (F.) ; Jenyns' Ordinary.

Owen, Griffith, LE FITZ WEN-UN-WEN (? FITZ OWEN-OWEN)—(E. III. Roll) bore, or, a lyon rampant gules ; Jenyns' Ordinary. Same as JOHN MUSCEGROS and WILLIAM POLE.

Oxcliff, William—(E. I. Roll) bore, argent, three bulls' heads cabossed sable ; Jenyns' Roll.

*[**Oxenden, Solomon** (E. III.)—bore, argent, a chevron gules between three oxen passant sable.—Shirley.] F., confirmed 24 H. VI. 1445-6.

Oxford, Earl of—(H. III. Roll) bore, quarterly, gules and or, a mullet argent (F.) ; Arden, Glover and Surrey Rolls ; carried also at the siege of Rouen 1418.

[**Oxford, Earl of,** ROBERT DE VERE, 9th, bore, azure, three crowns or, a bordure argent *quarterly with,* VERE ; grant 3 Jan. 1386, pat. I. m. 1 Cotton MS. Julius C. VII. fo. 237.]

Oysell, Richard and **Roger**—(E. III. Roll) bore, argent, a saltire engrailed between four " Choughes de Cornwaille " sable ; Grimaldi Roll and Jenyns' Ordinary.

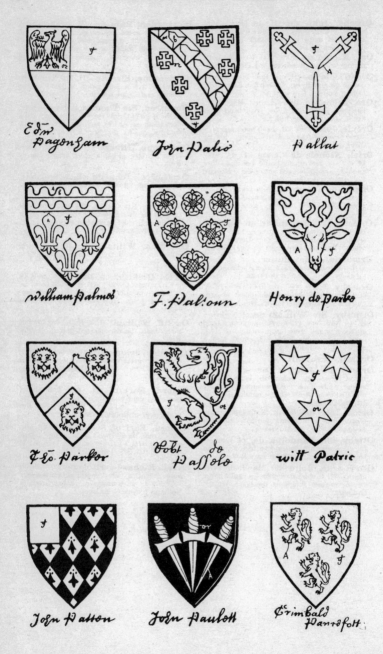

Edm̄
Pagonham

Jorn Palio

Pallat

william Palmes

F. Palioun

Henry de Parko

F. Eo. Parkor

Robt   do
Passolo

will Patric

John Patton

John Paulott

Grimbald
Panrdfott

P—Q

Pagenham, Sir Edward or **Sir Edmund,** of Suffolk, and **John**—(E. II. Roll) bore, quarterly or and gules, an eagle displayed vert; Ashmole and Parliamentary Rolls and Jenyns' Ordinary. F.

Pagham (——), an Essex ? Knight—(H. VI. Roll) bore, argent, three chevronels gules; Arundel Roll.

Pakenham, Sir John, of Beds.—(E. II. Roll) bore, barry (6) argent and azure, on a bend gules three mullets or. Sir JOHN LE FITZ, pierced mullets for difference; Parliamentary Roll; and so borne by LAWRENCE in Surrey Roll.

Pakenham, Myles—(E. I. Roll) bore, gules, a chevron between three crosses crosslet fitchée argent; Jenyns' Roll.

Palie, Sir John de, knighted at the capitulation of Calais 1348—bore, gules, a bend vair between six crosses potent or. F.

Palialogi, the; Emperors of Greece— bore, or, a sea lyon sable. Segar Roll. See Greece.

Pallat, ——, Kt., slain at the siege of Calais 1348—bore, gules, three swords, points to the centre argent. F.

Paltoun, Sir F., of Suffolk, Kt.—(H. VI. Roll) bore, argent, six roses 3, 2, 1 gules; Arundel Roll. Sir JOHN bore six-foyles; Ashmole Roll.

[Palmer, William (9 H. IV.)—bore, sable, a chevron or between three crescents argent.— Shirley.] F.

*[Palmes, William, 1300—bore, gules, three fleurs-de-lys argent, a chief vair.—Shirley.] F.

Pantu'e, James de—(H. III. Roll) bore, argent, six barrulets and a canton gules; Arden Roll. See PAUNTON.

Pappeworth, William de—(H. III. Roll) bore, gules, a fess dancettée argent; Surrey Roll.

Parys, Sir William de—bore, at the battle of Boroughbridge 1322, sable, crusily and a chevron argent. (F.) Arundel Roll and Jenyns' Ordinary.

‡Parke, Henry de (PERKE)—(H. III. Roll) bore, argent, a stag's head cabossed gules. (F.) Dering and Howard Rolls.

Parke, Richard del—(E. III. Roll)—bore, sable, an eagle displayed argent, a bordure azure—argent in trick; Jenyns' Ordinary.

*[Parker, Thomas, R. II.—bore, gules, a chevron between three leopards' faces or.— Shirley.] F.

Paslew, Sir John, of Essex, Kt.—(H. VI. Roll) bore, azure, a fess argent between three cups or; Arundel Roll. See WAKYRLEY.

Paslew, John—(E. I. Roll) bore, argent, a fess between three mullets pierced azure; Jenyns' Roll.

Paslew, Sir John (PASSELEWE), of Essex — (E. II. Roll) bendy (10) or and azure, on a canton argent a lyon passant gardant gules; Parliamentary Roll—or, four bends azure, &c. in Harl. MS. 6137 fo. 14.

Passele, Robert de—(H. III. Roll) bore, gules, a lyon rampant or; Surrey Roll.

Patishulle, Sir John (of Rutland)—bore, at the battle of Boroughbridge 1322, argent, a fess sable, between three crescents gules. Ascribed to Sir WALTER in the Ashmole Roll, and with the fess undée, to Sir WALTER, of Essex, in the Parliamentary Roll.

Pateshull, Sir Walter de—bore, at the battle of Boroughbridge 1322, argent, a fess engrélée between three crescents sable. (F.) Ascribed to SIMON, but with a plain fess in Jenyns' Ordinary.

Pateshull, John—(E. III. Roll) bore, ermine, a lyon rampant gules, crowned or; Jenyns' Ordinary.

‡Patrick, William—(H. III. Roll) bore, gules, three mullets (6) or. (F.) Arden and St. George Rolls—spur-rowells in Jenyns' Ordinary.

[Patten, John, 1376—bore, lozengy ermine and sable, a canton gules.—Shirley.] F.

Paule, John—(E. I. Roll) bore, ermine, on a fess azure three crosses crosslet or; Jenyns' Roll.

*[Paulet, Sir John, ob. 1356—bore, sable, three swords in pile points to the base proper —his son Sir JOHN bore (15 R. II.) gules, a pair of wings conjoined in lure argent—being the coat of his mother, the heiress of Reyney.— Shirley.] F.

Paulys, Sir Walter, of Stratton—(E. III. Roll) bore, gules, three lyons passant argent on a baston azure three mullets or; Ashmole Roll.

‡Pauncefot, Sir Grimbald—(H. III. Roll) bore, gules, three lyonceux rampant argent (F.) Dering and Howard Rolls. Sir GILBERT, of Gloucestershire, bore the same; Parliamentary Roll E. II.

Walt d' Paueli

Walt Paveley

ffoubo Payfoote

Jorn Paynoll

willia painoll

Edmond porgo

Jorn pogogo

Jon pogo

Tromab porgo

Rogor Pedwardin

monb. Polgam

Henry de pendobo

Pauncefot, William—(H. III. Roll) bore, azure, two bars or ; Arden Roll.

Paunton, (——), an Essex ? Knight—(H. VI. Roll) bore, barry (10) argent and gules, a quarter of the last ; Arundel Roll. JAMES DE PANTU'E (H. III. Roll) bore, argent, six barrulets and a canton gules ; Arden Roll.

Paunton, Sir Hugh, of the North—(E. II. Roll) bore, gules two bars and, in the cantel a fer-de-moulin ermine ; Parliamentary Roll.

Paveley, Sire Walter de—bore, at the battle of Boroughbridge 1322, azure, a cross florettée and a martlet or "in the quarter." (F.) JOHN, RENAUD and Sir WALTER bore it without the martlet ; Jenyns' Ordinary, St. George and Harl. Rolls. Sir JOHN bore the martlet argent ; knighted at the capitulation of Calais 1348. REGINALD and WILLIAM took up the cross in the last Crusade 1270.

Paveley, Sir Walter, K.G., a founder—(H. III. Roll) bore, azure, a cross patonce or ; Surrey Roll and K. 398 fo. 30.

Paveley, Edward — (H. III. Roll) bore, azure, a cross recercelée or ; Norfolk Roll.

Paveley, Sir Walter (of Oxon.), knighted at the capitulation of Calais 1348—bore, gules, three lyons passant argent, on a bend azure three mullets or (F.) ; a baston in Cotgrave Roll.

Pavent, John—(E. I. Roll) bore, argent, on a bend gules three eaglets or ; Jenyns' Roll and Ordinary.

Payfote, Sir Fouke—bore, at the first Dunstable tournament 1308, argent, five fleurs-de-lys 3, 1, 1, sable, a label (3) gules ; another florettée. (F.)

Payn, Sir Geoffrey and Sir John, both slain at the siege of Calais 1347—bore, argent, two bars and in chief three escallops, azure —sable for Sir JOHN. GEOFFREY took up the cross in the last Crusade 1270.

Payne, Walter—(E. I. Roll) bore, gules, a lyon rampant tail fourchée argent *quarterly with* PAVELEY, azure a cross florettée or ; Jenyns' Roll—called WALTER PAYUELI, in Jenyns' Ordinary.

Paynell, Sir Raffe, of Caythorpe, co. Linc. —(E. II. Roll) bore, argent, a bend sable ; Parly. Roll. Ascribed to RALPH PAYNE in Jenyns' Ordinary—STOPHAM bears the same.

Paynell, Sir John, of co. Linc.—(E. II. Roll) bore, gules, a cinquefoyle argent ; Parly. Roll.

Paynell, John—(E. III. Roll) bore, gules a cross argent ; STEPHEN PENCESTER bears the same arms ; Jenyns' Ordinary.

Paynell (Sir) John, DE KNAPTOFT— (E. III. Roll) bore, gules, a cross patonce argent ; Ashmole and Surrey Rolls.

Paynell, Sir William—bore, at the first Dunstable tournament 1308, argent, five bars sable, eight martlets in orle gules ; tricked also with 4 bars. F.

Paynell, Sir John, banneret—bore, at the battle of Falkirk 1298 and at the siege of Carla-verock 1300, vert, a maunch or (F.) ; but the reverse appears for JOHN, Baron of Otteley, in Nobility Roll 1300 ; and for WILLIAM in Nobility Roll 1310 ; and for JOHN in Harl. and Parly. Rolls. See next.

Paynell, William, lord of Fracynton, baron 1303-17, and his brother **John,** lord of Otteley, baron 1317-18, sealed the Barons' letter to the Pope 1301 (*the former on a lozenge*), with two bars and an orle of eight martlets. See next.

Paynell, Hugh, Sir Thomas, of Wilts, and **Sir William**—(H. III. Roll) bore, or, two bars azure, nine (8 or 6) martlets in orle gules. (F.) Arden, Howard, Parly. Har-lcian and other Rolls—(the field argent ascribed to WILLIAM in Jenyns' Ordinary) ; another Sir WILLIAM, of Wilts, bore the bars sable and the martlets "in manner of bordure assis" ; Parly. and Howard Rolls ; THOMAS‡ and WILLIAM (‡) in Dering Roll.

Paynell, Sir William—(E. I. Roll) bore, argent, three bars azure in chief three martlets gules ; Holland Roll.

Paynell, ffouke de—(H. III. Roll) bore, or, two lyons passant gules, crowned azure ; Howard Roll.

Paynell, John—(R. II. Roll) bore, gules, two chevronels and a bordure argent ; Surrey Roll.

Payver (PAYCUR) —— (H. III. Roll) bore, argent three martlets gules ; Arden Roll— surname uncertain. See PEYVERE.

Pecham *v.* **Peckam,** and **Petham.**

Peche, Sir Gilbert, of Corby, banneret, baron 1299—bore, at the battle of Falkirk 1298, and at the first Dunstable tournament 1308, argent a fess between two chevronels gules. (F.) Nobility and Howard Rolls ; another GILBERT (‡) in Dering Roll ; ascribed also to HAMOND in the St. George Roll, to JOHN in Jenyns' Ordinary and to Sir ROBERT, of Kent, banneret in Arundel Roll. (Sir WILLIAM, of Suffolk, bore the chevronels sable.) Sir HUGH, of Suffolk, differenced with a label (3) azure—to this, Sir ROBERT, also of Kent, perhaps a baron 1321, added a besant on each point of the label ; Parly. Roll. SIMON and WILLIAM took up the cross 1270.

Peche, Sir Edmund, of Suffolk—(E. II. Roll) bore, argent a fess between two chev-ronels gules, as many martlets in chief and one in base sable (F.) ; Parly. Roll. In Harl. MS. 6137, a semée of martlets sable is added.

Pecche, Sir John, of Warwickshire—bore, at the first Dunstable tournament 1308 and as a banneret at the battle of Boroughbridge 1322 gules, crusily and a fess argent (F.) ; at the latter Sir JOHN *soun fiz*, differenced with a label (3) azure ; ascribed also to THOMAS, but with six crosses crosslet (3 and 3) in Jenyns' Roll.

Peche, Sir (——), of Suffolk—(E. II. Roll) bore, argent, a chevron gules a bordure sable besantée ; Parliamentary Roll.

Peche, Sir Robert, an error for Sir GILBERT —bore, at the battle of Falkirk 1298, argent (a fess between) two chevronels gules. (F.) Jenyns' Ordinary.

Peche, John—(R. II. Roll) bore, azure, a lyon rampant tail fourchée ermine, crowned or ; Surrey Roll.

‡**Peche, John**—(H. III. Roll) bore, gules, a crescent or and on a chief argent two mullets (5) pierced of the field. (F.) Dering Roll ; spur-rowels in Howard Roll.

Peche, Baldwin—(H. III. Roll) bore, vaire or and gules ; Norfolk Roll.

A KNIGHT OF THE PEMBRIDGE FAMILY.

IN CLEHONGER CHURCH, HEREFORDSHIRE. *After Hollis.*

Peche, Sir Thomas, of co. Cambridge—(E. II. Roll) bore, azure an eagle displayed argent, on the dexter wing a maunch gules. Parliamentary Roll.

Peche, Sir Thomas—(E. III. Roll) bore, ermine, a gorge gules ; Ashmole Roll. F.

‡**Peckham, John de** (PECHAM)—(H. III. Roll) bore, azure, six annulets 3, 2, 1 or. (F.) Dering and Howard Rolls. See PETHAM.

Peckham (——) a Kentish Knight—(H. VI. Roll) bore, ermine a chief quarterly gules and or ; Arundel Roll. St. NICOLAS bears the same, with the chief reversed (?)

Peckham, Roger de (BECKHAM)—(R. II. Roll) bore, checquy or and sable, a fess ermine ; Surrey Roll.

Pedwardyne, Sir Roger—bore, at the battle of Boroughbridge 1322, or, crusily and three crescents gules, each charged with a plate. F.

Pedwardwyn, Thomas, Walter and **William**—(E. III. Roll) bore, gules, two lyons passant in pale or. (F.) Arden and Surrey Rolls, Jenyns' Ordinary. ROBERT differenced with a label (3) argent ; Surrey Roll.

Pedwardyne, Walter de—(H. III. Roll) bore, or, three lyons passant in pale gules ; Howard Roll.

***Pelham, (Sir John)**—bore, at the siege of Rouen 1418, azure, three pelicans argent 2 and 1 vulning themselves proper. F.

Pembroke *v.* **Marshall** and **Valence.**

Pembroke, Earl of—bore, at the siege of Rouen 1418, barry (10) argent and azure an orle of martlets gules, *quarterly with*, or a maunch gules. (F.) JOHN (HASTINGS) last Earl of Pembroke of that line was accidentally killed in a tournament at Woodstock 1389, aged about 17.

Penbrige, Sir John de (PENBRUGGE)—bore, at the first Dunstable tournament 1308, azure, a chief gules and a bend engrailed argent. F.

Pembrugge, (Sir John, of Cheshire)—bore, at the second Dunstable tournament 1334, argent, a chief azure, a bordure engrailed gules ; Parliamentary Roll.

Pembrugge, Fouk de—(E. I. Roll) bore, barry (6) or and azure ; Harleian Roll ; for HENRY, barry 6, 8 and 14 (F.) are tricked in Dering, Howard, St. George, and Camden Rolls (and differenced with a label (5) gules in Arden Roll). Sir RICHARD, K.G. 1369, barry of eight.

Penbryg, Sir Henry de—bore, at the first Dunstable tournament 1308, barry (6) or and azure, a bend gules (F.) ; Arden Roll ; barry (8) for Sir HENRY of Herefordshire in Parly. Roll.

Penbruge, Sir John, of Herefordshire—(E. II. Roll) bore, barry (8) or and azure, on a bend gules three mullets argent ; Parly. Roll. See Monumental Effigy of a member of this family, leopards' faces on the bend.

Penbrugge, John—(R. II. Roll) bore, or, a fess double cotised azure, a bendlet gules ; Surrey Roll.

‡**Pencestre, Stephen**—(H. III. Roll) bore, gules, a cross argent (F.) ; Dering Roll ; borne also by JOHN PAYNELL ; the cross or, for JOHN in Jenyns' Ordinary.

Penedoke, Henry de—(H. III. Roll) bore, sable, a lyon rampant argent (F.) ; St. George Roll.

Penley, Sir Richard—(E. III. Roll) bore, or, a lyon rampant purpure ; Ashmole Roll.

Penne. See DE LA PENNE.

***Pennyngton, Sir William de**—(E. II. Roll) bore, or, five fusils conjoined in fess azure ; Parly. Roll ; tricked also as a fess fusily and a fess indented. JOHN differenced with a label (3) gules (F.) ; Jenyns' Ordinary. Sir JOHN bore the field argent and a label (5) gules in the Ballard Roll.

Penzret, Sir John de, of Cumberland—(E. II. Roll) bore, gules, a bend battely argent ; Parliamentary Roll.

Percehay, Sir Wauter—bore, at the battle of Boroughbridge 1322, argent, a cross patonce gules and in the dexter chief point, an inescocheon of ATON—or, a cross sable ; the cross patonce is tricked patée in Ashmole MS. F.

Percehay, Sir Walter, knighted at the capitulation of Calais 1348—bore, argent, a cross patonce (flory in the trick) gules, in the cantel an inescocheon quarterly sable and or. F.

Percehay, Walter—(E. III. Roll) bore, argent, a cross patonce (flory in the trick) gules ; HENRY COLVILE of Cambridgeshire bears the same arms, which are in dispute ; Jenyns' Ordinary.

Percehay, Walter—(E. III. Roll) bore, argent a cross patonce (flory in the trick) gules, in the cantel a lozenge of the second all within a bordure engrailed of the last ; Jenyns' Ordinary.

*[**Perceval, Richard** (Hen. IV.)—bore, argent, on a chief indented gules three crosses patée of the first ; ascribed to Sir ROGER as per Seal E. I.—Shirley.] F.

Percy, Henry, of Topcliffe, banneret, baron 1298-9—bore, at the battle of Falkirk 1298, and at the siege of Carlaverock 1300, or, a lyon rampant azure.—F. (Nobility, Parly. and Arundel Rolls), being the arms of BRABANT, with which he sealed the Barons' letter to the Pope 1301. Ascribed also to THOMAS in the Surrey Roll, and to Sir PIERS at the first Dunstable tournament 1308. (1) HENRY differenced it with a label (3) gules ; (2) RAFFE with a mullet or, on the lyon's shoulder, both in the Surrey Roll ; and (3) WILLIAM differenced his brothers' arms with a bordure "recersele" gules ; Cotgrave Roll. See MONTFORT.

Percy, Henry de, SR. DE LUCY, Earl of Northumberland 1399-1408—(R. II. Roll) bore, or, a lyon rampant azure, *quarterly with* LUCY, gules, three lucies hauriant 2 and 1 argent ; Surrey Roll.

Percy, Sire Nichol—bore, at the battle of Boroughbridge 1322, undée (6) argent and azure. F.

Robt d' Perce

Robt de Perpound

Symon de Perpound

Rauf Parov

will'm de Port.

nicole peson

will Possun

Ego Potto

Richard de Povenese

Hue Peuerel.

John Poveroll

Roger Poytbyn

Percy, Henry, of Wiltshire—(E. I. Roll) bore, argent, five fusils conjoined in fess sable (or, in Camden); Jenyns' Ordinary; engrailed in Jenyns' Roll; JOHN bore the reverse, see below.

Percy, Walter de—(H. III. Roll) bore, azure, five fusils conjoined in fess argent; Arden and St. George Rolls. A WALTER took up the cross in the last Crusade 1270.

‡**Percy, Sir Henry,** of Spofford—(H. III. Roll) bore, azure, five fusils conjoined in fess or; Dering and Howard Rolls; indented in Grimaldi Roll; engrailed in Glover Roll, for HENRY.

Percy, Arnold, of Kildale—(E. III. Roll) bore, gules, five fusils conjoined in fess argent; Jenyns' Ordinary.

Percy, Robert, of Sutton-upon-Derwent—(E. III. Roll) bore, or, five fusils conjoined in fess azure; Jenyns' Ordinary; fess engrailed in Glover Roll.

Percy, Arnold and **Robert**—(H. III. Roll) bore, or, five fusils conjoined in fess sable (F.); Arden and St. George Rolls. Same arms as RICHARD DAUTREY; Jenyns' Ordinary.

‡**Percy, John de**—(H. III. Roll) bore, sable, five fusils conjoined in fess argent; Dering Roll; a fess of fusils in Howard Roll.

Perers, Sir Richard de—bore, at the first Dunstable tournament 1308, and at the battle of Boroughbridge 1322, quarterly argent and sable, in the cantel a mullet (vij. in Nativity Roll) gules (pierced or, at Dunstable) (F.); another Sir RICHARD (of co. Leic.) bore it when knighted at the capitulation of Calais 1348; Parly. and Harl. Rolls; EDWARD bore it undifferenced at the siege of Rouen in 1418.

Peres, Sir Thomas de (or PRYERS), of Essex—(E. II. Roll) bore, vert, a bend argent cotised or; Parliamentary Roll.

Periam (——) an Essex Knight—(H. VI. Roll) bore, gules, three crescents argent; Arundel Roll.

Perke, Henry de (or PARKE)—(H. III. Roll) bore, argent, a stag's head cabossed gules; Dering and Howard Rolls.

Perpont *v.* **Pierpont.**

Perpont (——), of Iklyng, and **Symon**—(H. III. Roll) bore, azure, a chief checquy or and gules; Howard and Ashmole Rolls. ROBERT ‡ bore the chief counter-compony (F.) in Dering Roll. SYMON ‡ bore the reverse, viz., checquy or and gules, a chief azure. (F.) Dering Roll; per fess in the tricks.

Perreres *v.* **Perers.**

Perrot, Rauf, baron 1297—bore, quarterly indented or and azure; Nobility Roll. To Sir RAUFE of Beds is ascribed quarterly per fess indented or and azure (F.), in Parly. and other Rolls; and to RAUF, dancettée in Dering Roll.

Pert, William de—(E. I. Roll) bore, argent, on a bend gules, three mascles or (F.); Jenyns' Roll.

Peshale, —— (R. II. Roll) bore, argent, a cross flory engrailed sable; Surrey Roll.

Peshale, Adam—(R. II. Roll) bore, argent, a cross flory sable, on a quarter gules a lyon's head erased of the first, crowned or; Surrey Roll.

†**Peson, Nicole de** — (H. III. Roll) bore, ermine, a fess azure. (F.) Dering Roll; thereon three lyonceux rampant argent (F.) in Howard Roll, and thus ascribed to WILLIAM in Arden Roll.

Petham, John de (POTHAM)—(H. III. Roll) bore, azure, six annulets or; Howard Roll. See PECHAM.

Petit, Thomas—(E. III. Roll) bore, gules, a fess between three annulets 2 and 1 or; Jenyns' Ordinary.

Pette, Thomas—bore, at the second Dunstable tournament 1334, ermine an engréle gules (F.)—tricked as a fess indented, dancettée is probably intended.

‡**Pevense, Richard de**—(H. III. Roll) bore, azure, a chevron or square fretted gules, between three crosses moline argent; Howard Roll—crosses recercelée (F.) in Dering Roll—square fretted may be an error in the trick for fretty.

Pevere *v.* **Peyvre.**

Peverell, —— (E. III. Roll) bore, quarterly 1 and 4, vaire or and vert—2 and 3, gules; Ashmole Roll.

Peverell, Sir John—bore, at the battle of Boroughbridge 1322, gyronny (8) argent and gules. F.

‡**Peverell, Thomas** — (H. III. Roll) bore, gyronny (12 or 16) argent and gules, a bordure sable bezantée; Dering and Howard Rolls.

Peverell, Henry—(E. III. Roll) bore, argent, on a saltire sable five mullets or pierced gules; Jenyns' Ordinary.

Peverell, Hugh—(H. III. Roll) bore, azure, three garbs argent banded gules, a chief or. (F.) St. George Roll.

Peverell, Sir Robert, of co. Leic.—(E. II. Roll) bore, gules, a fess argent between six crosses patonce or; Parliamentary Roll.

‡**Peyferer, William**—(H. III. Roll) bore, argent, three fleurs-de-lys 2 and 1 sable; Arden and Camden Rolls—six in Howard and Dering Rolls. Sir WILLIAM, of Kent (R. II. Roll) bore, argent, florettée sable; Parliamentary Roll. Sir FOUKE differenced with a label (3) gules.

Peyton, Sir John de, of Suffolk—(E. II. Roll)—bore, sable, a cross engrailed or, a mullet argent (Parliamentary, Arundel and Surrey Rolls) in the first and second quarter, in Jenyns' Ordinary—probably a mistake. One of these names took up the cross in the last Crusade 1270.

Peytwyn, Sir Roger, of Lincolnshire—(H. III. Roll) bore, ermine, three chevronels gules (four (F.) in Jenyns' Ordinary); Arden and Parliamentary Rolls.

Peyvere, Sir Philip, of Norfolk—(E. II. Roll) bore, or two bars sable between six martlets 3, 2, 1 argent; Parliamentary Roll — an addition.

Rog Pichard de standone

Ẃ̃ Pikworth

Henri Pirpund·

Goffrey pichford

Joan.d Pichford·

Goffory Pigot·

Pers Pigod·

will Pigott

Alox pilkinglon

Tomes de pin

Thomas d Pin

Ẃ̃ de pinkenoi

Peyvre, John, baron 1298-9—bore, argent, on a chevron gules three fleurs-de-lys or; Nobility Roll. Ascribed also to Sir JOHN and Sir ROGER, both of Beds. in Parliamentary Roll; THOMAS, in Jenyns' Ordinary, and WILLIAM in Glover Roll.

Phelip, Sir William, K.G. 1418—bore, quarterly gules and argent, in the first an eagle displayed or; K. 401 fo. 16.

Pichford, Geffrey—(H. III. Roll) bore, checquy, or and azure, on a fess gules three lyonceux rampant argent. (F.) Arden and Camden Rolls.

Pichford, John de—(H. III. Roll) bore, sable, semée of quartrefoyles and a cinquefoyle pierced or; St. George Roll—crusily (F.) in Arden Roll.

Pickard, Roger—(H. III. Roll) bore, argent, three lozenges sable; St. George Roll. JOHN differenced with a label (5)) gules. (F.) Segar Roll.

Pickarde, Sir Myles (or PICHARD), of Salop **Richard** and **Roger**—(E. II. Roll) bore, gules, a fess or between three escallops argent. (F.) Parliamentary and Jenyns' Roll. [Sir JOHN differenced with a label of 3 azure—sometimes or.] ROGER, of Stondon, bore the fess argent; Arden and St. George Rolls.

Pi(c)kenham, Raffe, of Thornton Watlass —(E. III. Roll) bore, or, on a chief indented azure three crescents of the field; cinquefoyles pierced in trick; Jenyns' Ordinary—see WATLOUS or WATLASS.

Pickenham, — (PYKNAM), a Knight — (H. VI. Roll) bore, azure, a lyon rampant holding in its fore-paws a cross patée fitchée all or; Arundel Roll.

Pickering, James le—(R. II. Roll) bore, ermine, a lyon rampant azure; Surrey and Ashmole Rolls. THOMAS bore the lyon crowned or, in Jenyns' Ordinary.

Pickering, Sir Thomas de—(E. II. Roll) bore, or (sometimes argent) a lyon rampant sable, a bordure gules bezantée; Harl. 6137. In Harl. 4033—argent, a lyon rampant sable, a bordure of the last bezantée.

Pi(c)kworth, Sir Thomas—(E. III. Roll) bore, argent, three picks gules; Ashmole and Surrey Rolls. ROBERT, differenced with an annulet; Surrey Roll.

Pickworth, John—(E. I. Roll) bore, gules, a bend between six picks (3 and 3) or. (F.) Jenyns' Roll—argent in Jenyns' Ordinary.

Pierpont, Henry (PERPUND)—(H. III. Roll) bore, burulée (16) argent and gules, a lyon rampant sable debruised of a baston or. (F.) Arden and St. George Rolls.

Pierpont, Sir Edmond, Henry and **Thomas**—(E. III. Roll) bore, argent, a lyon rampant sable, within an orle of six-foyles gules (the reverse ascribed to EDMOND in the Surrey Roll); Ashmole Roll and Jenyns' Ordinary—cinquefoyles in Cotgrave Roll, where to "the NEPIEW" is ascribed argent, a lyon rampant sable a baston gules.

Pierpont, Sir Robert—bore, at the first Dunstable tournament 1308, argent, a lyon rampant sable debruised by a baston or (F.); Cotgrave and Nativity Rolls.

Pierpont, Sir Robert (PEYPOUNDE)— (E. II. Roll) bore, argent, a lyon rampant sable (powdered with roses gules, Harl. 6137); a bordure of six roses gules, Harl. 4033; Parly. Roll.

Piers, Mons., LE CAPITOW DE BOUCH, K.G., *v.* Greilly.

Piers, Henry (PYERS)—(E. I. Roll) bore, azure, a bend argent, cotised or, between six martlets 3 and 3 of the second (F.); Segar Roll.

Pigot, Sir Robert (PYGOT), slain at the siege of Calais 1347—bore, gules, three picks 2 and 1 argent (F.), borne also by BALDWIN; Surrey Roll

Pigot, Geffrey, of Melmerby—(E. I. Roll) bore, sable three picks (picois) argent (F.); Grimaldi and Jenyns' Rolls; and by RANDOLF in Surrey Roll.

Pigott, Sir J. (PYGOTT)—(H. VI. Roll) bore, or, on a cross azure five crescents argent; Atkinson Roll.

Pigott (——), Sr, of Norfolk—(E. II. Roll) bore, argent, two bends engrailed gules; and in a marginal note, "3 molles sable"; Parly. Roll, an addition.

Pigott, Sir Baldwin, of Yorkshire, and **John** of Doddington—(E. II. Roll) bore, azure, two bars or in chief three besants; Parly. Roll and Jenyns' Ordinary.

Pigott, Sir Pyers de, of Notts—(E. II. Roll) bore, azure, a bend engrailed between six martlets 3 and 3 or (F.); Parly. Roll; bend indented Jenyns' Ordinary; dancettée or fusily in Arden Roll.

[**Pigott, William,** ob. 1376—bore, ermine, three fusils conjoined in fess sable.—Shirley.] F.

*[**Pilkington, Sir Alexander** 1301—bore, argent, a cross patonce voided gules.—Shirley.] F.

Pilkington —— (E. I. Roll) bore, argent, three bends gules and on a canton (or?) a cross voided sable; Harleian Roll.

†**Pin(e), Thomas de**—(H. III. Roll) bore, gules, a chevron argent, between three pine cones or (F.F.); Arden and St. George Rolls.

Pinkeney, Sir Henry de, of Northants, baron 1299—bore, at the battle of Falkirk 1298, or a fess "engréle" gules (F.) *i.e.* five fusils conjoined; Nobility Roll and Jenyns' Ordinary, with which he sealed the Barons' letter to the Pope 1301; a fess dancettée in Harl. MS. 6137 fo. 52ᵇ, and indented on fo. 22ᵇ.

Pinkenei, Robert—(E. I. Roll) bore, or, six fusils conjoined in fess gules, and THOMAS differenced with a baston sable (F.); Segar Roll.

GEOFFREY, COUNT OF ANJOU, FATHER OF HENRY II.

DIED 7TH SEPTEMBER, 1150.

From an enamelled tablet in the Museum at Mans, formerly in the Church of St. Julien. After Stothard.

The lyons on the shield are perhaps the earliest specimens of armorial bearings.

Pipard, Sir Rauff, baron 1299—bore, at the battle of Falkirk 1298, argent, a fess and a demi fess, on a canton azure a cinquefoyle or (F). In the Nobility and other Rolls—two bars; "une fees et demi" in Jenyns' Ordinary, the cinquefoyles pierced in Arden and St. George Rolls. Signed but did not seal the Barons' letter to the Pope 1301.

Pipe, Sir Thomas de la, of Staffs—(E. II. Roll) bore, azure crusily 3, 3, and a fess or; Parly. Roll; crusily fitchée; Jenyns' Roll.

Piritone, Joan de—(H. III. Roll) bore, or, a pear-tree vert fructed gules (F.); Arden and St. George Rolls.

Pitlysden (——) a Knight—(H. VI. Roll) bore, argent, a fess between three pelicans azure vulning themselves; Arundel Roll. JOHN DE PYVELSDON took up the cross in the last Crusade 1270.

Placetis *v.* **Plessetis.**

Plaice, Sir Edmond de—bore, at the first Dunstable tournament 1308, argent, a bend between six annulets 3 and 3 gules (F.); bend azure in H. 5848.

Planche, Sir James de la, of Bucks, Kt.— (E. II. Roll) bore, argent, billetty and a lyon rampant sable; Harleian and Segar Rolls; crowned or, in Parly. Roll; in Segar Roll the billets are more like guttée de poix, they even suggest ermine. F.

Playz, Giles de, baron 1297—bore, per pale or and gules, a lyon passant argent; Nobility Roll; borne also by his son Sir RICHARD, a baron 1317, at the battle of Boroughbridge 1322 (F.)—lyon passant gardant in Parly. Roll, ascribed also to JOHN in Ashmole and Surrey Rolls.

Plays, William—(E. III. Roll) bore, azure, on a chief argent, three chaplets gules; Ashmole Roll and Jenyns' Ordinary. F.

Plesington, Robert de—(E. III. Roll) bore, azure, a cross flory between four martlets argent; Jenyns' Ordinary.

Plessetis, Hugh de, baron 1299—bore, argent, six annulets gules (F.); Nobility and other Rolls; ascribed to Sir JOHN in Glover Roll—three annulets in Norfolk Roll, under PLACETIS, PLESCY, PLESCIS, and PLESSIS.

Plecy, Sir Henry or **Hugh de,** of Oxon— (E. II. Roll) bore, argent, six torteaux; Sir JOHN differenced with a label (3) azure, and his son with a baston azure; Parly. Roll.

*****[Plowden, John—**(E. III.) bore, azure, a fess dancettée florettée at the points or.— Shirley.] F.

Plugenett, Sir Alan de (or PLUKENET), banneret, baron 1295—bore, ermine, a bend engrailed gules (F.), Nobility Roll; a banneret, Arundel Roll; blasoned as a bend fusily in Segar and St. George Rolls; as a bend of fusils (F.) in the Howard Roll, and as a bend sinister fusily, probably erroneously, in Dering and Guillim Rolls. HUGO took up the cross in the last Crusade 1270.

Plumpton, Robert de and **Sir William** —(H. III. Roll) bore, azure, five fusils in fess or, on each an escallop gules; Ashmole, Arundel and Surrey Rolls, and Jenyns' Ordinary.

Plumpton, Sir Robert—(E. II. Roll) bore, azure, six fusils conjoined in fess or, on each a mullet gules; Parly. Roll – a fess indented in Harl. MS. 4033 fo. 51b.

‡**Poer, Robert le —** (H. III. Roll) bore, quarterly ermine and azure, two leopards' faces or. (F.) Dering Roll.

Pogeys, Sir Robert, of Bucks—(E. II. Roll) bore, lozengy argent and gules; Parly. Roll. (F.) YMBERT PUGEIS bore the reverse in the Howard Roll.

Poinings and **Pointz** *v.* **Poynings** and **Poyntz.**

Pole *v.* **de la Pole,** and **Pull.**

Pole, Michael de la, baron 1366—bore, or, a lyon rampant gules; Nobility Roll—borne also by Sir JOHN at the first Dunstable tournament 1308; ascribed to WILLIAM in Jenyns' Ordinary; borne also by JOHN MUSCEGROS and GRIFFITH OWEN, le fitz. Sir LEWIS, of Cheshire, differenced with a baston sable; Parliamentary Roll.

*****Poole, Sir Thomas of—**(E. IV. Roll) bore, azure, florettée and a lyon rampant argent, *quarterly with,* argent, a chevron sable between three bucks' heads cabossed gules — *with crest;* Ballard Roll.

*****[Pole, Sir John de la—**(E. III.) bore, argent, a chevron between three crescents gules.—Shirley.] F.

‡**Pole, Walter de la—**(H. III. Roll) bore, gules, a saltire argent, within a bordure sable bezantée. (F.) Dering Roll. POYLE in Howard Roll and PULLE in Arden and St. George Rolls.

Poley, Rauff—(R. II. Roll) bore, argent, on a bend gules, three crosses patée or; Surrey Roll.

Poleyn (——) a Knight—(H. VI. Roll) bore, or, a fess gules and a bendlet sable; Arundel Roll.

*****[Polhill, John—**(Hen. VI. Roll) bore, or, on a bend gules three crosses crosslet of the first.— Shirley.] F

Poltimore, Richard de—(H. III. Roll) bore, or, a lyon rampant vert; Arden Roll.

‡**Poltimore, Lucas de** and **Richard—** (H. III. Roll) bore, sable, a lyon rampant or. (F.) Dering and Howard Rolls.

Poltimore, Sir Richard de, of Devon— (E. II. Roll) bore, or, a cross engrailed gules, a baston gobony argent and azure; Parly. Roll.

*****[Polwhele, Richard de** (E. III.)—bore, sable, a saltire engrailed ermine.—Shirley.] F.

Pomerey, Sir Henry and **John Pomeray—**(E. III. Roll) bore, or, a lyon rampant gules, a bordure engrailed sable; Ashmole and Surrey Rolls.

(Pomfret ?) —— (R. II. Roll)—bore, argent, three cocks 2 and 1 sable; Surrey Roll.

Robt Pourtel.

Porcher

Porchester

Joan d. Pordone

W Porter

John Potonhold

Ormel Pomel

Wm de Pozo

Michael Poynings

Le Sire do Poynings

Robt. Pulsford

Sire Hulston

Ponchardon ?. **Punchardon.**

Popham, John de—(E. 1. Roll) bore, argent, a fess gules, in chief two bucks' heads cabossed or; Jenyns' Roll.

Popham, Raffe de—(E. 1. Roll) bore, argent, on a chief gules three bucks' heads cabossed or; Jenyns' Roll. POPHAM, a Suffolk Knight, carried a besant between the two bucks' heads; Arundel Roll.

Popham, John—bore, at the siege of Rouen 1418, gules, besantée (6, 4) and a chevron argent, *quarterly with*, argent, on a chief gules a besant between two stags' heads cabossed or. F.

Porcel, Robert—(H. III. Roll) bore, ermine three torteaux. (F.) Arden and St. George Roll.

Porcher —— (H. III. Roll) bore, argent, a cinquefoyle pierced gules. (F.) St. George Roll.

Porchester, Sr. —— knighted at the capitulation of Calais 1348—bore, or, eight barrulets sable. F.

Pordone, John de—(H. III. Roll) bore, gules, a fess or, between three mullets (6) argent. (F.) St. George Roll.

Porter, Sir W.—(H. VI. Roll) bore, sable, three bells 2 and 1 argent; Atkinson Roll. F.

Potenhall, Sir John—bore, at the siege of Calais 1345-8, or, on a fess azure three decrescents of the field. F.

Potenale, Sir John—(E. III. Roll) bore, argent, on a chevron azure three cinquefoyles pierced or; Ashmole Roll.

Pountney, John de—(E. III. Roll) bore, azure, a fess dancettée gules, in chief three leopards' faces sable—on the fess in trick; Jenyns' Ordinary.

Pouuel, Sir Ouuel—bore, at the battle of Boroughbridge 1322, paly (6) or and azure on a bend gules, three martlets argent. F.

Pouslyne, Sir William (PONSCYN, POUSCYN or PUSLINCH), of Herefordshire— (E. II. Roll) bore, quarterly argent and azure, a lyon rampant gules; Parliamentary Roll.

Powell, Sire Walter de, of Oxon—(E. II. Roll) bore, undée (6) or and sable a bend argent; Parly. Roll—tricked nebulée.

Power (——) a Suffolk Knight—(H. VI. Roll) bore, gules, on a chief argent three mullets pierced sable; Arundel Roll.

Power (PORE), **Richard de**—(H. III. Roll) bore, gules, a fess and in chief two mullets argent. (F.) Arden and St. George Roll.

Powis, Le Sr. de—(H. VI. Roll) bore, or, a lyon rampant gules; Nobility Roll. See Monumental Brass, JOICE, Lady TIPTOFT.

Powtrell, Sir Robert, of Derbyshire, and **Roger** (E. II. Roll) bore, or, on a bend azure three fleurs-de-lys argent; Parly. Roll and Jenyns' Ordinary.

Poyerd ——, (E. III. Roll) bore, azure a bend or between two indents (cotises indented) argent—and another with a label (3) gules; Ashmole Roll.

Poynings, Sir Michael, of Surrey - bore, at the first Dunstable tournament 1308, barry (6) or and vert, a bend gules. On the same occasion his brother Sir THOMAS bore on the bend three mullets argent (Parly. Roll); at the second tournament 1334, another THOMAS bore the undifferenced coat, when his brother MICHAEL differenced with a bordure engréle (indented) ermine.

Poynings, Sir Michael, baron 1339—bore, at the siege of Calais 1345-8, the paternal coat barry (6) or and vert a bend gules (F.) Sir JOHN (or CHRISTOPHER) bore the same, he and his brother Sir THOMAS were knighted at the capitulation (of Calais), when the latter differenced with a baston gobony argent and gules.

Poynings (**Robert**) lord—bore, at the siege of Rouen 1418, barry (6) or and vert, a bend gules, *quarterly with*, gules, three lyonceux passant argent debruised by a bend azure. F.

‡**Poynings, Lucas** (H. III. Roll), and **Thomas** (E. III. Roll) bore, barry (6) or and vert, a bend gules; Dering Roll and Jenyns' Roll, probably erroneous when tricked, or three bars vert, a baston (bend) gules in Howard Roll for LUCAS, and in Jenyns' Roll for JOHN.

Poyntz, Hugh, of Cory Malet, baron 1295— bore, barry (8) gules and or; Nobility Roll; the reverse is ascribed to him as having been borne at the battle of Falkirk 1298, and at the siege of Carlaverock in 1300 (F.); signed the Barons' letter to the Pope 1301; these being the arms of FITZALAN were disputed. Notwithstanding this Sir NICHOL (as banneret) appears to have borne them at the first Dunstable tournament 1308; (Arundel and Parly. Rolls), indeed, his seal with these arms and a label (5) is said to have been attached by his father to the Barons' letter to the Pope of 1301.

*****Predias, John**—(R. II. Roll) bore, argent, a chevron sable, a label (3) gules (F.); Surrey Roll.

Prendergast, Robert—(E. II. Roll) bore, gules, a bend cotised argent; Jenyns Ordinary.

Presmarsh, Sir Reynold de—(E. I. Roll) bore, bendy (8) or and azure, on a chief of the second two palets between as many esquires based of the first, over all an inescocheon argent; Holland Roll. (F.) See MORTIMER, which is barry.

Preston, Piers de (ioust) JUXTA WENDESLAWE (E. III. Roll) and **Sir William de** (E. I. Roll) bore, gules, crusily and a bend or (F.); Grimaldi and Holland Rolls; crusily fitchée in Howard Roll, and perhaps crusily potent in Dering Roll for a WILLIAM. ‡

Preston (——) a Suffolk Knight—(H. VI. Roll) bore, ermine, on a chief sable, three crescents or; Arundel Roll.

Preston, Thomas de—(R. II. Roll) bore, gules five fusils in chief and three in base argent; Surrey Roll.

Prestwolde, Hugh de—(E. III. Roll) bore, sable, a chevron or fretty gules, between three garbs argent; Jenyns' Ordinary.

Howgp de Poynt

Weynold de
Proshmarsh

will
de Preston

fgit de Preyb

John Prideaux

Oliver
Ponchardon

Rob
Pundolardo

will
de Quentin

Robt de Quincy

will   de
Quisanco

Roland Quetin

John de Quexley

Preyers, Sir Henry, of Rutland—(E. II. Roll) bore, gules, three escallops argent; Parly. Roll. F.

Preyers, Sir John, of Essex—(E. II. Roll) bore, gules, a fess double cotised argent; Parly. Roll.

Preyers, Sir Thomas de, of Essex—(E. II. Roll) bore, vert, a bend argent cotised or; Parly. Roll.

Preys, Sir Philip de—(E. III. Roll) bore, paly (6) or and azure, on a chief gules a lyon passant argent; Ashmole Roll. F.

Prideaux, John v. **Predias.**

Prowze, Sir William le (PREUZ), of Cornwall—(E. II. Roll) bore, sable, crusily and three lyonceux rampant argent; Parly. Roll.

Pudsay, John—(E. III. Roll) bore, vert, a chevron between three spur-rowells or; Jenyns' Ordinary and Ballard Roll.

Pugeis v. **Pogeys.**

Puleston, Sir Richard, of Cheshire—(E. II. Roll) bore, sable three mullets argent; Parly. Roll. JOHN DE PYVELSDON took up the cross in the last Crusade 1270; or PIT-LYSDEN. F.

Pulsford, Sir Robert, of co. Lancs.—bore, at the first Dunstable tournament 1308, sable, a cross flory or; patonce in Parly. and Jenyns' Rolls (F.), said to be same as ROBERT SWINNERTON who bore the cross florettée, which see.

Pull, William de—(H. III. Roll) bore, or, three eagles displayed azure; Howard Roll.

†**Punchardon, Oliver de**—(H. III. Roll) bore, sable platey 4, 3, 2, 1; Arden and St. George Rolls (F.); 3, 2, 1 in Jenyns' Ordinary.

Pundelarde, Robert—(H. III. Roll) bore, per pale argent and vert, a lyon rampant gules; Howard Roll. F.

‡**Queney, Robert** (or QUINCY)—(H. III. Roll) bore, gules, a cinquefoyle (ermine in Glover Roll) argent, in Howard and Camden Roll; pierced argent in Dering Roll. F.

Queney, Walder de (or QUERYNE)—(H. III. Roll) bore, or, a cinquefoyle gules; Glover Roll.

Quentin, Sir William—(E. III. Roll) bore, gules, on a chevron argent three martlets sable; Ashmole Roll.

Quilly, Sir Roger—(E. III. Roll) bore, argent, a chevron between three mullets sable; Ashmole Roll—pierced in Harl. Roll.

Quincy, Roger de, Earl of Winchester—(H. VI. Roll) bore, gules, seven mascles conjoined 3, 3, 1 or; Nobility Roll—3, 2, 1 in Ashmole (E. III.) Roll.

Quisance, William de—bore, at the second Dunstable tournament 1334, sable a bend engrailed argent, a label gules. F.

Quitricke, John (or WHITRICK)—(E. I. Roll) bore, argent a fret and a quarter gules—fretty in trick; Jenyns' Roll.

Qukin, Roland (or QUENKIN)—(E. I. Roll) bore, bendy (6) gules and ermine. (F.) Segar Roll.

Quixley, John de—(E. III. Roll) bore, gules, three greyhounds courant in pale argent, collared gobony or and sable. (F.) ADAM differenced this with an escallop sable on the shoulder of each hound—the collars, checquy or and sable.

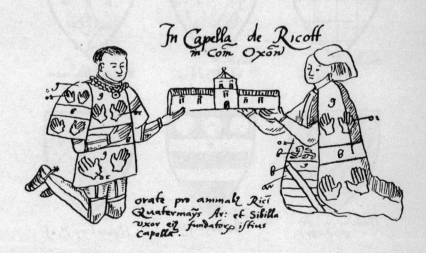

In Capella de Ricott in cõm Oxõn

orate pro animaḃ Riĉi Quatermayns Ar: et Sibilla uxor eiꝰ fundatorꝰ istius Capellæ.

John Vadcliffe   Henri d. Roleie.   Sire de Vamoine

John Vatclyffe   John Vavon Sholme   miles Vawdon

Walter de Vodeham   Will d. Redham   Richard Vodman

Baldwin de Vodverd.   John de Vaginghall   Howel ap Res

R

†**Rabayn, Ellis de**—(H. III. Roll) bore, argent, a fess between three escallops gules; Glover Roll.

Racel *v.* **Rocel.**

***Radcliffe, Sir John**—(E. III. Roll) bore, argent, two bends engrailed sable, a label (3) gules. (F.) JOHN of Ordsall bore the same, his brother ROBERT of Smithills bore it undifferenced and his son NICHOLAS of Chadderton, differenced with a fess gules; Harl. MS. 1481 fo. 68.

Ragan, John—(E. I. Roll) bore, argent, a chevron between three bucks' heads couped sable; Jenyns' Roll.

‡**Ralee, Henry** (or RALEY) and **Sir John de** —(H. III. Roll) bore, gules, crusily or, a bend vair. (F.) Dering (Ashmole copy), Howard and St. George Rolls—tricked also probably in error, (1) gules, a fess vair and (2) ermine a bend vair.

Ralee, Sir Simon, of Devon—(E. II. Roll) bore, gules, a bend lozengy (4) argent; Parly. Roll—engrailed in Harl. MS. 4033 fo. 33.

Raley, John—(E. III. Roll) bore, checquy or and gules, a chief undée (4) argent and azure; Jenyns' Ordinary—blasoned azure and argent in COTGRAVE.

Rayle, Sir Thomas de—(E. III. Roll) bore, checquy or and gules, a chief vair; Ashmole Roll.

Rame (——) an Essex Knight—(H. VI. Roll) bore, azure, three rams' heads cabossed argent; Arundel Roll.

Ramerne, Sire de ——, (E I. Roll) bore, argent, a lyon rampant sable, oppressed by a baston sable. (F.) Camden Roll.

Rameston, Thomas de—(R. II. Roll) bore, argent, a chevron sable, in the cantel a cinquefoyle pierced of the last; Surrey Roll. Ascribed also to Sir THOMAS RAMPSTON, K.G. 1402; K. 400 fo. 25.

Rande, William—(E. III. Roll) bore, gules, three chevronels argent, a bordure engrailed sable; Jenyns' Ordinary.

Randolph, Sir John, of Wilts—(E. II. Roll) bore, gules, on a cross argent five mullets sable; Parly. Roll.

Ratclyffe, Sir John—bore, at the siege of Calais 1345-8, argent, a bend engrailed sable. (F.) Borne also by RADCLIF of the Tower; Ballard Roll; and by Sir JOHN, K.G. H. VI. See also RADCLIFFE.

Ratelysdown —— (E. III. Roll) bore, azure, six escallops 3, 2, 1 or; Ashmole Roll.

Ravenscroft (——), of Cheshire—(F. IV. Roll) bore, argent, a chevron sable between three ravens' heads erased proper—with crest; Ballard Roll.

Ravensholme, Sir John—bore, at the siege of Calais 1345-8 vert, on a fess or a lyon passant gardant gules. (F.) Harl. MS. 3968 fo. 123; a marginal note in the Ashmole MS. ascribes to him—argent, on a fess double battely gules, a lyon passant gardant or, as in Jenyns' Roll and Ordinary.

[**Rawdon, Michael de** (E. III.)—bore, argent a fess between three pheons sable.— Shirley.] F.

Ray, John de—(E. III. Roll) bore, quarterly argent and azure, on a bend gules three fleurs-de-lys or; Jenyns' Ordinary.

Raynes, John (REYNES) and **Sir Thomas** —(R. II. Roll) bore, checquy or and gules, a canton ermine; Ashmole and Surrey Rolls. Another coat with a canton argent in Ashmole Roll.

†**Raynes, Roger de**—(H. III. Roll) bore, azure, fretty sable and a bend vaire potent counter potent or and gules; Howard Roll.

Raynsford, Henry — (E. I. Roll) bore, argent, a cross p'my and a bordure sable; Jenyns' Roll—another coat argent, a cross sable—with crest; Ballard Roll. For parmy see also CONSTABLE, and DACRE.

Rede (——) a Suffolk Knight—(H. VI. Roll) bore, azure, three pheasants 2 and 1 or; Arundel Roll.

Redisham, Sir Edmond, of Norfolk— (E. II. Roll) bore, argent, florettée gules; Parliamentary Roll, additional.

Redesham, Walter de—(E. I. Roll) bore, checquy argent and gules. (F.) Camden Roll.

Redford, Henry de (RYDFORD)—(R. II. Roll) bore, argent, fretty and a chief sable; Surrey Roll.

Redham, William de—(H. III. Roll) bore, gules, an inescocheon within an orle of martlets argent. (F.) Arden and St. George Rolls.

Redman, Richard—bore, at the siege of Rouen 1418, gules, three lozenge-cushions ermine tasselled or. (F.) Surrey Roll and Jenyns' Ordinary. In the Parliamentary Roll (E. II.) they are ascribed to Sir MATHEW of Cumberland, and tricked as three square cushions or; Parly. Roll, in Harl. MS. 4033; lozenge ermine, &c., in Harl. 6137. See also Glover Roll (H. III.).

PETER OF SAVOY, EARL OF RICHMOND.
IN THE COLLEGIATE CHURCH OF AQUABELLA, IN SAVOY, 1268.
From the "Archæologia."

Redman, Mathew—(R. II. Roll) bore, gules, a chevron argent between three lozenge-cushions ermine tasselled or ; Surrey Roll.

Rednesse, William de—(E. III. Roll) bore, sable, a chevron between three leopards' faces argent ; Cotgrave Roll.

Redvers, Earl of Devon and lord of the Isle of Wight. See DEVON and ISLE.

Redvers, Baldwin de—(E. II. Roll) bore, or, a lyon rampant azure ; Parly., Segar and St. George Rolls (F.) ; the LORD PERCY carries the same.

Rees, Howel ap—(H. III. Roll) bore, gules a chevron between three spur-rowells argent (F.) ; St. George Roll.

Reigate *v.* **Rygate.**

Rekell or REKETT —— a Kentish Knight— (H.VI. Roll) bore, gules two barrulets sable between three annulets argent ; Arundel Roll.

†**Renci, Sire de** (RENTI)—(H. III. Roll) bore, gules, three broad axes erect 2, 1, edges to the dexter argent ; or in Ashmole MS. ; Dering Roll.

Repinghall, John de—(E. I. Roll) bore, sable two bars argent, in chief three plates (F.) ; Camden Roll.

Repps, Sir John, of Norfolk—(E. II. Roll) bore, ermine, three chevronels sable ; Parly. (*additional*) and Ashmole Rolls and Jenyns' Ordinary.

Reresby, Sire Adam de—bore, at the battle of Boroughbridge 1322, gules, on a bend argent three crosses (patée) sable (F.) ; Jenyns' Roll and Ordinary ; usually tricked as the modern patonce. THOMAS and WILLIAM both LE FITZ differenced with a label (3) or ; Jenyns' Roll and Ordinary.

Reresby, Thomas—(R. II. Roll) bore, gules, on a bend argent three mullets pierced sable ; Surrey Roll.

Resonne, Sir John de—(E. II. Roll) bore, gules, a lyon rampant or, in the cantel a cross patonce vair—in another trick, a cross patonce vert on the shoulder of the lyon ; Parly. Roll.

Restwold, Richard—(E. I. Roll) bore, per saltire ermine and gules ; Jenyns' Roll.

Retford, John de—(E. III. Roll) bore, quarterly argent and gules a bordure engrailed sable ; Jenyns' Ordinary.

Retford, Thomas de, of Ashby—(E. I. Roll) bore, ermine, on a chevron sable three escallops argent ; Jenyns' Roll.

Retour, Richard—(E. I. Roll) bore, argent, three tree stumps (racynes) eradicated sable ; Jenyns' Roll.

Revel, Sir John—(E. III. Roll) bore, ermine, a chevron gules, a bordure engrailed sable ; Sir WILLIAM differenced with a mullet or on the chevron ; Ashmole Roll.

Rever, John, *v.* **Rider.**

Reveshall, John de—(H. III. Roll) bore, or, a cross gules, a label (5) of France (F.) ; Arden and St. George Rolls.

Reydon, Sir Robert de, of Suffolk—(E. II. Roll) bore, checquy argent and gules, a cross azure ; Parly. Roll ; another REYDON coat, azure, a cross counter-compony argent and gules ; Ashmole Roll.

†**Reymes, Roger de,** *v.* **Raynes.**

Reynell, John—(E. III. Roll) bore, ermine, a chevronel gules, a chief indented sable ; Jenyns' Ordinary.

Reynham, Edmund de — (R. II. Roll) bore, sable, three mallets 2 and 1 argent ; Surrey Roll.

Reythinge *v.* **Roynger.**

Ribbesford, Sir Henry, of co. Leic.— (E. II. Roll) bore, ermine, a chief gules fretty or (F.) ; Parly. Roll ; RIBEFORD in Arden and St. George Rolls.

Riboo, Richard, of Newbegging—(E. III. Roll) bore, argent, a chevron gules between three torteaux ; Grimaldi Roll ; RYBO in Jenyns' Ordinary.

Richmond, Roald le, Constable of the Honour of—(H. III. Roll) bore, gules, two gemelles and a chief or ; St. George Roll. SIR THOMAS DE RICHMONDE bore the same at the siege of Carlaverock 1300 (F.) ; Nativity and Parly. Rolls.

Richmond, Earl of, *v.* **John de Bretagne.**

[**Richmond, Earl of,** Peter of Savoy, maternal uncle to ELEANOR Consort of Hen. III.—bore, an eagle displayed within a bordure—died at Chillon, in the pays de Vaud 7 or 9 June 1268, buried in the Abbey of Hautecombe in Savoy, see Bookplate.]

Riddell, Sir William (RYDELL), of the North—bore, at the first Dunstable tournament 1308, and at the battle of Boroughbridge 1322, gules, a lyon rampant within a bordure indented argent (F.) ; Parly. Roll and Jenyns' Ordinary.

Riddell, Sir John (RYDELL), of Beds.— (E. II. Roll) bore, paly (6) argent and gules ; Parly. Roll.

Riddell, John (RYDELL)—(E. I. Roll) bore, argent, a fess azure between three garbs gules ; Jenyns' Roll.

Rider, John (REVER)—(E. I. Roll) bore, argent, on a bend azure cotised gules three crescents or ; Jenyns' Roll.

Ridemore, Sir Walter de (RYDEMOR)— bore, at the first Dunstable tournament 1308, gules, three stirrups argent (F.) ; also tricked as escallops.

Ridmer, Reynaud de—(E. III. Roll) bore, azure, a chief argent, a bend sable ; Grimaldi Roll.

Ridmer, Reynald de—(E. III. Roll) bore, argent, a chief indented azure, a baston sable ; Jenyns' Ordinary.

Ridware, Sir Thomas de, of co. Cambridge—(E. II. Roll) bore, azure, an eagle displayed argent ; Parly. Roll.

Rigby (——) a Knight—(H. VI. Roll) bore, argent, on a cross patonce sable five mullets or ; Arundel Roll.

Rigmayden, Thomas—(E. I. Roll) bore, argent three bucks' heads 2 and 1 cabossed sable ; Jenyns' Roll ; of Wedacre, in Ballard Roll.

Riley *v.* **Wrialeye.**

Ripley, Sir (——) Knighted at the capitulation of Calais 1348—bore, or, three lyons rampant azure.

walt de Vidmore

Ponnotub tivort

VobSart

Vaffe de Vochoford

Vobt de Vochoford

Thomaf Rocelin

Witt VeSSohyn

Theobald VorGrourt

Jon de Vobollo

Riĉ. d la rokele

VieGard Voboll

Vobt Voboby

Ripley —— (REPPLEY), an Essex Knight— (H. VI. Roll) bore, ermine, a fess or between three toads (tortoise in trick) sable; Arundel Roll.

Ripley, Sir John (RYPEL)—(E. III. Roll) bore, or, two chevrons and a canton gules; Ashmole Roll.

Rithre v. **Rythre.**

River v. **de la River.**

Rivers, Sir John de, of Aungre (Onger), banneret, baron 1299—bore, at the battle of Falkirk 1298 and at the siege of Carlaverock 1300, masculy or and gules—generally tricked six (or 7) mascles 3, 2, 1 (F.) but also as lozenges and also as fusils; Arundel and Parliamentary Rolls.

Rivers, Sir Donnet—bore, at the siege of Calais 1345-8, gules, a pale masculy or. (F.) For surname PAYNE ROET in Ashmole MS.; RUETT and RUVETT or RYVETT also occur as suggestions.

Rivers, Sir William de (RYZERE), of Lincolnshire—(E. II. Roll) bore, gules, a bend ermine, a label (3) or; Parliamentary Roll.

Roald, Constable of the Honour of Richmond —(H. III. Roll) bore, gules, two gemelles and a chief or; St. George Roll.

Robsart (——), knighted at the capitulation of Calais 1348, bore, vert, a lyon rampant or ("alii the reverse"); borne also by Sir JOHN, K.G., and Sir GEORGE, K.G. temp. H. V. F.

Roce v. **de la Roce.**

Rocel, Raf—(H. III. Roll) bore, argent, two bars fusily gules azure—in St. George Roll— sometimes dancettée. (F.) Arden Roll.

Roceline, Sir Peers (ROSSELYN), of Norfolk, and **Thomas**—(E. II. Roll) bore, gules, three buckles 2 and 1 argent, tongues to the dexter; St. George and Parly. Rolls. (F.) Another THOMAS, in Jenyns' Ordinary, the tongues to the sinister.

Roceline, Sir William (ROSSELYN), of Norfolk—(E. II. Roll) bore, azure, three buckles or, tongues to the dexter in Harl. MS. 6137 fo. 16ʰ, and to the base in Harl. MS. 4033; Parly. Roll. F.

Roch v. **de la Roch.**

Roche, Sir J.—(H. VI. Roll) bore, gules, three roach argent; Atkinson Roll.

Rochecourt, Sir Theobald—bore, at the siege of Calais 1345-8, sable, five fleurs-de-lys 2, 1, 2 in saltire or. F.

‡**Rocheford, Gyles de**—(H. III. Roll) bore, argent, burulée (9, 12) azure, a chief dancettée (4 indents) gules. (F.) Dering and Howard Rolls.

Rocheford, Guy le, le Poytevin—(H. III. Roll) bore, quarterly argent and gules; Glover Roll.

Rochford, Guy de—(H. III. Roll) bore, quarterly or and gules; Norfolk Roll.

Rochford, Sir Robert de—bore, at the first Dunstable tournament 1308, quarterly or and gules, a bordure indented sable (F.) on which occasion Sir ROGER bore the bordure indented argent.

Rochford, Sir Thomas de, knighted at the capitulation of Calais 1348—bore, quarterly or and gules a label (5) azure (F.); ascribed also to GUY in Howard Roll—and a label (3) azure to RAFFE in Jenyns' Ordinary.

Rocheford, Sir John and **Sir Raffe,** of Essex—(E. II. Roll) bore, quarterly or and gules, a bordure sable besantée; Ashmole, Atkinson and Surrey Rolls—another RAFFE, differenced with an annulet argent, on the gules quarters; Surrey Roll. Sir JOHN, of Essex, differenced with a martlet sable; Parliamentary Roll.

Rocheford, Raffe—bore, at the siege of Rouen 1418, gules, an eagle displayed or, *quarterly with,* quarterly or and gules, a bordure sable bezantée. (F.)

Rockley, Richard de (ROKELEY)—bore, at the siege of Carlaverock 1300, lozengy ermine and gules. (F.) JAMES of Wokingdon and Sir RICHARD of Suffolk bore the same; Jenyns' Ordinary and Parliamentary Roll; sometimes blasoned masculy, Glover Roll and Jenyns' Ordinary, and the tinctures reversed, as in Parly. and Ashmole Rolls.

‡**Rockley, Richard de la**—(H. III. Roll) bore, lozengy argent and gules, a bend azure. (F.) St. George Roll.

Rockley, Robert de—(R. II. Roll) bore, lozengy argent and gules, a fess sable; Surrey Roll.

Rockley —— (E. IV. Roll) bore, argent, a fess sable between seven lozenges 3, 3, 1 gules; with crest; Ballard Roll.

‡**Rocksley, John** and **Sir Richard,** of Kent (H. III. and E. II. Rolls) bore, azure, a fess gules between six lyonceux rampant argent. (F.) Dering, Howard, and Parly. Rolls.

Rocliffe, John de and **Sir Robert**— (E. II. Roll) bore, argent, a chevron between three lyons' heads erased 2 and 1 gules; Ashmole Roll and Jenyns' Ordinary. Sir RICHARD differenced with a chess-rook or; Ashmole Roll.

Rocliffe, Robert—(E. III. Roll) bore, argent, a chevron and in chief two lyons' heads erased gules, an annulet or for difference; Jenyns' Ordinary.

Rodes, Sir Gerard de, Chevr. de France— (E. I. Roll) bore, gules; Nativity Roll.

‡**Rodes, William de**—(H. III. Roll) bore, azure, a lyon rampant or; Dering Roll—debruised by a baston gules. (F.) Camden Roll.

Rodney, John de—(R. II. Roll) bore, or, three eagles displayed 2 and 1 gules; Surrey Roll. Sir WALTER bore the eagles purpure; Ashmole Roll.

Roet, Payne v. **Sir Donnet Rivers.**

Rohaut, Sir Roger—(E. II. Roll) bore, or, two chevronels gules on a canton of the last a mullet pierced argent; Ashmole Roll. F.

*****Rokeby, Sir Robert de,** knighted at the siege of Calais 1348—bore, argent, a chevron sable between three rooks proper (F.); ascribed also to ALEXANDER in Grimaldi Roll, and to THOMAS in Ashmole and Surrey Rolls.

MONUMENTAL EFFIGY OF ROBERT ROOS, BROUGHT TO THE TEMPLE CHURCH FROM YORK, 1682.

From Richardson.

Thomas de Hoanye

willt de Roß

Will d. Roſ

Thomas Roos
de bousobyo

Rolleston, John and **William de**—(E. III. Roll) bore, sable, a saltire argent ; Surrey Roll and Jenyns' Ordinary. ELYAS took up the cross 1270.

‡**Rome, Roger de** — (H. III. Roll) bore, argent, a fess sable and in chief a lyon passant gules. (F.) Dering Roll.

‡**Romenal, Roger de**—(H. III. Roll) bore, or, two chevronels gules, on a quarter of the second three cats' (or leopards') faces 2 and 1 or (F.) ; Dering Roll. Another, on the canton gules, a lyon passant of the field ; Howard Roll.

Romesbury, John de (or RONNEBURY)—(E. III. Roll) bore, argent, a saltire gules, between four pyes (birds) sable ; Jenyns' Ordinary.

Romsey, Walter—(E. I. Roll) bore, argent, a fess gules, a label (5) azure ; Jenyns' Roll.

Ronye, Sir Thomas le—bore, at the first Dunstable tournament 1308, ermine, on a chief indented gules two escallops argent. F.

Rookwood, Sir William, of Suffolk—(H. VI. Roll) bore, argent, six chess-rooks 3, 2, 1 sable ; Arundel Roll. F.

Ros, Sire George de—bore, at the battle of Boroughbridge 1322, argent, three water-bougets sable—borne also by Sir JOHN, of Notts, in Parliamentary Roll.

Roos, Robert and **Sir William,** banneret (both), of Ingmanthorpe—(E. III. Roll) bore, azure, three water-bougets or ; Norfolk Roll and Jenyns' Ordinary. Sir WILLIAM of Youlton, also Yorks., bore the water-bougets argent, and a label (3) or ; Parliamentary Roll.

Roos, John le—(R. II. Roll) bore, ermine, three water-bougets gules ; Surrey Roll.

Roos, William, of Hamlake, banneret, baron 1285—bore, at the battle of Falkirk 1298, and at the siege of Carlaverock 1300, gules, three water - bougets argent. (F.) Sealed the Barons' letter to the Pope 1301. Ascribed also to (‡) ROBERT in Dering, Norfolk and other Rolls. JOHN, 8th Lord, also bore the same at the siege of Rouen 1418. ROBERT fil WILLIAM bore a label (3) azure ; Glover Roll —another WILLIAM differenced, with a crescent sable on the first water-bouget ; Surrey Roll.

Roos and **Badlesmere, Le Sr. de**—(R. II. Roll) bore, gules, three water-bougets argent, *quarterly with,* BADLESMERE —argent, a fess double cotised gules ; Surrey Roll. Borne also by WILLIAM, Lord Roos, K.G. 1414.

Roos, James, Sir Robert, of Gedney, Notts, and **William**—(E. III. Rolls) bore, gules, three water - bougets ermine. (F.) Surrey, Parly. and St. George Rolls. THOMAS KNOVILE bore the same. ROBERT differenced with a label azure ; St. George Roll.

Roos, John, of Youlton, and **Sir Richard** —(E. III. Roll) bore, gules, three water-bougets or ; Ashmole Roll and Jenyns' Ordinary.

Roos, Robert, of Werke, and **Thomas,** of Kendale—(H. III. Roll) bore, or, three water-bougets sable ; Glover Roll and Jenyns' Ordinary. JOHN, differenced with a crescent sable ; Jenyns' Ordinary.

Ros, Sire Thomas de (of Yorkshire) — bore, at the battle of Boroughbridge 1322, gules, a fess vair between four water-bougets or—three (F.) only in Ashmole MS.—the latter borne also by Sir THOMAS and THOMAS DE BEUSEBY or BOUSEBYE ; Nativity Roll and Jenyns' Ordinary.

Roos, Sir John le (le filz)—bore, at the first Dunstable tournament 1308, gules, three lyonceux rampant argent, a label (3) azure *sic.* (F.)

*[**Roper, Edwin,** (E. I.)—bore, per fess azure and or, a pale counterchanged, three bucks' heads erased of the second.—Shirley.] F.

Rosehall, John de — (E. III. Roll) bore, azure, a fess between six martlets or (argent in trick) ; Jenyns' Ordinary.

Rosells, Henry—(E. III. Roll) bore, gules six roses 3, 2, 1, argent ; Jenyns' Ordinary. JOHN (H. III. Roll) bore, argent, ten roses gules, pierced or. (F.) St. George Roll.

Rotherfield, Adam de—(R. II. Roll) bore, gules, three fleurs-de-lys ermine ; Surrey Roll.

Roucliffe *v.* **Rocliffe.**

Rouge-Mayne, Charles de la, founder of the Abbey of Lakee in Ireland. *v.* **MacMoylin.**

Rous, Geoffrey, and **Sir John,** of co. Gloucester—(E. II. Roll) bore, per pale azure and gules three lyonceux rampant 2 and 1 ermine ; Parly. Roll and Jenyns' Ordinary.

Rous, Giles le—(H. III. Roll) bore, per pale gules and azure three lyonceux rampant 2 and 1 argent ; St. George Roll.

Rous, Roger le—(H. III. Roll) bore, per pale gules and azure a lyon rampant tail fourchée argent (F.) ; Arden and St. George Rolls.

Rous, Sir Roger, of co. Glouc.—(E. II. Roll) bore, per pale or and azure three lyonceux rampant gules ; Parly. Roll.

Rous, John de (or ROOS)—(E. III. Roll) bore, checquy gules and argent—tricked argent and gules ; Jenyns' Ordinary.

Rous, John (or ROOS), of Tyde –(E. III. Roll) bore, barry (8) gules and argent, a chief of the last over all a bend engrailed azure ; Jenyns' Ordinary.

Rous, Sir John de (ROOS), of co. Linc.— (E. II. Roll) bore, argent, three bars gules, a bend engrailed sable ; Parly. Roll.

Rous, Sir Richard le, of Beds.—(E. II. Roll) bore, quarterly argent and sable, a baston counterchanged—sable in trick ; Parly. Roll and Jenyns' Ordinary.

Rous, Sir Thomas le—(E. II. Roll) bore, ermine, on a chief dancettée gules three (sometimes two) escallops argent ; Parly. Roll.

*[**Rouse, Peter,** (E. III.)—bore, sable, a fess dancettée or between three crescents argent.— Shirley.] F.

Routh, John de—(R. II. Roll) bore, argent, on a bend cotised sable three mullets of the field ; Surrey Roll.

Routhe, John de—(E. III. Roll) bore, barry (6) or and azure on a bend argent three rooks proper ; Jenyns' Ordinary.

SIR WILLIAM DE RYTHER.

IN RYTHER CHURCH, YORKS, 1308. *After Hollis.*

Routhe, John de—(E. III. Roll) bore, barry (6) azure and or a bend gobony argent and of the first; Jenyns' Ordinary, Harl. MS. 6589 fo. 24.

Routhe, Piers de—(E. III. Roll) bore, argent, a chevron sable between three wolves' heads erased gules; Grimaldi Roll—lyons' heads instead of wolves' heads are ascribed to THOMAS in Jenyns' Ordinary.

Rowthings, —— (E. III. Roll) bore, argent, four palets gules; Ashmole Roll.

Roynge(r), Sir Rafe de, of Norfolk— (E. II. Roll) bore, argent, three bars and eight martlets in orle gules; Parly. Roll.

Rue, Amande de—(E. III. Roll) bore, argent, on a bend cotised sable three mullets of the field; Jenyns' Ordinary.

[**Rushall, Richard de**—bore, argent, a lyon rampant within a bordure engrailed sable, adopted by HARPUR.—Shirley.]

Russell —— an Essex? knight—(H. VI. Roll) bore, gules, three palets argent, a chief azure; Arundel Roll.

Russell, Sir Geffray (ROSSELL), of Northants or Rutland—(E. II. Roll) bore, argent, a chevron azure between three roses gules; Parly. Roll, (crosses crosslet instead of roses for THOMAS). Another THOMAS, bore it with the field or; Jenyns Roll and Ordinary.

Russell, Hugh and **Thomas**—(E. II. Roll) bore, or, a chevron azure between three roses gules a label (3) argent; Jenyns' Roll and Ordinary.

Russell, —— (E. III. Roll) bore, or, a fess between six martlets sable; Ashmole Roll.

Russell, Sir John—(F. II. Roll) bore, or, on a cross sable five martlets argent; mullets in Harl. MS. 6137 fo. 5[b].

Russell, Maurice and **Raufe**—(H. III. Roll) bore, argent, on a chief gules three besants; Howard and Jenyns' Rolls.

*[**Russell, Henry,** 1455—bore, argent, a lyon rampant gules, on a chief sable three escallops of the first.—Shirley.] F.

Russell, Robert—(R. II. Roll) bore, gules, on a bend sable, fimbriated or, two mullets of the last pierced of the field alternated with two swans argent; Surrey Roll.

Russival, Sire Thomas—bore, at the battle of Boroughbridge 1322; sable, a fess between six martlets 3 and 3 or. F.

Rutland, Earl of— ED. PLANTAGENET, K.G. 1390–1402—bore, France and England quarterly, a label (5) per pale argent (charged with nine torteaux) and gules, charged with three castles or; Surrey Roll; a label (3) per pale gules and argent, on the gules, six castles or, and on the silver, as many lyonceux rampant gules; K. 399 fo. 11.

Ryba, Richard—(E. III. Roll) bore, argent, a chevron gules between three torteaux; Grimaldi Roll and Jenyns' Ordinary.

Rydergens, Sir John, FRANCOYS—bore, at the battle of Boroughbridge 1322, azure, a bend argent, an inescocheon or charged with a bend engrailed sable; Ashmole MS. See LYDEVUSERS, another suggestion for this rather doubtful name is LYDERGAM.

Rye, Sir William de—bore, at the first Dunstable tournament 1308, gules, a bend ermine, a label (3) or (F.); azure in Nativity Roll.

Rygate, John, of Howke—(H. III. Roll) bore, argent a bend lozengy azure (bend engrailed in Harl. MS. 6589); Jenyns' Ordinary.

Rythre, Sir William de, banneret, baron 1299—bore, at the battle of Falkirk 1298, and also at the siege of Carlaverock 1300, azure, three crescents or (F.); Parly. Roll, &c. See Monumental Effigy. WILLIAM differenced with a label (5) gules. (F.) Arden and St. George Rolls.

Ryther, John de—(E. I. Roll) bore, argent, on a bend azure three crescents or (F.); Jenyns' Roll and Ordinary. See also WITHER or WYTHER.

ALMARIC,
LORD
ST. AMAND.

IN ELSING
CHURCH,
NORFOLK,
OB. 1382.

From a rubbing from the Hastings Brass.

S

Sacheverell —— (E. III. Roll) bore, argent, on a saltire azure five water-bougets or ; Jenyns' Ordinary.

Sackville, (Sir) Andrew (of Suffolk)—bore, at the first Dunstable tournament 1308, quarterly or and gules, a bend vair (F.) ; borne also by another (‡) ANDREW or ADAM in Dering Roll, by GEOFFREY of Sussex, and by JOHN, and THOMAS in Surrey Roll and Jenyns' Roll and Ordinary. An Essex knight bore the bend argent ; Arundel Roll H. VI.

Sackville, Bartholomew and **Thomas** —(H. III. Roll) bore, ermine, three chevronels gules ; Glover and Surrey Rolls.

St. Amand, Almaric, of Wodehay, banneret, baron 1299, sealed the Barons' letter to the Pope 1301, bore, at the siege of Carlaverock 1300, or, fretty sable, on a chief of the last three bezants (F.) See Monumental Brass ; the field argent in Nobility Roll. Sir WILLIAM bore the same in Jenyns' Ordinary, and the Lord St. AMAND is said to have borne them at the siege of Rouen in 1418, but the barony appears to have been in abeyance 1402-49. Curiously blasoned as, or a saltire and chevron interlaced—for fretty—but in Jenyns' Ordinary as, or three chevronels interlaced sable, &c., both in all probability erroneously tricked.

St. Amand, Sir Oliver de, of co. Glouc.— bore, at the first Dunstable tournament 1308, or, fretty sable, on a chief of the second two mullets argent pierced vert (F.)—three silver mullets unpierced in Parly. Roll.

St. Andrew, Sir John—(E. I. Roll) bore, gules, six mascles 3, 2, 1 or, a label (3) argent ; Ashmole Roll. ROGER bore 7 mascles and a label azure, in Jenyns' Ordinary ; and Sir ROGER of co. Leicester bore three mascles (sometimes lozenges) and the azure label ; Parly. Roll.

St. Andrew, John—(R. II. Roll) bore, argent, a cross flory engrailed sable, a bordure gules besanty ; Surrey Roll.

‡**St. Aubin, Gilbert de**—(H. III. Roll) bore, or, on a cross sable five plates (F.) ; Dering, St. George, and Surrey Rolls. Another GILBERT with bezants in Arden Roll. See ORKABLIN and WOLTAUBIN.

St. B——, Nicholl de—(H. III. Roll) wrongly blasoned burulée (15) argent and azure ; Howard Roll.

St. Clere, John and **Sir W.**—(E. I. Roll) bore, azure, a sun or ; Jenyns' and Atkinson Rolls.

St. Clere, Sir John de, of Suffolk—(E. II. Roll) bore, or, a lyon rampant, tail fourchée, gules collared argent ; Parly. Roll.

St. Cler, William—(H. III. Roll) bore, argent, a lyon rampant gules, a bordure sable (sometimes bezantée) (F.) ; St. George Roll ; lyon crowned or and bordure crusily or ; Arden Roll.

St. Cler, Thomas—(R. II. Roll) bore, gules, a fess between three leopards' faces or ; Surrey Roll.

St. Clere, William de—(H. III. Roll) bore, gules, a fess between three boars' heads or ; Howard Roll.

St. George, Sir Bawdwyn de, of co. Cambridge—(E. II. Roll) bore, argent, a cross patonce sable ; Parly. Roll.

St. George, Bawdwyn—(E. III. Roll) bore, argent, a chief azure, over all a lyon rampant gules, crowned or ; Surrey Roll and Jenyns' Ordinary—Sir WILLIAM, of co. Cambridge, bore the lyon uncrowned in Parly. Roll.

St. Helen, John de—(H. III. Roll) bore, gules, six lyonceux 3, 2, 1 rampant argent (F.) ; Arden and St. George Rolls.

St. Ive, John de (CEINTEYNO)—(H. III. Roll) bore, or, three lyons passant gules ; Arden Roll.

St. John, Sir John de, of Lageham, banneret, baron 1299—bore, at the battle of Falkirk 1298, and at the siege of Carlaverock 1300, argent, on a chief gules two mullets or, accompanied on the latter occasion by his son JOHN, who differenced with a label (3, 5) azure (F.), spur-rowells in Nicolas and in the Nobility Roll.

‡**St. John, John de**—(E. I. Roll) bore, argent * on a chief gules, two mullets pierced or ; Dering Roll (F.) ; spur-rowells in trick, not pierced for ROBERT in Grimaldi Roll.

+**St. John, Sir John de,** of Lageham—bore, * at the first Dunstable tournament 1308, or, on a chief gules, two mullets pierced vert, a bordure indented sable ; Parly. Roll—engrailed in Harl. 6137 fo. 36. He may be identical with JOHN junior, who differenced with a label at Carlaverock, and with Sir JOHN DE LAGE-HAM, who bore at the battle of Boroughbridge gules, on a chief argent two mullets sable.

St. John, John, brother of HUGH of Basing, ƒ JOHN—bore, argent, on a chief gules two mullets or pierced vert, a bendlet gules ; Harl. MS. 1481 fo. 73.

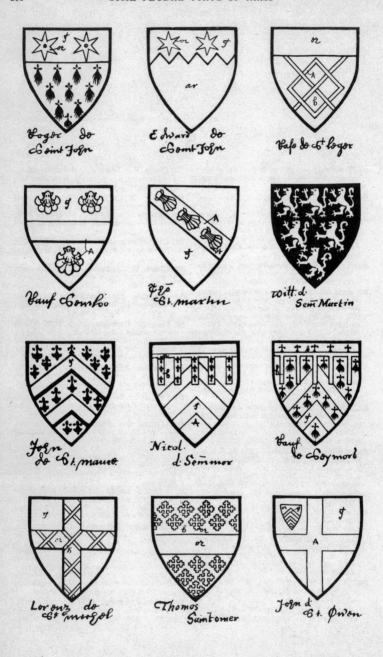

Roger de Saint John

Edward de Saint John

Vafe de St Leger

Pauf Combo

Et. martin

Will d. Sem Martin

John de St. maure

Nicol. d'Semmor

Pauf de Seymorb

Lorenz de St. mirgol

Thomas Saintomer

John d. St. Owen

St. John, John de, of Hanak (Halnaker), junior, baron 1300, sealed the Barons' letter to the Pope 1301—bore, (argent), on a chief (gules) two spur-rowells (or) ; a label (3) azure in Nobility Roll ; borne undifferenced by another JOHN and Sir R., in Norfolk and Harleian Rolls ; by others the mullets are pierced azure, sometimes vert.

St. John, Sir John—(H. III. Roll) bore, argent, on a chief gules two mullets (? in error) or a bordure indented sable ; Ashmole Roll. One of these names took up the cross 1270.

St. John, Sir Edward de—bore, at the battle of Boroughbridge 1322, argent, on a chief indented (dancettée, in the Surrey Roll) gules, two mullets (6) or (F.) ; pierced vert in Surrey Roll.

St. John, Sir Roger de (of Wilts)—bore, at the first Dunstable tournament 1308, ermine, on a chief gules, two mullets or pierced vert. (F.) Parly. Roll, borne by HUE and RICHARD, with mullets unpierced ; St. George and Segar Rolls.

St. John, St. Germyne (EYMIS), of Wilts —(F. II. Roll) bore, argent, crusily sable, on a chief gules two mullets or ; Parly. Roll.

St. John, Edmond, is said to have borne, at the second Dunstable tournament 1334, ermine. a chief gules—the blason is evidently imperfect.

St. John, Giles—(R. II. Roll) bore, gules, two bars argent, a quarter ermine ; Surrey Roll.

St. John, Hugh (SEINGEINE)—(H. III. Roll) bore, gules, three spur-rowells 2 and 1 and a chief dancettée or ; Norfolk Roll.

St. John, Walter de—(H. III. Roll) bore, azure, three buckles or ; Norfolk Roll.

‡**St. Leger, Sir Raffe,** of Kent, ‡**William and Robert**—(H. III. Roll) bore, azure, fretty argent and a chief or (F.) ; Dering Roll. ROBERT bore the same in Parly., Arundel, and Arden Rolls ; erroneously tricked with three chevronels interlaced in Jenyns' Ordinary.

St. Leger, Sir John, of Kent, and **William**—(H. III. Roll) bore, azure fretty argent and a chief gules ; Howard and Parly. Rolls. THOMAS bore the chief argent in Jenyns' Ordinary ; RENOLD and Sir THOMAS of Kent bore the chief or, in the cantel a spur-rowell gules ; Surrey Roll ; but a mullet in Parliamentary Roll.

St. Lo, Sire Rauf de (ST. LOUH)—bore, at the battle of Boroughbridge 1322, gules, a fess between three escallops argent (F.) ; borne also by ROGER and by Sir THOMAS of co. Lincs. ; Jenyns' Ordinary and Parly. Roll.

St. Lo, Hugh—(E. III. Roll) bore, azure, two bars argent, a chief gules ; Cotgrave Roll.

St. Loe, Sir John—(E. I. Roll), bore, gules vij fesses (barrulets) argent, three escallops of the second ; Nativity Roll.

St. Marcyl, William—(H. III. Roll) bore, gules, a fess argent, a label (5) or. (F.) Arden and St. George Rolls. ST. MARTILL in Harl. MS. 4965, the fess sometimes or. DE SAUTE MAREIS in St. George Roll.

St. Martin, John, Sir Renaud, of Wilts, and **William de.** (F.)—(H. III. Roll) bore, sable, six lyonceux rampant 3, 2, 1 or (F.) ; St. George and Parly. Rolls, Jenyns' Ordinary (gules for WILLIAM in the Arden Roll) ; the reverse of LAYBOURNE of the North and of THOMAS MALLORY.

St. Martin, John de—(H. III. Roll) bore, argent, two bars gules, a label (5) azure. St. George Roll. See also MARTIN and WINTERHULL.

St. Martin, Thomas de—(H. III. Roll) bore, gules, on a bend argent three escallops vert ; Arden Roll. F.

St. Maur v. Seymour.

St. Maure, Sir John de, knighted at the capitulation of Calais 1348, bore, ermine two chevronels gules. (F.) This coat also in Harl. Roll and 6th Nobility Roll (H. VI.) borne also by Sir RAUFFE, of Suffolk (E. II. Roll) differenced, with a label (3, 4 or 5) azure (F.), (the field argent in the Howard Roll), and by NICHOLAS, with a label of France, *i.e.* on each pendant three fleurs-de-lys or (F.) ; Harl. MS. 6137 *ff* 50, 81[b] ; Segar and Parly. Rolls—the field argent in Ashmole and St. George Rolls—the name is often spelt SEIMOR and SEYMOR in these entries.

St. Maur, Sir Lawrence and Sir Nicholas, of co. Glouc. (E. II. Roll) and **Sir William**—bore, argent, two chevronels gules a label (3 or 5) vert ; Holland and Parly. Rolls—the label azure for (‡) LAURENCE in Ashmole and Howard Rolls, and for HUE in Segar Roll—a label (4) azure. The name is often spelled SEIMOR and SEYMOR in these entries. LAWRENCE DE ST. MAUR took up the cross 1270.

‡**St. Michell, Lawrence de**—(H. III. Roll) bore, gules, a cross or fretty azure. (F.) Dering Roll, Ashmole MS. and Howard Roll.

St. Nicolas —— a Kentish Knight—(H. VI. Roll) bore, ermine, a chief quarterly or and gules ; Arundel Roll.

St. Omer, Sir John de—(E. I. Roll) bore, azure, on a cross or five mullets gules ; Nativity Roll.

St. Omer, Thomas and William—(H. III. Roll) bore, azure, crusily and a fess or. (F.) St. George Roll and Jenyns' Ordinary—(JOHN CLINTON bears the same arms)—a different trick in Ashmole Roll for THOMAS—crosses flory 3, 3.

St. Omer, William—(H. III. Roll) bore, azure, billettée and a fess or ; Glover and Grimaldi Rolls.

St. Omer, William—(E. I. Roll) bore, azure, a fess gules billettée (4, 3) or ; Jenyns' Roll.

St. Owen, Sir Gilbert de, of co. Glouc., and **Thomas**—(E. III. Rolls) bore, gules three chevronels or ; Parly. Roll and Jenyns' Ordinary.

St. Owen, John de—(H. III. Roll) bore, barry (6) gules and or. (F.) St. George Roll. RAF bore, or three bars gules ; Arden Roll.

St. Owen, Sir John de (of Herefordshire) —bore, at the first Dunstable tournament 1308, gules, a cross argent, in the cantel, a shield of CLARE (or rather GRANVILLE) or, three chevronels gules. (F.) Parliamentary Roll.

Joan de
St ffulbert

Urian d' St peire

Herebert d' Sentqumt

Joan d Semwaleri

Roger Calosbury

niccol Calforde

Prior Saltmarsh

Aubotyn Galbayn

Gerard de Galveyn

Will Calvey

Camfortt

Will de fiz Campson

St. Philibert, Hugh de, of Oxon, baron 1299 — bore, bendy (6) argent and azure; Nobility and Parly. Rolls. Sir JOHN, of Oxon., bore it also at the battle of Boroughbridge 1322. F. See SYUSIWARDE.

St. Pierre, Sir Uryan de, banneret—bore, at the first Dunstable tournament 1308, argent, a bend sable, a label (3) gules—of five points in H. III. Rolls (F.), Arden, Howard, and St. George Rolls; ascribed to Sir THOMAS in Ashmole Roll.

St. Pole, Count de—(E. I. Roll) bore— the arms of COUNT DE BLOIS (*i.e.* gules, three palets vair, a chief or) with a label (5) azure; Camden Roll.

St. Quintin, Sir Geffrey and William —(E. I. Roll) bore, or, a chevron gules, a chief vair; Nativity and Surrey Rolls. JOHN and THOMAS differenced with a mullet or; Jenyns' Ordinary and Surrey Roll.

St. Quintin, Edward—(E. III. Roll) bore, or, two chevronels gules, a chief vair; Jenyns' Ordinary.

‡**St. Quintin, Sir Herbert**—(E. II. Roll) bore, or, three chevronels gules, a chief vair (F.), Dering, Howard, and Parly. Rolls;. his brother (1) WILLIAM, of Fishide, bore two chevrons, and (2) ALEXANDER, of Harpham, bore one, as aforesaid.

‡**St. Quintin, Herbert**—(E. III. Roll) bore, argent, a lyon rampant rere-regardant purpure, sable in trick; Jenyns' Ordinary.

St. Valeri, Sir Richard de, of Oxon.— (E. II. Roll) bore, or two lyons passant gules; Parly. Roll. JOHN bore the lyon gardant (F.); Arden and St. George Rolls.

Salesbury, Roger—(E. I. Roll) bore, gules patée (patonce in trick) argent between four leopards' faces or; Jenyns' Roll. F.

Salford, Sire Neel de—bore, at the battle of Boroughbridge 1322, argent, on a chevron gules three escallops or. F.

Salisbury, Earls of, *v.* **Longespee** and **Montagu** or **Montacute.**

Salkeld, John—(E. I. Roll) bore, vert, a fret or; fretty in trick; Jenyns' Roll.

Salman, Thomas — (R. II. Roll) bore, argent, an eagle displayed sable, on its breast, a tyger's or leopard's face or; Surrey Roll.

•**Saltmarsh, Sir Piers de** (of Lincolnshire) —bore, at the battle of Boroughbridge 1322, argent, crusily and three six-foyles gules (F.); (roses in Parly. Roll)—ascribed also to THOMAS in Jenyns' Roll.

Saltmarsh, Sir Robert—(E. III. Roll) bore, argent, three six-foyles between four crosses crosslet fitchée within a bordure engrailed all gules; Ashmole Roll.

Salveyn, Sire Anketyn— bore, at the battle of Boroughbridge 1322, argent, a chevron between three boars' heads couped gules (F.); Jenyns' Ordinary.

•**Salvayn, Sir Gerard,** of Yorkshire—(E. I. Roll) bore, argent, on a chief sable two spur-rowells or, sometimes argent (unpierced mullets in Parly. Roll); Ashmole, Surrey, and Jenyns' Rolls and Ordinary.

Salveyn, Sire Gerard de (of co. Durham) —bore, at the battle of Boroughbridge 1322, argent, on a chief azure two mullets (6) or, a bordure indented gules (F.) tricked engrailed —the chief sable in the Arundel Roll.

*[**Salwey, William,** (E. I.)—bore, sable, a saltire engrailed or.—Shirley.] F.

Saly, William—(R. II. Roll) bore, quarterly argent and sable, a bendlet gules; Surrey Roll.

Samby, Sir John, knighted at the capitulation of Calais 1348, bore, argent fretty azure. F.

Samforde, Sir Thomas—(E. III. Roll) bore, argent, a chief gules; Ashmole Roll. See SANDFORD.

Samforth —, a Kentish Kt.—(H. VI. Roll) bore, per chevron sable and ermine, in chief two boars' heads erased argent (perhaps or) (F.) Arundel Roll.

Samson — (E. III. Roll) bore, paly (6) argent and azure a canton gules; Cotgrave Roll.

Samson, Sir John, of Yorkshire—(E. II. Roll) bore, or, a cross patonce sable; Parly. and Ashmole Rolls.

Samson, William, baron 1299—bore, argent, a cross moline sable (F.); Nobility Roll —probably father of

Sampson, Sir William, Da f? (? la f?) banneret—bore, at the battle of Falkirk 1298, sable, a fer-de-moulin or—(the reverse in Parly. Roll)—as a banneret, he carried, or a cross moline (recercelée) sable pierced of the field, in the Arundel Roll.

Samsson, William— (H. III. Roll) bore, argent, a fess and in chief two mullets (6) sable (F.); St. George and Arden Rolls.

Samur, Raufe de—(H. III. Roll) bore, azure, on a chief indented or, a crescent gules; Howard Roll.

Sancerlis, Piers de—(H. III. Roll) bore, gules, a fess or between six escallops 3, 3, argent; Arden Roll. Surname doubtful.

Sandacre, — **de**—(H. III. Roll) bore, argent, a lyon rampant purpure and a baston vert; Cotgrave Roll.

‡**Sandars, Thomas de**—(H. III. Roll) bore, or, on a chief azure, three lyonceux rampant argent (F.), Dering Roll; the colours, or, gules, or, in Ashmole MS.

Sandeby, Sir Robert, of Lincolnshire, and **Sir Thomas**—(E. III. Roll) bore, argent fretty azure; Parly. and Ashmole Rolls, and Jenyns' Ordinary.

Sandes, Richard de—(E. III. Roll) bore, argent, a fess dancettée (4) between three crosses crosslet fitchée gules; Jenyns' Roll.

Sandford, William de—(E. I. Roll) bore, ermine, on a chief gules two boars' heads couped argent; Jenyns' Roll.

*•**Saunford, Sire William de**—bore, at the battle of Boroughbridge 1322, quarterly indented azure and ermine. (F.) Probably per fess indented is intended.

Saunford, Gilbert—(H. III. Roll) bore, undée (6) argent and azure; Arden Roll; argent and gules for NICHOLAS and WILLIAM in Glover and Norfolk Rolls; NICHOLAS fil. WILLIAM differenced with a label gules; Glover Roll.

SIR JOHN SAY.

In Broxbourne Church, Herts, 1473.   *After Waller.*

‡**Sandwith, John de**—(H. III. Roll) bore, argent, a chief dancettée azure in Dering Roll ; the field or (F.) in Howard and Camden Rolls.

‡**Sandwith, Rauf de**—(H. III. Roll) bore, azure, a chief dancettée (4) or—another trick as if per fess dancettée ; Dering Roll ; THOMAS bore three lyons on the chief (no tinctures) ; Howard Roll ; he probably took up the cross 1270.

+**Sansaver, Hugh** and **Sir Raffe**, of Surrey + or Sussex —(H. III. Roll) bore, crusily and three crescents or (F.) ; Dering, Howard, and Parly. Rolls ; crusily fitchée for HUGH in Jenyns' Ordinary. RALPH LE SAUSER took up the cross 1270.

Sansaver, Robert—(H. III. Roll) bore, gules, a bend between six escallops argent ; Howard Roll.

Santon, Sir John de (SAUNTON or SAUM-SON), of Lincolnshire—(E. II. Roll) bore, or, a chief azure ; Parly. Roll.

Saperton, John de—(E. III. Roll) bore, or, an eagle displayed vert, membered gules, a baston gobony (6) argent and gules ; Jenyns' Ordinary.

Sapi, John—(E. I. Roll) bore, gules, three buckles, tongues to the dexter or ; Jenyns' Roll and Ordinary.

Sapi, John de—(H. III. Roll) bore, argent, billettée and a lyon rampant gules (F.) ; Arden Roll.

Sapie, Robert—(E. III. Roll) bore, argent, on a bend vert, cotised gules, three eaglets displayed or ; Jenyns' Ordinary.

Sarcilun, William—(H. III. Roll) bore, argent, a fess and in chief two mullets (6) sable ; Arden Roll. See SAMSSON.

Sarnesfeld, Nicoll and **Walter**—(H. III. Roll) bore, azure, an eagle displayed or (F.) ; Surrey and St. George Rolls. Sir NICHOLAS, K.G., 1387, bore the eagle crowned argent. K. 399 fo. 18.

Sarren, William de—(H. III. Roll) bore, azure, three crosses or ; Glover Roll.

Sassenau, Sir Otes de (CASANOVA) —bore, at the battle of Falkirk 1298, " d'or ou lez pies de sable."

Saunzaver, Ralph, baron 1294. See SAN-SAVER.

Savage, (Sir) Ernaud—bore, at the second Dunstable tournament 1334, argent, six lyon-ceux sable (F.) ; Ashmole and Surrey Rolls ; ascribed also to Sir ROGER of Kent in the Parly. Roll, and the reverse to LAWRENCE in Jenyns' Ordinary.

Savage, Sir John—(E. IV. Roll) bore, argent, a pale lozengy sable ; with crest ; Ballard Roll.

Savage, Sir John, of Kent—bore, at the first Dunstable tournament 1308, ermine, on a chief azure, three lyonceux rampant argent (F.) ; ascribed also to (‡)RAUF in the Dering Roll, and with the lyons or in the Howard Roll.

Savage, Sir Piers de—(E. I. Roll) bore, gules, a cross moline argent ; a cross argent in Glover Roll.

Savage, Robert de—(H. III. Roll) bore, barry or and gules ; Glover Roll.

*****Saville, John**—(R. II. Roll) bore, argent, on a bend sable, three owls of the field (F.) ; another JOHN differenced with a label (3) gules ; Surrey Roll.

Sawney, Amys de and **Henry de**—(E. I. Roll) bore, argent, an eagle displayed sable (F.) ; Camden Roll.

Saxton, —— (E. IV. Roll) bore, argent, three wreaths gules between two bastons sable ; with crest ; Ballard Roll.

‡**Say, Sir William de**—(H. III. Roll) bore—MANDEVILLE'S coat—quarterly or and gules (F.) ; Dering, Glover, and Howard Rolls ; borne also by Sir GEOFFREY, banneret (baron 1313) at the first Dunstable tournament 1308, and at the second (1334) by his son GEOFFREY who was possibly knight (? banneret) at the capitulation of Calais 1348, bearing the same coat. One of this surname, a Suffolk Knight, bore, in the first tournament, a lyon passant azure (gardant in Harl. 4033 fo. 39b) ; Parly. Roll.

[**Say, Sir John**, of Herts., 1473—bore, per pale (argent and gules) three chevrons voided all counterchanged. See Monumental Brass.]

Saye, Sir William de, NORREYS, (sic)—(E. III. Roll) bore, gules, a cross patonce argent ; Ashmole Roll. There seems probable confusion here with SYWARD.

Scales, Robert de, of Musells, banneret, baron 1299, bore, at the battle of Falkirk 1298, and at the siege of Carlaverock 1300, gules, six escallops argent (F.) — Nicolas names 3 only—9 in Harleian Roll, 10 in St. George Roll. See knights banneret in Arundel Roll ; sealed (with 6 escallops) in Barons' letter to the Pope 1301, and so ascribed to THOMAS, last Lord SCALES, K.G., in K. 402 fo. 4.

Scargill, Waryne and **William de**—(E. III. Roll) bore, ermine, a saltire gules ; Grimaldi and Surrey Rolls ; Sir WALTER differenced, with a mullet or, in Ashmole Roll.

Scargill, Sir William—(E. III. Roll) bore, ermine, a saltire engrailed gules ; Ashmole Roll.

Scarsbricke, James of—(E. IV. Roll) bore, gules, three mullets between two bendlets engrailed argent ; with crest ; Ballard Roll.

‡**Scorenci, John de**—(H. III. Roll) bore, argent (sometimes or), a chevron gules (F.) ; Dering Roll.

Scott, John le, Earl of HUNTINGDON — (H. III. Roll) bore, paly (6) or and gules a bend sable ; Glover and Jenyns' Rolls ; in Jenyns' Ordinary the arms are tricked, or three piles meeting in base gules ; and as Earl of CHESTER, 1232–7, azure, three garbs or, are ascribed to him in Jenyns' Ordinary.

‡**Scotto, Robert de**—(H. III. Roll) bore, ermine, on a cross gules five martlets, or (F.) Dering Roll — SCOTHE in Howard Roll, ESTOTOT and STOTTOT in Arden and St. George Rolls.

Scremby —— de (E. I. Roll) bore, azure, three barrulets and a bend or ; Jenyns' Roll.

SIR ROBERT DE SEPTVANS.

IN CHARTHAM CHURCH, KENT, 1306. *After Waller.*

*Scrope, Richard le—(R. II. Roll) bore, azure, a bend or ; Parliamentary and Surrey Rolls ; and so ascribed to WILLIAM, K.G., Earl of WILTSHIRE, in K. 399 fo. 13.

(1) HENRY, differenced with a label (3) argent.

(2) JOHN, with a label ermine ; Surrey Roll.

(3) HENRY LE, differenced with a label (3) argent, each charged with as many barrulets gules ; Surrey Roll.

(4) HUGH, of Ruthen, slain at the siege of Calais 1347—bore, a martlet for difference, and a label (5) or. F.

(5) STEPHEN, differenced with a mullet ermine ; Surrey Roll.

(6) THOMAS, differenced with a label (3) argent, charged with an annulet sable ; probably on the bend ; Surrey Roll.

(7) —— differenced with a lozenge ermine, on the bend ; Surrey Roll.

Scrope, Sir Henry le, of Bolton—(E. I. Roll) bore, azure, on a bend or, a lyonceux passant purpure ; Nativity and Parliamentary Rolls and Jenyns' Ordinary. Sir RICHARD LE SCROPE, 1st baron, was thrice challenged as to his arms—first (as to crest) at the siege of Calais 1347 ; second, by CARMINOW in Paris 1360 ; and third, by GROSVENOR in 1385, but was never worsted.

Scrope, William le—(R. II. Roll) bore, gules, three armed legs conjoined argent, garnished or a label (3) argent ; *quarterly with*, SCROPE and a label (3) gules ; Surrey Roll.

Scudamore, Walter—(E. I. Roll) bore, gules, three stirrups, or, with the "cuires" argent ; Jenyns' Roll. (F.) Sir PIERS bore the stirrups argent ; Ashmole Roll. F.

Scures, Sir John de (of Wilts.)—bore, at the first Dunstable tournament 1308, azure, fretty, or. (F.) Parliamentary Roll and Jenyns' Ordinary. Borne also by another Sir JOHN, knighted at the capitulation of Calais 1348.

*[Sebright, Peter, 1294—bore, argent, three cinquefoyles pierced sable.—Shirley.] F.

Seckford, Sir George, of Suffolk—(H. VI. Roll) bore, ermine, on a fess gules three escallops argent ; Arundel Roll. F.

Sees, Sir Diggory—(R. II. Roll) bore, azure, platey 4, 3, 2, 1 a chief or, issuant therefrom a demi-lyon rampant gules ; Jenyns' Ordinary —six plates and the demi-lyon sable in Arundel Roll.

Sefoule, Sir Ralph, of Norfolk—(E. II. Roll) bore, argent, a cross patonce vert, in the cantel a sea-fowl gules ; Parly. Roll. F.

Segni, Le Sire de—(H. III. Roll) bore, argent, a cross sable—"a merlos sable bordeaus" probably martlets — in orle sable ; Norfolk Roll.

†Segrave, Nicholas—(H. III. Roll) bore, sable three garbs argent (F.) ; borne also by GEOFFREY and GILBERT ; Dering, Norfolk, Glover, and Howard Rolls.

Segrave, Sir John de, banneret, baron 1296-1325, sealed the Barons' letter to the Pope 1301—bore, at the battle of Falkirk 1298 and at the siege of Carlaverock 1300, sable, a lyon argent crowned or ; as did his brother NICHOLAS, baron 1295-1322, with a label (3) gules, he signed but did not seal the famous

Barons' letter 1301 ; he bore the arms also at the first Dunstable tournament 1308 and at the battle of Boroughbridge 1322—a label (5) gules. F.

Segrave, Sir Stephen—bore, at the first Dunstable tournament 1308, sable, a lyon rampant argent, crowned or, charged on the shoulder with a fleur-de-lys gules (F) ; ascribed also to Sir JOHN, of co. Leic., in Segar and Parliamentary Rolls.

Segrave, Sir Henry de, of co. Leic.—bore, at the first Dunstable tournament 1308, sable, a lyon rampant argent, crowned or, debruised by a bendlet engrailed gules ; a baston gules (F.) in Harleian and Parly. Rolls ; and also for HUGH, whose brother JOHN (*f* John) differenced with a baston or, as did Sir SIMON also of co. Leic. (Harl. MS. 1481 fo. 77).

Segrave, Nicole de—(E. I. Roll) bore, sable, a lyon rampant argent ; Dering and Howard Rolls.

Segrey, John and **Simon de**—(H. III. Roll) bore, ermine, a lyon passant gardant gules ; Arden and St. George Rolls. (F.) SYMON bore a lyon rampant in Jenyns' Ordy.

Seilly, John de—(H. III. Roll) bore, azure, semée of mullets (6) and a lyon rampant or ; Howard Roll. See SULLY.

*Selby, Sir Walter—(E. III. Roll) bore, burrulée (14) or and sable. (F.) Ashmole Roll.

Senefylde, Sir Guy de, of Essex—(E. II. Roll) bore, vert, an eagle displayed or ; Parly. Roll. NENESFELD, NEVESFELD or STENEFELDE.

Seneschal, William le, *v.* Steward.

Sennyle, Sir Symon de (SENCILLE), knighted at the capitulation of Calais 1348, bore, azure, crusily fitchée (3, 3) and a bend or.

†Septvans, Sir Robert, of Kent—(H. III. Roll) bore, azure, three corn-fans or. (F.) Dering and Arundel Rolls – tricked crusily or, in Howard Roll – see Monumental Brass.

Servington, Sir Oliver—(E. III. Roll) bore, ermine, on a chief azure three bucks' heads cabossed or ; Ashmole Roll.

Seton, Sir John—(E. III. Roll) bore, gules, a bend argent between six martlets or ; Ashmole and Surrey Rolls.

*[Seimor, Sir Roger, 23 H. III.—(Seal), gules, two wings conjoined in lure of the first.—Shirley.] F.

Seymour *v.* St. Maur.

Seymour, Thomas—bore, at the second Dunstable tournament 1334, argent, three chevrons gules, a label vert. F.

Seymour, Sir Thomas (SEMOR)—(E. III. Roll) bore, argent, a chevron gules, a label (3) azure ; Ashmole Roll.

Seynanse, Sir William de—(E. III. Roll) bore, gules, on a chevron or three martlets sable ; Ashmole Roll. F.

Seys, Hemar (SCEYS)—(H. III. Roll) bore, gules, two palets vair and a chief or ; Howard Roll.

Shakerley, William—(E. IV. Roll) bore, argent, three shakebolts 2 and 1 sable—with crest ; Ballard Roll.

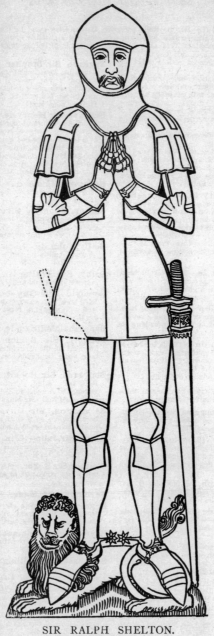

SIR RALPH SHELTON.

IN GREAT SNORING, NORFOLK, 1423. *After Cotman.*

Shardelow, Sir John—(E. III. Roll) bore, argent, a chevron gules between three crosses crosslet fitchée azure ; Ashmole Roll. JOHN CARBONELL bears the same arms.

Shardelow, Sir J.—(H. VI. Roll) bore, gules, a cross argent, a bordure engrailed or, Atkinson Roll. See also CARBONELL.

Shardeston, Fouke de—(H. III. Roll) bore, gules, a saltire engrailed argent ; Glover Roll.

Sharingbourne, Andrew de—(E. III. Roll) bore, gules, a lyon rampant or, a quarter ermine ; Ashmole Roll and Jenyns' Ordinary.

Sharnfield, John de—(E. III. Roll) bore, azure, an eagle displayed or membered gules ; Jenyns' Ordinary. JOHN DE WOLVERTON bears the same.

Sharshall, Sir William—(E. III. Roll) bore, undée (6)—now barry nebulée—argent and gules, a bordure sable besantée. Sir ADAM differenced with a mullet (6) or ; Ashmole Roll. See SARASSWELLE.

Shastowe, Robert de—(H. III. Roll) bore, gules, on a bend argent three mullets azure ; Glover Roll.

Sheffield, Sir Thomas de (SHEFELDE)—bore, at the first Dunstable tournament 1308, gules, a fess between three garbs banded or. (F.) (Sir ROBERT bore the reverse ; Parly. Roll.) JOHN and Sir THOMAS bore six garbs 3, 3. with the colours reversed ; Parly. Roll and Jenyns' Ordinary.

Sheffield, Thomas—(E. III. Roll) bore, argent, a chevron gules between three garbs 2 and 1 or—another with the field ermine ; Jenyns' Ordinary.

*[**Shelley, Sir William,** (R. II.)—bore, sable, a fess engrailed between three whelk-shells or. —Shirley.] F.

Sheme, Sir (——) of Sheppey, in Kent—(H. VI. Roll) bore, azure, four lyonceux rampant argent a canton ermine ; Arundel Roll. Surname doubtful, see SHIRLAND.

[**Shelton, Sir Ralph,** of Norfolk, 1423—bore (azure) a cross (or). See Monumental Effigy.]

Shepey, Sire John de—(E. II. Roll) bore, azure, a cross or fretty gules ; Parly. Roll. See STEPEY.

Shepey, Sir John—(E. III. Roll) bore, gules, a fess between three garbs argent ; Ashmole Roll.

*[**Sherard, Sir Robert,** 1343—bore, argent, a chevron gules between three torteaux.—Shirley.] F.

Sherborne, Sir John—bore, at the siege of Calais 1345-8, vert, a lyon rampant gardant argent. F.

Sherburne, Sir Richard, of Stonyhurst—(E. IV. Roll) bore, argent, a lyon rampant or *quarterly with*, vert, an eagle displayed argent ; with crest ; Ballard Roll.

Shillighelde, Yvon de, *v.* **Silligheld.**

Shillithorne, William—(E. III. Roll) bore, argent a cross checquy argent and sable,—counter-compony in trick ; Jenyns' Ordinary.

Shirbrook, Robert de—(H. III. Roll) bore, vair, a chief or, over all a bend gules (St. George Roll) charged with three mullets (6) ; Harl. MS. 6589.

Shirland, Sir Robert (of Kent)—bore, at the first Dunstable tournament 1308, azure, six lyonceux rampant argent, a canton ermine. (F.) & Monumental Effigy ; borne also by (‡) ROGER ; Dering and Howard Rolls.

Shirley, Sir Raffe, of Warwickshire—(E. II. Roll) bore, paly (6) or and sable ; Parly. Roll. *HUGH and Sir RALPH—with a canton ermine. (F.) in Surrey and Ashmole Rolls.

Sherley, William de—(H. III. Roll) bore, paly (6) or and azure, a bend gules ; Arden Roll.

Shottesbrooke, Sir Gilbert—(E. III. Roll) bore, ermine, a chief per pale indented or and gules ; Ashmole Roll (F.) ; Sir R. ermine (incomplete) ; Atkinson Roll.

*[**Shuckburgh, John de,** (Ed. III.)—bore, sable, a chevron between three mullets pierced argent.—Shirley.] F.

Shyryak, Sir John—(E. III. Roll) azure, an inescocheon within an orle of martlets argent ; Ashmole Roll.

Sibbeton, Sir John de, of Herefordshire—(E. II. Roll) bore, or, an eagle displayed, a baston gobony argent and gules ; Parly. Roll.

Sidney ——, an Essex ? Knight (H. VI. Roll) bore, or, a pheon azure ; Arundel Roll.

Sifrewast, Richard de—(H. III. Roll) bore, azure, twc gemelles and a chief or. (F.) St. George and Arden Rolls—NICHOLAS took up the cross 1270. See CIFREWAST.

Siggeston, Sir John—(E. III. Roll) bore, argent, a double-headed eagle displayed gules (sable, in Jenyns' Ordinary) ; Ashmole Roll.

‡**Silligheld, Ivon de**—(H. III. Roll) bore, azure, six cats' or leopards' faces 3, 2, 1 or (F.) ; Dering Roll ; men's heads couped in Howard Roll.

Silton, Sir John de—bore, at the first Dunstable tournament 1308, or, an eagle displayed vert, a bendlet gobony argent and gules. F.

Simeon, Robert—(R. II. Roll) bore, gules, a fess or between three lyons rampant argent ; Surrey Roll.

Sindlesham, Sir Robert de, of Berks—(E. II. Roll) bore, argent, on a fess between three escallops gules, as many martlets or Parly. Roll.

Skelton, Sir Rauf, (of Suffolk) – (E. II. Roll) bore, azure, a cross or ; Ashmole and Parly. Rolls. Another RAUFF with a label (3) argent ; Surrey Roll.

Skelton, Clement de—(E. I. Roll) bore, azure, a fess gules between three fleurs-de-lys or ; Jenyns' Roll.

Skette, John—(E. II. Roll) bore, argent, a cross crosslet sable ; Surrey Roll.

Skidburgh, Robert, of Saltfletby in Lincolnshire - (E. I. Roll) bore, azure, three closed helmets crested or ; Jenyns' Roll.

Skillithorne *v.* **Shillithorne.**

Skipton, John de—(E. I. Roll) bore, argent, an anchor erect sable ; Jenyns' Roll.

Skipton, John de—(E. III. Roll) bore, per base indented argent and purpure a lyon rampant of the last ; Jenyns' Ordinary. F.

SIR ROBERT DE SHURLAND.

IN MINSTER CHURCH, KENT.   *After Stothard.*

[**Skipwith, Sir William,** (E. III.)—bore, argent, three bars gules in chief a greyhound courant sable.—Shirley.] F.

Skirpenbeck, le Baron de—(E. I. Roll) bore, gules a cross patée (patonce in trick) argent, on a chief azure a lyon passant gardant or ; Jenyns' Roll.

Sleght, Robert—(R. II. Roll) bore, or, crusily (6, 4) and a chevron sable ; Surrey Roll.

Sleghtes, Henry—(E. III. Roll) bore, gules, six crosses moline 3, 2, 1 or, in chief a lyon passant argent ; Jenyns' Ordinary.

Sleghtes, Robert, of Legbourne in Lincs.—(E. I. Roll) bore, gules, a chevron between three crosses moline or ; Jenyns' Roll.

Smalborough, William—(R. II. Roll) bore, sable a chevron between three bears' heads couped or ; Surrey Roll.

Smareys, Sir Herbert de—bore, at the first Dunstable tournament 1308, argent, a lyon rampant sable (F.) ; as DES MAREYS.

Smyth, Sir John, of Essex—(H. VI. Roll) bore, ermines, three bezants ; Arundel Roll.

Snaves, John de—(H. III. Roll) bore, sable, a chevron between six lyons rampant argent ; Howard Roll.

*[**Sneyd, Richard de**—bore, gules, a scythe argent, the coat of his mother ROSIA DE PRAERS, his descendant RICHARD DE TUNSTALL DE SNEYD, had the fleur-de-lys sable for Poictiers 1356.—Shirley.] F.

Snotterley, Sir Roger de, of Norfolk—(E. II. Roll) bore, gules, a fess between three buckles, tongues to the dexter argent ; Parly. Roll.

Snylly, Robert — (E. III. Roll) bore, or, two bars gules ; Jenyns' Ordinary. See SULLY.

Soardeby, John, v. **Sywardby.**

‡**Sodon, Stephen,** (SOWDON)—(H. III. Roll) bore, azure, three bendlets argent (F.) ; Dering and Howard Rolls ; bendy (6) argent and azure in Ashmole MS.

Sofhongell, Raffe — (E. III. Roll) bore, argent, a cross flory sable—now patée flory—" boutes florettes " ; Jenyns' Ordinary.

Soleni, Averay de—(H. III. Roll) bore, quarterly argent and gules ; Arden Roll and Jenyns' Ordinary.

Solers, Henry de—(H. III. Roll) bore, paly (10) or and azure a bend gules (F.) ; St. George Roll.

Soleys, Richard—(H. III. Roll) bore, or, a fess gules (azure in Harl. MS. 6137) ; St. George Roll. F.

Soltone, Sir John de—(E. II. Roll) bore, or, a lyon rampant azure, a chief gules ; Harl. MS. 4033. In Harl. 6137—or, a chief gules, over all a lyon rampant azure ; Parly. Roll.

Somervile, Roger de—(E. I. Roll) bore, burulée (12) argent and gules, on a bordure, azure eight martlets or ; Jenyns' Roll and Ordinary.

Someri, Henry de—(H. III. Roll) bore, sable, a bend between six martlets 3, 3 argent (F.) ; Arden and St. George Rolls.

Someri, Sir John, of Kent—bore, at the first Dunstable tournament 1308, quarterly or and azure, a bend gules (F.) ; ascribed to JOHN of Herts. in Parly Roll.

Somery, Sir John, knight banneret—(H. VI. Roll), bore, argent two lyons passant azure—Arundel Roll. **Sir Percival,** of Warwickshire—(E. II. Roll)—bore, azure, two lyons passant or (F.) ; St. George and Parly. Rolls. (Sir HENRY DE ERDINGTON bears the same ; Arden Roll) ; Sir JOHN of Herts., a baron 1308, and ROGER (‡) bore the reverse ; Parly., Dering, and Norfolk Rolls.

Somery, Sir John—bore, at the first Dunstable tournament 1308, or, three lyons passant azure (F.) ; Segar Roll.

‡**Somery, Symon de**—(H. III. Roll) bore, azure, fretty argent, on a canton or a fleur-de-lys gules. (F.) Dering and Howard Rolls.

Sor, John le—(H. III. Roll) bore, checquy or and gules, a fess azure ; St. George Roll.

Sothill, Sire Henry de—bore, at the battle of Boroughbridge 1322, gules, an eagle displayed argent (F.) ; ascribed also to Sir JOHN, Ashmole Roll, and to WILLIAM—oppressed by a barrulet azure, in Segar Roll. F.

Souch v. **Zouch.**

Southbury, Sir John de, of Beds.—(E. II. Roll) bore, ermine, on a chief gules, three roses or ; Parliamentary Roll.

Southleye, John de (SUTHLEYE)—(E. I. Roll) bore, or, two bends gules ; Segar Roll.

Southworth, Thomas—(R. II. Roll) bore, sable, a chevron between three crosses patonce argent ; Surrey Roll. Sir CHRISTOPHER, of Samlesbury, bore the same, with crest ; Ballard Roll (E. IV.), in which crosses flory are intended.

Sowdan, Percyvall—bore, at the siege of Rouen 1418, gules, a man's head wreathed argent, *quarterly with,* sable three cinquefoyles argent. F. See also SODON.

Spalding, Michael de—(E. III. Roll) bore, gules, two bars and in chief three annulets argent ; Jenyns' Ordinary.

Spayne, Sir Peter, a captain—bore, at the siege of Calais 1345-8, gyronny (8) or and azure, an inescocheon argent. F.

Spaygne, William de—(R. II. Roll) bore, argent, a fess dancettée between three spaniels' heads erased sable ; Surrey Roll. See ESPAGNE.

*[**Speke, Sir John,** (H. VI.)—bore, barry (8) argent and azure over all a double-headed eagle gules.—Shirley.] F.

Spencer v. **Despencer** and **Le Despencer.**

*[**Spencer, John** and **Thomas,** 1504—bore, azure a fess ermine between six sea-mews' heads erased argent.—Shirley.]

Spencer, Philip—(E. III. Roll) bore, barry (6) or and azure, a canton ermine ; Surrey Roll and Jenyns' Ordinary.

Spencer, Sir William—(E. III. Roll) bore, gules, on a cross engrailed argent five torteaux Ashmole Roll.

RALPH,
LORD
STAFFORD,
K.G.

In Elsing
Church,
Norfolk, 1347,
21 E. III.

After a rubbing from the Hastings Brass.

Spenythorne, Thomas de—(E. I. Roll) bore, argent, on a bend sable three mullets or ; Jenyns' Roll—on a bend argent three mullets gules, in trick.

Spigurnell, Sir Henry, baron 1297—bore, gules, two gemelles and in chief a lyon passant or ; Nobility Roll.

Spigurnell, Sir John, of Bucks—(E. II. Roll) bore, gules, fretty argent, on a chief or a lyon passant gardant gules. Sir HENRY, of Bucks, bore this with a baston azure ; Parly. Roll ; not gardant in Cotgrave Roll.

Sprigurnel (Sir) Rauf—bore, at the second Dunstable tournament 1334, azure, three bars or, a mullet argent. (F.) Ashmole Roll.

Sporle (——) a Suffolk Knight—(H. VI. Roll) bore, azure, three estoyles of 16 rays, and a bordure engrailed or ; Arundel Roll. Spurrowells may have been originally intended.

Spring, Henry—(E. III. Roll) bore, azure an orle argent ; Jenyns' Ordinary.

Springe, Sir John, of Yorkshire—(E. II. Roll) bore, argent, a lyon rampant vert ; Parliamentary Roll.

Springhose, Roger—(H. III. Roll) bore, gules, two lyons passant argent, a label (5) azure. (F.) Arden and St. George Rolls.

Spysse, Sir Roger, of Essex, Kt.—(H. VI. Roll) bore, per fess argent and gules a pile counterchanged ; Arundel Roll.

Sqyrye (——) a Suffolk Knight (H. VI. Roll) bore, argent a squirrel sejant gules, cracking a nut or ; Arundel Roll.

Stackpoole, Sir Richard de, of co. Glouc. —(E. II. Roll) bore, argent, a lyon rampant gules, collared or ; Parly. and Harl. Rolls.

Stafford, Edmund, banneret, baron 1299 (sealed the Barons' letter to the Pope 1301)— bore, or a chevron gules (F.) ; Nobility Roll; (bore, or a chevron gules ermynée in Grimaldi Roll). RALPH, K.G., founder 1344, 2nd baron (1st Earl) bore it at the siege of Calais 1345–8. See Monumental Brass. Borne by (another ?) Sir RALPH, knighted at the capitulation in 1348, and by HUMPHREY, 6th Earl (Duke of BUCKINGHAM, K.G.), and then a youth of 16, at the siege of Rouen 1418, and on the same occasion by HUGH, within a bordure gules. F.

Stafford, Hugh, K.G. 1418–19, Baron BOURCHIER—bore, or, on a chevron gules, a mullet of the first for difference, *quarterly with*, argent, a cross engrailed gules between four water-bougets sable ; K. 401 fo. 27.

Stafford, Robert de—(H. III. Roll) bore, or, on a chevron gules three plates, Jenyns' Roll ; a label azure (F.) Arden and St. George Roll—ascribed in the latter Roll without the label to Baron de STAFFORD.

Stafford, Sir Robert de, of co. Cambridge —(E. II. Roll) bore, or on a chevron gules, three besants ; Parly. and Glover Rolls.

Stafford, Edmond de, clerk, and **Sir Richard,** of Pipe—(E. III. Roll) bore, or, a chevron gules between three martlets sable ; Ashmole and Surrey Rolls and Harl. MS. 1481 fo. 56.

Stafford (——) of Pipe, co. Staffs.—(E. III. Roll) bore, or, on a chevron between three martlets gules, as many besants ; Ashmole Roll.

Stafford, Humphrey de, of Hoke, *f* JOHN of Bromshall—(R. II. Roll) bore, or, a chevron gules within a bordure engrailed sable ; Surrey Roll. JOHN, of Frome, *f* RALPH, bore the bordure gules ; Harl. MS. 1481 fo. 56.

Stafford, Nicol de—(R. II. Roll) bore, or, a chevron gules, a chief azure ; Surrey Roll. RALPH, of Grafton (brother of HUMPHREY), bore a quarter ermine in lieu of the chief ; Harl. MS. 1481 fo. 56.

Stafford, Robert de—(R. II. Roll) bore, or, a chevron gules surmounted of a bendlet azure ; Surrey Roll.

Stafford, John de—bore, at the second Dunstable tournament 1334, argent, a chevron gules.

Stallingborn, Sir Walter—(E. III. Roll) bore, sable, a chevron engrailed between three crosses botonnée all argent ; Ashmole Roll— the trick may be intended for ordinary crosslets. Surname very indistinct in the MS.

Stallingburgh, William — (E. I. Roll) bore, sable, a chevron between three crosses crosslet fitchée argent ; Jenyns' Roll—"iij bottones fyches " in Harl. MS. 6589 fo. 48ᵇ. F.

Stamford —— an Essex Knight—(H. VI. Roll) bore, gules, a saltire vair between four leopards' faces or ; Arundel Roll. F.

Standish, Sir Alexander, of Standish— (E. IV. Roll) bore, sable, three standing dishes 2 and 1 argent, *quarterly with*, argent, a saltire engrailed sable, with crest ; Ballard Roll.

Standish, Sir Christopher, of Duxbury— (E. IV. Roll) bore, azure, three standing dishes 2 and 1 argent (with crest) ; Ballard Roll. HUGH bore this at the siege of Rouen 1418 differenced with a label (3) or. (F.) In the Ashmole MS. squirrels sejant are the charges.

Standon *v.* **Stanton** and **Staunton.**

Standon, Robert — (H. III. Roll) bore, ermine, *quarterly with*, gules a fret or. STANHOWE in St. George Roll ; STAUNDONE in Jenyns' Roll. See also STAUNDON.

Stangrave, Sir Robert (STONGRAVE)— bore, at the first Dunstable tournament 1308, and at the battle of Boroughbridge 1322, azure, billettée and a cross argent. (F.) Ashmole Roll, and of Kent in Parliamentary Roll.

∗[Stanhope, Sir Richard, (E. III.)—bore, quarterly ermine and gules.—Shirley.] F.

Stanhope, John (E. I. Roll)—bore, quarterly gules and ermine, in the first and fourth a goat's head erased argent ; Jenyns' Roll. F.

Stanhowe, Hervey—(H. III. Roll) bore, barry (6) or and azure, a bend ermine. (F.) St. George Roll.

Stanhowe, Robert—(H. III. Roll) bore, ermine, *quarterly with*, gules a fret or. (F.) St. George Roll. See STANDON.

Stanlade, Sir Rauf de (or STANLOWE, of co. Staff.) bore, at the first Dunstable tournament 1308, argent, a lyon rampant tail fourchée sable (F.)—and renowée, in Parliamentary Roll. See STANLOWE.

SIR WILLIAM STAUNTON.

IN STAUNTON CHURCH, NOTTS, 1326. *After Stothard.*

*Stanley, Sir Humphrey, of Aston—(E. IV. Roll), bore, argent, on a bend azure three bucks' heads cabossed or (BAMVILLE), with 3 quarterings; Ballard Roll. JOHN bore STANLEY (*i.e.* BAMVILLE) *quarterly with*, LATHOM, at the siege of Rouen 1418—ascribed also to THOMAS and to Sir THOMAS; Jenyns' and Atkinson Rolls.

Stanley, Sir William, of Horton—(E. IV. Roll) bore, STANLEY (*i.e.* BAMVILLE) *quarterly with*, argent, on a bend vert three mullets or—with crest; Ballard Roll.

Stanlowe, Gerard—(E. III. Roll) bore, or, a lyon rampant tail fourchée sable; Jenyns' Ordinary. See STANLADE.

Stanmarshe, Robert—(E. III. Roll) bore, gules, on a fess dancettée argent three crescents sable; Jenyns' Ordinary. F. See NEWMARCH.

Stanmarche, Thomas—(E. III. Roll) bore, argent, a fess dancettée gules; Jenyns' Ordinary. See NEWMARCH.

Stanton, Helis de, and Sir William, of co. Leic.—(E. II. Roll) bore, vaire argent and sable, a canton gules; St. George and Parly. Rolls. See STAUNTON.

Staple, le (——) bore, at the siege of Rouen 1418, argent, two bars undée sable, on a chief gules a lyon passant gardant or. (F.) See also RICHARD STAPLETON.

*Stapleton, Sir Richard—bore, at the siege of Calais 1345-8, argent, a lyon rampant sable —ascribed also to Sir MILES, of Yorkshire, and to NICHOLAS; Parliamentary Roll and Jenyns' Ordinary. In Ashmole Roll are two unidentified STAPLETON coats, the one differenced, with a label (3) gules, and the lyon in the other, with a fleur-de-lys or. MYLES, K.G. (founder 1344), and BRYAN, K.G. 1382, differenced with a mullet, (M) or (B) gules on the lyon, in the Surrey Roll : undifferenced in K. 398, 399. Another BRYAN and MYLES differenced with an annulet (B) argent (M) azure. Jenyns' Ordinary and Ashmole Roll.

Stapeltone, Robert de—(E. I. Roll), bore, azure, a lyon rampant or; Harleian Roll.

Stapleton, Sir Robert de (of co. Staff.) —bore, at the first Dunstable tournament 1308, azure, a lyon rampant tail fourchée or. (F.) Parly. and St. George Rolls. Borne also by JOHN, Jenyns' Ordinary.

Stapleton, Miles—(E. I. Roll) bore, sable, a lyon rampant tail fourchée argent. Harleian Roll.

Stapleton, Sir Richard de—(E. III. Roll) bore, argent, two bends undée (nebulée) sable; Ashmole Roll. WILLIAM DE HELLIFIELD bears the same arms, Jenyns' Ordinary; another coat for RICHARD in Jenyns' Ordinary is tricked, barry nebulée (6) sable and argent.

Stapleton, William, of Cumberland—(E. I. Roll) bore, argent, three swords conjoined at the pomel gules; Jenyns' Roll.

*[Starky, Geoffrey, E. I.—bore, argent, a bend between six storks sable.—Shirley.] F.

Staunton, Henry de, (STANDON)—(E. I. Roll) bore, argent, a bend double battaile sable; Jenyns' Roll and Ordinary.

Staunton, Robert de—(E. III. Roll) bore, sable, a cinquefoyle within an orle of martlets argent; Jenyns' Ordinary. F.

Staundone, Robert de—(H. III. Roll) bore, quarterly argent and gules fretty or, over all a baston sable; Arden Roll. Ascribed to HUGH LE DESPENCER in Glover Roll.

Staunton, Sir Robert—(E. III. Roll) bore, gules, three crosses patée 2 and 1 argent, in chief a lyon passant or; Ashmole Roll. See STAYNTON.

*Staunton, Sir Geoffrey de and Thomas de—(E. III. Roll) bore, argent, two chevronels sable, a bordure engrailed of the last (F.); Ashmole and Surrey Rolls; a plain border for Sir WILLIAM of Notts. 1326. See Monumental Effigy.

Staunton, Helis de and Sir William, of co. Leic.—(H. III. Roll) bore, vaire argent and sable, a canton gules (F.); St. George and Parly. Rolls.

Staveley, Adam de—(E. III. Roll) bore, barry (8) argent and gules, over all a fleur-de-lys sable; Jenyns' Ordinary; gules and argent in Grimaldi Roll.

Staveley, Sampson—(R. II. Roll) bore, paly (6) argent and azure; Surrey Roll.

Stavile, Sir Thomas de—bore, at the first Dunstable tournament 1308, gules, a fess between three escallops argent (F.); also tricked or.

†Staverton, John de—(H. III. Roll) bore, argent, fretty gules (F.); Dering Roll.

Stawel, Sir T.—(H. VI. Roll) bore, gules, a cross masculy argent, *quarterly with*, argent three bends azure; Atkinson Roll.

Stenefeld, Sir Guy de (NENESFELDE or SENEFYLDE), of Essex—(R. II. Roll) bore, vert, an eagle displayed or; Parly. Roll.

Stengrave, Sir John—(H. III. Roll) bore, ermine a lyon rampant gules (F.); St. George and Guillim Rolls.

Stepey, Sir John, of Notts.—(H. III. Roll) bore, azure, a cross or fretty gules (F.); Parly. Roll. WILLIAM DE STEPHEN bore the same; Arden and St. George Rolls. F. See SHEPEY.

Sterlyng (——) a Suffolk knight—(H. VI. Roll) bore, azure, a cross patée between four estoyles or; Arundel Roll.

Steward, Robert de—bore, at the siege of Carlaverock 1300, sable, a cross patée florettée argent (see also SYWARD), a cross flory in Nicolas.

Steward, William (LE SENESCHAL) — (H. III. Roll) bore, gules, on a cross argent five torteaux (F.); St. George Roll.

Steyngrave v. Stengrave.

Steynton, Sir Robert—(E. III. Roll) bore, gules, three crosses patée 2 and 1 argent, in chief a lyon passant or; Ashmole Roll.

Stockport, Waren, v. Warren.

Stodebuit, Raffe — (E. III. Roll) bore, burulée (12) argent and azure over all three lyonceux rampant gules—another purpure; Jenyns' Ordinary.

Stoddard°

Simon
d· Stodham

Henri de Stoke

Witt d· Estoke

Joan d· Estone

Richard de Stone

Rauf de Stopgam

Robt
d· Stotenile·

Robt
de Stotovillo

John
Stryrolin

Adam de Strode

John   de
Strutzeley

Stoddaw (——) an Essex Knight—(H. VI. Roll) bore, gules, a chevron argent between three Cornish choughs proper, a bordure engrailed of the last ; Arundel Roll. F.

Stodham, Simon de—(H. III. Roll) bore, per pale or and azure, barry of six counter-changed, a chevron gules (F.) ; St. George Roll.

Stokes, Henry de—(H. III. Roll) bore, bendy (10) or and azure, a canton gules (F.) ; Arden Roll.

Stokes, William—(H. III. Roll) bore, vair, a chief gules (F.) ; Arden and St. George Rolls.

Stokes, William, of Kent, Knight—(H. VI. Roll) bore, gules, a demi-lyon rampant, tail fourchée, argent, a bordure sable bezantée ; Arundel Roll.

Stone, John de—(H. III. Roll) bore, gules, crusily argent, a lyon rampant or (F.) ; St. George Roll ; no crusily in Arden Roll.

Stone, Sir Nicholas de (ETONE), of Warwickshire— (E. II. Roll) bore, gules a chevron between three eagles displayed argent ; Parly. Roll.

Stone, Richard de—(H. III. Roll) bore, azure, crusily a bend or surmounted of another gules (F.) ; Arden and St. George Rolls. ESTONE, STONE, or STOWE, crusily a bend argent, &c. in Glover Roll.

Stone, William de—(H. III. Roll) bore, argent, a lyon passant gardant sable ; Arden Roll.

Stongrave *v.* **Stangrave.**

*****Stonore, John**—(E. III. Roll) bore, azure, two bars dancettée and a chief or (F.) ; Jenyns' Ordinary.

Stopham, John, Thomas, and **Sir William,** of Yorkshire—(E. III. Roll) bore, argent, a baston sable ; another JOHN and Sir JOHN of Yorkshire differenced with a label (3, 5) gules (F.) ; Segar and Parly. Rolls and Jenyns' Ordinary.

†**Stopham, Rauf de**—(H. III. Roll) bore, argent, three crescents and a quarter gules (F.) ; Dering and Howard Rolls ; ascribed to Sir WILLIAM in Nativity Roll.

Stormyn *v.* **Sturmyn.**

Story, William—(E. III. Roll) bore, argent, a lyon rampant tail fourchée purpure ; Ashmole Roll—charged on the shoulder with a cross crosslet or ; Jenyns' Roll. RICHARD bore the cross patée or ; Surrey Roll.

Stoteville, Robert—(E. III. Roll) bore, burulée (10, 12, 14) argent and gules. (F.) Grimaldi and Jenyns' Rolls and Ordinary— six barrulets in St. George Roll.

Stotevile, Robert de—(H. III. Roll) bore, argent (5, 8, 9 or) 10 barrulets gules, over all a lyon rampant sable (F.) ; Dering and Howard Rolls.

†**Stottot, Robert le**—(H. III. Roll) bore, ermine, on a cross gules five martlets or ; Arden and St. George Rolls. ESTOTOT and SCOTTO in Dering Roll.

Strabolgi *v.* **Atholl.**

Stradling, Sir Edward—(E. III. Roll) bore, paly (6) argent and azure, on a bend gules three cinquefoyles pierced or ; Ashmole Roll.

Strange *v.* **Le Strange.**

Strangray, John and **Raffe de**—(E. III. Roll) bore, azure, billettée and a cross argent ; Jenyns' Ordinary.

Stratherne, the Earl of, in Scotland— (E. III. Roll) bore, two chevronels or. (F.) Camden Roll and Jenyns' Ordinary.

Stratton, Sr. le, (——) knighted at the capitulation of Calais 1348, bore, or, two bars and in the cantel an inescocheon gules. F.

Stretton, (——), a Suffolk Knight—(H. VI. Roll) bore, argent, on a cross sable five torteaux ; Arundel Roll.

Stratton, (——), a Suffolk Knight—(H. VI. Roll) bore, or, on a chief dancettée azure, three escallops argent ; Arundel Roll.

Strecche, Stephen — (E. I. Roll) bore, argent, a "chevron et demi " (2 chevronels in trick) azure, on a quarter of the last a fleur-de-lys or ; Jenyns' Roll.

Strechley, Sir John de (of Notts)—bore, at the battle of Boroughbridge 1322, argent, an eagle displayed sable. (F.) Parliamentary Roll ascribed also to THOMAS in Jenyns' Ordinary.

Strelley, —— (E. III. Roll) bore, paly (6) argent and azure ; Jenyns' Ordinary.

*****Strickland, Sir Thomas** and **Sir Walter** —(E. I. Roll) bore, sable, three escallops argent (F.) Jenyns', Ashmole, Nativity and Surrey Rolls ; see also Ballard Roll for quarterly coat.

Strickland, Sir Walter—(E. II. Roll) bore, argent, two bars and a quarter gules—in another trick three bars ; Parliamentary Roll.

[**Strode, Adam de,** E. I.—bore, argent, a chevron between three conies sable.—Shirley.] F.

Strother, Thomas de—(E. III. Roll) bore, gules, on a bend argent three eaglets displayed vert membered gules ; Jenyns' and Surrey Rolls.

Stryvelyn, Sir John de, baron 1342— bore, at the siege of Calais 1345-8, argent, on a chief gules three buckles, tongues to the dexter or. F.

Stryvelyn, Sir John—(E. III. Roll) bore, sable, crusily (fitchée in Cotgrave Roll) and three covered cups argent ; Jenyns' Ordinary—in Ashmole Roll three cups between three crosses fitchée.

Stukele, Nicoll—(R. II. Roll) bore, argent, on a fess sable three mullets of the field. Surrey Roll.

Sturmy, Sir Robert de—(E. I. Roll) bore, sable, a cross engrailed or, a label (3) argent ; Holland Roll.

Sturmyn, Sir Robert de, of Cheshire— (E. II. Roll) bore, gules, a chevron argent between three plates, Parliamentary Roll.

Sturmyn, —— (E. III. Roll) bore, gules, three inescocheons ermine ; Ashmole Roll.

Sturmin, Henry le — (H. III. Roll) bore, argent, three demi-lyons (rampant) gules ; St. George Roll MERVILLE in Harl. 6137 fo. 89b.

John Sturmy

John Sturton

John Sudbury

Joan d' Suteye

John de Suloy

&c̄ Surtoys

Erre de Susat

Hamond de Sutton

James de Sutton

John Sutton

John de Sutton

Roland Sutton

Sturmyn, Sir John, knighted at the capitulation of Calais 1348, bore, sable, a lyon passant gardant argent – blasoned saliant argent in Jenyns' Ordinary. F.

Sturmyne, Sir Roger, of Suffolk—(E. II. Roll) bore, quarterly or and gules, on a bendlet azure three besants ; Parliamentary Roll.

Sturton, Sir John—bore, at the siege of Rouen 1418, sable, a bend or between six fountains. F.

Sudbury, Sir John—bore, at the first Dunstable tournament 1308,—ermine, on a chief gules three cinquefoyles or. Another, argent, on a fess dancettée gules three cinquefoyles or (F.) ; Harl. 6137 fo. 37ᵇ.

Sudeston, — (E. I. Roll) bore, gules, fretty argent ; Harl. Roll.

Sudley, John de (SULLEE), banneret, baron 1299, sealed the Barons' letter to the Pope 1301—bore, or two bends gules. (F.) Nobility and Surrey Rolls. Borne also by his father, (‡) Sir BARTHOLOMEW SULEY and JOHN SULLEY, in many Rolls. (To BARTHOLOMEW and ROBERT bars are erroneously ascribed in Jenyns' Ordinary and Camden Roll). Another Sir BARTHOLOMEW SULEY, of co. Worc., and Sir WILLIAM SULE differenced with a label (3) azure ; Parliamentary and Harl. Rolls.

Sully, John—bore, at the second Dunstable tournament 1334, ermine, three torteaux. F.

Sully, Sir John (or SULBY), K.G., 1362—bore, ermine, four bars gules, K. 400 fo. 27. F.

Suley, Sir William de—bore, at the first Dunstable tournament 1308, gules, two bends or, a label (3) argent each pendant charged with 4 barrulets azure (F.) ; (another trick, or and gules)—the pendants gobony (4) argent and azure in the Parliamentary Roll.

Suneli, William de—(H. III. Roll) bore, azure, fretty or, a label (5) gules. (F.) St. George Roll.

Surrien, Sir Francis, K.G. (H. VI.)—bore, or three palets gules, on a chief argent three escallops sable ; K. 402 fo. 28.

Surteys, Thomas—(E. I. Roll) bore, ermine, on a quarter gules, an orle argent ; Jenyns' Roll. F.

‡**Susat, Sire de** (SUSANE)—(H. III. Roll) bore, sable, on a chief argent, a (demi) fleur-de-lys issuant gules. (F.) Dering Roll.

Sutton, Sir Avery de—(E. III. Roll) bore, quarterly argent and gules ; Ashmole Roll.

Sutton, Sir John de—bore, at the first Dunstable tournament 1308, azure, on a chief or, a lyon passant gules. F.

Sutton, Sir Hamond de (of Essex)—bore, at the first Dunstable tournament 1308, vert, crusily and three covered cups argent. (F.) Parliamentary Roll.

Sutton (James) de—(H. III. Roll) bore, ermine, a canton sable. (F.) Arden Roll ; as JAMES le fiz, in St. George Roll. *[ROLAND, (H. III.) bore, the field argent.— Shirley.] F.

Sutton, Sir John de, of Holderness, baron 1324, bore at the battle of Boroughbridge 1322, or, a lyon rampant azure, oppressed by a baston gobony argent and gules. (F.) Ashmole Roll and Jenyns' Ordinary.

Sutton, John de—bore, at the second Dunstable tournament 1334, or, a lyon rampant azure, oppressed by a baston gobony or and gules.

Sutton, Sir Richard, banneret—(E. II. Roll) bore, or, a lyon rampant tail fourchée vert ; Parliamentary Roll.

Sutton, Sir John de, of Lincolnshire—(E. II. Roll) bore, or, a lyon rampant vert, a label (3) gules ; Parly. Roll—probably also undifferenced by Sir RICHARD, knight banneret ; Surrey Roll.

Sutton, Sir John—(E. I. Roll) bore, or, a lyon gules and a chief vair ; Nativity Roll.

Sutton, John, BARON DUDLEY, K.G. (H. VI.) —bore, or, two lyons passant azure, *quarterly with*, argent, a cross patonce azure ; K. 402 fo. 43.

Sutton, John de—(E. III. Roll) bore, azure, five fusils conjoined in fess or, a baston gobony argent and gules ; Jenyns' Ordinary.

Sutton, Sir John de—bore, at the battle of Boroughbridge 1322, argent, a cross patonce azure (F.) ; ascribed also as a cross flory in trick and a cross patée in blason to RICHARD in Jenyns' Ordinary.

Sutton, John de—bore, at the second Dunstable tournament 1334, or three chevronels sable. (F.) Sir JOHN, knighted at the capitulation of Calais 1348, bore the same—as also JOHN, in Surrey Roll, and RICHARD, of Norfolk, in Jenyns' Ordinary. TERRY DE MANNY bore the same arms—Sir JOHN le fys differenced with a label (3) gules ; Ashmole Roll.

Sutton (——) a Knight—(H. VI. Roll) bore, azure, two chevronels between three mullets argent ; Arundel Roll.

Swalow, William—(R. II. Roll) bore, or, a fess between three swallows rising sable ; Surrey Roll. F.

Swillington —— (E. I. Roll) bore, gules, a gryphon segreant argent ; Cotgrave Roll. F.

Swillington, Adam, baron 1326, bore, argent, a chevron azure ; Jenyns' Ordinary. Sir ADAM, of Yorks., differenced with a label (3) gules ; Nativity and Parly. Rolls. ROBERT differenced with a label (3) ermine ; Surrey Roll.

Swillington, Sir Hugh, of Yorkshire— (E. II. Roll) bore, argent, on a chevron azure, a fleur-de-lys or ; Parly. Roll and a label (3) of the last ; Harl. MS. 6137 fo. 21ᵇ.

Swinburne, Adam de—bore at the second Dunstable tournament 1334, gules, crusily and a swine's head argent. F.

Swinburne, Sir Adam de, of Northumberland—(E. II. Roll) bore, gules, three swines' heads couped argent ; Parliamentary, Glover and Jenyns' Rolls.

Swinburne, Sir Robert, of Northumberland—(E. II. Roll) bore, gules crusily and three swines' heads couped argent ; Parly. and Surrey Rolls. THOMAS bore it with a label (3) or ; Surrey Roll. and Lansd. MS. 872 fo. 66ᵇ.

will E walon

de Swillington

Adam de Swynobourn

will de Swynobourne

John de Swynford

Robt Swyneserd

Roger de Swynerton

Roger de Swynerton

Robt. Swynd of Hilton

Th: Swynythwaite

Sydney

Richard Swynard

Swinbourne (——) bore, at the siege of Rouen 1418, or, a saltire engrailed sable, charged with an annulet, *quarterly with*, gules, crusily and three swines' heads couped argent.

*Swinbourne, William—(E. III. Roll) bore, argent, a chief gules and three cinquefoyles counterchanged 2 and 1 (F.); Jenyns' Ordinary. In the Surrey Roll it is blasoned per fess gules and argent, three roses counterchanged.

Swynford, Sir John de, of Hunts.—(E. II. Roll) bore, argent, three swines' heads couped gules; Parly. Roll. F.

Swynford, Norman and **Sir Thomas de**, of Hunts.—(E. II. Roll) bore, argent on a chevron sable three swines' heads couped or; Jenyns' and Parly. Rolls. THOMAS differenced with a cinquefoyle, and WILLIAM differenced with a quarter sable charged with a cinquefoyle or; Jenyns' Roll and Ordinary. In the coat for Sir THOMAS, Harl. MS. 6137 fo. 22, the swines' heads are gules and between the chevron.

Swynhowe, Robert—(E. I. Roll) bore, sable three swine passant argent; Jenyns' Roll. F.

Swinnerton, Sir Roger de, baron 1337, bore, at the first Dunstable tournament 1308, argent, a cross (patée) florettée sable (F.); another ROGER bore it at the second Dunstable tournament 1334. Sir THOMAS bore it at the siege of Calais 1345-8, and Sir ROGER, knighted at the capitulation of Calais 1348, differenced it with a label (5) gules.

Swinnerton, Sir Roger, of Cambridgeshire —(E. II. Roll) bore, argent, a cross patonce couped at the foot sable; Harl. 4033. In Harl. 6137, argent, a cross patée florettée fitchée at the foot sable; Parly. Roll. F.F.

Swinnerton, Adam de—(E. III. Roll) bore, argent, a cross flory sable (now patée flory) bouttes florettes; Jenyns' Ordinary. Sir ROGER bore argent, a cross patée sable;

Nativity Roll. ROBERT bore the reverse (in Jenyns' Ordinary), being the same as PULFORD; the probability is that the cross in these instances should be the same and are inaccurately tricked.

Swyne, Robert, of Hilton (in Holdernesse), founder of the abbey—(E. I. Roll) bore, or, three chaplets gules; Jenyns' Roll; HILTON bears the same. F.

Swynythwaite, Thomas — (E. I. Roll) bore, argent, a chevron between three swine passant sable; Jenyns' Roll and Ordinary. F.

Sydney (——) an Essex? knight—(H. VI. Roll) bore, or, a pheon azure; Arundel Roll.

Syfrewast, Robert — (E. I. Roll) bore, azure, three gemelles and a chief argent; Jenyns' Roll. See CYFREWAST and SIFREWAST.

Synsiwarde, Roger (SUISTYWARD)—(E. I. Roll) bore, bendy (6) argent and azure; Jenyns' Roll, (blasoned the reverse); same arms as St. PHILIBERT.

Syward, Sir Richard, banneret (of Scotland)—bore, at the battle of Falkirk 1298, sable, a cross florettée argent (F.) He bore the same (tricked cross patée florettée) at the siege of Carlaverock 1300; the cross is variously tricked and blasoned cross flory, cross patonce, and fer-de-moulin; Holland Roll, &c. Called ROBERT in Harl. 6137 fo. 38ᵇ.

Syward, Sir Richard, a banneret—(E. II. Roll) bore, sable a cross florettée fitchée at the foot argent,—in trick a cross patonce couped at the foot; Parly. Roll; for a similar cross see Sir ROGER SWINNERTON.

Syward, Sir William—(E. III. Roll) bore, gules, a cross patonce argent; Ashmole Roll, with a note Sir WILLIAM DE SAYE, NORREYS.

Sywardby, John—(E. III. Roll) bore, argent, a bend cotised sable between six lyonceux (3, 3) of the last; Surrey Roll and Jenyns' Ordinary.

Le C. de timo   Talbot   Robert Talbot

Lord Talbot dire   Ricz Talebot   Richard Talbott

will Talomarço   Giles de Tamworth   will Tanchard

Bertram Tancro   Robt d'Tateshale   John de ondring

T

Tadington, Sir Peres de (TATYNGTON), of Suffolk—(E. II. Roll) bore, sable, a cross (moline) recercelée or ; Parliamentary Roll.

Talbot, Richard—(H. III. Roll) bore, or five bendlet gules. (F.) St. George Roll and Harl. MS. 6137 ff. 83, 89 —bendy (10) argent and gules (F.) is the paternal coat of TALBOT, as attributed by the later Heralds. As Lord of ECKLESWELL, he sealed the Barons' letter to the Pope 1301, with the arms of RHESE AP GRIFFITH, Prince of South Wales, viz. : **a lyon rampant within a bordure engrailed.**

***Talbot, Sir Gilbert** (of co. Glouc.)—bore, at the first Dunstable tournament 1308, GIL-BERT, and his son RICHARD, with a label azure, bore at the second Dunstable tournament 1334, and RICHARD, lord steward of the King's Household, bore at the siege of Calais 1345–8, gules, a lyon rampant within a bordure engrailed or (F.) being the bardic arms of RHYS, Prince of South Wales ; the border is often blasoned and tricked indented. GILBERT, K.G. (5th lord), bore at the siege of Rouen 1418, RHYS, *quarterly with* STRANGE, argent, two lyons passant in pale gules ; these are also ascribed to RICHARD, in the Surrey Roll (R. II.). In the 6th Nobility Roll, LE SR. TALBOT bears the arms of STRANGE only and the Earl of SHREWSBURY those of BELISME only, azure, a lyon rampant within a bordure or.

Talbot, Sir John, knighted at the capitulation of Calais 1348, bore, gules, a lyon rampant or, a bordure engrailed of the last, and a bendlet azure. Jenyns' Ordinary, ascribes to another JOHN, the coat without the bendlet, the lyon charged with a mullet (argent).

Talbott, Richard—(H. III. Roll) bore, or, a lyon gules collared or, a bordure vert besantée ; Norfolk Roll.

Talbot, Sir Edmond—bore, at the first Dunstable tournament 1308, argent, three lyonceux rampant gules,—purpure, for another Sir EDMUND, of Lanc., in Parliamentary Roll and Jenyns' Ordinary.

Talbot, Sir (? EDMUND), of Bashall, in Lanc., knighted at the capitulation of Calais 1348, bore, argent, three lyonceux rampant 2 and 1 azure (F.) *vel* purpure. Sir JOHN, of Salebury, Sir EDMOND and Sir THOMAS, of Bashall, bore, the lyonceux purpure ; Ballard, Parliamentary and Surrey Rolls.

Talbot, Sir Richard—bore, at the battle of Boroughbridge 1322, gules, two bars vair. (F.) Ascribed also to Sir JOHN and WILLIAM ; and with a mullet pierced argent to GILBERT ; Ashmole and Surrey Rolls and Jenyns' Ordinary.

Talbot, Gilbert—(H. III. Roll) bore, vaire, gules and or, a bordure azure ; Arden Roll.

Talbot, Sir John—(E. III. Roll) bore, argent, crusily fitchée (5, 7), and three fleurs-de-lys gules ; Ashmole and Surrey Rolls.

Talbot, Gilbert and (‡) **Robert**—(H. III. Roll) bore, barry (6) argent and gules ; Howard and Ashmole copy of Dering Roll—or and gules for ROBERT in Dering Roll.

Talboys, Walter—(R. II. Roll) bore, argent, a saltire gules, on a chief of the last, three escallops of the field ; Surrey Roll. HENRY bore the field or, in Jenyns' Ordinary.

Talboys, Sir William, SR. DE KYME—bore, at the siege of Rouen 1418, gules, crusily and a cinquefoyle or, *quarterly with*, KYME ; azure, crusily and a chevron or. F.

Talmache, Sir Hugh, of Suffolk—(H. III. Roll) bore, argent, fretty sable ; Arden and Parliamentary Rolls. Sir WILLIAM differenced with a label (3, 5) gules. (F.) Harleian and Segar Rolls.

Talworth, Sir William, of Essex, Kt.—(H. VI. Roll) bore, barry (6) or and azure, on a chevron gules three mullets (6) of the first ; Arundel Roll.

‡**Tamworth, Giles de**—(H. III. Roll) bore, argent, a fess dancettée between three cocks' heads erased sable ; Dering Roll. F.

*[**Tanckard, William,**(H. III.)—bore, argent, a chevron between three escallops gules.— Shirley.] F.

‡**Tancre, Bartram** (TANQUERAY)—(H. III. Roll) bore, azure, two bends argent. (F.) Dering and Howard Rolls.

Tany, Sir John, of Essex, and **Lucas**—(H. III. Roll) bore, azure, three barrulets argent ; Parliamentary and Howard Rolls and Jenyns' Ordinary.

Tany, Sir Richard, of Essex—(H. III. Roll) bore, or, six eaglets displayed sable ; Guillim, Howard and Parliamentary Rolls — three eaglets in Jenyns' Ordinary.

Tarent, the Duke de—(E. IV. Roll) bore, quarterly gules and argent in the first an eagle displayed of the second ; Jenyns' Ordinary.

SIR EDMUND DE THORPE.

IN ASHWELLTHORPE CHURCH, NORFOLK, 1418. *Stothard.*

Tateshall, Sir Robert (TATTESHALL), of Buckenham, baron 1295—bore, at the battle of Falkirk 1298, as did his son Sir ROBERT at the siege of Carlaverock 1300, checquy or and gules, a chief ermine. (F.) Arden, St. George and other Rolls;—this ROBERT the son differenced with a label (3) azure at Falkirk 1298, and so sealed the Barons' letter to the Pope 1301. ROBERT or ROGER LE FITZ differenced with a label (3) or, in Jenyns' Ordinary. Ascribed to RAFFE undifferenced, in Norfolk Roll.

Tateshal, Sir Hue de—(E. I. Roll) bore, checquy or and gules, a canton ermine ; Harl. Roll.

ᵃ[**Tatton, Robert,** E. III.—bore, quarterly argent and gules four crescents counterchanged. —Shirley.] F.

Tempest, —— (E. III. Roll) bore, argent, a chevron gules, between three martlets sable ; Cotgrave Roll.

*** Tempest, Richard and William**—(E. III. Roll) bore, argent, a bend between six martlets 3, 3, sable ; Surrey Roll and Jenyns' Ordinary—bend engrailed for RICHARD also in Jenyns' Ordinary ; the birds are sometimes blasoned stormy petrels and storm finches.

Temple, the Auntient of the—(H. III. Roll) bore, argent, a cross passant gules and a chief sable.—The ANCIENT DEL HOSPITALL, bore, gules, a cross formée argent ; Norfolk Roll.

Tendring, Sire John—bore, at the battle of Boroughbridge 1322, sable, a fess between two chevronels or, a label (3) of France ; gules, on each pendant three fleurs-de-lys argent. F.

Tendring, Sir John, a Suffolk Knight— (E. II. Roll) bore, azure, a fess between two chevronels or, a label (3) gules, on each pendant a fleur-de-lys argent. (F.) Parly. Roll.

Tendring, Sir William, a Suffolk Knight —(E. III. Roll) bore, azure, a fess between two chevronels argent ; Arundel, Ashmole and Surrey Rolls.

Tendring, Sir John, of Brenthall, Essex— (H. VI. Roll) bore, argent, on a fess between two chevronels azure three crescents or ; Arundel Roll, Harl. MS. 4205 fo. 20.

Terby, John, (TEREBY)—(E. III. Roll) bore, argent, an estoile or, on a chief azure three water-bougets of the second ; Jenyns' Roll.

Teringham v. **Tyringham.**

Teyes, Sir Walter de, of Stangreve, in Yorks., knight banneret, baron 1299—bore, at the battle of Falkirk 1298, or on a fess between two chevronels gules three mullets of the first ; argent in Arundel, Ashmole and Nobility Rolls ; (see also TYES), spur-rowells on his seal, attached to the Barons' letter to the Pope 1301.

Teye (TAY) **——** an Essex Knight—(H. VI. Roll) bore, argent, a fess between three martlets in chief and a chevron in base all azure ; Arundel Roll.

Thaine, Gilbert de—(H. III. Roll) bore, gules, three mullets (6) argent (F.) ; ascribed also to GILBERT or GILES HAUNSARD or HASSELL ; St. George Roll.

Thaine, Henry de—(H. III. Roll) bore, or, three crescents gules, each charged with a spur-rowell argent. (F.) St. George Roll.

†**Thani, Lucas de**—(H. III. Roll) bore, azure, three bars argent ; St. George Roll.

Thani, Richard de—(H. III. Roll) bore, argent, six eagles displayed sable ; St. George Roll.

Thimbleby —— Knight—(H. VI. Roll) bore, gules, a chevron engrailed and a chief argent ; Arundel Roll.

Thirkeld —— (E. III. Roll) bore, argent, a maunch gules ; Ashmole Roll.

Thirkeld, William—(E. I. Roll) bore, argent, a maunch gules, a label (3) vert ; Jenyns' Roll—another, argent, a maunch burulée or and gules—or, three bars gules, in trick ; Jenyns' Ordinary.

Thirlewall, Raphe de—(E. I. Roll) bore, gules, a chevron between three boars' heads couped bendways argent. (F.) Jenyns' Roll.

Thoresby, William, late Keeper of the Privie Seale—bore, at the siege of Calais 1345-8, argent, a chevron between three lyonceux rampant sable (F.) ; ascribed also to HUGH and PIERS ; Grimaldi Roll and Jenyns' Ordinary.

Thornburgh, William de—(E. I. Roll) bore, ermine fretty and a chief gules—tricked as three chevronels interlaced in base ; Jenyns' Roll.

Thornbury, John — (R. II. Roll) bore, argent, a chief or, surmounted by a lyon rampant azure, over all two bendlets gules ; Surrey Roll.

Thorne, Sir William de—(E. III. Roll) bore, azure, a fess argent between three lyonceux rampant or ; Ashmole Roll.

Thorneham, Robert, founder of Beigham Monastery, in Sussex—(E. I. Roll) bore, gules, a lyon passant between two lozenges in pale or. (F.) Jenyns' Roll.

[**Thornes, Robert,** 1357—bore, sable, a lyon rampant gardant argent.—Shirley.] F.

***Thornhill, Sir Bryan**—(E. III. Roll) bore, gules, two gemelles and a chief argent ; Ashmole Roll and Jenyns' Ordinary.

Thornton, Sir Piers de, knighted at the capitulation of Calais 1348, bore, argent on a bend gules three escarbuncles or. F.

Thornton —— a Knight—(H. VI. Roll) bore, sable, a chevron and a chief dancettée all argent ; Arundel Roll.

*[**Thorold, Sir Richard,** (E. III.)—bore, sable, three goats' salient argent.—Shirley.] F.

Thorpe (Sir) Edmond—bore, at the siege of Rouen 1418, azure, three crescents 2 and 1 argent. (F.) Ashmole, Surrey and Jenyns' Roll. See Monumental Effigy, THORPE quarterly with BAYNARD.

Thorp, John, baron 1309—bore, gules, a fess between six fleurs-de-lys argent ; Nobility Roll ; checquy or and gules a fess ermine ; Parly. Roll.

Thorpe, Sir George de (of Norfolk)—bore, at the first Dunstable tournament 1308, checquy or and gules on a fess argent three martlets sable, as did Sir ROGER at the battle of Boroughbridge 1322. F.

John Throckmorton

Marmadue Thynge

Payn Foqotot

Jo do Tichbourne

Roger do Tilmanston

Erro Tymporley

Tobe

Robert Fonyo

walter do Torpigni

Guillia do Tochollos

walter Fouke

Sir Townley

Thorp, John de—(R. II. Roll) bore, azure, a fess dancettée ermine ; Surrey Roll.

Thorp, William de—bore, at the second Dunstable tournament 1334, burulée, or and sable. F.

*[**Throckmorton, John**, (E. III.)—bore, gules, on a chevron argent three gemelles sable.—Shirley.] F.

Thurston (——) of Anderton—(E. IV. Roll) bore, sable, three shackbolts 2 and 1 argent *quarterly with*, vert, three bugles 2 and 1 argent stringed or—with crest ; Ballard Roll.

Thwaites, Thomas, of Coupland—(E. III Roll) bore, argent, a cross fretty sable and argent ; Jenyns' Ordinary.

Thweng, Marmaduke, of Kilton, banneret, baron 1310—bore. gules, a fess argent between three popinjays vert ; Nobility Roll. All other Rolls give the reverse, viz., argent a fess gules, &c.

Thweng, Marmaduke de (called JOHN in the Roll), a baron 1307—bore, at the battle of Falkirk 1298, argent, a fess gules between three popinjays vert. See also FITZ MARMADUKE— ascribed also to Sir WILLIAM ; Ashmole Roll and Jenyns' Ordinary. F.

Thweng, Marmaduke, of Cornburgh— (E. I. Roll) bore, argent, on a fess gules between three popinjays vert as many escallops or ; Jenyns' Roll.

Tibetot, Sir Payn de, (TIPETOFT), banneret baron 1308—bore, at the first Dunstable tournament 1308, argent, a saltire engrailed gules (F.) ; Nobility and Arundel Rolls ; borne at the second Dunstable tournament 1334, by JOHN, the probable grandfather of John (baron 1426) who differenced with a label (3) azure at the siege of Rouen 1418. Ascribed also to ROBERT(‡) in the Dering and Howard Rolls. A JOHN and ROBERT took up the cross in the last Crusade 1270.

Tibtot, Paine—(E. III. Roll) bore, argent, a cross engrailed gules ; Jenyns' Ordinary —borne also by JOHN DE LA LINDE ; the cross probably a mistake for the saltire.

*[**Tichborne, Sir John de**, (E. II.)—bore, vair, a chief or.—Shirley.] F.

Tichesie *v.* **Tychesie**.

Tillioll, Piers and **Sir Robert**—(E. I. Roll) bore, gules, a lyon rampant argent, a baston azure ; Jenyns' and Ashmole Rolls.

Tilly, John—(E. III. Roll) bore, argent, a cross patonce (flory in trick) between four crescents argent ; Jenyns' Ordinary.

‡**Tilmanston, Roger de**—(H. III. Roll) bore, gules, six lyonceux rampant ermine (F.) ; Dering Roll ; argent in Howard Roll.

Tilney, Sir John — (E. III. Roll) bore, azure, three cinquefoyles pierced argent ; Ashmole Roll.

Timperley (——) knighted at the capitulation of Calais 1348—bore, gules, three inescocheons argent. F.

Tochelles *v.* **Touches**.

Todenham, Oliver—(H. III. Roll) bore, barry lozengy (6) argent and azure (F.); St. George Roll. JOHN bore it argent and gules. See TUDENHAM.

***Toke** (——) an Essex Knight—(H. VI. Roll) bore, per chevron sable and argent, three gryphons' heads erased counterchanged (F.) ; Arundel Roll. See also TOOKES and TOUKE.

Toni, Sir Robert de, of Castle Matill, banneret, a baron 1299, sealed the Barons' letter to the Pope 1301—bore, at the battle of Falkirk 1298, at the siege of Carlaverock 1300, and at the first Dunstable tournament 1308, argent, a maunch gules (F.) ; Nobility Roll ; ascribed also to RAFE (‡) in Dering and Howard Rolls.

Tookes, Sir Robert (TOUK), of co. Cambridge—(E. II. Roll) bore, barry (6) argent and sable ; Parly. Roll, the reverse in Jenyns' Ordinary.

Torboc, Sir Richard, of Torboc—(E. IV. Roll) bore, or, an eagle's claw couped gules, on a chief dancettée azure three plates ; with crest ; Ballard Roll.

‡**Torpigni, Walter de**, (TURPIGNI)—(H. III. Roll) bore, azure, an inescocheon within an orle of escallops (9) argent (F.) ; Dering Roll, no escallops in Ashmole Roll.

Torrell — an Essex Knight—(H. VI. Roll) bore, gules, a fess engrailed argent between three bulls' heads couped or, perhaps argent ; Arundel Roll.

Torry *v.* **Corry**.

Torts, Sir Raffe de, of Dorset—(E. II. Roll) bore, gules, a gryphon segreant or ; Parly. Roll.

Totesham —— (E. III. Roll) bore, sable, billettée and a cross argent ; Ashmole Roll.

Touches, Emlam—bore, at the siege of Carlaverock 1300, gules, six martlets or ; 10 martlets (F.) are ascribed to WILLIAM TOCHELLES in Harl. MS. 6137.

Touchet, William, lord of Levenhales 1299–1306, sealed the Barons' letter to the Pope 1301—crusily patée fitchée a lyon rampant ; Cott. Julius C vii. 277. The coat of martlets is ascribed to him in the Nobility Roll, and ermine a chevron gules in the Parliamentary Roll

Touchet, Robert — (E. II. Roll) bore, ermine a chevron gules ; Jenyns' Roll and Ordinary, Surrey and Ashmole Rolls ; ascribed to Sir THOMAS of Northants., and to ROBERT (or ROGER) LE FITZ with a label (3) azure ; Parliamentary Roll.

Touchet, Sir William—(E. I. Roll) bore, gules, ten martlets 4, 3, 2, 1 or ; Parly. Roll ; six in the Arundel Roll—this latter is ascribed to EMLAM TOUCHES in the Carlaverock Roll 1300 and to WM. TOCHELLES in Harl. MS. 6137. F.

Toukes, Sir Walter, of Notts.—(E. II. Roll) bore, sable, billettée or, a canton ermine (F.) ; Parly., Holland, and St. George Rolls.

Tours, Eustace de—(H. III. Roll) bore, gules, an orle argent, in the cantel an inescocheon azure charged with a lyon rampant of the second crowned or, a label (5) of the last ; Glover Roll ; (this blason is rather obscure), identical with EUSTACE DE BALIOL DE TEAS.

*[**Townley, Richard de**, alias DE LA LEGH 1375—bore, argent, a fess and in chief three mullets sable. —Shirley.] F.

SIR ROGER DE TRUMPINGTON.

IN TRUMPINGTON CHURCH, CAMBS, 17 E. I, 1289.   *After Waller.*

*[**Townshend, Sir Walter de,** c. 1400— bore, azure, a chevron ermine between three escallops argent.—Shirley.] F.

Tracheon v. **Treveynour.**

Tracy, Sir William, (co. Worcr.)—bore, at the first Dunstable tournament 1308, or, two bends and an escallop gules (F.); Ashmole and Parly. Rolls. Sir JOHN, knighted at the capitulation of Calais 1348, differenced with a label (5) azure. F.

Tracy, William—(H. III. Roll) bore, or, two bends between nine or ten escallops gules (F.); Arden and St. George Rolls.

***Trafford, Edmund,** of Trafford—(E. IV. Roll) bore, argent, a gryphon segreant gules; with crest. (F.) Ballard Roll.

‡**Traseme, Otes,** (TRAISINE)—(H. III. Roll) bore, or, three bends azure, within a bordure gules (F.); Dering Roll; bendy (6) or and azure in Ashmole MS.

Travers, John de—(R. II. Roll) bore, argent, a chevron between four butterflies sable; Surrey Roll.

Trayley, Sir (John) de, of Beds.—(H. III. Roll) bore, or, a cross between four martlets gules; Arden, Parly. and Surrey Rolls.

*[**Trefusis, Peter de,** 10 E. III.—bore, argent, a chevron between three wharrow spindles sable.—Shirley.] F.

Tregoz, Sir John—bore, at the battle of Falkirk 1298, or, two gemelles and in chief a lyon passant gardant gules (GEOFFREY bore the same in the Norfolk Roll), and in all Rolls save the Nobility Roll, in which the colours are azure and or. The lyon is not gardant in the Dering nor Guillim Rolls. F.

Tregoz, Sir Henry, banneret, baron 1305— bore, azure, two gemelles and in chief a lyon passant gardant or; Nobility, Dering and other Rolls; gardant in Arden and Howard Rolls and Jenyns' Ordinary. Sealed the Barons' letter to the Pope 1301.

Tregoz, Robert de—(H. III. Roll) bore, gules, three gemelles or, in chief a lyon passant of the first (sic) probably or; Glover Roll; two gemelles in St. George Roll.

Trehampton, Ralph de—(H. III. Roll) bore, argent, a bend gules; Glover and Grimaldi Rolls.

Trehampton, John de—(E. III. Roll) bore, argent, on a bend gules three cinquefoyles or; Jenyns' Roll.

Trekingham, Sire Walter de—bore, at the battle of Boroughbridge 1322, argent, two bars gules, in chief three torteaux, over all a baston sable; ascribed to JOHN (F.) in Jenyns' Ordinary.

*[**Trelawny, John,** E. I.—bore, argent, a chevron sable.—Shirley.] F.

Trellowe, Robert — (R. II. Roll) bore, azure, a chevron between three escallops argent; Surrey Roll. See TRILLON.

*[**Tremayne, Perys,** E. I.—bore, gules, three dexter arms conjoined and flexed in triangle or, hands clenched proper.—Shirley.] F.

Trenton, Sir Raffe de (TREAUNTON), of co. Lincs.—(H. III. Roll) bore, argent, a bend gules; Arden and Parly. Rolls.

*[**Trevelyan, Nicholas de,** E. I.—bore, gules, a demi-horse maned and unguled or, issuing out of waves proper.—Shirley.] F.

Trevet, Thomas—bore, at the siege of Rouen 1418, argent a trevet sable (F.); ascribed to Sir JOHN TRYVETT in Ashmole Roll. JOHN bore it within a bordure engrailed sable; Surrey Roll.

Treveynour, Sir John—(E. III. Roll) bore, argent, a fess azure between two chevronels gules; Ashmole Roll. TRACHEON bears the same in PAPWORTH.

Trewent, Steven de—(E. III. Roll) bore, argent, a chevron between three double-headed eaglets gules; Jenyns' Roll and Ordinary.

Trewlove, Robert—(E. I. Roll) bore, argent on a chevron sable three quartrefoyles or; Jenyns' Roll.

Trigot, Sir Henry — (E. I. Roll) bore, azure, two bars and in chief a lyon passant gardant or; Harleian Roll.

Trillon, Sir John—(E. III. Roll) bore, argent, a chevron engrailed sable between three escallops of the last; Ashmole Roll.

Triminell, Sir Nicholas, of co. Leicr.— (E. II. Roll) bore, or, a cross engrailed gules, a baston azure; Parly. Roll.

Tromyn, Roger—(R. II. Roll) bore, sable, a saltire engrailed or; Surrey Roll; ascribed to JOHN TRUMWY in Jenyns' Ordinary.

Tromyn, Sir Humphrey—(E. III. Roll) bore, sable a saltire engrailed or, a bordure argent; Ashmole Roll.

Troutbeck, Sir William, of Dunham— (E. IV. Roll) bore, azure three troutbeck intertwined argent, quarterly with, argent, a trefoyle sable between three moors' heads couped proper; Ballard and Arundel Rolls.

Trumpington —— bore, at the siege of Rouen 1418, azure, crusily and two hautboys (or trumpets) addorsed or. F.

Trumpington, Sir Giles, of co. Cambridge (E. II. Roll) bore, azure, crusily and two hautboys chevronwise or; Parly. Roll.

Trumpington, Sir Roger—bore, at the battle of Boroughbridge 1322, azure, crusily and two hautboys pileways or, a label (3) argent (F.); borne undifferenced by JAMES and Sir ROGER (see Mon. Brass); Camden and Howard Rolls. Sir JAMES bore it crusily fitchée in the Harleian Roll. A ROGER took up the cross in the last Crusade 1270.

Trumpington —— a Suffolk Kt.—(H. VI. Roll) bore, azure, crusily and two trumpets pileways or, quarterly with, argent, fretty sable, a canton gules, over all a label (3) azure; Arundel Roll.

Trussebut, Robert—(H. III. Roll) bore, argent, three water-bougets gules (F.); Arden and St. George Rolls. One of these names Hereditary Standard-bearer temp. R. I. See Introduction.

Trussebut, Robert and **Sir William**— —(E. III. Roll) bore, argent, a fess dancettée between three water-bougets 2 and 1 sable. Sir ROBERT differenced with a label (3) gules; Ashmole Roll and Jenyns' Ordinary.

Trussell, Sir William—bore, at the battle of Boroughbridge 1322, argent, a cross patée florettée gules (F.); Ashmole MS.; ascribed also to Sir JOHN who was knighted at the capitulation of Calais 1348; Ashmole Roll, &c.

Rob̃ le uffebut   will Trufsoll   waren. d Truffel

math. de Tryo   R̃ğõ Tunftall   Hug de Torpinton

Johan Turnoy   will Twyor   Robert Tyas

Tyndale   Roger Tyroll   will Tyrwhitt

Trussell, Sir Waren and **Sir William,** of Cublesdon, (Northants).—bore, at the siege of Calais 1345-8, argent, fretty gules, bezanty at the joints (F.) ; (Sir WILLIAM differenced with a label (3) azure) and also Sir — TRUS-SELL knighted at the capitulation 1348 ; ascribed also to Sir JOHN, RICHARD and Thomas ; Ashmole and St. George Rolls and Je yns' Ordinary. AVERY bore the field or ; Surrey Roll.

*Trye, Mathew de—(H. III. Roll) bore, or, a bend azure. (F.) Dering Roll. REGINALD differenced with a label gules in Norfolk Roll.

Try, Seigneur de, DE BILEBATIA—(H. III. Roll) bore, or, a bend gobony argent and azure ; Norfolk Roll.

Tryvett, John—(R. II. Roll) bore, argent, a trivett within a bordure engrailed sable ; Surrey Roll. THOMAS bore it without the bordure at the siege of Rouen 1418, and it is so ascribed to Sir JOHN in Ashmole Roll. See TREVET.

Tudenham, John de—(H. III. Roll) bore, barry lozengy (6) argent and gules ; St. George Roll and Jenyns' Ordinary, in which latter it is blasoned barry (8) argent and gules endented counterchanged. OLIVER bore it argent and azure. See TODENHAM.

Tunstall, Richard, of East Bolton—(E. III. Roll) bore, argent, on a chief azure three besants. In Jenyns' Ordinary, argent, on a chief indented azure four besants, three in trick.

Tunstall, Thomas—bore, at the siege of Rouen 1418, sable, three combs 2 and 1 argent. (F.) Surrey Roll and Jenyns' Ordinary.

Turbervile, Sir Gilbert—bore, at the siege of Calais 1345-8, checquy or and gules a fess ermine (F.) ; ascribed to Sir PAINE, of co. Glouc., in Parly. Roll — fess sable in Jenyns' Ordinary.

Turbervile, Hugh de—(H. III. Roll) bore, argent, a lyon rampant gules. (F.) Arden, Dering and Camden Rolls.—crowned or in Howard Roll and Jenyns' Ordinary. ROBERT took up the cross in the last Crusade 1270.

Turbervile, Thomas de—(H. III. Roll) bore, ermine, a lyon rampant gules ; Howard Roll.

Turberville, Thomas—(E. III. Roll) bore, argent, billettée and a lyon rampant gules ; Jenyns' Ordinary.

Turbervile, Geoffrey—(H. III. Roll) bore, sable, three lyons rampant or. (F.) St. George Roll.

Turbervile, Henry *v.* **Haberville.**

Turk, Robert—(R. II. Roll) bore, argent, on a bend azure between two lyons rampant gules three besants ; Surrey Roll.

Turpinton, Sire Hugh de—bore, at the battle of Boroughbridge 1322, argent, on a bend triple cotised sable six mullets or, on an inescocheon, the arms of MORTIMER azure and or. F.

Turvey, Sire John—bore, at the battle of Boroughbridge 1322, gules, a chevron between three bulls (passant) or. F.

Turvile, Sir Nicholas, of Warwickshire, and **Robert**— E. II. Roll) bore, gules, two chevronels vair ; Parliamentary Roll and Jenyns' Ordinary.

*Turvile, Sir Richard, of Warwickshire— (E. II. Roll) bore, gules, three chevronels vair ; Parliamentary Roll.

Tutcham, Oliver de—(H. III. Roll) bore, checquy argent and gules a fess azure ; ROBERT, on the fess three escallops or ; Howard Roll.

Tuyley *v.* **Cuilly.**

Twyer, Robert and **William**—(E. III. Roll) bore, gules, a cross vair ; Howard Roll and Jenyns' Ordinary. F.

Twyford, Sire John de (of co. Leicr.)— bore, at the first Dunstable tournament 1308 and at the battle of Boroughbridge 1322, argent, two bars sable, on a quarter of the second a cinquefoyle or. (F.) Another JOHN bore it at the second tournament 1334 on which occasion his son differenced with a label gules (the cinquefoyle pierced in Ashmole Roll) ; ascribed also to RICHARD ("une barre et demi") and to ROBERT—in Jenyns'Ordinary and Surrey Roll.

*[Twysden, Adam de, (E. I.)—bore, per saltire argent and gules, a saltire between four crosses crosslet all counterchanged.—Shirley.] F.

‡Twytham, Aleyn de—(H. III. Roll) bore, argent three cinquefoyles pierced sable. (F.) Dering Roll ; six-foyles in Howard Roll.

Tyas, Francis, (TYEYS)—(H. III. Roll) bore, argent, a fess and in chief three mallets gules ; Arden Roll.

Tyas, Robert—(E. I. Roll) bore, gules, a fess between three mallets bendways or—argent in trick. (F.) Jenyns' Roll.

‡Tychesy, Thomas de—(H. III. Roll) bore, gules, fretty vair. (F.) Dering & Howard Rolls.

Tyes, Sir Henry, of Chilton, banneret, baron 1299, sealed the Barons' letter to the Pope 1301—bore at the siege of Falkirk 1298 and at the siege of Carlaverock 1300, argent, a chevron gules ; (F.) as did his son HENRY (banneret) at the first Dunstable tournament 1308, at the battle of Boroughbridge 1322, and at the siege of Calais 1345-8 ; ascribed also to JOHN in Jenyns' Ordinary.

Tyndale, Sir William—(E. III. Roll) bore, argent, on a fess sable three garbs or ; Ashmole Roll and Jenyns' Ordinary.

Tyndale (——) a Knight—(H. VI. Roll) bore, argent, three nails erect 2 and 1 sable ; Arundel Roll. F.

Tyringham, Sir Roger de, of Bucks, and **John**—(E. II. Roll) bore, azure, a saltire engrailed argent ; Parliamentary, Surrey and Arundel Rolls.

Tyrrell, Sir Roger (of co. Hereford) bore, at the first Dunstable tournament 1308, azure, a lyon rampant argent, a bordure indented or (engrailed Harl. MS. 6137 fo. 31^b). (F.) Parliamentary and Ashmole Rolls.

Tyrrell, Roger (TIREL)—(H. III. Roll) bore, gules, a fess and in chief three annulets argent. (F.) Arden and St. George Rolls.

Tyrrell (——) an Essex Knight—(H. VI. Roll bore, argent two chevronels azure and a bor dure engrailed gules ; Arundel Roll. F.

*Tyrwhit, Sir William, of Kettilby, co. Lincs.—(E. IV. Roll) bore, gules three tyrwhits 2 and 1 or (F.), with crest ; Ballard and Arundel Rolls.

Robert de Offord

Joan d' Offord

Vaux: Incised Slab, Newton Rigney,
Cumberland. *Boutell.*

Ingram d' Umfrauile

Rob. de Umfrayville

Johan de Orsalo

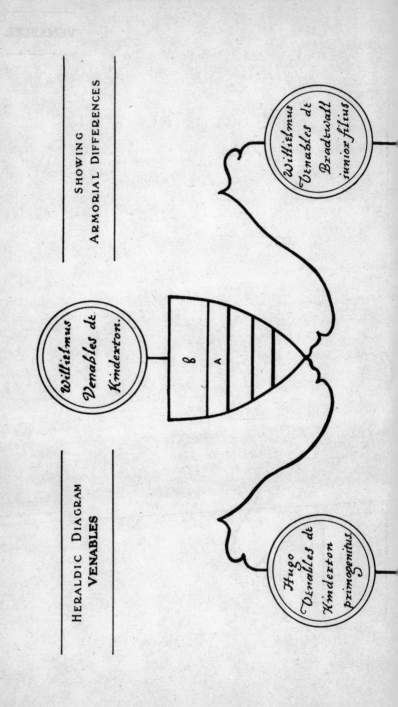

HERALDIC DIAGRAM
VENABLES

SHOWING
ARMORIAL DIFFERENCES

Willielmus Venables de Kinderton.

Willielmus Venables de Bradwall iunior filius

Hugo Venables de Kinderton primogenitus

B
A

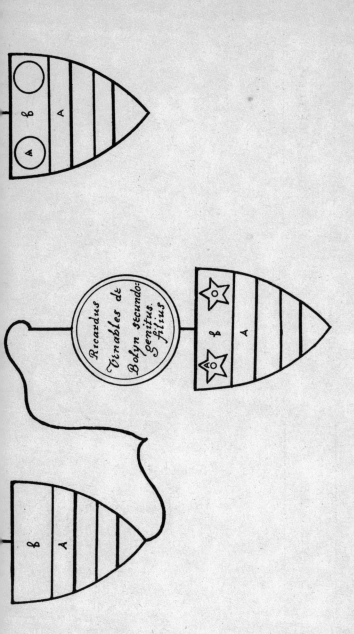

Ricardus Vinables de Bolyn secundo-genitus. filius

U–V

Ufflete, Sir Gerard—(E. II. Roll) bore, argent on a fess azure three fleurs-de-lys or ; Parly. Roll and Jenyns' Ordinary—F.—fess sable in Nativity Roll. In the Surrey Roll— or, a bend between six martlets gules *quarterly with*, argent on a fess azure three fleurs-de-lys or, for another GERARD.

Ufford, Sir Robert de, baron 1309—bore, at the first Dunstable tournament 1308, sable, a cross engrailed or (F') ; as did his son ROBERT (after Earl of SUFFOLK, K.G.) at the battle of Boroughbridge 1322, at the second Dunstable tournament 1334, and at the siege of Calais 1345–8 (blasoned the reverse in Segar and Grimaldi Rolls). His brothers (1) Sir EDMUND differenced with a crown in the cantel argent and (2) Sir JOHN as in the next ; Harl. MS. 1481 fo. 34. A ROBERT DE UFFORD took up the cross in the last Crusade 1270 ; see also Dering Roll.

Ufford, Sir Thomas de—bore, at the first Dunstable tournament 1308, sable, a cross engrailed or, surmounted of a baston argent (F.) ; as did JOHN, at the second Dunstable tournament 1334 ; Ashmole Roll.

Ufford, Sir Edmund—(E. III. Roll) bore, sable, a cross engrailed or, a baston gobony argent and gules ; Ashmole Roll.

Ufford, Rauf de—bore, at the second Dunstable tournament 1334, sable, a cross engrailed or, an annulet argent. Sir THOMAS differenced with a label (3) argent and Sir WALTER with a ducal coronet or, in the cantel ; Ashmole Roll.

Ufford, John de—(H. III. Roll) bore, sable, a cross engrailed in the 1st and 2nd an escallop argent ; Arden Roll.

Ufford, John de—(H. III. Roll) bore, azure, on a cross engrailed or five escallops gules. (F.) St. George Roll.

Ughtred, Sir Thomas, K.G., baron 1343— bore, at the siege of Calais 1345–8, gules, on a cross patonce or five mullets of the field (F.) ; spur-rowells in Ashmole and Surrey Rolls and Jenyns' Ordinary. See OUGHTRED.

Ughtred, Sir John or **Robert**, (OUTREDE), of Yorkshire—(E. II. Roll) bore, or, on a cross patonce gules three mullets of the field ; four in tricks ; Parliamentary Roll.

Ulgham, Reinould de, of Northumberland —(E. I. Roll) bore, gules a cinquefoyle pierced or a bordure azure entoyre of horse-shoes argent.—Jenyns' Roll.

Ulster, Earl of, Walter de Burgh—bore, or, a cross gules, the ancient arms of (BIGOD) Earl of NORFOLK ; Ashmole Roll and Jenyns' Ordinary.

Umfraville, Gilbert, Earl of ANGUS—bore, at the battle of Falkirk 1298, gules crusily and a cinquefoyle or—in some Rolls the cinquefoyle is pierced (F.) ; (crusily patée in Guillim Roll), borne also by ROBERT, at the siege of Rouen 1418 (with a crescent for difference), and ascribed also to THOMAS,—crusily patée in Jenyns' Ordinary. Sir ROBERT, K.G., 1409–13, differenced with a baston azure and Sir THOMAS, of Harbottle, Northumberland, differenced with a baston engrailed argent ; Harl. MS. 1481 fo. 75.

Umfreville, Gilbert de—(H. III. Roll) bore, or, a cinquefoyle gules, a bordure azure entoyre of horse-shoes of the second ; Glover Roll.

Umfrevile, Sir R.—(H. VI. Roll) bore, gules, a bend between six crosslets or ; Atkinson Roll.

Umfraville, de —— (E. III. Roll) bore, party per fess or and gules 12 seysfoyles 3, 3, 3, 2, 1 counterchanged pierced ; Ashmole Roll.

Umfraville, Sir Ingram de—(H. III. Roll) bore, gules, an orle ermine, a label (3, 5) azure. (F.) St. George and Ashmole Roll and Jenyns' Ordinary—no label in Arden Roll. See INGRAM DE BALIOLL.

Upsale, Sir Geffrey and **John de**—(E. I. Roll) bore, argent, a cross sable. (F.) Segar, Nativity and Parly. Rolls ; Jenyns' Ordinary.

Upsale, Michel de, (OPSHALE)—(H. III. Roll) bore, argent, a cross sable fretty or ; Arden and St. George Rolls.

Upton v. Hopton.

*Upton —— (E. III. Roll) bore, sable, a cross recercelée (now moline) argent. (F.) Ashmole Roll.

Urswicke, Robert de—(R. II. Roll) bore, argent, on a bend sable three lozenges of the field each charged with a saltire gules. WALTER, differenced with a crescent of the second ; Surrey and Ballard Rolls.

Uvedale v. Dowdale.

Vache, Hugh le—(E. III. Roll) bore, gules, three lyonceux rampant 2 and 1 argent ; GRIMBALD PAUNCEFOTE bore the same ; Jenyns' Ordinary—lyons crowned or in Arundel and Surrey Rolls. See DE LA VACHE.

Vale v. De la Val.

WILLIAM DE VALENCE, EARL OF PEMBROKE.
IN S. EDMUND CHAPEL, WESTMINSTER, 1296. *After Gough.*

Vale, Nicol de—(E. I. Roll) bore, argent, on a cross gules five escallops or ; Harleian Roll.

Valenan *v.* **Velemane.**

Valence *v.* **Earl of Pembroke.**

Valence, Aymer de, of Mountenake, banneret, baron 1299, Earl of PEMBROKE 1308, sealed the Barons' letter to the Pope 1301—bore, at the battle of Falkirk 1298 and at the siege of Carlaverock 1300, barry (10) argent and azure, ten martlets in orle 3, 2, 2, 3 gules, on his banner ; Nobility and Parliamentary Rolls—burulée 12, 14, 16 or 20 ; ascribed also to WILLIAM (his father) Earl of PEMBROKE, who took up the cross in the last Crusade 1270 ; Grimaldi Roll (see Monumental Effigy)—(azure and argent) also to WILLIAM in Camden Roll and argent and gules in Glover Roll. (F.) For differences see Harl. MS. 1418 fo. 29.

Valence, Sir William de—(E. II. Roll) bore, argent, a chief dancettée (3) azure ; Parliamentary Roll.

Valeys, William de—(H. III. Roll) bore, burulée (14) argent and azure, over all a saltire gules ; Howard Roll.

‡**Valoines, Sire William de**, of Kent—(E. I. Roll) bore, paly wavy (ounde de longe of 6, argent and gules. (WILLIAM le fitz differenced with a label (3) or) ; RAFFE bore it within a bordure, ermine ; all, Jenyns' Roll—three palets wavy in Dering and Camden Rolls.

Valoines, Sire Henry—bore, at the battle of Boroughbridge 1322, pale undée (6) or and gules, a label (6) argent. F.

Valoines, Stephen (VALONS)—(R. II. Roll) bore, or three palets wavy gules, a bordure ermine ; Surrey Roll.

Valoines, Theobald—(E. I. Roll) bore, six peus undée or and gules—*vel*—or, three undées gulez—tricked, or three piles wavy meeting in base gules ; Jenyns' Roll (and also for WILLIAM in Jenyns' Ordinary) ; oundée (6) or and gules, in Grimaldi Roll.

Valoines, John de—(E. I. Roll) bore, sable, a maunch argent. (F.) Segar Roll.

Valoines, Richard de—(H. III. Roll) bore, burulée (14) argent and azure on a bend gules three mullets of six points (perhaps estoiles) or. (F.) St. George Roll.

Valoines, Richard de (DAVEREIGNES)—(E. III. Roll) bore, argent, a cross gules, a bordure engrailed sable ; Jenyns' Ordinary.

Valoynes, Theobald—(E. III. Roll) bore, or, a cross gules a bordure azure entoyre of martlets of the first ; Jenyns' Ordinary.

‡**Valoynes, Walrois de**—(H. III. Roll) bore, gules, fretty ermine. (F.) Dering Roll—WERREIS in Camden Roll and WILLIAM in Howard Roll—WARREN gules, fretty engrailed ermine ; Ashmole Roll.

Van Halle, Sir Francis, K.G., 1360—bore, gules, a wyvern or, from its neck an escocheon pendent gules charged with a double-headed eagle argent, all within a bordure azure florettée alternated with lyons passant gardant all or. K. 398 fo. 53. F.

Varley, Sir Philip de (VERLEY), of Essex (E. II. Roll) bore, or, six eaglets displayed 3, 2, 1 sable, over all a bend gules ; Parliamentary Roll.

Vascoil, Sir John (VASTOYLE), of Essex—(E. II. Roll) bore, argent, on a cross sable five mullets or ; Parliamentary Roll.

Vauncy, Sire John (WANNCY)—bore, at the battle of Boroughbridge 1322, argent, an eagle displayed purpure.

Vauncy, William—(E. III. Roll) bore, argent, an eagle displayed azure, membered or ; Jenyns' Ordinary.

‡**Vautour, John le**—(H. III. Roll) bore, or, a saltire gules. (F.) Dering and Surrey Rolls.

[**Vaux** (——) of Catterlen in Cumberland—bore, a fess checquy between six garbs. See incised slab at Newton Rigney.]

‡**Vaux, John** and **Robert**—(H. III. Roll) bore, checquy argent and gules. (F.) Dering and Norfolk Rolls. [SIR JOHN, of Notts, bore a label (3) azure ; Parly. Roll.] FOULKE differenced with a quarter azure.

Vaux, Sir William de—bore, at the first Dunstable tournament 1322, or, an inescocheon within an orle of (8) martlets gules—the field argent for Sir WILLIAM, of Norfolk in Parliamentary Roll.

Vaux, Sir John de—bore, at the battle of Boroughbridge 1322, argent, an inescocheon within an orle of mullets gules. (F.) JAMES bore the same, blasoned argent an orle of martlets gules, a false escocheon ; Jenyns' Ordinary.

Vaux, Sir John de, of co. Worc.—(E. II. Roll) bore, gules, on an inescocheon or two lyons passant azure, eight martlets in orle or ; Parliamentary Roll.

Vaux, John and **Roland**—(H. III. Roll) bore, argent, a bend checquy argent and gules, counter-compony in trick ; Glover and Jenyns' Rolls.

Vavasour, Sir William, banneret, baron, 1299—bore, at the battle of Falkirk 1298 and at the siege of Carlaverock 1300, or, a fess dancettée (3) sable. (F.) Nobility and Parly. Rolls—ascribed to HENRY in Jenyns' Ordinary.

Vavasour, Sir William—(E. I. Roll) bore, argent, a fess dancettée azure ; Holland Roll —a label (5) for another WILLIAM ; St. George Roll.

Vavaseur, John le—(E. I. Roll) bore, or, fretty sable, a label (5) gules. (F.) Segar Roll.

‡**Vele, Robert le**—(H. III. Roll) bore, argent on a bend sable three calves passant of the field. (F.) Dering and Howard Rolls.

Velemane, Raffe, otherwise AUGUST or RUSTEN VALENAN — bore, at the siege of Rouen 1418 gules three birds in bend between two cotises argent. (F.) In the Ashmole MS. the trick is, gules, a bend cotised between two peahens argent.

Venables, Sir Hugh—(E. III. Roll) bore, azure, two bars argent ; Ashmole Roll, and with crest in Ballard Roll. RICHARD of Bolyn (son of HUGH) differenced with two mullets pierced argent in the chief—and WILLIAM of Bradewall (brother of HUGH) bore two plates in chief ; Harl. MS. 1481 fo. 35.

Venables, Richard—(R. II. Roll) bore, argent, two bars azure, on a bend gules three arrows of the field ; Surrey Roll.

ROBERT DE VERE, EARL OF OXFORD.

IN HATFIELD BROAD OAK CHURCH, ESSEX, OB. 1221. *After Stothard.*

Erected at a later date.

Vene, Sir Leysen de, of co. Glouc.—(E. II. Roll) bore, gules, three chevronels argent; Parliamentary Roll.

Venour, Sir Robert de, of co. Linc.—(E. II. Roll) bore, argent, crusily and a lyon rampant tail fourchée gules; Parly. Roll.

‡**Verdon, Sir Theobald de,** of Alton, banneret, baron 1295, sealed the Barons' letter to the Pope 1301—bore, at the first Dunstable tournament 1308, or, fretty gules (F.); ascribed also to JOHN in Surrey and Cotgrave Rolls, as or, a fret gules; who perhaps took up the cross in the last Crusade 1270.

Verdon, Sir Theobald de, of Webley, junior baron 1299—bore, at the battle of Falkirk 1298, or, fretty gules a label (3, 5) azure; Nobility and Guillim Rolls.

Verdon, Theobald de—(E. III. Roll) bore, or, fretty gules platey at the joints; Jenyns' Ordinary.

Verdon, Sir Thomas de (of Northants) bore, at the first Dunstable tournament 1308, sable, a lyon rampant argent; Parly. Roll—borne also by JOHN (F.) at the second Dunstable tournament 1334 (and on the same occasion by his brother THOMAS—on the lyon's shoulder a chess-rook gules) and by Sir JOHN, knighted at the capitulation of Calais 1348; Jenyns' Ordinary.

Verdon, Christopher de, knighted at the capitulation of Calais 1348—bore, sable, a lyon rampant argent, on his shoulder a chess-rook gules. (F.) Borne also by THOMAS at the second Dunstable tournament 1334.

Verdon, Thomas de—(E. III. Roll) bore, sable, a lyon argent, holding in his paw a chess-rook gules; Cotgrave Roll.

Verdon, Sir Robert de (of Warwickshire) —(E. II. Roll) bore, argent, a cross azure fretty or Parly. Roll (Harl. 4033) and argent, on a cross azure five fleurs-de-lys or, Parly. Roll, Harl. MS. 6137.

Vere, Robert de, banneret, Earl of Oxford 1296—bore, at the battle of Falkirk 1298, quarterly gules and or, a mullet argent. (F.) Nobility and Parly. Rolls. See Monumental Effigy. Borne by an Earl of Oxford (? RICHARD 11th Earl, K.G. 1415) at the siege of Rouen 1418. This coat is often erroneously blasoned the reverse.

Vere, Hugh de, of Swanscombe, banneret (brother of ROBERT), baron 1299, sealed the Barons' letter to the Pope 1301—bore, at the siege of Carlaverock 1300, quarterly gules and or, a mullet argent, all within a bordure engrailed sable. (F.) Harl. MS. 6137. (In NICOLAS, the field tinctures are reversed, the bordure indented.) Nobility, Arundel and Segar Rolls—indented, Parly. and Guillim Rolls.

Vere, Sir Thomas de—bore, at the first Dunstable tournament 1308, quarterly gules and or, a mullet argent, a label (3) azure; differenced with a label sable (F.), by Sir THOMAS le fiz le Count de Oxenford, at the battle of Boroughbridge 1322.

Vere, Aubrey le and **Sir Aufonso de,** of Essex—(E. II. Rolls) bore, quarterly gules and or, a mullet ermine; Surrey and Parly. Rolls; argent, in H. 4033 fo. 38.

Vere, Sir Richard de, knighted at the capitulation of Calais 1348, bore, quarterly or and gules a bordure vair. F.

Vere, Robert de — (H. III. Roll) bore, argent, a cross gules; Glover Roll. Nichol differenced with a label (3) azure; Jenyns' Ordinary.

Vere, Robert de—(E. I. Roll) bore, sable, three boars' heads couped or; Jenyns' Roll. F.

Vere, Simon de—(H. III. Roll) bore, gules three cinquefoyles (sixfoyles ermine in Glover Roll) argent (F.); Jenyns' Ordinary—pierced in Arden and St. George Rolls.

Verney, Sir Philip de—(E. III. Roll)—bore, argent, a fess gules fret'y in chief three mullets of the second; Ashmole Roll. F.

***Vernon, John** and **Richard**—(E. III. Roll) bore, argent, a fret (fretty) sable, a quarter gules. (F.) Atkinson and Surrey Rolls and Jenyns' Ordinary. Lord VERNON bears it without the quarter.

Vernon —— (R. II. Roll) bore, or, on a fess azure three garbs of the field, *quarterly with,* argent a fret sable; Surrey Roll. VERNON quartering VERNON. F.

✝**Vesci, John, Eustace** and **Sir William,** banneret—(H. III. Roll) bore, or, a cross sable; Jenyns' Ordinary, Dering and Arundel Rolls. Another WILLIAM (‡) differenced with a label (5) gules. (F.) Dering and St. George Rolls.

Vescy, William de—(H. III. Roll) bore, gules, a cross patonce argent; Glover Roll. F.

Vescy, William—(E. III. Roll) bore, or, a lyon rampant azure, a baston gules; Jenyns' Ordinary.

Videlon, Sir William, of Berks—(E. II. Roll) bore, argent, three wolves' heads erased gules; Parliamentary Roll. F.

Vile, Ansel de—(H. III Roll) bore, argent, a fess between six spur-rowells gules; Dering Roll. See DEYVILE.

Villers, Sir Francis de, of Notts—(E. II. Roll) bore, gules, billettée and a cross or; Parliamentary Roll.

***Villers, Sir Nicholas de,** of co. Glouc. —(E. II. Roll) bore, argent, on a cross gules five escallops or. (F.) Ashmole and Parly. Rolls and Jenyns Ordinary.

Villers, Nichol de—(E. III. Roll) bore, azure, on a cross or five escallops gules; Jenyns' Ordinary—same as RANDOLF DACRE.

*[**Vincent, Miles,** (10 E. II.)—bore, azure, three quatrefoyles argent.—Shirley.] F.

Vipount, Sir John de—bore, at the first Dunstable tournament 1308, or, six annulets 3, 2, 1 gules a label (3) azure. (F.) Nativity and Parly. Rolls.

Vipount, Sir Nicholas, banneret (E. II. Roll), and **Sir Robert** and **John,** of Westmoreland (E. III. Roll) bore, or six annulets 3, 2, 1 gules; Ashmole, Arundel and Parly. Rolls, Jenyns' Ordinary.

Vyan, Sire le —— (E. I. Roll) bore, or, billettée and a lyon rampant gules. (F.) Camden Roll.

‡**Vyan, Lucas de,** (VYENNE)—(H. III. Roll) bore, azure, a fess dancettée argent; Howard Roll—in the Dering Roll azure, crusily and a fess dancettée or. F.

*[**Vyvyan, Sir Vyell,** 13th cent.—bore, argent, a lyon rampant gules.—Shirley.] F.

Sire de Madripun   Simon d' Waddone   Robert de Wadevile

Hue. Wake   Johan Wake   Thomas Wake

John Walcot   Alex Waldon   Alan d' Waldesef

Johan de Waleis   Richard de Walleis   Will le Waleis

W

Wachesham, Sir Gerard—(E. II. Roll) bore, argent, a fess and in chief three crescents gules. Sir JOHN of Suffolk bore it with a baston azure ; Parliamentary Roll.

Waddone, Simon de—(E. II. Roll) bore, sable, a cross engrailed or, in the first and second an escallop argent ; St. George Roll. F.

Wadesley, Sir Robert de, of Yorkshire—(E. II. Roll) bore, argent, on a bend between six martlets 3 and 3 gules, three escallops or ; Parliamentary Roll.

Wadeville, Sire Robert de—bore, at the battle of Boroughbridge 1322, argent, three chevrons gules within a bordure sable. F.

‡**Wadripun, Sire de**—(E. I. Roll) bore, or, two lyons rampant addorsed gules. Camden Roll (F.) ; called WATERIBONT in Dering Roll.

Wahull, Thomas de, of Beds., a baron 1297—bore, or, three crescents gules ; Nobility and Parliamentary Rolls.

*****Wake, Sir John de**, banneret, a baron 1295 —bore, at the battle of Falkirk 1298, or, two bars gules in chief three torteaux—borne also by BALDWIN(‡) and HUGH (F.) ; Dering and Glover Rolls. In the Arden Roll a Wake coat is tricked, azure two bars or and in chief three besants ; this in Camden Roll with the field, gules for HUE WAKE.

Wake, Sire Thomas de Blisworth—bore, at the battle of Boroughbridge 1322, argent, two bars gules and in chief three torteaux, a bordure indented sable ; as did THOMAS of Blisworth at the second Dunstable tournament 1334 ; the border is usually tricked engrailed ; ascribed to THOMAS of Deeping, but with ogresses in lieu of torteaux, in Jenyns' Ordinary. F.

Wake, Sir Hugh, of Yorkshire—(E. II. Roll) bore, or, two bars gules, in chief three torteaux, a baston azure. Sir HUGH, the uncle, bore, gules two bars argent, in chief three plates ; Parliamentary Roll.

Wake, Hue—(H. III. Roll) bore, argent fretty sable besanty at the joints ; Arden Roll. F.

Wake, Jon—(H. III. Roll) bore, or, a fess gules in chief three torteaux ; Arden Roll.

Walcote, John de—(R. II. Roll) bore, argent, on a cross patonce azure five fleurs-de-lys or ; Surrey Roll.

*[**Walcot, John**, (H. v.)—bore, argent, a chevron between three chess-rooks ermine.— Shirley.] (F.) Checkmated the king with a rook, and so had these arms given him.

*****Waldegrave, Richard**—(R. II. Roll) bore, per pale argent and gules ; Surrey Roll. Sir RICHARD DE bore this coat with a bend engrailed sable ; Ashmole Roll, E. III.

Walden, Alexander—(R. II. Roll) bore, sable, two bars ermine, in chief three cinque-foyles pierced argent ; Surrey Roll.

Waldeseuf, Alain de (or WALDESEFTH)— (H. III. Roll) bore, gules, two chevrons argent a label (5) of France ; St. George Roll—borne also by EDMUND, in the Arden Roll.

Wale v. **Waleus.**

Wale, Sir Thomas, K.G., a founder—(E. III. Roll) bore, argent a cross sable ; Surrey Roll. Sir THOMAS of Rutland bore, on the cross, five lyonceux or ; Parliamentary Roll, E. II.

Wales, Prince of; Edward; v. **England.**

Wales, Prince of—(H. VI. Roll) bore, or, a lyon passant gules, *quarterly with*, gules, a lyon passant or ; Nobility Roll.

Waleis, Sir Steven—bore, at the siege of Calais 1345-8, gules, a fess ermine ; borne also by Sir RICHARD of Sussex, a baron 1321 ; Parliamentary Roll (F.) ; ascribed to another RICHARD (‡) in the Dering Roll. HENRY bore gules a fess sable ; Arden Roll.

Waleys, Sir Simon de, of Sussex—(E. II. Roll) bore, gules, a fess ermine, in chief a lyon passant gardant or ; Parliamentary Roll.

Waleys, Sir John de, of Somerset—bore, at the first Dunstable tournament 1308, ermine, a bend gules. Sir JOHN knighted at the capitulation of Calais 1348, bore the reverse (F.) ; he is sometimes called Sir JOHN WALWAYNE.

‡**Waleis, Henry de**—(H. III. Roll) bore, burulée (14) argent and azure, a bend gules ; St. George Roll. F.

Waleis, John de—(E. II. Roll) bore, gules, billettée or an orle ermine. (F.) Arden Roll. Called WALHOPE in St. George Roll.

JOHN WANTLEY.

IN AMBERLEY CHURCH, SUSSEX, C. 1424, 2 H. VI. *After Stothard.*

Waleis, Stephen le, and Sir Richard le—(H. III. Roll) bore, quarterly gules and argent a bendlet or—F. (engrailed in Jenyns' Ordinary); Parliamentary and St. George Rolls and Jenyns' Ordinary. Sometimes tricked and blasoned argent and gules.

Waleis, William le—(H. III. Roll) bore, argent a fess between six martlets sable; St. George Roll. F.

Waleis, William de (GALEYS)—(E. I. Roll) bore, gules, a fess between two chevronels or; Segar Roll.

Walesborough, Sir John—(E. III. Roll) bore, gules, three bendlets a bordure engrailed sable; Ashmole Roll. See also WHALESBOROUGH.

Waleus, Sir John—(E. III. Roll) bore, vert, a lyon rampant or; Ashmole Roll.

Walkfare, Sir Robert de, of Norfolk— (E. II. Roll) bore, argent, a lyon rampant sable, on the shoulder a mullet or; Parliamentary Roll.

Walkingham, Sir John de—(E. II. Roll) bore, vair, two bars gules; Parliamentary Roll.

Walkington, William de—bore, at the second Dunstable tournament 1334, gules, a chevron argent. F.

Walkington, Sir William, knighted at the capitulation of Calais 1348—bore, gules on a chevron azure three mullets pierced argent. (F.) Another Sir WILLIAM bore, gules, a chevron between three mullets argent; Ashmole Roll.

Walhope *v.* **Welhopp.**

*****Wallop, Richard de**, (2 Ed. III.) formerly BARTON, great-grandson of PETER (E. I.) who bore, argent, a bend wavy sable. See JOHN DE BARTON. Surrey Roll.

*****[Walpole, Sir Henry,** (E. I.)—bore, or on a fess between two chevrons sable three crosses crosslet of the first.—Shirley.] F.

*****[Walrond, John,**(E. I.)—bore, argent, three bulls' heads cabossed sable.—Shirley.] F.

Walrond, John and Robert—(H. III. Roll) bore, argent a bend fusily gules; Arden Roll; endented, tricked lozengy — Jenyns' Ordinary; engrailed in Glover Roll—all intended for one and the same—fusily.

Walsh, John—(R. II. Roll) bore, argent, a chevron between three fleurs-de-lys sable; Surrey Roll.

Walshe, Thomas—(R. II. Roll) bore, gules, two gemelles surmounted of a bendlet all argent; Surrey Roll.

Walsingham, Sir Richard de, of Norfolk—(E. II. Roll) bore gules, three chessrooks argent; Parliamentary Roll.

Walsingham, Roger de—(E. I. Roll) bore, sable a chevron argent between three cinquefoyles pierced or; Jenyns' and Surrey Rolls— not pierced in Jenyns' Ordinary.

Waltham, Ratcliff—(E. III. Roll) bore, gules, besantée and a lyon rampant argent; Jenyns' Ordinary.

Walton, William, of Essex, Knight — (H. VI. Roll) bore, argent, on a chief dancettée sable three besants ; Arundel Roll.

Walton, Sir Adam de, of the North — (E. II. Roll) bore, argent, a cross patonce sable a bordure indented gules; Parly. Roll.

[Wantley, John, of Sussex, 1424, bore vert three leopards' faces argent. See Sepulchral Brass.]

Wanton *v.* **Wauton** and **Wawton.**

Wanton, Sir William de, of Essex — (E. II. Roll) bore, argent, a chevron sable; Norfolk and Parliamentary Rolls. Another WILLIAM (‡) in the Dering Roll.

Wanton, Sir William, knighted at the siege of Calais 1348, **Thomas** and **Sir John**—bore, argent, a chevron sable, in the cantel a martlet gules. (F.) Jenyns' Ordinary and Ashmole Roll. Another THOMAS differenced with an annulet sable; Surrey Roll.

Wanton, Sir William (of co. Glouc.)— bore, at the first Dunstable tournament 1308, argent, on a chevron sable three eaglets displayed or. (F.) Jenyns' and Parly. Rolls.

Wanton, William de—bore, at the second Dunstable tournament 1334, or, on a chevron sable three eaglets displayed of the field.

Wanton, John de—(H. III. Roll) bore, argent, on a bend sable three buckles, tongues to the dexter or. (F.) Arden and St. George Rolls.

Wapaile, Roger de—(H. III. Roll) bore argent two chevrons ("a chevron et demy") gules over all a quarter of the last. (F.) Another differenced with a martlet sable; St. George and Jenyns' Rolls.

‡**Warbleton, Thomas de**—(H. III. Roll) bore, lozengy or and azure. (F.) Dering, Arden and Howard Rolls.

Warburton —— bore, at the siege of Rouen 1418, argent, three birds sable (F.) ; supposed to be cormorants.

Warburton, Geoffrey—(R. II. Roll) bore, argent, two chevronels gules, on a quarter of the last a mullet or; Surrey Roll.

Warcop, Thomas de—(E. III. Roll) bore, sable, a chevron between three covered cups argent; Jenyns' Ordinary. F.

Warde *v.* **de la Warde.**

Warde, Sir John—bore, at the siege of Calais 1345-8, azure, a cross flory or. (F.); (a cross patonce ascribed to JOHN in Surrey Roll)—a cross patée for Sir SYMON, banneret, patonce in trick in Parly. Roll, and flory in Jenyns' Ordinary.

Warde, Henry, of Swynythwaite—(E. III. Roll) bore, argent, crusily fitchée, 3, 3 and a fess sable; Jenyns' Ordinary.

Wardewick, John—(F. III. Roll) bore, vert, three lyonceux rampant tails fourchée 2 and 1 argent; Jenyns' Ordinary.

Ware, William de—(E. I. Roll) bore, gules, a lyon rampant tail fourchée argent, debruised by a baston sable; Segar Roll.

Warre *v.* **de la Warr.**

Countes de Warren

John de Wayz

Rog d'Wasseburne

Hugh de Wasonham

Estephe Wossingtono

Will de Wassington

Hardolf de Waslonoys

Will de Watonald

Henge Walterton

Geofferay Watervillo

Johan d'Waunei

Geofray d'Waunei

Warren, John, Earl of, and a banneret; sealed the Barons' letter to the Pope 1301—bore at the battle of Falkirk 1298 and at the siege of Carlaverock 1300, checquy or and azure (F.); (his only son WILLIAM was killed at a tournament at Croydon 15 Dec. 1285), as did his grandson JOHN Earl of Warren at the first Dunstable tournament 1308—colours reversed in the Arden and Guillim Rolls.

Warren, Reginald (brother of Earl WILLIAM) founder of the abbey of Castlecombe, bore checquy or and azure, a bordure engrailed gules; Harl. MS. 1481 fo. 32ᵇ.

Warren, Sir William—bore, at the siege of Calais 1345-8, checquy or and azure on a canton gules, a lyon rampant argent. F.

Warren, Sir William, le filz, knighted at the capitulation of Calais 1348—bore, checquy or and azure, a chief argent. F.

Warren, Sir John, of Poynton—(E. IV. Roll) bore, checquy or and azure, on a canton gules a lyon rampant argent (ermine in Ashmole Roll) with two quarterings and crest; Ballard Roll.

Warryne, Sir William — (E. III. Roll) bore, argent, a chief counter-compony or and azure; Ashmole Roll.

Waren (——) de Stockport—(H. III. Roll) bore, azure, crusily and three lozenges or; Arden Roll.

†**Warwick, (Thomas) de,** Earl of, " le veyl escu "—checquy or and azure, a chevron gules; Howard and other Rolls—a bend ermine in Reg. MS. 14 cvii. fo. 134. See also BEAUCHAMP.

Wasenham, Sir Hugh de—(E. III. Roll) —bore, sable, a fess dancettée (3) between three mullets argent; Ashmole Roll. F.

Washington v. **Wassington.**

Wassand, John—(E. I. Roll) bore, argent, a fess and in chief two crescents gules; Jenyns' and Ashmole Rolls. F.

Wasse, Sir John de (WAYZ)—bore, at the first Dunstable tournament 1308, gules, on an inescocheon or two lyons passant azure, all within 8 martlets in orle of the second. F.

Wasse, William de—(E. III. Roll) bore, " argent, an orle of martlets gules, a false escocheon of the same "; Jenyns' Ordinary.

Wasse, Sir William, of Bucks—(R. II. Roll) bore, barry (6) argent and gules on a canton of the last a mullet pierced of the first; Parliamentary Roll.

Wasseburne, Roger de—(H. III. Roll) bore, gules, besantée on a canton or a raven proper. (F.) St. George Roll.

Wassington, William de—(R. II. Roll) bore, argent, two bars in chief three mullets pierced gules; Surrey Roll—colours reversed in Jenyns' Roll. F.

Wassington, Walter (WESSINGTON) — (E. III. Roll) bore, gules, a lyon rampant argent, a bendlet gobony azure and argent; Jenyns' Ordinary. F.

Wassington, Stephen de—bore, at the second Dunstable tournament 1334, azure, " un rase " or. F.

Wasteneys, Sir William (of co. Staff.)—bore, at the first Dunstable tournament 1308, sable, a lyon rampant argent collared gules. (F.); ascribed also to EDMUND and SIR THOMAS; Segar and Ashmole Rolls.

Wasteneys, Hardolf de—bore, at the second Dunstable tournament 1334, sable a lyon rampant tail fourchée argent (F.); ascribed also to Sir EDMUND and ROBERT in Parliamentary Roll and Jenyns' Ordinary.

Watenald, Sir William de, knighted at the capitulation of Calais 1348—bore, sable, a bend fusily or (F.) *alii* argent.

‡**Wateribont, Sire de**—(H. III. Roll) bore, or, two lyons rampant addorsed gules; Dering Roll—called WADRIPUN in Camden Roll. (F.)

‡**Wateringbury, Bartholomew de** — (H. III. Roll) bore, argent, six lyonceux rampant sable. (F.) Dering and Howard Rolls.

*****Waterton, Hugh** — bore, at the siege of Rouen 1418, barry (6) argent and gules, over all three crescents 2, 1 sable (F.); ascribed to ROBERT in Jenyns' Roll; borne ermine and gules by (*Sir* ROBERT) a Yorkshire Knight Arundel Roll; (H. VI.).

Wateville, Sir Geoffrey—bore, at the first Dunstable tournament 1308, sable, crusily and a lyon rampant argent. F.

Watervile, Sir Robert, of Hunts, and **John de** (E. III. Roll) bore, argent, crusily (5, 5) and a fess dancettée gules; Parly. Roll and Jenyns' Ordinary.

Watevile, Sir John de, of Essex—(E. II. Roll) bore, argent, three chevronels gules; Parly. Roll—inescocheons tricked in Harl. MS. 6137 fo. 13, and for Sir ROBERT and Sir ROGER named below.

Wateville, Sir Robert (of Essex) baron 1326—bore, at the first Dunstable tournament 1308, argent, three chevrons gules, a bordure indented sable—engrailed (F.) in trick; Harl. MS. 6137 fo. 34, and so ascribed to ROGER in Jenyns' Ordinary.

Wateville, Sir Roger de (of Essex)—bore, at the first Dunstable tournament 1308, argent, three chevrons gules, in the cantel a martlet sable.

Watlass, Hervey de—(E. III. Roll) bore, or, on a chief indented azure three crescents of the field; Grimaldi Roll and Jenyns' Ordinary. See PICKENHAM.

Wauncy, Sire John—bore, at the battle of Boroughbridge 1322, argent, an eagle displayed purpure. (F.) See VAUNCY.

Waunci, Gefrai de—(H. III. Roll) bore, gules, three dexter gauntlets aversant argent. (F.) St. George Roll; ascribed to JOHN in Arden Roll.

Wauncy, Nichole de—(H. III. Roll) bore, gules, three dexter gauntlets argent; Howard Roll.

Wauncy, Sir Robert de, of Rutland—(E. II. Roll) bore, sable, three sinister gauntlets aversant 2, 1 argent; Parliamentary Roll.

Wauncye, Sir William de, of Suffolk—(E. II. Roll) bore, gules, six sinister gauntlets 3, 2, 1 argent; Parliamentary Roll.

walbowrk

will welby

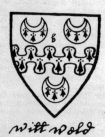

will wold

*Jorn
Woto wango*

SIR RICHARD DE WHATTON.

IN WHATTON CHURCH, NOTTS, TEMP. H. III.   *From Stothard.*

Wauton *v.* **Wanton.**

Wauton, John de—(H. III. Roll) bore, argent, on a bend sable three buckles tongues to the dexter or. (F.) Arden and St. George Rolls.

Wawton, John, and also **Gilbert de,** of Kerperby—(E. I. Roll) bore, gules. on a chief argent three torteaux; Howard Roll and Jenyns' Ordinary; no torteaux in the Ashmole and Grimaldi Rolls.

Wawton, Henri de (WAUTON)—(H. III. Roll) bore, argent, on a chief gules, a maunch of the field ; Howard Roll.

Wedone, Sir Raffe de, of Bucks—(E. II. Roll) bore, argent, two bars gules in chief three martlets sable; Parliamentary Roll.

Welbewik —— (E. III. Roll) bore, azure, a fess engrailed argent between three escallops of the last ; Ashmole Roll. F.

*[**Welby, Sir William,** (E. I.)—bore, sable, a fess between three fleurs-de-lys argent.— Shirley.] F.

*[**Weld, William,** Sheriff of London 1352— bore, azure, a fess undée between three crescents ermine.—Shirley.] F.

Welhopp, John de—(E. III. Roll) bore, gules, billettée or, an orle ermine; Jenyns' Ordinary, same as JOHN DE WALEIS.

Welles, Sir Adam de, banneret, baron 1293, sealed the Barons' letter to the Pope 1301—bore, at the battle of Falkirk 1298 and at the siege of Carlaverock 1300, a lyon rampant tail fourchée sable (F.); as did JOHN, 5th baron, at the siege of Rouen in 1418.

Wells, Sir Philip de, of Lincolnshire— (E. II. Roll) bore, argent, a lyon rampant tail fourchée sable, a baston gules; Parly. Roll.

Welle, Sir John de, of Kent—(E. II. Roll) bore, gules, six crescents 3, 2, 1 argent, a baston gobony or and azure; Parly. Roll.

Wells, Sir Richard—(E. II. Roll) bore, paly (6) or and gules on a canton argent a spur-rowell sable. (F.) Ashmole Roll—argent and gules in Dering Roll—three pales for Sir RICHARD of Herts. in Parly. and Howard Rolls.

Welle, Robert de—(H. III. Roll) bore, argent, two bastons gules, besantée; Glover Roll.

Well, Roger de—(E. I. Roll) bore, or, a male gryphon segreant vert ; Jenyns' Roll.

Wellesburne —— of the Montfort, slain at the siege of Calais 1347—bore, (purpure?) a lyon rampant tail fourchée argent.

Wellesbourne, Sir Armine, together with his namesake the Captain of Dover, were slain at the siege of Calais 1347—bore, gules, a gryphon segreant or, a chief checquy of the first and second, over all a bendlet ermine. (F.) The gryphon and the metal checque may be argent in the coat of the Captain of Dover, the colour has faded. This is a doubtful coat.

Wellesby, John — (E. I. Roll) bore, "amptie" = enté = per chevron sable and argent a lyon passant gardant or; Jenyns' Roll. See also WILSHIRE.

Wellington *v.* **Willington.**

Welnetham, Sir John (WELWETHAM), of Suffolk—(E. II. Roll) bore, or, on a fess azure three plates ; Parliamentary Roll.

Welse, Sir John—(E. I. Roll) bore, ermine, a bend gules ; Harleian Roll.

Weltdene, Simon—(E. I. Roll) bore, argent, a cinquefoyle pierced gules, on a chief of the last a demi-lyon rampant issuant of the first a bordure counterchanged of the first and second. (F.) Jenyns' Roll.

Welton *v.* **Weston.**

Welwike *v.* **Welbewik.**

Wene, Sire William—bore, at the battle of Boroughbridge 1322, ermine, on a bend gules three escallops or. F.

Wenlock, Sir Roger, slain at the siege of Calais 1348—bore, argent, on a chevron (sable) between three moors' heads erased proper those in chief regarding each other, an escocheon quarterly sable and argent. F.

Wennesley, Thomas de—(R. II. Roll) bore, ermine, on a bend gules three escallops or ; Surrey Roll.

Wentworth, William, of Wentworth, Yorkshire—bore, sable, a chevron between three leopards' faces or; his brother, JOHN of Elmshall bore it within a bordure argent; Harl. MS. 1481, fo. 69b.

Wentworth, Sir (——), of Suffolk—(H. VI. Roll) bore, gules, on a fess argent between three escallops azure, a spur-rowell of the second ; Arundel Roll.

Werintone —— —(E. I. Roll) bore, azure, a bend between six escallops (3, 3) or ; Harleian Roll.

Weste, Thomas—(E. I. Roll) bore, probably at the second Dunstable tournament 1334, azure, three leopards' faces jessant-de-lys or (F.); Jenyns' and Surrey Rolls. ROBERT bore it within a bordure gules; engrailed in the trick ; Jenyns' Roll.

*[**West, Sir Thomas,** (E. II.)—bore, argent, a fess dancettée sable.—Shirley.] F.

Weston, Sir John de—bore, at the first Dunstable tournament 1308, argent, a fess sable within a bordure indented (engrailed Harl. 6137) gules, besantée (F.); (a plain bordure in the Parly. Roll). Sir JOHN, LE FIZ (of Hants. or Wilts.) bore it also at the battle of Boroughbridge 1322, as did THOMAS at the second Dunstable tournament in 1334, on which occasion his brother JOHN bore, a plain bordure and without the besants. WILLIAM (E. I. Roll) bore a plain bordure platey ; Jenyns' Roll. A JOHN DE WESTON took up the cross in the last Crusade 1270.

Weston, Roger de—(E. III. Roll) bore, gules, crusily fitchée or, a lyon rampant argent, a baston engrailed sable ; Cotgrave Roll.

*[**Weston, Sir William,** (E. II.)—bore, sable, a chevron or between three leopards' faces argent crowned or.—Shirley.] F.

Wetewang, John—(E. I. Roll) bore, sable, three lamps argent. (F.) Jenyns' Roll.

Wetwang, Sir Walter, "thresorer of the Wares," at the siege of Calais, 1345-8, bore, azure, a lyon rampant gardant tail fourchée argent, crowned or. F.

EFFIGY IN ATHERINGTON CHURCH, DEVON, TEMP. R. II.
PERHAPS FOR WILLINGTON. *After Stothard.*

Weyer, Sir William de, of Staffs.—(E. II. Roll) bore, argent, a fess between three crescents gules ; Parly. Roll.

Weyland, Sir John de—bore, at the first Dunstable tournament 1308, azure a lyon rampant or oppressed by a bendlet gules (perhaps the lyon argent in the Harl. Roll) ; ascribed also to ROGER (F.) in St. George Roll, and with a baston or, to Sir RICHARD of Suffolk, in Parly. Roll.

Weyland, Sir Nicholas de, of Suffolk—(E. II. Roll) bore, argent, on a cross gules five escallops or ; Sir WILLIAM differenced with a label (3) azure ; Parly. Roll.

Whalesborough (——) an Essex Knight—(H. VI. Roll) bore, argent, three bendlets gules, a bordure sable besantée ; Arundel Roll. See also WALESBOROUGH.

Wharton, Thomas de, of Westmoreland—(E. III. Roll) bore, sable, a maunch argent; Jenyns' Ordinary.

[**Whatton, Sir Richard de**, of Notts., temp. H. III. bore, argent crusily gules on a bend sable three bezants. See Monumental Effigy.]

[**Whichcote, John**, (6 E. IV.)—bore, ermine, two boars passant in pale gules.—Shirley.] F.

Whitacre *v.* **Witacre.**

White, Sir John (WHYGHT) of Norfolk—(E. II. Roll) bore, gules, a chevron between three boars' heads couped argent ; Parly. Roll, additional.

Whitfeld, Sir William de—bore, at the battle of Boroughbridge 1322, sable, a bend engrailed or (F.) RICHARD bore five fusils in bend ; Arden Roll.

‡**Whitfeld, Robert de**—(H. III. Roll) bore, sable, crusily and a bend fusily or (F.) ; Dering and St. George Rolls ; a bend of lozenges conjoined in Howard Roll.

*[**Whitgrave, Robert**, 13 Aug. 1442 (20 H. VI.)—bore, azure, a cross quarterly pierced or between four chevronel gules, *per* grant from HUMPHREY Earl of Stafford.] F.

*[**Whitmore, John**, H. III.—bore, vert, fretty or.—Shirley.] F.

Whitney *v.* **Witney.**

Whitrick, (QUTRIKE) **John** — (E. I. Roll) bore, argent, a fret (fretty in trick) gules, a quarter of the last ; Jenyns' Roll.

Wickston, John and **Robert de**, (E. III.—Roll) bore, argent, a chevron gules, in chief three torteaux ; Jenyns' Ordinary. See WISTOWE.

Widdrington, Gerard and **John de**—(H. III. Roll) bore, quarterly argent and gules a baston sable; Jenyns' Ordinary ; a bend in Ashmole—a bendlet in Surrey Roll.

Wigington, John de—(E. III. Roll) bore, argent, three mascles gules, sable in trick; Jenyns' Ordinary.

†**Wigton, Walter de**—bore, at the siege of Carlaverock 1300, sable, three mullets and a bordure indented or ; (NICOLAS)—engrailed in H. 6137 fo. 4ᵇ (F.) three fleurs-de-lys and the bordure engrailed Harl. MS. 6137 fo. 40 ; the latter also in Arden, Jenyns' Nobility and St. George Rolls ; ascribed also to Sir JOHN, banneret, in Nobility and Parly. Rolls.

*[**Wilburgham, Richard de**, 43 H. III.—bore, argent, three bends wavy azure.—Shirley.] F.

Williamscott, Sir Henry, of co. Glouc.—(E. II. Roll) bore, argent, three bars azure over all a lyon rampant gules, crowned or; Parly. Roll.

Willisthorpe, John—(E. I. Roll) bore, azure, a chevron between three lyons passant gardant argent ; Jenyns' Roll.

Willington, Sir John de, banneret, baron 1329—bore, at the first Dunstable tournament 1308, (and by Sir HENRY at the battle of Boroughbridge 1322) gules, a saltire vair (F.) (see Monumental Effigy);—his son RAUF differenced at the second Dunstable tournament 1334, with a label or ; ascribed to another RAUF (‡) in the Dering and Howard Rolls. Sir EDMOND, of co. Glouc. differenced with a mullet or ; Parly. Roll. Sir JOHN, knight banneret, (H. vi.) bore, gules, a saltire sable (*sic*), in Arundel Roll.

Willington —— (E. III. Roll) bore, or, a saltire lozengy vair and gules ; another differenced with a label (3) argent ; Ashmole Roll.

Willington—(WELYNGTON)—(E. III. Roll) bore, sable, a bend engrailed argent cotised or ; Ashmole Roll.

*∗**Willoughby, Robert de** — bore, at the siege of Carlaverock 1300, or, fretty azure.

Willoughby, Sir Robert, knighted at the capitulation of Calais 1348 —bore, gules, a cross recercelée argent, a bendlet sable (F.), and without the bendlet for Sir ROBERT, banneret (H. VI. Roll) as a cross moline ; Arundel Roll ; a fer-de-mouline in Parly. Roll.

Willoughby (Robert, 6th) Lord de— bore, at the siege of Rouen 1418, gules, a cross moline argent, *quarterly with*, or a cross engrailed sable (F.) ; the quarterings reversed in the Surrey Roll.

Willoughby, Richard de—(E. III. Roll) bore, argent, two bars azure, on each three cinquefoyles or ; in another three cinquefoyles 2 and 1 ; Jenyns' Ordinary.

Willoughby, Edmund—(R. II. Roll) bore, or, two bars gules, charged with three waterbougets 2 and 1 argent ; Arundel, Ashmole and Surrey Rolls.

Willoughby, William de—bore, at the second Dunstable tournament 1334, gules, a fer-de-mouline ermine. F.

Willoughby, Robert de—(H. III. Roll bore, argent, a chevron sable. (F.) Arden and Segar Rolls. WILLIAM fil. ROBERT took up the cross in the last Crusade, 1270.

Wilshire, Sir John, slain at the siege of Calais 1347, bore, per chevron gules and argent the chief crusily patée (5, 2) of the second. RAFE bore it argent and azure (and another azure and argent—with crosses crosslet 4, 2) blasoned—argent and azure amptiz le chief crusily or ; Jenyns' Roll. See WELLESBY.

Wilton, John de—(R. II. Roll) bore, gules, on a chevron argent three crosses crosslet fitchée of the field ; Surrey Roll—colours reversed in Ashmole Roll.

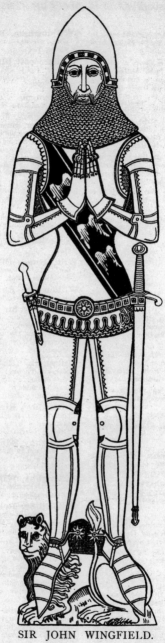

SIR JOHN WINGFIELD.

IN LETHERINGHAM CHURCH, SUFFOLK, C. 1400, 2 HEN. IV. *From Boutell.*

Winceles, Edmond de (or WINSELES)— (H. III. Roll) bore, per pale argent and sable a fess counterchanged; St. George Roll— borne also by FITZ PAINE.

Winchester, Earl of, *v.* **Quincy.**

Windlesore, Hugh de—(H. III. Roll) bore, gules, a bend vair; Howard Roll.

Windsor — a Suffolk Knight—(H. VI. Roll) bore, sable, a saltire argent; Arundel Roll.

Windsor, Sir Richard de, of Berks— (E. II. Roll) bore, gules, crusily or, a saltire argent; Parliamentary Roll.

Wingfield, William—(R. II. Roll) bore gules, two wings conjoined in lure argent; Surrey Roll.

*[**Wingfield, Sir Henry,** (H. VI.)—bore, argent, on a bend gules cotised sable three pair of wings conjoined of the field.—Shirley.] F. See Monumental Brass for Sir JOHN.

*Winnington — (E. IV. Roll) bore, argent, an inescocheon voided sable within an orle of martlets of the last (F.); crest: a retort azure; Ballard Roll. LYDULPH, E. I. Shirley.

Winsington, Sir John de, of co. Gloucr. —(E. II. Roll) bore, sable, three boars' heads couped argent; Parliamentary Roll.

Wintershulle, John de—(H. III. Roll) bore, or, two bars gules, a label (5) sable. (F.) St. George Roll. See MARTIN and JOHN ST. MARTYN.

Wisemale, Ernaud de—(E. I. Roll) bore, gules, three fleurs-de-lys argent. JOHN bore the lys, or; Camden Roll. F.

Wisham, Sir John de, (of co. Glouc.)— bore, at the first Dunstable tournament 1308, sable, a fess between six martlets 3 and 3 or— argent (F.) in Jenyns' and Parly. Rolls—and so borne by WILLIAM at the siege of Rouen 1418.

Wistowe, John and **Robert de**—(E. I. Roll) bore, argent, a chevron gules, in chief three torteaux; Jenyns' Roll and Ordinary.

Witacre, Richard—(H. III. Roll) bore, argent, on a fess gules three besants, in chief two mullets (6) of the second. (F.) St. George Roll.

Withacre, Sir Richard, of Warwickshire —(E. II. Roll) bore, sable three mascles argent, —lozenges in trick; Parliamentary Roll.

Wither, Sire Thomas (WYTHER)—bore, at the battle of Boroughbridge 1322, argent, a fess between three crescent gules. (F.) Jenyns' Ordinary.

Wither, William—(H. III. Roll) bore, argent, three crescents gules. (F.) St. George Roll. See also RYTHER.

Witleburye, Aubrey de—(E. I. Roll) bore, azure; Camden Roll.

Witney, Sir Eustace de, of Cheshire— —(E. II. Roll) bore paly (6) or and gules, a chief vair; Parliamentary Roll.

Witney, Eustace and **Robert de Whit- neye**—(H. III. Roll) bore, azure, a cross counter-compony or and gules. (F.) St. George and Surrey Rolls; argent and gules in Arden Roll.

✝**Wodeburgh, Rafe de**—(E. I. Roll) bore, burulée (10, 12, 14) argent and azure over all three lyons rampant gules. (F.) Jenyns' Ordinary—6, 7 barrulets in Arden and St. George Rolls (crowned or in Dering and Howard Rolls); THOMAS burulée 12 (5 barru- lets in trick), WILLIAM 14, Jenyns' Ordinary and St. George Roll; 9 barrulets and crowned or in Howard Roll. See also WOODEBURNE.

*[**Wodehouse, John,** 1415—bore, sable, a chevron or, guttée de sang between three cinquefoyles ermine.—Shirley.] (F.) Said to have been granted for valour at Agincourt.

Wodhull, John de and **Symon**—(H. III. Roll) bore, or, three crescents gules. (F.) Arden, Jenyns' and St. George Rolls.

Wodvyle, Sir Richard, of Kent—(H. VI. Roll) bore, argent a fess and a quarter gules; Atkinson Roll—(differenced in Arundel Roll— with a crescent of the first); and *quarterly with,* gules, an eagle displayed or; Jenyns' Ordinary; Lord RIVERS, K.G.; K. 402 fo. 32.

Wogges, Thomas de (? of Suffolk, Knight) —(E. III. Roll) bore, argent, a fess engrailed between three annulets sable; Jenyns' Ordi- nary and Arundel Roll.

Wokingdon, Sir Thomas, of Essex—(E. II. Roll) bore, gules, a lyon rampant argent crowned or; Cotgrave, Harleian and Parly. Rolls—ascribed to NICOLE in Segar Roll. F. See WYFRYNGDON.

Wokingdon, Sir Nicholas, of Essex— (E. II. Roll) bore, gules, a lyon rampant barry (8) or and azure; Parly. Roll—barry of six in Harl. Roll.

Wolterston — an Essex ? Knight—(H. VI. Roll)—bore, sable, a fess nebulée between three wolves' heads couped or—a Suffolk Knight of the name bore lyons' heads; Arundel Roll.

Wolford, Sir William, a Gascoyne—bore, at the siege of Calais 1345-8, sable a fess, and in chief three fleurs-de-lys or. F.

Wol(l)aston, Sire John de—bore, at the battle of Boroughbridge 1322, sable, a chevron between three escallops argent (F.); estoyles of many points (F.) in the Ashmole MS. pro- bably in error.

*[**W(o)lseley, Robert de,** 1281—bore, argent, a talbot passant gules.—Shirley.] F.

Woltaubin, Gilbert de—(H. III. Roll) bore, or, on a cross sable five besants; Arden Roll. See ORKABLIN.

Wolverton, Sir John de, of Bucks—(E. II. Roll) bore, azure, an eagle displayed or, a baston gules; Parliamentary Roll.

Wolwardington, Sir Peers de, of War- wickshire—(E. II. Roll) bore, bendy (10) argent and sable; Parliamentary Roll.

Wombewell, Thomas—(E. I. Roll) bore, argent, on a bend between six martlets (3, 3) gules, three besants; Jenyns' Roll.

*[**Wombwell,** *alias* **Tawnell, Hugh** (6 H. IV. 1404-5)—bore, gules, a bend between six unicorns' heads couped argent.—Shirley.] F.

Witt. Wodeburh.

will wolrycff

worsley

Robert
morsewik

Roger wrey

Hugh
Wrottesley

Nicol.
d Wunhale

will wyborgh

will do
wifringdono

will d. Wiwile

John wywill

Roger. d Wiwile

Woodeburne, John—(E. III. Roll) bore, burulée (12) argent and azure, over all three lyonceux rampant (2 and 1) gules; Jenyns' Ordinary. See WODEBURGH.

Woodstock, Thomas of, v. **Gloucester, Duke of.**

*[**Woolryche, William,** 1403—bore, azure, a chevron between three swans' wings elevated argent.—Shirley.] F.

*[**Worsley** —— a Lancashire Knight—(H. VI. Roll) bore, argent, a chief gules; Arundel and Ballard Rolls. F.

Worswick, Robert—(E. III. Roll) bore, argent, on a bend sable three lozenges of the first each charged with a saltire gules. (F.) Jenyns' Ordinary.

Wortley, Sir Nicholas de, of Yorkshire, and **Robert de**—(E. II. Roll) bore, argent, on a bend between six martlets (3, 3) gules, three besants; Parly. Roll and Jenyns' Ordinary —being the arms of FURNIVALL and three besants on the bend.

*[**Wrey, Roger,** (19 E. III.)—bore, sable, a fess between three poleaxes argent, helved gules.—Shirley.] F.

Wrialeye, Pers—(H. III. Roll) bore, azure, two bars or charged with five martlets, 3, 2, gules; Arden Roll—? being the arms of LEY with the martlets.

Wrokeshall, Geoffrey—(E. III. Roll) bore, ermine, two bars gules; Jenyns' Ordinary.

Wrokeshall, Geoffrey de—(H. III. Roll) bore, gules, two bars ermine over all a bend azure; Howard Roll.

Wroth —— a Kentish Knight—(H. VI. Roll) bore, argent, on a bend sable three tygers' (probably leopards') faces argent crowned or; Arundel Roll.

***Wrottesley, Sir Hugh,** K.G., founder 1344 —bore or, three piles, meeting in base sable and a quarter ermine—being the coat of his mother JOAN BASSET. K. 398 fo. 23. To another HUGH, or, a bend engrailed gules, is ascribed in Surrey Roll.

Wroughton —— a Somersetshire Knight— (H. VI. Roll) bore, argent, chevron between three boars' heads couped gules; Arundel Roll.

*[**Wybergh, William de,** (38 E. III.)—bore, sable, three bars or, in chief two estoyles of the last.—Shirley.] F.

Wycliffe, Robert — (E. III. Roll) bore, argent, a chevron between three crosses crosslet gules; Grimaldi Roll—the chevron sable and crosses botonnée in Jenyns' Ordinary.

Wyfryngdon, Sir Nichol de—bore, at the first Dunstable tournament 1308, gules, a lyon rampant argent crowned or. F. See WOKINGDON.

Wykes, Richard de—(H. III. Roll) bore, azure, a lyon rampant argent (Arden Roll); checquy argent and gules. (F.) St. George Roll—Sir JOHN, slain at the siege of Calais 1348—arms gone from Roll.

Wymale, Nicholas—(H. III. Roll) bore, argent, three cushions 2 and 1 gules. (F.) St. George and Jenyns' Rolls.

*[**Wyndham, John,** (38 H. VI.)—bore, azure, a chevron between three lyons' heads erased or.—Shirley.] F.

Wynseles v. **Winceles.**

Wythe, Sir Geffrey and Oliver de— (E. II. Roll) bore, azure, three gryphons passant in pale or membered gules; Arundel, Ashmole and Cotgrave Rolls. See FITZ WYTHE.

Wyther, Sire Thomas—bore, at the battle of Boroughbridge 1322, argent, a fess between three crescents gules. See RYTHER and WITHER.

Wivile, William de—(H. III. Roll) bore, argent, two bars sable, a bordure engrailed (gules). (F.) St. George Roll.

Wyvile, William—(E. I. Roll) bore, gules, fretty or, a quarter of the first (*sic*); Jenyns' Roll.

***Wyvill, John**—(E. III. Roll) bore, gules, three chevronels interlaced in base vair, a chief or (F.); Jenyns' Ordinary—erroneously blasoned, gules, fret vair, a chief or.

Wyville, Roger, slain at the siege of Calais 1347, bore, azure, three chevronels interlaced in base argent. F.

Rich. d' Wikes

John Wyndham

Alloyn la zouch

Alain d'La Souche

Amory de la Zouch

York, Duke of, Richard Plantagenet, 1415–60—bore, France and England—a label (3) on each pendant three torteaux; Surrey Roll—these arms appear on the Rouen Roll 1418—this Duke born in 1412 succeeded in 1415!

Ypre, John de—(R. II. Roll) bore, argent, a chevron between three bulls' heads cabossed gules. RAUFF differenced with a mullet; Surrey Roll.

Zevelton, Robert le—(R. II. Roll) bore, argent, two bars undée sable, a label (3) gules; Surrey Roll.

Zouche, Roger de la, at the second Dunstable tournament 1334, and Sir Simon (la), knighted at the capitulation of Calais 1348— bore, azure, besantée 4, 3, 2, 1 (F.); ascribed also to JOHN, of Sibthorpe (Jenyns' Ordinary), Sir ROGER (Ashmole Roll) and WILLIAM, of Haringworth, baron 1308 in Cotgrave Roll; 6 bezants in Howard Roll; ascribed to another WILLIAM (‡) in Dering Roll. Sir WILLIAM, of Leic., differenced with a label (3) gules in Ashmole and Parly. Rolls.

Zouche, Roger la—(H. III. Roll) bore, ermine, on a fess gules three besants; Howard Roll.

Zouche, Sir Alan la, of Ashby, baron 1299, sealed the Barons' letter to the Pope 1301, bore at the battle of Falkirk 1298, and at the siege of Carlaverock 1300, gules, besantée (4, 3, 2, 1) (F.); Parly. Roll; as did also his son Sire WILLIAM, banneret, of Haringworth, baron 1308, at the battle of Boroughbridge 1322 (six besants in Howard Roll)—ascribed also to HUGH and ROGER in Surrey and Arden Rolls, and to another ALAN (‡) in the Dering Roll. Sir WILLIAM bore it with a label (3) azure, at the first Dunstable tournament 1308; Parly. Roll.

Zouche, Sire Roger la—bore, at the battle of Boroughbridge 1322, and WILLIAM (5th baron) of Haringworth; bore, at the siege of Rouen 1418, gules, besantée and a quarter ermine (borne by one of the name with a mullet of 6 sable on the canton or quarter; Harl. Roll); ascribed also to Sir YVON (F.) in various Rolls, though he seems to have borne it with a label (3) azure at the battle of Boroughbridge 1322.

Zouche, John la—bore, at the siege of Rouen 1418, gules, besantée, a canton ermine, quarterly with, argent, a fess dancettée sable besantée. F.

Zouche, Sir William la, banneret, knighted at the capitulation of Calais 1348 – bore, gules, besantée or, a canton "endente in base" ermine (F.),—a quarter ermine in Parly. Roll.

Zouche, Richard and Thomas la— (E. III. Roll) bore, gules, besantée and a chief ermine; Surrey and Ashmole Rolls and Jenyns' Ordinary.

Zouche, Sir Amory de la—bore, at the first Dunstable tournament 1308, gules besantée and a bend azure—though argent (F.) at the battle of Boroughbridge 1322; Parly. Roll. In Jenyns' Ordinary the coat is gules platey and a bend argent.

Zouche, Alan and Roger la—(H. III. Roll) bore, gules, besantée, and a fess ermine; Arden and St. George Rolls. F.

Zouche, Sir Oliver, of co. Leic.—(E. II. Roll) bore, gules, besantée and a chevron ermine; Parliamentary Roll.

Zouche, Sir Thomas, of co. Leic.—(E. II. Roll) bore, gules, besantée on a canton argent a mullet sable; Parly. Roll.

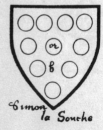

Simon la Souche

Will la Zouch

Sir Yvon la Zouch